Proceedings

Graphics **Interface** 2000

Sidney S. Fels and Pierre Poulin
Program Co-Chairs

www.graphicsinterface.org

Montréal, Québec
15-17 May 2000

ISSN 0713-5424
ISBN 0-9695338-9-6

Proceedings Graphics Interface 2000, Sidney S. Fels and Pierre Poulin (Program Co-Chairs), Montréal, Québec, 15-17 May 2000.

Graphics Interface is sponsored by:
The Canadian Human-Computer Communications Society (CHCCS)

Membership Information for CHCCS is available from:
     Canadian Information Processing Society (CIPS)
     One Yonge Street, Suite 2401
     Toronto, Ontario
     Canada M5E 1E5
     Telephone: 416 861-CIPS (2477)
     Fax: 416 368-9972
     Web: http://www.cips.ca/

Additional copies of the proceedings are available from:
     Canadian Information Processing Society (in Canada)

     Morgan Kaufmann Publishers
     340 Pine Street, Sixth Floor
     San Francisco, CA 94104 USA
     Telephone: 800 745-7323 or 415 392-2665
     Email: orders@mkp.com
     Web: http://www.mkp.com/

Published by the Canadian Human-Computer Communications Society
Printed in Canada by Graphics Services at the University of Waterloo, Waterloo, Ontario.
Cover Credits
     Wireframes: Front cover, Karan Singh and Evangelos Kokkevis. Back cover, Roger Fernandes. Computer Program: Jan Kautz. Colour images: Left to right (starting on back left): Normand Brière and Pierre Poulin; James O'Brien, Bobby Bodenheimer, Gabriel Brostow, and Jessica Hodgins; Frank Dachille and Arie Kaufman; Bernhard Preim, Felix Ritter, Oliver Deussen, and Thomas Strothotte; Alexandre Meyer and Fabrice Neyret; Martin Isenburg; Ronald Metoyer and Jessica Hodgins; Eric Marchand and Nicolas Courty. Top to bottom (skipping joint): Normand Brière and Pierre Poulin; Frank Dachille and Arie Kaufman; Karan Singh and Evangelos Kokkevis; Jeffrey Smith, Andrew Witkin, and David Baraff. Design: Christine Goucher.

Message from the Program Co-Chairs

Sidney S. Fels
Department of ECE
University of British Columbia

Pierre Poulin
Département IRO
Université de Montréal

This year marked the return to Montréal of the Graphics Interface conference after 15 years of being held in different cities across Canada. Graphics Interface 2000 was held at the Palais des Congrès on May 15th to 17th in conjunction with four other conferences (Artificial Intelligence 2000, Vision Interface 2000, International Symposium on Robotics 2000, and the Annual PRECARN-IRIS Conference), as well as two trade shows (Robotics of Tomorrow and Montréal Machine Tool and Factory Automation).

We received 90 paper submissions on a wide range of topics related to computer graphics and human-computer interaction. From these, after considerable deliberation, the program committee selected the 27 papers that appear in these proceedings. With the very high overall quality of the submissions, the selection was very difficult. Each submission was reviewed by at least four experts, including two who sat on the program committee. The reviewing process was double-blind; no reviewer was informed of the authors or affiliations of any paper, even during the selection process at the program committee meeting. The program committee paper selection meeting was held in Toronto in January and was attended by 15 of the 19 committee members; each committee member paid their own expenses. Each committee member actively participated in discussing all submitted papers, except for those for which they had a conflict of interest, to try to ensure the fairness of the process. We greatly appreciate the enormous contribution the program committee made to keep GI an excellent, high quality conference.

We extend our gratitude to our three invited speakers: Henry Fuchs, University of North Carolina; Hiroshi Ishii, MIT Media Laboratory; and Demetri Terzopoulos, University of Toronto, who came to share their inspiration in their respective fields.

We wish to thank all the committee members for their strong involvement, all the reviewers for their critical analysis, James Stewart for developing all the necessary scripts for the electronic submission, reviewing, and final submission process, Michael McCool for the production of the printed proceedings, Wolfgang Stuerzlinger for taking care of everything involved in organizing the posters, Paul Johnston for bringing all these events together, Hélène Lamadeleine and Golden Planners Inc. for the organization of the joint conferences, Laurent Lefebvre for supporting the local web site, and Luc Leblanc for lending his personal computer to the project for several months. All of these people took time out of their busy schedules to make this event a memorable success, and we sincerely regret if any omissions have been made in these acknowledgements. The devotion of these volunteers to fellow researchers and to their fields demonstrates the importance granted to Graphics Interface. Finally, we wish to extend our appreciation to all the authors whose papers could not be included in these proceedings. The quality of your work often deserved the honour of appearing in these proceedings, and we regret that time and space constraints prevented us from accepting more of the submitted papers.

With its wide distribution throughout the world and the quality of the scientific contributions of its papers, we expect these proceedings to become an invaluable resource for computer graphics and human-computer interaction researchers and practitioners. We invite you to visit our website and strongly encourage you to contribute to future Graphics Interface conferences:

http://www.graphicsinterface.org/

Organization

Conference and Program Chairs
Sidney Fels, University of British Columbia
Pierre Poulin, Université de Montréal

Posters Chair
Wolfgang Stuerzlinger, York University

Videos Chair
Pierre Poulin, Université de Montréal

Program Committee
Kadi Bouatouch, Université de Rennes 1
Mathieu Desbrun, Caltech
Frédo Durand, Massachusetts Institute of Technology
Deborah Fels, Ryerson Polytechnic University
Mark Green, University of Alberta
Carl Gutwin, University of Saskatchewan
Christopher G. Healey, North Carolina State University
Kori Inkpen, Simon Fraser University
Paul Lalonde, Electronic Arts
Michael McCool, University of Waterloo
Dimitris N. Metaxas, University of Pennsylvania
Chris Shaw, University of Regina
Mikio Shinya, Nippon Telegraph and Telephone Corporation
James Stewart, University of Toronto
Wolfgang Stuerzlinger, York University
Benjamin Watson, University of Alberta
Shumin Zhai, IBM Almaden Research Center

Webmasters
James Stewart, University of Toronto
Laurent Lefebvre, Université de Montréal

Proceedings Editor
Michael McCool, University of Waterloo

Referees

Mark Ackerman
John Amanatides
Steve Anderson
Jim Arvo
Norman Badler
Rui Bastos
Ben Bederson
Mark Billinghurst
Jules Bloomenthal
kadi Bouatouch
Armin Bruderlin
John W. Buchanan
Emilio Camahort
Marie-Paule Cani
Sheelagh Carpendale
Jim Carter
Frederic Cazals
Chun-Fa Chang
Anastasia Cheetham
Sean Cocks
Jonathan D. Cohen
Daniel Cohen–Or
Matt Conway
Satyan Coorg
Edward H. Cornell
Donald Cox
Sara Czaja
Rudy Darken
Doug DeCarlo
Gilles Debunne
Mathieu Desbrun
Ralph Deters
Jean-Michel Dischler
George Drettakis
Frédo Durand
Daniel C. Fain
François Faure
Paul Fearing
Deborah Fels
Paul Ferry
Alain Fournier
Laure France
Issei Fujishiro
Michael Garland
Ricki Goldman-Segall
Ardeshir Goshtasby
Ambarish Goswami
Craig Gotsman
Mark Green
Saul Greenberg

Jonathan Grudin
Eduard Grller
Yves Guiard
Thierry Guiard-Marigny
Stefan Gumhold
Carl Gutwin
James Hall
Li-Wei He
Christopher G. Healey
Pheng Ann Heng
Ken Hinckley
Jessica Hodgins
Scott Hudson
Kori Inkpen
Horace H.S. Ip
John Isidoro
Robert Jacob
Frederik W. Jansen
Ioannis Kakadiaris
Kazufumi Kaneda
Rob Kooper
Cyriaque Kouadio
Steve LaValle
David Laidlaw
Paul Lalonde
Joseph Laszlo
James Lester
Bruno Levy
Bob Lewis
Erik Lindholm
David Luebke
Scott MacKenzie
Jock Mackinlay
Eric Maisel
Stephen Mann
Dave Martindale
Claude Martins
David McAllister
Michael McCool
Leonard McMillan
Daniel Meneveaux
Mark Meyer
Eric Neufeld
Fabrice Neyret
Tomoyuki Nishita
Jun-Yong Noh
Ming Ouhyoung
Marc Olano
Mark Peercy
Catherine Plaisant
Zoran Popovic

Patrick Ratto
Penny Rheingans
George Robertson
Randy Rohrer
Martin Rumpf
Takafumi Saito
Gernot Schaufler
Eric Schenk
Christophe Schlick
Carlo Sequin
Ehud Sharlin
Chris Shaw
Mikio Shinya
John Sibert
Maryann Simmons
Barton Smith
Tony C. Smith
Jim Spohrer
Robert St. Amant
Jos Stam
Marc Stamminger
James Stewart
Wolfgang Stuerzlinger
Ching Y. Suen
Tamara Sumner
Hanqiu Sun
Tokiichiro Takahashi
Jim Tam
Toshimitsu Tanaka
Russell M. Taylor II
Demetri Terzopoulos
Joelle Thollot
Judi Thomson
Eric Tosan
Xiaoyuan Tu
Jack Tumblin
Michiel van de Panne
Bill Verplank
Pascal Volino
John W. Senders
Benjamin Watson
Carolynn Whiteley
Turner Whitted
Laurel Williams
David Wong
Brian Wyvill
Shigeki Yokoi
R. Michael Young
Robert Zeleznik
Shumin Zhai

Table of Contents

Invited Speaker

Tangible Bits: Designing the Boundary between People, Bits, and Atoms 1
    Hiroshi Ishii

Issues and Techniques for Interactive Information Spaces

Multi-resolution Amplification Widgets 3
    Kiril Vidimce and David Banks
Navigating Complex Information with the ZTree 11
    Lyn Bartram and Axel Uhl
The Effects of Feedback on Targeting Performance in Visually Stressed Conditions 19
    Julie Fraser and Carl Gutwin

Modeling

Fast and Controllable Simulation of the Shattering of Brittle Objects 27
    Jeffrey Smith, Andrew Witkin, and David Baraff
Skinning Characters using Surface-Oriented Free-Form Deformation 35
    Karan Singh and Evangelos Kokkevis

Invited Speaker

Artificial Animals (and Humans): From Physics to Intelligence 43
    Demetri Terzopoulos

Animation

Dynamic Time Warp Based Framespace Interpolation for Motion Editing 45
    Golam Ashraf and Kok Cheong Wong
Automatic Joint Parameter Estimation from Magnetic Motion Capture Data 53
    James O'Brien, Bobby Bodenheimer, Gabriel Brostow, and Jessica Hodgins
Animating Athletic Motion Planning By Example 61
    Ronald Metoyer and Jessica Hodgins

Image-based Modeling and Rendering

Image-Based Virtual Camera Motion Strategies 69
    Eric Marchand and Nicolas Courty
Analysis and Synthesis of Structural Textures 77
    Laurent Lefebvre and Pierre Poulin
High-Quality Interactive Lumigraph Rendering Through Warping 87
    Hartmut Schirmacher, Wolfgang Heidrich, and Hans-Peter Seidel

Collaborative and Community Spaces

Effects of Gaze on Multiparty Mediated Communication 95
    Roel Vertegaal, Gerrit van der Veer, and Harro Vons
Towards Seamless Support of Natural Collaborative Interactions 103
    Stacey Scott, Garth Shoemaker, and Kori Inkpen
The ChatterBox: Using Text Manipulation in an Entertaining Information Display 111
    Johan Redström, Peter Ljungstrand, and Patricija Jaksetic

Rendering

Approximation of Glossy Reflection with Prefiltered Environment Maps 119
    Jan Kautz and Michael D. McCool
Adaptive Representation of Specular Light Flux 127
    Normand Brière and Pierre Poulin
Multiscale Shaders for the Efficient Realistic Rendering of Pine-Trees 137
    Alexandre Meyer and Fabrice Neyret

Image Processing and Visualization

Anisotropic Feature-Preserving Denoising of Height Fields and Images 145
    Mathieu Desbrun, Mark Meyer, Peter Schroeder, and Alan Barr
A Fast, Space-efficient Algorithm for the Approximation of Images by an Optimal Sum of Gaussians 153
    Jeffrey Childs, Cheng-Chang Lu, and Jerry Potter
Oriented Sliver Textures: A Technique for Local Value Estimation of Multiple Scalar Fields 163
    Chris Weigle, William Emigh, Geniva Liu, Russell Taylor, James Enns, and Christopher Healey

Advances in HCI Design and Applications

Using a 3D Puzzle as a Metaphor for Learning Spatial Relations 171
    Bernhard Preim, Felix Ritter, Oliver Deussen, and Thomas Strothotte
Affordances: Clarifying and Evolving a Concept 179
    Joanna McGrenere and Wayne Ho
Are We All In the Same "Bloat"? 187
    Joanna McGrenere and Gale Moore

Geometry

Triangle Strip Compression 197
    Martin Isenburg
Incremental Triangle Voxelization 205
    Frank Dachille and Arie Kaufman
Dynamic Plane Shifting BSP Traversal 213
    Stan Melax
Model Simplification Through Refinement 221
    Dmitry Brodsky and Benjamin Watson

Tangible Bits:
Designing the Boundary between People, Bits, and Atoms

Hiroshi Ishii
Tangible Media Group
MIT Media Laboratory
`http://www.media.mit.edu/~ishii`

People have developed sophisticated skills for sensing and manipulating our physical environments. However, most of these skills are not employed by traditional Graphical User Interface (GUI). Tangible Bits, our vision of Human Computer Interaction (HCI), seeks to build upon these skills by giving physical form to digital information, seamlessly coupling the dual worlds of bits and atoms. Guided by the Tangible Bits vision, we are designing "tangible user interfaces" which employ physical objects, surfaces, and spaces as tangible embodiments of digital information. These involve foreground interactions with graspable objects and augmented surfaces, exploiting the human senses of touch and kinesthesia. We are also exploring background information displays which use "ambient media" – ambient light, sound, airflow, and water movement. Here, we seek to communicate digitally-mediated senses of activity and presence at the periphery of human awareness. Our goal is to realize seamless interfaces between humans, digital information, and the physical environment taking advantage of the richness of multimodal human senses and skills developed through our lifetime of interaction with the physical world.

In this talk, I will present a variety of tangible user interfaces the Tangible Media Group has designed and presented within the CHI, SIGGRAPH, IST, and CSCW communities in the past years.

More information can be found on the web site at `http://tangible.media.mit.edu/`.

2

Multi-resolution Amplification Widgets

Kiril Vidimce
vkire@erc.msstate.edu
NSF Engineering Research Center
Mississippi State University

David C. Banks
banks@csit.fsu.edu
Computational Science & Information Technology
Florida State University

Abstract

We describe a 3D graphical interaction tool called an amplification widget that allows a user to control the position or orientation of an object at multiple scales. Fine and coarse adjustments are available within a single tool which gives visual feedback to indicate the level of resolution being applied. Amplification widgets have been included in instructional modules of The Optics Project, designed to supplement undergraduate physics courses. The user evaluation is being developed by the Institute of the Mid-South Educational Research Association under the sponsorship of a 2-year grant from the National Science Foundation.

Nous décrivons un outil graphique de l'interaction 3D q'on appele un "widget d'amplification" qui permet à un utilisateur de contrôler la position ou l'orientation d'un objet aux échelles divers. Les réglages fins et approchés sont disponibles dans un outil simple qui donne le feedback visuel pour indiquer le niveau de la résolution étant appliquée. Des widgets d'amplification ont été inclus dans des modules d'instruction de The Optics Project, conçus pour compléter des cours de physique. L'évaluation d'utilisateur est développée par l'Institute of the Mid-South Educational Research Association sous le patronage du National Science Foundation.

Key words: 3D widgets, user interface, interactive control.

1 Introduction

This paper describes amplification widgets that deliver to the user an amplified version of changes that occur in a 3D object. Instead of offering just one level of amplification, these 3D widgets [Conner] allow multiple scales of operation. Our reason for creating such widgets was specific and practical, but the widgets themselves can be used in more general and even fanciful settings.

During the past four years we have developed several interactive 3D graphical tools as part of The Optics Project (TOP) to teach principles of optics to undergraduate physics students. The student sometimes needs to apply very fine control to an optical element in a simulated system. For example, moving a mirror or changing the wavelength in a Michelson interferometer produces large changes in the interference patterns on an observation screen. The resolution of a mouse is insufficient for providing satisfactory control.

Fine control is important in other application areas of computer graphics. A surgeon makes precise cuts with a scalpel, and a surgical simulation should offer such precision. Tele-operation of robotic controls may require precision beyond what a typical input device can afford. For individuals with motor disabilities, it is desirable to construct a user interface that improves the resolution of a non-dextrous hand.

If you want to translate an object with precision, one standard strategy is to zoom, move, and unzoom. If you don't zoom, the resolution of the mouse maps a 1-pixel motion into a relatively large translation. But when you zoom, the 1-pixel motion of the mouse converts to a small translation. It would be nice to have fine control without demanding the zoom/unzoom sandwich around the translation.

One strategy is – by fiat – to decree that the 1-pixel motions of the cursor are converted to tiny translations of the object. But that sacrifices the virtuous goal of direct manipulation: the object should move together with the cursor. How can you simultaneously provide direct manipulation and fine control?

Rotation creates similar problem. To exercise fine control over the orientation of an object you might use a knob. When you rotate the knob, the object rotates too. But how do you make the object turn by a millionth of a degree? You might make the knob be *really* big; then a 1-pixel motion on the knob would only rotate by a millionth of a degree. But there is not enough screen to make the knob that big. Alternatively, you could decouple the knob's rotation from the object's, so one degree on the knob becomes a millionth of a degree for the object. But that seems to sacrifice direct manipulation of the object. A solution to one problem promises a solution to the other.

The single most influential work that inspired our efforts was the 1992 paper by the group at Brown University on 3-dimensional widgets [Conner], which demonstrated how effectively a 3D object can be manipulated through geometric elements that visually connect a representation of the input device (a cursor for a mouse, a hand for a 3D tracker) to the object being manipulated. When the object undergoes a simple 1-to-1 motion that tracks the device, such widgets may be gratuitous. But indirect control is mediated very effectively by an intervening widget.

Other researchers have addressed the general problem of how to design a "natural" 3D interaction technique that allows a user to manipulate an object without demanding a 1-to-1 correspondence to the input device. Poupyrev's "go-go interaction" applies a non-linear mapping of the user's hand position to the world, so that a reaching gesture will grab objects that are much farther than an arm's length away [Poupyrev]. Mark Mine took the idea a step further by automatically stretching the manifestation of the user's arm as long as is required to grab the object beyond the hand [Mine].

Bier's group developed "magic lenses" to permit multiple styles of display and interaction through a see-through interface [Bier]. They designed several overlay tools for 2D displays. They describe the notion of composing a widget with a lens:

> ... consider a click-through button on top of a magnifying lens. Mouse events pass through the button, are annotated with a command, and then pass through the lens, which applies the inverse of its transformation to the mouse coordinates.

Although they did not illustrate this idea for multiple scales of translational or rotational control, the notion was certainly part of their overall view of a modular layered interface.

Mackinlay's perspective wall [Mackinlay] and Furnas's fish-eye view [Furnas] share the strategy of warping a display in order to selectively scale (zoom) a region of interest. We depart from this scheme by restricting the deformations to the widgets rather than to the entire display, and by concentrating on translation and rotation rather than scale.

Ahlberg and Masui both addressed the problem of positioning a slider bar during a search of a large dataset [Ahlberg] [Masui]. Both coarse-scale seeking (finding the right chapter of a book) and fine-scale seeking (finding the right sentence or word) can occur within moments of each other. Masui's rubber-band slider offers two levels of resolution. Ahlberg's offers two or three levels.

Mackinlay's work on rapid controlled movement demonstrated that an exponential relation between fine control and coarse control is effective in navigating a 3D environment [Mackinlay2]. We pursue a similar approach, although for manipulation rather than navigation.

Stoakley's worlds-in-miniature addresses a complementary problem to ours [Stoakley]. Rather than apply micro-scale changes to sensitive objects, his users manipulate physical props to speed up interaction, providing a means to produce large changes in translation. We have not yet applied amplification widgets to produce gross translations (or rotations for that matter, but rotations are essentially bounded by 360 degrees which makes them uninteresting for coarse control), but we plan to do so in the future.

2 Amplification Widgets

A 3D "amplification widget" is a cascade of 3D components, one controlling the next, with one component directly controlling a given object in a scene. The hierarchy of these components propagates increasingly fine control outward from the object being manipulated so that direct manipulation occurs at the object. For example, a box can be positioned at a scale of 1:1 by a widget component, but can also be translated at a scale of 2:1 by the neighboring component, which in turn is translated at a scale of 2:1 by its neighbor, and so on. In a similar fashion, an object can be rotated at a 2:1 ratio; the rotating element can be similarly rotated by another, and so forth, until the outermost component amplifies a minuscule rotation of the object into a large sweep of the mouse or tracker.

The benefit of amplification widgets is that they (1) eliminate the requirement that a user zoom, micromanipulate, then unzoom (a situation that arises when small changes are made within large environments); (2) preserve the spirit of direct manipulation by visually connecting the point of control with the point of attachment; and (3) provide multiple scales of resolution for manipulation.

2.1 Translation Amplifiers

Our strategy for giving interactive control works like this. A widget has a sequence of components to govern the movement of the object they are attached to. The position of component number u is $p(u)$, with $p(0)$ indicating the point of attachment that provides direct control of the object. The user grabs component number

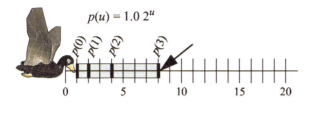

$p(u) = 1.0\ 2^u$

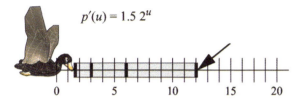

$p'(u) = 1.5\ 2^u$

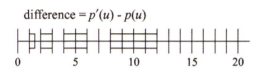

difference $= p'(u) - p(u)$

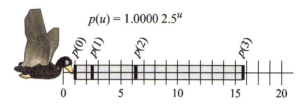

$p(u) = 1.0000\ 2.5^u$

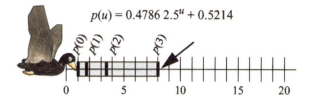

$p(u) = 0.4786\ 2.5^u + 0.5214$

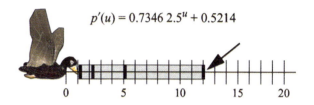

$p'(u) = 0.7346\ 2.5^u + 0.5214$

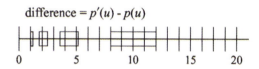

difference $= p'(u) - p(u)$

Figure 1. (Top) The mouse (indicated by the arrow) drags knuckle number 3, beginning at position 8. Other knuckles in the widget move according to the equation shown.
(Middle) When the mouse reaches position 12, an appropriate scale factor is computed to maintain the form of Equation 1. As a consequence, the other knuckles move too.
(Bottom) The gray regions show how much each knuckle moved. The duck moves with knuckle 0; the other knuckles amplify this small translation.

Figure 2. Changing the sensitivity of the transAmp without changing its overall appearance.
(Top) The base of the exponent in figure 1 is increased from 2.0 to 2.5, making the widget longer and more sensitive at the rightmost end.
(Upper middle) The widget is scaled and offset to match the length of the transAmp in figure 1. This requires calculating a different scale and offset.
(Lower middle) The user again moves the transAmp's right end from position 8 to 12, but the duck moves less than in figure 1 because the exponent is now larger.
(Bottom) The gray regions show how much each knuckle moved.

u and drags it. Direct manipulation applies to the component of the widget, not to the object itself. The sequence of widget elements ties the cursor to the object in a natural, visual way.

There are many mathematical functions that exaggerate motion away from the zero point, but the exponential function

$$p(u) = sb^u - q \qquad (1)$$

is perhaps the most convenient way to capture this desired behavior. We chose this equation since it can be used to encapsulate the notions of widget scale s, exponential base b, and the widget's point of attachment q to the object. The base b of the exponent produces the multi-resolution effect: the kth knuckle amplifies the object's motion by b^k. The scale term is applied to the ensemble of knuckles as a whole so that the user can dictate how large the entire collection is on the screen.

The translation amplifier (transAmp) has n segments that stretch or squish and $n+1$ knuckles that can be dragged by the cursor. Since (by Equation 1) the widget attaches at the point $p(0) = s - q$, changes made in the scale s produce translation of this point of attachment. Changes to the exponential's base b have a different effect: the point of attachment $p(0)$ is independent of b, but the relative lengths of the segments change. When b is large, the uth knuckle moves considerably compared to the motion of the attachment point.

Figures 1 and 2 illustrate a transAmp with three segments. The putative goal is for the user to move the duck by a small amount. The left end of the transAmp attaches to the duck at position $p(0) = 1$. With the scale $s = 1$ and the base $b = 2$, we must have $q = 0$. Thus the other knuckles lie at $p(1) = 2$, $p(2) = 4$, and $p(3) = 8$.

We leave the base b and the offset q fixed, allowing s to vary. When the rightmost knuckle $p(3)$ is dragged to a new position $p'(3) = 12$, the scale s is no longer valid and must be recalculated. According to Equation 1, this knuckle lies at $p'(3) = s' 2^3 - q = 12$, which is satisfied by a new scale factor $s' = 1.5$. The positions of the other knuckles are updated accordingly using the new s'. The point of attachment therefore changes from $p(0) = 1$ to $p'(0) = 1.5$, moving 0.5 units, while the rightmost knuckle moves 4 units. The third knuckle amplifies the object's motion by a factor of 8. This is how the motion of the transAmp is amplified with respect to the motion of the object. The second knuckle at point $p(2)$ only moves 2 units, so if it had been selected and dragged the cursor's motion would amplify the object's motion by a factor of 4. Similarly, point $p(1)$ amplifies by a factor of 2.

We can calculate this amplification factor by writing the position of the uth knuckle in terms of the 0th knuckle. Substituting in Equation 1 for the scale s when $u = 0$ we have

$$p_u = (p_0 + q) b^u - q,$$

where p_u denotes $p(u)$. When p_0 changes, so does p_u. The amplification is the rate of change of one with respect to the other and is given by the derivative

$$\frac{dp_u}{dp_0} = b^u$$

So the knuckles exhibit exponentially increasing amplification. We can limit the maximum amount of amplification for a given configuration of the widget. A transAmp with n knuckles and total length l, having a maximum amplification of B, satisfies $b^n = B$, so the desired base of the exponent is $b = B^{1/n}$. Furthermore, we note that $s = l/(B-1)$ and $q = p_0-s$. Thus the scale, the base, and the offset can be easily calculated to satisfy a desired configuration for the widget.

When a knuckle is dragged, the new value of s is computed as $s = p_u/b^u$. We also allow the user to drag a knuckle for the purpose of changing the base b, rather than for producing a translation via a change of the scale s. In that case, the new value of b is given by the equation $b = (p^u/s)^{1/u}$.

2.2 Look and Feel

As the components move, the transAmp's shape distorts because they move by unequal amounts. The *object* moves rigidly, the *cursor* moves rigidly, each *knuckle* moves rigidly, but not the widget as a whole. When the user releases the widget, how should it return

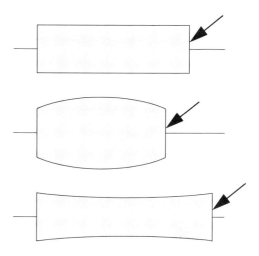

Figure 3. (Top) A cylindrical component of the translation amplifier in its rest state is grabbed (arrow).
(Middle) The cylinder bulges when it is compressed.
(Bottom) The cylinder squeezes in when it is extended.

to its undistorted rest state? One choice is to simply switch from the stretched state to the rest state discontinuously. But a smoother transition is produced by briefly animating the widget's return (as a visual inverse operation of the dynamic stretching the widget undergoes when it is in use). This strategy gives the widget a more physical look and feel than does a discontinuous pop. The only issue is how to provide a reasonable animation. To restore the widget to its original shape, we animate the transition from distorted to undistorted when the user completes the drag (releasing the mouse). We experimented with a damped spring and various other oscillating behaviors to animate the dragger's return to its rest state, but we were eventually the most satisfied with a simple cubic "return function"

$$c(t) = 2t^3 - 3t^2 + 1$$

which has velocity zero at the endpoints of the interval [0,1]. This cubic is the lowest-degree polynomial that has zero-derivatives at both ends of the interval, which makes it the simplest choice for animating the widget's return to its rest state. The point of attachment remains fixed at p'_0 during the animation, while the other knuckles return to their original rest positions, translated by p'_0. The behavior is given by the equation

$$p_u = c(t) p'_u + (1-c(t)) (p'_0 + p_u).$$

To give additional visual feedback during dragging, we make the widgets bulge outward when compressed and squeeze inward when stretched (figure 3). This is the appropriate behavior for a cylinder of constant volume as its length changes. We give the cylinder a parabolic profile that preserve its original volume. Why parabolic? Because a second-degree polynomial is the quickest non-linear shape to compute on the fly. In normalized units, the axis of a cylinder runs from -1 to 1 in the x-direction, its radius is r, and its volume v is $2\pi r^2$. When the length of the axis is changed to some other value l, the radius is found by the quadratic expression $r = au^2+b$, where a and b are chosen to preserve the volume of the cylinder as it bulges or contracts. This quadratic is chosen so that the radius at the endpoints of the cylinder remains fixed.

We apply texture mapping to the cylinders forming the transAmp segments so that each local neighborhood looks like it is stretching or contracting. Ideally the texture would stretch non-linearly to match the exponential stretching, but for segments of modest length the difference is not objectionable. We created periodic texture maps so that there would be no visible seam where they wrap, and constructed the textures from multi-frequency noise so their appearance would remain acceptable throughout varying degrees of expansion or compression.

We experimented with segments whose lengths formed a geometric progression so that segment k has length $l_k = b\, l_{k-1}$. The visual effect is not appreciably different from the exponential function already described, but the math is considerably more tedious.

After we used the transAmp for awhile, three improvements to the widget became immediately evident. First, there is no need to scale the knuckles beyond the one being dragged. This is especially obvious when the knuckle at the point of attachment is moved. All the other knuckles spread out exponentially, which really isn't their purpose. We therefore restrict the scaling to the knuckles between the one being dragged and the one at the point of attachment. The others simply translate by the same amount as the dragged knuckle.

The second improvement is an implementation detail. Rather than calculate the absolute position of each knuckle, it is more convenient to calculate the relative position of one knuckle with respect to its neighbor. Since the scale s and the base b are actually variables, the change of position p is given by the total derivative

$$dp = \frac{\partial}{\partial u}sb^u du + \frac{\partial}{\partial s}sb^u ds + \frac{\partial}{\partial b}sb^u db$$

$$= s\ln b b^u du + b^u ds + sub^{u-1} db$$

Therefore

$$dp(u-1) = \frac{1}{b}(dp(u) - sb^{u-1} db)$$

Thus we have an expression for the change in position of component u-1 (which is closer to the object) as a function of the change of its neighboring component u. In this way, the motion of the mouse can be propagated from knuckle to knuckle, all the way back to the point of attachment to the object.

When the user is not adjusting the value of the base b, then $db = 0$ and the right hand side is simply $dp(u)/b$. This means that the knuckles can be recalculated progressively toward the object by moving each one by a fraction $1/d$ of the distance its neighbor moves. The knuckles can be recalculated progressively outward from the dragged knuckle by moving each one the same distance $dp(u)$ that the point p_u moved.

The third improvement exploits the relative calculation of distance from knuckle to knuckle. The calculations were designed to agree with the exponential function for the positions p_u. But we can continue to blithely use these relative calculations even if the initial positions of the knuckles result from a completely different distribution. For example, the knuckles can be evenly spaced rather than crowding together near the point of attachment (as in figure 2), but still retain the exponential scaling of their motion amplification. In other words, they may be displayed as if $b = 1$, but have an effect as if $b = 10$. At first blush this may seem jarring: why should we be justified in applying phoney derivatives that don't match the actual set of positions? But the idea is actually familiar in a different guise. Bump mapping assigns "fake" tangents to a polygon in order to produce more complicated reflectance effects than a flat surface can afford. So there is a precedent in cheating on a derivative in computer graphics.

As a final note, two 1-dimensional transAmps can be attached to an object to permit fine control in two different dimensions. Likewise, three transAmps can be fitted to it to permit three degrees freedom for precise translation.

2.3 Rotation Amplifiers

If you can amplify translation, you can amplify rotation. This is useful in cases when small rotations produce large results, because unlike translation (where zooming provides a simple scheme for converting mouse motion into small absolute motion in world space), rotation angles do not change when a scene is zoomed. Let $\theta(u)$ represent the angle as a function of the distance u from the point of attachment connecting a rotation amplifier (rotAmp) to an object. Initially we set $\theta(u) = \theta(0)$ for every knuckle u (which means that the scale s is zero for all the knuckles). When one knuckle is rotated by some amount $d\theta(u)$, the neighboring knuckles (working

8

inward toward the object) are updated in the same manner as for the transAmp:

$$d\theta(u-1) = \frac{1}{d}(d\theta(u) - sb^{u-1}db)$$

Just as for transAmps, knuckles on a rotAmp may be placed according to an arbitrary initial distribution θ(*u*); the values of *u* need not even be uniformly spaced. For knuckles outside the one being dragged, we apply the same incremental rotation as that of the dragged point. The inner ones are adjusted according to the iterative scheme described in the section above. Figure 4 shows

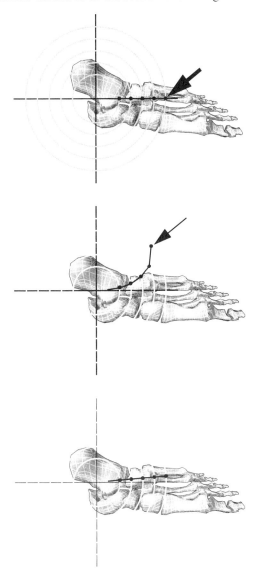

Figure 4. (Top) The outermost knuckle of the rotation amplifier is selected and dragged (arrow). The outer knuckle is rotated, changing the scale of the governing equation and producing a slight rotation of the object.
(Bottom) The knuckle is released and the widget returns to its straight-line rest state, but rotated now by a slight amount..

an example of a rotAmp before, during, and after the outermost knuckle is moved.

3 Implementation and Evaluation

The original motivation for the amplification widgets was very practical – we wanted students to exert extremely fine control over sensitive elements in a 3D simulation of optical experiments. Sometimes the user wants to quickly move from a blue wavelength (400 nm) to a red wavelength (700 nm); however, the user also needs to be able to commit minute changes (on the order of one or less than one nanometer) in the wavelength in order to observe the rapid changes in the interference patterns. For this reason we inserted amplification widgets into components of The Optics Project where they are most needed.

The Optics Project now contains more than 10 modules and is being field-tested in physics courses at several universities. Our analysis of the students' performance using the amplification widgets will not be available until after the spring semester of 2000; we plan to include the results on the Optics Project home page at www.webtop.org. The user evaluation is being developed by the Institute of the Mid-South Educational Research Association under the sponsorship of a 2-year grant from the National Science Foundation.

We developed these amplification draggers on top of the Open Inventor framework from SGI. Open Inventor provides a convenient environment for designing new widgets. It already has translation widgets (called draggers) and rotation widgets that can control 3D objects in a scene. We have also implemented the widgets using VRML and Java as part of our Web-based deployment of The Optics Project.

We have applied the widgets in several test domains. These are summarized briefly below and illustrated in figures 5-7. (1) The Optics Project: Amplification widgets allow the user to control the wavelength of light at very fine resolution in the Michelson Interferometer module, but also permit gross changes in wavelength from blue to red. The widgets allow the user to make micro-adjustments to the optical elements along the workbench in the Geometrical Optics module, but also allow elements to be moved large distances out of the way. (2) Text scrollbar: The translation amplifier has been converted into a variable-resolution scrollbar to allow either fast sweeps through a document or slower line-by-line scrolling. (3) 3D control: Multiple translation amplifiers and multiple rotation amplifiers have been combined to provide multi-resolution control of 3D position and 3D orientation.

Figure 5. TransAmp scrollbar for browsing text. Top knuckle scrolls a pixel at a time, while bottom knuckle scrolls entire pages.

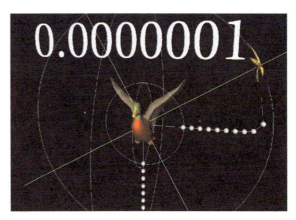

Figure 7. 3D rotation. The three gimbals provide 3D orientation control of the duck. The outermost knuckle of each rotAmp provides control at the resolution of less than a millionth of a degree.

4 Conclusions

Amplification widgets balance (1) the need for direct manipulation with (2) the need to control the position or orientation at resolutions finer than a screen cursor ordinarily permits. An amplification widget deforms when it is in use, then recovers its initial shape for repeated usage. The widgets permit a user to translate or rotate an object at fine, coarse, and in-between levels of resolution. The widgets can be composed in 1D, 2D, and 3D. We implemented translation and rotation amplification widgets for instructional modules in The Optics Project, where both fine and coarse adjustments are needed.

Acknowledgments

This work was supported in part by the National Science Foundation (grant numbers 9555053, 9624325, and 9950569). The authors gratefully acknowledge equipment provided by Intergraph Corporation. We thank Martin Reddy for his helpful suggestions on how to improve the readability of the paper.

References

[Ahlberg] C. Ahlberg and B. Shneiderman, "The Alphaslider: A Compact and Rapid Selector," Proceedings of ACM CHI '94, pp. 365-371.

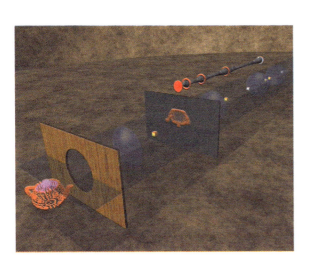

Figure 6. Simulation of geometrical optics. The transAmp (with red knuckles) allows the user to position the observation screen along the workbench, and then micro-position the screen precisely in order to bring the image into sharp focus.

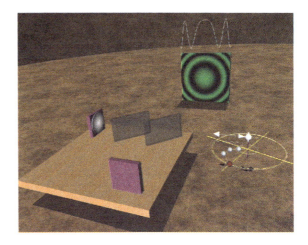

Figure 8. Simulation of the Michelson interferometer. A minuscule rotation of the elements of the apparatus produces a substantial change in the interference fringes on the observation screen. The rotAmp on the right has 4 knuckles the user can control, providing 4 levels of rotational resolution.

10

[Bier] E. Bier, M. Stone, K. Pier, W. Buxton, and T. DeRose, "Toolglass and Magic Lenses: The See-through Interface," Proceedings of ACM SIGGRAPH '93, pp. 73-80.

[Conner] D. B. Conner, S. Snibbe, K. Herndon, D. Robbins, R. Zeleznik, A. van Dam, "Three-Dimensional Widgets," Proceedings of the 1992 Symposium on Interactive 3D Graphics, pp. 183-188.

[Furnas] G. Furnas, "Generalized fisheye views." Proceedings of ACM CHI '86, pp. 16-23, 1986.

[Mackinlay] J. Mackinlay, G. Robertson, S. Card, "The perspective wall: detail and context smoothly integrated," Proceedings of ACM CHI '91, pp. 173-176.

[Mackinlay2] J. Mackinlay, S. Card, G. Robertson, "Rapid Controlled Movement Through a Virtual 3D Workspace," Proceedings of ACM SIGGRAPH '90, pp. 171-176.

[Maui] T. Masui, K. Kashiwagi, G. Borden, "Elastic Graphical Interfaces for Precise Data Manipulation," CHI '95 Conference Companion, pp. 143-144. Addison-Wesley, May 1995.

[Mine] M. Mine, F. Brooks, C. Sequin, "Moving Objects in Space: Exploiting Proprioception in Virtual-Environment Interaction" Proceedings of ACM SIGGRAPH '97, pp. 19-26.

[Poupyrev] I. Poupyrev, M. Billinghurst, S. Weghorst, T. Ichikawa, "Go-Go Interaction Technique: Non-Linear Mapping for Direct Manipulation in VR." Proceedings of UIST '96, pp. 79-80.

[Stoakley] R. Stoakley, M. Conway, R. Pausch, "Virtual Reality on a WIM: Interactive Worlds in Miniature," Proceedings of ACM CHI '95 (Denver, CO, USA, 1995), ACM Press, pp. 265-272.

Navigating Complex Information with the ZTree

Lyn Bartram
School of Computing Science
Simon Fraser University
Burnaby, BC, V5A 1S6
CANADA
lyn@cs.sfu.ca

Axel Uhl
ABB Corporate Research[†]
Heidelberg

GERMANY
axel.uhl@io-software.com

Tom Calvert
Technical University of British Columbia
Surrey, BC, V3R 7P8

CANADA
calvert@techbc.ca

[†] Current address: InterActive Software Objects GMBH, Freiburg, GERMANY

Abstract

This paper discusses navigation issues in large-scale databases and proposes hypermap visualizations as effective navigational views. We describe the ZTree, a technique that allows users to explore both hierarchical and relational aspects of the information space. The ZTree uses a fisheye map layout that aids the user in current navigational decisions and provides a history of previous information retrieval paths.

Key words: Information visualization, interactive techniques.

1 Introduction

Complex information systems demand different interface approaches from the usual desktop paradigm. People increasingly get lost in electronic space. Navigation is a familiar activity in the real world but a bewildering process in abstract information spaces which lack analogous cues and tools to situate and guide the user along desired routes. The challenge facing us is how to facilitate navigation in such systems without imposing extra cognitive overhead.

Complexity in these spaces is a function of size, scope and organisation. One taxonomy defines information structures as anarchic (arbitrary organization) vs. moderated (imposed organization) and known (fully defined) vs. unknown (constantly changing) [16]. However, even well-structured and fully-defined spaces can be "unknowable". In many applications it is the relationships between elements of information that are as interesting as the information itself, and these relationships may be both fixed (imposed by the information model) and dynamic (created by the user as part of the information assimilation task). Further, in many complex spaces it is the user's path through them (the trace of the information retrieval "dialogue") that is of interest rather than individual nodes. We use Tweedie's concept of *derived* [24] rather than *fully known* structure to express this accumulated set of retrieval paths. A user may derive different structures from the same underlying space in the context of different searches and problem-solving tasks.

While much work in information navigation has been in the well-known domain of the World Wide Web ([6,9,10]), many other information spaces present equally challenging problems. The project described in this paper concerns large-scale databases for engineering applications in which the information submits to a defined structure but is of such a size and scope that it cannot be fully known by any one user. Simple query-based approaches are insufficient: users need to understand the information in given contexts and quickly find relevant relationships to other such contexts. We are interested in discovering which elements of information visualization techniques apply well to navigational support in such systems.

Navigational approaches in large information space visualization tend to fall into two categories. Multiscale interfaces such as Pad++ [5] and EPS [7] operate on the information space directly and allow variable levels of exploration. More common are *structure views:* abstractions of the underlying structure which provide the user with selectable points to deliver detailed information in another display area (such as file system views). Our research focuses on the use of explicit map-based representations as structure views.

This paper describes the ZTree, a fisheye view based on the Continuous Zoom [3] which provides a 2D navigational map. A major issue in applying such techniques as mapping tools is the layout of the structure. An automatic layout algorithm was developed to accommodate dynamic structure accumulated as the user moves through the information space.

The paper is organized as follows. We discuss general issues of navigation and define the *hypermap*, an effective navigational tool for complex spaces. A overview of related work follows. We then briefly describe a large-scale engineering logistics application (SiLog) and the issues in navigating the information space as context for the description of the ZTree

12

interface based on the CZ and the `Grid` automatic layout algorithm. We conclude the paper with some open research questions and suggestions for further investigation and development.

2 From Structure Views To Hypermaps

How do people find information in a complex space? Furnas defines navigation as "moving oneself sequentially around an environment, deciding where to go next based on the task and the parts of the environment seen so far" [16]. Effective view navigation requires small views and short and discoverable paths [13]. Users need support in constructing an overview of the information space [16]. This helps them construct a mental map of the information structure and topology. In addition, they need history: where they've been and the set of connections and traverses they have made. A study of WWW navigation found that visualizing the entire structure was less important than being able to re-find interesting pages one had previously visited and retrace associations [10]. Finally, because navigation is a cognitive activity that requires context, users need a persistent representation of the overall space.

Humans rely on maps to navigate in the physical world. We believe that graphical maps of the information structure which elicit the familiar process of map-based navigation will be most useful in our complex environment. We extend the definition of a GIS *hypermap* [18] to be any 2D or 3D structure view which evokes three key aspects of paper-based maps: persistent overview of navigation possibilities; identification and retrieval of key features; and identification of how features relate to one another.

A 2D fisheye map of a WWW space was found to be useful because it evoked two key characteristics of paper-based maps: identification of key features, and identification of relationships between those features [10]. Map layouts exploit human spatial cognition abilities, and it appears that substantial distortion can be applied as long as relative positional constraints are respected [11].

3 Related Work

Many approaches use tree models to organize information space hierarchically and variants of tree structures to display them. TreeMaps [2] used a 2D space-filling approach to lay out a tree-structure, in which higher nodes in the tree got more space in the tree map. The resulting display gave effective contextual information and elicited the immediate perception of distribution in the tree, but individual features were difficult to discriminate once the tree was reasonably populated. Cone Trees [21] are a 3D extension to traditional 2D tree layouts, allowing a much greater amount of information to be concurrently shown at the cost of some occlusion. The user may have to rotate a node to get access to a subtree, but smooth animation

greatly reduces the cognitive transition of re-orienting the tree. Several database visualization systems incorporate Cone Tree approaches. WINONA models class-object structure in a Cone Tree view [20]. LyberWorld, a hypertext document database, uses Cone trees to represent the information retrieval history by building up a view of query paths [14]. Of particular interest is PadPrints [5], a 2D multiscale hypermap of a user's path through the WWW based on Pad++[6]. PadPrints dynamically builds up a tree structure of nodes corresponding to pages accessed which allows the user to maintain as much context as desired (by zooming in and out of the structure view) while viewing detail in the standard browser window.

All of the above are constrained by an inherent limitation of tree views: relational information that does not correspond to hierarchical structure cannot be easily shown. Thus there is great interest in exploring the flexibility and extensibility of graph visualizations. Both OFDAV [9] and NicheWorks [25] are examples of graph layouts for WWW navigation that manage arbitrarily large graphs. OFDAV does so by only rendering a subgraph around a current focus node and giving cues that lead "off-screen": the user never sees the entire context. NicheWorks employs specialized layout algorithms to cluster related elements in a graph closely together in perceptual clumps, highlighting only a few elements of interest. Design Gallery Browser [1] uses 2D and 3D graphs to layout semantically organized clusters of similar images. Thumbnails of the images surround the graph and are connected to their relevant node by links. Users navigate to a cluster by panning and zooming in the space to select full size image views, so overall context can be lost.

The lack of hierarchical structure in such graph-based approaches makes them harder to navigate than trees. Moreover, moving around the graph and adding nodes results in often disorienting reconfiguration of the layout which seriously perturbs any perceptual map the user may have had of the space, complicating feature retrieval.

A detail-in-context approach which models both hierarchical and relational structure is the Continuous Zoom [3] (CZ). Parts of the information space are summarized by being contained in closed cluster nodes, while the user can open other clusters to successively examine finer levels of detail. Such fisheye approaches[12] have been generally shown to have advantages whenever users find themselves in an information space which is too complex to easily render on one small display or window [23]. However, they tend to suffer from problems of distortion [15,22]. Our intuition is that such techniques may hold more potential as hypermaps than for their previously explored applications of direct information visualization.

Most CZ applications have been to direct

visualization of the underlying information space in which detail was mapped onto the leaf nodes. The resulting screen space issues limited the technique. However, recent approaches which use a CZ basis as structure views for network management and the WWW [10,11] have proven successful. A sample visual programming application built with the Hyper Mochi interface [27] (a CZ-based technique) suggests that the combination of hyperlinks and hierarchy provides an intuitive navigational model.

4 The Silog Project: Large-scale Logistics

Building turnkey power generation installations is an enormously complex logistical undertaking, requiring the coordination of hundreds of suppliers, thousands of shipments and millions of parts within tight time and quality constraints. An important aspect is the flow of information between all participants along the supply chain. The ABB *SiLog* (Site Logistics) application is designed to streamline processes on-site. These include handling on-site material delivery and reception, purchase requests, providing feedback on missing and broken parts and communicating changes in due dates.

Visualization and navigation of the complex logistical data must support different information retrieval and management strategies for people in different roles. For example, the project manager puts in a request like "by when do we have all parts for assembly group #123?", whereas the material handling manager might ask "where in our outdoor storage is the crate with ID #987?". Role needs are modeled as *use cases*, each with differing requirements for how the data is visualized, grouped and arranged. Not only is there an enormous amount of object data, there are also a variety of relationships between the different entities like delivery items, purchase orders or transport items. A lot of them are *one-to-many* relations where, for example, a purchase order knows the set of all delivery items it subsumes. At the same time, each delivery item pertains to a particular shipping bill of materials, which, in turn, belongs to a purchase order. Thus entities can be reached in a variety of ways. This makes visualizing the available information and streamlining the navigation a challenging task for two reasons. First, the scope and size of the information space exceeds the scope of any individual user (complexity), so the space is essentially "unknowable". Second, users need to see only the subset of the information in context to their roles. The standard query-filter-requery approach provides detail but quickly strands them in space. Thus they need a graph of both entity and structural information; more precisely, they need the derived structure [24] of the information space that fits their roles and expands to accommodate information retrieval activities.

Because large graphs are inherently difficult for humans to navigate [13,25], SiLog maps the object graph onto a hierarchy, interpreting certain edges as a containment relation. Hierarchical views tailored for particular use cases are defined for the object graph. The hierarchies are arranged so that the user gets a view that corresponds with the use case's terminology and logic. This lets us present the graph as a familiar tree view and gives the user a simplified representation of the space. Tree views allow the user to drill down and roll up specific branches of the tree (by expanding nodes and collapsing subtrees) and are generally considered to be an effective navigational tool when the underlying structure is moderately balanced [13]. However, the tree model is problematic because the structure is not exclusively hierarchical, but is also a graph with links that are not modeled by containment in the hierarchy.

To handle this problem SiLog models *canonical paths*. Each object contained in a hierarchy view has exactly one canonical path associated with it leading from the root of the hierarchy to that object. Other non-canonical paths may exist in the hierarchy leading to the same object. This conceptualizes the fact that there is a way to reach an object that is more usual to a user in a given context than any other way, but that there are other potentially relevant paths to that information. We use this concept to handle links that run across the hierarchy. Tracing a selected node in the tree view back to the root of the tree results in the navigation path leading to that node. Whenever a node in the hierarchy offers a link to an object whose canonical path does *not* start with the current navigation path, traversing this link will expand the canonical path for the reached object in the tree view and display the object there. This way, each object is represented at most once in the whole tree, but can be related to and accessed from many other parts of the tree.

While this approach provides a more tractable model of the underlying information space, it is problematic at the interface. The original SiLog interface comprises two views: a detailed *content view*, usually tables and lists of data at each node, and a tree-based structure view. The structure view supports "coarse" navigation to the node required: the user can see appropriate attributes and details in the `content view`. Selecting items in the `content view` is analogous to exploring a relationship (a cross-hierarchy link) and may result in new paths being opened in the structure view. Figure 1 shows the initial design of the structure view: an indented scrolling list akin to familiar file system viewers, called the `JTree` after the Java widget used to implement it.

The `JTree` is inadequate for visualizing and navigating even small prototype projects. The list rapidly gets large and is awkward as soon as the user needs to manipulate or discover entries that may have scrolled off the page. The user quickly loses context. Moreover, there is no clear way to emphasize or even detect relations between entities that are not hierarchical. In the prototype of Figure 1, the user

14

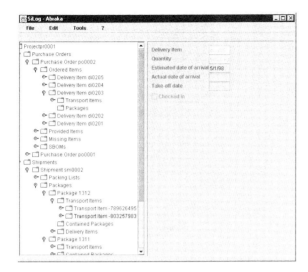

Figure 1. The *Jtree* SiLog interface

explored the **Shipments** subtree to reach **Transport Item 803257983.** Selecting a delivery item from the accompanying content view resulted in an abrupt change to the structure view: a path was opened in the **Purchase Order** subtree to the related element and the focus "jumped" to it with no accompanying visual cue to indicate the relationship and explain the sudden change to the structure view.

Our goal was the design of better navigation support for the SiLog application by combining the power of hypermapping techniques with the flexibility of detail-in-context offered by multiscale approaches. We identified the following criteria for a SiLog structure view.

- Effective view traversal and navigation: users didn't want to expend too much effort tracking down information.

- Preservation of context: information can be reached by several paths.

- Explicit visualization of relations between information elements. Derived structure must involve both paths (tree descents) and relationships (cross-hierarchy traverses).

- Automatic layout. Users do not need to see the entire space but only the subset of interest. Thus the structure view gets populated "on the fly" by user queries and needs to be dynamically reconfigured in such a way that the transitions are easily followed. Since the user's task is to find information and not to reorganize the view, this reconfiguration should not require user intervention.

Because it supports simultaneous detail and contextual views, hierarchical and associative structure, and spatial cognition [11], these criteria led us to select the Continuous Zoom as a basis for a hypermap.

5 The Ztree: A Continuous Zoom Hypermap

CZ models a hierarchical data structure with added links between arbitrary nodes in the hierarchy. Nodes represent discrete points in the information space: links represent relationships. Therefore CZ can effectively represent combinations of trees and graphs. Parts of the information space are summarized by being contained in closed *cluster* nodes while other clusters can be opened to successively examine finer levels of detail.

As described in [3], CZ manages a rectangular 2-D display space by recursively breaking it up into smaller rectangular areas, creating a hierarchy of nested rectangles. The user controls the amount of detail in different areas of the display by opening and closing clusters. The contents of an open cluster are visible, allowing one to see the deeper (more detailed) levels of the hierarchy. Closing a cluster effectively prunes a portion of the tree from the display, reducing the detail shown for that part of the system. Open clusters are allocated more space than closed clusters. In addition to this automatic resizing of cluster nodes, the user can enlarge or reduce any node on the display. Through opening and closing clusters, and resizing nodes, the user has complete control over the amount of detail seen in each part of the display. Since the entire hierarchy is visible at all times, the detailed portions always appear in context. Multiple areas can be zoomed simultaneously.

Our previous experience with the CZ in network visualization [4] indicated it was effective for navigating large, hierarchically structured graphs. The CZ effectively supports both the hierarchical and associative (topological) thinking which are essential components of information searching [17,19]. Another reason is the explicit support the CZ provides the user for recognizing and understanding her present location in the information space, a feature targeted as a major need in other complex, multiply-linked information spaces such as hypertext [26]. Finally, CZ layouts appear to exploit the spatial cognition aspects of graphical maps [11] without suffering from the excessive distortion drawbacks of other 2D fisheyes. We have hypothesized two reasons for this. First, CZ layouts do not violate relative layouts: that is, essential "left of", "inside", "on top of" relationships which are fundamental to cognitive consistency [11]. Second, smooth animations perceptually guide the user through the view transition.

5.1 ZTree Description

The ZTree is a general-purpose widget responsible for specifying an initial CZ layout, responding to application-specific events and defining how the CZ view controller interacts with other application views (in the SiLog application, the content view.) It renders some subset of the data model up to and including the entire data model based on the user's and/

or programmer's specification. When the information space is too large, application-defined heuristics can control what subset of the space is initially presented. In the SiLog case, the initial structure view only contains nodes with less than 10 children to reduce the starting complexity. This prunes large branches of the tree. Users build up a richer derived structure view through subsequent queries and browsing in the detailed view.

When the SiLog application is launched two windows appear: one with the standard SiLog view, and one with the initial `ZTree` view. Using the `ZTree` is somewhat similar to using the `JTree`. The user can open and collapse parts of the tree view; can select what to display in the Content pane from the tree view; and can select something in the `content view` which will add an open path to the tree view (perhaps dynamically changing the structure of the tree itself). The `ZTree` expands in 2D rather than in 1D, and zooming and shrinking interactions can be applied to make individual nodes larger and smaller. However, when the user causes a node to be opened, a degree-of-interest algorithm (DOI) tracks the user's attention and devotes more size to the most recent node. Thus manual sizing is possible but not necessary: desirable behaviour from the user's point of view as indicated in the Hyper Mochi study [27].

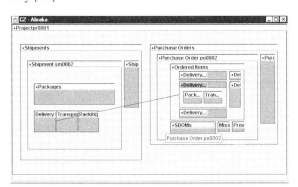

Figure 2. Expanding the `ZTree` structure through detail selections.

Items can be selected in the `ZTree` to view in more detail in the Content Pane. The `ZTree` node whose contents are currently displayed in the `content view` is considered to be the current *focus node* and its title bar is highlighted. Items selected in the `content view` affect the `ZTree` view in different ways. If the item has already been rendered (i.e., it has been laid out and specified), then the `ZTree` is opened along the relevant path in the tree structure to that item. However, if the appropriate item has not been specified and rendered it will be dynamically added to the `ZTree` structure and the `ZTree` layout will change to reflect the new node. If the item's canonical path is different from the path by which it was selected, the canonical path will be opened as well and a link drawn between the two related

elements. This behaviour causes an incrementally derived structure view to be accumulated over the user's session as she explores other parts of the information space. In the current example, when the user selects item **di0203** in the `content view`, the `ZTree` will open up the associated path for that item and indicate the relationship between the two with a link (Figure 2).

It is important to note that this behaviour is supported by the `ZTree` but must be programmatically invoked: that is, the `ZTree` has no concept of a "canonical path", but it does have methods to define and render links based on related path criteria. The resulting view both explicitly renders the relation and reduces the navigational overhead required to explore the related context (in this example, the Purchase Order). Occasionally a diagnostic message will indicate that there is not enough space to actually open the nodes: the user can then close some other nodes to free up space or can resize the `ZTree` window .

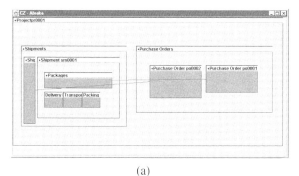

(a)

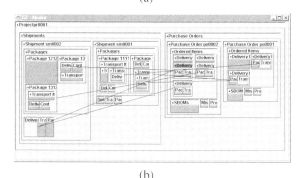

(b)

Figure 3. Virtual links in the `ZTree`.

Previous versions of the CZ supported only simple links, which could cross levels of the hierarchy but were always rendered in detail. The resulting web quickly grew too cluttered. In the ZTree, links are themselves hierarchical and selectable objects.When a cluster node is closed, any links to its children will also be "closed" and rendered as a single *virtual link*. Just as one can drill down into the space by successively opening cluster nodes, one can also explore relations in successively more detail by opening the virtual links. Figure 3a shows a a `ZTree` view with virtual links: opening the links results in the more detailed view in Figure 3b. In the interface these links are rendered in magenta and blue respectively. Finally, links also have a DOI which influences how much space they can have. This ensures that important links never get "squashed" between adjacent nodes.

The `ZTree` and CZ libraries support saving and restoring views. The derived structure displayed in the graphical map represents a composited history of the user's information forays (a graphical map of their information retrieval and problem-solving strategies). Users can thus recall their contexts over sessions, and can in fact share the maps with other users to highlight aspects of the information.

Layout: The `Grid` algorithm

The CZ algorithm has two inputs: the initial layout of the space, or *normal geometry*, and a set of scale factors (one for each node). The normal geometry and the scale factors are combined to produce the *zoomed geometry*, which is then displayed. In previous applications the normal geometry has remained constant (i.e., the space has been fully defined at runtime.) However, in hypermap applications such as the `ZTree` and CzWeb [11], the information structure can change over time as the user builds up successive paths through the information space. One approach would be to model the entire space and only render subsets of it. Indeed, the original CZ approach required the layout of the 2D space to be defined in an external map file. This is generally undesirable, as it restricts flexibility and introduces computational overhead. Instead we recalculate the normal geometry at each reconfiguration using an automatic `grid`-based layout algorithm.

2D automatic layout is an open research area in graph visualization (see [8] for an review). Force-directed (spring) layouts are common. However, in the `ZTree`, nodes are not necessarily fully connected by edges, necessitating a lattice structure to be superimposed to use a spring approach. Moreover, force-directed layouts cannot avoid overlap in all cases and do not distribute nodes aligned well with the axes of a bounding box. Instead, the `ZTree` layout problem can be seen as a variant of the bin-packing problem where the sizes of the bins are not known until the children are laid out.

We separate logical layout (topology and location) from pixel (x,y) layout. The CZ normal space consists of hierarchically organized clusters of nodes. We break this problem down into sub-problems of automatically laying out each group of siblings within a larger parent. Our logical layout approach (the `Grid` algorithm) partitions space into a rectangular `grid` of cells in which each cell is one logical unit. This `grid` is initially as close to square as possible, as we have observed that most reasonable layouts are achieved in `grids` that are either $x \times x$ or $x \times (x+1)$ units.

`Grids` can contain other `Grids` and have a 2D array of cells, a capacity (how many cells can be occupied in total), a weight (where $weight = \sum childCapacities$) and an orientation, since a `Grid` may need to be rotated to fit in the parent's available space. Each `grid` is optionally associated with some external (domain) object.

Child `Grids` can be added to the parent at any time. Children are sorted by size and inserted into the parent in a modified first-fit algorithm. Adding a child `Grid` to a parent may cause a "refit" of the parent: if there is not enough space in the parent, it will resize itself to accommodate the child and so on recursively up the hierarchy of `Grids`. If there is enough space in the parent to incorporate a rotated child, the child `Grid` will be rotated, and so will its children recursively down the tree. Nodes can be deleted in a similar fashion. There is no restriction on the size or number of `Grids` in a tree. Although theoretically this algorithm is potentially very costly, in practice the "close-to-squareness" constraint and the hierarchical partitioning of the solution space render it tractable, producing automatic layout calculation of `ZTree` spaces with no apparent performance lag.

We apply this in the `ZTree` by giving each node in the tree a `Grid`, laying out the space logically by recursively adding the child `Grids` associated with the `ZTree` node's children to that `Grid`, and then mapping the logical layout to pixel space (to account for borders, gaps between nodes, and other rendering issues.) The resulting layouts seem extremely workable. Overlap is impossible. All the layouts in the screen images in this paper were generated by this approach.

One potential disadvantage of this approach relates to the sorting of child nodes on size, since it can result in changed relative locations as new nodes are added. This can violate the consistency principle of maps discussed earlier. We are investigating variants which maintain relative layouts wherever possible.

6 Discussion, Issues and Future Work

At first inspection the `ZTree` seems to address the issues we identified for this application. It supports navigational maps which include both hierarchical and relational information (Figure 5). It allows users to drill down in the information space without sacrificing context using both node-centric (entity) and link-centric (relation) access. View traversal and navigation are aided both by persistent context and an automatic layout which preserves relative positioning necessary for effective perceptual processing. User intervention in resizing views or in re-arranging the automatic layout is supported but unnecessary. Composite graphs are built up of user information retrieval allowing the user to recall higher-level problem solving contexts and to share them with other users.

However, this is very preliminary work, and many questions remain. The obvious one is: Do the users like

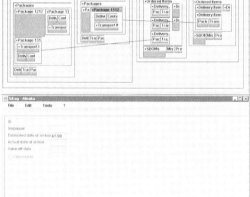

Figure 4. `JTree` and `ZTree` maps for the same paths.

it? Is it useful? We have added the `ZTree` as an alternative user interface technique to the existing SiLog application based on initial user feedback. We are hoping to arrange more detailed studies with field-based IT managers in the future. In the interim, we raise some open questions about the extent of `ZTree` utility.

Node representation and DOI: Each object (node or link) has an interest measure associated with it which is altered by user attention or by application specific factors. The DOI affects an object's chances of getting screen space. In previous CZ applications that has been useful since we use the node itself to contain information. However, as a structure view, it may make more sense to tune the DOI to other measures such as how many elements it contains, or how important it is with respect to the application, or how many times the user has visited it. Moreover, it introduces the potential for using the object space to convey information about the detailed view. How can we exploit this in a database

application, and would it be useful?

Space requirements: As Figure 5 shows, the `Ztree` can accommodate more contextual information than a scrolling list. Eventually, however, it requires more screen space than is available.Thus previously accessed nodes and links may have to be pruned from the view. There are issues to be decided in how we go about this. Do we automatically prune the view based on factors like age (least recently accessed), DOI, or distance from current focus point? Do we prompt the user to free up space and let her make the decision? This will have to be tested.

Representing links: While we feel that link manipulation and representation has great potential for facilitating database navigation and comprehension, there is as yet little knowledge and experience on how best to approach this. We hypothesize that in many complex information worlds, relations between entities are more interesting than the entities themselves. We anticipate much interesting research in this area.

7 Acknowledgments

This work was supported by a research grant from ABB Corporate Research, Heidelberg. We are indebted to our colleagues Anne Tissen at ABB and Dr. Thomas Strothotte at the Technical University of Magdeburg for their interest and feedback.

References

[1]   Andalman, B.A., Ryall, K., Ruml, W., Marks, J. and Shieber, A. "Design Gallery Browsers Based on 2D and 3D Graph Drawing", in *Proceedings of the 5th International Symposium on Graph Drawing*, ed. DiBattista,G. , Springer, 1997, pp. 322-329.

[2]   Asahi, T., Turo, D., Shneiderman, B. "Using Treemaps to Visualize the Analytic Hierarchy Process", Information Systems 6(4), Dec. 1995, pp. 357-375.

[3]   Bartram, L., Ho, A., Dill, J. and Henigman, F. "The Continuous Zoom: A Constrained Fisheye Technique for Viewing and Navigating Large Information Spaces", in *Proceedings of UIST '95*,ACM, NY 1995, pp. 207-214.

[4]   Bartram, L., R. Ovans, J. Dill, J. Dyck, A. Ho and W. Havens. "Contextual Assistance in User Interfaces to Complex, Time-Critical Systems: The Intelligent Zoom." *Proceedings of Graphics Interface '94*, pp. 216-224, May 1994.

[5]   Bederson, B.B. and J.D. Hollan. "Pad++: A Zooming Graphical Interface for Exploring Alternate Interface Physics," *Proceedings of UIST '94*, November 1994.

18

[6] Bederson, B. B., Hollan, J.D., Stewart, J., Rogers, D., Druin, A., and Vick, D. "A Zooming Web Browser", SPIE Multimedia Computing and Networking **2667**, 1996, pp.260- 271.

[7] Carpendale, M.S., Cowperthwaite, D and Fracchia,F.D. "Editing in Elastic Presentation Spaces". Submitted to UIST '99.

[8] di Battista, G., Eades, P., Tamassia, R. and Tollis, I. Algorithms for Drawing Graphs: An annotated bibliography." Computational Geometry Theory and Applications, 4(5):235-282, 1994.

[9] Eades, P., Cohen, R.F., and Huang, M.L. "Online Animated Graph Drawing for Web Navigation", in Proceedings of the 5th International Symposium on Graph Drawing, Springer, 1997, pp. 330-335.

[10] Fisher, B., Agelidis, M,. Dill, J., Tan, P., Collaud, G., and Jones,C. "CZWeb: Fish-Eye Views for Visualizing the World-Wide Web", in Proceedings of HCI International '97.

[11] Fisher, B. and Dill, J. "Application of theories of indexical cognition to a Web-based workspace." *American Association for Artificial Intelligence Symposium on Smart Graphics*, May 2000.

[12] Furnas, G.W. "Generalized Fisheye Views." *Proceedings of ACM SIGCHI'86*, pp. 16-12, April 1986.

[13] Furnas, G. "Effective View Navigation", in *Proceedings of CHI '97 Human Factors in Computing Systems*, ACM/SIGCH, N.Y., 1997.

[14] Hemmje, M., Kunkel, C., and Willet, A. "Lyber-World - A Visualization User Interface Supporting Fulltext Retrieval". in *Proceedings of ACM SIGIR 94*, ACM Press, New York, 1994.

[15] Hollands, J.G., T.T. Carey, M.L. Matthews and C.A. McCann. "Presenting a Graphical Network: A Comparison of Performance Using Fisheye and Scrolling Views." In *Designing and Using Human-Computer Interfaces and Knowledge-Based Systems*,. G. Salvendy and M. Smith (Eds), Elsevier, pp. 313-320, 1989.

[16] Jul, S. and Furnas, G. "Navigation in Electronic Worlds", *Report on the CHI 97 Information Navigation Workshop*I. ACM/SIGCHI 1997.

[17] Lai, Y. and Waugh, M. "The Effects of Three Different Hypertextual Menu Designs on Various Information Searching Activities". *Journal of Educational Multimedia and Hypermedia*, **4(1)**, March 1995.

[18] Laurini, R. and Thompson, D. Fundamentals of Spatial Information Systems. Academic Press, London 1992.

[19] Mukherjee, S., Foley, J. and Hudson, S. "Visualizing Complex Hypermedia Networks Through Multiple Hierarchical Views." *Proceedings of CHI '95*, pp. 331-339, 1995.

[20] Rapley, M. H.and Kennedy, J. B. "Three Dimensional Interface for an Object Oriented Database" in I*nterfaces to Database Systems. Lancaster 1994*, Sawyer, P., Ed.; Springer: 1995, 143.

[21] Robertson, G.G., Mackinlay, J.and Car, S.K. "Cone Trees: Animated 3D visualizations of hierarchical information." *Proceedings of CHI '91 Human Factors in Computing Systems*, ACM/SIGCHI, 1991, pp. 189-194.

[22] Sarkar, M., S.S. Snibbe, O.J. Tversky and S.P. Reiss. "Stretching the Rubber Sheet: A Metaphor for Viewing Large Layouts on Small Screens." *Proceedings of ACM UIST*, pp. 81-92, Nov. 1993.

[23] Schaffer, D., Z. Zuo, Greenberg, S., Bartram, L., Dill, J. Dubs, S and Roseman, M. "Navigating hierarchically clustered networks through fisheye and full-zoom methods. ACM Transactions on Computer-Human Interaction, 3(2):, 1996, pp. 162-188.

[24] Tweedie, L. "Characterizing Interactive Externalizations", in *Proceedings of CHI '97 Human Factors in Computing Systems*, ACM/SIGCH, N.Y., 1997, pp. 375-381.

[25] Wills, G.J. "NicheWorks - Interactive Visualization of Very Large Graphs", in Proceedings of the 5th International Symposium on Graph Drawing, Springer, 1997, pp. 404-414.

[26] Nielsen, J. "The Art of Navigating Through HyperText". *Communications of the ACM*, **33(3)**, March 1990.

[27] Toyoda, M. and Shibayama,E. "Hyper Mochi Sheet: A Predictive Focusing Interface for Editing and Navigating Nested Networks Through a Multi-Focus Distortion-Oriented View". *Proceedings of CHI '99 Human Factors in Computing Systems*, ACM/SIGCHI, 1999, pp. 504-511.

The Effects of Feedback on Targeting Performance in Visually Stressed Conditions

Julie Fraser and Carl Gutwin

Department of Computer Science, University of Saskatchewan
57 Campus Drive, Saskatoon, SK, S7N 4J2
+1 306 966-8646
[jdf804, gutwin]@cs.usask.ca

Abstract

In most graphical user interfaces, a substantial proportion of the user's interaction involves targeting screen objects with the mouse cursor. Targeting tasks with small targets are visually demanding, and can cause users difficulty in some circumstances. These circumstances can arise either if the user has a visual disability or if factors such as fatigue or glare diminish acuity. One way of reducing the perceptual demands of targeting is to add redundant feedback to the interface that indicates when the user has successfully acquired a target. Under optimal viewing conditions, such feedback has not significantly improved targeting performance. However, we hypothesized that targeting feedback would be more beneficial in a visually stressed situation. We carried out an experiment in which normally-sighted participants in a reduced-acuity environment carried out targeting tasks with a mouse. We found that people were able to select targets significantly faster when they were given targeting feedback, and that they made significantly fewer errors. People also greatly preferred interfaces with feedback to those with none. The results suggest that redundant targeting feedback can improve the usability of graphical interfaces for low-vision users, and also for normally-sighted users in visually stressed environments.

Key words: Extraordinary HCI, accessibility, low-vision users, targeting, redundant targeting feedback.

1 Introduction

The vast majority of current graphical user interfaces involve manipulation of onscreen artifacts with a mouse-controlled pointer (Johnson et al. 1995). The core activity in these manipulations, one that users carry out over and over again, is targeting— the act of moving the pointer onto a manipulable region of the screen such as a button, a window border, a selection handle, or a scrollbar arrow. For most users, targeting does not present many problems; however, for users in a visually stressed environment, targeting can be an arduous task. For example, a person with reduced visual perception may be unable to locate the pointer to begin

with, may lose track of the pointer en route to the target, or may have difficulty determining that the pointer is correctly placed on the target.

In this paper, we investigate the problem of making targeting tasks easier for visually stressed users— in particular, users who have reduced visual acuity. Two main groups of users in this category are people with visual disabilities and the elderly, but it also includes ordinary users in settings where bad lighting, fuzzy displays, or fatigue reduce visual acuity in normally-sighted users. As Alan Newell (1995) has pointed out, many situations exist where ordinary users are artificially disabled by environmental factors, and considering the design of interfaces for people with visual disabilities can have unexpected benefits for all users.

Our approach is to simplify targeting by providing the user with additional feedback during the targeting process. In particular, we consider the usefulness of feedback that indicates when the pointer enters or leaves a target. Although this kind of targeting feedback not been found to cause significant improvements in visually optimal settings (Akamatsu, MacKenzie, and Hasbrouq 1995), we believe that it will have a greater effect in a visually stressed situation. To test the usefulness of assistive feedback, we carried out an experiment where users in visually stressed conditions carried out targeting tasks with and without targeting feedback. The experiment is described below. First, however, we briefly discuss three areas that underlie the research: targeting, low-vision users, and redundant feedback.

1.1 Targeting

Targeting is the act of pointing to and selecting an object on the screen (Baecker et al. 1995). All direct-manipulation actions in graphical interfaces begin with a targeting task: for example, pressing a button, selecting text in an editor, or choosing a menu item all begin with the same user action of moving and positioning the mouse pointer. When the pointing device in the interface has an on-screen pointer (as opposed to a touch-screen or a light pen), we can divide targeting into three distinct stages: locating, moving, and acquiring.

Locating is the act of finding the mouse pointer on the computer screen when its position is unknown. Moving is the act of bringing the pointer to the general vicinity of the target, requiring the user to stay aware of the pointer's position as it travels across the screen. Acquiring is the final phase, and is the act of precisely setting the pointer over the target and determining that the pointer is correctly positioned. Acquisition requires greater fine motor control and attention to visual detail, and is the phase that we concentrate on in this work.

According to Fitts' law, targeting difficulty is determined by the size of the target and its distance from the starting location (e.g. Mackenzie 1995). Acquisition, however, is primarily affected by target size. In a standard Windows environment, there are several interface elements that are small enough to become potential targeting problems. The smallest common targets are window border at four pixels wide, and window splitters and tab stop markers at six pixels wide (see Figure 1). Other small targets include object selection handles in drawing programs (seven pixels) and window close buttons (12 pixels). Icons may also appear to have a small selectable region depending upon the visible picture, although the actual area of an icon is generally a larger region around the picture.

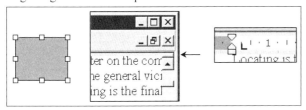

Figure 1. Small targets in the Windows environment. Left: object selection handles. Middle: window close buttons and window splitter (at arrow). Right: tab stop and indent markers.

1.2 Low-vision users

Low vision users are those people with a profoundly reduced degree of visual perception, but with enough usable eyesight to operate computer applications (Jacko and Sears 1998). There are a wide range of visual disabilities, but one of the main factors that affects people's use of graphical interfaces is visual acuity. A person with normal eyesight has a visual acuity of 20/20—from a distance of twenty feet they are able to see what any other person with normal vision can see from the same distance. However, a person with a visual acuity of 20/70 (for example) has significantly less eyesight. At twenty feet they are only able to see the level of detail that a person with normal vision sees from seventy feet. Acuity in the range of 20/70 to 20/160 constitutes moderate vision loss, while an acuity in the range of 20/160 to 20/400 constitutes severe vision loss (Levack

1994). We will use the term "low vision" to refer to both groups.

Although some assistive technologies exist for low vision users (e.g. screen magnification software), most users carry out their tasks with standard hardware and software, and most operate in a graphical interface environment (Fraser 1998). Graphical user interfaces are widely regarded as a significant step forward in the usability of computer systems. However, the shift from command line interfaces to graphical interfaces implies a trade-off for all types of computer users: while direct manipulation reduces the cognitive load placed on the user, it puts an increased demand on the perceptual systems. Graphical environments thus present a particular challenge for the sight impaired, and targeting is one of the major problems. The mouse cursor is a small, fast-moving object that can disappear against a non-contrasting background or can become lost in screen clutter. Target acquisition is particularly problematic because it requires precise visual discernment of pointer and target.

1.3 Redundant targeting feedback

Graphical user interfaces, by definition, provide a basic level of visual feedback to support targeting tasks—namely, the visual representations of the on-screen pointer and the target object. However, several applications have gone beyond this basic level to provide additional targeting feedback. This assistive information has been primarily visual, but can also be auditory or tactile information.

A common visual technique involves highlighting a selectable object when the mouse pointer enters the object's boundary. The highlight indicates that the pointer is correctly positioned to select the target. The technique can be seen in menus (see Figure 2) and more recently in application toolbars (see Figure 3). A second visual approach changes the appearance of the on-screen pointer rather than the appearance of the target. For example, when the pointer moves over a selectable window border in MS Windows, the cursor changes to indicate the resizing operation that can be performed (see Figure 4).

Auditory and tactile targeting feedback is less common in commercial applications, but has been used in assistive technology for the blind, and in a few research systems (Kline & Glinert 1995; Vanderheiden 1989). For example, Kline and Glinert explored the application of feedback intended specifically for the partially sighted. They used sounds to indicate such system events as the mouse pointer crossing a window boundary, and employed redundant visual information to assist the user in locating the pointer when it became lost.

Their additions were well received in user evaluations. Another example not designed specifically for low vision users is Gaver's (1989) Sonic Finder, which provided a range of auditory feedback to users interacting with a desktop environment. Similarly, "force-feedback" mice are available that provide tactile information when the mouse pointer passes into or out of a screen region such as a window, button, or menu item (e.g. Logitech 1998).

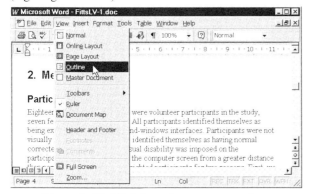

Figure 2. Highlighting of current menu item

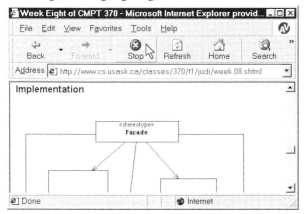

Figure 3. Highlighting (border and colour) of current button on toolbar

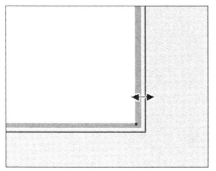

Figure 4. Cursor change over selectable window border

The usefulness of targeting feedback has been studied in a laboratory setting by Akamatsu, MacKenzie, and Hasbrouq (1995), where they examined the effects of different types of targeting feedback on traditional Fitts' law target selection tasks. The authors looked at four types of feedback: visual, auditory, tactile, and a combination of all three together. Although they did not find a significant improvement in target acquisition times or error rates for any of the feedback conditions, users expressed a preference for feedback over no feedback.

The research carried out by Akamatsu, MacKenzie, and Hasbrouq suggests that redundant targeting feedback is not useful for improving performance. However, their experiments involved normally-sighted users in an optimal viewing environment; we believe that targeting feedback will be of much more value to individuals with reduced visual acuity or individuals operating in a poor visual environment. Our overall hypothesis is that the addition of redundant feedback will make targeting tasks less visually demanding and thus easier for users with limited eyesight. The following sections describe an experiment we carried out to test this hypothesis.

2 Methodology

2.1 Participants

Eighteen undergraduate students were volunteer participants in the study, seven females and eleven males. All participants identified themselves as being experienced with mouse-and-windows interfaces. Participants were not visually disabled; all participants identified themselves as having normal corrected vision. An artificial visual disability was imposed on the participants by having them view the computer screen from a greater distance than normal. We used normally-sighted participants for two reasons. First, it would have been difficult to recruit enough visually-impaired users for the study. Second, visually-impaired users have a wide range of particular visual problems, and the wide variance in the participant population would substantially reduce the precision of our measurements. The ramifications of our choice of participants are discussed in greater detail in later sections.

2.2 Simulated visual disability

Participants were seated further from the computer screen than normal, in order to induce a simulated visual impairment. As discussed above, reduced visual acuity is one major component of visual disability, and visual acuity decreases with distance. Viewing a computer screen from a distance results in many of the types of problems experienced by real low vision users. In the study, participants were positioned by moving them back from the screen until they could no longer read text in the title bar of the application. At this distance, all participants could still see and differentiate between the objects in the test software (start region, target, and mouse pointer). This method of positioning meant that each participant sat at a different distance from the screen; however, most people were placed between five and ten feet. Although the method is imprecise, it does provide a roughly equivalent visual disability for all participants.

2.3   Apparatus

Custom software (see Figure 5) was built for the study to allow participants to carry out standard two-dimensional Fitts'-law tasks. The software was implemented with Tcl/Tk (Ousterhout 1995) and the SNACK sound extension (Sjölander 1999). The software displayed two circles on a grey background: a start region and a target. The start region was 40 pixels in diameter; the target was six pixels in diameter. Target size was chosen to roughly match the size of the smaller targets in standard Windows applications (see discussion above). The display was a nineteen-inch monitor set to a resolution of 1024 x 768 pixels; this means that the targets were 2.1 mm in actual diameter.

A single trial consisted of moving the pointer to the start region and clicking the mouse button, then moving the pointer to the target and clicking again. If the target was successfully selected, the start region was redrawn at the pointer's current position, the target would be redrawn at a new location, and a new trial would begin. Participants were instructed to continue attempting to select the target until they were successful.

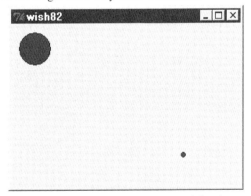

Figure 5. Target-selection software used for the study. The large circle is the start region; the small circle is the target (the window is considerably reduced in extent).

2.4   Study design and conditions

Three experimental conditions were implemented, providing different types of targeting feedback:

- No additional feedback: the target did not change when the mouse pointer entered it.

- Visual feedback: the target changed from blue to red and was highlighted with a red circle whenever the mouse pointer was inside the target (see Figure 6).

- Auditory feedback: when the pointer entered the target a 440Hz tone (approximately 'tock') was played for a duration of 0.009 seconds; on exit, a 1760Hz tone (approximately 'tick') was played for the same duration.

We used a repeated-measures within-participants design, where participants carried out trials in each of the three experimental conditions. Condition order was counterbalanced. We had three hypotheses in the study:

1. targeting feedback will reduce completion time in targeting tasks

2. targeting feedback will reduce errors (incorrect selection) in targeting tasks

3. targeting feedback will be preferred by participants over no feedback

However, we did not have a prior hypothesis about which type of feedback (visual or auditory) would be more beneficial.

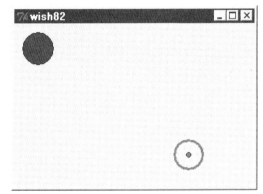

Figure 6. Visual feedback provided when the pointer was inside the target (pointer not shown).

2.5   Procedure

The experimenter positioned the participant at a suitable distance from the screen (as described above) and introduced the task. Participants completed 25 practice trials with no feedback to learn how the trials would work. Participants then carried out trials in each of the three experimental conditions: ten practice trials in order to become accustomed to the feedback, and then 32 test trials in that condition. Participants were instructed to be both as fast and as accurate as possible. The order of the conditions was randomized and counterbalanced. When all the trials were completed, participants were asked questions about their preferences and experiences.

2.6 Data collection

For each trial the following data were recorded: start position and time, end position and time, mouse clicks where the target was missed, and coordinates and time-stamps for all mouse moves. After all trials, participants were asked to rank the three conditions in terms of how easy it was to select the targets, and were asked to provide general opinions and comments about their experiences.

3 Results

We collected data to explore each of our three hypotheses— that feedback would improve completion time, error rates, and preference. Our results are organized below into these three areas.

3.1 Completion time

Each participant carried out 32 trials in each of the three conditions. Completion times were calculated using raw start and end times recorded by the software. Times for each set of 32 trials were added together to give a total time for each condition. These data are summarized in Table 1 below and illustrated in Figure 7 (error bars show standard deviation).

Condition	N	Mean	SD
No feedback	18	89.93	21.21
Auditory feedback	18	78.06	12.93
Visual feedback	18	81.91	13.46

Table 1. Mean completion times to carry out 32 trials (in seconds). N = number of participants.

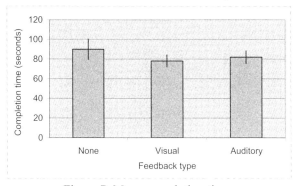

Figure 7. Mean completion times

These data show that participants selected targets more quickly with either visual or auditory feedback. When participants received visual feedback, they completed each trial about three tenths of a second faster than with no feedback; with auditory feedback, they were approximately four tenths of a second faster than with no feedback. Analysis of variance (ANOVA) indicated a main effect of feedback (F = 5.94, p < 0.05). We con-

ducted followup t-tests on each pair, using a Bonferroni correction to maintain alpha at 0.05. These tests showed significant differences between auditory feedback and no feedback (p < 0.0167) and between visual feedback and no feedback (p < 0.0167); no difference was found between auditory and visual feedback (p = 0.026).

3.2 Errors

Errors were calculated by counting the number of incorrect target selections (mouse clicks). Error data are shown below: Table 2 shows the mean error rate per trial, and these means are illustrated in Figure 8. In Figure 8, error bars show standard deviation.

Feedback type	N	Mean	SD
None	18	10.55	8.55
Auditory	18	3.00	2.30
Visual	18	4.12	3.70

Table 2. Error rates (total errors per 32 trials)

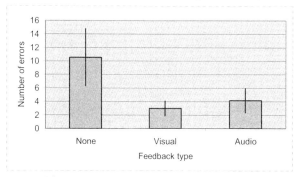

Figure 8. Mean error rates over 32 trials

Participants made fewer errors in selecting the targets when they received visual or auditory feedback. ANOVA again indicated a main effect of feedback (F = 11.72, p < 0.05). Followup t-tests showed significant differences between auditory feedback and no feedback (p < 0.0167) and between visual feedback and no feedback (p < 0.0167); no difference was found between auditory and visual feedback (p = 0.11).

3.3 Preference

Preferences were determined by asking participants to rank the three conditions in order of preference once all trials were complete. Table 3 below shows the number of participants who placed the different conditions as first, second, and third in their rankings. Figure 9 shows the totals for participants' top preference.

As is obvious from the data, the number of participants preferring some type of feedback is significantly larger than those preferring no feedback. In addition to these results, informal observations of frustration (e.g.

swearing, exclamations) were much more frequent when participants had no targeting feedback.

Feedback Type	First choice	Second choice	Third choice
None	0	3	15
Auditory	6	9	3
Visual	12	6	0

Table 3. Participant preference (cells show number of participants)

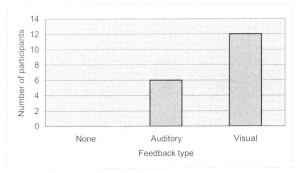

Figure 9. First preference (number of participants)

4 Discussion

Our overall hypothesis was that targeting feedback would assist users who were in a visually stressed condition with targeting tasks. Our results indicate that when users are positioned at a distance from the screen, both visual and auditory feedback lead to decreased task completion time, decreased errors, and increased satisfaction. Targeting time was reduced by three to four tenths of a second for a single task, and errors were reduced from one error in every three targeting attempts to about one in every ten. These results stand in contrast to those of Akamatsu, MacKenzie, and Hasbrouq (1995), where no significant benefits of feedback were found under optimal viewing conditions. In the following sections we discuss reasons why feedback was found to be useful in this situation, comment on how the results will generalize to real users, and suggest guidelines for adding targeting feedback to real-world interfaces.

4.1 Explanation of the results

In general terms, feedback works by providing an indication that some particular event has occurred. In this study, that event was the correct positioning of the mouse pointer over the target. The extra feedback provided in the auditory and visual conditions could lead to improved performance only when the normal feedback— that is, the visual images of the pointer and the target— was inadequate for determining that the pointer

was correctly positioned. This was the case for the participants in the study; it was clear from our observations that they found it more difficult to see the pointer and the target from a distance.

The most likely reason why we found an effect when previous studies did not is that previous targeting tasks did not approach this threshold of difficulty. People will generally maintain performance in a test situation simply by expending more effort on the task (Monk 1995); however, it appears that our tasks were difficult enough that additional effort alone could not maintain performance without additional feedback. All participants in our study sat at least twice as far from the screen as they normally would, and so they were working with objects that were considerably reduced in actual size. Doubling the viewing distance reduces the angular width of an object to half of normal and the area of the object to one quarter of normal. In addition, this reduction applies equally to the target and to the mouse pointer, further complicating the task.

Although people do not often sit far away from their displays in real life, our results suggest a continuum of difficulty where redundant feedback can be valuable to users carrying out demanding targeting tasks. The next questions to be answered are whether these kinds of demanding tasks will ever occur in the real world, and if so, what kind of feedback should be provided.

4.2 Generalizing the results to the real world

We consider the generalization of our results to two communities: first, low-vision users, and second, normally-sighted users. In each discussion, we consider how often users will have difficulty with targeting tasks, and consider how well the study participants correspond to users in the real world.

Low-vision users

Reduced visual acuity is one of the defining characteristics of a low-vision computer user. All users with moderate or severe vision loss (20/70 to 20/400) will experience difficulty in determining whether an onscreen pointer is correctly positioned over a target; therefore, targeting feedback should be particularly useful for this group and should increase in value as acuity decreases. For many low-vision users, it is *always* difficult to determine target acquisition with ordinary interface objects, and so any strategy that lessens perceptual demands will be extremely useful.

Although the simulated visual impairment used in this study does not perfectly capture the experience of users with actual impairments, we believe that our results are applicable to the low-vision user community. We chose to manipulate visual acuity specifically because it is defined in terms of distance and therefore affects all users regardless of their eyesight. Reduced acuity is a component of many visual disabilities, and so solutions that aid acuity-sensitive tasks like targeting are worth further attention, even if they must be considered in conjunction with other demands presented by a specific visual condition. As an aside, we note that many of the normally-sighted participants in the study began to exhibit behaviour and characteristics common to low-vision users (e.g. Fraser 1998) when seated at a distance from the screen. For example, people would trap the mouse pointer in the corner of the screen when it became lost, or would shake the mouse to locate the cursor. In addition, participants commented that their eyes became tired quickly and that it was hard to see the white mouse pointer against a grey background; several people stated that they would have preferred a darker background, a scheme used widely by low vision users.

Normally-sighted users

Our results can also be used to inform the design of interfaces for normally-sighted users. Although the particular situation used in our study— users sitting at a distance from the computer— will rarely happen in real life, normally-sighted users often impose other kinds of artificial visual impairments on themselves by operating computers in less-than-optimal visual settings.

As Newell (1995) states, ordinary users often find themselves in situations where they are artificially disabled by factors in the environment. A variety of these factors can contribute to reductions in visual acuity, including fatigue, eyestrain, incorrect eyeglass prescription, fuzzy or flickering displays, poor contrast, or screen glare from overhead lighting. These environmental conditions put people into a visually stressed condition similar to that imposed on the participants in this study, reducing their abilities to see mouse pointers and small targets. Any computer user who has stared at a screen all day after a poor night's sleep can attest that the mouse cursor is not always as visible as it should be. In these situations, our experimental results are likely to generalize well.

Artificial visual impairments, however, are unlikely to profoundly affect acuity; therefore, normally-sighted users are most likely to see benefits in targeting feedback for small targets that are closer to the limit of the user's visual abilities. Our discussions with users suggest that targets of about the size we studied (2-3 mm wide) are good candidates for targeting feedback: this includes interface elements such as object handles, window borders, small icons, and ruler markers. Of these elements, only window borders currently provide feedback in the Windows environment. In addition to

small targets, feedback becomes more useful when the cost of error— that is, the cost of erroneously clicking outside the target— is high. For example, there is a considerable cost in mistakenly clicking the close button of a Windows application instead of the maximize button (see Figure 1); in these cases, feedback can improve usability even with larger targets.

4.3   Type, amount, and presentation of feedback

There are many ways to provide targeting feedback, varying widely in type, amount, and presentation. Our discussions with the study participants suggest that flexibility and subtlety will be extremely important considerations when adding targeting feedback to real world applications.

A majority of the participants preferred visual feedback to auditory feedback, but many people in both camps had extremely strong preferences that are not represented in our quantitative data. Some participants were adamant that auditory feedback was the easiest condition to work under, while others remarked that the sound was distracting and made it difficult to concentrate. One user remarked that the visual feedback was too dramatic, and also somewhat distracting. These strong views suggest that feedback type should be controllable by the user. Most people were equally discerning in discussing the amount of information that should be part of targeting feedback (e.g. duration of a sound, area of a visual signal) and its presentation characteristics (e.g. volume, pitch of a sound; colour of visual feedback). There was general agreement, however, that feedback should be subtle, for the simple reason that the user's attention is already focused on the act of acquiring the target.

Since all of our participants were normally-sighted users, we cannot comment on the characteristics of feedback that will be most successful for low-vision users. This question is part of our future work in the area; however, given the wide variety of visual disabilities, it is unlikely that a single inflexible solution will be appropriate for the low-vision community.

5   Future work

Our next steps in this area will be to test the idea of redundant targeting feedback in realistic applications and with real low vision users. Realistic applications will likely demand a more subtle approach to targeting feedback, and we will re-test our hypotheses under these conditions. We are currently building a simple word processor in which targeting feedback will be available for a variety of interface elements.

One additional question to be considered in this application is how to present targeting feedback when there

26

are multiple potential targets (such as the buttons on a tool palette). To avoid confusing or distracting the user, the system must determine when a targeting action is taking place, and only provide feedback for the intended target. Pointer velocity is one possible indicator of the stage of targeting. When complete, the word processor application will be used in a longer-term realistic evaluation of targeting support, with the participation of real low-vision computer users. Although the work described here focuses on support for the acquisition phase of targeting, we are also planning to include support for locating and moving the mouse cursor.

6 Conclusion

In this paper we considered the problem of targeting, where interface elements are selected with an on-screen pointer. Under visually stressed conditions caused by small targets, visual disability, or environmental factors, targeting can become a difficult task. We hypothesized that targeting feedback could improve performance in these conditions. In contrast to studies using optimal viewing conditions, we found that auditory and visual feedback led to improved performance time and lower error rates. We conclude that targeting feedback has considerable potential both for low-vision computer users and for the normally-sighted community as well.

7 References

1. Akamatsu, M., MacKenzie, I. S., and Hasbrouq, T. *A Comparison of Tactile, Auditory, and Visual Feedback in a Pointing Task using a Mouse-type Device.* Ergonomics, 38, 816-827. 1995.

2. Baecker, R., Buxton, B., Grudin, J., and Greenberg, S. Chapter Introduction: Touch, Gesture, and Marking. In: *Readings in human-computer interaction (2nd ed.).* R. M. Baecker, W. A.S. Buxton, J. Grudin, and S. Greenberg eds. Kaufmann, Los Altos CA, 1995.

3. Fraser, J.D. *Human Computer Interaction and the Low Vision User.* Unpublished Report, Technical University of Nova Scotia, Halifax NS, 1998.

4. Gaver, W.W. The SonicFinder, An Interface that Uses Auditory Icons, *Human Computer Interaction*, 4, 67-94, 1989.

5. Jacko, J.A, and Sears, A. Designing Interfaces for an Overlooked User Group, *Assets 98: Preeedings of the Third International ACM Conference on Assistive Technologies*, (Marina del Rey CA, April 1998), ACM Press, 75 - 77.

6. Kline, R.L., and Glinert, E.P. Improving GUI Accessibility for People with Low Vision, *Proceedings of ACM CHI'95 Conference on Human Factors in Computing Systems* (Denver CO, May 1995), ACM Press, 14 - 121.

7. Levack, N. *Low Vision : A Resource Guide with Adaptations for Students with Visual Impairments.* Texas School for the Blind and Visually Impaired, Austin TX, 1994.

8. Logitech Corporation, Logitech WingMan Force-Feedback Mouse. Press release at: http://www.logitech.ch/de/about/al_006_29.html

9. MacKenzie, I.. S. Movement Time Prediction in Human-Computer Interfaces. In: *Readings in human-computer interaction (2nd ed.).* R. M. Baecker, W. A.S. Buxton, J. Grudin, and S. Greenberg eds. 483-493. Kaufmann, Los Altos CA, 1995.

10. Monk, A., McCarthy, J., Watts, L., and Daly-Jones, O., Measures of Process, in *CSCW Requirements and Evaluation*, P. Thomas ed., 125-139, Springer-Verlag, London, 1996.

11. Newell, Alan F. Extra-Ordinary Human Computer Interaction, in *Extra-Ordinary Human Computer Interaction*, A.D. Edward ed., Cambridge University Press, New York NY, 1995.

12. Ousterhout. Tcl and the Tk Toolkit. Addison-Wesley Publishing Co., Reading MA, 1995.

13. Sjölander, Kåre. The Snack Sound Extension for Tcl/Tk 1999. www.speech.kth.se/SNACK/

14. Vanderheiden, G. Nonvisual Alternative Display Techniques for Output from Graphics-Based Computers. Journal of Visual Impairment and Blindness, 1989.

Fast and Controllable Simulation of the Shattering of Brittle Objects

Jeffrey Smith
Robotics Institute
Carnegie Mellon University

Andrew Witkin
Pixar Animation Studios

David Baraff
Pixar Animation Studios

Abstract

We present a method for the rapid and controllable simulation of the shattering of brittle objects under impact. An object to be broken is represented as a set of point masses connected by distance-preserving linear constraints. This use of constraints, rather than stiff springs, gains us a significant advantage in speed while still retaining fine control over the fracturing behavior. The forces exerted by these constraints during impact are computed using Lagrange multipliers. These constraint forces are then used to determine when and where the object will break, and to calculate the velocities of the newly created fragments. We present the details of our technique together with examples illustrating its use.

Key words: Physically-based modeling, computer animation, impact, brittle materials.

1 Introduction

Realistic animation of breaking objects is difficult to do well using the traditional computer animation techniques of hand modeling and key-framing. This difficulty arises from the fact that the breaking of an object typically creates many small, interlocking pieces. The complexity and number of these fragments makes modeling them by hand all but impossible, but the distinctive look of a shattered object prevents the use of simple short-cuts, such as slicing the surface of an object into faces or the use of RenderMan shaders.

Consequently, the simulation of breaking and shattering has received some attention within the graphics community. An early attempt at modeling fracture is given in Terzopoulos and Fleischer[12], where they presented a technique for modeling viscoelastic and plastic deformations. While not specifically intended to model the breaking of brittle objects, their work allowed the simulation of tearing cloth and paper with techniques that could conceivably have be applied to this task. In 1991, Norton et. al. [7] described a technique specifically for modeling the breaking of three-dimensional objects wherein the object to be broken was subdivided into a set of equally-sized cubes attached to one another with springs. Unfortunately, their use of an elastic network invited massive

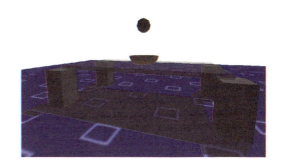

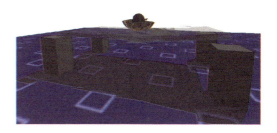

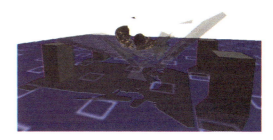

Figure 1: *A bowling ball is dropped onto a ceramic bowl that is sitting on a thick glass table. Images are roughly 0.33 seconds apart*

computational expense for large objects. Most recently, O'Brien and Hodgins[8] used continuum mechanics techniques developed in mechanical and civil engineering to model flexible objects, which included crack initiation and propagation. This method was rather slow, however, due to a combination of high physical realism and a complex system for dynamically re-meshing the solid during simulation.

Unsurprisingly, the fields of condensed-matter physics and materials science have examined this topic more thoroughly. Within the past decade many papers have been published on the subject of the simulation of brittle[1] fracture. A commonly used approach in these papers is the lattice model (Arabi[1], Chung[3], Donze[4]). This method models objects as a lattice of points or point-masses connected by stiff springs. During simulation, the extension of each spring, or some other potential function of the particle displacements, is computed. Depending on the model, either every element exceeding its extension or potential limit, or only the most egregious violator, is removed. The state of the system is cleared and the process repeated until the object falls apart, or until no new elements are being broken.

Although simple and general, the simulation methods outlined in the materials science literature are inappropriate for graphics applications. In general, materials scientists are interested in predicting with great accuracy how and when an object will shatter, whereas a computer animator is more concerned with generating realistic-looking behavior in a reasonable amount of time. Consequently, the level of physical detail used in materials science simulations is much higher, and often of a different nature, than we require.

A significant disadvantage of material science lattice solutions is that they almost universally use three-dimensional systems of stiff springs combined with explicit numerical integration methods The step sizes for this type of simulation must be on the order of the inverse of the speed of sound in the material being simulated, and thus the computational expense can be high. (Even with the use of implicit integration methods, the simulation of a lattice of stiff springs entails a computational cost as least equal to that of Lagrange multipliers.) For example, in Chung[3], the simulation of an object with 2701 lattice-links is done in 137 time-steps, each taking 86 seconds on a 75MHz MIPS R8000, for a total of three and a half hours. A comparable simulation with our method on the same hardware would take roughly five and a half

minutes.

The continuum mechanics approach used by O'Brien and Hodgins[8] does not explicitly use a lattice of springs attached to point masses, but their method suffers from some of the same computational slow-downs. Specifically, their use of Euler and second-order Taylor integrators restricts the time step of simulation to extremely small values. Due to their re-meshing technique, the timing of the examples presented in their paper is difficult to directly compare with our own. As a rough comparison, their "wall #2" mesh, with a final total of 8275 elements, took an average of 1098 seconds of computation per simulation second on an 195 MHz R10000 processor. Running a similarly sized model with the same impact and fragmentation characteristics took roughly 90 seconds for a complete simulation with our technique.

In this paper, we present a fast and controllable method for simulating the fracture of brittle objects for animation. This method differs from the majority of the reviewed literature in that we use a system of point-masses connected by workless, distance-preserving constraints to represent the object, rather than a lattice of stiff springs. Our use of rigid constraints follows from an abstraction of brittle material properties and allows us to solve for the forces exerted by these elements during impact much more quickly than using explicit methods and an elastic mesh. We compute our solution by constructing a large, sparse, linear system which we solve using conjugate gradient methods. The constraint forces, once calculated, indicate when and where the object will break. This information is then used to construct the fragments of the broken object from the original geometry and to solve for the final linear and angular velocities of these bodies. In addition to advantages of speed, our system retains a great deal of user controllability while still yielding realistic-looking output, making it well-suited for use in animation.

2 Modelling

As mentioned above, our lattice method is roughly based on the elastic networks common in material science literature. However, instead of a three-dimensional mesh of springs we use a lattice of rigid constraints to connect point-masses. We are motivated in this choice by both speed considerations and the nature of ideal brittle materials.

Consider the naive system of points and springs. Since we are simulating brittle objects, these springs must be very stiff: stiff enough that no visible flexing (plastic deformation) takes place during high-momentum impact. As the brittleness of an object increases, the stiffness of these springs increase, and the displacements they under-

---

[1]The term "brittle," as used in materials science literature (and in this paper) means that the substance does not undergo significant plastic (reversible) deformation before breaking[2]. That is, a brittle object will not bend much under stress, but either will resist almost completely or break catastrophically.

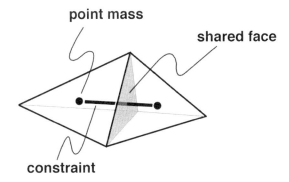

point mass

shared face

constraint

Figure 2: Two tetrahedra and their point/constraint complement

go during impact decrease. In the limit, then, for an ideally brittle material we would be forced to model springs which are infinitely stiff and undergo infinitesimal displacements.

Instead, we idealize these stiff springs as distance-preserving constraints and, rather than calculating displacements, calculate the forces that these constraints exert in response to an applied impulse. As mentioned earlier, a significant problem with simulating large systems of springs is the computational expense of explicit numerical integration. Our use of distance-preserving constraints allows a faster method of solution (discussed in section 3) while retaining both realism and a large amount of user-controllability.

2.1 Constructing the Model

The first step in our simulation is the construction of a solid model — consisting of a collection of simple polyhedra — from the initial description of the object to be shattered. Since this initial description is usually a set of points and faces describing only the surface, we first add a large number of well-distributed points inside this surface.

The addition of internal points is followed by a constrained Delaunay tetrahedralization. This operation yields our solid model, which consists of a set of connected tetrahedra. We then transform this solid model into a lattice representation — our final model. This lattice representation is simply the Voronoi complement (or "dual") of the solid object, which represents the tetrahedra as point-masses and their connections (shared faces) as rigid constraints (figure 2). Each point-mass is placed where the center of the tetrahedra it represents was located and the mass of each point is determined by the volume of the tetrahedra and the density of the object in that volume.

The rigid constraints connecting these point-masses

have an associated ultimate strength which corresponds physically to the strength of the bond between two "micro-fragments" of the original object. If the tensile or compressive forces across a constraint exceeds this strength then the bond will be broken.

The breaking strength of a constraint is determined though a combination of user-specified functions and a pair of simple heuristics based upon the the geometry of the two tetrahedra the constraint is "gluing" together. In our model, the strength of a constraint scales with the volume of the connected tetrahedra and with the area of their shared face. By relating the strength of a constraint to the size and shape of the tetrahedra it connects, the breaking behavior will be influenced by the geometry of the object, which is necessary for physically realistic results.

In addition to these simple geometry-based heuristics, the user may add a procedural variation to the constraint strengths. For example, simple cleaving planes may be added by systematically reducing the constraint strength along a cross-section of the object, or nodes of great strength may be created which will result in intact nodules remaining after the rest of the object is shattered. We have also achieved good results using noise and turbulence functions, as described in Perlin[9]. Much of the flexibility of our model comes from an appropriate choice of the function that determines the constraint strengths.

3 Simulation

Our approach to the simulation of fracture is a simple one, intended to avoid the computational expense and complexity of a full dynamic simulation while preserving physical realism. Although the time course of impacts can be as little as 100 microseconds, the speed of sound is brittle materials is typically several thousand meters per second[2]. Given that the objects we wish to shatter are of moderate size (usually on the order of 10 cm on a side), the time to equilibrate internal forces (transmitted at the speed of sound) is on the order of one microsecond. Because the duration of a typical impact is so much longer than the time it takes the internal stresses to reach equilibrium, we make a quasi-static loading approximation, and can safely use global solution methods to calculate the forces between elements of the solid.

3.1 Fundamentals of the Simulation

We formulate the problem of calculating the forces being exerted by the rigid constraints as one of solving for Lagrange multipliers in the following simplification of the constraint force equation (For a derivation of this equation, see Witkin and Baraff[13] or Witkin, Gleicher and

---

[2]5100 meters/second in common glass and between 3500 and 7000 meters/second in hard stone.

30

Welch[14]):

$$JWJ^T \vec{\lambda} = -JWQ^T \qquad (1)$$

where W is the inverse mass matrix and Q is the global force vector, containing information on what forces are being exerted on which particles by the impact.

The matrix J is defined as

$$J = \frac{\partial C}{\partial p}$$

where C is the "constraint vector": a vector of functions — one for each constraint in the system — whose values are zero if the constraint is being satisfied and non-zero otherwise. If we wish to introduce prior material stresses, the initial constraint vector may be given non-zero entries and equation 1 must then be changed to

$$JWJ^T \vec{\lambda} = -JWQ^T - kC$$

where k is some unit-normalizing factor.

Each constraint function is of the form

$$C_i(p_a, p_b) = \|p_a - p_b\| - d_i$$

where p_a and p_b are the locations of the two particles connected to constraint i, and d_i is the length of the constraint.

After solving equation 1 for $\vec{\lambda}$, we can calculate $\hat{Q}$

$$\hat{Q} = J^T \vec{\lambda}$$

which is the vector containing the forces being exerted by each constraint in reaction (and opposition) to the applied forces, Q. These values of $\hat{Q}$ are then used to determine which constraints should be broken. Specifically, if a constraint is found to be exerting a force greater than its strength, it is removed. It should be noted that intergranular bonds in brittle materials are eight times stronger under compression than during extension [5], and this must be accounted for in our breaking decision-rule.

3.2 Physically Realizable Solutions

The system which we are solving:

$$JWJ^T \lambda = b \qquad (2)$$

is underconstrained in the sense that for a given b, there are any number of $\vec{\lambda}$'s which satisfy the equation. However, an arbitrary vector $\vec{\lambda}$ does not necessarily correspond to a physically realizable set of constraint forces between connected particles. Given this fact, how can we be certain that our solution to equation 1 is the physically realizable one?

First we note that those solutions which are physically meaningful have a particular structure. Consider again

the connections between particles to be stiff springs. In this case, the only internal forces that can arise are those that have been generated due to some displacement δp of the particles. These displacements in turn correspond to a vector of spring tensions $\vec{\lambda} = J\delta p$. We can therefore see that all physically realizable $\vec{\lambda}$'s can be written as $\vec{\lambda} = J\delta p$ for some displacement δp. (We could parameterize by δp, but our solution would still have to satisfy equation 2 and our system would be more complex.) Stated a different way, any physically realizable $\vec{\lambda}$ must lie within the column-space of J and thus also in the column space of JWJ^T (regardless of J's rank; see Strang[11] for details).

Note, though, that any solution $\vec{\lambda}$ of equation 2 that lies in the column space of JWJ^T is a minimum-norm solution. Thus, physically realizable solutions are equivalent to minimum-norm solutions, and since the minimum-norm solution to a linear equation is unique (Strang[11]), so is the physically realizable solution. Therefore, a solution method which finds a minimum-norm solution of equation 2 is guaranteed to give us the unique physically realizable solution $\vec{\lambda}$.

We use the conjugate gradient method to solve for the minimum-norm solution of our system. Not only will it give us the correct solution, as shown above, but it exploits the sparsity of the JWJ^T matrix to give us fast solution times[10].

3.3 Multiple-Step Solutions

It would appear that the simulation of an impact could be done with a single-step solution for $\hat{Q}$. However, our use of a global solution method would permit constraints to "transmit" forces of arbitrary strength before being removed, whereas we desire the constraints to be able to transmit no more force than their breaking strength would allow. Visually, a single-iteration solution results in the pulverization of a large volume surrounding the impact without the distinctive shards and fragments we desire.

Instead of a single iteration, however, we can solve for $\hat{Q}$ in multiple steps, increasing the impact force with each iteration. In this way we can slowly ramp up the magnitude of the impact so that we are certain that no constraint transmits a force greater, to within some ϵ, than its breaking strength. By gradually increasing the magnitude of the impact force, we are impressing a pseudo time-course upon our simulation. That is, rather than simulating an impact as a single, zero-time impulse, we are creating a more realistic impact history. For all examples given in this paper, we used the simple piecewise linear function shown in figure 3 as our impact schedule.

Since, as mentioned before, the time to equilibrate the forces within a brittle object is much less than the duration of the impact we can safely chop this duration into

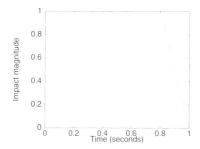

Figure 3: Impact magnitude versus time

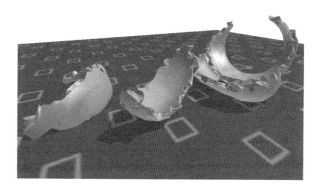

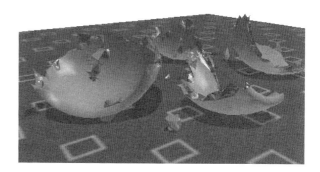

Figure 4: Glazed ceramic bowl, before (top) and after being broken with two different constraint-strength distributions

smaller segments without losing the ability to solve with a global method. In practice, we have found that around 50 iterations of this loop generally yields acceptable results. Increasing the number of iterations beyond this brings little or no change in the fracturing behavior.

3.4 Crack Growth

Another important feature of brittle fracture that we would like to capture in our simulation is the growth of cracks. In brittle materials, the energy required to start a new crack of length *l* is significantly higher than the energy required to lengthen an existing crack by the same distance[6]. This behavior is the major reason why glass — despite its material homogeneity — breaks into large, polygonal shards under impact rather than turning into a cloud of tiny fragments.

In order to encourage the growth of pre-existing cracks, we modify our multi-step algorithm. When we remove a newly-broken constraint, we weaken the constraints around it that correspond to faces which adjoin the just-broken constraint. Thus, in the next iteration it is more likely that these constraints will break than constraints with an equal initial breaking-strength that are not connected to a pre-existing crack. By specifying what form this function takes the desirability of creating new cracks versus spreading existing flaws can be easily controlled.

To illustrate this effect, three examples were generated using the same model — a simple rectangular plank — the only difference between the simulations being the crack growth function used. The model used contained 3962 tetrahedra with 7096 shared faces. Constraint strengths varied between 90.2 and 541.0, having been generated with a combination of a turbulence function and the geometric heuristics described in section 2.1 Although these objects all have the same initial geometry and constraint values and are broken with the same impact, significantly different results were produced. Figure 5 shows (from the top) the aftermath of this test solid being fractured with no crack growth function. Here, dark lines show the edges of the top-facing tetrahedral faces and white lines indicate crack boundaries. We can

 Graphics **Interface** 2000

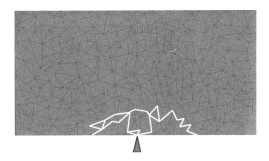

Figure 5: Top view of broken plank, showing cracks between tetrahedra

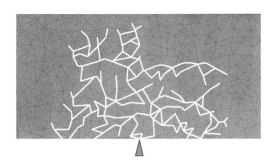

Figure 7: Top view of broken block, showing dramatic crack growth

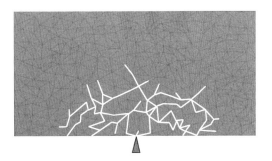

Figure 6: Top view of broken plank, showing moderate crack growth

see from this picture that the cracks which resulted in the fragmentation of this object have not spread far beyond the immediate impact location (the tip of the triangle).

Figure 6 shows the results of the same object being broken, but with a crack growth function that reduces constraint strengths by up to a factor of two. Specifically, the function

$$s_{new}^i = s_{old}^i (1.0 - \frac{1}{2}\sin(2\theta + \frac{\pi}{2}))$$

where θ is the angle between some constraint broken in the previous time-step and the neighboring constraint i (between $-\frac{\pi}{2}$ and $\frac{\pi}{2}$). s_{old}^i and s_{new}^i are the old and new constraint strengths respectively. This crack growth function has encouraged the creation of more fragments, and has permitted parts of the object further from the impact site to break.

Finally, figure 7 shows the results our test object being broken again, but with a more extreme crack growth function. This function reduces constraint strengths by up to a factor of 1000:

$$s_{new}^i = s_{old}^i (0.5005 - 0.4995\sin(4\theta + \frac{\pi}{2})) \quad (3)$$

Not surprisingly, cracks have propagated deeply into the solid and have caused it to break into many more pieces.

As can be seen from the three examples, even simple changes in the crack growth function can significantly alter our results, allowing the user further control over the material properties of the object.

3.5 Using the Results

Our algorithm produces as its output a large set of solids, each of which corresponds to a fragment of the original object. From the force of the impact and the individual masses of these fragments, we can easily compute their resulting angular and linear velocities.

Given a point i, we know that

$$\dot{p}_i = v_i + \omega_i \times p_i$$

where $\dot{p}_i$ is the velocity of the point, v_i is the strictly linear velocity, ω_i is the angular velocity and p_i is its position. Thus, if we have a solid with three distinct points on its surface, p_0, p_1 and p_2, (trivial, since our most primitive solid is a tetrahedra), we can separate v_{solid} from ω_{solid} by solving the following simultaneous equation:

$$\begin{bmatrix} I & -p_0^* \\ I & -p_1^* \\ I & -p_2^* \end{bmatrix} \begin{bmatrix} v_{solid} \\ \omega_{solid} \end{bmatrix} = \begin{bmatrix} \dot{p}_0 \\ \dot{p}_1 \\ \dot{p}_2 \end{bmatrix}$$

where I is the 3 by 3 identity matrix and p^* is the dual matrix:

$$\begin{bmatrix} 0 & -p_z & p_y \\ p_z & 0 & -p_x \\ -p_y & p_x & 0 \end{bmatrix}$$

With these velocities in hand, we can perform a dynamic physical simulation to produce an animation of the aftermath of shattering.

4 Results and Discussion

We have described a simple, physically-motivated model for the rapid simulation of brittle fracture. The following examples illustrate the output of our work and demonstrate some of the different fracturing behaviors and material properties that can be simulated.

4.1 Wine glass

The examples shown in figure 8 were generated from the same geometric data: a wine glass modeled as 3422 tetrahedra with 6447 shared faces. Differences in fracturing behavior were produced by changing the function that determined the strengths of the constraints. More specifically, the constraint strengths were determined by a combination of a thresholded turbulence function and the geometric heuristics outlines in section 2.1. Each glass was broken with a single impact at the point where it struck the floor after falling.

4.2 Clay pot

Figure 4 shows before and after images of a pot, made from glazed earthenware. This model was constructed from 6902 tetrahedra, with 13150 shared faces. In the middle image, the initially homogeneous constraints were alternately strengthened and weakened along the vertical axis. This variation yields the the characteristic breaking behavior of pottery created without a wheel, out of a single coil of clay. The lower image shows the same geometric model, but with constraints modified only by geometric factors and a mild turbulence function, which yields a very different set of fragments.

4.3 Glass table

Figure 1 shows a sequence of six images of a ceramic bowl, sitting on a thick glass table, broken by the impact of a falling bowling ball. For this example, the strength of the constraints in both broken objects (the bowl and the table-top) were homogeneous; modified only by the standard geometric factors. The crack growth function used in the table was that described in equation 3 which contributed to the formation of the long, narrow glass-like fragments.

4.4 Timing

Two major steps are involved in the destruction and subsequent animation of a shattered object: the impact calculation, and the reconstruction of the new fragments' surfaces afterwards. The left graph in figure 9 shows the amount of time required for each impact step calculation as a function of the the number of constraints (shared faces) in the lattice model. (All timing was done on a 195 MHz R10000 SGI Octane.)

As can be seen, even for relatively large objects the impact simulation is computationally inexpensive. Since we are repeatedly solving a sparse linear system with the conjugate gradient method, our computational cost varies between $O(mn\log n)$ and $O(mn\sqrt{n})$ depending on the structure of JWJ^T.

Reconstruction of the fragments after impact requires similarly few resources. The right-hand graph in figure 9 shows the time required to construct the surfaces and ve-

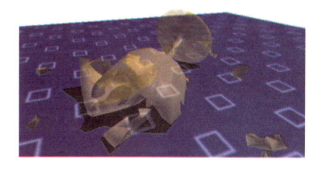

Figure 8: Three broken wine glasses, demonstrating different fracture behavior

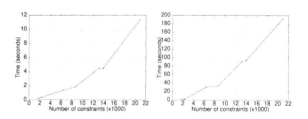

Figure 9: Time per impact step versus total number of constraints (left) and time required to construct fragments versus total number of constraints (right)

34

locities of the new fragments after impact. We find, then, that the total the time required to break and reconstruct models of moderate size (several thousand constraints) is only a few minutes.

5 Conclusion

We have presented a fast and controllable method for the simulation of the shattering of brittle objects. By framing the problem in terms of distance-preserving constraints rather than stiff springs, we have avoided expensive explicit solution methods while retaining physical accuracy. Furthermore, our method allows simple control over the ultimate number, size and shape of the fragments by adjusting the strength of the constraints throughout the body or by changing the nature of crack growth within the material. Combined with speed and accuracy, this controllability makes our method useful for the otherwise difficult task of animating complex, realistic shattering.

A significant limitation of our method, however, is the fact that, before fracturing behavior can be simulated, we must have a fully tetrahedralized model of the object to be broken. This requirement entails several disadvantages. First, the files describing the geometry of the object to be broken can become quite large, although compression of the text files, or storage in a compact binary form will offset this to a large degree. More significantly, a complete prior meshing means that fractures will only occur along mesh boundaries. Thus, if we wish to avoid meshing artifacts and "jaggy" fracture boundaries, the tetrahedralization must be done at a high resolution, which increases the computational expense (see figure 9). A solution to this shortcoming which we plan to pursue is to use a hierarchical approach along with fracture-boundary re-meshing such as that described in O'Brien and Hodgins[8]. This planned improvement, combined with more realistic crack-propagation functions, should substantially increase the realism of our method, which still allowing a great deal of user control over the fracture process.

References

[1] S. Arbabi and M. Sahimi. Elastic properties of three-dimensional percolation networks with stretching and bond-bending forces. *Physical Review B*, 38(10):7173–7176, 1988.

[2] G.P. Cherepanov. *Mechanics of Brittle Fracture*. McGraw-Hill, 1979.

[3] J.W. Chung, A. Roos, and J. Th. M. De Hosson. Fracture of disordered three-dimensional spring networks: A computer simulation methodology. *Physical Review B*, 54:15094–15100, 21.

[4] F. Donze and S.-A. Magnier. Formulation of a 3-d numerical model of brittle behavior. *Geophysical Journal International*, 122(3):709–802, 1995.

[5] A.A. Griffith. The theory of rupture. *The Proceedings of The First International Congress of Applied Mechanics*, 1924.

[6] B. Lawn. *Fracture of Brittle Solids*, chapter one: "The Griffith concept". Cambridge University Press, 1993.

[7] A. Norton, G. Turk, B. Bacon, J. Gerth, and P. Sweeney. Animation of fracture by physical modeling. *Visual Computing*, 7(4):210–219, 1991.

[8] J. O'Brien and J. Hodgins. Graphical modeling and animation of brittle fracture. *SIGGRAPH 99 Conference Proceedings*, 33:287–296, 1999.

[9] K. Perlin. An image synthesizer. *SIGGRAPH 85 Conference Proceedings*, 19(3):287–296, 1985.

[10] Jonathan R. Shewchuk. An introduction to the conjugate gradient method without the agonizing pain. Technical Report CMU-CS-94-125, Aug. 1994.

[11] G. Strang. *Linear Algebra and its Applications*. Harcourt Brace Jovanovich, 1988.

[12] D. Terzopoulos and K. Fleischer. Modeling inelastic deformation: Viscoelasticity, plasticity, fracture. *SIGGRAPH 88 Conference Proceedings*, 22:287–296, 1988.

[13] A. Witkin and D. Baraff. *Physically Based Modeling: Principles and Practice*, chapter Physically Based Modeling. SIGGRAPH Course Notes, ACM SIGGRAPH, 1997.

[14] A. Witkin, M. Gleicher, and W Welch. Interactive dynamics. In *Proceedings of the 1990 Symposium on Interactive 3D Graphics*, volume 24, pages 11–21, March 1990.

Skinning Characters using Surface-Oriented Free-Form Deformations

Karan Singh
karan@paraform.com

Evangelos Kokkevis
vangelisk@home.com

Alias|wavefront
210 King St. E., Toronto, Canada M5A 1J7

Abstract

Skinning geometry effectively continues to be one of the more challenging and time consuming aspects of character setup. While anatomic and physically based approaches to skinning have been investigated, many skinned objects have no physical equivalents. Geometric approaches, which are more general and provide finer control, are thus predominantly used in the animation industry. Free-form deformations (FFD) are a powerful paradigm for the manipulation of deformable objects. Skinning objects indirectly using an FFD lattice reduces the geometric complexity that needs to be controlled by a skeleton. Many techniques have extended the original box-shaped FFD lattices to more general control lattice shapes and topologies, while preserving the notion of embedding objects within a lattice volume. This paper in contrast, proposes a surface-oriented FFD, where the space deformed by the control surface is defined by a distance function around the surface. Surface-oriented control structures bear a strong visual semblance to the geometry they deform and can be constructed from the deformable geometry automatically. They also allow localization of control lattice complexity and deformation detail, making them ideally suited to the automated skinning of characters. This approach has been successfully implemented within the *Maya2.0* animation system.

Key words: Character animation, skinning, deformers, free-form deformations.

1 Introduction

A layered approach [1] to the modeling and animation of articulated figures is a widely adopted methodology. The layers may be broadly classified into skeletal, muscle, underlying tissue and skin. These layers are largely symbolic of their contribution to the visual appearance of the animated character, since physical equivalents of bones or muscles for characters modeled from inanimate objects such as a lamp, need not exist. Hair, clothes and accessories form further layers on many characters. Layers are often omitted, collapsed together, or further classified depending on the sophistication of the application.

The *skin* is particularly important since it largely establishes the visual appearance of a character. A number of techniques for the modeling and animation of the *muscle* and *skin* layers have been investigated [1, 5, 10, 11, 13, 16, 17, 18]. The typical workflow for setting up an articulated character involves building a model representing the geometric skin of the character in some pose. An underlying skeletal structure comprising of reference frames at joints is also constructed to control the movement of the articulations. More sophisticated methodologies sometimes also model underlying bones and muscles using geometry. The skinning algorithm is responsible for deforming the geometric skin to respond to the motion of the underlying skeleton. Skinning approaches can be classified as geometric or physically based. While a number of physical models for muscle and skin [4, 11, 16, 18] exist, techniques used in the animation industry continue to be predominantly geometric [1, 5], because of their generality and control.

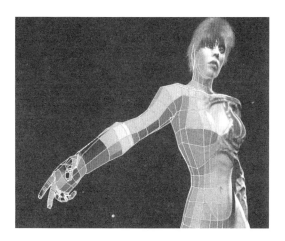

Figure 1: Surface-oriented FFD overlaid on a character

It is worth noting that characters are often modeled using a number of adjacent parametric surface patches, for reasons of smoothness and ease of modeling, texturing and rendering. Animators, however, would rather deal with a single contiguous skin surface since it obviates issues of continuity between adjacent pieces of skin during animation. A geometric skinning approach that presents a single skin interface for setup and animation is thus desirable. Subdivision surfaces provide the smoothness and parameterization characteristics of surface patches while presenting a single control mesh as an animation interface [5]. We aim to provide the animation interface and control of a subdivision surface to an underlying skin of arbitrary geometric representation.

A good skinning algorithm needs to provide an automated attachment of points representing the skin surface of a character to an underlying skeletal and muscle structure. Subsequently, it should be easy for an animator to edit the default attachments, as it is difficult to universally predict how an arbitrarily shaped object is intended to be controlled by its skeleton. Once pieces of skin are attached to corresponding pieces of muscle and bone, the strength with which pieces of the skin are deformed by parts of the skeleton should be easy to control. The effect on skin from changes in underlying layers, such as muscle shape or bone position should be easy to overlay. We avoid an explicit bone and muscle model since the range of articulated deformable objects and skin deformation effects is as vast as the animator's imagination. Instead we emphasize a system where any localized deformation can be easily specified and controlled by underlying skeletal motion. The resulting skin deformation should be smooth and predictable. Finally, the approach should be efficient allowing real-time interactivity for at least a low resolution model of the geometric skin. Empirical geometric approaches to skinning [1, 10, 13, 17] have shown realistic results at interactive rates.

A number of techniques have advanced the box-shaped lattices of the original FFD formulation [12], to allow for greater generality in the shapes and topologies of the control lattice. This is in accordance with the general trend for the control structures of higher level deformation techniques to bear a visual correlation to the geometry they deform [5, 14]. Most FFD approaches, however, preserve the notion of a volume enclosed by the control lattice, within which objects are embedded.

In contrast, we propose here a deformation technique that is surface-oriented. The region of space deformed by the control point structure is not the volume enclosed by the control points but is based on a distance metric from a surface defined by the control point structure. Surface-oriented deformation control structures provide a better visual representation of the geometry they deform and can typically be constructed from the deformable geometry itself (See Figure 1). They allow better localization of control lattice complexity and deformation detail as illustrated by the results in our implementation.

Our surface-oriented FFD thus aims to represent and control any underlying object by a single control polymesh. Unlike subdivision surfaces the control polymesh does not have a limit surface that represents the object. Our goal instead is to allow the advantages of a single control mesh to represent and control an object that has an alternate surface model (such as a set of surface patches, a different control mesh or even a subdivision surface). The control mesh can be used to both visually represent the surface model and to drive the deformation of the object. The control mesh can be user created or automatically synthesized from data, for example by tesselating and stitching various surface patches that define the deformed skin. In addition to their application in skinning characters, surface-oriented FFDs are a useful tool for the multi-resolution modeling and animation of objects.

The remainder of this paper is organized as follows: Section 2 describes characteristics of existing free-form deformation techniques and motivates the surface-oriented free-form deformation approach. Section 3 presents the surface-oriented deformation algorithm. Section 4 provides an analysis of the properties of the algorithm and describes an extension of it. Section 5 describes the implementation of an automated skinning workflow based on surface-oriented free-form deformations, within the modeling and animation system *Maya2.0*. Section 6 concludes with a discussion of the results obtained.

2 Free-form Deformation Techniques

In this section we present an overview of a number of existing free-form deformation techniques and contrast their properties with the characteristics of our surface-oriented deformation algorithm described in Section 3.

Free-form deformations (FFD) were originally introduced by Sederberg and Parry [12] as a general technique where objects are deformed by warping a volume of space within which the objects are embedded. The volume of space is typically defined using a structure connecting a set of control points. Spatial deformations are then accomplished by the manipulation of these control points. A one-to-one correspondence is established between points within the original and deformed volumes of space. Objects embedded within the original volume are thus deformed by mapping the point-set representing the object to their corresponding points in the deformed volume. This process typically involves calculating a parameterization of the volume based on the topology of its control point structure. The actual mapping of an undeformed point to a point in the deformed volume is then a function of the deformed positions of the control points for the given parameterization. Continuity of the correspondence function is crucial to the smoothness properties of the deformed object.

Sederberg and Parry [12] used a parallelopiped lattice of control points to define a trivariate Bezier volume. The mapping of points within the parallelopiped volume to a trivariate basis is straightforward. Evaluating the deformed point is simply a matter of evaluating the Bezier equation for the deformed set of control points. Griessmair and Purgathofer [6] extended this technique to employ a trivariate B-spline basis. While these methods are simple, efficient and in popular use they suffer from the drawback of a restrictive original volume shape. Parallelopiped volumes rarely bear any visual correlation to the objects they deform and typically have a globally uniform lattice point structure that is larger than is required for the deformations to which they are applied.

Coquillart [3] extended the box-shaped lattices to allow for a richer set of shapes (EFFD), constructed by join operations applied to paralleloped lattices. The parameterization of a point within the original trivariate volume is calculated numerically, making the technique less stable than the original FFD [12] in the general case.

Chang and Rockwood [2] present an approach where a deCasteljau approach of repeated affine transformations defines the deformable space around a Bezier curve. The approach is intuitive and fast but restricted in the range and local control of the deformations it can capture.

MacCracken and Joy [7] use a volume equivalent of the Catmull-Clark subdivision scheme for surfaces to iteratively define a volume of space based on a control point structure of arbitrary topology. This is a significant step in increasing the admissible set of control lattice shapes. The technique is powerful and its only real shortcoming are the potential continuity problems of the mapping function (a combination of subdivision and interpolation) of points within the volume. The approach also suffers from the same discontinuity problems as Catmull-Clark surfaces at extraordinary vertices.

Dirichlet free-form deformations [9] is an approach based on the Voronoi structure defined within the convex hull of a set of points. While there is no restriction on the shape of the volume, the deformations are controlled solely by the parameterization defined by natural neighbour interpolants. These interpolating functions have singularities that result in unwanted deformation artifacts.

All the above approaches are strongly volume-oriented. The structure of the control points explicitly defines a volume of deformable space. The deformation function $D(P)$ for a point P can be typically represented by $D(P) = \sum_{i=1}^{n} W_i(P)P_i$, where P_i is a control point and W_i a function that maps a point P to a weight value for the control point P_i. For FFDs $W_i(P) = B_i(s, t, u)$,

where B is the Bezier basis function and s, t, u the parameterization of P within the parallelopiped volume.

The property that affine transformations to the control lattice are transmitted as such to the deformed points is desirable. Suppose an affine transformation M were applied to the lattice. $D(P) = PM = \sum_{i=1}^{n} W_i(P)(P_iM)$ or $P = \sum_{i=1}^{n} W_i(P)P_i$, where P_i are the positions of the control points in the original lattice. Thus for affine transformations to be captured by the deformation, the weighted average of control points for any point in space point should be the point itself. Additionally $\sum_{i=1}^{n} W_i(P) = 1$ for the convex hull property of the deformation to hold. These properties can be verified for the approaches described thus far.

Singh and Fiume [14] provided a different direction to free-form deformations by making them surface-oriented, in that there was no explicit mapping of points between two deformable volumes. Instead points in space were associated with surface elements, parametric curves called wires. Transformation of these associated surface elements result in a deformation of space surrounding the surface element. The control structure of a surface-oriented deformer typically bears a strong visual correlation to the object it deforms. Local control over the deformation is easier and the arbitrary nature of the control point structure makes it possible to introduce detail locally without a global change to the object. At the same time it is harder to ensure continuity properties and perfectly transmitted affine transformations for surface-oriented deformations. This paper addresses these issues for a polygon based deformer.

3 Surface-oriented deformations

The surface-oriented deformation algorithm described in this paper, binds the surface S of a deformable object to a deformer object O. Manipulation of O is then tracked by S. Formally, we define the deformer O as a triple $\langle D, R, local \rangle$ where D and R are surfaces, referred to as the *driver surface* and *reference surface* and *local* a scalar value. R is a congruent copy of the deformer surface D, that is made when surface S is bound to O. Subsequent manipulation of D causes a deviation relative to R that drives the deformation of surface S. The parameter *local* provides control over the locality of the deformation.

For the purpose of our algorithm we need to be able to compute localized orientation and scaling information at points on the surfaces D and R. We also require a unique and intuitive correspondence between points on D and R. This section treats D and R to be polygon based surfaces of matching topology, for which these calculations are straightforward and efficient.

Graphics **Interface** 2000

3.1 Overview of the Algorithm

There are three phases to the deformation process: The bind phase, the registration phase and the deformation phase. The bind phase takes place once whereas the registration and deformation phases are repeated as needed. During the bind phase, the user-specified deformer surface becomes the driver surface D. An identical copy of it becomes the reference surface R, which along with a user-specified *local* value define the deformer object O.

Let the driver D, and reference surface R of a deformer object be represented by a collection of enumerated *control elements*. These control elements are the triangular facets of polygon based surfaces D and R (non-triangular faces of D are triangulated before the creation of R during the bind phase). There is thus a simple bijective correspondence between the control elements of D and R based on element index.

The registration phase computes how much each control element of the deformer object affects the deformation of each point P representing the surface S. This scalar value, referred to as the *influence weight* of the control element for P, is calculated using a distance metric. Control elements closer to P have a higher influence weight, and therefore affect the deformation of P more than elements further away from P. The registration phase typically takes place once, right after the bind phase and needs to be repeated only if the position of the reference surface R changes relative to the surface S.

The deformation phase follows the registration and is repeated every time the deformer object's driver surface D is manipulated. The influence weights calculated in the registration phase as well as the spatial difference between the control elements of the reference and driver surfaces are used to determine the deformation of each point P on the surface S.

The registration and deformation phases are now described in greater detail.

3.2 Registration

During the registration phase, the influence weights for all the control elements and points P of the deformable surface S are computed. Typically, the surface S is represented by the set of points P^S that are necessary to construct or approximate S. P^S could therefore be a set of vertices in a polygonal mesh, a set of control vertices in a free form surface or an unstructured set of points in space. The deformation is applied to points P of this set. Of the two surfaces of the deformer object O, only the reference surface R is used in this phase. In our implementation, a distance metric represented as a scalar function $f(d, local)$, is employed to compute the influence weights. The first parameter, d, is the distance of P from the control element. The second parameter, *local*,

controls the rate at which the function f decays in value with an increase in distance d. We define the function $f(d, local)$ for any $d, local \geq 0$ to be:

$$f(d, local) = \frac{1}{1 + d^{local}}. \tag{1}$$

We define the distance of point P from a triangular facet to be the length of the vector $\overrightarrow{PP'}$ where P' is the point on the surface of the facet that is the closest to point P. For each point P and each control element k of the deformer object's reference surface R we define the corresponding weight $w_k^P = f(d_k^P, local)$, where d_k^P is the distance of point P from control element k. The influence weights for a point P are normalized to preserve the convex hull property described in Section 2. The normalized weight vector for point P is defined as $U^P = \{u_1^P, u_2^P, \ldots, u_n^P\}$, where n is the number of control elements of the influence object's surfaces and u_k^P is the normalized weight of control element k for point P defined as $u_k^P = \frac{w_k^P}{\sum_1^n w_k^P}$. Section 5 will show that in practice u_k^P is set to zero for all but a few control elements making the approach quite efficient.

The control elements as used for this algorithm define not only a local position in space but also a local coordinate frame with axes $\overrightarrow{e_1}, \overrightarrow{e_2}, \overrightarrow{e_3}$. In other words, each control element defines its own coordinate system that can be represented compactly with a 4×4 transformation matrix Q. We denote transformation matrices of elements on the driver and reference surface as Q^D and Q^R respectively.

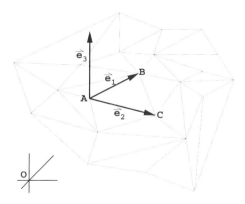

Figure 2: The coordinate system of a polymesh face.

The position vector and the attached coordinate system of a control element corresponding to a triangular facet of a polygonal surface are derived directly from the vertices and edges of the facet (See Figure 2). An arbitrary ordering may be assigned to the three vertices of the triangular facet. Referring to these three vertices as vertices A, B and C we define the coordinate system for the control element with its origin at A and axes as :

$$\vec{e_1} = \vec{B} - \vec{A}, \vec{e_2} = \vec{C} - \vec{A}, \vec{e_3} = \frac{\vec{e}_1 \times \vec{e}_2}{||\vec{e}_1 \times \vec{e}_2||}. \quad (2)$$

In addition to the influence weights, the registration phase computes a representation of undeformed points P of surface S in the coordinate system defined by each control element k of the reference surface R. This operation can be easily carried out by inverting the transformation matrix Q_k^R of the control element. $P_k^R = P(Q_k^R)^{-1}$, where P_k^R is the representation of the point P in the local coordinate system of control element k of the reference surface R.

During the deformation phase the point P is deformed to preserve its local position, P_k^R, in the coordinate frame of the control element k of the driver surface D.

3.3 Deformation

The deformation procedure maps each point P in the set of points P^S defining the undeformed surface S to a point P_{def}. The set P_{def}^S of all points P_{def} defines the deformed object surface.

As the user manipulates the driver surface D of the deformer object, control elements on D change shape, position and orientation. Comparing the coordinate system defined by the element k on the reference surface and the element k on the driver surface makes it possible to calculate the deformation effect of element k on a point P. The effect of each control element k is weighted by the corresponding normalized weight factor u_k^P and is added to the contributions of all the other control elements.

During the registration phase, the representation of point P in the local coordinate system of the control element k on reference surface R was calculated to be P_k^R. In the deformation phase, we deform the point to have the same local representation in the coordinate system of the corresponding driver surface control element. The world space position of the point P as deformed by control element k is thus, $P_k^{def} = P_k^R Q_k^D$, where Q_k^D is the transformation matrix corresponding to the local coordinate system of the control element k of the driver surface. The effect on point P of each control element is weighted by the corresponding normalized weight value stored in vector U^P. The weighted effects are added to compute the resulting point P_{def} on the deformed surface:

$$P_{def} = \sum_{k=1}^{n} u_k^P P_k^{def}. \quad (3)$$

The algorithm can be adapted to allow parametric surface patches to represent the driver and reference surface by specifying control elements as a parametric sampling of points. The sampling density is a trade-off between computational efficiency and the fidelity with which the surface is represented. Sampling at knot vector parameter values provides good local control on manipulation of the control vertices of the driver surface. The local coordinate system in Equation 2 at a sample point G, is defined as $\vec{e_1} = \vec{t_u}, \vec{e_2} = \vec{t_v}, \vec{e_3} = \vec{n}$, where $\vec{t_u}$ and $\vec{t_v}$ are the tangents at G along two parameter curves, and $\vec{n}$ is the surface normal at G.

4 Algorithm Analysis

The algorithm imposes no restriction on the topology of the deformer object or its position relative to the deformable surface S. There are, however, implicit assumptions that greatly influence the quality and control that the deformer object has over the resulting deformation.

For a control element to provide good local control of the deformation of a region of the surface S, its spatial position on the reference surface R should be closer to the surface S than other control elements of R.

Also for the deformation of the region of surface S to appear intuitive it should be proximal to the control element in absolute terms. Non-intuitive behavior may be observed for points whose projection onto the plane of the triangle does not lie within the triangle. A point P on the deformed surface can be visualised as being anchored to its projection point P_k^{proj} on the plane of the triangle k offset at a fixed distance, normal to the plane. The deformation of P thus has a clear visual correlation to the deformation of the triangle if and only if P_k^{proj} lies within this triangle.

These observations place an implicit assumption on the nature of R relative to S, in that every point P of S should be proximal to some triangle k of R and have its projection onto the plane of triangle k lie within it. This is in accordance with the motivation for our deformer to provide a lower resolution visual model of our original surface S.

4.1 Algorithm Properties

- The surface S does not deform upon being bound to a deformer object. Since the driver and the reference surfaces of the deformer object are spatially identical when bound, $P_{def} = P_k^{def} = P$ for all control elements k.

- The deformation of space defined by the algorithm is continuous and intuitive. The parameter *local* provides good control over the localization of deformation effects.

- Rotations and translations applied to the entire driver surface are imparted precisely to the surface S, since the weight values used in equation 3 are normalized.

- Warping of space normal to the plane of the control elements is captured as a constant offset from the control element, since $\vec{e_3}$ is a normalized vector, normal to the plane of the triangle in both R and D.

4.2 Extending the Algorithm

We now look at shortcomings of the approach described thus far. The first deals with non-intuitive deformations resulting from a point P being anchored to its projection P_k^{proj} on the plane of a triangle k of the reference surface, where P_k^{proj} does not lie within the triangle. It is conceivable to clamp P_k^{proj} to the closest point on the triangle boundary P_k^{close} and calculate the deformed point as two offsets from the point corresponding to P_k^{close} on the driver surface. The first offset is $P_k^{proj} - P_k^{close}$ in the plane of the triangle and the second, $P - P_k^{proj}$ normal to the plane of the triangle. While this addresses the shortcoming, the change introduces a first order discontinuity of deformation as P_k^{proj} for points P transitions across the triangle boundary.

The second shortcoming deals with the fact that the algorithm does not capture the warping of space in a direction normal to the plane of its control elements. Uniform scaling of the driver surface D, for example will scale the object precisely in the plane of the control elements of D, but maintain a constant distance from the elements in a direction perpendicular to them.

Both of these shortcomings can be attributed to the ambiguities in the perception of the behavior of space around the deformer object on manipulation of the driver surface. There are infinitely many ways by which a user can deform space such that the discrete set of points of a driver surface are manipulated to the same position. In each case, however, the behavior of the spatial neighbourhood of the points of the driver surface is different.

This ambiguity can be reduced by defining a coordinate system by introducing three additional points for every given point on the deformer surface. These points form mutually independent axes with the point on the deformer surface as the origin. The three points are subsequently subjected to the same manipulation function as the corresponding point on the deformer surface. While this coordinate system represents the space of a local linear transformation accurately, non-linear deformations are once again only approximated. This gives us some insight into the nature of spatial deformations and solutions to them by providing the user with additional control.

Every triangle k in our extended model has three local coordinate systems instead of one, centered at each vertex of the triangle and constructed during the bind phase. We register the point P by computing the local position of the point within each of the three coordinate system as

described in Section 3.2. We also generate a deformed point with respect to each of the three coordinate systems of triangle k. The three deformed points are then weight averaged to a single resultant P_k^{def}. The weights in this case are provided by the barycentric coordinates of P_k^{close} (the closest point to P from triangle k). The deformed result of the various control elements are combined as in Section 3 to determine the final position of a point. It is straightforward to see that the range of deformation behavior captured above encompasses that of the the algorithm in Section 3.

5 Skinning Workflow

It is a fairly common practice in the animation industry to model articulated figures using a number of surface patches. Joint regions such as the shoulder in Figure 3 are particularly problematic to skin. This is because the range and degrees of freedom of the joint cause large variations in the motion of points. It is also the case that often a number of patches converge in the region around a joint, making the problem of skinning the geometry while maintaining smoothness and continuity across the patches a formidable task.

Figure 3: Shirt skinned using surface-oriented FFDs

A single surface-oriented deformer can abstract this underlying patch complexity so the user has to deal with the more tractable problem of skinning a single lower resolution object that bears a close visual semblance to the actual geometry. We prescribe a simple workflow that largely automates the entire skinning process. The shirt in Figure 3 was skinned with such a deformer.

The basic skinning workflow involves the construction of a single surface-oriented deformer around a character. This deformer is essentially a low-resolution representation of the character (See Figure 1). More importantly the resolution is adaptive, to allow a greater resolution of control points in the region of character joints.

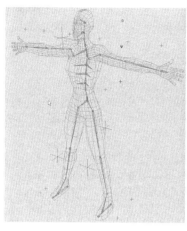

Figure 4: Skinning workflow: polyhedral deformer bound to skeleton(left), deformed surface (right)

Geometric representations such as parametric surface patches and implicit functions have well established tesselation algorithms. Polymesh decimation algorithms have also been well studied [8, 15]. For the common case where the underlying geometric skin comprises of a number of surface patches, the patches are tesselated independently and then stitched together to form a single deformer object. The stitched mesh represents all or a large section of the skin of an articulated character. The underlying geometry is bound to and controlled by the deformer object using the algorithm described in Section 3. The deformer object is bound to the underlying skeleton using any number of techniques [1, 14, 18]. We find that in practice it is often worthwhile to define the motion of individual points by keyposing them against various joint angle positions. The reduced point complexity of the deformer object makes this a reasonable task that allows complete customizability to be layered over the basic motion of the points of the deformer object as dictated by the basic binding technique used (See Figure 4). Finer local control may also be achieved at any point of time by subdividing triangles in a problematic region to generate a larger number of control elements. Non-triangular deformer polymeshes are internally triangulated, so as not to subject a user to unnecessary visual clutter.

A common problem with techniques that use Euclidean distance to determine correspondence between the deformed and deformer object, is that quite often regions of the deformer object will strongly influence regions of the deformable surface which happen to be spatially proximal but are quite distinct in the eyes of the user. A clear example of this can be seen in Figure 5 where the deformer region of the right thigh pulls on part of the left thigh geometry even though it should not affect

it at all. Our implementation, therefore constructs, for each point P, a subset of contributing control elements C_P, from the set of control elements of the deformer object for a given point. As can be seen from Equation 1 the function f rapidly decays in value with distance such that the normalized influence weights are likely to be significantly larger than zero for only a small number of control elements. By default the control elements with a significant non-zero influence define C_P. The set, however, is under user control and may be edited if necessary. Thus by removing the control elements of the right thigh from the contributing control element sets for points of the left leg we can get the desired behavior.

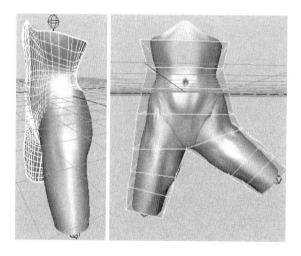

Figure 5: Deformation using a surface-oriented FFD

The algorithm described in this paper has been implemented as a general deformation technique within our modeling and animation system *Maya2.0*. The skinning of geometry has been automated as summarized below.

1. Polygonize surface patches or other geometric representation of objects to be skinned. Decimate and weld polygon objects as required to generate a few low resolution deformer objects.

2. Bind the deformer driver surface points to the skeleton. Points are rigidly attached to the Euclidean closest limb by default.

3. The control points of the deformer can be then keyposed against various skeletal and muscle attributes to generate custom skinning behavior.

4. The various parameters of the surface-oriented free-form deformation and the contributing element sets for various points may also be edited.

42

6 Results and Conclusion

We find in practice that surface-oriented free-form deformations address many requirements of geometric skinning. The deformer object itself provides a reasonably accurate low resolution representation of the skinned geometry, making it perfectly suitable as a stand-in for highly interactive animation tasks. The process is largely automated and may be all an animator needs for a quick setup. More importantly, however, the animator still has control at the finest level, through increasing degrees of detail. An analysis of the algorithms in Section 3 and 4, show them to be robust, efficient and of predictable deformation behavior and continuity. This is corroborated by the practical results shown in this paper and on a few of the characters of the animation short Bingo.

Our implementation combines multiple deformers on an object as described by Singh and Fiume [14]. Surface-oriented FFDs have also been used as a compelling modeling and animation tool with much of the appeal and control of a subdivision surface. Figure 6 shows the physical simulation of a polymesh deformer draping over a table top controlling a NURBS surface rendered with a checker texture.

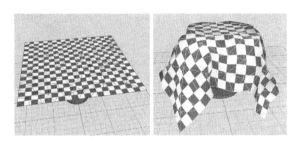

Figure 6: Physical simulation of a polyhedral mesh controlling a superposed NURBS tablecloth

While the extended algorithm in Section 4 gives us greater control and the property that all affine transformations to the deformer object are imparted perfectly to the underlying geometry, we find the algorithm of Section 3 to be simpler for an animator to understand and sufficient for the skinning application discussed in this paper.

Acknowledgements

We thank Barbara Balents and the *Maya* team for their help in the design and implementation of this technique and Paul Thuriot for providing us with invaluable case studies of character setup using surface-oriented FFDs.

References

[1] J. Chadwick, D. Haumann and R. Parent. Layered construction for deformable animated characters. *Computer Graphics*, 23(3):234–243, 1989.

[2] Y.K. Chang and A.P. Rockwood. A generalized de Casteljau approach to 3D free-form deformation. *Computer Graphics*, 28(4):257–260, 1994.

[3] S. Coquillart. Extended free-form deformations: A sculpting tool for 3D geometric modeling. *Computer Graphics*, 24(4):187–196, 1990.

[4] D. Chen and D. Zeltzer. Pump it up: Computer animation of a biomechanically based model of muscle using the finite element method. *Computer Graphics*, 26:89–98, 1992.

[5] T. DeRose, M. Kass and T. Truong. Subdivision surface for character animation. *Computer Graphics*, 85–94, 1998.

[6] J. Griessmair and W. Purgathofer. Deformation of solids with trivariate B-splines. *Eurographics 89*, 137–148.

[7] R. MacCracken and K. Joy. Free-form deformations with lattices of arbitrary topology. *Computer Graphics*, 181–189, 1996.

[8] A. Lee, W. Sweldens, P. Schroder, L. Cowsar and D. Dobkin. MAPS: Multiresolution adaptive parametrization of surfaces. *Computer Graphics*, 95–105, 1998.

[9] L. Moccozet and N. Magnenat Thalmann. Dirichlet free-form deformations and their application to hand simulation. *Computer Animation*, 93–102, 1997.

[10] N. Magnetat-Thalmann, D. Thalmann. Human body deformations using Joint Dependent Local Operators and Finite Element Theory. *Making Them Move*, Morgan Kaufmann, 243–262.

[11] F. Scheepers and R. Parent and W. Carlson and S. May Anatomy-Based Modeling of the Human Musculature. *Computer Graphics*, 163–172, 1997.

[12] T. Sederberg and S. Parry. Free-form deformation of solid geometric models. *Computer Graphics*, 20:151–160, 1986.

[13] K. Singh, J. Ohya and R. Parent. Human figure synthesis and animation for virtual space teleconferencing. *IEEE VRAIS*, 118–126, 1995.

[14] K. Singh and E. Fiume Wires: A geometric deformation technique. *Computer Graphics*, 405–414, 1998.

[15] G. Taubin, A. Gueziec, W. Horn and F. Lazarus Progressive forest split compression. *Computer Graphics*, 123–133, 1998.

[16] Y. Lee, D. Terzopoulos and K. Waters. Realistic modeling for facial animation. *Computer Graphics*, 55–62, 1995.

[17] M. Walter and A. Fournier. Growing and animating polygonal models of animals. *Eurographics*, 151–158, 1997.

[18] J. Wilhelms and A. Van Gelder. Anatomically Based Modeling. *Computer Graphics*, 173–180, 1997.

Artificial Animals (and Humans):
From Physics to Intelligence

Demetri Terzopoulos
Department of Computer Science
University of Toronto

The confluence of computer graphics and artificial life has produced virtual worlds inhabited by realistic "artificial animals". These synthetic organisms possess biomechanical bodies, sensors, and brains with locomotion, perception, behavior, learning, and cognition centers. Artificial animals, including artificial humans, are of interest because they are self-animating creatures that dramatically advance the state of the art of character animation and interactive games. As biomimetic autonomous agents situated in realistic virtual worlds, artificial animals also foster a deeper, computationally oriented understanding of complex living systems.

44

Dynamic Time Warp Based Framespace Interpolation for Motion Editing

Golam Ashraf   Kok Cheong Wong

Center for Graphics and Imaging Technology
Nanyang Technological University, Singapore

Abstract

Motion capture (MOCAP) data clips can be visualized as a sequence of densely spaced curves, defining the joint angles of the articulated figure, over a specified period of time. Current research has focussed on frequency and time domain techniques to edit these curves, preserving the original qualities of the motion yet making it reusable in different spatio-temporal situations. We refine Guo et. al.'s[6] framespace interpolation algorithm which abstracts motion sequences as 1D signals, and interpolates between them to create higher dimension signals. Our method is more suitable for (though not limited to) editing densely spaced MOCAP data, than the existing algorithm. It achieves consistent motion transition through motion-state based dynamic warping of framespaces and automatic transition timing via framespace frequency interpolation.

Key words: motion editing, framespace interpolation, blending, concatenation, motion correspondence.

1 Introduction

With increasing availability of motion capture devices and high fidelity motion requirements in the entertainment industry, realistic animation has become possible without need for dynamic simulation or laboriously crafted keyframed data. However, *motion reuse* is as relevant as captured motion data, since it is not always feasible to retake motions or record transitions between two desired motions. Simple basis motions are created and then interpolated or extrapolated through various techniques, to yield a large variety of motions. Motion editing broadly encompasses *reshaping, blending, concatenation* and *retargetting* of basis motions. In this paper, we deal with consistent blending and concatenation, both of which are referred to as motion transition problems by several authors[3, 12].

Interactivity in motion editing research has been assigned paramount importance, since it is necessary to avoid clogging up the animators' workflow through undesirably long waits between edits. Ease of editing specification is also very important and requires minimiz-ing the number of control parameters. Framespace interpolation is a time domain motion-transition technique which allows such interactivity through minimal user-specification and simple computation needs. Guo and Roberge[6] use parametric framespace interpolation for transitions between human running and walking, where inter-motion correspondences are developed between key states of the lower half of the body. We reformulate their framespace interpolation technique, specifically keeping motion editing of densely spaced signals in mind, while establishing motion correspondences. The rest of this paper has been organized as follows: a survey of motion editing techniques, an analysis of the existing framespace interpolation algorithm, consistent framespace interpolation via dynamic time warping, results and analysis, and a summary of contributions.

2 Survey of Motion Editing Techniques

Most researchers[3, 5, 6, 16] have treated motion data as a 'blackbox' set of 2D C^2 continuous signals, without differentiating the degrees of freedom (DOF) in terms of relevance to the motion, or hierarchy of structure. Bindiganavale and Badler[2] introduced some heuristics based on end-effector acceleration zero-crossings, to isolate significant events and abstract constraints from an agent's action. This approach cuts down unnecessary constraint checks, hence saving valuable computation. We build on this motion abstraction paradigm and achieve significant savings in pre-blend/pre-concatenation motion-warping.

Motion editing in frequency domain has been proposed by a few researchers. Bruderlin's[3] application of Gaussian and Laplacian pyramids to motion data, provides a way to transform motion by adjusting the gains of the different bands, before reconstruction. Unuma et. al.[14] proposed a Fourier transform of discrete motion signals. From a given set of Fourier coefficients for two motion clips, they achieve *interpolation, extrapolation* and *transition* between these motions, by linearly varying the interpolant weights of the Fourier coefficients and phase angles. Though these methods drastically reduce the number of control parameters, a domain transform makes

Graphics **Interface** 2000

control less intituitive as a priori knowledge is needed about which frequencies contain the essential motion-characteristics.

Several time domain motion editing techniques have evolved. Guo and Roberge[6, 7] proposed a parametric framespace interpolation paradigm for motion blending and concatenation. By employing a user-specified curve to interpolate entire sequences of articulated figures, animator-effort is minimized. Rose et. al.[11] employ radial basis functions to interpolate and extrapolate actions. Bruderlin[3] used displacement mapping, as a means of editing densely spaced motion curves. The method involves specifying a smooth curve, through a few keyframes (*constraints*), and adding it to the original curve. This way, the original motion characteristics are preserved, yet achieving a change in the motion via a low frequency offset curve. Luo[9] and Gleicher[5] use displacement curves as a constraint specification tool. Witkin[16] uses a similar concept in the form of motion warping.

Witkin and Kass[15] introduced motion synthesis as a constraint optimization problem, where given a set of constraints, the problem is to find a valid motion that best satisfies the goal. Cohen[4] proposed a more interactive system, where the solution is guided by the user. Gleicher[5] simplified the formulation for interactive performance, by using *Sequential Quadratic Programming* (SQP) techniques. SQP solvers perform efficiently because they accept quadratic optimization metrics and only linear constraints. Motion retargetting[5, 8] and concatenation[12] can be viewed as spacetime problems, in that given a length of motion, the problem is to find the best motion which satisfies the constraints and maximizes the goal. Unlike pure IK based re-positioning, the spacetime approach ensures that the constraints affect neighboring frames as well.

3 Analysis of Existing Framespace Algorithm

3.1 Interpolation Algorithm

In simple terms, framespace interpolation is a way of specifying postural blends via an input curve (*interpolant*), drawn within *frames* which enclose a rectangular area or a cubic volume. Basis motions (*primitives*) which are to be interpolated, are each represented by one such frame. Mapping the entire clip of an animated figure with normalized times, on to this frame yields a *1D framespace*. In Eqn.(1) m dimensional point, Q, represents the body posture at a given time instant. Eqn.(2) represents the motion curve of DOF_i as an interpolation function ($\phi_i(s)$) of a time-sequence of a_i points. $F(s)$ abstracts the m motion curves as a 1D framespace, parameterized by arc length s.

$$Q = \{a_1, a_2, \ldots, a_m\}^T \qquad (1)$$

$$F(s) = \{\phi_1(s), \phi_2(s), \ldots, \phi_m(s)\}^T, \; 0 \le s \le 1 \quad (2)$$

Combining 2^{n-1} such framespaces, interpolation can be done in n dimensional framespace. As a practical interpolation tool, 2D and 3D framespaces are adequate, since user-interaction in higher dimensional interpolation of 1D framespaces has no direct visual mapping. Eqns.(3) & (4) express 2D and 3D linear parametric interpolation, where x (time), y and z (weights) are cartesian coordinates of points, $P(x, y, z)$, of the interpolant. $F_{1,\ldots,4}$ are parametric 1D framespaces, which represent the basis motions.

$$F'(x, y) = (1 - a)\, F_1(x) + a\, F_2(x) \qquad (3)$$

$$\begin{aligned} F'(x, y, z) = {}& (1 - a)(1 - b)\, F_1(x) + a(1 - b)\, F_2(x) \\ & + (1 - a)b\, F_3(x) + ab\, F_4(x) \end{aligned} \qquad (4)$$

where $\quad a = \dfrac{y - y_1}{y_2 - y_1}, \quad b = \dfrac{z - z_1}{z_2 - z_1}$

y_1, y_2, z_1, z_2 are physical bounds of the interface.

Bruderlin[3] points out that arbitrary interpolation between un-correlated motions could give rise to severe inconsistencies in the result. Such correlation has not been established between the primitives in [7]. Guo and Roberge address this limitation, by implementing *consistent 3D framespace interpolation*[6]. Two styles of human walking and running are chosen as primitives and key locomotion postures are chosen as correspondence points (*states*). The 3D interpolation space (see Fig.1) is divided into sub-volumes by *event surfaces* (S_n) constructed between corresponding states from the four primitives ($\{s_n^1 s_n^2 s_n^3 s_n^4\}$ in Eqn.(5)) . These surfaces are non-planar in the general case. Every point on the interpolant, $P(x, y, z)$, is first projected (along the time axis) on all event surfaces to determine whether it lies on a surface. If true, then the four states defining the surface are used for interpolation (as in Eqn.(5)). Otherwise, if P belongs to a sub-volume, v_i then its eight bounding states are used (as in Eqn.(6)).

$$F'(x, y, z) = \sum_{i=1}^{4} a_i F_i(s_n^i) \qquad (5)$$

$$F'(x, y, z) = \sum_{i=1}^{4} \left(a_i F_i(s_n^i) + a_{i+4} F_i(s_n^{i+1}) \right) \quad (6)$$

where

s_n^i : Correspondence state n of framespace F_i

$\quad \{s_n^1 s_n^2 s_n^3 s_n^4\}$ define event surface S_n in Fig.1

$a_{1,\ldots,8}$: coefficient functions $f\{x, y, z, \sigma_n(z), \sigma_{n+1}(z)\}$

$\sigma_n(z)$: $P(x, y, z)$ projected along x axis, on surface S_n

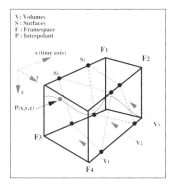

Figure 1: Guo and Roberge's[6] consistent interpolation.

3.2 Drawbacks of Existing Technique

An important difference between Eqns.(3) & (4) and Eqns.(5) & (6) can be observed. While the domain of the former set of equations is the entire framespace ($F_i(x), 0.0 \leq x \leq 1.0$), the domain of the latter set comprises only of the keyframes ($F_i(x), x \in \{s_0^i, \ldots, s_m^i\}$). Though the coefficients a_i are functions of the entire framespace, it is important to note that these coefficients are merely used to weigh the values of the bounding keyframes, and hence, joint angle values of the entire framespace are *not* used. Thus the algorithm does not exploit the high frequency information in the framespaces constructed from MOCAP data, since only key correspondence points are interpolated. This formulation seems more suited to sparsely placed keyframes rather than dense motion curves, where the premise of keyframes being equivalent to *key events* does not hold.

Secondly, a generic framework has not been proposed for the automatic generation of timing for the resulting motion. The default time mapping proposed is specifically related to human locomotion, and does not cater to general motion transition.

Lastly, the arc length parameterization of the m-D interpolation function in Eqn. (2) overlooks a basic drawback. Referencing a point at arc distance s along $\phi_i(s)$ curves ($1 \leq i \leq m$), would yield points at different time instances t_i, and not t as we normally expect in parametric keyframe animation. This is because the arc-lengths for the m ϕ_i curves at a given time, will be different due to their characteristic shapes. Besides being an unconventional parameter in keyframe animation, this undesirable feature makes it tedious to validate postures on the fly.

4 Consistent Framespace Interpolation via Dynamic Time Warping

We propose a more efficient algorithm which improves on the above-mentioned drawbacks. A modified framespace interpolation technique is described in this section, which exploits the entire framespace information and

provides a generic method of default transition-timing generation. Arc length parameterization is not used for reasons mentioned in the last section.

4.1 Algorithm Overview

The proposed algorithm hinges on ideas drawn from Bruderlin's[3] *dynamic time warping* and correspondence based on high level events[2, 6, 10]. Instead of projecting $P(x, y, z)$ on event surfaces (Sec.3.1), the irregular bounding volumes (Fig.1) are regularized by weighted scaling of inter-state time gaps in the basis motions. The source frames are then extracted from the regularized framespaces and blended using weights drawn from $P(x, y, z)$. Further, these weights are used to interpolate the frequencies of the primitives, to yield smooth timing transition in the resulting curves. Weight coefficients a and b in all equations in these sections, are the same as in Eqns.(3) & (4). Assigning $y_1 = z_1 = 0$ and $y_2 = z_2 = 1$, saves on unnecessary division and yields $a = y$ and $b = z$. The following sections will explain the concepts in greater detail. Fig.2 summarizes the algorithm.

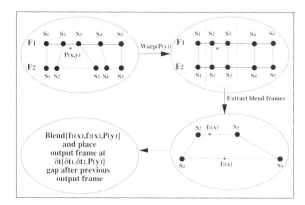

Figure 2: Proposed Consistent Interpolation Framework

4.2 Dynamic Time Warp Preliminaries

Bruderlin[3] uses dynamic time warping to align signals before performing blending. He uses Sederberg's[13] physically based signal correspondence techniques to establish this time warp. The algorithm solves the correspondence problem by exhaustive graph traversal, where the vertices represent all possible combinations of inter-point correspondence between two signals. This is an expensive O(mn) operation (if the two signals have m and n samples each). We simplify the correspondence problem by identifying samples where *key events* occur, and then use these as reference points to apply time warps to entire sections of the signal, instead of warping the samples individually, as in Sederberg's method. Such a motion-abstraction assisted warp method is much more economical than Sederberg's low level warping algorithm.

48

4.3 Pre-blend Warping of Primitives

In our problem formulation, motion states are pre-classified. The system then automatically identifies corresponding states, based on a best match between event labels of analyzed primitives. What needs to be resolved now is, by how much should each of the primitives be warped to enable consistent blending. Warping the rest of the primitives to one primitive leads to inconsistent results, since the net frequencies of the other primitives are changed completely. Consider a simple 2D interpolation case of transition from *run* to *walk*. If the walk action is warped to match the run, we have a much faster walk parametric space, with the run frequency untouched. When the interpolant meets the *walk frame* (run has no effect), the result will be a funny fast shuffle, which is neither a walk nor a run.

To solve this problem, we propose a regularization warp function for aligning all primitives. The function is driven by $P(x, y, z)$, where y & z provide weights and x makes the function time-variant (dynamic). Let us explain this concept in the 2D interpolation case first. A single cycle of two hypothetical 1D framespaces can be represented as shown in Fig.3. Δt refers to the elapsed time between successive motion states. Then the problem of changing the Δt between successive states so that all the framespaces are *consistently* affected, can be solved by a weighted interpolation of these curves. This can be easily generalized to the 3D interpolation case. Eqns.(7) & (8) define dynamic time warp functions for 2D and 3D framespaces respectively. Δt_n^m represents time elapsed between states n and $n-1$, for framespace F_m, and y & z are interpolant weights. $dT'(n, y)$ and $dT'(n, y, z)$ represent the new Δt values for 2D and 3D interpolation respectively, which will be applied to all the primitives, resulting in regular subspaces.

$$dT'(n, y) = (1-a)\Delta t_n^1 + a\Delta t_n^2 \qquad (7)$$
$$dT'(n, y, z) = (1-a)(1-b)\Delta t_n^1 + a(1-b)\Delta t_n^2$$
$$+ (1-a)b\Delta t_n^3 + ab\Delta t_n^4 \qquad (8)$$

The problem of dynamic time warping has thus been elegantly solved by interpolating the Δt curves based on the weights derived from $P(x, y, z)$. In other words, the warp operation tantamounts to stretching and squeezing inter-state times of the framespaces to achieve regular volumes, where the magnitude of transformation depends on $P(y, z)$, at time instance x. So in the special case of $P(x, y, z)$ lying on a primitive frame, $F_n(x)$, the corresponding states in the other primitives ($F_i(x), i \neq n$) are warped to follow the inter-state gaps of $F_n(x)$.

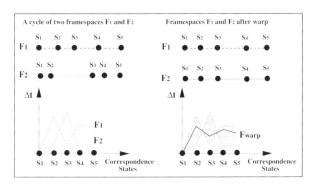

Figure 3: Regularization Warp of Primitives

4.4 Linear Parametric Blending

The previous section describes how pre-blend time warping is done to align the primitives. However, it must be noted that we *do not* actually warp the framespaces for each point $P(x, y, z)$ on the interpolant, since it would incur a lot of meaningless computation. The reason for warping the framespaces is to yield a regular subspace, and extract the *bounding states* for the current interpolant sample $P(x, y, z)$. The bounding state check is done in the warp compensated regular subspaces.

Once the bounding states have been identified, the next step is to extract the reference frames from the primitives. This can be achieved through linear coordinate geometry, as expressed by Eqns.(9) & (10).

$$T'(n) = x - s_{n-1}^* \qquad (9)$$
$$f_i(x) = F_i\left(s_{n-1}^i + \frac{\Delta t_n^i}{dT'(n)}T'(n)\right) \qquad (10)$$

where

x	:	Current cycle time
$T'(n)$	:	Relative time in warped subspace w.r.t. state n-1
$dT'(n)$	:	Differential time in warped subspace w.r.t. state n-1, from Eqns.(7) & (8)
s_n^*	:	Time of state n after warp compensation
s_n^i	:	Time of state n of framespace F_i, i = 1,2,3,4

$f_i(x)$ are the reference frames from primitives F_i, which are used for the linear weighted blending operation shown in Eqns.(11) & (12). $F'(x, y)$ and $F'(x, y, z)$ are the results of 2D and 3D framespace interpolation.

$$F'(x, y) = (1-a) f_1(x) + a f_2(x) \qquad (11)$$
$$F'(x, y, z) = (1-a)(1-b) f_1(x) + a(1-b) f_2(x)$$
$$+ (1-a)b f_3(x) + ab f_4(x) \qquad (12)$$
where $f_i(x)$ from Eqn.(10)

4.5 Frequency Transition

Having calculated the value of the result frame, it is equally important to place it at an appropriate distance from the last calculated frame. This is how default frequency calculation of the resulting motion can be described at a micro level. Though the framespace time axis is normalized, the time periods of the original cyclic motions are used to calculate the inter-sample durations of F_i, as shown in Eqn.(14). These are linearly blended with weights derived from $P(x, y, z)$ in Eqn.(13), to yield the gap between the current and previous output samples.

$$\delta'(x,y,z) = (1-a)(1-b)\delta_1 + a(1-b)\delta_2$$
$$+(1-a)b\delta_3 + ab\delta_4 \qquad (13)$$
$$\delta_i = \frac{\Pi_i}{n}, \qquad i = 1, \ldots, 4 \qquad (14)$$

where

Π_i : Time period of motion clip i

n : Resolution of interpolation curve samples

Thus a transition from a low frequency motion to a high frequency motion is accompanied with equivalent changes in joint angular values as well as motion frequency. This simple yet generic method does away with the need for a procedural frequency transition formulation or user defined time warps for natural motion transitions.

4.6 Special Treatment of Pelvis Translatory DOFs

The range of angular DOFs is finite, governed by joint limits. However, the translatory DOFs of the root (pelvis) are not bound by any limits. So interpolating *changes*[12] in translatory motion has two benefits: it does not require the basis motions to start at the same global position, and it eases interpolation across many cycles using only one cycle of each primitive. We build instantaneous velocity curves for each participating pelvis (translatory DOFs) by differencing neighboring samples. The interpolation procedure is the same as the rest of the DOFs, except that the source frames are drawn from the velocity curves, and instantaneous velocities have to be scaled down by δ_i in Eqn.(14) before blending. The interpolated value is then added to the previously calculated sample of the result curve to yield the spatial value.

5 Experimental Results

The algorithm has been implemented in Alias/Wavefront Maya^{TM} API and run on Intergraph TDZ2000 (450MHz CPU with 128MB RAM). Though the basis motions are cyclic, we use a single cycle extracted from the MOCAP data. Desired number of cycles are generated through repeated self-concatenation of the primary cycle after smoothing the start and end regions. Our results are obtained from four basis motions, namely, *walking, running, a common dance step (dance1)* and *the "Egyptian rap" (dance2)*. Fig.4 shows the key postures of these basis motions, the time progression being from left to right. We have specifically chosen the dance motions to show that our algorithm can handle motion transitions between widely varying classes of full bodied motions.

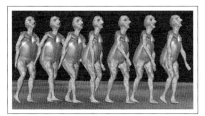

(a) Walk cycle

(b) Run cycle

(c) Dance1 (common dance) cycle

(d) Dance2 (Egyptian rap) cycle

Figure 4: Key postures of basis motions

We present here both 2D and 3D interpolation test cases. Table 1 presents a state classification of the basis motions, based on which correspondences are automatically established as shown in Table 3. Table 2 explains the meanings of the abbreviations used in labelling states. Note that a state can contain more than one characteristic event and is taken care of during state matching. From Table 1, it is evident that the upper and lower body coordination of *dance2* is 180° out of phase with the rest of the motions. A possible solution to such state-sequence clashes is to perform decoupled blending in the two halves of the body, and is a subject of ongoing research. We have presented some preliminary results of such decoupled blending in sequences involving *dance2*.

Fig. 5 shows examples of concatenation and blend

Run	Walk	Dance1	Dance2
Cycle Time	*Cycle Time*	*Cycle Time*	*Cycle Time*
0.77s	1.24s	2.43s	3.07s
Lowerbody	*Lowerbody*	*Lowerbody*	*Lowerbody*
L._et (0.0)	L._et (0.0)	R.HI_flex (0.0)	L._mt (0.0)
R.HI_flex (0.22)	R.HI_flex (0.22)	R.H_gnd (0.14)	L._et (0.36)
R._mt (0.26)	R._mt (0.26)	L.HI_flex (0.41)	R.HI_flex (0.41)
R._et (0.48)	R._et (0.49)	L.H_gnd (0.69)	R._mt (0.49)
L.HI_flex (0.78)	L.HI_flex (0.88)	R.HI_flex (1.0)	R._et (0.76)
L._mt (0.83)	L._mt (0.9)		L.HI_flex (0.84)
L._et (1.0)	L._et (1.0)		L._mt (1.0)
Upperbody	*Upperbody*	*Upperbody*	*Upperbody*
L.S_ext (0.0) R.S_flex	L.S_ext (0.0) R.S_flex	R.S_ext (0.0) L.S_flex	R.S_ext (0.0) L.S_flex
L.S_msw (0.17) R.S_msw	L.S_msw (0.24) R.S_msw	R.S_msw (0.16) L.S_msw	R.S_msw (0.38) L.S_msw
L.S_flex (0.44) R.S_ext	L.S_flex (0.44) R.S_ext	R.S_flex (0.41) L.S_ext	R.S_flex (0.54) L.S_ext
L.S_msw (0.57) R.S_msw	L.S_msw (0.73) R.S_msw	R.S_msw (0.62) L.S_msw	R.S_msw (0.82) L.S_msw
L.S_ext (1.0) R.S_flex	L.S_ext (1.0) R.S_flex	R.S_ext (1.0) L.S_flex	R.S_ext (1.0) L.S_flex

Table 1: Meta data of basis motions

Code	Description
{L,R}._[j]_e	{ left or right joint }_[optional joint name]_event name e.g. L.S_flex represents maximum flexion of the left shoulder joint
flex	Local maxima in joint flexion
ext	Local minima in joint flexion
mt	Mid transfer (refer to [6])
et	End transfer (refer to [6])
msw	Mid swing or half way between flexion and extension
gnd	End effector touches ground plane after being in air
joints	S: Shoulder; HI: Hip; H: Heel

Table 2: Index to state label abbreviations

Run, Walk	Dance1, Dance2	Run, Walk, Dance1, Dance2
Lowerbody	*Lowerbody*	*Lowerbody*
{L._et} {0.0, 0.0}	{R.HI_flex} {0.0, 0.41}	{L._et} {0.0, 0.0, 0.69, 0.36}
{R.HI_flex} {0.22, 0.22}	{R.H_gnd} {0.14, 0.76}	{R.HI_flex} {0.22, 0.22, 1.0, 0.41}
{R._mt} {0.26, 0.26}	{L.HI_flex} {0.41, 0.84}	{R._mt} {0.26, 0.26, 0.14, 0.49}
{R._et} {0.48, 0.49}	{L.H_gnd} {0.69, 1.0}	{L.HI_flex} {0.78, 0.88, 0.41, 0.84}
{L.HI_flex} {0.78, 0.88}	{R.HI_flex} {1.0, 0.41}	{L._et} {1.0, 1.0, 0.69, 0.36}
{L._mt} {0.83,0.9}		
{L._et} {1.0,1.0}		
Upperbody	*Upperbody*	*Upperbody*
{L.S_ext, R.S_flex} {0.0, 0.0}	{R.S_ext, L.S_flex} {0.0, 0.0}	{L.S_ext, R.S_flex} {0.0, 0.0, 0.41, 0.54}
{R.S_msw, L.S_msw} {0.17, 0.24}	{R.S_msw, L.S_msw} {0.16, 0.38}	{R.S_msw, L.S_msw} {0.17, 0.24, 0.62, 0.82}
{R.S_ext, L.S_flex} {0.44, 0.44}	{L.S_ext, R.S_flex} {0.41, 0.54}	{R.S_ext, L.S_flex} {0.44, 0.44, 1.0, 1.0}
{R.S_msw, L.S_msw} {0.57, 0.73}	{R.S_msw, L.S_msw} {0.62, 0.82}	{R.S_msw, L.S_msw} {0.57, 0.73, 0.16, 0.38}
{L.S_ext, R.S_flex} {1.0, 1.0}	{R.S_ext, L.S_flex} {1.0, 1.0}	{L.S_ext, R.S_flex} {1.0, 1.0, 0.41, 0.54}

Table 3: Correspondence results yielded by system

Operation(Participants)	Execution Time (secs)	Result Duration (secs)
ζ(Run,Walk)	5.06	12.33
β(Run,Walk)	4.97	11.53
ζ(Dance1,Dance2)	5.22	32.67
β(Dance1,Dance2)	5.08	33.43
ζ(Run,Dance2)	5.42	22.83
β(Run,Dance2)	4.87	25.86
ζ(Run,Walk,Dance1,Dance2)	5.61	21.87
β(Run,Walk,Dance1,Dance2)	5.93	18.33

Table 4: Statistics for 1200 interpolation operations

shapes of the interpolant. The interface allows the animator to manipulate control vertices of the B-Spline interpolant curve to shape the transition function. The curve is automatically constrained to lie within the framespace bounds. The physical length of the framespace time axis is transformed via logical mapping of a user-specified number of cycles onto it, to achieve transitions over variable durations. The resolution of the time axis is made proportional to the number of cycles, to maintain a constant number of samples per cycle and avoid aliasing effects. Fig. 6 shows the results of blending (β) and concatenation (ζ) between the basis motions. Running and walking are somewhat similar in motion characteristics, so the real challenge was in trying to blend different genres of actions like the *Egyptian rap* and running. The concatenations are seamless and yield consistent motion. Blending via 3D framespace interpolation yielded a curious mix of the two different dance styles and jogging, something which looks like a happy jive. Thus framespace interpolation can achieve the same *emotional qualities* as cited in [14] by using appropriate basis motions. For example, a cyclified angry gesticulation blended with walking would yield an angry walk. Performance statistics are presented in Table 4. Concatenation (ζ) and blending (β) operations (decided by the interpolant shape) are both presented for the four chosen combinations of primitives. The experiments use a 63 DOF articulated figure. For identical primitive combinations and number of operation cycles, the lengths of the results are different for concatenation and blending because of the frequency blending component, which is used to achieve natural transition timing. Fig.7 illustrates the timing transition mechanism and velocity interpolation of translatory DOFs (monotonic curves in Fig.7). The smooth change in cyclic duration is clearly evident in the rotational DOFs. Animation clips of results presented in Table 4 are available at [1].

6 Discussion

Having explained the algorithm and presented the results, we now address some critical questions to compare our methods with related research, and evaluate the role of some of the employed techniques. Pertinent issues about why and how we modify existing techniques and what gains are achieved, are outlined below:

- **Simplified Time Warp vs Physically based Correspondence**: We have simplified Bruderlin's approach of using physically based correspondence techniques[13] to correlate and warp motions. We refer to our warp algorithm as *dynamic* because it constantly changes with time, unlike that in[3, 9].

- **Necessity of framespace warps in identifying reference blend frames**: While it is relatively simple to determine the bounding region of interpolant P in 2D using coordinate geometry, doing so for irregular 3D sub-spaces is non-trivial and computation-intensive[6]. In our case, regularizing the subspaces via framespace warping, provides a common reference and corresponding blend frames can be easily extracted.

- **Performance considerations**: The performance of our proposed pre-blend framespace warp is highly efficient, since only a few event-reference points (states) are shifted along the time axis, instead of the entire set of signal samples. The warp is used to calculate the blend frames' locations, instead of physically adjusting all the samples at every juncture. Each transition operation involves three linear blending operations, namely, *framespace warp, DOF value interpolation* and *frequency interpolation*.

- **Quality considerations**: By using blend frames from the entire framespace, we exploit high frequency information in the basis motions, unlike[6]. Even dropping some of the correspondence events used in[6] yields no visible degradation, since the angular-blend resolution is not hampered. We use event states from the entire body and not just locomotion states (e.g. unlike[6]), to develop correspondence between actions. This widens the application of our algorithm in interpolating *significantly different* motions (eg. running and dancing). Lastly, though linear blending is being used, a tight coupling between framespace warping, DOF value interpolation and frequency blending, achieves a fluid transition.

Though our algorithm is efficient, it only tackles a subset of motion editing problems. For instance, it does not take care of motion retargetting. Though smooth interpolations are achieved, self collision may occur and additional validation needs to be done. Lastly, if basis motions are drastically different, results might not be acceptable due to the lack of adequate correspondence.

7 Summary and Future Work

We have presented a refined framespace interpolation algorithm, which is better suited (but not limited to) editing MOCAP data. Consistent interpolation is achieved by corresponding labelled states from different basis motions. Weights drawn from the interpolant drive a dynamic regularizing warp function, parametric interpolation and transition timing. Velocity interpolation is performed for pelvic translations. Four basis motions, *run,*

walk, dance1 and *dance2* have been used to illustrate blending and concatenation results.

Our chief contributions can be summarized as follows: a) Refined existing algorithm to exploit high frequency information of MOCAP data. b) Efficient computation via simplified dynamic framespace warps and linear blending. c) Fluid transition with minimal user specification, achieved via weight-coupled *framespace warp, DOF value interpolation* and *frequency interpolation*. d) Generalization of framespace interpolation to involve different classes of motions.

We are currently investigating a generalized decoupled blending mechanism, and seamless mixing of acyclic and cyclic primitives. Work remains on developing a robust IK assisted cyclification algorithm and motion validation scheme. The results we have achieved so far, are extremely encouraging. The framespace interpolation technique, though based on simple principles, promises to be an efficient, expressive and powerful animation tool, very much feasible for practical use.

8 Acknowledgements

We gratefully acknowledge our GI2000 reviewers, whose valuable feedback has improved the presentation of our paper and demo-clips[1] significantly.

References

[1] Golam Ashraf. Framespace interpolation results. *http://www.cgit.ntu.edu.sg/~ashraf/framespace/*.

[2] Rama Bindiganavale and Norman I. Badler. Motion abstraction and mapping with spatial constraints. In *Modelling & Motion Capture Techniques for Virtual Environment,CAPTECH'98 Proceedings*, pages 70–82, 1998.

[3] Armin Bruderlin and Lance Williams. Motion signal processing. In Robert Cook, editor, *SIGGRAPH 95 Conference Proceedings*, Annual Conference Series, pages 97–104. Addison Wesley, August 1995.

[4] Michael F. Cohen. Interactive spacetime control for animation. In Edwin E. Catmull, editor, *Computer Graphics (SIGGRAPH '92 Proceedings)*, volume 26, pages 293–302, July 1992.

[5] Michael Gleicher. Retargeting motion to new characters. In Michael Cohen, editor, *SIGGRAPH 98 Conference Proceedings*, Annual Conference Series, pages 33–42. Addison Wesley, July 1998.

[6] S. Guo and J. Roberge. A high-level control mechanism for human locomotion based on parametric frame space interpolation. *Eurographics Computer*

Animation and Simulation EGCAS'96, pages 95–107, 1996.

[7] S. Guo, J. Roberge, and T. Grace. Controlling movement using parametric frame space interpolation. In N. Magnenat Thalmann and D. Thalmann, editors, *Models and Techniques in Computer Animation*, pages 216–227. Springer, Tokyo, 1994.

[8] Jehee Lee and Sung Yong Shin. A hierarchical approach to interactive motion editing for human-like figures. In Alyn Rockwood, editor, *Proceedings of SIGGRAPH '99*, Computer Graphics Proceedings, Annual Conference Series, pages 39–48. Addison Wesley, August 1999.

[9] Yongping Luo. Handling motion processing constraints for articulated figure animation. *Masters Thesis, School of Computer Science, Simon Fraser University*, November 1997.

[10] Roberto Maiocchi. A knowledge-based approach to the synthesis of human motion. In *IFIP Conference on Graphics Modeling*, pages 157–178, 1991.

[11] Charles Rose, Michael F. Cohen, and Bobby Bodenheimer. Verbs and adverbs: Multidimensional motion interpolation. *IEEE Computer Graphics & Applications*, 18(5):32–40, September - October 1998.

[12] Charles F. Rose, Brian Guenter, Bobby Bodenheimer, and Michael F. Cohen. Efficient generation of motion transitions using spacetime constraints. In Holly Rushmeier, editor, *SIGGRAPH 96 Conference Proceedings*, Annual Conference Series, pages 147–154. Addison Wesley, August 1996.

[13] Thomas W. Sederberg and Eugene Greenwood. A physically based approach to 2D shape blending. In Edwin E. Catmull, editor, *Computer Graphics (SIGGRAPH '92 Proceedings)*, volume 26, pages 25–34, July 1992.

[14] Munetoshi Unuma, Ken Anjyo, and Ryozo Takeuchi. Fourier principles for emotion-based human figure animation. In Robert Cook, editor, *SIGGRAPH 95 Conference Proceedings*, Annual Conference Series, pages 91–96. Addison Wesley, August 1995.

[15] Andrew Witkin and Michael Kass. Spacetime constraints. In John Dill, editor, *Computer Graphics (SIGGRAPH '88 Proceedings)*, volume 22, pages 159–168, August 1988.

[16] Andrew Witkin and Zoran Popović. Motion warping. In Robert Cook, editor, *SIGGRAPH 95 Conference Proceedings*, Annual Conference Series, pages 105–108. Addison Wesley, August 1995.

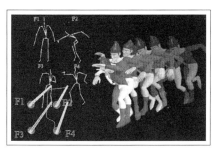

(a) Interface

(b) 2D concatn.   *(c) 3D blend*

Figure 5: *Framespace Interpolation interface.*

(a) $\beta\{Run, Walk\}$

(b) $\zeta\{Dance2, Run\}$

(c) $\beta\{Run, Walk, Dance1, Dance2\}$

Figure 6: *2D & 3D Interpolation results*

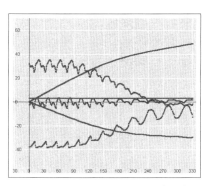

Figure 7: *Pelvis DOFs of $\zeta\{w,r\}$*

Automatic Joint Parameter Estimation from Magnetic Motion Capture Data

James F. O'Brien   Robert E. Bodenheimer, Jr.   Gabriel J. Brostow   Jessica K. Hodgins

College of Computing and Graphics, Visualization, and Usability Center
Georgia Institute of Technology
801 Atlantic Drive
Atlanta, GA 30332-0280
e-mail: [obrienj|bobbyb|brostow|jkh]@cc.gatech.edu

Abstract

This paper describes a technique for using magnetic motion capture data to determine the joint parameters of an articulated hierarchy. This technique makes it possible to determine limb lengths, joint locations, and sensor placement for a human subject without external measurements. Instead, the joint parameters are inferred with high accuracy from the motion data acquired during the capture session. The parameters are computed by performing a linear least squares fit of a rotary joint model to the input data. A hierarchical structure for the articulated model can also be determined in situations where the topology of the model is not known. Once the system topology and joint parameters have been recovered, the resulting model can be used to perform forward and inverse kinematic procedures. We present the results of using the algorithm on human motion capture data, as well as validation results obtained with data from a simulation and a wooden linkage of known dimensions.

Keywords: Animation, Motion Capture, Kinematics, Parameter Estimation, Joint Locations, Articulated Figure, Articulated Hierarchy.

1 Introduction

Motion capture has proven to be an extremely useful technique for animating human and human-like characters. Motion capture data retains many of the subtle elements of a performer's style thereby making possible digital performances where the subject's unique style is recognizable in the final product. Because the basic motion is specified in real-time by the subject being captured, motion capture provides a powerful solution for applications where animations with the characteristic qualities of human motion must be generated quickly. Real-time capture techniques can be used to create immersive virtual environments for training and entertainment applications.

Although motion capture has many advantages and commercial systems are improving rapidly, the technology has drawbacks. Both optical and magnetic systems suffer from sensor noise and require careful calibration[6]. Additionally, measurements such as limb lengths or the offsets between the sensors and the joints are often required. This information is usually gathered by measuring the subject in a reference pose, but hand measurement is tedious and prone to error. It is also impractical for such applications as location-based entertainment where the delay and physical contact with a technician would be unacceptable.

The algorithm described in this paper addresses the problem of calibration by automatically computing the joint locations for an articulated hierarchy from the global transformation matrices of individual bodies. We take motion data acquired with a magnetic system and determine the locations of the subject's joints

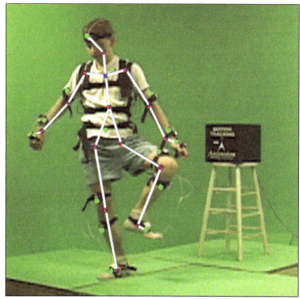

Figure 1: *Test subject and generated model. The subject is wearing the motion capture equipment during a capture session; the superimposed skeletal model is generated automatically from the acquired motion capture data. The chest and pelvis sensors are located on the subject's back.*

and the relative sensor locations without external measurement. The technique imposes no constraints on the sensor positions beyond those necessary for accurate capture, nor does it require the subject to pose in particular configurations. The only requirement is that the data must exercise all degrees of freedom of the joints if the technique is to return an unambiguous answer. Figure 1 shows a subject wearing magnetic motion capture sensors and the skeletal model that was generated from the motion data in an automatic fashion.

Intuitively, the algorithm proceeds by examining the sequences of transformation data generated by pairs of sensors and determining a pair of points (one in the coordinate system of each sensor) that remain collocated throughout the sequence. If the two sensors are attached to a pair of objects that are connected by a rotary joint, then a single point, the center of the joint, fulfills this criterion. Errors such as sensor noise and the fact that human joints are not perfect rotary joints, prevent an exact solution. The algorithm solves for a best-fit solution and computes the residual error that describes how well two bodies "fit" together. This metric makes it possible to infer the body hierarchy directly from the motion data by building a minimum spanning tree that treats the residuals as edge weights between the body parts.

In the following sections, we describe related work in the fields of graphics, biomechanics, and robotics, and our method for computing the joint locations from motion data. We present the results of processing human motion capture data, as well as validation results using data from a simulation and from a wooden linkage of known dimensions.

2 Background

Computer graphics researchers have explored various techniques for improving the motion capture pipeline including parameter estimation techniques such as the algorithm described in this paper. Our technique is closely related to the work of Silaghi and colleagues[18] for identifying an anatomic skeleton from optical motion capture data. With their method, the location of the joint between two attached bodies is determined by first transforming the markers on the outboard body to the inboard coordinate system. Then, for each sensor, a point that maintains an approximately constant distance from the sensor throughout the motion sequence is found. The joint location is determined from a weighted average of these points. The sensor weights are determined manually, and because the coordinate system for the inboard body is not known it must be estimated from the optical data. Our technique takes advantage of the orientation information provided by magnetic sensors. The computation is symmetric with respect to the joint between two bodies and does not require any manual processing of the data.

Inverse kinematics are often used to extract joint angles from global position data. In the animation community, for example, Bodenheimer and colleagues[2] discussed how to apply inverse kinematics in the processing of large amounts of motion capture data using a modification of a technique developed by Zhao and Badler[24]. The method presented here is not an inverse kinematics technique: inverse kinematics assumes that the dimensions of the skeleton for which joint angles are being computed is known. Our work extracts those dimensions from the motion capture data, and thus could be viewed as a preliminary step to an inverse kinematics computation.

Outside of graphics, the problem of determining a system's kinematic parameters from the motion of the system has been studied by researchers in the fields of biomechanics[15, 16] and robotics[9]. Biomechanicists are interested in this problem because the joints play a critical role in understanding the mechanics of the human body and the dynamics of human motion. However, human joints are not ideal rotary joints and therefore do not have a fixed center of rotation. Even joints like the hip which are relatively close approximations to mechanical ball and socket joints exhibit laxity and variations due to joint loading that cause changes in the center of rotation during movement. Instead, the parameter that is often measured in biomechanics is the instantaneous center of rotation, which is defined as the point of zero velocity during infinitesimally small motions of a rigid body.

To compute the instantaneous center of rotation, biomechanicists put markers on each limb and use measurements from various configurations of the limbs. To reduce error, multiple markers are placed on each joint and a least squares fit is used to filter the redundant marker data[4]. Spiegelman and Woo proposed a method for planar motions[19], and this method was extended to general motion by Veldpaus and colleagues[22]. Their algorithm uses multiple markers on a body measured at two instants in time to establish the center of rotation.

We are primarily concerned with creating animation rather than scientific studies of human motion, and our goals therefore differ from those of researchers in the biomechanics community. In particular, because we will use the recorded motion to drive an articulated skeleton that employs only simple rotary joints, we need joint centers that are a reasonable approximation over the entire sequence of motion as opposed to an instantaneous joint center that is more accurate but describes only a single instant of motion.

The biomechanics literature also provides insight into the errors inherent in a joint estimation system and suggests an upper bound on the accuracy that we can expect. Because the joints of the human body are not perfect rotary joints, the articulated models used in animation are inherently an approximation of human kinematics. Using five male subjects with pins inserted in their tibia and femur, Lafortune and colleagues found that during a normal walk cycle the joint center of the knee compressed and pulled apart by an average of 7 mm, moved front-to-back by 14.3 mm, and side-to-side by 5.6 mm[11]. Another source of error arises because we cannot attach the markers directly to the bone. Instead, they are attached to the skin or clothing of the subject. Ronsky and Nigg reported up to 3 cm of skin movement over the tibia during ground contact in running[14].

Roboticists are also interested in similar questions because they need to calibrate physical devices. A robot may be built to precise specifications, but the nominal parameters will differ from those of the actual unit. Furthermore, because a robot is made of physical materials that are subject to deformation, additional degrees of freedom may exist in the actual unit that were not part of the design specification. Both of these differences can have a significant effect on the accuracy of the unit and compensation often requires that they be measured[9]. Taking these measurements directly can be extremely difficult so researchers have developed various automatic calibration techniques.

The calibration techniques relevant to our research infer these parameters indirectly by measuring the motion of the robot. Some of these techniques require that the robot perform specific actions such as exercising each joint in isolation[25, 13] or that it assume a particular set of configurations[10, 3], and are therefore not easily adapted for use with human performers. Other methods allow calibration from an arbitrary set of configurations but focus explicitly on the relationship between the control parameters and the end-effector. Although our technique fits into the general framework described by Karan and Vukobratović for estimating linear kinematic parameters from arbitrary motion[9], the techniques are not identical because we are interested in information about the entire body rather than only the end-effectors. In addition, we can take advantage of the position and orientation information provided by the magnetic motion sensors whereas robotic calibration methods are generally limited to the information provided by joint sensors (that may themselves be part of the set of parameters being calibrated) and position markers on the end-effector.

3 Methods

For a system of m rigid bodies, let $\mathcal{T}^{i \to j}$ be the transformation from the i-th body's coordinate system to the coordinate system of the j-th body ($i, j \in [0..m-1]$). The index $\omega \notin [0..m-1]$ is used to indicate the world coordinate system so that $\mathcal{T}^{i \to \omega}$ is the global transformation from the i-th body's coordinate system to the world coordinate system.

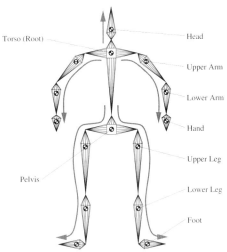

Figure 2: *Example of an articulated hierarchy that could be used to model a human figure. The torso is the root body and the arrows indicate the outboard direction. For rendering, the skeleton model shown here would be replaced with a more realistic graphical model.*

A transformation $\mathcal{T}^{i \to j}$ consists of an additive, length 3 vector component, $\mathbf{t}^{i \to j}$, and a multiplicative, 3×3 matrix component, $\mathbf{R}^{i \to j}$. We will refer to $\mathbf{t}^{i \to j}$ as the translational component of $\mathcal{T}^{i \to j}$ and to $\mathbf{R}^{i \to j}$ as the rotational component of $\mathcal{T}^{i \to j}$, although in general $\mathbf{R}^{i \to j}$ may be any invertible 3×3 matrix transformation.

A point, $\mathbf{x}^i$, expressed in the i-th coordinate system may then be transformed to the j-th coordinate system by

$$\mathbf{x}^j = \mathbf{R}^{i \to j} \mathbf{x}^i + \mathbf{t}^{i \to j}. \tag{1}$$

A transformation from the i-th coordinate system to the j-th coordinate system may be inverted so that given $\mathcal{T}^{i \to j}$, $\mathcal{T}^{j \to i}$ may be computed by

$$\mathbf{R}^{j \to i} = (\mathbf{R}^{i \to j})^{-1} \tag{2}$$

$$\mathbf{t}^{j \to i} = (\mathbf{R}^{i \to j})^{-1} (-\mathbf{t}^{i \to j}), \tag{3}$$

where $(\cdot)^{-1}$ indicates matrix inverse.

Because in general the bodies are in motion with respect to each other and the world coordinate system, the transformations between coordinate systems change over time. We assume that the motion data is sampled at n discrete moments in time called frames, and use $\mathcal{T}_k^{i \to j}$ to refer to the value of $\mathcal{T}^{i \to j}$ at frame $k \in [0..n-1]$.

An articulated hierarchy is described by the topological information indicating which bodies are connected to each other and by geometric information indicating the locations of the connecting joints. The topological information takes the form of a tree[1] with a single body located at its root and all other bodies appearing as nodes within the tree as shown in Figure 2. When referring to directions relative to the arrangement of the tree, the *inboard* direction is towards the root, and the *outboard* direction is away from the root. Thus for a joint connecting two bodies, i and j, the parent body, j, is the inboard body and the child, i, is the outboard body. Similarly, a joint which connects a body to its parent is that body's inboard joint and a joint connecting

---

[1]We discuss the topological cycles created by loop joints in Section 5.

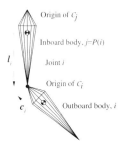

Figure 3: *Joint diagram showing the location of the rotary joint between bodies i and $j = P(i)$. The location of the joint is defined by a vector displacement, $\mathbf{c_i}$, relative to the coordinate system of body i, and a second vector displacement, $\mathbf{l_i}$, in the coordinate system of body j.*

body to one of its children is an outboard joint. All bodies have at most one inboard joint but may have multiple outboard joints.

The hierarchy's topology is defined using a mapping function, $P(\cdot)$, that maps each body to its parent body so that $P(i) = j$ will imply that the j-th body is the immediate parent of the i-th body in the hierarchical tree. The object, $\tau \in [0..m-1]$, with $P(\tau) = \omega$ is the root object. To simplify discussion, we will temporarily assume that $P(\cdot)$ is known *a priori*. Later, in Section 3.3, we will show how $P(\cdot)$ may be inferred when only the $\mathcal{T}^{i \to \omega}$'s are known.

The geometry of the articulated hierarchy is determined by specifying the location of each joint in the coordinate frames of both its inboard body and its outboard body. Because each body has a single inboard joint, we will index the joints so that the i-th joint is the inboard joint of the i-th body as shown in Figure 3.

Let $\mathbf{c}_i$ refer to the location of the i-th joint in the i-th body's (the joint's outboard body) coordinate system, and let $\mathbf{l}_i$ refer to the location of the i-th joint in the $P(i)$-th body's (the inboard body's) coordinate system (see Figure 3). The transformation of equation (1) that goes from the i-th coordinate system to its parent's, $P(i)$, coordinate system can then be re-expressed in terms of the joint locations, $\mathbf{c}_i$ and $\mathbf{l}_i$, and the rotation at the joint, $\mathbf{R}^{i \to P(i)}$, so that

$$\mathbf{x}^{P(i)} = \mathbf{R}_k^{i \to P(i)} (\mathbf{x}^i - \mathbf{c}_i) + \mathbf{l}_i \tag{4}$$

$$= \mathbf{R}_k^{i \to P(i)} \mathbf{x}^i - \mathbf{R}_k^{i \to P(i)} \mathbf{c}_i + \mathbf{l}_i. \tag{5}$$

3.1 Finding Joint Locations

The general transformation given by equation (1) applies to any arbitrary hierarchy of bodies. When the bodies are connected by rotary joints, the relative motion of two connected bodies must satisfy a constraint that prevents the joint between them from coming apart. Comparing equation (5) with equation (1) shows that although rotational terms are the same, the translational term of equation (1) has been replaced with the constrained term, $-\mathbf{R}_k^{i \to P(i)} \mathbf{c}_i + \mathbf{l}_i$. Using equation (5) to transform the location of $\mathbf{c}_i$ to the $P(i)$-th coordinate system will identically yield $\mathbf{l}_i$, and equation (5) enforces the constraint that the joint stay together.

The input transformations for each of the body parts do not contain any explicit information about joint constraints. However, if the motion was created by an articulated system, then it should be possible to express the same transformations hierarchically using equation (5) and an appropriate choice of $\mathbf{c}_i$ and $\mathbf{l}_i$ for each of the joints. Thus for each pair of parent and child bodies, $i \neq \tau$ and $j = P(i)$, there should be a c_i and l_i such that equation (1) and equation (5) are equivalent and

$$\mathbf{R}_k^{i \to P(i)} \mathbf{x}^i + \mathbf{t}_k^{i \to P(i)} = $$
$$\mathbf{R}_k^{i \to P(i)} \mathbf{x}^i - \mathbf{R}_k^{i \to P(i)} \mathbf{c}_i + \mathbf{l}_i \quad (6)$$

for all $k \in [0..n-1]$. After simplifying, equation (6) becomes

$$\mathbf{t}_k^{i \to P(i)} = -\mathbf{R}_k^{i \to P(i)} \mathbf{c}_i + \mathbf{l}_i \quad (7)$$

for all $k \in [0..n-1]$. Later, it will be more convenient to work with the global transformations. By applying $\mathcal{T}^{P(i) \to \omega}$ to both sides of equation (7) and simplifying the result, we have

$$\mathbf{R}_k^{i \to \omega} \mathbf{c}_i + \mathbf{t}_k^{i \to \omega} = \mathbf{R}_k^{P(i) \to \omega} \mathbf{l}_i + \mathbf{t}_k^{P(i) \to \omega} \quad (8)$$

for all $k \in [0..n-1]$. Equation (8) has a consistent geometric interpretation: the location of the joint in the outboard coordinate system, $\mathbf{c}_i$, and the location of the joint in the inboard coordinate system, $\mathbf{l}_i$, should transform to the same location in the world coordinate system; in other words, the joint should stay together.

Equation (8) can be rewritten in matrix form as

$$\mathbf{Q}_k^{i \to P(i)} \mathbf{u}_i = \mathbf{d}_k^{i \to P(i)}. \quad (9)$$

where $\mathbf{d}_k^{i \to P(i)}$ is the length 3 vector given by

$$\mathbf{d}_k^{i \to P(i)} = -(\mathbf{t}_k^{i \to \omega} - \mathbf{t}_k^{P(i) \to \omega}), \quad (10)$$

$\mathbf{u}_i$ is the length 6 vector

$$\mathbf{u}_i = \begin{bmatrix} \mathbf{c}_i \\ \mathbf{l}_i \end{bmatrix}, \quad (11)$$

and $\mathbf{Q}_k^{i \to j}$ is the 3×6 matrix

$$\mathbf{Q}_k^{i \to j} = \begin{bmatrix} (\mathbf{R}_k^{i \to \omega}) & (-\mathbf{R}_k^{P(i) \to \omega}) \end{bmatrix}. \quad (12)$$

Assembling equation (9) into a single linear system of equations for all $0..n-1$ frames gives:

$$\begin{bmatrix} \mathbf{Q}_0^{i \to P(i)} \\ \vdots \\ \mathbf{Q}_k^{i \to P(i)} \\ \vdots \\ \mathbf{Q}_{n-1}^{i \to P(i)} \end{bmatrix} \begin{bmatrix} \mathbf{c}_i \\ \mathbf{l}_i \end{bmatrix} = \begin{bmatrix} \mathbf{d}_0^{i \to P(i)} \\ \vdots \\ \mathbf{d}_k^{i \to P(i)} \\ \vdots \\ \mathbf{d}_{n-1}^{i \to P(i)} \end{bmatrix}. \quad (13)$$

The matrix of $\mathbf{Q}$'s is $3n \times 6$ and will be denoted by $\widehat{\mathbf{Q}}$; the matrix of $\mathbf{d}$'s is $3n \times 1$. The linear system of equations in equation (13) can be used to solve for the joint location parameters, $\mathbf{c}_i$ and $\mathbf{l}_i$.

Unless the input motion data consists of only two frames of motion, $\widehat{\mathbf{Q}}$ will have more rows than columns and the system will, in general, be over-constrained. Nonetheless, if the motion was generated by an articulated model, an exact solution will exist. Realistically, limited sensor precision and other sources of error will prevent an exact solution, and a best-fit solution must be found instead.

Despite the fact that the system will be over-constrained, it may be simultaneously under-constrained if the input motions do not span the space of rotations. In particular, if two bodies connected by a joint do not rotate with respect to each other, or if they do so but only about a single axis, then there will be no unique answer. In the case where they are motionless with respect to each other, any location in space would be a solution. Similarly, if their relative rotations are about a single axis, then any point on that axis could serve as the joint's location. For reasons of numerical accuracy, in either of these cases the desired solution is chosen to be the one closest to the origin of the inboard and outboard body coordinate frames.

The technique of solving for a least squares solution using the singular value decomposition is well suited for this type of problem[17]. Because there is no numerical structure in our problem that we can exploit (such as sparsity), our use of this technique to solve equation (13) is straightforward. In later sections, we will use the residual vector from the solution of this system to show the translational difference between the input data and the value given by equation (5).

3.2 Single-axis Joints

If a joint rotates about two or more non-parallel axes, enough information is available to resolve the location of the joint center as described above. However, if the joint rotates about a single axis, then a unique joint center does not exist, and any point along the axis is an equally good solution to equation (13). In these cases the solution to equation (13) found by the singular value decomposition will be an essentially arbitrary point on the axis.

This situation can be detected by examining the singular values of $\widehat{\mathbf{Q}}$ from equation (13). If one of the singular values of $\widehat{\mathbf{Q}}$ is near zero, i.e., if $\widehat{\mathbf{Q}}$ is rank deficient, then that joint is a single-axis joint, or at least in the input motion it rotates only about a single axis. The first three components of the corresponding column vector of $\mathbf{V}$ from the singular value decomposition are the joint axis in the inboard coordinate frame; the second three are the axis in the outboard coordinate frame

While we were able to verify this method for detecting single-axis joints using synthetic data, none of the data from our motion capture trials indicated the presence of a single-axis joint. We believe that single-axis joints did not appear in the data because our subjects were specifically asked to exercise the full range of motion and all degrees of freedom of their joints. As a result, the system was able to determine a location even for joints such as the knee and elbow that are traditionally approximated as one degree-of-freedom joints.

3.3 Determining the Body Hierarchy

In the previous sections, we assumed that the hierarchical relationship between the bodies given by the parent function, $P(\cdot)$, is known. In some instances, however, determining a suitable hierarchy automatically by inferring it from the input transformation matrices may be desirable. Our algorithm does this by finding the parent function that minimizes the sum of the ε_i's for all the joints in the hierarchy.

The problem of finding the optimal hierarchy is equivalent to finding a minimal spanning tree. Each body can be thought of as a node, joints are the edges between them, and the joint fit error, ε_i, is the weight of the edge. The hierarchy can then be determined by evaluating the joint error between all pairs of bodies, selecting a root node, τ, and then constructing the minimal spanning tree. See [5] for example algorithms.

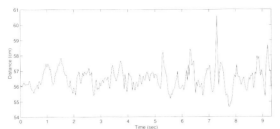

Figure 4: *Calibration data showing the distance between two markers attached rigidly to one another and moved through the capture space. If the sensors are not moved, the data is much less noisy.*

3.4 Removing the Residual

After we have determined the locations of the joints, we can use this information to construct a model that approximates the dimensions of the subject. This model can then be used to play back the original motion data. Unless the residual errors on the joint fits were all near zero, the motion will cause the joints of the model to move apart from each other during playback in a fashion that is typical of unconstrained motion capture data. If, however, we use the inferred joint locations to create an articulated model with kinematic joint constraints and then play back the motion through this model, the joints will stay together. Playing back motion capture data by applying only the rotations to an articulated model is common practice; the difference here is that the model itself has been generated from the motion data. Essentially, we have projected the motion data onto a parametric model and then used the fit to discard the residual.

4 Results

To verify that our algorithm could be used to determine the hierarchy and joint parameters from motion data, we tested it on both simulated data and on data acquired from a magnetic motion capture system. First, the technique was tested on a rigid-body dynamic simulation of a human containing 48 degrees of freedom. The simulated figure was moved so that all of its degrees of freedom were exercised. The algorithm correctly computed limb lengths within the limits of numerical precision (errors less than 10^{-6} m) and determined the correct hierarchy.

We next tested our method in a magnetic motion capture environment. Magnetic motion capture systems are frequently noisy, and the Ascension system we used has a published resolution of about 4 mm[1]. To establish a baseline for the amount of noise present in the environment, two sensors were rigidly attached 56.5 cm apart and moved through the capture space. The results of this experiment are shown in Figure 4. A scale factor exists when converting from units the motion capture system reports to centimeters, and we calculated this scale factor to be 0.94 based on the mean of this data set. The scaled standard deviation of the data is 0.7 cm.

To test the algorithm on something less complicated than biological joints, we constructed a wooden mechanical linkage with five ball-and-socket joints. That linkage is shown in Figure 5. Six sets of data were captured in which all the degrees of freedom were exercised. Before Set 6 was captured, the marker positions were moved to evaluate the robustness of the method to changes in marker locations. The results are shown in Table 1 along with the measured values of the joint-to-joint distances. The maximum error across all trials is 1.1 cm, and the hierarchy was computed correctly for each trial. Another way of eval-

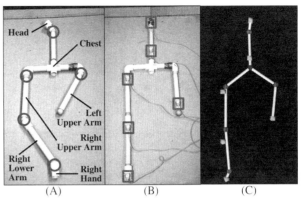

Figure 5: *Wooden mechanical linkage. (A) Labels indicate the terms that we used to refer to the body parts; circles highlight the joint locations. (B) The motion capture sensors (highlighted squares) have been attached to the linkage. (C) The model computed automatically from the motion data using our algorithm. The joints are shown with spheres, and the sensors with cubes. Links between joints are indicated with cylinders.*

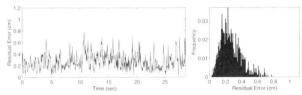

Figure 6: *Residual errors of the right shoulder joint for the data from Set 1 for the mechanical linkage (Table 1). The left graph shows the magnitude of the residual vector. The right graph shows the distribution of the frequency of the magnitudes.*

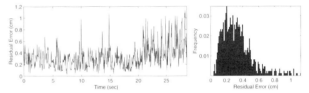

Figure 7: *Residual errors of the left shoulder joint for the data from Set 6 for the mechanical linkage (Table 1).*

uating the fit is to examine the residual vectors from the least squares process. The norms of the residual vectors for the best fit (Set 1, Right Shoulder) and the worst fit (Set 6, Left Shoulder) are shown in Figures 6 and 7, respectively. The right-hand graph has an asymmetric distribution because it is the distribution of an absolute value. We regard these results as very good because the error is on the order of the resolution of the sensors.

The important test case, of course, is to verify that we are able to estimate the limb lengths of people. This task is more difficult because human joints are not simple mechanical linkages. To provide a basis for comparison, we measured the limb lengths of our test subjects. As mentioned previously, this process is inexact and prone to error, but it does provide a plausible estimate. We measured limb lengths from bony landmark to bony landmark to provide repeatability and consistency in our measurements. For example, the upper leg of a subject was measured as the distance from the top of the greater trochanter of the femur to the lateral condyle of the tibia. Because the head of the femur extends upward and inward into the innominate, this measurement will be inaccurate by a few centimeters. Nonetheless,

	Meas.	Set 1	Set 2	Set 3	Set 4	Set 5	Set 6	Δ 1	Δ 2	Δ 3	Δ 4	Δ 5	Δ 6
Neck — Left Shoulder	39.0	39.4	38.8	39.8	39.1	39.1	40.1	-0.4	0.2	-0.8	-0.1	-0.1	-1.1
Neck — Right Shoulder	39.7	39.8	39.8	40.3	40.0	39.9	40.3	-0.1	-0.1	-0.6	-0.3	-0.2	-0.6
Between Shoulders	34.3	34.3	33.7	34.5	34.3	34.3	34.8	0.0	0.6	-0.2	0.0	0.0	-0.5
Right Upper Arm	28.6	29.2	29.0	28.8	28.9	29.0	29.1	-0.6	-0.4	-0.2	-0.3	-0.4	-0.5
Left Upper Arm	31.4	31.5	31.7	31.9	31.5	31.1	31.2	-0.1	-0.3	-0.5	-0.1	0.3	0.2

Table 1: *A comparison of measurements and calculated limb lengths for six data sets of the mechanical linkage. The units are centimeters and the columns labeled Δ show the difference in measured and calculated values. Joint names follow the analogy with human physiology used in Figure 5(A).*

because the greater trochanter is the only palpable area at the upper end of the femur, this measurement is the best available. The difficulty in obtaining accurate hand measurements is one of the primary reasons that we chose to develop our automatic technique.

Our test subjects performed two different sets of motions for capture. We refer to the first set as the "exercise" set. In it the subjects attempted to move each joint essentially in isolation to generate a full range of motion for each joint. Thus the routine consists of a set of discrete motions such as rolling the head around on the neck, bending at the waist, high-stepping, lifting each leg and waving it about, lifting the arms and waving them about, bending the elbows and the wrists, etc. This exercise set mimics the way we gathered data for the mechanical linkage. We refer to the second set of motions captured as the "walk" sets. In it the subjects try to move as many degrees of freedom at once as they can while walking. This routine is perhaps best described as a "chicken" walk, consisting of highly exaggerated leg movements coupled with bending the waist and waving the arms about.

A male subject performed the two types of motion and the results of the limb length calculations are shown in Tables 2 and 3. As expected, the residual errors for a human are much larger than for the mechanical linkage. A representative example is shown in Figure 8. For this subject, the maximum difference between measured and calculated values is 4.1 cm, and occurs at the left upper arm during one of the exercise sets. The mean of the differences between calculated and measured values is less than one centimeter for every limb except the upper arms where it is 1.4 cm and 2.2 cm for the right and left arms, respectively. The algorithm consistently finds a longer length for the left upper arm than what we measured, and that difference may be due, in part, to an error in the value measured by hand. However, the shoulder joint is poorly approximated by a rotary joint: an accurate biomechanical rigid-body model would have at least seven degrees of freedom[21, 20], and it is not surprising that the worst fit occurs there.

The same motions were repeated with a female subject, and the results are shown in Table 4. The largest difference between calculated and measured values is 2.4 cm and again occurs for the left upper arm. The algorithm also finds a longer length for the left upper arm than we measured. The maximum error is less than that for the male test subject, but less consistency was found among the results for the female test subject. The mean of the differences between the calculated and measured values is greater than one centimeter for the right lower leg, left upper leg, and left upper arm.

The system also computed a hierarchy for each trial. For all "exercise" trials for both male and female subjects the computed hierarchy was correct; however, results from the "walk" data were less satisfactory. For three of the five "walk" trials, the algorithm improperly made one of the upper legs a child of the other instead of the pelvis. This error may have occurred be-

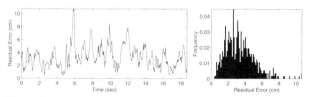

Figure 8: *Residual errors of the left shoulder for the data from Walk 2 of a male subject (Table 3). The scale of the residual vectors is larger than that of the residual vectors for Figures 6 and 7.*

cause the pelvis sensor was mounted on the system's battery pack worn on the subject's hip. Motion in this sensor caused by rotating the thigh upwards may have contributed to the error. The limb length results we report are, of course, for the correct hierarchy assignments.

In addition to the joint measurements we reported, our algorithm determines information for joints (such as between the chest and pelvis) that model the bending of the torso but which are gross approximations to the way the human spine bends. Our algorithm reports limb lengths for these joints within the torso, and these are generally consistent with the dimensions of the torsos of the subjects. However, because we have no reasonable way of measuring these lengths for comparison, we have omitted them from the results. The locations computed for these joints can be seen in Figure 1 and in the animations that accompany this paper.

The algorithm is quite fast. On an SGI O2 with a 195 MHz R10000 processor, less than 4 seconds are required to process 45 seconds of motion data for 16 sensors with the hierarchy specified, and less than 14 seconds when the hierarchy was not specified.

5 Discussion and Conclusions

This paper presents an automatic method for computing limb lengths, joint locations, and sensor placement from magnetic motion capture data. The method produces results accurate to the resolution of the sensors for data that was recorded from a mechanical device constructed with rotary joints. The accuracy of the results for data recorded from a human subject is consistent with estimates in the biomechanics literature for the error introduced by approximating human joints as rotational and assuming that the skin does not move with respect to the bone.

Measuring and calibrating a performer in a production animation environment is tedious. Because this algorithm runs very quickly, it provides a rapid way to accomplish the calibration for magnetic motion capture systems. Detecting and correcting for marker slippage are additional complications in the motion capture pipeline. Because this technique looks for large changes in the joint residual, it provides a rapid way of determining if a marker slipped during a particular recorded segment, thus allowing the segment to be performed again while the subject is still suited with sensors.

	Meas.	Exer. 1	Exer. 2	Exer. 3	Exer. 4	Δ 1	Δ 2	Δ 3	Δ 4
Right Lower Leg	40.0	40.8	40.9	42.2	42.5	-0.8	-0.9	-2.2	-2.5
Left Lower Leg	40.3	37.3	38.4	41.2	41.5	3.0	1.9	-0.9	-1.2
Right Upper Leg	41.6	41.5	42.1	42.9	42.2	0.1	-0.5	-1.3	-0.6
Left Upper Leg	43.2	41.4	41.8	43.2	43.0	1.8	1.4	0.0	0.2
Right Lower Arm	27.0	26.3	26.7	27.7	27.0	0.7	0.3	-0.7	0.0
Left Lower Arm	26.7	26.5	27.0	26.7	27.1	0.1	-0.3	-0.1	-0.4
Right Upper Arm	29.5	32.1	31.3	29.3	28.8	-2.6	-1.8	0.2	0.7
Left Upper Arm	29.5	33.7	32.9	30.1	29.9	-4.1	-3.4	-0.6	-0.4

Table 2: *A comparison of measurements and calculated limb lengths for four data sets of a male subject attempting to exercise each degree of freedom essentially in isolation.*

	Meas.	Walk 1	Walk 2	Walk 3	Δ 1	Δ 2	Δ 3
Right Lower Leg	40.0	40.7	40.3	38.9	-0.6	-0.3	1.1
Left Lower Leg	40.3	40.8	38.9	39.8	-0.4	1.4	0.5
Right Upper Leg	41.6	40.7	40.6	42.6	0.9	1.0	-1.0
Left Upper Leg	43.2	45.1	42.7	43.1	-1.9	0.5	0.1
Right Lower Arm	27.0	27.3	27.5	25.8	-0.3	-0.5	1.2
Left Lower Arm	26.7	26.2	24.9	25.6	0.5	1.7	1.0
Right Upper Arm	29.5	31	31.1	32.7	-1.4	-1.6	-3.2
Left Upper Arm	29.5	32.3	32.3	30.8	-2.7	-2.7	-1.3

Table 3: *A comparison of measurements and calculated limb lengths for three data sets of a male subject attempting to exercise all degrees of freedom simultaneously.*

	Meas.	Exer. 1	Walk 1	Walk 2	Δ_e 1	Δ_w 1	Δ_w 2
Right Lower Leg	36.8	39.1	38.0	38.1	-2.3	-1.2	-1.3
Left Lower Leg	36.5	37.6	37.0	37.4	-1.1	-0.5	-0.9
Right Upper Leg	42.2	42.9	43.3	42.2	-0.7	-1.1	0.0
Left Upper Leg	41.9	42.4	44.1	42.9	-0.5	-2.2	-1.0
Right Lower Arm	24.8	25.5	25.3	22.4	-0.7	-0.5	2.3
Left Lower Arm	24.8	25.1	24.8	23.0	-0.3	0.0	1.8
Right Upper Arm	27.6	27.5	27.5	28.7	0.2	0.1	-1.0
Left Upper Arm	27.6	28.5	30.0	29.0	-0.9	-2.4	-1.3

Table 4: *A comparison of measurements and calculated limb lengths for four data sets of a female subject. The column labeled "Exercise" denotes a performance attempting to exercise each degree of freedom in isolation. Columns labeled "Walk" denote a performance attempting to exercise all degrees of freedom simultaneously. The units are centimeters, and the columns labeled Δ show the difference in measured and calculated values for the appropriate set.*

The parameters computed by this method can be used to create a digital version of a particular performer by matching a graphical model to the proportions of the motion capture subject. The process does not require the subject to assume a particular pose or to perform specific actions other than to exercise their joints fully. Therefore, the method can be incorporated into applications where explicit calibration is infeasible. A cleverly disguised "exercise" routine, for example, could be part of the pre-show portion of a location-based entertainment experience.

The algorithm would also be of use in applications where the problem is fitting data to a graphical model with dimensions different from those of the motion capture subject. The algorithm presented here could be used in a pre-processing step to provide the best-fit limb lengths for the data and modify the data to have constant limb lengths. Then constraint-based techniques could be applied to adapt the resulting motion to the new dimensions of the graphical character.

Passive optical systems often have problems with marker identification because occlusion causes markers to appear to swap. For example, when the hand passes in front of the hip during walking, the marker on the hand and the one on the hip may become confused. If this happens, the marker locations may change relatively smoothly but the joint center of the inboard and outboard bodies for each marker will change discontinuously. This error should be identifiable when the data is processed, allowing the markers to be disambiguated.

For relatively clean data, this algorithm can be used to extract the hierarchy automatically. Specifying the hierarchy is not burdensome for magnetic motion capture data because the markers

are uniquely identified by the system. However, automatic identification of the hierarchy might be useful in situations where connections between objects are dynamic such as pairs dancing or a subject manipulating an instrumented object.

We have assumed that the hierarchy is a strict tree and does not contain cycles or loop joints such as the closed chain that is created when the hands are clasped. If the hierarchy is known *a priori*, the location of a loop joint is found just as it is for any other joint. If the hierarchy is not known, the method of Section 3.3 will not find cycles and the hierarchy it returns will be missing the additional joints required to close the loops. This problem could be detected by informing the user that a joint fit with a low error was not used in building the tree.

The algorithm we have described is statistically equivalent to fitting a parameterized model to a distribution. The rotary joint model that is commonly used for skeletal animation is linear, but more complex models that explicitly model the errors introduced by the non-rotational nature of the joints, the slippage of skin, or the noise distribution seen in the magnetic setup would be non-linear. Non-linear models have been used in robotics research to model elastic deformation of robot limb segments, joints that do not have a fixed center of rotation, and dynamic variation due to system inertial properties[12, 7, 23, 8, 9]. Reconstructing the motion based on the joint locations, as described in Section 3.4, is a first step towards identifying the components of the motion that are due to actual motion and those that are due to errors. The addition of more sophisticated models could allow us to separate components of the data attributable to the motion of the subject from components that are due to other sources. This separation might allow accurate data to emerge even from systems where the sensors are only loosely attached to the subject.

Acknowledgements
The authors would like to thank Victor Zordan for helping with the motion capture equipment and the use of his software. Christina De Juan also helped with various phases of the motion capture process. We also thank Len Norton for his assistance during the early stages of this project.

This project was supported in part by NSF NYI Grant NSF-9457621, Mitsubishi Electric Research Laboratory, and a Packard Fellowship. The first author was supported by a Fellowship from the Intel Foundation, the second author by an NSF CISE Postdoctoral award, NSF-9805694, and the third author by NSF Graduate Research Tranineeships, NSF-9454185. The motion capture system was purchased with funds from NSF Instrumentation Grant, NSF-9818287.

References
[1] Ascension Technology Corporation, http://www.ascension-tech.com.

[2] B. Bodenheimer, C. Rose, S. Rosenthal, and J. Pella. The process of motion capture: Dealing with the data. In D. Thalmann and M. van de Panne, editors, *Computer Animation and Simulation '97*, pages 3–18. Springer NY, Sept. 1997. Eurographics Animation Workshop.

[3] J.-H. Borm and C.-H. Menq. Experimental study of observability of parameter errors in robot calibration. In *Proceeding of the 1989 IEEE International Conference on Robotics and Automation*, pages 587–592. IEEE Robotics and Automation Society, 1998.

[4] J. H. Challis. A procedure for determining rigid body transformation parameters. *Journal of Biomechanics*, 28(6):733–737, 1995.

[5] T. H. Cormen, C. E. Leiserson, and R. L. Rivest. *Introduction to Algorithms*. McGraw–Hill Book Company, fourth edition, 1991.

[6] B. Delaney. On the trail of the shadow woman: The mystery of motion capture. *IEEE: Computer Graphics and Applications*, 18(5):14–19, 1998.

[7] A. A. Goldenberg, X. He, and S. P. Ananthanarayanan. Identification of inertial parameters of a manipulator with closed kinematic chains. *IEEE: Transactions on Systems, Man, and Cybernetics*, 22(4):799–805, 1992.

[8] R. Gourdeau, G. M. Cloutier, and J. Laflamme. Parameter identification of a semi-flexible kinematic model for serial manipulators. *Robotica*, 14:331–319, 1996.

[9] B. Karan and M. Vukobratović. Calibration and accuracy of manipulation robot models – an overview. *Mechanism and Machine Theory*, 29(3):479–500, 1992.

[10] D. H. Kim, K. H. Cook, and J. H. Oh. Identification and compensation of robot kinematic parameters for positioning accuracy improvement. *Robotica*, 9:99–105, 1991.

[11] M. A. Lafortune, P. R. Cavanaugh, H. J. Sommer, and A. Kalenka. Three-dimensional kinematics of the human knee during walking. *Journal of Biomechanics*, 25(4):347–357, Apr. 1992.

[12] J. Lai and H. X. Lan. Identification of dynamic parameters in lagrange robot model. In *Proceedings of 1988 IEEE International Conference on Systems, Man, and Cybernetics*, pages 90–93, 1988.

[13] R. Liscano, H. El-Zorkany, and I. Mufti. Identification of the kinematic parameters of an industrial robot. In *Proceedings of COMPINT '85: Computer Aided Technologies*, pages 477–480, Montreal, Quebec, Canada, 1985. National Research Council of Canada, IEEE Computer Society Press. Held in Montreal, Quebec, Canada, 8–12 September 1985.

[14] B. M. Nigg and W. Herzog, editors. *Biomechanics of the Musculo-skeletal system*. John Wiley, New York, 1998.

[15] M. M. Panjabi, V. K. Goel, and S. D. Walter. Errors in kinematic parameters of a planar joint: Guidelines for optimal experimental design. *Journal of Biomechanics*, 15(7):537–544, 1982.

[16] M. M. Panjabi, V. K. Goel, S. D. Walter, and S. Schick. Errors in the center and angle of rotation of a joint: An experimental study. *Journal of Biomechanical Engineering*, 104:232–237, Aug. 1982.

[17] W. H. Press, B. P. Flannery, S. A. Teukolsky, and W. T. Vetterling. *Numerical Recipes in C*. Cambridge University Press, second edition, 1994.

[18] M.-C. Silaghi, R. Plänkers, R. Boulic, P. Fua, and D. Thalmann. Local and global skeleton fitting techniques for optical motion capture. In N. Magnenat-Thalmann and D. Thalmann, editors, *Modelling and Motion Capture Techniques for Virtual Environments*, volume 1537 of *Lecture Notes in Artificial Intelligence*, pages 26–40, Berlin, Nov. 1998. Springer. Proceedings of CAPTECH '98.

[19] J. J. Spiegelman and S. L.-Y. Woo. A rigid-body method for finding centers of rotation and angular displacements of planar joint motion. *Journal of Biomechanics*, 20(7):715–721, 1987.

[20] F. C. T. van der Helm. Analysis of the kinematic and dynamic behavior of the shoulder mechanism. *Journal of Biomechanics*, 27(5):527–550, May 1994.

[21] F. C. T. van der Helm. A finite element musculoskeletal model of the shoulder mechanism. *Journal of Biomechanics*, 27(5):551–569, May 1994.

[22] F. E. Veldpaus, H. J. Woltring, and L. J. M. G. Dortmans. A least-squares algorithm for the equiform transformation from spatial marker co-ordinates. *Journal of Biomechanics*, 21(1):45–54, 1988.

[23] D. W. Williams and D. A. Turcic. An inverse kinematic analysis procedure for flexible open-loop mechanisms. *Mechanism and Machine Theory*, 27(6):701–714, 1992.

[24] J. Zhao and N. Badler. Inverse kinematics positioning using nonlinear programming for highly articulated figures. *ACM Transactions on Graphics*, 13(4):313–336, 1994.

[25] H. Zhuang and Z. S. Roth. A linear solution to the kinematic parameter identification of robot manipulators. *IEEE: Transactions on Robotics and Automation*, 9(2):174–185, 1993.

Animating Athletic Motion Planning By Example

Ronald A. Metoyer   Jessica K. Hodgins

College of Computing and Graphics, Visualization, and Usability Center
Georgia Institute of Technology
801 Atlantic Drive
Atlanta, GA 30332-0280
e-mail: [metoyer|jkh]@cc.gatech.edu

Abstract

Character animation is usually reserved for highly skilled animators and computer programmers because few of the available tools allow the novice or casual user to create compelling animated content. In this paper, we explore a partial solution to this problem which lets the user coach animated characters by sketching their trajectories on the ground plane. The details of the motion are then computed with simulation. We create memory-based control functions for the high-level behaviors from examples supplied by the user and from real-world data of the behavior. The control function for the desired behavior is implemented through a lookup table using a K-nearest neighbor approximation algorithm. To demonstrate this approach, we present a system for defining the behaviors of defensive characters playing American football. The characters are implemented using either point-masses or dynamically simulated biped robots. We evaluate the quality of the coached behaviors by comparing the resulting trajectories to data from human players. We also assess the influence of the user's coaching examples by demonstrating that a user can construct a particular style of play.

Key words: animation, behavioral control, physical simulation, machine learning

1 Introduction

No matter how realistic a character may look, if it behaves in an unnatural way, the illusion of reality is lost. Animated shorts, video games, interactive virtual environments, and training simulation environments all require animated characters whose high-level behavior conveys an appearance of intelligence. For example, the opponent agents in Quake are most appealing when they appear as proficient in combat as a skilled human opponent. In a sports training environment, unrealistic behaviors are unacceptable because they can lead to negative training.

High-level behaviors govern the way a character moves within the environment to achieve its goals in the presence of obstacles and other characters. Two-dimensional navigation control is necessary in any three-dimensional

Figure 1: Two teams of dynamically simulated bipeds playing American football. The offensive players (blue) are tracking pre-defined offensive routes from real football data. Seven defensive players (yellow) are also tracking pre-defined routes while the four red defensive players are controlled by the behavior function table. Collisions are enforced between all players.

scene with locomoting characters. For example, path planning algorithms allow a character in a video game to avoid collisions with other moving characters and static obstacles. High-level behaviors can also tell a character how to move to accomplish a task such as defending a soccer goal.

We need intuitive interfaces for creating compelling and realistic high-level behaviors because the people who would like to create the content are not always experts in animation, control, or computer programming. For example, a quarterback training simulator should allow a football coach to set up a scenario that is appropriate for a particular trainee. A sports video game could allow the user to demonstrate defensive maneuvers and customize the playing style of his team. Similarly, a child might want to create an animation by directing a swarm of bugs to navigate a particular terrain. Architectural visualizations would benefit from a two-dimensional interface for creating animated figures that navigate through a particular three-dimensional architectural structure.

In this paper, we explore a data-driven approach to defining navigation control where much of the data is supplied directly by the user via an intuitive mouse interface. We use a real-time, memory-based technique that builds local approximations of the appropriate action based on data stored in a table. The data is obtained from coaching examples provided by the user and from observations of real-world scenes[11]. We use point-mass simulations as well as three-dimensional dynamically simulated characters that possess low-level locomotion primitives (Figure 1) to execute the output of the navigation control. We have used this system to implement defensive behaviors for a man-to-man defense and a limited zone defense in American football. We demonstrate the effectiveness of coaching examples by comparing the performance of the coached behaviors to recorded human behavior. We also show that the user can provide coaching examples to create particular styles of defensive play.

2 Background

We build on a considerable history of work in memory-based techniques for creating both high and low-level controllers. In the machine learning community, memory-based learning has been used successfully in robot control. Atkeson and colleagues survey the use of locally weighted learning for robot control tasks[2]. Moore investigates efficient memory-based techniques for robot control[13]. Aha and Salzberg explore the use of nearest-neighbor algorithms for a robot that learns to catch a ball[1]. Researchers have also explored the use of learning from examples to develop road-following controllers for vehicles. The ALVINN system uses a neural network to train off-line on examples of road-following[14]. The ELVIS system learns the eigenvectors of an input image and steering commands for road following examples and projects new examples into this eigenvector feature space to determine steering commands for new situations[8]. In computer graphics, Grzeszczuk, Terzopoulos, and Hinton used neural networks to learn the dynamics and control of several dynamic systems including a rocket ship, a car, and a dolphin[7].

Many other researchers in computer graphics have explored data-driven approaches that combine multiple motion sequences to produce new motion. Unuma, Anjyo, and Takeuchi use Fourier interpolation to generate walking and running gaits that express a variety of emotions[16]. Wiley and Hahn use a tri-linear interpolation pyramid and time warping to create generalized pointing as well as walking on sloped terrain[17]. Rose, Cohen, and Bodenheimer use a radial basis function model to generalize behaviors such as walking and running for speed and angle of the terrain[15]. Their work also emphasizes parametric control of emotional expressiveness for a set of base behaviors.

The goal of our research is to explore whether intu-

itive interfaces can be designed that allow the novice to construct animations effectively. Recently, superb work has been done on a related problem, intuitive interfaces that allow the novice to build three-dimensional graphical models. These systems used a pen and/or mouse to provide the user with intuitive control within a constrained domain. Both Eggli and Zeleznik and their colleagues explored free-hand sketching techniques for creating three-dimensional rectilinear models[5, 18] while Igarashi, Matsuoka, and Tanaka provided an intuitive interface for modeling rounded freeform objects[10]. Our interface builds on these ideas by using a mouse to provide the high-level control examples in the two-dimensional plane and a dynamic simulation as a constraint to produce the details of the low-level animated motion.

Several researchers have explored intuitive interfaces for animation or character direction in virtual environments. Blumberg and Galyean allow the user to direct a character at the motivational, task, and motor levels[4]. Johnson and his colleagues embedded an instrumented skeleton within a plush toy and allowed users to manipulate the toy. Their system recognized common gestures made by the user and interpreted them as commands for the control of an interactive animated character[12]. Each of these techniques constrains the number of degrees of freedom that the user must control to make the problem tractable.

3 American Football

In this paper, we explore a mouse-based interface for coaching reactive behaviors for the defensive-back positions in American football. We first develop a behavior function table based on an existing database of tracked football plays[11]. We then allow the user to modify the behavior by adding coaching examples of the desired behavior. We also build behaviors starting from an empty table for other tests. We present the behavior results with both an offensive/defensive pair of point-masses and two full teams of biped robots. The offensive players and some of the defensive players run pre-defined routes from the database of football plays while the actions of selected defensive players are determined by the behavior function table.

We focus on two types of defense in football: man-to-man and zone. The characteristics of each defensive strategy determine the features that are used to index into the behavior function table as well as the actions that result from the function query. The man-to-man strategy requires that the defender focus on a single offensive receiver and maintain a position near the receiver as he moves down the field. The defender must stay close enough to the receiver to prevent the completion of a short pass but allow enough space to prevent the receiver from getting behind him to complete a long pass[3, 6]. The zone strategy requires that the defender focus on defending any pass within a given area of the field rather than focusing on a specific player. When the play begins, the defender observes the offensive players and takes the

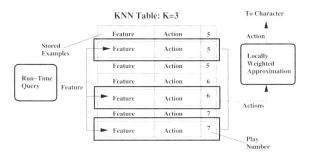

Figure 2: *During training, the algorithm stores all data. At query time, it finds the K-nearest neighbor examples in the table and uses them to compute a local approximation to the appropriate action.*

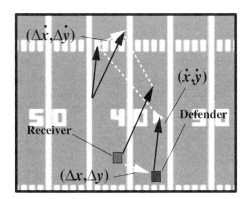

Figure 3: *The man-to-man defensive strategy depends on the absolute velocity of the defender($\dot{x},\dot{y}$), his position with respect to the receiver ($\Delta x,\Delta y$), and his velocity with respect to the receiver ($\Delta\dot{x},\Delta\dot{y}$). The corresponding action is the desired position of the defender with respect to the receiver ($\Delta x_d, \Delta y_d$).*

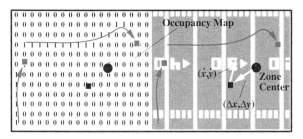

Figure 4: *The zone defensive strategy depends on the absolute velocity of the defender ($\dot{x},\dot{y}$), the relative position of the defender with respect to the zone center ($\Delta x,\Delta y$), and a measure of the offensive activity in the assigned zone area (occupancy map). The corresponding action is the desired position of the defender with respect to the zone center ($\Delta x_d, \Delta y_d$).*

appropriate position within his assigned zone based on the movement of the offensive players[3, 6].

4 Behavior Representation

Memory-based learning is a lazy learning technique because all behavior examples are stored in a table and

actual learning or function approximation does not take place until a query has been made. The query is a feature vector that represents the current state or situation. When a query is made, the K feature vectors that are closest to the query are retrieved from the table along with their accompanying actions. These K feature/action pairs are used to build a distance-weighted local approximation of the action (Figure 2).

Figure 3 illustrates the three features used in the man-to-man defensive strategy: the defensive player's absolute velocity ($\dot{x},\dot{y}$), his position relative to the receiver ($\Delta x,\Delta y$), and his velocity relative to the receiver ($\Delta\dot{x},\Delta\dot{y}$). The action is the desired relative position of the defender with respect to the receiver: ($\Delta x_d, \Delta y_d$).

Figure 4 shows the three features used in the zone defensive strategy: the defender's absolute velocity ($\dot{x},\dot{y}$), his position relative to the zone center ($\Delta x,\Delta y$), and the general offensive activity in his zone area. The general activity within a zone area is determined with a low resolution occupancy map (16x24 m) of the offensive players within the general zone area. If an offensive player occupies a discretized position on the field over the course of a play, a value of one is assigned to that position, creating a map of offensive player travel within the zone area. The maps are compared in a bitwise fashion and the distance between two maps is the number of entries that differ. The corresponding action is the desired position of the defender with respect to the zone center: ($\Delta x_d, \Delta y_d$).

A feature vector p is represented as $(a_1(p), a_2(p), \ldots, a_n(p))$ where $a_r(p)$ denotes the rth attribute of the feature vector p. The distance between two feature vectors p_i and p_j is

$$d(p_i,p_j) = \sqrt{\sum_{r=1}^{n}(a_r(p_i) - a_r(p_j))^2}$$

The weighting for a particular neighbor i given a query, q, is $w_i = 1/d(p_q,p_i)^2$ The distance-weighted action is then

$$f(p_q) = \frac{\sum_{i=1}^{K} w_i f(p_i)}{\sum_{i=1}^{K} w_i}$$

where K is the number of nearest neighbors used in the approximation and $f(p_i)$ is the action associated with instance p_i. This locally approximated action is then used as the output.

5 Sources of Data

The K-nearest neighbor table is built on examples of the desired behavior. These examples can come from measurements of the real world or from data sketched by the user. In Section 7, we describe experiments that use these sources of data both independently and together. A behavior example is defined as a player's defensive trajectory over time. Regardless of the source, the behavior example is sampled at 30Hz and these samples define the

64

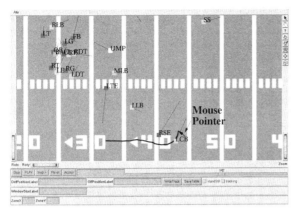

Figure 5: The database contains each player's (x,y) field position sampled at 30Hz. Velocity vectors for the players are computed using finite differences and shown as lines in the image. Labels for each position are also included in the database. Our interface allows the user to draw a path for the defensive player over time in response to the movement of the receiver. Non-coached players move according to the tracked data.

features and actions that are stored contiguously in the table so that continuous pieces of examples can be easily recalled. A 5 second play, then, would contain 150 feature/action pairs.

The real-world data that we used was extracted from an existing database of digitized football plays[11]. This database consists of approximately 100 plays from the 1993 season of the New England Patriots. The plays contain the two-dimensional position of each player on the field sampled at 30Hz as well as the name of the player's position within the offensive or defensive scheme (Figure 5).

The user can supplement the data from the real world by creating time-dependent behavior examples for the defender. The user drags the mouse to sketch out the defensive trajectory on the two-dimensional plane of the field as the play advances in time (Figure 5). The interface allows the user to coach an entire play or only a portion of a play. The user's mouse pointer does not determine the defensive player's position directly; instead it defines the endpoint of a spring and damper system that is connected to the defensive player (Figure 6). The position of the defensive player in x is

$$x_{t+1} = x_t + \dot{x}_t dt + 0.5\frac{f_x}{m}dt^2$$

and the force is $f_x = k_p(x_d - x) - k_v\dot{x}$ where k_p is a position error gain, k_v is a velocity damping gain, x is the current position and x_d is the desired position represented by the mouse pointer. Similar equations hold for y. The velocity of the defender is clamped at 10m/s, a reasonable limit for a football player and the position and velocity are sampled at 30Hz. The dynamics of the spring and damper model serve as a filter on the user's actions

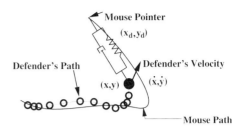

Figure 6: The user tugs at the defender with a spring and damper connected to the mouse pointer.

with the mouse. Using the mouse position and differentiated velocity directly does not provide reasonable feature vectors.

As the user creates a behavior example, each new feature is compared to the closest features in the table. If the new feature is one for which there is no nearby feature/action pair in the table, the new data is added to the table. If the area has been explored, the data is added only if the action is within a threshold distance of the actions for similar features. This process helps to avoid unwanted interference between old and new feature/action pairs and reinforces existing feature/action pairs with similar ones. This culling may also prevent the replacement of bad feature/action pairs with new, radically different feature/action pairs. Instead, replacements are handled by clearing the table or deleting particular behavior examples.

5.1 Run-Time Algorithm

We demonstrate the performance of the K-nearest neighbor table by placing the defensive character in game situations and using the behavior function table to determine his actions during a play. At run-time, a feature vector is computed for the current state of the defensive player. The feature vector is used to find the K-nearest feature/action pairs that come from different behavior examples with a simple linear search through the table ($O(N)$ time). Using a kd-tree would improve searching performance to $O(logN)$. The behavior lookup is performed every T time-steps. For the intervening $T - 1$ time-steps, the system builds the local approximation using the feature/action pair that occurred next in time in the play examples that were originally selected. Switching examples only every T time steps creates more continuous actions. A new query is performed sooner if a play example ends or if the distance error between the current feature in the play example and the current query becomes larger than a threshold value. We used $T = 10$ with a time step of 0.033s for the experiments reported in this paper.

The value of K affects the performance of the system. High frequency changes associated with $K = 1$ lead to poor feature values for subsequent lookups. A higher value for K smooths the actions and consequently the features for subsequent queries. The experiments reported here use a value of $K = 3$.

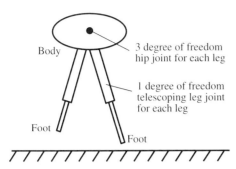

Figure 7: *The biped robot consists of a body and two telescoping legs. Each leg has three degrees of freedom at the hip and a fourth degree of freedom for the length of the leg.*

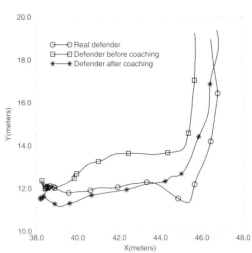

Figure 8: *The line marked with squares shows the performance of the point-mass using a behavior built from the database of football plays. The line marked with stars shows the performance after the table has been augmented with coaching examples while the line marked with circles shows the response of the digitized actual defender. The symbols represent time stamps as the play moves down the field from left to right.*

6   Simulations for Low-Level Behaviors

We demonstrate the performance of the behavior function table on both point-mass simulations and dynamically simulated biped robots. The point-masses have a mass of 100kg and a maximum velocity of 10m/s. A spring and damper connect the point-mass to the desired position on the field. The spring and damper position gain, k_p, was 7000 and the velocity damping gain, k_v, was 700 in our experiments.

The dynamically simulated biped consists of 5 body parts and 8 degrees of freedom (Figure 7). The biped has a leg length of 0.9 meters (approximately the length of the leg of a person 2 meters tall) and uses control laws described in [9]. Because the biped robots are not as agile as human football players, the features are scaled before lookup in the behavior function table and the inverse of the scaling factor is applied to the resulting action. The tracked humans reach maximum velocities of 10m/s whereas the biped robot has a maximum velocity of approximately 4m/s resulting in a scaling factor of 2.5.

7   Results

We ran several tests to evaluate the performance of the system. The first test illustrates the improvement provided by combining coaching with a baseline behavior function table built from the database of tracked football plays. We extracted 30 examples of man-to-man defensive behavior as played by the outside linebacker and cornerback positions. The corresponding feature/action pairs for 29 of these examples were entered into the table to serve as the baseline for man-to-man defensive behavior. Although this table performs reasonably well on many plays, in some cases, the performance is not particularly good.

When the user provides partial or full examples of the desired behavior for several of the 29 plays, the performance improves for the test play that was withheld from the table (Figure 8). The user provided 8 example sequences that were the equivalent of approximately 2 full plays of 3s each. Of the actions used in the final trajectory, 30% were from coached data while the remaining

70% were from the original table data.

Figure 9 shows the results of coaching a character to play a generic man-to-man defense. Starting from an empty table, the character was coached on a set of randomly chosen plays from the database of real football plays. The graph depicts the defender's performance for a play that was not included in the coaching drills. The performance of the coached player is similar to that of the real player not just in the path taken but also in the timing of the play.

To be useful as a tool, the system must allow the user to mold the behavior of the character. We ran two tests to exercise this aspect of the system performance. In each test, the user was to create two distinctly different styles of man-to-man defense. Figure 10 shows a defender coached to have an inside defensive bias and another coached to have an outside defensive bias. This graph is for a play that was not in the coaching set. A defender might take such a bias if a defensive strategy provides him with support from other defensive players on either side. We ran a similar experiment to create both a tight and a loose man-to-man defensive style. The need for these two styles might arise in a football training environment where the content creator would want a defender who plays a tight man-to-man defense for a "goal line" scenario but a loose man-to-man for a scenario of "third down and long."

For this experiment, we ran user tests to determine if subjects other than the authors could use the coaching interface to create the two styles of defense. The subjects were given approximately five minutes to fa-

66

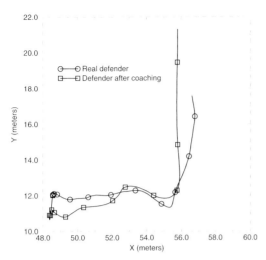

Figure 9: A point-mass character coached to play generic man-to-man competitive defense. Performance against a play from the database is similar to that of the real defender that was recorded for this particular play. The play moves down the field from left to right.

miliarize themselves with the dynamics of the coaching interface. They were then presented with two separate movies of biped robots playing a man-to-man defense against biped receivers. One video represented a tight man-to-man defense while the other represented a loose man-to-man defense. The subjects were asked to coach a point-mass character to play a loose man-to-man defense against a point-mass receiver for six plays. After training on these six plays, the resultant behavior table was applied to an unseen and uncoached play to determine if the subject was satisfied with the resulting loose man-to-man defensive behavior. The process was repeated for the tight man-to-man defense.

On a scale of 1-5, all of the subjects ranked their ability to control the point-mass a 3 or above, and rated their satisfaction with the resulting behavior on the unseen play a 3 or above. Figure 11 shows a graph of the point-mass performance on an unseen play after being coached by one of our subjects. The loose variation was coached for a total of 1015 feature/action pairs, the equivalent of approximately 11 plays of 3s each. The tight variation was coached for a total of 1332 feature/action pairs, the equivalent of approximately 15 plays of 3s each.

Figure 12 shows a graph of the average separation distance between the defender and the receiver for both the loose and tight version of the man-to-man defense for each test subject as well as for the demonstrated man-to-man play that they were attempting to imitate. Subjects 2-6 clearly demonstrate the two distinct styles of man-to-man defense, but subjects 7 and 8 were unable to produce the two styles of defense. Both subjects 7 and 8 are left-handed, but use their right hands for typical mouse manipulations. All other subjects are right-handed.

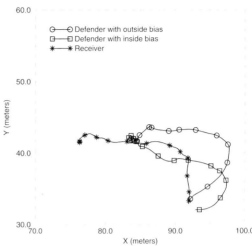

Figure 10: The line marked with circles represents a point-mass defender coached to play a man-to-man defense with an outside position bias. The line marked with squares represents a defender coached to play with a bias to the inside of the receiver. Both behaviors were coached starting from an empty table. The play moves down the field from left to right. The sideline is at the top of the graph, and the player with the outside bias defends closest to the sideline.

Among the right-handed subjects, those with better control over the character were clearly able to produce more consistent examples and this consistency was reflected in the resulting behavior. The subject's level of football knowledge appeared to have little effect as long as the subjects were consistent in their examples.

In the next example, we show that the user can train the character for a limited zone defense. The defender was drilled on three types of plays, with multiple variations of each type. There are three basic zone defensive rules for a linebacker [3]. First, if the halfback to the linebacker's side runs a wide route, the defender must stay wide to protect against the pass to the halfback. Second, if the halfback runs a stop route, the wide receiver will be running a route to the outside. The defender must move to a wide position in the zone to protect against the wide receiver outside route. And finally, if the halfback runs an angle route, the wide receiver is running a deep-inside route. The defender must get to a deep position in the zone and fade to the inside to protect against the wide receiver inside route.

Figure 13 shows an example of the second rule. The offensive player routes were synthetically created for each of the zone examples because the database of football plays did not contain a sufficient number of examples. The defender reacts correctly for a play that was not used in the coaching drills. He moves to a wide position to protect against the wide receiver out route as stated in the second rule.

All of the preceding examples used a point-mass sim-

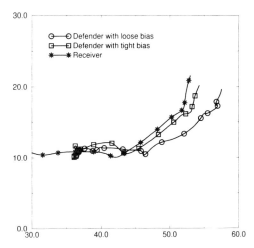

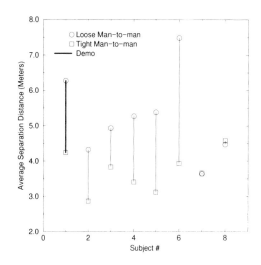

Figure 11: The line marked with circles represents a point-mass defender who was coached to play a loose man-to-man. The line marked with squares represents a defender who was coached to play a tight man-to-man. Both behaviors were coached starting from an empty table. The play moves down the field from left to right.

Figure 12: Average separation distance between defender and receiver for user test subjects coaching a loose man-to-man and tight man-to-man defense. The bold line represents the average separation distance for the demonstration play.

ulation to compute the low-level motion but we can also use simulated bipeds as the football players. Figure 14 shows the performance of a simulated biped robot defender. The robot is controlled with a behavior function table that did not include this particular play. The biped trajectory is compared to that of the human player where the human data has been scaled by $1/2.5$ to match the abilities of the biped.

In each of these examples, the offensive characters are not responsive to the defense and are running predefined routes from the database of football plays or from hand-drawn routes in the case of the zone. This simplification is often reasonable for receivers because their routes must be followed closely after a play has started. The quarterback will often throw the ball to a predetermined spot on the field before the receiver arrives or even looks toward the quarterback.

8 Discussion

This paper illustrates how coaching can be used to create or refine high-level behaviors for animated characters and demonstrates the approach in American football. We built a man-to-man defense behavior based on an initial database of examples and applied it to both a point-mass and a biped robot. We demonstrated the power of the user interface by using coaching to modify this baseline behavior function table as well as to define man-to-man and zone defense behaviors from an initially empty table. We performed user tests and showed that subjects could produce both a tight and a loose man-to-man defense.

The selection of appropriate features is an important aspect of our approach because it determines the dimen-

sionality of the table and therefore the amount of data necessary to populate the table. Unnecessary features result in wasted storage space while too few features can result in an inability to model the desired function. We selected a small set of appropriate features based on our domain knowledge. Given sufficient data, techniques such as principal components analysis might compute the appropriate features automatically. Scaling of the features also affects the performance of our system. We do not normalize the features for the man-to-man or for the zone examples because they were on the same order of magnitude. We did, however, weight the relative position by a factor of 3.0 to increase its importance. For the zone example, our occupancy map feature is potentially subject to noise problems because offensive situations that are shifted with respect to the zone center may not appear similar. This problem could be addressed by using pattern matching techniques that are invariant with respect to shift.

Although we have used only real-world and coaching examples to control the characters in this paper, we believe that the next step towards easily programmed and controlled characters is a combination of several techniques including coaching examples, real-world data, hand-programmed reactive behaviors, and finite state machines for switching between behaviors. Combining coaching with other techniques would allow the animator to influence behavior when desired but would free the animator from providing examples for every situation.

68

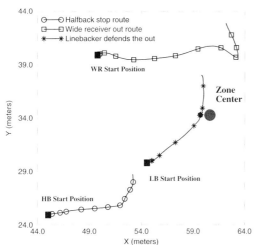

Figure 13: After coaching on several zone play examples, the character effectively defends the zone for this play where the halfback runs a stop pattern. The linebacker retreats to his zone area and correctly moves to the outside to guard against the wide receiver out route.

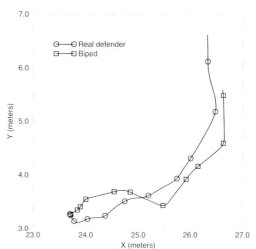

Figure 14: The biped defensive trajectory compared to the recorded human defensive trajectory.

Acknowledgements

We thank Eugene Zhange for the biped collision detection and response implementation. This project was supported in part by a Lucent Technologies Fellowship, NSF NYI Grant No. IRI-9457621, and a Packard Fellowship.

References

[1] D.W. Aha and S. L. Salzberg. Learning to catch: Applying nearest neighbor algorithms to dynamic control tasks. In *Fourth International Workshop on Artificial Intelligence and Statistics*, pages 363–368, 1993.

[2] C.G. Atkeson, A. W. Moore, and S. Schaal. Locally weighted learning for control. *Artificial Intelligence Review*, pages 75–113, 1996.

[3] T. Bass. *Play Football the NFL Way*. St. Martin's, New York, NY, 1992.

[4] B.M. Blumberg and T.A. Galyean. Multi-level direction of autonomous creatures for real-time virtual environments. *Proceedings of SIGGRAPH 95*, pages 47–54, August 1995.

[5] L. Eggli, C. Hsu, G. Elber, and B. Bruderlin. Inferring 3D models from freehand sketches and constraints. *Computer Aided Design*, 29(2):101–112, 1997.

[6] T. Flores and B. O'Conner. *Coaching Football*. Masters Press, Indianapolis, IN, 1993.

[7] R. Grzeszczuk, D. Terzopoulos, and G. Hinton. Neuroanimator: Fast neural network emulation and control of physics-based models. *Proceedings of SIGGRAPH 98*, pages 9–20, July 1998.

[8] J. Hancock and C. Thorpe. ELVIS: Eigenvectors for land vehicle image system. In *Proceedings of the International Conference on Intelligent Robots and Systems(IROS 95)*, pages 35–40, 1995.

[9] J. K. Hodgins, J. Koechling, and M. H. Raibert. Running experiments with a planar biped. In *Robotics Research: The Third International Symposium*, 1986.

[10] T. Igarashi, S. Matsuoka, and H. Tanaka. Teddy: A sketching interface for 3D freeform design. *Proceedings of SIGGRAPH 99*, pages 409–416, August 1999.

[11] S. Intille and A.F. Bobick. MIT Media Lab football trajectory database. http://vismod.www.media.mit.edu/vismod/demos/football,1998.

[12] M.P. Johnson, A. Wilson, B. Blumberg, C. Kline, and A. Bobick. Sympathetic interfaces: Using a plush toy to direct synthetic characters. In *Proceedings of CHI '99*, pages 152–158, 1999.

[13] A.W. Moore. *Efficient Memory-based Learning for Robot Control*. PhD thesis, University of Cambridge, 1990.

[14] D. Pomerleau. *Knowledge-based Training of Artificial Neural Networks for Autonomous Robot Driving*. Kluwer Academic Publishing, 1993.

[15] C. Rose, M. Cohen, and B. Bodenheimer. Verbs and adverbs: Multidimensional motion interpolation. *IEEE Computer Graphics and Applications*, 18(5):32–40, 1998.

[16] M. Unuma, K. Anjyo, and R. Takeuchi. Fourier principles for emotion-based human figure animation. *Proceedings of SIGGRAPH 95*, pages 91–96, August 1995.

[17] D. J. Wiley and J. K. Hahn. Interpolation synthesis for articulated figure motion. In *Proceedings of IEEE Virtual Reality Annual International Symposium*, pages 156–160, March 1997.

[18] R.C. Zeleznik, K.P. Herndon, and J.F. Hughes. Sketch: An interface for sketching 3D scenes. *Proceedings of SIGGRAPH 96*, pages 163–170, August 1996.

Image-Based Virtual Camera Motion Strategies

Eric Marchand   Nicolas Courty

IRISA - INRIA Rennes
Campus de Beaulieu,
35042 Rennes Cedex, France

Abstract

This paper presents an original solution to the camera control problem in a virtual environment. Our objective is to present a general framework that allows the automatic control of a camera in a dynamic environment. The proposed method is based on the *image-based control* or visual servoing approach. It consists in positioning a camera according to the information perceived in the image. This is thus a very intuitive approach of animation. To be able to react automatically to modifications of the environment, we also considered the introduction of constraints into the control. This approach is thus adapted to highly reactive contexts (virtual reality, video games). Numerous examples dealing with classic problems in animation are considered within this framework and presented in this paper.

Key words: Automatic camera motion, Automatic cinematography, Visual servoing, Animation

1 Overview

Issues. There are numerous issues related to the control of a camera in a virtual environment. Typically, the control of the camera is handled by Lookat/lookfrom techniques associated with the definition of 3D trajectories. The camera must, usually, first position itself wrt. to its environment, and must then react in an appropriate and efficient way to modifications of the environment. As regards with the first issue, even if a full knowledge of the scene is available, as in the computer animation context, the positioning task is not a trivial problem (see [2]). There is a need for precise control of the 6 degrees of freedom (d.o.f) of the camera in the 3D space. The second issue, that can be defined as the introduction of constraints in the camera trajectory, is even more complex. In order to be able to consider unknown or dynamic environments and to achieve real-time camera motion control, these constraints must be properly modeled and "added" to the positioning task.

Related work. Visual servoing has proved, within the robotics context, to be an efficient solution to these problems. Visual servoing or image-based camera control consists in specifying a task (mainly positioning or target tracking tasks) as the regulation in the image of a set of visual features [17, 6, 8]. A good review and introduction to visual servoing can be found in [10]. As the task specification is carried out in 2D space, it does not require a 3D relationship between objects. However, since the approach is local, it is not *a priori* possible to consider planning issues. If the control law computes a motion that leads the camera to undesired configurations (such as occlusions, obstacles), visual servoing fails. Control laws taking into account these "bad" configurations therefore have to be considered. Framework that allows the consideration of such constraints has been presented in, for example, [13, 12]. It combines the regulation of the vision-based task with the minimization of cost functions reflecting the constraints imposed on the trajectory.

Viewpoints computation also has received attention in computer graphics. The main difference wrt. computer vision or robotics is that the problem is no longer ill-posed. Indeed, in that case a full knowledge of the scene is available. Even in an interactive context, the past and current behavior of all the objects is fully known. Ware and Osborn [16] consider various metaphors to describe a six d.o.f. camera control including "*eye in hand*". Within this context, the goal was usually to determine the position of the "eye" wrt. its six d.o.f in order to see an object or a set of objects at given locations on the screen. User interfaces such as a 3D mouse or a six d.o.f joystick could be considered to control such virtual device. Obtaining smooth camera motions required a skilled operator and has proved to be a difficult task. The classical lookat/lookfrom/vup parameterization is a simple way to achieve a focusing task on a world-space point. However specifying a complex visual task within the lookat/lookfrom framework is quite hopeless. Attempts to consider this kind of problem have been made by Blinn [2], however the proposed solutions appear to be dedicated to specific problems and hardly scaled to more complex tasks. Image-based control has been described within the computer graphics context by Gleicher and Witkin in [7], who called it "*Through-the-lens camera control*". They proposed to achieve very simple tasks such as positioning a camera with respect to objects defined by static "virtual" points. This technique, very similar to the visual servoing framework, considers a local inversion of the nonlinear perspective viewing transformation. A constraint optimization is used to compute the camera velocity from the desired motion of the virtual point in the image. Another formulation of the same problem has been proposed in [11]. In both case, the image Jacobian (that links the motion of the features to camera motion) is proposed only for point features. Furthermore, the introduction of constraints in the camera trajectory is not considered within the proposed framework.

The introduction of constraints has received great attention in both the robotics (e.g. [15, 4]) and computer graphics [5] communities. The resulting solutions are often similar. Each constraint is defined mathematically as a function of the camera parameters (location and orientation) to be minimized using deterministic (e.g. gradient approaches) or stochastic (e.g. simulated annealing) optimization processes. These approaches feature numerous drawbacks. First they are usually time consuming (the search space is of dimension six) and the optimization has to be considered for each iteration of the animation process (i.e. for each new frame). It is then difficult to consider these techniques for reactive applications such as video games. As already stated, visual servoing allows the introduction of constraints in the camera trajectory [14, 13, 12]. These constraints are modeled as a cost function to be minimized. The resulting motion, also named secondary task, is then projected in the null space of the main task; it has then no effect on the main visual task. In this framework, as the camera trajectory that ensures both the task and the constraints is computed locally, it can be handled in real-time as required by the considered applications.

Presented system and contributions. The aim was to define the basic camera trajectories for virtual movie directors as well as the automatic control of a camera for reactive applications such as video games. We assume that we fully know the model of the scene at the current instant. Within this context, we present a complete framework, based on visual servoing, that allows the definition of positioning tasks wrt. to a set of "virtual visual features" located within the environment (these features can be points, lines, spheres, cylinders, etc.). When the specified task does not constrain all the camera d.o.f, the method allows the introduction of secondary tasks that can be achieved under the constraint that the visual task is itself achieved. Furthermore the considered features are not necessarily motionless. Using this approach we present solutions to various non-trivial problems in computer animation. Some of these tasks are more concerned with reactive applications (target tracking and following, obstacles and occlusion avoidance) while others deal with cinema application (panning, camera traveling, lighting conditions optimization, etc).

The remainder of this paper is organized as follows: Section 2 recalls the visual servoing framework within the task function approach. Section 3 presents methods allowing navigation in cluttered dynamic environments. Section 4 handles constraints more closely related to the cinema industry.

2 Image-based camera control

Image-based visual servoing consists in specifying a task as the regulation in the image of a set of visual features [6][8]. Embedding visual servoing in the task function approach [14] allows the use of general results helpful for the analysis and the synthesis of efficient closed loop control schemes. A good review and introduction to visual servoing can be found in [10].

2.1 Camera positioning wrt. visual targets

Let us denote $\mathbf{P}$ the set of selected visual features used in the visual servoing task measured from the image, or by projection in the computer graphics context, at each iteration of the control law. To ensure the convergence of $\mathbf{P}$ to its desired value $\mathbf{P_d}$,

we need to know the interaction matrix (or image Jacobian) $\mathbf{L_P}^T$ that links the motion of the object in the image to the camera motion. It is defined by the now classic equation [6] :

$$\dot{\mathbf{P}} = \mathbf{L_P}^T(\mathbf{P}, \mathbf{p})\mathbf{T_c} \qquad (1)$$

where $\dot{\mathbf{P}}$ is the time variation of $\mathbf{P}$ (the motion of $\mathbf{P}$ in the image) due to the camera motion $\mathbf{T_c}$. The parameters $\mathbf{p}$ involved in $\mathbf{L_P}^T$ represent the depth information between the considered objects and the camera frame. A vision-based task $\mathbf{e_1}$ is defined by:

$$\mathbf{e_1} = \mathbf{C}(\mathbf{P} - \mathbf{P_d}) \qquad (2)$$

where $\mathbf{C}$, called combination matrix, has to be chosen such that $\mathbf{C}\mathbf{L_P}^T$ is full rank along the desired trajectory $r \in SE^3$. If $\mathbf{e_1}$ constrains the 6 d.o.f, it can be defined as $\mathbf{C} = \mathbf{L_P}^{T+}(\mathbf{P}, \mathbf{p})$. We will see in Section 2.3 how to define C if the 6 d.o.f are not constrained. $\mathbf{L}^+$ is the pseudo inverse of matrix $\mathbf{L}$.

To make $\mathbf{e_1}$ decreases exponentially and behaves like a first order decoupled system, the camera velocity given as input to the virtual camera is given by:

$$\mathbf{T_c} = -\lambda\mathbf{e_1} \qquad (3)$$

where λ is a proportional coefficient.

Within this framework we can easily perform positioning tasks wrt. to any object of the scene. The main advantage of this approach is that even if the task is specified within the 2D image space, control is performed in 3D.

2.2 Building new skills

One of the difficulties in image-based visual servoing is to derive the image Jacobian $\mathbf{L}^T$ which corresponds to the selected control features. A systematic method has been proposed to analytically derive the interaction matrix of a set of control features defined upon geometrical primitives [6]. Any kind of visual information can be considered within the same visual servoing task (coordinates of points, line orientation, surface or more generally inertial moments, distance, etc).

Knowing these interaction matrices, the construction of elementary visual servoing tasks is straightforward. A large library of elementary skills can be proposed. The current version of our system allows to define X-to-X feature-based tasks with X = {point, line, sphere, cylinder, circle, etc.}. Using these elementary positioning skills, more complex tasks can be considered by stacking the elementary Jacobians. For example if we want to build a positioning task wrt. to a segment, defined by two points $\mathbf{P_1}$ and $\mathbf{P_2}$, the resulting interaction matrix will be defined by:

$$\mathbf{L_P}^T = \left[\begin{array}{c} \mathbf{L_{P_1}}^T \\ \mathbf{L_{P_2}}^T \end{array} \right] \qquad (4)$$

where $\mathbf{L_{P_i}}^T$ is defined, if $\mathbf{P_i} = (X, Y)$ and z is its depth, by (See [6] for its derivation):

$$\mathbf{L_P}^T = \left(\begin{array}{cccccc} -1/z & 0 & X/z & XY & -(1+X^2) & Y \\ 0 & -1/z & Y/z & 1+Y^2 & -XY & -X \end{array} \right) \qquad (5)$$

More positioning skills can thus be simply defined.

2.3 Introducing constraints

If the vision-based task does not constrain all the n robot d.o.f, a secondary task (that usually represents a camera trajectory constraint) can be performed. $\mathbf{C}$ is now defined as $\mathbf{C} = \mathbf{CL}_\mathbf{P}^T$ and we obtain the following task function:

$$\mathbf{e} = \mathbf{W}^+\mathbf{e_1} + (\mathbf{I_n} - \mathbf{W}^+\mathbf{W})\mathbf{e_2} \qquad (6)$$

where

- $\mathbf{e_2}$ is a secondary task. Usually $\mathbf{e_2}$ is defined as the gradient of a cost function h_s to be minimized ($\mathbf{e_2} = \frac{\partial h_s}{\partial \mathbf{r}}$). This cost function is minimized under the constraint that $\mathbf{e_1}$ is realized.

- $\mathbf{W}^+$ and $\mathbf{I_n} - \mathbf{W}^+\mathbf{W}$ are two projection operators which guarantee that the camera motion due to the secondary task is compatible with the regulation of $\mathbf{P}$ to $\mathbf{P_d}$. $\mathbf{W}$ is a full rank matrix such that Ker $\mathbf{W} =$ Ker $\mathbf{L}_\mathbf{P}^T$. Thanks to the choice of matrix $\mathbf{W}$, $\mathbf{I_n} - \mathbf{W}^+\mathbf{W}$ belongs to Ker $\mathbf{L_P}$, which means that the realization of ***the secondary task will have no effect on the vision-based task*** ($\mathbf{L}_\mathbf{P}^T(\mathbf{I_n} - \mathbf{W}^+\mathbf{W})\mathbf{e_2} = 0$). Let us note that, if the visual task constrains all the n d.o.f of the manipulator, we have $\mathbf{W} = \mathbf{I_n}$, which leads to $\mathbf{I_n} - \mathbf{W}^+\mathbf{W} = 0$. It is thus impossible in that case to consider any secondary task.

The control is now given by:

$$\mathbf{T_c} = -\lambda\mathbf{e} - (\mathbf{I_n} - \mathbf{W}^+\mathbf{W})\frac{\partial \mathbf{e_2}}{\partial t} \qquad (7)$$

2.4 Tracking a mobile target

A target motion generally induces tracking errors that have to be suppressed in order to always achieve the tracking task perfectly.

In that case, the motion of the target in the image can be rewritten as:

$$\dot{\mathbf{P}} = \mathbf{L}_\mathbf{P}^T\mathbf{T_c} - \mathbf{L}_\mathbf{P}^T\mathbf{T_0} \qquad (8)$$

where $\mathbf{L}_\mathbf{P}^T\mathbf{T_c}$ and $\mathbf{L}_\mathbf{P}^T\mathbf{T_0}$ are respectively the contribution of the camera velocity and of the autonomous target motion to the motion of the target in the image. The new camera velocity that suppresses the tracking errors is then given by:

$$\mathbf{T_c} = -\lambda\mathbf{e} - (\mathbf{I_n} - \mathbf{W}^+\mathbf{W})\frac{\partial \mathbf{e_2}}{\partial t} - \alpha\mathbf{T_0} \qquad (9)$$

where $\alpha \in [0, 1]$ is a scalar. If $\alpha = 1$, the tracking errors are fully suppressed while if $\alpha = 0$, they are not handled.

3 Reactive viewpoint planning

The positioning tasks that can be considered within the framework presented in the previous section are quite simple. As we did not consider the environment, the target was assumed to be "alone". We now present a method that makes it possible to achieve far more complex tasks in dynamic "*cluttered environments*". In this difficult context we will propose a purely reactive framework in order to avoid undesirable configurations in an animation context.

3.1 Avoiding obstacles

Obstacle avoidance is a good example of what can be easily given within the proposed framework. Let us assume that the camera is moving in a cluttered environment while focusing on a visual target. The goal is to ensure this task while avoiding all the obstacles in the scene.

There are in fact multiple solutions to this problem: one solution is to planify a trajectory that avoids the obstacles using a trajectory planning process. Another solution is to consider a secondary task that uses the redundant d.o.f of the camera to move away from obstacles. This function will tend to maximize the distance between the camera and the obstacle. A good cost function to achieve the goal should be maximum (infinite) when the distance between the camera and the obstacle is null. The simplest cost function is then given by:

$$h_s = \alpha\frac{1}{2\|C - O_c\|^2} \qquad (10)$$

where $C(0, 0, 0)$ is the camera location and $O_c(x_c, y_c, z_c)$ are the coordinates of the closest obstacle to the camera, both expressed in the camera frame (note that any other cost function that reflects a similar behavior suits the problem). If $O_s(x_s, y_s, z_s)$ are the coordinates of the obstacle within the scene frame (or reference frame) and $M_c(RT)$ the homogenous matrix that describes the camera position within this reference frame, the obstacle coordinates within the camera frame are given by $X_c = R^T X_s - R^T T$.

The components of the secondary task are given by:

$$\mathbf{e_2} = -(x_c, y_c, z_c, 0, 0, 0)^T\frac{h_s^2}{\alpha} \quad \text{and} \quad \frac{\partial \mathbf{e_2}}{\partial t} = 0 \qquad (11)$$

Multiple obstacles can be handled considering the cost function $h_s = \sum_i \alpha\frac{1}{\|C - O_{c_i}\|^2}$.

3.2 Avoiding occlusions

The goal here is to avoid the occlusion of the target due to static or moving objects (with unknown motion). The virtual camera has to perform adequate motion in order to avoid the risk of occlusion while taking into account the desired constraints between the camera and the target. There are actually many situations that may evolve in an occlusion. The first and most simple case is a moving object that crosses the camera/target line (see Figure 1.a). Two other similar cases may be encountered: in the first one (see Figure 1.b) the target moves behind another object in the scene while in the second one (see Figure 1.c) the camera follows an undesirable trajectory and is hidden behind an object.

We will now present a general image-based approach that make it possible to generate adequate camera motion automatically to avoid occlusions [12]. In a second time we will see a simple method to determine the risk of occlusion in order to weight adequately the camera response (i.e. its velocity).

Automatic generation of adequate motions

Let us consider $\mathcal{O}$ the projection in the image of the set of objects in the scene which may occlude the target T: $\mathcal{O} = \{O_1 \ldots O_n\}$. According to the methodology presented in

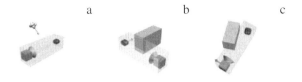

Figure 1: Occlusion issues (a) occlusion due to a moving object (b) occlusion due to the target motion (c) occlusion due to the camera motion

paragraph 2.3 we have to define a function h_s which reaches its maximum value when the target is occluded by another object of the scene. In fact this occlusion problem can be fully defined in the image. Indeed, if the occluding object is closer than the target, when the distance between the projection of the target and the projection of the occluding object decreases, the risk of occlusion increases.

We thus define h_s as a function of this distance in the image:

$$h_s = \frac{1}{2}\alpha \sum_{i=1}^{n} e^{-\beta\left(\|T-O_i\|^2\right)} \qquad (12)$$

where α and β are two scalar constants. α sets the amplitude of the control law due to the secondary task. The components of $\mathbf{e_2}$ and $\frac{\partial \mathbf{e_2}}{\partial t}$ involved in (7) are then:

$$\mathbf{e_2} = \frac{\partial h_s}{\partial \mathbf{r}} = \frac{\partial h_s}{\partial \mathbf{P}}\frac{\partial \mathbf{P}}{\partial \mathbf{r}}, \qquad \frac{\partial \mathbf{e_2}}{\partial t} = 0$$

Computing $\frac{\partial h_s}{\partial \mathbf{P}}$ is seldom difficult. $\frac{\partial \mathbf{P}}{\partial \mathbf{r}}$ is nothing but the image Jacobian $L_{\mathbf{P}}^T$.

Let us consider the case of a single occluding object here considered as a point. The generalization to other and/or to multiple objects is straightforward. We want to see the target T at a given location in the image. Thus we will consider the coordinates $\mathbf{P} = (X, Y)$ as its center of gravity. If we also consider the occluding object $\mathcal{O}$ by a point $\mathbf{P}_{\mathcal{O}} = (X_{\mathcal{O}}, Y_{\mathcal{O}})$, defined as the closest point of $\mathcal{O}$ to T, we have:

$$h_s = \frac{1}{2}\alpha e^{-\beta\|\mathbf{P}-\mathbf{P}_{\mathcal{O}}\|^2}$$

and $\mathbf{e_2}$ is given by:

$$\mathbf{e_2} = \frac{\partial h_s}{\partial \mathbf{r}} = \frac{\partial h_s}{\partial X}\mathbf{L}_X^T + \frac{\partial h_s}{\partial Y}\mathbf{L}_Y^T \qquad (13)$$

with

$$\frac{\partial h_s}{\partial X} = -\alpha\beta(X - X_{\mathcal{O}})e^{-\beta\|\mathbf{P}-\mathbf{P}_{\mathcal{O}}\|^2}$$

and

$$\frac{\partial h_s}{\partial Y} = -\alpha\beta(Y - Y_{\mathcal{O}})e^{-\beta\|\mathbf{P}-\mathbf{P}_{\mathcal{O}}\|^2}$$

In fact $\mathbf{e_2}$ as defined in (13) is an approximation of $\frac{\partial h_s}{\partial \mathbf{r}}$. Indeed $\mathbf{L}_{\mathbf{P}}^T = \left[\mathbf{L}_X^T, \quad \mathbf{L}_Y^T\right]^T$ is the image Jacobian related to a physical point. In our case, since the point is defined as the closest point of $\mathcal{O}$ to T, the corresponding physical point will change over time. However considering $\mathbf{L}_X^T$ and $\mathbf{L}_Y^T$ in (13) is locally a good approximation.

Risk of occlusion

Using the presented approach to compute the camera reaction is fine if the occluding object moves between the camera and the target [12] as depicted in Figure 1. Indeed, in that case occlusion will occur if no action is taken. However, it is neither necessary nor desirable to move the camera in all the cases (if the occluding object is farther than the target). A key point is therefore to detect if an occlusion may actually occur. In that case we first compute a bounding volume $\mathcal{V}$ that includes both the camera and the target at time t and at time $t + ndt$ assuming a constant target velocity (see Figure 2 and Figure 3). An occlusion will occur if an object is located within this bounding box. The time-to-occlusion may be computed as the smallest n for which the bounding box is empty. If an object $\mathcal{O}$ of the scene is in motion, in the same way, we consider the intersection of the volume $\mathcal{V}$ with a bounding volume that includes $\mathcal{O}$ at time t and at time $t + ndt$.

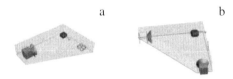

Figure 2: Computing the risk of occlusion

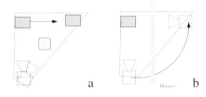

Figure 3: Detection of a future (a) occlusion (b) collision with an obstacle

Let us point out two other interesting issues:

- Obstacle avoidance may be considered in this context. Indeed, if an obstacle is on the camera trajectory, it will be located in the created bounding box (see Figure 3.b). The system will therefore forbid the camera to move in that direction.

- Some cases are more difficult to handle. A good example is a target moving in a corridor (see Figure 4). In that case, the only solution to avoid the occlusion of the target by one of the walls and to avoid the contact with the other wall is to reduce the camera/target distance. This can only be done if the z axis is not controlled by the primary task.

In conclusion, let us note that in this paragraph, we have just proposed a method to detect and quantify the risk of occlusion. The method proposed in paragraph 3.2 must be, in all cases, used to generate the adequate motion that will actually avoid occlusion. The time-to-occlusion computed here will in fact be

Figure 4: Occlusion issues: camera in a corridor

used to set the parameter α (see equation (12)) that tunes the amplitude of the response to the risk.

4 Virtual director for automatic cinematography

Whereas the issues considered in the previous section are more related to reactive applications such as video games, the problems considered in this paragraph are more concerned with camera control for movie making applications. The question considered here is the following: where should we place the camera to ensure film constraints within a given *shot* [1]. Our goal here is not to provide a director with a language that describes scenes and shots such as in [3][9] but to propose some elementary skills to be used afterwards by the director.

4.1 Cinematographic basic camera placement

Panning and Tracking Panning and tracking, certainly the most common camera motions, are straightforward to consider within the image-based framework, and have been widely considered in the previous sections of this paper. In fact the only difficulty is to choose the visual features (virtual or not) on which we want to servo. This choice is very important as it will determine the d.o.f of the virtual camera that will be used to achieve the task. For example for panning issues, the users are likely to choose one or two virtual points or a straight line as visual features (for these features the pan axes of the camera will be controlled). For tracking issues, the adequate features may depend on the desired camera motion. For example, if the camera motion has to be "parallel" to the target trajectory, the 6 d.o.f must be constrained in order to achieve a rigid link between the camera and the target (4 points or 4 lines – or any other combination of visual features such that $\mathbf{L}^T$ is a full rank 6 matrix – are then suitable for such a purpose).

Trajectory tracking As regards with the trajectory tracking issue, the problem is fairly simple. We want the camera to move on a curve $\mathcal{V}(t) = (x(t), y(t), z(t))$ defined in the camera frame. We consider a secondary task that is nothing but a function of the distance between the camera and the point $\mathcal{V}(t)$. A good solution is to define the secondary task as the function h_s simply defined as:

$$h_s = \|\mathcal{V}(t)\|^2. \tag{14}$$

Many other basic cinematographic issues exist (see [1] or [9]), e.g. building apex camera placement (that can be defined by two segments or two points for example), external or internal view (that has to consider the target and a virtual line of interest). Our goal is not to describe these tasks here. However, as they are described within the image space, image-based camera control is suitable for such issues.

4.2 Controlling lighting conditions

Controlling lighting condition (i.e. the "photography" problem), is a fundamental and non trivial issue for a film director. The main problem is to define what a good shot is wrt. these conditions. Two different functions are proposed to achieve this goal: one is directly based on the intensity within the image while the second is based on the intensity gradient (that gives information about the contrast in the image).

Our goal is to position the camera wrt. the lit aspect of the object. Therefore, we want to maximize the quantity of light (re)emitted by this object to ensure good lighting conditions. Applying the proposed methodology, we want to maximize the following cost function:

$$h_s = \frac{1}{n} \sum_X \sum_Y I(X, Y)$$

where $I(X, Y)$ represents the intensity of the 2D point (X, Y). The points (X, Y) belong to the object. The secondary task is then given by:

$$\frac{\partial h_s}{\partial \mathbf{r}} = \frac{1}{n} \sum_X \sum_Y \left(\frac{\partial h_s}{\partial X} \frac{\partial X}{\partial \mathbf{r}} + \frac{\partial h_s}{\partial Y} \frac{\partial Y}{\partial \mathbf{r}} \right)$$
$$= \frac{1}{n} \sum_X \sum_Y \left(\nabla_X \mathbf{L}_X^T + \nabla_Y \mathbf{L}_Y^T \right) \tag{15}$$

where $\nabla I_X = \frac{\partial I}{\partial X}$ and $\nabla I_Y = \frac{\partial I}{\partial Y}$ represents the spatial intensity gradient.

If our goal is to maximize the contrast within the image, one possible criterion will be to maximize the sum of the spatial intensity gradient within the image. The corresponding cost function is given by:

$$h_s = \frac{1}{n} \sum_X \sum_Y \left[\nabla I_X^2 + \nabla I_Y^2 \right] \tag{16}$$

We therefore need to compute the gradient $\frac{\partial h_s}{\partial r}$ that is in fact given by

$$\frac{\partial h_s}{\partial r} = \frac{1}{n} \sum_X \sum_Y \left(\frac{\partial h_s}{\partial X} \mathbf{L}_X^T + \frac{\partial h_s}{\partial Y} \mathbf{L}_Y^T \right) \tag{17}$$

After some rewriting, we finally get:

$$\frac{\partial h_s}{\partial r} = \frac{2}{n} \sum_X \sum_Y \left[\left(\frac{\partial^2 I}{\partial X^2} \nabla I_X + \frac{\partial^2 I}{\partial Y \partial X} \nabla I_Y \right) \mathbf{L}_X^T \right. $$
$$\left. + \left(\frac{\partial^2 I}{\partial X \partial Y} \nabla I_X + \frac{\partial^2 I}{\partial Y^2} \nabla I_Y \right) \mathbf{L}_Y^T \right]^T \tag{18}$$

5 Results

In this section some results are presented to illustrate our approach. Most of the images are generated in "real-time" (i.e. less than 0.1 s/frame) on a simple SUN Ultra Sparc (170Mhz) using Mesa GL (the images produced using this process can be seen in, for example, Figure 6 or Figure 8). The animations of Figure 7 or Figure 9 are computed afterwards using Maya from Alias Wavefront.

74

5.1 Avoiding occlusions: museum walkthrough.

In this example, we applied the proposed methodology to a navigation task in a complex environment. The target to be followed is moving in a museum-like environment. The goal is to keep the target in view (i.e. to avoid occlusions) while considering *on-line* the modifications of the environment (i.e. other moving objects). In this example, we consider a focusing task wrt. an image centered virtual sphere. This task constrains 3 d.o.f of the virtual camera (i.e. to achieve the focusing task and to maintain the radius constant in the image). The reader can refer to [6] for the complete derivation of the image Jacobian related to a sphere. Figure 5 shows the camera trajectories for various applied strategies. Obstacles appear in yellow. The target trajectory is represented as a red dotted line, while the trajectory of another moving object is represented as a blue dotted line. The red trajectory represents the simplest strategy: just focus the object. As nothing is done to consider the environment, occlusions and then collisions with the environment occur. The blue trajectory only considers the avoidance of occlusions by static objects; as a consequence, the occlusion by the moving object occurs. The green trajectory considers the avoidance of occlusions by both static and moving objects.

A bird's eye view of some key-frames are given in Figure 6. The yellow volume (associated to the camera-target couple) corresponds to the bounding volumes used to predict the occlusions. The green volume is only used to detect the occlusions by the moving object as explained in Section 3.2. Figure 6 (A2, A3, B1) shows three views "acquired" during the avoidance of the occlusion by the *wall 1*. Between view B1 and view B2 the occlusion by the moving object is avoided. As for the first wall the problem of *wall 2* in the center of the room is handled as shown in images B3, C1 and C2. Final position is reached on C3. Figure 7 shows six views acquired by the virtual camera and rendered by using Maya.

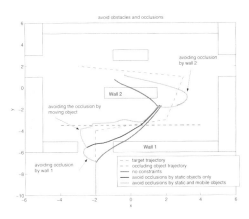

Figure 5: *Museum walkthrough: camera trajectories for various strategies*

5.2 Walking in a corridor: Merging multiple constraints

In this experiment the considered task is the same but the target is moving within a narrow corridor and is turning right (see

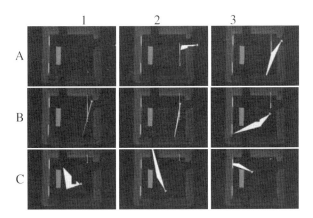

Figure 6: *Museum Walkthrough: bird's eye views with the bounding volumes used for occlusion predictions*

Figure 7: *Museum Walkthrough: bird's eye views and corresponding camera views*

Figure 8). In this experiment it is not possible to achieve this task if the distance between the camera and the target remains constant. If one wants the camera to keep the target in view an occlusion avoidance process has to be avoided. The problem is that the motion computed to avoid the occlusion moves the camera toward the red wall. An obstacle avoidance process is then necessary. We then have three secondary tasks: one related to the camera-target distance, one related to obstacle avoidance (see paragraph 3.1) and the last one related to occlusion avoidance (see paragraph 3.2). The resulting control law automatically produces a motion that moves the camera away from the wall and reduces the camera-target distance. This distance, initially set to 3.5 m, decreases and reaches less that 2.5 m to ensure the task.

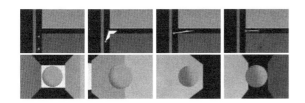

Figure 8: Moving in a corridor: bird's eye views and camera views

5.3 Trajectory tracking

In the experiment described in Figure 9, the camera focuses on the tower (i.e. we want to see this tower vertically and centered in the image). Let us note here that a similar task has been considered in [7].

Let us first consider the positioning task itself. It can be handled in various ways according to the chosen visual features. The simplest way to define a segment is to consider its two extremities. In that case $\mathbf{L_P}^T$ is a full rank 4 matrix. In that case, the distance between the camera and the middle of the segment must remain constant. If we want to follow a trajectory that does not ensure this constraint, we will have to modify the focal length of the camera to ensure both the main task and the trajectory tracking [7]. This solution is usually not suitable for cinematographic issues. The other way to consider this segment is to choose the segment support straight line as visual feature. In that case, the image Jacobian is a full rank 2 matrix and only two d.o.f are then constrained. Figure 9.a and Figure 9.b show the beginning and the end of this focusing task. Once this is achieved, the camera follows a given 3D trajectory. Results are shown on Figure 9(b–f).

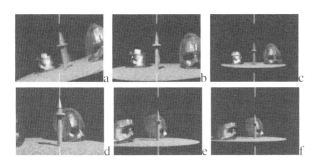

Figure 9: Positioning wrt. a segment and trajectory tracking

5.4 The "photography" problem

As regards this issue, we first perform a positioning experiment wrt. to a sphere lit by a positional light source. Results of this positioning task are presented on Figure 10(a-b). It is worth noting that the average intensity increases very smoothly (see Figure 10.c). We also plot the distance between the camera and the object-light axis (see Figure 10.d). We can note that this distance tends towards zero, i.e., the camera is located between the sphere and the light as can be predicted by theory (see Fig-

ure 10.e).

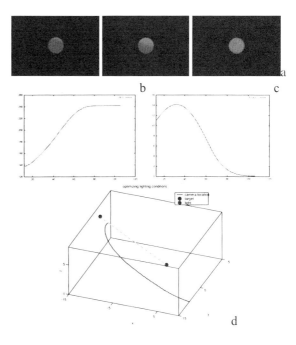

Figure 10: Positioning wrt. a sphere under good lighting conditions: (a) scene observed by the camera (illumination increases) (b) average intensity in the image (c) distance to sphere-light axis (d) camera/sphere/light position over time

Other experiments involve more complex objects (here a teapot has been used). The results presented (see Figure 11) show the validity of our approach. Only a focusing task has been considered. This explains that the teapot turned upside down.

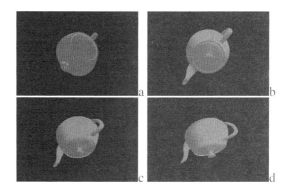

Figure 11: Teapot sequence: considering lighting conditions

6 Conclusion

There are many problems associated with the management of a camera in a virtual environment. It is not only necessary to be able to carry out a visual task (often a focusing task or more generally a positioning task) efficiently, but it is also necessary to be able to react in an appropriate and efficient way to modifications of this environment. We chose to use techniques widely considered in the robotic vision community. The basic tool that we considered is visual servoing which consists in positioning a camera according to the information perceived in the image. This image-based control constitutes the first novelty of our approach. The task is indeed specified *in a 2D space*, while the resulting camera trajectories are *in a 3D space*. It is thus a very intuitive approach of animation since it is carried out according to what one wishes to observe in the resulting images sequence.

However, this is not the only advantage of this method. Indeed, contrary to previous work [7], we did not limit ourselves to positioning tasks wrt. virtual points in static environments. In many applications (such as video games) it is indeed necessary to be able to react to modifications of the environment, of trajectories of mobile objects, etc. We thus considered the introduction of constraints into camera control. Thanks to the redundancy formalism, the secondary tasks (which reflect the constraints on the system) do not have any effect on the visual task. To show the validity of our approach, we have proposed and implemented various classic problems from simple tracking tasks to more complex tasks like occlusion or obstacle avoidance or positioning wrt. lit aspects of an object (in order to ensure good "photography"). The approach that we proposed has real qualities, and the very encouraging results obtained suggest that the use of visual control for computer animation is a promising technique. The main drawback is a direct counterpart of its principal quality: the control is carried out in the image, thus implying loss of control of the 3D camera trajectory. This 3D trajectory is computed *automatically* to ensure the visual and the secondary tasks but is not controlled by the animator. For this reason, one can undoubtedly see a wider interest in the use of these techniques within real-time reactive applications.

Acknowledgements

The authors wish to thank François Chaumette for is valuable comments and Rémi Cozot for submitting us the lighting problem.

Animations on-line.

Most of the animations presented in this paper can be found as mpeg film on the VISTA group WWW page (http://www.irisa.fr/vista then follow the "demo" link).

References

[1] D. Arijon. *Grammar of the Film Language*. Communication Arts Books, Hastings House, New York, 1976.

[2] J. Blinn. Where am I ? what am I looking at ? *IEEE Computer Graphics and Application*, pages 76–81, July 1998.

[3] D.B. Christianson, S.E. Anderson, L.-W. He, D.H. Salesin, D.S. Weld, and M.F. Cohen. Declarative camera control for automatic cinematography. In *Proc of AAAI'96 conference*, pages 148–155, Portland, Oregon, 1996.

[4] C.K. Cowan and P.D. Kovesi. Automatic sensor placement from vision task requirements. *IEEE trans. on Pattern Analysis and Machine intelligence*, 10(3):407–416, May 1988.

[5] S.M. Drucker and D. Zeltzer. Intelligent camera control in a virtual environment. In *Graphics Interface'94*, pages 190–199, Banff, Canada, 1994.

[6] B. Espiau, F. Chaumette, and P. Rives. A new approach to visual servoing in robotics. *IEEE Trans. on Robotics and Automation*, 8(3):313–326, June 1992.

[7] M. Gleicher and A. Witkin. Through-the-lens camera control. In *ACM Computer Graphics, SIGGRAPH'92*, pages 331–340, Chicago, July 1992.

[8] K. Hashimoto. *Visual Servoing : Real Time Control of Robot Manipulators Based on Visual Sensory Feedback*. World Scientific Series in Robotics and Automated Systems, Vol 7, World Scientific Press, Singapor, 1993.

[9] L.-W. He, M.F. Cohen, and D.H. Salesin. The virtual cinematographer: a paradigm for automatic real-time camera control and directing. In *Proc. of ACM SIGGRAPH'96, in Computer Graphics Proceedings*, pages 217–224, New Orleans, August 1996.

[10] S. Hutchinson, G. Hager, and P. Corke. A tutorial on visual servo control. *IEEE Trans. on Robotics and Automation*, 12(5):651–670, October 1996.

[11] M.H. Kyung, M.-S. Kim, and S. Hong. Through-the-lens camera control with a simple jacobian matrix. In *Proc. of Graphics Interface '95*, pages 171–178, Quebec, Canada, May 1995.

[12] E. Marchand and G.-D. Hager. Dynamic sensor planning in visual servoing. In *IEEE Int. Conf. on Robotics and Automation*, volume 3, pages 1988–1993, Lueven, Belgium, May 1998.

[13] B. Nelson and P.K. Khosla. Integrating sensor placement and visual tracking strategies. In *IEEE Int. Conf. Robotics and Automation*, volume 2, pages 1351–1356, San Diego, May 1994.

[14] C. Samson, M. Le Borgne, and B. Espiau. *Robot Control: the Task Function Approach*. Clarendon Press, Oxford, United Kingdom, 1991.

[15] K. Tarabanis, P.K. Allen, and R. Tsai. A survey of sensor planning in computer vision. *IEEE trans. on Robotics and Automation*, 11(1):86–104, February 1995.

[16] C. Ware and S. Osborn. Exploration and virtual camera control in virtual three dimensional environments. In *Proc. 90 Symposium on Interactive 3D Graphics*, pages 175–183, March 1990.

[17] L.E. Weiss, A.C. Sanderson, and C.P. Neuman. Dynamic sensor-based control of robots with visual feedback. *IEEE Journal of Robotics and Automation*, 3(5):404–417, October 1987.

Analysis and Synthesis of Structural Textures

Laurent Lefebvre   Pierre Poulin

Département d'informatique et de recherche opérationnelle
Université de Montréal
{lefebvla, poulin}@iro.umontreal.ca

Abstract

With the advent of image based modeling techniques, it becomes easier to apply textures extracted from reality onto virtual worlds. Many repetitive patterns (structural textures) in human constructions can be parametrized with procedural textures. These textures offer a powerful alternative to traditional color textures, but they require the artist to program the desired effects. We present a system to automatically extract from photographs values for parameters of structural textures, giving the user the possibility to guide the algorithms. Two common classes of procedural textures are studied : rectangular tilings and wood. The results demonstrate that synthesizing textures similar to their real counterpart can be very interesting for computer-augmented reality applications.

Key words: procedural textures, texture mapping, image based modeling, feature extraction, wood texture, rectangular tiling, brick layout, computer-augmented reality.

1 Introduction

Repetitive patterns such as layouts of bricks and tiles are ubiquitous in human constructions. It is therefore not surprising to observe their frequent apparition as textures in computer graphics scenes. These textures are mainly produced by two methods : color textures created by artists or extracted from photographs, and procedural textures generated by algorithms.

1.1 Color Textures

Traditional texture mapping takes an image (often a photograph) of a pattern and applies it to 3D models [10]. We refer to these as *color textures* in this paper. While popular, the technique suffers from several shortcomings. First, the extracted texture presents perspective deformations that must be corrected. The texture must fit exactly the 3D model, otherwise extending or tiling the texture can be noticed even if adjacent tiles are seamless. The color for each texel results also from the real scene illumination, and it is very difficult to factor out the illumination effects from these colors. Finally, the texture remains of a fixed resolution.

With the advent of image based modeling for aug-mented reality applications, textures and models are both extracted from photographs of a real scene, leading to a closer relationship between the model and its texture. Several methods to exploit this relationship have been introduced [9, 3, 4, 20, 18, 19].

They give good results, but are not perfect. For example, visibility discontinuities on two adjacent faces would produce artifacts (see Figure 12 left). Consider also the situation where objects occlude at least partly the desired object from all angles. It is virtually impossible to remove the occluders from the extracted textures, or to determine what lies behind. Lighting artifacts due to camera flash, or shadows and reflections of the cameraman can occur in photographs. Extracting the texture augmented with its BRDF [24] can reduce the artifacts, unfortunately without removing them all. Moreover, extracting the BRDF is a difficult and lengthy operation that can currently be done only in highly controlled environments.

1.2 Procedural Textures

Procedural textures [16, 17] are generated by algorithms. As repetitive patterns are often easily defined by such algorithms, it falls under the responsibility of the artist to design the proper algorithm to reach his goal. Unfortunately, not all computer artists are necessarily efficient programmers.

Another direction consists in analyzing a texture to extract its parameters in order to synthesize a new texture with similar characteristics. All undesired features can thus be removed during the analysis phase, and a potentially smaller set of parameters is kept to generate the new texture at the desired resolution.

This approach is popular in image processing and texture recognition, and has been extended by multi-resolution techniques or by non-parametric sampling [11, 12, 2, 5, 6]. These techniques give very good results on a large class of stochastic or semi-stochastic textures such as rocks, grass, stucco, etc. They have been applied to replace portions of textures in reconstructed 3D scenes [15]. Their generality frees the user from any intervention. However they usually fail in the case of a repetitive pattern such as bricks, where the semantics of the features

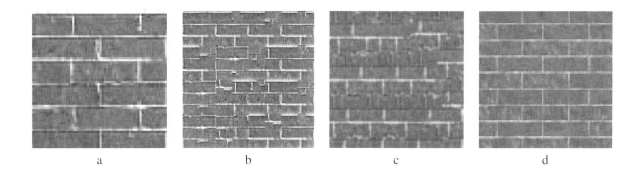

Figure 1: Synthesizing a wall of bricks : (a) Original image; (b) Synthesis from De Bonet [2]; (c) Synthesis from Efros and Leung [6], implementation of Wei [22]; (d) Synthesis from our algorithm

(mortar lines, brick size and shape, regular tiling) is lost (see Figure 1).

Very little work has been devoted to synthesize structural textures with a priori information on the structure of the texture [23, 25]. The situation is similar in the feature extraction from structural textures, except on specialized applications such as road tracking by vehicles [8, 14].

1.3 Extraction and Synthesis of Structural Textures

We present in this paper our solution to the problem of generating textures adapted to a scene reconstructed from photographs. We are not attempting to generate a procedural texture identical to its corresponding color texture. However our textures should be sufficiently similar to them to adequately replace the color texture in order to remove its artifacts such as illumination from the real scene, occlusions, fixed texture resolution, etc. Because of their frequent use, we concentrate our efforts on algorithms for the analysis and synthesis of rectangular tilings and wood textures.

The process can be summarized by the following steps. A 3D model is created from photographs using our interactive photogrammetry reconstruction software [18], and a color texture is associated with each polygon. For each texture, the user selects the texture type and produces with various image processing tools [21] a binary mask representing the texture with black and white pixels. Given the color texture, the binary mask, and the texture class, the system analyzes the features and fits values to the parameters associated with this texture class. Finally a new procedural texture can generate adapted high resolution textures for the 3D models. The system allows user intervention at all steps, while automatically providing extracted values for all parameters.

Our system can create quality structural textures free from artifacts generally present in the photographs. Because of our knowledge of the structure of the texture, the resulting procedural texture can be further refined in

several ways, including the addition of a full reflection model, a bump or displacement map, etc.

In the next two sections, we detail our procedural models for rectangular tilings and wood. Section 4 shows how these models can be augmented to create more sophisticated textures. Finally we conclude and discuss extensions for this work.

2 Rectangular Tiling

The first texture class we present is the rectangular tiling. Because of its ubiquity in most man-made constructions, many textures fall in this category : brick walls, ceramic tiles, skyscraper windows, hanging ceilings, etc.

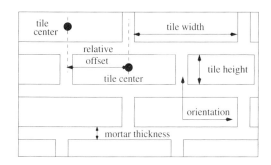

Figure 2: Our rectangular tiling model

We start by segmenting the color texture into a binary mask in order to facilitate parameter extraction. Several tools, including Sobel and pyramidal edge detectors, histogram segmentation thresholding, and morphological operators (opening, closing, eroding, etc.) are provided to the user to segment and clean up the color texture in order to create the binary mask. Most of these tools are interfaced from the C image processing library CVIP [21]. This segmentation step is fundamental because some of our parameter extraction algorithms can be sensitive to noise. Fortunately, the user can observe the quality of his mask and refine it if necessary. Typically, an experienced user would not require more than a few minutes to produce a reasonable mask.

Our tiling model is simple enough to automatically extract all its parameters from a binary mask (created by the user) representing the texture. Our model consists of 6 scalar parameters (some illustrated in Figure 2) : width and height of the tiles, orientation of the pattern, mortar thickness, number of bricks along a wall, and relative offset between adjacent tiles on successive rows.

The Fourier transform (actually FFT) of the binary mask (see Figure 3) gives important clues in relation to the height of the tiles and their orientation.

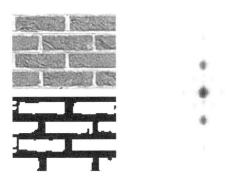

Figure 3: Color texture, segmented texture (binary mask), and scaled negative of the FFT of the mask

2.1   Height and Orientation

In a FFT image of resolution $2R \times 2R$, the center of the brightest group of points $(\hat{x}, \hat{y})$ other than the center of the image (DC frequency), corresponds to the major frequency in the texture. In a tiling pattern, this frequency is associated with the repetition of the base lines of the tile layers. The relation between the spectral and the frequency domains provides the height of the tiles measured as a proportion of the total image height as

$$\text{Height} = \frac{R}{2\sqrt{(\hat{x} - R)^2 + (\hat{y} - R)^2}}. \quad (1)$$

Because the orientation of the base lines in the tiling pattern is invariant under the Fourier transform, the brightest point $(\hat{x}, \hat{y})$ in the FFT image also provides the orientation angle of the tiling pattern as

$$\text{Angle} = \arctan\left(\frac{\hat{x} - R}{\hat{y} - R}\right) \quad \text{(in radians).} \quad (2)$$

The sign of the angle is given by the sign of $(\hat{x} - R)$.

The height and orientation of the tiles are extracted with very good precision because the FFT is a global transformation which resists well to noise. These two values are the first extracted and serve as a basis for the extraction of the remaining parameters.

The pattern formed by the vertical mortar lines is usually more difficult to extract accurately from the FFT image, as illustrated by finding the second brightest cluster of points in Figure 3. The next section describes our spatial algorithms to extract the remaining information. While filters applied vertically or autocorrelation techniques could prove useful, these spatial algorithms have shown to be sufficiently reliable and efficient for our purpose.

2.2   Width and Relative Offset

The remaining parameters are extracted using local and more efficient spatial algorithms, even though they are more prone to the effects of noise. For simplicity in subsequent steps, we rotate the mask backward by the angle previously measured in order to align it with the axes of the image.

To estimate the width of the tiles, we trace a number of horizontal scanlines, counting the number of continuous white pixels (tiles) separated by black pixels (mortar). Scanlines within the mortar horizontal regions are discarded as well as tiles not bounded by mortar. Every tile width is sorted and the median is taken as the width of the tiles.

In presence of patterns formed with tiles of a small set of different lengths, this approach can find the length of each type of tile by separating them into categories. Although we did not investigate further this direction, one should be able to apply results in pattern detection [13] to determine more sophisticated tiling patterns.

The mortar thickness is similarly computed, but instead with vertical scanlines. This orientation is less affected by noise due to the segmentation. If horizontal and vertical thicknesses are different, this approach can easily be extended to satisfy a new model.

The relative offset between successive rows of tiles is also extracted with horizontal scanlines. A tile is selected randomly and its width is estimated as above with horizontal scanlines. An adjacent tile on a row above or under is found by tracing a vertical scanline crossing only one mortar region. The width of this second tile is also estimated like for the first tile. The relative offset is computed from the center of both tiles. The process is repeated for several tiles, discarding outliers, and averaging the median offsets over several selected tiles. If the relative offset divided by the tile width is close to zero, we assume we are in presence of an aligned tiling pattern often occurring in ceramic tiles.

2.3 The Number of Tiles

The number of tiles on the 3D polygon is not always automatically extracted. For instance, we often use a close-up view of the texture which includes more details than the extracted texture. In this case, the number of tiles in the close-up view is different from the actual number of tiles on the wall. Also, in many photographs taken to reconstruct a scene, the mortar regions are often too small to automatically and reliably determine the number of tiles.

The user therefore might want to specify how many tiles should appear in a row on the 3D polygon. Once this value is detected or entered, the system can lay tiles with the right width and the proper aspect ratio over the 3D polygon.

2.4 Filling the Interior

Interiors of tiles and mortar regions have often a more stochastic nature, and are therefore more suitable for automatic analysis and synthesis algorithms [11, 2, 6]. We use the C implementation by El-Maraghi [7] of the Heeger and Bergen algorithm [11].

The user selects one or more regions to represent tiles and one or more regions to represent mortar. He should avoid unsatisfactory regions with artifacts such as occlusions, highlights, shadows, poor resolution, aliasing, etc. The Heeger and Bergen algorithm then processes automatically the selected regions to generate similar high quality textures at the desired resolution.

Sometimes, the distribution of tiles presents itself a special color pattern, or tiles in some regions might be more dirty than others. Once all parameters of the tiling model are extracted, it is easy to decide which selected region to generate from, according to the location of the current tile being treated.

2.5 Results of Rectangular Tiling

The results in this section use our method to analyze and synthesize tiling textures. Roughness, specularity, and reflectance are not currently extracted, but represent one of our topics for future work. At this moment, the user must enter values to set the corresponding parameters.

The left part of Figure 4 shows a bump mapped synthesized brick wall generated from the real wall of Figure 1a. All parameters were automatically extracted from the photograph. In the right part of the figure, some noise is added to displace the surface in order to increase the realism.

The same method is applied on a real ceramic wall on the left of Figure 5. The user selected analysis regions outside the specular highlight, thus avoiding mixing these colors in the synthesis. The presence of such highlights introduces difficulties to most analysis and synthesis algorithms [11, 2, 6], having a direct impact on the quality

Figure 4: Synthesized bricks with bump map (left) and synthesized bricks with displacement map (right)

of the resulting synthesized textures. A bump map function and a specular coefficient are applied on the generated tiles, which then behave properly under new illumination (Figure 5 right).

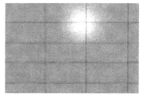

Figure 5: Real and synthesized ceramic walls

3 Wood

Wood textures, although not as frequent as rectangular tilings, represent nevertheless a great deal of textures in our environments. Wood is used for floors, doors, furniture, stairs, window frames, etc. It can be modeled from a simple growth pattern that can be extracted from photographs, and then generated onto 3D models. Another approach consists of creating an anisotropic 3D texture volume using a pair of orthogonal photographs [5] and mapping this volumetric texture onto 3D models.

While more sophisticated and complete wood models exist [1], we chose to keep our model simple enough to automatically extract values for its parameters from a single photograph.

The trunk of a tree oriented along the Z axis is modeled as a series of identical thickness concentric rings with alternating colors between *early* and *late* wood types. The distribution of colors follows a periodic sine function of frequency ω, starting from the central axis (x_c, y_c, z) of the trunk. The color of any 3D point (x, y, z) is computed by thresholding the following equation :

$$\sin\left(\omega\sqrt{(x - x_c)^2 + (y - y_c)^2}\right).$$

A wood plank is modeled as a rectangular cut into this trunk. A tilt angle and a rotation angle are associated with

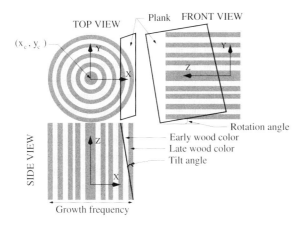

Figure 6: Our simple wood model

the plank, as illustrated in Figure 6.

The 10 scalar parameters of our wood model are sufficient to reproduce a fair range of wood types, notwithstanding knots. They are : trunk center (x_c, y_c), tilt and rotation angles, growth frequency, early/late wood ratio and colors, and turbulence intensity and frequency.

Once again, the user starts by converting the original texture into a binary mask image with thresholding and edge detection operators (see Figure 7).

 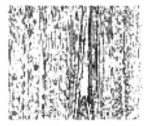

Figure 7: Real wood texture and segmented mask

3.1 Early and Late Wood Colors and Ratio

The binary mask is first traversed to determine the ratio of early wood pixels in the texture. In this paper, late wood is represented as black pixels and early wood as white pixels.

While traversing the corresponding pixels in the original texture, we sort the colors for each wood type. The 25th percentile of the early wood color and the 75th percentile of the late wood color provide satisfying colors for each wood type. This empirical solution avoids to wash out the colors resulting from the binary thresholding, and they are modifiable by the user if necessary.

3.2 Wood Growth Frequency and Rotation Angle

The center of the brightest group of points (other than the DC frequency) in the Fourier transform of the mask corresponds to the major frequency in the texture. It provides the growth frequency. The orientation of this frequency determines the rotation angle of the plank in the trunk. These computations are given by Equations (1) (actually its inverse) and (2) of Section 2 to determine the principal frequency and orientation of the wood.

Once the orientation is determined, the mask and its texture are rotated backward to be aligned with the image axes for the extraction of the tilt angle and other parameters.

3.3 Tilt Angle

The appearance of the wood texture is highly influenced by the tilt angle of the plank in the trunk. The tilt angle controls mainly the shape of ellipses in the texture, and therefore these ellipses can be used to determine this angle.

Our wood model does not handle the presence of knots in the texture. Detecting and synthesizing knots is part of our future work. Unfortunately, large knots can considerably bias most automatic algorithms because they behave similarly to the trunk itself, but at a smaller scale.

Our current solution is approximative, but simple and efficient. It is based on the observation that as the ellipses curve, less and less late wood (or respectively of early wood) appear in successive horizontal scanlines. If the tilt angle is null, the texture shows only straight lines with an identical number of early wood pixels. We therefore proceed by counting the number of late wood pixels in successive horizontal scanlines, and associate an empirically measured factor with this variation.

Obviously, this method is sensitive to noise in the mask and suffers in presence of a large number of knots. However on our test set of wood textures, the results were surprisingly visually satisfying.

We are currently investigating another direction, where the wood grain is traced in the mask. If an elliptic path is identified, we compute its center and eccentricity. By randomly selecting paths in the mask, we expect that statistics on the resulting ellipses should more reliably estimate the tilt angle.

3.4 Turbulence Intensity and Frequency

We observe that turbulence in wood patterns has usually a fairly low frequency. We set a typical value by default, that the user can modify if necessary.

The intensity of this turbulence is estimated in regions outside high curvature ellipses. We compute the variation of wood type between vertical scanlines of pixels. If there is no variations, we are in presence of parallel vertical wood grain, thus the intensity of the turbulence is set to null. Otherwise, it is set according to the degree of variation.

3.5 Trunk Center

The coordinates of the trunk center (x_c, y_c) relative to the plank are also estimated statistically.

Assume one tangent of the plank is oriented along Y. If the plank is tilted, ellipses will appear in the image. The center of these ellipses corresponds to the Y coordinate (y_c) of the center of the trunk. To find this center, we compute the color variance of each column of pixels in the image. The column with the largest variance (*i.e.*, intersecting more ellipses) is associated with the trunk center. If the variance is smaller than a certain threshold, a default value outside the image is assigned to the Y coordinate.

The X coordinate is more difficult to extract accurately. For a trunk located at $x_c \neq 0$, the width of successive layers of wood type varies, as illustrated in Figure 8. Once again, statistics on rows of pixels in the image are used to indicate the location of the X coordinate (x_c) of the trunk center. As a general rule of thumb, except for the central layer which can be thinner, the larger the widths become, the closer to the center we are.

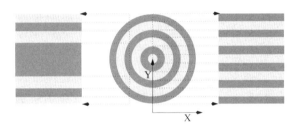

Figure 8: Setting the X coordinate of the trunk center

3.6 Results of Wood Textures

Although our extraction algorithms are only approximative for a number of parameters, and that many of these parameters are closely interrelated, they usually perform very well when visually comparing real wood textures and the synthesized textures. Figure 9 shows a typical result of our method.

An attractive aspect of this model is that the values we extract from a single 2D image of wood, are producing a complete 3D procedural texture, which has an infinite resolution and can be applied on any surface, even curved surfaces.

In order to evaluate the precision of our parameter extraction algorithms, we generated a number of textures with our procedural wood model, and compared the values extracted with the real values. We generated ten dif-

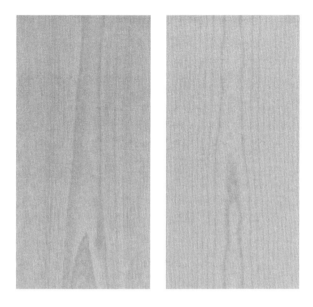

Figure 9: Real wood and synthesized wood

ferent wood patterns for which we modified each parameter, one at a time. After each session, we kept the difference between the estimated value and the real one. The results appear in Table 1 as percentages of the difference with the real value. Note that these percentages are computed on the maximum scale values for most of the parameters. For all our generated textures, we found that the error was proportional to the real value for the tilt angle and the frequency. For these two parameters, the percentages are computed with respect to the real value instead of the maximum scale value.

The parameter with the worst estimated value is the intensity of the turbulence. While some perturbation appears in wood, the exact value of this perturbation is less important. We observed that our extracted values were usually quite visually satisfying. Since the early/late wood ratio, the early wood color, and the late wood color are all extracted using the mask, errors are caused mainly by differences between the masks created by the user for each texture.

Real wood planks are usually cut either almost parallel or almost perpendicular to the wood grain. Considering this fact in our generated textures, we only made small modifications to the tilt angle around $0°$ and $90°$ to evaluate the tilt angle extraction algorithm. Our extraction algorithm is less precise when the cut is made at angles not near $0°$ or $90°$. For example, we generated a texture in which the tilt angle was $30°$ and the extracted value had an error of 36% (this result is not included in Table 1). In such cases, since the shape of the ellipses is defined by the tilt angle, the user can modify the tilt value to achieve

Wood Model Parameter	Maximum Scale Value	Statistics on Differences (%)		
		Average	STD	Max
Tilt	*	8.09	4.56	14.29
Orientation	$180°$	0.35	0.24	0.6
Frequency	*	2.47	4.81	12.34
Ratio Early/Late	8	5.5	3.5	10.5
Turbulence Intensity	30	10.3	7.16	20.63
x_c	512	2.71	2.46	6.56
y_c	512	2.27	2.21	6.50
Early Intensity	256	3.18	0.76	4.94
Late Intensity	256	2.79	0.94	3.38

* Proportional to the real value.

Table 1: Extracting values for simulated wood

the desired effet.

For the remaining parameters, our algorithm is usually sufficiently precise with average errors around 2-5% (see Table 1). In the case of an unusual error, the user can correct the problem in a few steps. For example, for the parameter y_c, the user can easily specify the center of the ellipses in the original image.

4 Improving the Procedural Models

Modifying the appearance of a digitized texture requires much work by the artist. Once we have extracted values for our simple models, adding new features specific to the resulting textures is much simpler because we have a structural definition of the texture. It is therefore simple to add a mirror reflection only on the interiors of tiles, to displace the mortar lines below the tiles depth, to raise the roughness of early wood type, etc.

4.1 Augmenting the Realism with Various Maps

Bump or displacement maps can be applied to the structural models according to the nature of each structure. For instance, one can apply a bump map on individual bricks, while forcing a deeper displacement map on the mortar regions. Figures 5 and 11 (right) show bump maps applied to a ceramic wall and a hardwood floor. Figure 10 shows a displacement map on brick walls.

Similarly, different specularity coefficients and roughnesses can be applied on specific elements of a structural model to create highlights on tiles but not on mortar. Mirror reflections on hardwood floors can provide a clean varnished appearance (Figure 13).

4.2 Matching Textures on Adjacent Polygons

Another advantage of a procedural texture is that one can set constraints to satisfy the structural nature of the texture, or parameters that must be shared by several instances of the texture.

Figure 10 shows a brick layout texture ensuring all

mortar lines match, as well as setting the relative offset of the bricks to match the width of a brick.

Figure 10: Brick walls on a tower and close-up view

4.3 Procedural Textures and Color Textures

While procedural textures offer a powerful method to generate structural textures, many textures such as paintings or text cannot be modeled by procedures.

When this happens, we give the user the possibility to choose in the texture space which part should be generated procedurally, and which part should be extracted as a traditional color texture. This is achieved by letting the user paint a mask to indicate the regions associated with each texture. The picture frame in Figure 12 and the metal screen of the fireplace in Figure 13 are color textures. Tiles, bricks, and the hardwood floor in these figures are procedural.

4.4 Multiple Structural Textures

On appropriate models, multiple structural textures can be applied on the same 3D surface. Hardwood floors exploit the two texture types described in this paper.

The rectangular tiling method extracts fairly reliably with the FFT the width of the planks, and the wood modeling method fills in the interior of each plank. Because less information can be extracted from a plank than from a large wood panel, the similarity of the generated wood texture might not be as precise. However we found that the nature of wood leads to satisfying results even with narrow planks. Figure 11 gives an example of this method.

When the photographs do not provide enough information to generate detailed wood textures, one can extract the necessary information from different photographs, and apply the result on the floor layout.

5   Conclusion

Color textures extracted from photographs can suffer from several artifacts resulting from different resolutions, misalignments, undesired occluding objects, missing portions in the texture, shadows, highlights, etc.

We have presented a technique to extract structural textures from photographs, and synthesize similar new textures from the corresponding procedural textures. Unlike random textures which can be generated automatically, the features in structural textures are significant and must be modeled accurately.

We focused our efforts on tiling patterns and wood patterns, both frequent in man-made constructions. For both patterns, we presented techniques to determine automatically values for their parameters, while giving the user the possibility to guide the algorithms or modify any value that was extracted. Structural textures inspired by photographs were generated as examples. Other results can be accessed from the web site associated with this paper from `www.iro.umontreal.ca/labs/infographie/papers`.

Our simple textural models lead to good results where no satisfying color textures could have been extracted. The procedural generation of these textures has many advantages. It can be adapted to the desired resolution, compressed more efficiently than color textures of similar quality, manipulated to generate different results, and augmented by other familiar rendering techniques to increase their realism.

While our parameter extraction techniques were developed specifically for our structural models, many features of these techniques could remain appropriate for parameter extraction in other structural models. For instance, the FFT is frequently used to find orientations and frequencies in image processing. We have tried our algorithms on several different tile patterns and wood styles, and we are confident that they should apply well to other such patterns.

Procedural textures cannot replace all color textures in computer graphics applications. However when they can be used, they offer great advantages that should be exploited. Although advanced synthesis algorithms such as the one proposed by Efros and Leung [6] are more general, they often take hours to synthesize structural textures and the results are not always semantically correct. Our algorithm running on an SGI Onyx R4400 processor takes only a few minutes for both tuning the parameters and synthesizing new textures. All the textures contained in this paper were created with at most three iterations for extracting the parameters (in the case of the hardwood floor of Figure 11). The longest time for texture synthesis was one hour for the fireplace, mainly because many bricks had to be synthesized using the Heeger and Bergen algorithm [11].

6   Future Work

While the current results are encouraging, we feel there is still much information in photographs that could be exploited to improve our structural textures.

The geometry recovered by our image based modeling tool can easily indicate regions in umbra, potential highlights, reflections, etc. These phenomena can significantly alter the colors of the extracted procedural textures. Rather than just neglecting these regions, one could develop techniques to extract values for these phenomena, thus obtaining a more complete structural model from the photographs.

Acknowledgements

We acknowledge financial support from NSERC, and an equipment donation from the DiTER of the Université de Montréal. Martin Blais developed an important portion of our current reconstruction system. We thank Jeremy De Bonet for providing the original and the synthesized textures in Figure 1. We also thank Li-Yi Wei [22] and T. El-Maraghi [7] for making available their respective implementations of Efros [6] and Heeger and Bergen [11] algorithms.

Figure 11: Real (left) and synthesized (center and right) hardwood floor. A small bump map is applied to curve the edges of each linear piece in the right figure.

Projected color textures   Synthesized view   Substituting the floor texture

Figure 12: Reconstruction of structural textures (synthesized tiles) from three photographs of a showcase bathroom. The system lets the user try out other combination of tiling patterns onto the image-based modeled 3D scene.

Real fireplace   Synthesized views

Figure 13: Reconstruction of structural textures (bricks and varnished hardwood floor) synthesized from a single photograph of a fireplace. The metal screen in front of the fireplace is a color texture extracted from the photograph. Small objects on the chimney are properly removed from the photograph without causing any holes.

86

References

[1] J.W. Buchanan. Simulating wood using a voxel approach. *Eurographics '98*, 17(3):C105–C112, 1998.

[2] J.S. De Bonet. Multiresolution sampling procedure for analysis and synthesis of texture images. In *SIGGRAPH 97 Conference Proceedings*, Annual Conference Series, pages 361–368, August 1997.

[3] P.E. Debevec, C.J. Taylor, and J. Malik. Modeling and rendering architecture from photographs: A hybrid geometry- and image-based approach. In *SIGGRAPH 96 Conference Proceedings*, Annual Conference Series, pages 11–20, August 1996.

[4] P.E. Debevec, Y. Yu, and G.D. Borshukov. Efficient view-dependent image-based rendering with projective texture-mapping. In *Ninth Eurographics Workshop on Rendering*, pages 105–116, Vienna, Austria, June 1998.

[5] J.M. Dischler, D. Ghazanfarpour, and R. Freydier. Anisotropic solid texture synthesis using orthogonal 2d views. *Eurographics '98*, 17(3):C87–C95, 1998.

[6] A.A. Efros and T. K. Leung. Texture synthesis by non-parametric sampling. In *IEEE International Conference on Computer Vision (ICCV'99)*, sep 1999.

[7] T. El-Maraghi. An implementation of Heeger and Bergen's texture analysis/synthesis algorithm. *University of Toronto, www.cs.utoronto.ca/~tem/2522/texture.html*, September 1997.

[8] D. Geman and B. Jedynak. An active testing model for tracking roads in satellite images. *IEEE Trans. on Pattern Analysis and Machine Intelligence*, 18(1):1–14, January 1996.

[9] P. Havaldar, M.-S. Lee, and G. Medioni. View synthesis from unregistered 2-D images. In *Graphics Interface '96*, pages 61–69, May 1996.

[10] P.S. Heckbert. Survey of texture mapping. *IEEE Computer Graphics and Applications*, 6(11):56–67, November 1986.

[11] D.J. Heeger and J.R. Bergen. Pyramid-based texture analysis/synthesis. In *SIGGRAPH 95 Conference Proceedings*, Annual Conference Series, pages 229–238, August 1995.

[12] A.N. Hirani and T. Totsuka. Combining frequency and spatial domain information for fast interactive image noise removal. In *SIGGRAPH 96 Conference Proceedings*, Annual Conference Series, pages 269–276, August 1996.

[13] R. Karp, R. Miller, and A. Rosenberg. Rapid identification of repeated patterns in strings, trees, and arrays. In *Proc. of the ACM Symposium on the Theory of Computing*, pages 125–136, 1972.

[14] W. Kasrpzak and H. Niemann. Adaptive road recognition and ego–state tracking in the presence of obstacles. *International Journal of Computer Vision*, 28(1):5–26, 1998.

[15] C. Loscos, M.-C. Frasson, G. Drettakis, B. Walter, X. Granier, and P. Poulin. Interactive virtual relighting and remodeling of real scenes. In *Tenth Eurographics Workshop on Rendering*, pages 329–340, Granada, Spain, June 1999.

[16] D.R. Peachey. Solid texturing of complex surfaces. *Computer Graphics (SIGGRAPH '85 Proceedings)*, 19(3):279–286, July 1985.

[17] K. Perlin. An image synthesizer. In *Computer Graphics (SIGGRAPH '85 Proceedings)*, volume 19, pages 287–296, July 1985.

[18] P. Poulin, M. Ouimet, and M.-C. Frasson. Interactively modeling with photogrammetry. In *Ninth Eurographics Workshop on Rendering*, pages 93–104, Vienna, Austria, June 1998.

[19] C. Rocchini, P. Cignoni, and C. Montani. Multiple textures stitching and blending on 3D objects. In *Tenth Eurographics Workshop on Rendering*, pages 119–130, Granada, Spain, June 1999.

[20] Y. Sato, M.D. Wheeler, and K. Ikeuchi. Object shape and reflectance modeling from observation. In *SIGGRAPH 97 Conference Proceedings*, Annual Conference Series, pages 379–388, August 1997.

[21] S.E. Umbaugh. *Computer Vision and Image Processing*. Prentice-Hall inc., 1998.

[22] L. Wei. An implementation of Alyosha Efros' texture synthesis algorithm. *Stanford University, www.graphics.stanford.edu/~liyiwei/project/texture/efros*, January 2000.

[23] R. Yokoyama and R.M. Haralick. Texture synthesis using a growth model. *Computer Graphics and Image Processing*, 8(3):369–381, December 1978.

[24] Y. Yu, P. Debevec, J. Malik, and T. Hawkins. Inverse global illumination: recovering reflectance models of real scenes from photographs. In *SIGGRAPH 99 Conference Proceedings*, Annual Conference Series, pages 215–224, 1999.

[25] S.W. Zucker. Toward a model of texture. *Computer Graphics and Image Processing*, 5(2):190–202, June 1976.

High-Quality Interactive Lumigraph Rendering Through Warping

Hartmut Schirmacher, Wolfgang Heidrich, and Hans-Peter Seidel

Max-Planck-Institut für Informatik

Saarbrücken, Germany

http://www.mpi-sb.mpg.de

email: {schirmacher,heidrich,hpseidel}@mpi-sb.mpg.de

Abstract

We introduce an algorithm for high-quality, interactive light field rendering from only a small number of input images with dense depth information.

The algorithm bridges the gap between image warping and interpolation from image databases, which represent the two major approaches in image based rendering. By warping and blending only the necessary parts of each reference image, we are able to generate a single view-corrected texture for every output frame at interactive rates.

In contrast to previous light field rendering approaches, our warping-based algorithm is able to fully exploit per-pixel depth information in order to depth-correct the light field samples with maximum accuracy.

The complexity of the proposed algorithm is nearly independent of the number of stored reference images and of the final screen resolution. It performs with only small overhead and very few visible artifacts. We demonstrate the visual fidelity as well as the performance of our method through various examples.

Key words: computer graphics, image based rendering, light fields, Lumigraphs, image databases, image warping, blending

1 Introduction

Image based rendering has received a lot of attention during the last few years, since it provides a means to render realistic images without generating, storing, and processing complex models of geometry, material, and light present in a scene.

Currently there are two major approaches for generating novel views from a set of reference images. One such approach, which can be best described by the term *image databases*, usually resamples and stores the reference images in some way that allows a very efficient interpolation of arbitrary views of the scene. The main problem of these techniques is that in order to obtain satisfactory results, they require enormous amounts of data for storage and display.

The second approach is called *image warping*. These kind of algorithms usually store the input data as a scattered (and relatively sparse) set of images together with their arbitrary camera parameters. The lack of structure implies higher rendering costs, and also introduces a number of artifacts that are not easily overcome.

In this paper, we propose an algorithm which combines aspects of both image databases and warping. We use a light field data structure with quantized, per-pixel depth values. For reconstructing a novel view, we first estimate which region of which reference image will contribute to the final image. Then, we forward-project all the pixels in these regions into the original image plane, but as observed from the novel view point. We interpolate the final pixel color from all unoccluded pixels that have been reprojected into the same image plane location.

Our approach has several advantages over previous methods. Since only parts of each reference image are reprojected, the complexity of our algorithm is almost independent of the number of reference images. In addition, the reprojection into the reference image plane minimizes distortion and undersampling artifacts. And finally, we can exploit dense depth information in order to perform maximum-accuracy depth-correction without reconstructing a 3D model. This is why the new algorithm can produce high quality views at interactive rates from a relatively small set of images.

2 Previous Work

The work presented in this paper combines the light field and Lumigraph approaches with warping-based techniques. In the following we briefly summarize both areas of image-based rendering.

2.1 Light Fields and Lumigraphs

Light fields and Lumigraphs are two related representations that have been independently introduced in [9] and [5]. Both approaches are based on storing samples of the so-called *plenoptic function*[1] describing the directional radiance distribution for every point in space. Since the radiance is constant along a ray in empty space, the

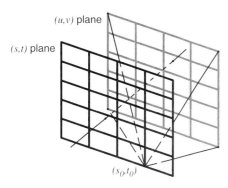

(u,v) plane

(s,t) plane

(s_0,t_0)

Figure 1: Schematic view of a two-plane parameterized light slab. Rays passing through a scene are characterized by a pair $[(s,t),(u,v)]$ of points in the two planes. The set of all rays passing through (s_0,t_0) is a sheared perspective image in the (u,v) plane.

plenoptic function of an object seen from outside its convex hull can be represented as a 4D function by using an appropriate parameterization.

This 4D function is called the *light field*, and the usual parameterization uses two parallel planes as depicted in Fig. 1. Every ray passing through the scene is characterized by a pair of points (s,t) and (u,v) on the two planes. The set of all (u,v) samples through a single point (s_0,t_0) on the (s,t) plane is an image created by a sheared perspective projection from (s_0,t_0). In what follows, we refer to the (s,t) plane as the *view point plane* and to the (u,v) plane as the *image plane*. The set of rays passing through the two planes is called a *light slab*. In order to view a scene from any point in the surrounding space, six light slabs are combined so that the six view point planes cover some box surrounding the scene.

Other light field parameterizations have also been proposed in the past [7, 2], but the two-plane parameterization has the advantage of simplicity and, as shown in [6], it also allows for insertion of new images with an efficient and reliable warping algorithm that we will also make use of in this paper.

The "light database" can be queried very efficiently in order to create arbitrary views of the scene. With the two-plane parameterization and regularly sampled image and view point plane, the radiance along a viewing ray can be reconstructed via quadri-linear interpolation from the rays through all combinations of the 2×2 closest grid points on the (s,t) and (u,v) planes (cf. Fig. 1). This is a constant time algorithm.

It is often desirable to use an *adaptive sampling* of the view point plane, e.g. for adjusting the amount of texture memory needed for the display [17], or for adding arbitrary new view points/images to the light field structure [15]. In that case, a triangulation of the view point

plane domain is used, and ray casting-based algorithms are logarithmic in the number of view points, since the view plane triangle through which the ray passes has to be determined. However, both regular and adaptive samplings can also be rendered very efficiently in hardware, using texture mapping and alpha blending [5, 17].

Unfortunately, simple interpolation will blur objects that are off the image plane. This can be avoided if the correct 3D location of the point, that is, its distance to the image plane, is known. Therefore, the *Lumigraph* uses an additional polygonal mesh that allows for *depth-correcting* the viewing rays before the interpolation step, as shown in Fig. 2.

The depth correction can be performed for each viewing ray if the rendering is done in software, or for the vertices of each textured triangle when using graphics hardware. Since the latter approximation is only valid if the depths of a triangle's vertices do not differ too much, the textured triangles in [5] are subdivided until all depth values for each triangle are similar.

Since the depth correction requires intersecting depth rays with the scene geometry, the approximate polygonal mesh should contain as few polygons as possible. On the other hand, the coarser the mesh, the lower the quality of the depth correction, and the larger the blurring artifacts. In [8], this fact has been used to simulate depth-of-field effects with arbitrary camera apertures using light fields and a very small number of polygons $(1 - 3)$ as approximate geometry. These polygons act as the focal plane(s) of the camera. This shows that the use of depth information is in no way a yes or no decision; rather a smooth tradeoff between rendering time and image quality becomes possible, depending on the amount and quality of geometric information used.

In [6], instead of using raycasting and polygonal meshes, per-pixel depth information is stored as an additional channel in the light field images. This information allows for refining the resolution of a light field during a display pre-process using image warping. In [15], the same kind of warping is used for estimating the amount of missing information for differnt view plane regions, and acquiring new synthetic reference images where necessary.

2.2 Image Warping Techniques

Image warping [4, 12, 11] is the process of taking individual pixels from one or more images and projecting them onto the image plane for a new eye-point location. This process requires geometric information in the form of per-pixel depth values or disparities, describing pixel motion in the image plane per unit camera motion.

One interesting variant of image warping has been introduced recently [13]. Here, the warping process is fac-

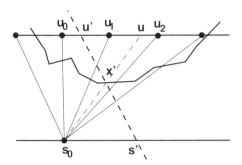

Figure 2: Depth correction scheme sketched in 2D. The viewing ray (s', u') intersects the geometry at x'. For some nearby view point s_0, instead of interpolating the color from u_0 and u_1 (which are the neighbors of u'), it is more appropriate to use u_1 and u_2, since they represent color information for points closer to x.

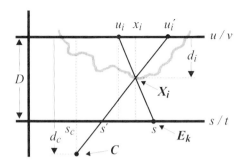

Figure 3: Schematic situation on the s/t and u/v planes when warping a pixel u_i from a reference view $\mathbf{E}_k$ with coordinate s to its new location u_i' for an arbitrary view point $\mathbf{C}$. $\mathbf{X}_i$ denotes the scene point corresponding to the pixel. The depth d_i of a pixel is measured as illustrated.

tored into a relatively simple *pre-warping* step and a traditional texture mapping step that can be performed by standard graphics hardware. As we will see later, we employ a similar technique here.

The most serious problem of image warping is that holes may occur in the destination image due to two different reasons. In the case of *undersampling*, the sampling rate required in the destination image is larger than that provided by the source images. *Disocclusion* occurs when some part of the scene has been occluded in the reference images, but becomes visible in the destination image.

There are several strategies for removing these holes, e.g. splatting and multi-scale approaches [4, 6], or connecting neighboring pixels in the source images by polygons [10, 14]. However, none of these methods can make up for the missing information.

Layered depth images [16, 3] deal with disocclusion artifacts by storing information about the visible as well as the occluded surfaces. Each pixel in such an "image" is actually a linked list of positions and colors, representing all intersections of surfaces with the viewing ray through that pixel.

3   Interactive Lumigraph Warping

The proposed algorithm generates an arbitrary view of the Lumigraph slab for any given output camera or view point in 3D space. Instead of reprojecting directly into the output camera plane, we compute a single texture to be mapped on the Lumigraph's image plane. The textured polygon is rendered using OpenGL's standard polygon drawing features. This allows us to keep our algorithm independent of the output image size, and exploits the graphics hardware for the resampling to the final image

resolution.

This section gives details about several aspects of the algorithm. First, we look at how to warp single pixels within the image plane for arbitrary view points. Then we show how to determine the regions to be warped in each reference image. After that, we explain the interpolation of the final pixel colors, and show how the different parts of the algorithm are put together.

3.1   Lumigraph Warping for Arbitrary Eye Points

The Lumigraph contains a set $\{I_0, I_1, \ldots, I_{N-1}\}$ of N images. Each image I_k is associated with an eye point $\mathbf{E}_k$ which is the center of projection used to generate the image. Warping a pixel (u, v) from a reference image I_k into the image plane texture T means determining the corresponding pixel location (u', v') in T. This correspondence is established by the depth value of the pixel.

Fig. 3 depicts the basic situation. The pixel u_i observed from a reference eye point $\mathbf{E}_k$ corresponds to the color of a scene object at $\mathbf{X}_i$. The output camera $\mathbf{C}$ observes this same point through the pixel u_i' in the texture image T. D defines the distance between the two planes of the slab, and d_i is the depth value of pixel i, measured from the image plane towards the eye point plane.

From the triangles in Fig. 3 we can derive these two basic relations:

$$\frac{u_i' - x_i}{d_i} = \frac{u_i' - s_c}{d_c} \quad . \quad \frac{s - x_i}{D - d_i} = \frac{s - u_i}{D}. \quad (1)$$

Solving the two equations for x_i, substituting one into the other, and solving again for u_i' gives the following:

$$u_i' = \frac{u_i d_c D + d_i d_c s - d_i d_c u_i - d_i D s_c}{D(d_c - d_i)}. \quad (2)$$

Eq. 2 computes the view-corrected coordinate u_i' of a pixel i, given its coordinate u_i in the reference image, its

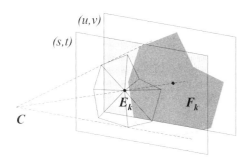

Figure 4: Texture partitioning: The reference image associated with eye point E_k has to contribute to the region F_k, which results in projecting the triangle fan around E_k from the current view point C and intersecting it with the image plane domain.

depth d_i, the reference eye point s, and the depth d_c and plane coordinate s_c of the output camera C. Since some of these variables are constant through all pixels for a pair (C, E_k), it makes sense to isolate some terms:

$$u'_i = \frac{1}{D(d_c - d_i)} \left[A_c u_i + d_i (d_c u_i + B_k) \right],\qquad(3)$$
$$A_c := d_c D, \quad B_k := d_c s - D s_c.$$

For each output image, A_c is constant, and B_k varies with the reference eye point E_k. The same equations also apply to the second pixel coordinate v'_i, by substituting v for u and t for s.

If the ray through a reference pixel does not intersect any scene object, the pixel does not need to be reprojected. We simply determine this by marking such background pixels with an "infinite" depth value.

3.2 Partitioning of the Image Plane Texture

Now that we know how to warp single pixels, the remaining task is to determine which pixels from which reference images we need to warp in order to obtain an output image of high quality at minimal cost.

In order to support the general case of a non-uniform view point plane, we use a Delaunay triangulation of the eye points $\{E_k\}$ in the Lumigraph's (s, t) planes (cf. Sec. 2). This means that the radiance values observed through each eye point triangle (E_a, E_b, E_c) will be interpolated from pixels in the three associated images I_a, I_b, I_c. In other words, each reference image I_k should contribute to all those triangles containing E_k as a vertex. One such triangle *fan* F_k is depicted in Fig. 4. After projecting the fan onto the image plane, we know to which texture region I_k has to contribute to. But since the pixels will be forward-projected, we also need to know the *source* region R_k in image I_k from which all pixels have to be projected so that the whole destination region will be covered. The source and destination regions are not

identical in general because the pixels "flow" through the image. In order to compute a conservative bound, the region has to be extended by the maximal flow that can occur when warping *into* the destination region (which does not need to be the same as when warping *from* the region).

Looking again at Fig. 3, we can re-formulate the warping equations in terms of the "virtual" view point s' on the eye point plane. This corresponds to the formulae presented in [6] and leads to:

$$u'_i - u_i \;=\; \frac{d_i}{D - d_i}(s' - s).\qquad(4)$$

We see that the pixel flow $(u'_i - u_i)$ is simply the product of the *virtual camera movement* $(s' - s)$ on the view point plane and the source pixel's *disparity* $z_i := d_i/(D - d_i)$ that denotes the flow of pixel i for a unit camera movement on the eye point plane.

The easiest way to find a conservative bound is to use the absolute values of the global maximum disparity $z_{max} := \max\{|z_i|\}$ within all images, and a per-fan bound F_k on the longest distance $|s' - s|$ within any triangle (e.g. the longest fan edge). The maximal flow f_k^{max} is obtained as the product of the two:

$$f_k^{max} \;=\; z_{max} F_k.\qquad(5)$$

In order to define a conservative warping region, we grow the triangle fan around E_k by this distance f_k^{max} in each direction. It is clear that this bound is far from optimal, so that more pixels will be warped than are needed. On the other hand, it guarantees that all the required pixels will be reprojected.

One can tighten the bound (and reduce the overhead) by partitioning the reference images into smaller blocks B (e.g. 16x16 pixels each) and storing the maximal disparity z_B for each block in each image. In order to determine f_k^{max}, one must iteratively determine from which "nearby" blocks B pixels could flow into the target region F_k. This is the case if

$$\min\{||X - E_k|| ; X \in B\} - F_k \leq z_B \cdot F_k,\qquad(6)$$

meaning that the maximal flow within the block is large enough to reach the boundary of the target region.

3.3 Blending

In addition to finding the relevant samples and reprojecting them according to the current view, we have to interpolate each texel's final color from all the visible samples that have been projected into the texel's domain.

In contrast to many warping-based algorithms, it is not sufficient to determine the frontmost sample per texel.

```
C ← output camera for this frame
for all front-facing slabs S do
  init buffers {(L_i, d_i)}
  for all eye points E_k ∈ S do
    /** partitioning **/
    R_k ← triangle fan around E_k
    f_k^max ← max. pixel flow into R_k
    grow R_k by f_k^max
    /** warping + blending **/
    for all pixels u_i in R_k
      if d_i ≠ ∞ then
        u'_i ← warp(u_i, d_i, E_k, C)
        j ← pixel_index(u'_i)
        blend (L_j, d_j) with (L_i, d_i)
    /** texture display **/
    specify {L_i} as texture
    draw textured image plane polygon
end
```

Figure 5: Pseudo code of the basic rendering algorithm, putting together the parts explained in Sec. 3.1 – 3.3.

We rather have to find the whole *set* of samples that represent visible scene features, discard all other samples, and interpolate the final color from the remaining ones. We do this along the lines of [6], by comparing the sample's depth values d_i, and keeping all those samples within an ϵ-environment around the frontmost depth value. In the case of quantized, discrete depth values, we can choose $\epsilon = 0$.

In order to guarantee a smooth reconstruction of colors across triangle boundaries, the interpolation weight for a sample from reference image I_k should be 1 in the triangle vertex corresponding to the eye point E_k, and 0 on the boundary of fan F_k. This corresponds to the sample's barycentric coordinate with respect to E_k. Alternatively, one can choose a computationally simpler weight which is 1 in E_k and falls off linearly or quadratically with the distance to E_k [6].

3.4 Overall Algorithm and Complexity

The rendering algorithm combines the parts that have been explained in the previous sections. Its pseudo code can be found in Fig. 5. It iterates through all eye points E_k of the current slab, computes the corresponding fan F_k, and extends it for obtaining the warping source region R_k (Sec. 3.2). All pixels in this region are then warped into the image plane texture (Sec. 3.1), and blended with the other valid samples (Sec. 3.3). After doing this for all eye points, the resulting textured polygon is drawn on the slab's image plane using graphics hardware.

The worst-case complexity of the algorithm is propor-

tional to the number of pixels in the image plane texture, which has the same resolution as the reference images. Every image only contributes to a texture region that is inversely proportional to the number of images, so the computation time does not increase significantly with the number of eye points. The region growing (cf. Sec. 3.2) adds some overhead, but since the grow factor scales with by the triangle size, this overhead roughly remains constant, regardless of the number of reference images.

4 Results

In order to validate our approach, we show some results produced with our experimental implementation. First, we analyze the image fidelity and performance for different numbers of reference images and different image plane resolutions. Next, we discuss the issue of quantizing the depth values used for warping. Last, we compare the new algorithm with implementations of the light field interpolation and depth-corrected Lumigraph rendering techniques.

4.1 Rendering Quality

Using the adaptive acquisition approach proposed in [15], we have generated images of a ray-traced elephant for building Lumigraphs of the same scene with any number of eye points from 4 – 164. We have rendered the same views of the elephant for an increasing number of view points (4, 25, 50, 100, 164, see [15] for the structure of the view point meshes). Figure 7 shows a view computed with our new method from a 2x2-image Lumigraph with 256x256 image plane pixels. Despite the small amount of input images, the resulting view appears very sharp. Due to the very sparse sampling of the scene, disocclusion artifacts near the legs and the trunk of the elephant are clearly visible. The glossy highlights on the surface also generate some artifacts, appearing as color seams.

Figure 8 shows the same view, but generated from a Lumigraph containing 25 images. This version of the Lumigraph already provides enough information to avoid the disocclusion problems as well as most of the glossy artifacts when using our algorithm. Only a few stronger artifacts can be detected from some viewing positions, mostly small disocclusions caused by the trunk.

If the viewer moves behind the eye point plane and gets very close to the image plane, the camera can be very close to the actual scene object, and undersampling artifacts appear (cf. Fig. 9). Since the gaps are very small, they could be removed quite easily by simple gap filling approaches as often used in image warping (cf. Sec. 2), or by adapting the image plane resolution accordingly.

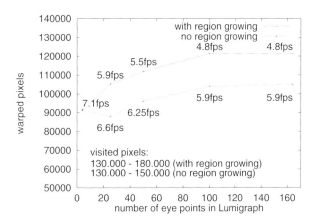

Figure 6: Warped pixels / frame rate plotted against the number of eye points in the 'elephant' Lumigraph. For the lower curve, warping source regions have not been extended at all. The upper curve was obtained using the global maximum (cf. Sec. 3.2). Rendering times are given for a 270 MHz SGI O2 (R12K). On a 300 MHz Octane, the rate goes up by 1.5–1.9.

4.2 Performance Issues

The rendering time of the algorithm depends on several factors. The resolution of the image plane texture plus the region growing overhead determine the upper bound for the number of pixels to be processed. However, since the algorithm discards background pixels immediately, it is obvious that the main computation time is spent on the actually warped foreground pixels (cf. algorithm in Fig. 5). As discussed in Sec. 3.4, the number of processed pixels is nearly independent of the number of reference images.

Figure 6 shows the number of foreground pixels as well as the frame rate for the "elephant" Lumigraph, for different numbers of reference images. The image plane resolution is 256x256 pixels, the maximum disparity 0.3. It can be observed that the rendering time increases sublinearly with the number of eye points, and the frame rate is proportional to the number of warped pixels. The difference of the two plotted curves nicely visualizes the constant overhead added by the region growing (cf. Sec. 3.2).

Figure 11 shows a different artificial scene, rendered into a 36-image Lumigraph with 512x512 image plane pixels. The rendering time for this Lumigraph increases as expected due to the four times higher image plane resolution, but since the number of foreground pixels is similar to that in the elephant scene, we still obtain 4.8 frames/s for 95.000 warped pixels with region growing, and 5.5 fps for 70.000 pixels without region growing on an O2 (max. disparity is 0.5). The average number of vis-ited pixels (including background) per frame is 212.000, as opposed to 140.000 for the elephant Lumigraph.

We viewed the images at full screen resolution. As expected, the this does not affect the rendering time since the final texture mapping step is done in hardware.

4.3 Depth Quantization

In all the example in this paper, the depth values have been uniformly quantized in the range $[-D : D]$ before using them for the warping. Choosing a quantization of 8 bit does not affect the quality or performance of the algorithm at all, and it removes the need for a blending depth threshold ϵ as explained in Sec. 3.3. In our experiments we found that even with 6 bit, the images appear quite sharp and clean. Only the extreme edges in the scene become a bit blurry (e.g. the elephant's ear). When using less than 6 bit, the artifacts are similar to, but not as strong as those of light field interpolation.

4.4 Comparison with Previous Approaches

Fig. 10 depicts the same view as Fig. 8, but computed through interpolation from a light field without depth information [9]. Even though we used twice the number of images than for Fig. 8, very strong blurring and ghosting artifacts appear. These are even visible for the 164-eye point light field.

Fig. 12 shows the same scene as in Fig. 11, but rendered using depth-corrected Lumigraph rendering along the lines of [5]. The algorithm casts depth rays towards a coarse geometric model of the scene. If the three depth values for an eye point triangle differ, the triangle is subdivided adaptively, and more depth rays are used. If the algorithm does not detect any depth discontinuities using the initial depth rays, the adaptive scheme fails. This leads to the blurred edges similar to those in Fig. 12. Also, if a discontinuity is detected, quite a large number of depth rays (up to one per pixel along an edge) has to be cast in order to adapt the triangles to the edge. The computational cost of the approach depends on the depth continuity of the scene as well as on the number of geometric primitives used for approximating the scene. More experiments would be necessary in order to analyze these aspects in detail. From the tests with the implementation at hand, we learned that the algorithm becomes noninteractive as soon as more than 1000 triangles are used.

Figure 7: A view of an elephant Lumigraph generated from only 2x2 images. You can see that the elephant appears very sharp, but there are visible disocclusions and highlight artifacts.

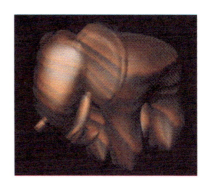

Figure 10: A view generated by the light field interpolation scheme from a 50-image Lumigraph. Despite the large number of images, there are very strong blurring and ghosting artifacts.

Figure 8: The same view, generated from a 25-image Lumigraph. The disocclusion artifacts are gone, and the highlight artifacts are only barely visible.

Figure 11: Lumigraph view of a simple scene, computed by warping from 6x6 images of 512x512 pixels resolution.

Figure 9: 25-image elephant Lumigraph, viewed from very close to the image plane. Gaps with the maximal width of 1 pixel can be observed (white spots).

Figure 12: Depth-corrected rendering of the same scene as in Fig. 11, according to the original Lumigraph hardware rendering algorithm [5]. Since the depth rays do not detect all edges, there is still a large amount of blurring.

5 Conclusions and Future Work

We presented an algorithm for rendering high-quality views of a Lumigraph at interactive rates. Using only a very small number of reference images (e.g. 25) and quantized depth values (6-8 bit), the algorithm produces no serious artifacts except when zooming in very close to the image plane. Furthermore, the method's computation time depends mainly on the number of pixels actually drawn on the image plane. The frame rate is nearly independent of the number of reference images used for the Lumigraph.

The algorithm presents a hybrid method, bringing together the best of warping and image databases, since it organizes and restricts the reference images in such way that the artifacts and overhead are minimized for the rendering.

Together with the adaptive acquisition scheme presented in [15], the algorithm can be employed for progressive transmission of Lumigraphs, for example in the world wide web. After loading only the first four images, the slab can be displayed, and the user can navigate around the object while some background process refines the Lumigraph by inserting the missing images as they are transferred. Standard image compression techniques can be applied to the Lumigraph images, and on-the fly decompression of pixel rows for warping seems to be feasible with our approach.

It is very important to test how the algorithm performs on real-world data, which is a major aspect of image based rendering. The quantization of depth values is a first step in that direction and shows promising results. Furthermore, it would be interesting to see which parts of the algorithm could be implemented using advanced features of contemporary graphics hardware.

We believe that our method may inspire many directions of future research. The most important and promising goal is to find an fully adaptive and hierarchical Lumigraph data structure that stores only little redundant information, but still allows for interactive rendering at multiple resolutions.

Acknowledgements

Thanks to Christian Vogelgsang (University of Erlangen) for his implementation of the Lumigraph rendering along the lines of [5], and to Pere-Pau Vazquez (University of Girona), who provided continuous encouragement and helped debugging a critical part of the implementation. Annette Scheel, Marc Stamminger, and Katja Daubert (Max-Planck-Institut für Informarik) provided kind support for acquiring the Lumigraph data using the in-house rendering system ANTELAO. The code for Delaunay triangulation was taken from Jonathan Richard Shewchuk's TRIANGLE package, available from http://www.cs.cmu.edu/~quake/triangle.html.

6 References

[1] E.H. Adelson and J.R. Bergen. *Computational Models of Visual Processing*, chapter 1 (The Plenoptic Function and the Elements of Early Vision). MIT Press, Cambridge, MA, 1991.

[2] E. Camahort, A. Lerios, and D. Fussell. Uniformly sampled light fields. In *Proc. 9th Eurographics Workshop on Rendering*, pages 117–130. Springer Verlag, 1998.

[3] C.-F. Chang, G. Bishop, and A. Lastra. LDI tree: A hierarchical representation for image-based rendering. In *Proc. SIGGRAPH 99*, pages 291–298. Addison-Wesley, 1999.

[4] S.E. Chen and L. Williams. View interpolation for image synthesis. In *Proc. SIGGRAPH '93*, pages 279–288. Addison-Wesley, 1993.

[5] S.J. Gortler, R. Grzeszczuk, R. Szeliski, and M.F. Cohen. The Lumigraph. In *Proc. SIGGRAPH '96*, pages 43–54. Addison-Wesley, 1996.

[6] W. Heidrich, H. Schirmacher, and H.-P. Seidel. A warping-based refinement of Lumigraphs. In V. Skala, editor, *Proc. WSCG '99*, pages 102–109, 1999.

[7] I. Ihm, S. Park, and R.K. Lee. Rendering of spherical light fields. In *Proc. Pacific Graphics '97*, 1997.

[8] A. Isaksen, L. McMillan, and S. J. Gortler. Dynamically reparameterized light fields. Technical Report MIT-LCS-TR-778, MIT LCS, May 1999.

[9] M. Levoy and P. Hanrahan. Light field rendering. In *Proc. SIGGRAPH '96*, pages 31–42. Addison-Wesley, 1996.

[10] W.R. Mark, L. McMillan, and G. Bishop. Post-rendering 3D warping. In *Proc. 1997 Symposium on Interactive 3D Graphics*, pages 7–16. ACM Press, 1997.

[11] L. McMillan. *An Image-Based Approach to Three-Dimensional Computer Graphics*. PhD thesis, Department of Computer Science, University of North Carolina at Chapel Hill, Chapel Hill, North Carolina, 1997.

[12] L. McMillan and G. Bishop. Plenoptic modeling: An image-based rendering system. In *Proc. SIGGRAPH '95*, pages 39–46. Addison-Wesley, 1995.

[13] M. M. Oliveira and G. Bishop. Factoring 3-D image warping into a pre-warp followed by conventional texture mapping. Technical Report TR99-002, Dept. of Computer Science, University of North Carolina at Chapel Hill, 1999.

[14] G. Schaufler. Nailboards: A rendering primitive for image caching in dynamic scenes. In *Proc. 8th Eurographics Workshop on Rendering*, pages 151–162. Springer Verlag, 1997.

[15] H. Schirmacher, W. Heidrich, and H.-P. Seidel. Adaptive acquisition of Lumigraphs from synthetic scenes. In *Proc. EUROGRAPHICS '99*, pages 151–159. Blackwell Publishers, 1999.

[16] J. W. Shade, S. J. Gortler, L. He, and R. Szeliski. Layered depth images. In *Proc. SIGGRAPH '98*, pages 231–242. Addison-Wesley, 1998.

[17] P.-P. Sloan, M.F. Cohen, and S.J. Gortler. Time critical Lumigraph rendering. In *Proc. 1997 Symposium on Interactive 3D Graphics*, pages 17–24. ACM Press, 1997.

Effects of Gaze on Multiparty Mediated Communication

Roel Vertegaal
Department of Computing and
Information Science
Queen's University, Canada
E-mail: roel@acm.org

Gerrit van der Veer
Computer Science Department
Vrije Universiteit Amsterdam
The Netherlands
E-mail: gerrit@cs.vu.nl

Harro Vons
Usability Consultancy
Baan Apps
The Netherlands
E-mail: hvons@baan.nl

Abstract

We evaluated effects of gaze direction and other non-verbal visual cues on multiparty mediated communication. Groups of three participants (two actors, one subject) solved language puzzles in three audiovisual communication conditions. Each condition presented a different selection of images of the actors to subjects: (1) frontal motion video; (2) motion video with gaze directional cues; (3) still images with gaze directional cues. Results show that subjects used twice as many deictic references to persons when head orientation cues were present. We also found a linear relationship between the amount of actor gaze perceived by subjects and the number of speaking turns taken by subjects. Lack of gaze can decrease turn-taking efficiency of multiparty mediated systems by 25%. This is because gaze conveys whether one is being addressed or expected to speak, and is used to regulate social intimacy. Support for gaze directional cues in multiparty mediated systems is therefore recommended.

Keywords: CSCW, videoconferencing, gaze direction.

1 INTRODUCTION

Humans exhibit great sensitivity to the look (or *gaze*) of others [2]. Most notably, gaze at one's eyes reveals one is being observed. From a distance of about 1 m, people can discriminate gaze at their eyes by someone facing them with an accuracy of approximately .6 degrees [6]. Head orientation can also reveal one's visual interest for others. From 1.5 m distance and at right angles to two interactors, humans can discriminate one person looking at the eyes of the other in 60% of cases, simply by judging the angle of head orientation [29]. However, the video-mediated communication systems we use are much less effective in conveying gaze directional cues [21]. This is because each user has only one camera (allowing a single frontal picture), and because that camera is typically placed well above the eyes of the other person on the screen. Due to the resulting parallax, eye gaze appears lowered. Isaacs & Tang [9] and O'Connaill et al. [14] observed that single-camera video mediated systems may cause problems in mediating multiparty communication. They noticed difficulties in floor control, and in referring to other participants. Our assumption was that these problems were directly caused by the lack of information about the gaze direction of the participants. Gaze directional cues code who is talking or listening to whom with great accuracy [28], and we expected the lack of such information to have a great effect on the management of group conversations. However, the isolated effect of gaze directional cues on multiparty conversation was never demonstrated empirically. We therefore conducted an experiment in which we gauged the effect of such cues on a variety of

dependent variables in a triadic video-mediated setting. To estimate the relative importance of these cues, we compared effects to those of other visual cues conveyed by video mediated systems. We will first discuss our independent variables, and how they were used to constitute experimental conditions. For each dependent variable, we will then discuss why it was measured, how this was done, and predictions toward treatment effects.

2 INDEPENDENT VARIABLES

We tried to isolate the effect on multiparty communication of three independent variables: (a) the presence of head orientation information; (b) the amount of gaze at the eyes conveyed; (c) the presence of other non-verbal visual cues such as facial expressions and lip movements, as conveyed by motion video. We used levels of variables (a) and (c) to constitute the following three conditions:

1) A condition in which all moving visual upper-torso cues were presented, except for head orientation (hereafter referred to as *motion video-only*, see Fig. 1a).

2) A condition in which all moving visual upper-torso cues were presented, including head orientation (hereafter referred to as *motion video with gaze direction*, see Figures 1a, 1b and 1c).

3) A condition in which no *moving* visual upper-torso cues were presented other than head orientation (hereafter referred to as *still images with gaze direction*, see Figures 1a, 1b and 1c).

As Sellen [18] showed, the use of different mediated systems to create these conditions is not possible without introducing other, potentially confounding, differences. Instead, we controlled our factors towards subjects using the same system in all conditions, by using actors as their conversational partners. These actors would alter their behavior towards subjects according to experimental conditions. Using triads of one replaceable subject and two reusable actors, we thus constituted the simplest form of multiparty communication, keeping the number of subjects and actors required to an absolute minimum. However, control over variable (b), the amount of gaze at the eyes of subjects, proved more difficult. Our experiment was aimed at evaluating the effect of human cues, rather than the technology used to convey them. As said, however, video mediation does not allow gaze at the eyes to be conveyed due to the parallax between camera and screen. Rosenthal [16] tried to solve this problem by placing a half-silvered mirror at a 45° angle between camera and screen. This way, the camera could be virtually positioned behind the eyes of the person on the screen [1]. The great drawback of this *video tunnel* technology is that subjects would have to sit perfectly still – their heads in a tunnel construction – to keep their eyes exactly aligned with the lens of an actor's camera [21]. This limitation, in turn, would impair individual gaze at their eyes by the other actor, blocking head orientation cues and restricting the natural behavior of subjects. To ensure subjects were able to perceive gaze at their eyes we therefore had to take a different approach, borrowed from TV presenters. We instructed the actors to look into the camera as much as possible when looking at their video monitors, thus simulating gaze at the eyes of subjects. This did mean the amount of gaze at the eyes was allowed to potentially vary between conditions. We controlled for this confounding influence retroactively by measuring the amount of gaze at the eyes perceived by subjects, using this as a covariate in our statistical tests. Predictions with regard to most dependent variables were therefore difficult to make, requiring post-hoc testing in most cases.

3 DEPENDENT VARIABLES & PREDICTIONS

We measured treatment effects on three dependent variables: task performance; the number of deictic references to persons; and turn frequency.

3.1 Task Performance

As Monk et al. [13] demonstrate, results obtained in comparing different mediated settings may depend very much on the experimental task used. Tasks that are highly personal and/or involve conflict are much more sensitive to differences in mediation than, e.g., problem-solving tasks. Thus, they are more likely to affect dependent variables other than task performance itself. We therefore devised a collaborative problem-solving task based on language puzzles. For each problem, each participant would obtain one of three pieces of information required to solve that problem. Participants would need to put these pieces in the correct order to score a point. By verbal communication of pieces and permutations of pieces, participants would collaborate to perform the task. Performance measure was the number of correct permutations given per session.

3.2 Deictic Verbal References

In their usability studies on video-mediated vs. face-to-face communication, Isaac and Tang observed many instances in face-to-face interaction when people used their eye gaze to indicate whom they were addressing [9]. However, when using a video-mediated system, participants would often use each other's names to indicate whom they were addressing. In general, the use deictic references to persons may be problematic when visuo-spatial cues are not conveyed. For example, if "You can try" is a direct response to something the addressed person just said, the meaning of the word "*you*" is easily disambiguated by knowledge about the identity of the previous speaker. If "You can try" is used imperatively, extra information is needed to ascertain whom is being addressed. This can be provided by head pointing. We believed it likely the availability of head orientation cues would thus affect the use of deictic referencing [10]. We measured the ability to use deixis towards persons by counting singular deictic use of second-person pronouns (i.e., the *you* in "Do *you* think so?"). As we did not expect a confounding influence of our covariate, we planned the evaluation of the following hypothesis:

Predictions Regarding Deictic Verbal References "The presence of head orientation cues causes the number of personal deictic verbal references used to rise significantly."

3.3 Speaker Switching and Turn Frequency

Isaacs and Tang [9] also observed that during video conferencing, people would control the turn-taking process explicitly by requesting others to take the next turn. In face-to-face interaction, however, they saw many instances where people used their eye gaze to indicate whom they were addressing and to suggest a next speaker. Kendon [12] suggested gaze directional cues play an important role in keeping the floor, taking and avoiding the floor, and suggesting who should speak next. As such, Short et al. [20] attributed problems in turn-taking behavior with mediated systems to a lack of gaze directional cues. We therefore decided to measure the number of turns taken by participants. Like Sellen [19], we did this by automated analysis of participants' speech patterns. There is little comparable evidence on which to base predictions regarding the effect of gaze directional cues on multiparty speaker switching. Firstly, there is only one study, by Sellen [18], in which gaze directional cues were part of the experimental treatment. Sellen failed to find significant differences in the number of turns between several multiparty conversational contexts: face-to-face, video-mediated with gaze direction, video-mediated without gaze direction, and audio-only communication. Secondly, most studies, particularly the early ones, were based on dyadic (two-person) communication. Finally, most studies, including Sellen's, compared communication settings that differed on too many variables at once. The most confirmed result from dyadic studies is a significant increase in the number of turns in face-to-face conditions, as compared with audio-only conditions [4, 17]. These results may well be explained by a lack of gaze directional cues yielding a worse synchronization of turn-taking in audio-only conditions [12]. Most studies suggest that with regard to turn-taking, adding motion video to speech communication has little effect (see Sellen [18] for an overview).

4 METHOD

We used an independent samples design for our experiment, comparing performance between three matched groups of subjects, each group treated with one of the three conditions. We treated this design as single-factor, using post-hoc testing for most dependent variables.

4.1 Conditions

In each condition, actors used exactly the same video-mediated system to communicate with the subject. Differences on treatment variables were presented only to the subject. As actors were seated in the same room, they did not use a video-mediated system to communicate with each other. As will be explained, care was taken that this would not confound the experiment. The subject assumed the actors were in two separate rooms, and that everyone was using the same type of video mediation to

Figure 1. *Three different directions of actor gaze as experienced by the subjects: a) facing the subject; b) looking at computer screen; and c) looking at other actor.*

communicate. For each condition, we will now describe how differences in the behavior of actors and system constituted the experimental treatment:

1) *Motion video-only.* In this condition, the subjects saw a full-motion video image of the actors, with the actors always facing the subject (Figure 1a).

2) *Motion video with gaze direction (Motion+GD).* In this condition, the subjects saw a full-motion video image of the actors. Actors were allowed to turn their heads in different directions, indicating whom or what they looked at: the subject (Figure 1a), their computer screen (Figure 1b), or the other actor (Figure 1c). As actors were in the same room, it would have been possible to achieve eye contact between them in this condition. To avoid this potentially confounding effect, when looking at each other, they looked at a common reference point instead.

3) *Still images with gaze direction (Still+GD).* At any moment in time, actors would manually select one of three still images for display to the subject: actor looking at subject (Figure 1a), actor looking at computer screen (Figure 1b), or actor looking at other actor (Figure 1c). Actors were instructed to base their selection on whom or what they would actually be looking at. This looking behavior essentially replicated that of condition 2. Note that the frontal picture was taken with the actors looking straight into the camera lens.

4.2 Experimental Subjects and Actors

Our experimental subjects were paid volunteers, mostly university students from a variety of technical and social disciplines. Prior to the experiment, we tested all subjects on eyesight and a number of relevant matching variables: Dutch language competence (using a pen-and-paper aptitude test [8]); age; sex; and field of study. We allocated each subject to a treatment group in a way that matched groups on these variables. The 56 subjects used for further analysis were assigned to treatment groups as follows:

- Motion video-only group. 20 subjects (13 male, 7 female, mean age 21.4);
- Motion video with gaze direction group. 19 subjects (13 male, 6 female, mean age 21.7);
- Still images with gaze direction group. 17 subjects (11 male, 6 female, mean age 22.2).

Subjects believed the actors were subjects also. None of the subjects in this subset knew or had any suspicion regarding the actors. None had any previous experience with video-mediated communication. Subjects believed we were interested in how people cooperate via the Internet, and were only informed of the true purpose of the experiment after treatment. We used one female and one male actor, seated in a separate room from the experimental subject. The difference in sex between the actors may have aided identification of voices in the still images with gaze direction condition. Both actors were about the same age as the subjects.

4.3 Task

We constructed a group problem-solving task in which each subject was asked to join the actors - perceived as being subjects also - in solving as many language puzzles as possible within a time span of 15 minutes. For each language puzzle, each participant (the subject and each actor) was presented a different fragment of a sentence (yielding a total of 3 fragments per puzzle). To solve each puzzle, they had to construct as many meaningful and syntactically correct permutations of the sentence fragments as possible (yielding a theoretical 6 possible solutions per puzzle). After having given all correct answers to a particular language puzzle, another set of fragments would be presented. For the creation of each permutation, participants had to use the following rules:

1) Each permutation had to be grammatically correct.
2) Each permutation had to be meaningful.
3) They were allowed to add punctuation marks, as long the permutation remained one sentence.
4) The order of the words inside each fragment could not be altered.

For the subject, each sentence fragment appeared on a computer screen. The actors pretended this was the case for them also, having their fragments listed on paper instead. To prevent a practice effect, this paper listed all correct answers to each puzzle. It prescribed which correct solutions they were allowed to give away, and when to give incorrect solutions. This was done to minimize the influence of actors on task performance while keeping their act credible towards the subject. In order to ensure an exchange of information between the subject and each actor:

1) No one could see the sentence fragment of the other participants.
2) Each fragment remained on the subject's screen for only 10 seconds.
3) Each participant had a specific role. The subject's role was to submit each solution they collectively agreed to be correct. Actor 1 would pretend to enter this solution for verification by computer, while Actor 2 would report its correctness, pretending this was indicated on her computer screen.

When all correct permutations were given, a computer would provide a new sentence fragment on the subject's computer screen, generating an audio signal to inform the actors. The number of correct permutations generated per 15 minute session was used as a measure of task performance. Correct permutations that were given more than once counted only once, and uncompleted language puzzles were discarded.

4.4 Instructions and Session Procedure

Prior to the experiment, actors were instructed with regard to their behavior in the different conditions, which they practiced in several training sessions. Actors memorized all answers to all problems solved in the experimental task prior to the experiment. They were not informed until after the experiment of the purpose of the experiment or reasons behind the experimental treatments. Actors were instructed to behave as if they were subjects, with a similar system setup. However, actors were told to allow the actual subject to take the initiative. This resulted in a situation in which much of the interaction was between the subject and one of the actors, rather than between actors only. For each subject, the session was structured in the following way. After introducing the subject to the system, the session would start with the participants seeing and hearing each other. After introducing themselves, the experimenter explained the role of each participant using a simple practice game. After exactly one minute, the experimenter interrupted the game to explain the rules of the actual task. The session proceeded with the first puzzle, ending after 15 minutes. After each session, subjects filled in a questionnaire and were debriefed by the host.

5 MATERIALS

All equipment was set up in a way that minimized differences between conditions to treatment variables only. All video and audio equipment was analog, with no discernable lag. All video and audio signals were recorded in sync on video tape using a video splitter device and two audio tracks.

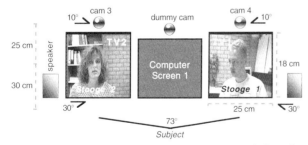

Figure 2. *The video-mediated system used by the subjects.*

5.1 Subject Configuration

Figure 2 shows the setup as experienced by subjects. The subject was seated in front of two video monitors, with the right monitor (TV1) displaying the image of Actor 1 and the left monitor (TV2) the image of Actor 2. Between these video monitors, a computer monitor (Screen 1) was placed, used to display the subject's sentence fragment. The average distance from the head of the subject to each

monitor was approximately 60 cm. From the subject's point of view, the angle between the center of the left monitor image and the center of the right monitor image was approximately 73°.

5.2 Actor Configuration

The equipment for each actor was about half the subject configuration. Actors each had only one video monitor (TV3 and TV4) on which they always saw live video images of the subject. An Apple videoconferencing camera was placed on top of each monitor, with its lens 17 cm above the center of the monitor. The cameras pointed almost horizontally at the eyes of the actors, seated about 80 cm away. In all conditions, Actor 1 got the live image of camera 4, and Actor 2 got the live image of camera 3. The actors each had a unidirectional microphone placed in front of them. The signal from each microphone was amplified and fed to the respective speaker in the subject room. Actors used a numeric keyboard for selecting images in Powerpoint in the still-image condition. These images looked identical to the live camera feeds. Actor 1 had a disconnected computer keyboard with which he pretended to feed answers into a computer for verification.

6 ANALYSIS

We will now discuss how we analyzed the video tape recordings to obtain measurements for each dependent variable.

6.1 Analysis of Deictic Verbal References

The experimenter and an independent observer scored the number of deictic verbal references used by subjects and actors during each full 15 minute session. Both observers were blind to experimental conditions. The independent observer was also blind to any experimental predictions or details. Before scoring, rules were agreed on what constituted a correct reference. Only deictic second-person pronouns were scored (i.e., the words *you* and *your* in "Are *you* sure that was *your* sentence?"), using these criteria:

- the reference was to one person only.
- the reference was not preceded or followed by a name.
- the reference was not used in a generic way.
- repetitions were scored only once (e.g., "You, you said").
- references in puzzle sentences were not scored.

Before scoring, both observers practiced the use of the above criteria on a subset of sessions not used for further analysis. After the training, the inter-observer reliability was determined on a new set of unused data. We obtained a significant correlation of r=.86 between observers (p<.001, 2-tailed). Subsequent analysis of 56 sessions, averaged between observers, yielded a mean number of deictic verbal references per session for the subject and each actor.

6.2 Turn-taking Analysis

We analyzed the first five minutes of each session for turn-taking behavior of subjects and actors. We used an automated procedure to analyze the speech patterns of individual speakers. As automated analysis could only be carried out on the isolated speech data of individual speakers, the two-track recordings were separated by hand into three separate digital audio tracks (22 KHz, 8- bit) for each session (inter-observer reliability r=.97, p<.001, 2-tailed). Like Sellen [18], we then used a fuzzy algorithm that counted the number of turns by each speaker [25]. First, this algorithm filled in 240 ms pauses to account for stop consonants, effectively removing pauses within words [5]. Then, the algorithm removed pauses between consecutively spoken words to identify talkspurts, series of phonemic clauses uttered by the same speaker. The phonemic clause is regarded as the basic syntactic unit of speech. On average, it consists of 2-10 words with a duration of approximately 1.5 s, providing an estimate for finding the shortest uninterrupted vocalizations (see [11, 19] for a discussion). To identify talkspurts, a 13-sample (1.56 s) window moved over the speech data, filling samples within a 70% confidence interval around its mean position with speech energy if more than half of the samples in the window indicated speech activity, and if this speech activity was balanced within the window. Finally, a turn was assigned if one of the speakers had a talkspurt longer than an average phonemic clause (i.e., 1.56 s), with everybody else being silent for the same length of time. The total number of turns by all participants, minus one, constituted the number of speaker switches. We checked the validity of the above turn-taking analysis algorithm by calculating the correlation over time between a turn classification produced by the algorithm and that produced by a trained linguist (see [25] for details). With a correlation of r=.64 (p<.001, 2-tailed) between classification methods the algorithm, which identified phonemic clauses simply by checking the duration of consecutive speech, did well against the human expert, who used intonation and semantics of speech to identify phonemic clauses.

6.3 Analysis of Gaze at the Eyes of Subjects

Since we allowed the amount of gaze at the eyes perceived by subjects to vary between and within conditions, we needed to measure and control for this factor after the fact. We used an independent observer, with no knowledge about the experiment, to score the number of video frames in which actors appeared to gaze at the eyes of the subject. Before scoring, both the observer and the experimenter practiced observation on a subset of experimental data not used for further analysis. Inter-observer reliabilities averaged across conditions (Fisher Z transformed) were r=.94 for Actor 1 gaze and r=.87 for Actor 2 gaze (both p<.001). Subsequent scoring by the independent observer of the first 5 minutes of each of the 56 used sessions yielded a mean percentage of gaze at the subject's eyes per actor per session.

7 RESULTS

Results for each variable were calculated over the same 56 sessions. Where appropriate, analyses of variance (one-way ANOVAs) were carried out, evaluated at an α=.05 level. Post-hoc comparisons were carried out using Student-Newman-Keuls (SNK) tests evaluated at an α=.05 level. One planned comparison was carried out using a one-tailed t-test evaluated at an α=.05 level. All data was normally distributed (Kolmogorov-Smirnov test, p>.05) with equal variances between conditions (Levene test, p>.05) unless indicated.

7.1 Task Performance

Analysis of variance showed no significant differences between conditions in the number of problems solved ($F_{(2, 53)}$=1.39, p=.26).

Variable	Deictic 2nd pers. Pronouns *mean (s.e.)*		
	Motion	Motion+GD	Still+GD
Subject number of references	1.3 (.3)	2.6 (.7)	3.6 (.9)
Mean actor # of references	1.8 (.3)	2.4 (.3)	2.2 (.3)

Table 1. *Means and standard errors for the number of deictic verbal references per first 5 session minutes.*

7.2 Deictic Verbal References

Table 1 presents the data summary for the number of deictic verbal references using second-person pronouns during the first five session minutes. A planned comparison showed that subjects used twice as many deictic verbal references in the condition conveying motion video with gaze direction than in the condition conveying motion video only (t(26.93)=1.82, p<.04, uneq. var., 1-tailed), thus confirming our hypothesis. Analysis of variance showed no significant differences between conditions in the mean number of deictic verbal references made by the actors ($F_{(2, 53)}$=.88, p=.42).

Variable	Speaker Turns *mean (s.e.)*		
	Motion	Motion+GD	Still+GD
Number of speaker switches	14.7 (1.0)	15.1 (1.1)	18.9 (1.5)
Subject number of turns	5.9 (.4)	6.3 (.5)	7.7 (.7)
Actor 1 number of turns	6.1 (.5)	5.3 (.4)	7.8 (.7)
Actor 2 number of turns	3.8 (.4)	4.6 (.5)	4.5 (.5)

Table 2. *Means and standard errors for the number of speaker turns per first 5 session minutes.*

7.3 Turn-taking Behavior

Table 2 shows the data summary for the number of speaker switches and individual turns during the first five session minutes. Analysis of variance showed the number of speaker switches differed significantly across conditions ($F_{(2, 53)}$=3.75, p<.03). Post-hoc comparisons showed this difference lay in the condition conveying still images with gaze direction (SNK, p<.05). There were over 25% more speaker switches in this condition. Differences across conditions in the number of individual turns by subjects showed a similar trend ($F_{(2, 53)}$=3.17, p=.05). Here, post-hoc comparisons showed that the still image with gaze direction condition was different from the motion video-only condition (SNK, p<.05). Differences across conditions in the number of turns by Actor 1 were significant ($F_{(2, 53)}$=5.39, p<.01). Post-hoc comparisons showed the still image with gaze direction condition was different from the other conditions (SNK, p<.05). There was no significant difference across conditions in the number of turns by Actor 2 (F(2, 53)=.94, p=.40). Actor 2 did show a practice effect over sessions (correlation between session order and number of turns per session r=.46, p<.001).

	Amount of Actor Gaze *mean (s.e.)*		
Variable	Motion	Motion+GD	Still+GD
Amount of gaze (% time)	13.8 (1.2)	6.6 (.8)	31.6 (1.5)

Table 3. *Means and standard errors for the percentage of actor gaze at the eyes of subjects per first 5 session minutes.*

	Estimated Means Adjusted for Gaze		
Variable	Motion	Motion+GD	Still+GD
Number of speaker switches	15.4	17.1	16.3
Subject number of turns	6.2	7.3	6.3

Table 4. *Means and standard errors for the number of speaker switches and subject turns, corrected for actor gaze, per first 5 session minutes.*

7.4 Removing Effects of Gaze at the Eyes

Table 3 shows the data summary of the percentage of actor gaze at the eyes of subjects during the first five session minutes. Analysis of variance showed differences in the mean percentage of actor gaze were significant across conditions (F(2, 53)=112.05, p<.0001). Post-hoc comparisons showed differences were significant between all conditions (SNK, p<.05). Subjects experienced about four times more actor gaze in the still image with gaze direction condition than in the motion video with gaze direction condition. There was a modest, but significant, linear relationship across conditions between the percentage of actor gaze at the eyes of subjects and the number of speaker switches (r=.37, p<.01 2-tailed) and between the percentage of actor gaze at the eyes of subjects and the number of subject turns (r=.34, p<.02 2-tailed). To adjust for this confounding effect, we performed a covariance analysis (Roy Bargman Stepdown test). All assumptions for the analysis were met. Table 4 shows the resulting adjusted mean number of speaker switches and subject turns. With the effect of gaze at the eyes of subjects removed, differences between conditions in the number of speaker switches (F(2, 52)=.56, p=.58) or subject turns (F(2, 52)=.92, p=.41) were no longer significant.

7.5 Questionnaire

Analysis of variance (one-way Kruskal-Wallis) on the ranked response categories of the questionnaire showed answers to only one question were significantly different across conditions. Subjects rated the *still image with gaze direction* condition as superior to the other conditions

with regard to the clarity with which they could observe whom their conversational partners were talking to ($\chi^2(2)$=10.8, p<.005).

8 DISCUSSION

We will first consider potential confounding effects of actor behavior. For each of our dependent variables, we will then discuss possible explanations for our findings.

8.1 Confounding Effects of Actor Behavior

For the main dependent variables, we will now discuss to what extent results could have been due to differences in actor behavior other than treatment.

Confounding Effects on Deixis

On average, we found no significant differences between conditions in the number of deictic verbal references made by actors, making it unlikely they induced subject behavior by verbal means. We therefore believe it likely effects were in fact due to treatment variables.

Confounding Effects on Turn-taking

Most of the speaker switches occurred between subjects and Actor 1. Although Actor 2 demonstrated no treatment effect, like the subjects, Actor 1 did have more turns in the still image condition (see Table 2). One might therefore suspect that treatment effects on subject turn-taking were due to the turn-taking behavior of Actor 1. The positive linear relationship between the amount of actor gaze at the eyes of subjects and the number of subject turns, across conditions, makes this unlikely. Firstly, Actor 1 did not see this information. Secondly, if the act of looking at the camera lens confounded his turn-taking behavior in both motion video conditions, we would have found a *negative* linear relationship in those conditions. We therefore believe it likely effects were in fact due to treatment variables.

8.2 Explaining Findings on Task Performance

We found no significant differences in task performance between conditions. Monk et al. [13] already suggested that measures of task performance are typically sensitive only to gross manipulations of experimental treatment. Our task may simply not have been very sensitive to experimental treatment. This does, however, suggest that effects with regard to other dependent variables were in fact due to differences between conditions in the communication process itself, rather than to differences in the nature of the experimental task. It also means we can generalize findings to other task situations in which efficiency of the turn-taking process is the parameter of interest.

8.3 Explaining Effects on Deixis

Results regarding the number of deictic verbal references to persons were in line with expectations. Subjects used twice as many references when head orientation was conveyed. Our hypothesis was confirmed, stating that the presence of head orientation cues causes the number of personal deictic verbal references used to rise significantly. The actual ability of subjects to use deixis towards the actors did not differ between conditions. We believe subjects judged the usefulness of deixis by assessing visuo-spatial properties of the system on the basis of actor head orientation behavior.

8.4 Explaining Effects on Turn-taking

Results with regard to the turn-taking variables ran contrary to expectations. We might have expected the motion video-only condition to show fewer speaker switches and consequently fewer turns than conditions in which gaze directional cues of the head were conveyed. Instead, the still image condition scored over 25% more speaker switches than *both* motion video conditions. Differences across conditions in the number of individual turns by subjects showed a similar trend. It is evident that the explanation for these results cannot lie in the absence of non-verbal visual cues in the still image condition. Both literature and earlier presented arguments suggest that any potential effects of this treatment variable would have gone in the opposite direction, with fewer turns when there are fewer nonverbal visual cues [4]. The sense of anonymity in the still image condition may have had a positive effect on turn-taking, but only one subject stated this in the questionnaire. As the analysis of covariance demonstrates, a much more satisfactory explanation for our findings is the confounding influence of actor gaze at the eyes of subjects. The linear relationship between the amount of gaze at the eyes perceived by subjects and their turn-taking behavior was sufficiently strong to explain our findings. In the still image condition, whenever the frontal image was selected, the actors would *always* appear to gaze at the eyes of the subject. This was not the case in the other conditions. When differences in the amount of gaze at the eyes of subjects were removed, differences in turn-taking behavior disappeared also. As discussed, people are very good at judging the angle of frontal eye gaze at their faces. One the one hand, we can therefore regard our covariate as a measure of the subjects' ability to discriminate whether they *themselves* were being looked at. On the other hand, our covariate was a measure for the *amount* of visual attention subjects received. This yields two, possibly complementary, explanations as to why there were more speaker switches in the still image condition:

1) *Knowing Your Turn.* According to a study by Vertegaal [25, 28], in multiparty conversation, gaze at the eyes codes whom is being addressed or listened to with great certainty. This information is not coded by other non-verbal means. Although head orientation might be used to see whom others address, this cue was not vital to the turn-taking process. Instead, subjects used gaze at their eyes to see when they *themselves* were addressed or expected to speak. Difficulties in conveying gaze at the eyes caused deficiencies in subjects obtaining and yielding the floor in both motion video conditions. This explanation is consistent with Kendon's findings regarding the functions of gaze in dyadic turn synchronization [12].

2) *Keeping Your Distance.* According to Argyle and Dean's Equilibrium of Intimacy theory [3], like proximity, people use gaze at the eyes to regulate social distance to each other. When the level of intimacy between people is disturbed (either too high or too low), they feel uncomfortable [2]. The mean percentage of gaze at the eyes in the still image condition was almost exactly that found by Exline for triadic face-to-face conversations [7]. In the other conditions percentages were much lower, yielding a much lower level of intimacy. As this lower level of intimacy could not easily be compensated by other means, subjects were less inclined to take the floor in those conditions.

With regard to our explanations for the mechanism behind the effect of gaze at the eyes on turn-taking, we found clear support for our first explanation in the questionnaire. Subjects found it significantly easier to observe who was talking to whom in the still image condition. Other qualitative observations, including comments by subjects, seemed mostly in line with our empirical findings.

9 CONCLUSIONS AND RECOMMENDATIONS

We first present our empirical conclusions, after which we outline our recommendations for the design of multiparty mediated systems.

9.1 Empirical Conclusions

In this paper, we presented an empirical evaluation of the effects of gaze directional and other non-verbal visual cues on multiparty mediated communication. Groups of three participants (two actors and one subject) solved language puzzles in three mediated communication conditions. In addition to speech, each condition presented a different selection of images of the actors' upper torsos to subjects: (1) frontal motion video showing gaze at the eyes 14% of time; (2) motion video with head orientation and 7% gaze at the eyes; (3) still images with head orientation and 32% gaze at the eyes. Effects of the amount of gaze at the eyes perceived by subjects were isolated retroactively. Results show the presence of head orientation cues caused subjects to use twice as many deictic verbal references to persons. We believe this was due to differences between conditions in the subjects' estimate of the effectiveness of head pointing in disambiguating deixis. Across conditions, we also found a significant positive linear relationship between the amount of actor gaze at the eyes of subjects and the number of subject turns (r=.34) and speaker switches (r=.37). We did not find a similar effect on turn frequency of the presence of other non-verbal upper-torso visual cues, including head orientation. As evidenced by subject performance in our still image condition, the potential increase in turn frequency may be in the order of 25% when gaze at the eyes is conveyed in a manner that preserves face-to-face characteristics. We believe there are two reasons why the presence of gaze at the eyes has a positive effect on turn frequency in multiparty mediated communication. Firstly, gaze at the eyes is used to determine when a person is speaking or listening to you. In group communication, it not obvious who will be the next speaker when the current speaker falls silent. Seeing when they were being addressed or expected to speak made it easier for subjects to obtain or yield the floor. We found clear support for this in our questionnaires. Subjects found it easier to observe who was talking to whom in the condition with normal percentages of gaze at the eyes. Secondly, gaze at the eyes seems to be used to regulate social distance. Subjects may have felt the level of intimacy with their conversational partners was disturbed when there was not enough gaze at their eyes, making them less inclined to take the floor.

9.2 Design Recommendations

We believe that a higher turn frequency is an indication of a more natural, and perhaps more efficient, turn-taking process. As discussed, most empirical studies seem to confirm this rationale. Although effects of a higher turn-taking efficiency may be dependent on the task situation, we believe one *can* generalize that synchronous interactive group communication systems should preserve gaze directional cues, especially gaze at the eyes. With respect to the design of such systems, we therefore formulated the following incremental requirements:

1) Preservation of relative position. Relative viewpoints of participants should be based on a common reference point (e.g., around a shared workspace), providing basic support for the use of a common external context in deictic referencing.

2) Preservation of head orientation. The ability to use head pointing eases the use of deictic references to persons.

3) Preservation of gaze at the eyes. Allowing participants to perceive gaze at each other's eyes eases management of turn-taking and may aid tele-presence.

Our findings do *not* suggest that motion video should not be conveyed. Rather, they suggest that when developing software for group communication, one should consider conveying gaze directional cues first. Whether it is for highly personal or business communication, participants need to be able to seek or avoid gaze at each other's eyes according to their own personal or cultural preferences. We will now briefly discuss how the above requirements could be implemented in group communication systems. If motion video *is* conveyed, we suggest the use of a multiple camera setup, in which each participant has a camera for each other participant. By placing each camera behind a semi-transparent screen displaying the image of that participant, basic support for the above requirements can be provided [1]. The larger the distance of the head to the screen, or the smaller the projected images, the more head movement of users is tolerable without impairing conveyance of gaze at the eyes. We believe office-size systems such as MAJIC [15] therefore provide the best implementation of our requirements currently possible with motion video. Note that the need for multiple video streams in such systems does mean bandwidth use will not scale well with the number of users [23]. When still images are used, our requirements can be implemented using very little bandwidth indeed. The GAZE Groupware System [23] implements all requirements in a transparent and noncommand fashion. It measures whom participants look at using a desktop eyetracking system. It then orients their picture so that it faces the person they look at [22-27].

10 REFERENCES

1. Acker, S. and Levitt, S. Designing videoconference facilities for improved eye contact. Journal of Broadcasting & Electronic Media 31(2), 1987, pp. 181-191.
2. Argyle, M. and Cook, M. Gaze and Mutual Gaze. London: Cambridge University Press, 1976.
3. Argyle, M. and Dean, J. Eye-contact, distance and affiliation. Sociometry 28, 1965, pp. 289-304.
4. Argyle, M., Lalljee, M., and Cook, M. The effects of visibility on interaction in a dyad. Human Relations 21, 1968, pp. 3-17.
5. Brady, P.T. A statistical analysis of on-off patterns in 16 conversations. The Bell System Technical Journal (Jan.), 1968.
6. Cline, M.G. The perception of where a person is looking. American Journal of Psychology 80, 1967, pp. 41-50.
7. Exline, R.V. Explorations in the process of person perception: Visual interaction in relation to competition, sex and need for affiliation. Journal of Personality 31, 1963, pp. 1-20.
8. Fokkema, S.D. and Dirkzwager, A. Ruimtelijk Inzicht; Taalgebruik II, Zinnen. Amsterdam: Swets & Zeitlinger, 1960.
9. Isaacs, E. and Tang, J. What video can and can't do for collaboration: a case study. In Proceedings of ACM Multimedia '93. Anaheim, CA: ACM, 1993.
10. Ishii, H. and Kobayashi, M. ClearBoard: A seamless medium for shared drawing and conversation with eye contact. In Proceedings of CHI'92. Monterey, CA: ACM, 1992.
11. Jaffe, J. and Feldstein, S. Rhythms of Dialogue. New York, NY USA: Academic Press, 1970.
12. Kendon, A. Some functions of gaze direction in social interaction. Acta Psychologica 32, 1967, pp. 1-25.
13. Monk, A., McCarthy, J., Watts, L., and Daly-Jones, O. Measures of process. In Thomas, P. (Ed.), CSCW Requirements and Evaluation. Berlin: Springer Verlag, 1996, pp. 125-139.
14. O'Connaill, B., Whittaker, S., and Wilbur, S. Conversations over video conferences: An evaluation of the spoken aspects of video-mediated communication. Human Computer Interaction 8, 1993, pp. 389-428.
15. Okada, K.-i., Maeda, F., Ichikawaa, Y., and Matsushita, Y. Multiparty videoconferencing at virtual social distance: MAJIC design. In Proceedings of CSCW '94. Chapel Hill, NC: ACM, 1994, pp. 385-393.
16. Rosenthal, A.H. Two-way television communication unit. United States Patent 2 420 198, 1947.
17. Rutter, D.R. and Stephenson, G.M. The role of visual communication in synchronising conversation. European Journal of Social Psychology 7, 1977, pp. 29-37.
18. Sellen, A.J. Remote conversations: the effects of mediating talk with technology. Human Computer Interaction 10(4), 1995.
19. Sellen, A.J. Speech patterns in video-mediated conversations. In Proceedings of CHI'92. Monterey, CA: ACM, 1992.
20. Short, J., Williams, E., and Christie, B. The Social Psychology of Telecommunications. London: Wiley, 1976.
21. Stapley, B. Visual Enhancement of Telephone Conversations. PhD Thesis. Empirial College, 1972.
22. Vertegaal, R. Conversational awareness in multiparty VMC. In Extended Abstracts of CHI'97. Atlanta, GA: ACM, 1997.
23. Vertegaal, R. The GAZE Groupware System: Mediating joint attention in multiparty communication and collaboration. In Proceedings of CHI'99. Pittsburg, PA: ACM, 1999.
24. Vertegaal, R. GAZE: Visual-spatial attention in communication. Video Paper. In Proceedings of CSCW '98. Seattle, WA USA: ACM, 1998.
25. Vertegaal, R. Look Who's Talking to Whom. PhD Thesis. Enschede, The Netherlands: Cognitive Ergonomics Department, Twente University, 1998.
26. Vertegaal, R., Velichkovsky, B., and Van der Veer, G. Catching the eye: Management of joint attention in cooperative work. SIGCHI Bulletin 29(4), 1997.
27. Vertegaal, R., Vons, H., and Slagter, R. Look who's talking: The GAZE Groupware System. In Summary of CHI'98. Los Angeles, CA: ACM, 1998.
28. Vertegaal, R., Slagter, R., Van der Veer, G., and Nijholt, A. Why conversational agents should catch the eye. In Summary of CHI'2000. The Hague, The Netherlands: ACM, 2000.
29. Von Cranach, M. and Ellgring, J.H. The perception of looking behaviour. In Von Cranach, M. and Vine, I. (Ed.), Social Communication and Movement. London: Academic Press, 1973.

Towards Seamless Support of Natural Collaborative Interactions

Stacey D. Scott   Garth B. D. Shoemaker   Kori M. Inkpen

EDGE Lab
School of Computing Science
Simon Fraser University
Burnaby, BC V5A 1S6 Canada
+1 604 291 3610
{sdscott, garths, inkpen}@cs.sfu.ca

Abstract

In order to effectively support collaboration it is important that computer technology seamlessly support users' natural interactions instead of inhibiting or constraining the collaborative process. The research presented in this paper examines the *human-human* component of computer supported cooperative work and how the design of technology can impact how people work together. In particular, this study examined children's natural interactions when working in a physical medium compared to two computer-based environments (a traditional desktop computer and a system augmented to provide each user with a mouse and a cursor). Results of this research demonstrate that given the opportunity, children will take advantage of the ability to interact concurrently. In addition, users' verbal interactions and performance can be constrained when they are forced to interact sequentially, as in the traditional computer setup. Supporting concurrent interactions with multiple input devices is a first step towards developing effective collaborative environments that support users' natural collaborative interactions.

Key words: Computer supported cooperative work (CSCW), computer supported collaborative learning (CSCL), single display groupware (SDG), user interfaces, multiple mice, and synchronous interaction.

1 Introduction

Collaboration with colleagues, friends, and/or classmates is often an important part of our daily activities. Whether working together to write a paper, brainstorming a software engineering design, consulting on a medical diagnosis, or for the enjoyment of playing with others, we often need or want to be able to collaborate with others. When these activities require the use of computer technology, we are limited by the underlying one-person/one-computer paradigm of typical computers found in homes, schools and workplaces. Existing alternatives include working together on networked workstations (presuming that collaborative support has been facilitated through software) or gathering around a single workstation. The research presented in this paper explores ways to more effectively support natural collaborative interactions of people working together in small, co-located groups. Specifically, this work addresses the importance of providing multiple input devices to support multiple concurrent interactions and the impact this has on the effectiveness of the collaboration.

An investigation was undertaken into the behaviours of school-aged children performing a puzzle-solving task under different experimental conditions: (1) a physical paper-based condition; (2) a one-mouse one-cursor condition; and (3) a two-mice two-cursor condition, that allows for synchronous independent interactions. It is important to explore issues of collaboration for the domain of education given that many traditional classroom activities utilize computers. These environments must support the strong social interactions both within groups of students and between students and teachers. It is essential that the natural collaborative interactions that exist for traditional learning settings be supported in modern computer-based learning environments. This will help ensure that the benefits associated with this rich form of interaction are not lost. Computer technology should support, and not interfere with, users' natural collaborative tendencies.

This paper presents a review of related research in Section 2, followed by a discussion of the methodology in Section 3. Section 4 reports on preliminary results gathered from this work, published previously, and Section 5 presents more in-depth analysis of the results. Section 6 provides an overall discussion relating to the underlying goals of this research. Finally, in Section 7, conclusions are presented as well as implications on future research in this area.

2 Related Work

It is becoming apparent that the conventional computer does not support some desired types of collaborative activities. To deal with this, many researchers are exploring alternative technologies to improve support for collaboration.

2.1 Alternative Collaborative Technologies

One approach to the support of collaborative activities is the development of alternative technologies based on real-world artifacts that facilitate collaborative interactions. This approach combines existing collaborative tools from the physical world (e.g. a whiteboard), with the benefits of traditional computer technology. Interactive displays, such as electronic whiteboards [9, 13] and tabletop displays [14], are two alternative technologies based on real-world counterparts.

Electronic whiteboards and tabletop displays are natural choices since they are based on a shared surface metaphor, such as a typical office whiteboard or a table surface. This allows researchers to take advantage of the fact the most users are familiar with collaborating around whiteboards and tables. More importantly, these metaphors facilitate collaboration by providing surfaces large enough for multiple people to collaborate around without crowding, allowing unrestricted drawing and erasing that is essential for many informal collaborative tasks, and giving all group members access to the shared workspace [13].

2.2 Alternative Interaction Devices

Beyond display, the design of input devices and interaction styles can also help support natural collaborative interactions. Researchers have begun to look at alternative input devices that support computer interaction through the manipulation of physical objects.

LEGO/Logo [10] was an early system that utilized physical manipulation of programmable blocks in a collaborative process. With this system, children could write programs using the Logo programming language, allowing them to control machines that they built with LEGO toy construction pieces. This system, though, required an intermediate interaction involving a traditional computer to perform the Logo programming before the LEGO pieces became interactive.

Tangible user interfaces (TUIs) [4] is a research area that investigates the manipulation of physical objects to interact with computers and can be a means of supporting face-to-face collaboration. Tangible user interfaces take advantage of the fact that physical objects naturally afford certain interactions [4]. These affordances help make the interfaces more intuitive to interact with than indirect manipulation devices such as a mouse. Manipulating TUIs requires body movement and body positioning within a physical space which provides a rich source of non-verbal communication to help manage the collaborative process [15]. For example, in a user study utilizing AlgoBlocks[1], it was found that a user's body movement, such as picking up a block, focused the attention of the user, drew the attention of the other group members, allowed the group to see the user's intention, and allowed the members of the group to monitor that user's progress.

2.3 Multiple Input Devices

Along with the development of alternative input devices, several researchers have explored the use of multiple input devices to facilitate multi-user interaction. This has been a main research direction in the area Single Display Groupware (SDG), which examines ways to support small groups of people collaborating around a shared display [11]. One of the first SDG systems was the Multi-Device, Multi-User, Multi-Editor (MMM) [1] which allowed up to three mice to be used to synchronously interact with a shared application. Since then, other researchers have investigated the technical issues surrounding support for simultaneous multi-user interaction [2, 3, 8].

Motivation behind the development of technology that supports multi-user interaction stems from previous research that has suggested that supporting co-located collaboration can provide positive achievement and social benefits for children in educational learning environments. Inkpen *et al.* [5] found that children were more motivated to play a commercial problem-solving computer game and were more successful in the game when playing together on a single machine as opposed to playing on side-by-side computers or by themselves. Inkpen *et al.* [7] and Stewart *et al.* [12] have also shown increased achievement and motivational benefits by providing support for multi-user interactions to children collaborating in a computer environment.

3 METHOD[2]

The study involved pairs of children playing a puzzle-solving activity using three different experimental setups: (1) a paper-based version of the game with physical pieces; (2) a computer-based version of the game with one mouse and one cursor; and (3) a computer-based version of the game with two mice and two cursors.

3.1 Participants and Setting

The study took place in a public elementary school on the east side of Vancouver, British Columbia, Canada. The school is located in a lower-economic, culturally diverse area of Vancouver. The participants included

---

1 AlgoBlocks is a tangible programming language developed as a collaborative learning tool for children [15].

2 The method presented here was also reported in an earlier paper discussing preliminary results gathered from the study [6].

forty children (22 girls and 18 boys) between the ages of nine and eleven from three grade four and five classes. Parental consent was obtained for all children who participated in the study. The study ran for three consecutive days in April 1999 in a small conference room that was located in the school library. The research area included two experimental setups, each consisting of an IBM-compatible PC, a video camera with two lavaliere microphones to capture the children's interactions, and a scan-converter to capture the computer screen. The two experimental setups were configured back-to-back so children working on one computer could not easily see the other computer.

3.2 Alien pattern game

The puzzle-solving game developed for use in this study involved placing alien faces with varying attributes in a row according to a specific pattern. The alien faces had three possible head colours (blue, green, or red), three possible eye colours (black, green, or red), and two possible mouth styles (happy or sad). Each puzzle began with nine squares positioned in either a horizontal or vertical row with an alien face placed in each of the three center squares. The remaining six alien faces were randomly scattered around the playing screen. The object of the game was to place the remaining six alien faces in the correct squares according to a specific pattern (see Figure 1). Three sets of twenty different patterns were created where each set had the same patterns with only the colour of the attributes changing between each set.

The paper-based version of the game was played on a 14" X 8" sheet of laminated paper (see Figure 2). The alien faces were mounted on 1" X 1" magnets to make them easy to handle. The alien faces were moved into place by physically positioning them on the paper. To check a solution, the players were required to ask a researcher whether or not it was correct. If the pattern was incorrect, the researcher asked the children to keep trying. If the pattern was correct, the researcher provided the children with the next puzzle in the game.

The computer versions of the game were played on IBM-compatible PCs with 14" monitors. The alien faces were moved into place using a mouse. To check a solution, the players were required to click the "check-answer" button located on the top left-hand corner of the screen. If the pattern was incorrect, an error message appeared, asking the children to try again. If the pattern was correct, a congratulation screen appeared and the players advanced onto the next puzzle. The software was developed using C++ and Microsoft DirectX and displayed a different colour cursor for every Universal Serial Bus (USB) mouse attached to the computer.

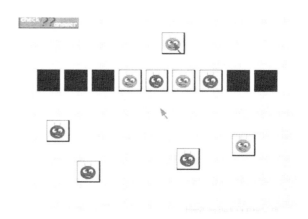

Figure 1. Sample puzzle screen from the computer version of the Alien Pattern game.

Figure 2. A pair of children playing the paper-based version of the Alien Pattern game.

3.3 Experimental Variables

A repeated measures design was used in this study with two independent variables: gender and collaborative condition. Both males and females participated in the study but only same-gender pairs were used. The collaborative conditions included: (1) paper-based; (2) one-mouse/one-cursor; and (3) two-mice/two-cursors. In the paper-based condition, pairs of children played using the paper version of the alien puzzle game. In the one-mouse/one-cursor condition, pairs of children played on a computer with one mouse and one cursor. In the two-mice/two-cursor condition, pairs of children played on a computer with two mice and two cursors. All pairs of children played the paper-based version of the game first and the order of the remaining two conditions was counterbalanced. This allowed all children to become familiar with the game before playing the computer-based version to minimize the effect that learning may have had on the computer-based conditions. It also provided information on how each pair of

106

children interact given a medium that affords multiple users interacting simultaneously.

The dependent variables analyzed included engagement, activity, concurrent interaction, verbal discussion, and puzzle duration. Engagement was measured by the amount of off-task behaviour exhibited by the children, gathered through video analysis. Activity was measured by the number of actions performed by each partner and by the pair as a whole, collected through computer logs and video analysis. These results were reported in an earlier paper on this study [6]. The amount of concurrent interaction was gathered through video analysis for the paper condition and through computer logs for the two computer-based conditions. For each pair, three categories of activity were recorded: (1) the amount of time both children were active (i.e. holding/placing pieces in the game); (2) the amount of time one of the partners was active (i.e. only one of the children holding/placing pieces in the game); and (3) the amount of time neither partner was interacting with the game. Verbal discussion was analyzed, for each user, through video analysis, recording the amount of on-task discussion initiated with his/her partner. Puzzle duration was the length of time it took the pairs of children to solve each puzzle in each of the experimental condition. Other data gathered included background information for the children, a post-session questionnaire, and qualitative observations gathered through video analysis.

3.4 Procedure

The children were randomly assigned a partner of the same gender from their class. Two pairs of children at a time were excused from regular class activities for one hour to take part in the study. The study began with welcoming remarks from the researchers, followed by the children filling out a short background questionnaire. The paper-based alien game was then described to the children and they were asked to play the game for ten minutes. All children played the same set of puzzles in the paper-based version. Following this, the children were told that they would be playing the same game two more times using a computer. It was explained that one computer had two mice while the other computer had one mouse, and that it was up to the children to decide how they would coordinate their play. In the one-mouse/one-cursor condition, the pair of children were free to share control of the mouse as they wished. One pair of children was randomly selected to begin with the one-mouse/one-cursor setup while the other pair began with the two-mice/two-cursors setup. A random assignment procedure was also used to select which puzzle set each pair would use in their first computer condition (out of two possible sets). The children

were allowed to play for ten minutes. After the ten-minute session, the pairs of children switched computers and played the game for another ten minutes using the alternate collaborative setup and puzzle set. Following the last experimental condition, the children filled out a post-session questionnaire and engaged in casual discussion with the researchers before returning to class.

4 Preliminary Results

Preliminary qualitative and quantitative analyses from the study described in this paper were previously reported [6]. These results revealed three main benefits of providing multi-user interaction to the children. First, the children exhibited a significantly higher level of engagement when allowed to synchronously interact with the computer. Second, the children tended to be more active when multi-user interaction was supported. Finally, the children significantly preferred playing on a computer that supported concurrent multi-user interaction.

5 Results

This paper presents an in-depth analysis of users' concurrent interactions, verbal communications, and performance, and how these variables differed across the three experimental conditions.

5.1 Concurrent Activity

One of the benefits provided by the physical world is the ability that people have to interact simultaneously. The issue of concurrent interaction was explored by examining how often people chose to work simultaneously when completing a collaborative task. Data was gathered from 14 pairs of children[3] on the amount of time users interacted concurrently (i.e. both players active at the same time), the amount of time users interacted sequentially (i.e. only one player active), as well the amount of time when neither partner was active. The results for the three experimental conditions are shown in Table 1. Figure 3 shows three segments from the video annotation system timeline that illustrates the concurrent nature of interactions in the paper condition and the two-mice condition, compared to the forced sequential interactions in the one-mouse condition.

Not surprisingly, in the paper condition, users were frequently active at the same time (37.5% of the time). This tangible medium, combined with the fact that the puzzles had several distinct physical pieces, enabled users to hold/place pieces simultaneously if desired. In the two mice condition, users also exhibited a high

---

[3] Data is only available for 14 of the 20 pairs of children, due to problems with video quality.

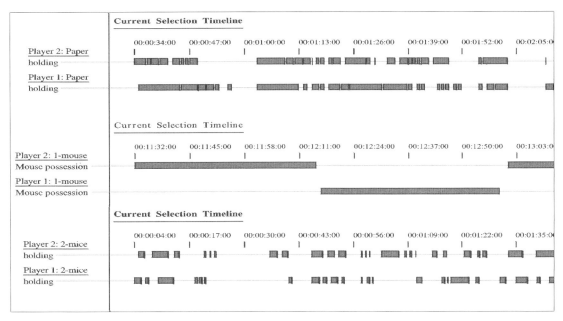

Figure 3. Three segments from an activity timeline illustrating when each user is holding and/or placing an object in the game, for the paper and two-mice conditions, and mouse possession for the one-mouse condition.

degree of concurrency, with simultaneous interactions 27% of the time. In this condition, providing each user with an input device and cursor enabled both children to interact with the game simultaneously, when desired. In contrast to the paper and the two-mice conditions, the one-mouse condition did not support simultaneous interaction. Therefore, users were forced to interact sequentially, taking turns with the mouse. Users tended to resist surrendering the mouse to their partners, even during idle periods. As a result of this behaviour, there was a significantly larger amount of time when neither partner was active than compared to the paper and two-mice conditions, F(1,13) = 54.35, p<.05 and F(1,13) = 67.67, p<.05 respectively.

Table 1. Average length of time both players were active (concurrent interaction), one player was active (sequential interaction), or neither player was active. Note, the total session time was 600 seconds.

	n (pairs)	Concurrent Interaction	Sequential Interaction	No Activity
Paper	14	225 sec. (37.5%)	102 sec. (17%)	273 sec. (35.5%)
One-Mouse	14	0 sec. (0%)	225 sec. (37.5%)	375 sec. (62.5%)
Two-Mice	14	162 sec. (27%)	214 sec. (36%)	224 sec. (37%)

It is important to recognize that interacting directly with the game via an input device is only one aspect of a user's "activity". In the one-mouse condition, the children performed both verbal and physical actions to provide input when not in control of the mouse. For example, each pair of children was observed physically pointing to the screen an average of 15.6 times per session in the one-mouse condition[4]. This was significantly more than the average 2.6 times in the two-mice condition, F (1,19) = 27.38, p<.05, however, pointing with the mouse cursor was not recorded in either computer conditions. Physical pointing in the paper version was comparable to the one-mouse condition, with an average of 12.2 times per session, F(1,19) = 1.85, ns. Children may have also remained active by issuing verbal instructions to their partner. In the one-mouse condition, this occurred an average of 3.75 times for each child per session, although this number was not statistically different from the number of instructions issued during the two-mice condition, F(1,23) = .553, ns.

5.2 Verbal Interactions

The amount of verbal interaction between participants was measured to gain insight into the impact each experimental condition had on collaborative dialogue. The amount of on-task verbal communication per user was

---

[4] Data from all 20 pairs of children was used for this analysis.

recorded for twelve of the twenty pairs of children[5], for each of the three experimental conditions and is shown in Table 2. A statistically significant difference was observed for experimental condition, $F(1,20) = 5.19$, $p<.05$. The two between-subject factors, gender and first computer condition, also produced marginally significant results, $F(1,20) = 4.35$, $p=.05$ and $F(1,20) = 3.413$, $p=.08$, respectively.

Table 2. Mean number of times users engaged in on-task discussion with his/her partner for each of the three experimental conditions.

		n (children)	On-Task Discussion
Paper Condition	Girls	16	17.25
	Boys	8	34.13
	Total	**24**	**22.88**
1-Mouse Condition	Girls	16	26.38
	Boys	8	36.00
	Total	**24**	**29.58**
2-Mouse Condition	Girls	16	27.38
	Boys	8	42.50
	Total	**24**	**32.42**

Figure 4 illustrates the average number of verbal communication events, per user for each experimental condition, based on which computer condition they played first. This result is interesting given the significant interaction effect uncovered in the preliminary results of this work [6][6], as illustrated in Figure 5. In both cases, playing the one-mouse condition first resulted in an increase (in number of actions and verbal events between players) when playing the follow-up two-mice condition. In contrast, playing the two-mice condition first caused no such increase (in number of actions and verbal events between players) in the follow-up one-mouse condition.

5.3 Puzzle Duration

A third measure of effective collaboration is related to the pairs' ability to solve puzzles in the game. The length of time the users took to solve each puzzle for each collaboration condition was recorded[7]. A marginally significant interaction effect for the first computer

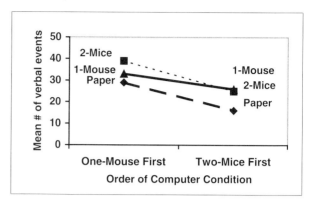

Figure 4. Mean number of verbal communication events for each user, in each condition, categorized by which computer condition they played first.

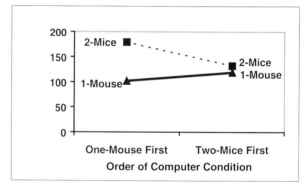

Figure 5. Mean number of actions (placing pieces or clicking on the guess answer button) for each user, in the two computer conditions, grouped by which computer condition the users played first.

condition was found, $F(1,17) = 4.280$, $p=.054$. As a result, the data was analyzed separately for each starting computer condition. Figure 6 shows the average length of time to complete puzzles in each of the experimental conditions. For each user pair, only puzzles that were completed in all three conditions were included in this analysis. For users who played the one-mouse condition first, a marginally significant improvement in times to complete puzzles was found when they played in the subsequent two-mice condition, $F(1,7) = 5.404$, $p=.053$. This improvement may have been related to the users' increase in activity and/or increase in verbal communication as reported in the previous section. For users who played the two-mice condition first, no such improvement was found in the subsequent one-mouse condition, $F(1,10) = 0.14$, *ns*.

---

[5] Data is only available for 12 of the 20 pairs of children, due to time constraints and problems with video quality.

[6] [6] reported an interaction effect between the average number of actions exhibited by each user in the one-mouse and two-mice condition, and which of these conditions they played first.

[7] Data is only available for 19 of the 20 pairs of children, due to problems with video quality.

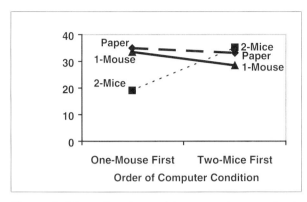

Figure 6. Mean time (seconds) to complete puzzles in the three experimental conditions, categorized by which computer condition the users played first.

6 Discussion

The results presented in this paper clearly demonstrate that users interact concurrently when the medium they are working with supports it. This is a significant finding given that typical desktop computers do not support simultaneous input from multiple users. Concurrent interaction frequently occurs in the real world but is constrained (by technology) when collaborating in a face-to-face computer environment.

An interesting result from this study is the interplay of dependent measures with the computer condition the children played first. It suggests that children's behaviour and performance are impacted by whether or not they first play on a traditional, one-mouse computer, or they instead play first on a computer equipped with two mice. In general, children who played using the one-mouse computer first increased their level of activity in the game, and were able to solve puzzles significantly faster, when they then moved to a computer with two mice. In contrast, children first exposed to the computer with two mice showed no difference in their level of activity or time to solve puzzles when they played in the subsequent one-mouse condition. The children's verbal interactions also exhibited a similar trend, although it was not statistically significant. Improvement over the three sessions, may be natural, given that the children have become more familiar with the game, the puzzles, the experimental setup, and with each other. However, it is also possible that performance may decrease in the third session if the children get bored of the activity.

We hypothesize that these interaction effects may be related to the fact that after playing in a constrained environment (one-mouse), the children flourish when provided with an environment that better supported their desired concurrent interactions. In contrast, when children are switched from the two-mice environment to the traditional computer, they may be frustrated with their inability to interact as naturally as they had in the previous sessions.

An interesting informal observation from this study was the difference observed in the children's physical activity between the non-computer and computer-based conditions. When children played in the paper condition, they were physically and mentally engaged in the activity. Figure 7(a) shows two boys with their arms intertwined, placing pieces all over the board, both working towards a solution. In every paper-based session, both children chose to physically hold and place pieces, and the physical sharing of the pieces occurred naturally. In contrast, children were less physically engaged, when interacting with a mouse, in the computer-based conditions (b & c). They often sat still, directing their view primarily towards the computer screen. Passing objects between the participants was also less intuitive. This lack of physical engagement may impact the overall effectiveness of the collaboration, through decreased user performance, motivation, and naturalness of interactions (both human-computer and human-human interaction).

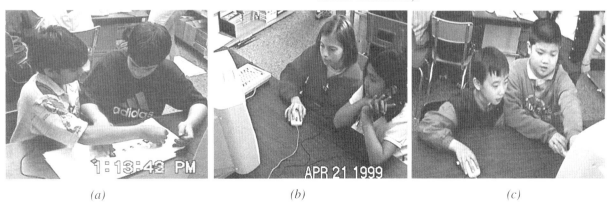

(a)   (b)   (c)

Figure 7. Children playing in each condition: (a) paper condition, (b) one-mouse condition, and (c) two-mice condition.

7 Conclusion and Future Work

The results presented in this paper, along with the preliminary results of this work, provide a strong justification for research in the area of Single Display Groupware (SDG). Existing computer technology does not effectively support the richness and complexity of users' face-to-face interactions and often, natural interactions are stifled as users conform to the constraints of traditional computing environments. This work is a first step in understanding how the introduction of alternative technologies affects users' collaborative interactions. An important next step includes performing similar studies in different environments. Distinct user groups have different interaction dynamics and therefore it is important to examine each individually.

This research examined the results of allowing different types of interaction, however, the precise reasons *why* behaviours differed under these conditions are still unknown. We plan to explore fundamental reasons why user behaviour changes when different interaction possibilities are provided. Isolating the factors that affect behaviour will make it possible to form a set of guidelines for the development of groupware applications. Moreover, it is desirable to extend this research to include interaction techniques that do not have physical world counterparts, but also do not conflict with users' natural interactions. Augmented workspaces are an example where, often, the interaction styles do not have a physical world counterpart, but could potentially be included in a work environment without compromising natural interactions.

8 Acknowledgments

This project was funded by Simon Fraser University, the Natural Sciences and Engineering Research Council of Canada, and the TeleLearning Networks Centres of Excellence. We would like to thank the students and teachers from Lord Nelson Elementary School, Dr. S. Carpendale, L. Bartram, Dr. K. Booth, Dr. C. MacKenzie, C. Blohm, and members of the EDGE Lab for their valuable assistance in this research project.

9 References

[1] Bier, E.A., and Freeman, S. (1991). MMM: A user interface architecture for shared editors on a single screen. *Proceedings of UIST '91*, 79-86.

[2] Bricker, L.J., Tanimoto, S.L., Rothenberg, A.I., Hutama, D.C., and Wong, T.H. (1995). Multiplayer Activities that Develop Mathematical Coordination. *Proceedings of CSCL '95*, 32-39.

[3] Hourcade, J.P., and Bederson, B.B. (1999). Architecture and Implementation of a Java Package for Multiple Input Devices (MID). Tech Report HCIL-99-08, CS-TR-4018, UMIACS-TR-99-26, Computer Science, University of Maryland, College Park, MD.

[4] Ishii, H. and Ullmer, B. (1997). Tangible Bits: Towards Seamless Interfaces between People, Bits and Atoms. *Proceedings of CHI '97*, 234-241.

[5] Inkpen, K., Booth, K.S., Klawe, M., Upitis, R. (1995). Playing together beats playing apart, especially for girls. *Proceedings of CSCL '95*, 177-181.

[6] Inkpen, K.M., Ho-Ching, W., Kuederle, O., Scott, S.D., Shoemaker, G.B.D. (1999). "This is fun! We're all best friends and we're all playing.": Supporting children's synchronous collaboration. *Proceedings of CSCL '99*, 252-259.

[7] Inkpen, K., McGrenere, J., Booth, K.S., and Klawe, M. (1997). The effect of turn-taking protocols on children's learning in mouse-driven collaborative environments. *Proceedings of GI '97*, 138-145.

[8] Myers, B.A., Stiel, H., and Gargiulo, R. (1998). Collaboration using multiple PDAs connected to a PC. *Proceedings of CSCW '98*, 285-294.

[9] Moran, T.P., van Melle, W., & Chiu, P. (1998). Tailorable Domain Objects as Meeting Tools for an Electronic Whiteboard. *Proceedings of CSCW '98*, 295-304.

[10] Resnick, M. (1993). Behavior Construction Kits. *Communications of the ACM*. 36(7), 64-71.

[11] Stewart, J., Bederson, B.B., and Druin, A. (1999). Single display groupware: A model for co-present collaboration. *Proceedings of CHI '99*, 286-293.

[12] Stewart, J., Raybourn, E.M., Bederson, B., and Druin, A. (1998). When two hands are better than one: Enhancing collaboration using single display groupware. *Proceedings of CHI '98*, 287-288.

[13] Streitz, N.A., Geibler, J., Haake, J. M., Hol, J. (1994). DOLPHIN: Integrated Meeting Support across Local and Remote Desktop Environments and Liveboards. *Proceedings of CSCW '94*, 345-358.

[14] Streitz, N. A., Geibler, J., Holmer, T., Konomi, S., Miiller-Tomfelde C., Reischl, W, Rexroth, P., Seitz, P., Steinmetz, R. (1999) i-LAND: An interactive Landscape for Creativity and Innovation. *Proceedings of CSCW '99*, 120-127.

[15] Suzuki, H. and Kato, H. (1995). Interaction-Level Support for Collaborative Learning: AlgoBlock – Open Programming Language. *Proceedings of CSCL '95*, 349-355

The ChatterBox: Using Text Manipulation in an Entertaining Information Display

Johan Redström, Peter Ljungstrand and Patricija Jaksetic
PLAY: Applied research on art and technology
Interactive Institute

Abstract

The ChatterBox is an attempt to make use of the electronic "buzz" that exists in a modern workplace: the endless stream of emails, web pages, and electronic documents which fills the local ether(-net). The ChatterBox "listens" to this noise, transforms and recombines the texts in various ways, and presents the results in a public place. The goal is to provide a subtle reflection of the local activities and provide inspiration for new, unexpected combinations and thoughts. With the ChatterBox, we have tried to create something in between a traditional application and a piece of art: an entertaining and inspiring resource in the workplace. This poses several interesting questions concerning human-computer interaction design, e.g., information and display design. In this paper, we present the ChatterBox, its current implementation and experiences of its use.

Keywords: Art, entertainment, awareness, ambient displays, text transformation, calm technology.

1   Introduction

Within computing science and interaction design, there is a long tradition of using text processing for various purposes, such as creating interfaces based on natural language, and work on how documents can be processed and transformed for better information retrieval (cf. [9, 20]). The ambition of this work has not been to use text processing to develop more efficient information processing and interaction. Instead, we wanted to use text processing to explore technology designed to be more like the works of art, posters and pictures that furnish our homes and offices, than a "traditional" application.

Inspired by the work of writers and artists, we have explored how the texts produced at an office can be transformed in various ways to be used in a public information display aimed to entertain and inspire. Dadaists and Surrealists, such as Tristan Tzara, Brion Gysin and William S. Burroughs [23], used more or less random creation of texts to create works of art. For instance, Tzara created a poem by pulling words out of a hat, and in the 1950's, Gysin cut and rearranged sections of articles in a newspaper at random to create a novel piece. This technique was called "cut-up" and Gysin later even used a computer as an aid in the process. Burroughs used the cut-up technique in several works, e.g., "Naked Lunch".

Figure 1: An installation of the ChatterBox in a corridor using projection on several layers of fabric. The first layer is very thin and moves as people passes by.

Approximately at the same time as Gysin was working with cut-ups, other writers and artists were experimenting with using words and texts as graphical elements in the composition of a work of art [12]. Transformations of texts were employed to various degrees. If the texts still could be considered as meaningful texts, although presented in a visually striking way, they were called "pattern poetry". If the visual aspects of the poem were so emphasized that it was no longer possible to read the text at all, it was called "concrete poetry". More recent contributions in these directions are, for instance, the "Digital Landfill" and the "Shredder" at Potatoland [17] which are both based on the processing of material available on the WWW.

Artists have long been using computers and information technology as media for expression (cf. [11, 21]). Making ideas go the other way, i.e., adopting ideas and concepts from art and design in interaction design, has often taken a bit longer. However, there are examples of such cross-fertilization: Arnowitz et al. employed concepts developed in art to improve interface usability [1]; Kirby et al. used techniques developed in painting to create multi-layered visualisations; and Gaver and Dunne used public electronic

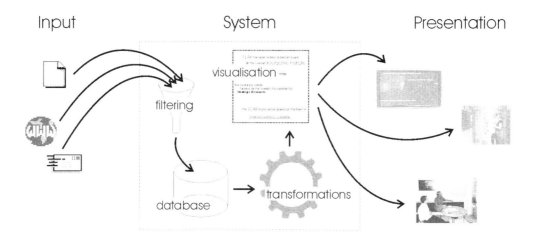

Figure 2: Figure showing the architecture of the ChatterBox system.

displays to enable people to express their opinions and other information [8], to name a few. We believe that, as computers continuously enters new situations of use and interaction designers have to face new constraints, ideas and concepts from the world of art and design will be increasingly important. The ChatterBox is an attempt to explore work in this direction and to expose issues relevant to human computer interaction.

2 The ChatterBox

While waiting for the coffee machine in the lunchroom to finish, you take a quick glance at the ChatterBox display "We believe the SONY PlayStation to be an important part of HCI research". You recognise the structure of the sentence - it looks like something you were working on last week - but it has obviously been transformed since what you were writing was not at all about the PlayStation. Nevertheless, it makes you think about the usefulness of game consoles in HCI research. You point out the sentence on the display to a colleague who just entered the room. After a short discussion, you agree that using a number of game consoles might be an interesting alternative to using workstations for a project, since they are much less complex to a novice end-user and more easily moved between different locations.

The scenario above describes what an encounter with the ChatterBox can be like. The ChatterBox generates and presents texts based on written material produced by a group of people working at an office. Texts are created by recombining material, e.g., substituting words and parts of sentences, while trying to keep the resulting text readable and grammatically correct. The ChatterBox is designed to be more similar to a poster, a picture or a potflower, than a traditional application, as we wanted it to be seen as a part of the environment in a sense similar to

we use decorative objects to furnish our homes, offices, etc.

The ChatterBox relies on being fed with material that can be used to generate texts. This is primarily done by sending emails to it, e.g., by making it subscribe to mailing-lists such as the mails sent to a group of collaborators or a project. The ChatterBox is designed to reflect long-term activities, such as interests or projects that are represented in the material that users submit to it. By continuously adding new material to the ChatterBox, its presentation will reflect changes in the activities taking place (in as much as these changes are evident in the material submitted to it). The aim is to provide inspiring and entertaining variations of mostly familiar texts that can act as inspiration to think about the material in novel ways, and act as an incitement for occasional communication by serving as an information resource in public places.

The need for users to explicitly interact with the system has been eliminated as much as possible. This is similar to the aim with *calm technology* [25]. However, while calm technology often has been about creating something that remains in the background and only calls for attention when certain events or changes take place, the ChatterBox is continuously changing presenting new material, even though at a relatively slow pace. In order not to disturb users despite being dynamic, its location is crucial. Besides the purpose of making it a public resource, this is the primary reason for locating it in public spaces where people move about and, presumably, not tend to sit and work for longer periods. This stands in contrast to, for instance, the ambientROOM where the goal was to integrate a number of ambient displays in a personal office [14].

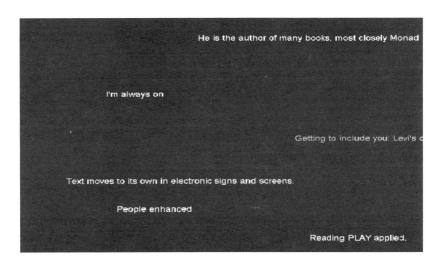

Figure 3: Screen shot showing the "floater" visualisation.

2.1 System

An early prototype of the ChatterBox was presented in [18]. This prototype generated random "phrases" consisting of 3-5 random non-frequent words occurring in a collection of texts. Experiments indicated that while the generated "phrases" certainly were novel combinations of words, they were rather difficult to make any sense of. Therefore, a second prototype that makes use of more advanced text-processing saving more of the original context of material (thus keeping more of the original semantics), was developed.

The current implementation of the ChatterBox accepts text based input, such as documents, emails and www pages, from users via a dedicated email account. The architecture of the system is illustrated in Fig. 2. When a piece of text is submitted, it is first fed into a text filter component for preprocessing, to remove parts that are not proper sentences, e.g. email headers, HTML tags, and signatures. The extracted sentences are passed on to a Link Grammar parser [22]. The basic idea with this parser is that words are connected to each other via grammatical links, e.g., if a noun is a subject to a certain verb, there exists a link, or a grammatical relation, between them. The parser takes one sentence at a time and identifies the syntactical function of the words and their grammatical interrelationships. The sentences are stored in a database along with the grammatical information and a timestamp.

A continuously running text synthesizer is generating a new sentence about every 10 seconds. It picks a sentence from the database and randomly selects a relation, or grammatical link, in it. Then, another sentence in the database, which contains the same relation, is retrieved. Both, or just one of the words in the selected relation are

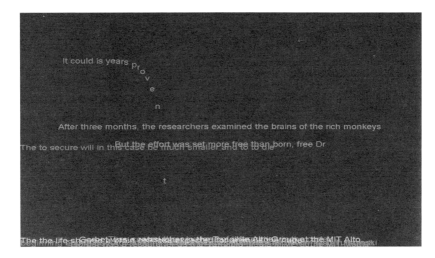

Figure 4: Screen shot showing the "falling leaves" visualisation.

then swapped between the two sentences. This substitution is repeated up to four times before one or both of the sentences are passed on to the visualisation module. Unlike the use of totally random re-combinations used in the original "cut-up" technique, this enables the system to keep some of the original context of the material, and to increase readability by having almost grammatically correct sentences. However, since the Link Grammar parser is not always accurate, the generated sentences sometimes end up being syntactically and semantically ill-formed.

Each sentence in the database has a certain probability to be selected by the text synthesizer. The probability slowly decays as a function of time, meaning that sentences that were recently submitted have a higher probability to be selected than older ones. The probability within a certain time period, such as a few days, does not decay much. Using a scheme like this allows the Chatter-Box to keep up with ongoing changes, while still using old material to keep in contact with its history.

Finally, the generated sentences are passed on to a visualisation module. Several different visualisations have been used. The first visualisation used continuously scrolling text, similar to how text is displayed at the end of a movie. Another visualisation used sentences printed in different colours appearing as floating around on a large display. Some sentences would fade in or out, some would move slowly across the screen, and sometimes different sentences would overlap (Fig. 3). Still another visualisation was based on a "falling leaves" metaphor in which the sentences were printed in different colours (typically in the colours leaves get in the fall) and appeared as slowly "falling" from the top of the screen (Fig. 4). Some sentences would fall faster than others, and some would have its letters fall off individually. The "leaves" would then whirl around at the bottom of the screen for a while before fading away. Generally, all visualisations have a relatively slow appearance in order not to attract too much attention. Several different display techniques have been used, including large plasma screens and projections on a variety of surfaces (cf. Fig. 1 and Fig. 5).

2.2 "Users"

The notion of "users" becomes somewhat problematic with the ChatterBox since it, being designed to be a part of the design of an environment, is hardly "used" at all in the sense more traditional applications are used. Considering what role people have in relation to the Chatterbox, it is possible to make a distinction between submitters and spectators. Submitters are the ones who contribute to the ChatterBox by sending in material. What material to send, is entirely up to the submitter. Spectators, on the other hand, are the ones watching the ChatterBox displays. Thus, both people working where the ChatterBox is located as well as occasional visitors can act as spectators. While most submitters also will take on the role as spectators, visitors are likely to be spectators only.

Being both a submitter and a spectator might be different from being an occasional spectator. The main reason for this assumption, is that since the texts are transformations of submitted material, knowledge about the original material can play an important role in how to make sense of the generated texts and to what extent this can be done at all. Someone who is familiar with the original material or domain will in some cases be able to see what sources have been combined or transformed (in case the transformation is not too extensive). A visitor, on the other hand, will perhaps only be able to recognise in what context or interest domain the material has its origin, for instance if it comes from an information technology research facility, a marketing company or a college school class. Still, its presentation can provide useful or entertaining cues to the local office culture. When we use the term "user" below, we refer to the people taking on both roles as submitters and spectators, in case not otherwise noted.

2.3 Privacy

The difference between an awareness system and a surveillance system is often a matter of degrees. Important aspects are, for instance, the degree of user control, the nature of the information displayed and how symmetrical the system is, i.e., if all users give and obtain the same amount and kind of information or if someone has greater access than others (cf. [13]). To the ChatterBox, users are anonymous to some extent: who submitted what and when, is not very interesting to know since everything the ChatterBox generates will be combinations of material from a number of different sources.

One way to deal with privacy issues is to rely on abstractions in some form to protect the privacy of the users, the abstract representation as such making the difference between a surveillance system and an awareness support system [6, 10, 16]. In the case of the ChatterBox, this might be a more or less efficient action, depending on the extent of the transformations, sometimes making it necessary to use other methods as well.

Although automatic collection of text material would have eliminated the need for explicit actions on behalf of the users, reducing worries about unwanted submissions is usually more important. In order to prevent private or otherwise delicate information from turning up on the display in the lunchroom, the control over the submission is put in the hands of the users in terms of sending texts to a specific email address. Still, automatic collection of material might be a possibility in some cases, especially if transformations are extensive or if the source material already is official, e.g., web pages, reports, and other public documents.

2.3.1 Groups

There are also privacy issues associated with groups of users. For instance, there might be information that is happily shared within a group, that they do not want others to see, such as corporate secrets or work in progress. To address this, one could either limit the access to the displays in question, shut them down during external visits or only use the ChatterBox with official material. All these variants have their drawbacks. The last one perhaps most notably so, since it will decrease the usefulness of the ChatterBox the most, in particular to the people who potentially benefit the most. However, given the way the ChatterBox works, it is probably difficult to infer detailed information about what is going on unless the original material and its context is partly known. This, in combination with the fragmentary nature of the Chatter-Box texts, reduces the risks of showing it to external visitors, should the texts be based on any non-official material.

Another problem is how to deal with offensive material. In the present prototype, problems with how to, for instance, filter out offensive submissions to the Chatter-Box have not been considered. However, a user group might have to take actions against submissions of offensive nature, or restricting who are allowed to contribute. It is more difficult to do something about the ChatterBox own text-generation. As the system is not to be considered as an intentional agent, any such offensive material should be seen as a coincidence.

3   Awareness, Ambience and Art

The ChatterBox can be seen as related to work on novel information display strategies such as ambient displays, since there is an intention not only to create random texts, but to create texts about something related to the environment the Chatterbox is located in. This also makes it related to work on how to support awareness about different aspects of a workplace. Below, we discuss some of the ChatterBox properties in relation to these lines of work.

3.1   Awareness

A variety of applications have been developed to support communication within physically distributed groups of people working together, by providing both a channel for communication and a context that enables users to determine when and how to engage in communication (cf. [4]). Displaying information about presence when sup-

porting communication among physically collocated people will often not be of great importance, unless there are for example obstacles in the environment that hinder people from obtaining that information. Instead, information about who is doing what, what is happening and where, is of greater interest [6, 7]. A number of applications have been developed to support awareness in virtual environments as well, for instance applications that visualise the development of communities on the web, or how the content of on-line discussion groups change over time [5, 6].

Compared to awareness support systems, the ChatterBox presentation is based on information aggregated over longer periods of time. Further, since the original material is transformed in various ways, it will never be an accurate source of information about what has actually happened. However, it might support occasional or "informal" [3, 27] communication by providing incitements for various discussions (as were illustrated in the scenario described earlier). By placing the ChatterBox at places such as in the lunchroom or in the corridors of an office, we aim to make it readily available for people moving around. "Serendipitous" or "informal" communication is often part of the reason for people's local mobility, or "local area roaming", i.e., when people move around in order to get a sense of what is going on [2, 3, 27].

Common to several applications supporting awareness is that they can be seen as a way of enabling users to see a "trace" of what has happened. This trace is often visualised as some sort of history, with chronologically ordered events. In the ChatterBox, events also leave a trace in the sense that information is aggregated over time and only slowly decays. While the actual phrases and sentences that are shown on the display change relatively quickly (a new sentence every 20 seconds or so), the underlying text data evolves and changes much more slowly. Compared to the transient nature of the information presented in many awareness systems, the ChatterBox has a rather slow appearance, especially in terms of how the content changes over time.

3.2   Abstract and Ambient Information Displays

An important aspect of how the information is represented to the user is what level of abstraction is being used to present it. In the case of information displays, abstraction often means a transformation of the original signal or information that reduces the level of detail in the presented information. The reasons for using abstract representations might be to create a presentation that is more easily perceived, that protects the privacy of users by not presenting too much information about them (e.g., "availability" instead of activity and location), or in order to create an aesthetically pleasing or entertaining way of showing the information.

Creating displays that are easily perceived and more "calm", at least compared to traditional GUIs, is the course taken by work on ambient media and ambient displays [14, 28 cf. also 16, 25]. Ambient displays make use of a re-mapping from the media of the original information to another, and presumably, less obtrusive media. In some cases the re-mapping itself, for instance from the number of hits on a web site to the intensity of a rain-like sound [14], constitutes such an abstraction.

A problem with abstraction through re-mapping is how to create an intuitive connection between the original information and its abstract representation. One of the seemingly more successful examples is the Dangling String [25]. In this design, the connection is rather strong: the dangling of an Ethernet cable hanging from the roof reflects the traffic frequency on the adjacent network cable. In many cases, the re-mapping seems less self-evident and thus, at least before some learning has taken place, associated with greater cognitive load (cf. [14, 16, 28]).

With the ChatterBox, we have taken a different path towards more abstract representations of the original information. Perhaps "abstraction" is a misleading description of what the ChatterBox does, but its transformation of texts serves many of the same purposes: it creates something that reflects but not necessarily presents the original information and it leaves room for protecting the privacy of the source of the presented information. Re-mapping the content of the texts submitted to the ChatterBox to, for instance, an ambient display like the Waterlamp [28] would have been a radical abstraction that would not likely have been of much use. Instead, we chose to stay with using texts, as these have been claimed to have a calm nature due to their ubiquity [24]. Another interesting property is that while the texts generated by the ChatterBox might be a bit strange and difficult to trace back to original material, this is an intended part of its design, i.e. to provide a novel view of the material.

There is at least one important difference between the strategy explored with the ChatterBox and that of ambient displays: while abstraction through re-mapping to an ambient display focuses on how to provide information about the main character of some set of information, for instance to what extent a continuous flow of information changes (e.g., [28]), the ChatterBox is all about manipulating the details of some information; the ChatterBox does not provide an overview. Further, it should not be

Figure 5: Picture showing the ChatterBox projecting the text transformations on the wall at one of the test locations.

considered as a reliable source of information, but rather as a source of inspiring, entertainingly mind-boggling "one-liners" that, nevertheless, have a strong connection to the place where it is being displayed.

3.3 Art

Art and design can influence technology design in many ways (cf. [1, 8, 11, 15]). While the ChatterBox was influenced by the work of artists as presented in the introduction, the purpose was not to create an artistic installation *per se*, but to explore issues in human computer interaction from a slightly different perspective [19]. Given these constraints, the ChatterBox is related to work halfway between applications and art such as Gaver and Dunne's Projected Realities [8], The Interactive Poetic Garden [26], and the Dangling String [25].

4 Experiences

The prototype was tested at two different locations, for approximately one week each: at the IT-department of a large manufacturing company and at an IT-consultant company. The ChatterBox display was placed in the local lunchroom and could be seen by 30-50 people at each site, most of them working at that location. Both places see a lot of both local mobility and occasional visitors. In both cases, a projector was used to display the Chatter-Box on a wall.

The ChatterBox was presented at the time of the installation, but since people are rather mobile, many potential "users" were not present at the time of the introduction. Thus, a complementary poster describing its purpose and how to submit material to it, was available next to the ChatterBox display. Since the parser we are using only accepts English texts, the users were informed that they should only submit text in English.

After a week, semi-structured interviews with eleven users were performed. As a complement, a questionnaire was sent out via email. We received 19 answers to the questionnaire. The purpose with these experiments was to find out more about the ChatterBox and to gain knowledge for future development. A common, and anticipated, comment from the users at the two offices was that the tests were too short: they did not have the time to use it long enough to evaluate it properly.

As a comparison, the ChatterBox was also tested in a setting more oriented towards entertainment and leisure, i.e., at two reception parties. Due to the rather brief nature of the experiments, the following findings should be seen as indicators that have to be followed up in future evaluations.

4.1   Results

There were numerous comments on the benefits of the ChatterBox. For instance: "It's like a scribble board that makes you think in new ways"; "It's a cool thing that gave rise to discussions"; "The poster said the ChatterBox should be seen as similar to a piece of art or a pot-flower. I think that describes it well. I see it as an installation. And as such, a pretty fun one."; "Fun idea to share thoughts, questions, ideas etc.". The ChatterBox ability to act as an incitement for discussions also received many positive comments.

Especially at the two offices, many users considered the transformation as problematic: "It is not very serious"; "What's the real use of this?"; "How do you know what is true and what is not?" Several users complained about the meaninglessness of technology that could not be trusted. One user expressed that the ChatterBox would add to the information overload since she felt she would have one more thing to attend to.

Some of these more sceptical users also seemed to think that the text transformations would be more useful to people working in more "creative" domains, for instance: "This random transformation of the messages seems to me more suitable to for instance an advertising agency. In that case, one could imagine to feed the system with different words and hopefully get something that can support new directions for slogans etc."

Several users expressed their interest in having public displays providing information that they did not want, or needed, on their PC. Other users commented that they wanted to have the ChatterBox running on their personal computers, either in the background or as a screen saver. Users also felt that the visual presentation of the Chatter-Box could be improved in order to make it more appealing.

While there were a number of remarks about privacy concerns, there were in fact fewer than we had anticipated. One user asked about assuring the security of the system, e.g., who would control what would be submitted, but several users expressed an interest in even using automatic collection of information, for instance from the local intranet. Many users thought that using already official material would be an interesting option.

Generally, it seems that the entertaining or inspiring properties of the ChatterBox were more successful than its support for awareness in the workplace. It also seemed that the introduction of the ChatterBox was crucial to how people perceived it. This is especially evident in the general difference between how people at the offices and at the parties perceived it. Whereas people at the offices commented about uselessness due to the lack of seriousness and accuracy, people at the parties found the very same properties entertaining. This is probably due to the fact that people do not seem to be as focused on usefulness and efficiency, properties which the ChatterBox at large lacks, at a party, as when at work. Investigating the trade-off between creating something entertaining and inspiring while still keeping its relevance and strong connection to a certain context, e.g., the work conducted at an office, is important in order to further develop strategies for how to design this type of applications.

5   Concluding Remarks

We have presented the ChatterBox as an application somewhere between a tool and a piece of art. It has not been designed to solve a particular problem, but rather to be an entertaining and inspiring resource in public spaces. We have tried to show that these aims are associated with a number of problems relevant to HCI research by discussing the properties of the ChatterBox and relating it to other work. We have also presented and discussed experiences of its use.

Future work will include more long-term studies of the ChatterBox. By comparing how it can be used, how it is perceived in different workplaces or settings and how to balance the trade-offs between creating entertaining and inspiring technology while still keeping its relevance and connection to the activities taking place where it is located, we hope to gain more knowledge about the ChatterBox and similar applications. We believe explorations in these domains of usercentered technology will play an important part in the development of the next generation of human computer interfaces.

6   Acknowledgments

The ChatterBox has its roots in a system envisioned by Lars Erik Holmquist, that would create random texts based on material collected from various web-pages, by for instance associating sentences that contain similar words.

References

[1] Arnowitz, J. S., Willems, E., Faber, L. & Priester, R. Mahler, Mondriaan, and Bauhaus: using artistic ideas to improve application usability. In: *Proceedings of DIS (Designing Interactive Systems) '97*, pp. 13-21. ACM Press, 1997.

[2] Bellotti, V. and Bly, S. Walking Away from the Desktop Computer: Distributed Collaboration and Mobility in a Product Design Team. In: *Proceedings of CSCW '96*, pp. 209-218. ACM Press, 1996.

[3] Bergqvist, J., Dahlberg, P., Ljungberg, F. and Kristoffersen, S. Moving Out of the Meeting Room; Exploring support for mobile meetings. In: *Proceedings of ECSCW '99*, pp. 81-98. Kluwer Academic Publishers, 1999.

[4] Buxton, B. Integrating the Periphery and Context: In: *Proceedings of Graphics Interface Conference '95*. ACM Press, 1995.

[5] Donath, J. S. VisualWho: Animating the affinities and activities of an electronic community. In: *Electronic Proceedings of ACM Multimedia '95*. ACM Press, 1995.

[6] Erickson, T., Smith, D. N., Kellogg, W. A., Laff, M., Richards, J. T. and Bradner, E. Socially Translucent Systems: Social Proxies, Persistent Conversation and the Design of "Babble". In: *Proceedings of CHI '99*, pp. 72-79. ACM Press, 1999.

[7] Fitzpatrick, G., Mansfield, T., Kaplan, S., Arnold, D., Phelps, T. and Segall, B. Augmenting the Workaday World with Elvin. In: *Proceedings of ECSCW '99*, pp. 431-450. Kluwer Academic Publishers, 1999.

[8] Gaver, W. & Dunne, A. Projected Realities; Conceptual Design for Cultural Effect. In: *Proceedings of CHI'99*, pp. 600-607. ACM Press, 1999.

[9] Gazdar, G. and Mellish, C. *Natural Language Processing in PROLOG*. Addison-Wesley, 1989.

[10] Gutwin, C. and Greenberg, S. Design for individuals, design for groups: tradeoffs between power and workspace awareness. In: *Proceedings of CSCW '98*, pp. 207-216. ACM Press, 1998.

[11] Harris, C. *Art and Innovation - The Xerox Artist-In-Residence Program*. MIT Press, 1999.

[12] Higgins, D. *Pattern Poetry: Guide to an Unknown Literature*. New York, State University of New York Press, 1987.

[13] Hudson, S. E. and Smith, I. Techniques for Adressing Fundamental Privacy and Disruption Tradeoffs in Awareness Support Systems. In: *Proceedings of CSCW '96*, pp. 248-257. ACM Press, 1996.

[14] Ishii, H. and Ullmer, B. Tangible Bits: Towards Seamless Interfaces between People, Bits and Atoms. In: *Proceedings of CHI '97*, pp. 234-241. ACM Press, 1997.

[15] Kirby, R. M., Marmanis, H. & Laidlaw, D. H. Visualizing Multivalued Data from 2D Incompressible Flows Using Concepts from Painting. In: *Proceedings of IEEE Information Visualization 1999*. IEEE, 1999.

[16] Pedersen, E. R. and Sokoler, T. AROMA: abstract representation of presence supporting mutual awareness. In: *Proceedings of CHI '97*, pp. 51-58. ACM Press, 1997.

[17] *Potatoland*: www.potatoland.org

[18] Redström, J., Jaksetic, P. and Ljungstrand, P. The ChatterBox. In: *Proceedings of Handheld and Ubiquitous Computing (HUC '99)*, Lecture Notes in Computer Science No. 1707, pp. 259-261, poster presentation. Springer-Verlag, 1999.

[19] Redström, J., Skog, T. and Hallnäs, L. Informative Art: Using Amplified Artworks as Information Displays. To appear in: *Proceedings of DARE 2000 (Designing Augmented Reality Environments)*, ACM Press, 2000.

[20] Salton, G. *Automatic Text Processing*. Addison-Wesley, 1988.

[21] Schweppe, M. & Blau, B. (eds). *Electronic Art and Animation Catalog, SIGGRAPH 99*. ACM Press, 1999.

[22] Sleator, D. and Temperly, D. Parsing English with a Link Grammar. In: *Proceedings of the Third International Workshop on Parsing Technologies (IWPT'93)*, Tilburg, The Netherlands, 1993.

[23] Vale (ed.). *RE/SEARCH #4/5: A Special Book Issue: William S. Burroughs, Brion Gysin and Throbbing Gristle*. San Fransisco, RE/SEARCH, 1982.

[24] Weiser, M. The Computer for the 21st Century. In: *Scientific American*, pp. 933-940, 1991.

[25] Weiser, M. and Seely Brown, J. Designing Calm Technology. In: *PowerGrid Journal 1.01*. Available at: http://www.powergrid.com/1.01/calmtech.html. 1996.

[26] White, T. and Small, D. An Interactive Poetic Garden. In: *Summary of CHI '98*, pp. 303-304. ACM Press, 1998.

[27] Whittaker, S., Frohlich, D. and Daly-Jones, O. Informal Workplace Communication: What is it Like and How Might We Support it? In: *Proceedings of CHI '94*, pp. 131-137. ACM Press, 1994.

[28] Wisneski, C., Ishii, H., Dahley, A., Gorbet, M., Brave, S., Ullmer, B. and Yarin, P. Ambient Displays: Turning Architectual Space into an Interface between People and Digital Information. In: *Proceedings of International Workshop on Cooperative Buildings (CoBuild '98)*, pp. 22-32. Springer Verlag, 1998.

Approximation of Glossy Reflection with Prefiltered Environment Maps

Jan Kautz
Max-Planck-Institut für Informatik
Saarbrücken, Germany

Michael D. McCool
Department of Computer Science
University of Waterloo, Waterloo, Canada

Abstract

A method is presented that can render glossy reflections with arbitrary isotropic bidirectional reflectance distribution functions (BRDFs) at interactive rates using texture mapping. This method is based on the well-known environment map technique for specular reflections.

Our approach uses a single- or multilobe representation of bidirectional reflectance distribution functions, where the shape of each radially symmetric lobe is also a function of view elevation. This approximate representation can be computed efficiently using local greedy fitting techniques. Each lobe is used to filter specular environment maps during a preprocessing step, resulting in a three-dimensional environment map. For many BRDFs, simplifications using lower-dimensional approximations, coarse sampling with respect to view elevation, and small numbers of lobes can still result in a convincing approximation to the true surface reflectance.

Key words: Environment map, glossy reflection, texture mapping, bidirectional reflectance distribution function.

1 Introduction

The environment map technique [2] is widely used to approximate reflections in real-time rendering. Environment maps are an approximation technique because they make an assumption that is often not true, namely that the environment is far from the reflecting surface. Despite this, they are effective and efficient, and can be used to build more sophisticated techniques.

Heidrich and Seidel [12] preblurred environment maps with the Phong model [18] to approximate glossy reflectance in real time. However, the technique was limited to Phong lobes. Variation of lobe shape with incident angle was not supported, although self-shadowing and Fresnel scale factors that varied with the incident and view direction have been demonstrated.

We have extended and refined this idea to support the generation of glossy reflections with a relatively general class of isotropic bidirectional reflectance distribution functions (BRDFs). For a number of elevation angles we approximate the given BRDF with a sum of radially symmetric lobes. In our representation each lobe must be symmetric around some axis, but need not be a Phong lobe: the radial shape function is arbitrary, and is derived from the data. Furthermore, the axis of each lobe may be offset from the reflection direction.

For "glossy" BRDFs with large peaks, lobe-fitting can be performed using a greedy technique that is more efficient than the global optimization techniques previously used for multilobe BRDF representations [15]. While not optimal, the greedy fitting technique is easy to implement and produces usable results quickly.

Once the lobes have been obtained we prefilter a specular environment map with each one. This results in a set of prefiltered two-dimensional environment maps, for each lobe and for each sampled elevation angle.

Lobes are then tracked over multiple elevation angles, to find consistent and coherent sequences of lobes that can be interpolated. The resulting stacks of prefiltered two-dimensional environment maps (each stack resulting from a sequence of coherent lobes filtered against the original environment map) can be stored in three-dimensional environment maps.

The new third dimension corresponds to the view elevation angle while the other two dimensions correspond to the incident elevation and azimuth angles. Use of three-dimensional environment maps permits the representation of important and common effects such as increased reflection sharpness at glancing angles.

By summing up multiple lobes an arbitrary BRDF can be approximated to whatever precision is desired; for the isotropic examples we have tested, a small number of lobes (less than 5, often as few as 1) have been visually satisfactory. Furthermore, for machines that do not support three-dimensional filtering, we have found that ignoring the dependence of the shape of the lobe on elevation angle is adequate for some BRDFs.

2 Prior Work

In Heidrich and Seidel's technique [12], specular environment maps are prefiltered with view-independent, radially symmetric Phong (exponentiated cosine) lobes. During rendering, view-dependent Fresnel scale factors are applied but the basic shape of the lobe is not varied.

Each entry of the Phong-prefiltered environment map

contains not only the radiance coming from $\hat{\omega}_i$ (like normal environment maps do), but also the radiance from a larger region integrated against the Phong lobe, as depicted in Figure 1.

The original Phong model was chosen because (after weighting by the cosine of the incident angle) Phong lobes are symmetric around the reflected view direction and the shape does not change with view elevation. However, Phong lobes are not realistic *exactly*

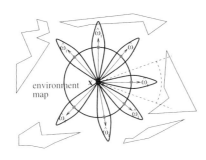

Figure 1: *Phong environment maps.*

because their shape does not change! In particular, at glancing angles Heidrich and Seidel's technique actually includes energy from below the horizon in the reflection. Normally, the lobe should become thinner and sharper.

Cabral et al. [3] proposed a technique that uses a set of prefiltered environment maps, which they call radiance environment maps. An original specular environment map is prefiltered with a BRDF using a specific viewing position. This is done for a number of viewing positions, generating a set of intrinsically view-dependent prefiltered environment maps.

In order to render a reflective object a new environment map is generated for every new viewpoint using three of the prefiltered environment maps, which are warped and blended together. This new environment map is then applied to the reflective object. In order to compute the warping the central reflection direction of the BRDF's lobe has to be known, and an assumption is made that the BRDF is radially symmetric about this direction. This technique also assumes an orthographic viewer. See the conclusions section for a comparison with our method.

Other researchers have looked at deriving multilobe representations for BRDFs. Lafortune et al. [15] used a generalized Phong lobe model and Walter et al. [21] used multiple Phong lobes to approximate the reflection of a global illumination solution from a surface with an arbitrary BRDF. Fournier [5] used Phong lobes to approximate the distribution of normals. Our work differs from these: we drop the restriction to Phong lobes entirely, and use local greedy fitting techniques rather than global optimization.

There have been other techniques for representing interactive glossy reflections that are not as closely related

to our work as the previous methods. We will briefly mention and comment on a few that attempt to target high-performance rendering.

Stürzlinger and Bastos [19] used photon maps for interactive glossy reflections; photons were "splatted" and weighted with an arbitrary BRDF. Diefenbach and Badler [4] used multi-pass methods (stochastic multi-sampling) to generate glossy reflections; this performs the filtering of the environment map (that we do in a prepass) using Monte Carlo integration at runtime. Miller et al. [17] used surface light fields to store and reconstruct glossy reflections. Lischinski and Rappoport [16] used layered depth images to produce glossy reflections. Bastos et al. [1] used a space-variant convolution filter in screen-space to produce glossy reflections; we apply our convolution in environment-map space during a preprocess, and so have fewer image quality limitations.

Finally, previous work by Kautz and McCool [14] addressed the problem of computing local illumination and reflectance from point sources in real time from surfaces with arbitrary BRDFs, using a separable decomposition of the BRDF. The current technique is complementary to that work, in that we address the problem of using arbitrary BRDFs in real-time rendering, but with environment maps instead of point sources for illumination.

The algorithm we will present has three phases: multilobe BRDF approximation (which is done once per BRDF), environment map prefiltering (which is done once per BRDF for each new specular environment map), and rendering. These are presented separately in the following sections, and will be followed by a sampling of the resulting images.

3 BRDF Approximation

A shift-invariant BRDF $f(\hat{\omega}_o, \hat{\omega}_i)$ can be approximated using a sequence of lower-dimensional approximations for a set of sampled viewing directions $\hat{\omega}_o$. The viewing direction $\hat{\omega}_o$ is set to a number of different values and then a two-dimensional approximation algorithm is run for each value. We will denote a BRDF "slice" with $\hat{\omega}_o$ fixed as $f_{\hat{\omega}_o}(\hat{\omega}_i)$, which we will call a *lobe*; this is in fact a two-dimensional function of $\hat{\omega}_i$.

For the prefiltering of environment map we *must* use radially symmetric lobes for each approximation. Assume we are given a BRDF with a non-radially symmetric lobe for a given local viewing direction $\hat{\omega}_o$, as seen on the left side of Figure 2. Assume the reflected viewing vector is used to index the environment map. The environment map stores the radiance prefiltered with (integrated against) that BRDF. If we rotate the surface and look at it from a different viewpoint so that we get the same reflected viewing vector (see right side of Figure 2),

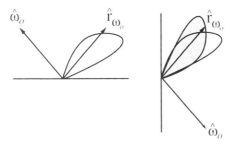

Figure 2: *Radially symmetric lobes are necessary.*

we will of course obtain the same value from the environment map, as we are indexing it with the same texture coordinates. However, the orientation of the actual lobe (grey) now differs from the orientation of the lobe with which the environment map was filtered. To avoid this problem we have to use lobes which are radially symmetric.

The use of only radially symmetric BRDFs might seem to limit this approach, but in practice many BRDFs have lobes that are close to radially symmetric for fixed viewing angles. We can use multiple radially symmetric lobes as basis functions to approximate BRDFs that do not show this symmetry.

3.1 Approximation with a Single Lobe

An existing *isotropic* BRDF $f(\hat{\omega}_o, \hat{\omega}_i)$ can be approximated with a separate lobe for each $\hat{\omega}_o = (\theta_o, 0)$, $\theta_o \in \{\theta_{o,1}, \theta_{o,2}, \ldots, \theta_{o,k}\}$, where $\theta_o = \hat{n} \cdot \hat{r}_v$; see Figure 6. In this paper we only consider isotropic BRDFs to keep the dimensionality of the result under control.

The actual fitting uses a greedy, heuristically-driven algorithm. This approach works in this case because "glossy" surfaces that give a recognizable reflection of the environment will be likely to have a peak near the direction of the reflection vector.

First, we find the maximum peak of $f_{\hat{\omega}_o}(\hat{\omega}_i)$; denote the direction in which the maximum lies using $\hat{\omega}_{i/\text{peak}}$. The offset elevation angle will be denoted by $\theta_{i/\text{off}}$ and the offset azimuth by $\phi_{i/\text{off}}$. These angles are the difference between the expected reflection direction (i.e. the reflected viewing direction) and the actual peak direction. For a single lobe approximation and an isotropic BRDF, the offset azimuth angle $\phi_{i/\text{off}}$ must in fact must be 0, but this will not be true for multilobe approximations.

We assume that $\hat{\omega}_{i/\text{peak}}$ lies in the center of the lobe given by $f_{\hat{\omega}_o}(\hat{\omega}_i)$, and create profile curves for the lobe by taking samples in radial directions away from the peak; see Figure 3. Every curve that is generated by the intersection of a plane going through $\hat{\omega}_{i/\text{peak}}$ and the lobe itself is a profile curve; see Figure 3. Then we average all the profile curves and create a mean profile. This

mean profile is used as the profile curve for our radially symmetric approximation lobe. The approximation lobe $p_{\theta_o}(\vartheta_i) \approx f_{\hat{\omega}_o}(\hat{\omega}_i)$ (where $\vartheta_i = \hat{\omega}_{i/\text{peak}} \cdot \hat{\omega}_i$) is computed by rotating the mean profile around $\hat{\omega}_{i/\text{peak}}$. This obviously makes the lobe radially symmetric; see Figure 3. The approximation is compact: the approximation's parameters consist of the profile curve and peak offset angles. The profile curves are stored using discrete samples.

Because of the averaging process the overall energy of our approximation lobe might be different from the original BRDF lobe, which results in reflections with the wrong brightness. To correct that error we compute the total hemispherical reflectivity of the approximation, compare this with the original BRDF, and scale our approximation accordingly.

3.2 Using a Single 2D Lobe

We can further approximate a given BRDF to save memory. Some glossy BRDFs maintain roughly the shape of their lobe as θ_o changes. When $\hat{\omega}_o$ varies, only a scale factor change is required. So another obvious approximation calculates only *one* average lobe $p(\vartheta_i)$, either by averaging all profile curves or by choosing a "characteristic" profile for a specific $\hat{\omega}_o$. To approximate the actual lobes $f(\hat{\omega}_o, \hat{\omega}_i)$ we assign a weight for each $\hat{\omega}_o$ to the single lobe $p(\hat{\omega}_i)$, to get $f(\hat{\omega}_o, \hat{\omega}_i) \approx k(\theta_o)p(\vartheta_i)$.

This representation has the advantage that it can be rendered with only a single two-dimensional environment map. The weights can be either assigned as colors at the vertices or put in an extra one-dimensional texture map—much like the Fresnel term used by Heidrich [12]. However, with this approximation we will not be able to capture such effects as increased sharpness or reflections at glancing angles.

3.3 Using Multiple Lobes

Some BRDFs might be difficult to approximate by a single lobe. In that case we can use multiple lobes. Each of these "basis lobes" has to be radially symmetric, as explained earlier, but may be offset by various amounts from the reflection vector.

There are two different approaches to fit multiple lobes to a BRDF: global methods and greedy iterative methods.

We tried two global techniques (simulated annealing and branch and bound), which both failed to yield a satisfying solution, even when we restricted ourselves to Phong lobes[1]. Therefore, we will only present an extension to the greedy technique that we have found works well in practice.

Our iterative greedy fitting scheme works almost like the single shape lobe fitting. First, find the maximum peak at $\hat{\omega}_{i/\text{peak}}$ of $f_{\hat{\omega}_o}(\hat{\omega}_i)$ and represent this direction us-

---

[1]This has also been noted by Walter et al. [21] in a similar situation.

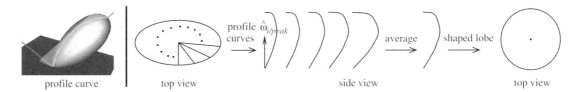

Figure 3: *Single lobe approximation.*

ing the offset angles $\theta_{i/\text{off}}$ and $\phi_{i/\text{off}}$, as described earlier. Then, create profile curves around $\hat{\omega}_{i/\text{peak}}$ and choose the *minimum* profile curve for the approximation lobe $p_{\theta_o}(\vartheta_i)$. A minimum profile curve is defined as the profile curve that generates a lobe $p_{\theta_o}(\vartheta_i)$ which is smaller than $f_{\hat{\omega}_o}(\hat{\omega}_i)$ for all ϑ_i. We are going to use additional lobes that can pick up the not-yet approximated parts, but we do not want negative residuals[2]. This lobe is subtracted from the original BRDF (both are represented using samples). On the remaining unapproximated energy, we rerun the algorithm to get another lobe; see Figure 4. We stop the algorithm when we reach a given number of lobes.

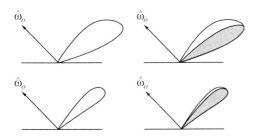

Figure 4: *Approximation with multiple lobes.*

As explained earlier, approximation is performed for each $\hat{\omega}_o$ separately, then we blur an existing environment map and store stacks of these maps in three-dimensional environment maps. In the multiple-lobe case we will get more than one lobe and therefore we will need to create more than one three-dimensional environment map. Each of these three-dimensional environment maps should be generated using a consistent and coherent selection of lobes.

What this means is shown in Figure 5. You can see a lobe varying over θ_o. In our representation this variation in shape is approximated by linearly interpolating approximations found for specific values of $\hat{\omega}_o$. We want the variation in shape to be gradual, and to do this we have to interpolate the "right" approximations. Profile lobes that are consistent and spatially coherent are marked with

the same letter (L, M, and R). Each of the three environment maps should be generated with only spatially coherent profile lobes, i.e. environment map one only with L lobes, environment map two only with M lobes, and so on.

This means that after finding different lobes for different $\hat{\omega}_i$, we cluster them by similar $\theta_{i/\text{off}}$ and $\phi_{i/\text{off}}$ values.

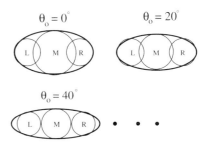

Figure 5: *Spatial coherence of multiple lobes.*

4 Prefiltering

Once we have a BRDF approximation an existing high-dynamic range specular environment map $E(\hat{r}_v)$ needs to be filtered by it. A specular environment map only depends on the reflected viewing vector. We integrate these against the radially symmetric lobes to obtain the three-dimensional environment map representation of the glossy reflection:

$$E_{\text{glossy}}(\hat{r}_v, \hat{n} \cdot \hat{r}_v) =$$

$$\int_{\Omega} p_{\hat{n} \cdot \hat{r}_v}(\hat{r}_v \cdot \hat{l}) \, (\hat{n} \cdot \hat{l}) E(\hat{l}) \, d\sigma(\hat{l}) \approx \quad (1)$$

$$(\hat{n} \cdot \hat{r}_v) \int_{\Omega} p_{\hat{n} \cdot \hat{r}_v}(\hat{r}_v \cdot \hat{l}) E(\hat{l}) \, d\sigma(\hat{l}) \quad (2)$$

All the vectors are depicted in Figure 6; $\hat{n}$ is the surface normal, $\hat{v} = \hat{\omega}_o$ in world coordinates, $\hat{l} = \hat{\omega}_i$ in world coordinates, and the reflection vector $\hat{r}_v = 2(\hat{v} \cdot \hat{n})\hat{n} - \hat{v}$, $d\sigma(\hat{l})$ is the projected solid angle measure. The lobes $p_{\hat{n} \cdot \hat{r}_v} = p_{\theta_o}$ actually only depend on the angle between the reflected viewing direction and the incident direction because they are by definition radially symmetric around $\hat{r}_v$ (we will *index* the new maps by the offset vectors, but filter them with the reflection vector).

---

[2]If signed arithmetic is supported, approximation techniques that generate signed lobes would be appropriate. Hardware is starting to become available which will be capable of this.

As you can see in Equation 1, we need not only to filter the environment map with the approximation lobe, but also have to include the cosine between the normal $\hat{n}$ and the incident direction $\hat{l}$.

Fortunately, we can approximate $\hat{n} \cdot \hat{l}$ with $\hat{n} \cdot \hat{r}_v$; otherwise, we would have another dependence on $\hat{n}$, which we cannot capture with a three dimensional environment map. At first sight, this approximation of $\hat{n} \cdot \hat{l}$ seems to be very crude. We assume, however, that BRDFs yielding interesting glossy reflections will have a fairly slim lobe in the direction of $\hat{r}_v$. In the cases of interest, $\hat{n} \cdot \hat{l}$ is therefore usually close to the constant value $\hat{n} \cdot \hat{r}_v$ where the integrand is large.

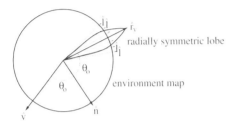

Figure 6: *The vector $\hat{n}$ is the surface normal, $\hat{v}$ is the viewing direction, $\hat{r}_v$ is the reflected viewing direction, and the $\hat{l}$ are the incident directions.*

5 Rendering

For our three different approximation methods (single lobe, single 2D lobe, multiple lobes), we basically use the same rendering algorithm. For each vertex of the reflective object, compute appropriate texture coordinates to represent the appropriate offset of the vector $\hat{r}_v$ and the value of $\hat{n} \cdot \hat{r}_v$. The actual representation of the offset vector as texture coordinates depends on the way the view-independent environment map was stored, e.g. as a parabolic map [11] on standard hardware, or as a cube map on hardware which supports them. Then we render our object with texture mapping turned on, and sum multiple lobes using either the accumulation buffer, multitexturing, or compositing, as appropriate.

5.1 Single Lobe Approach

Assume that we have already filtered an existing environment map $E(\hat{r}_v)$ with a shaped lobe approximation of the BRDF, so we have a three-dimensional environment map $E_{\text{glossy}}(\hat{r}_v, \vec{n} \cdot \hat{r}_v)$; see Equation 2.

This three-dimensional environment map consists of several two-dimensional environment maps, each of which depends only on $\hat{r}_v$. The value $\hat{n} \cdot \hat{r}_v$ is the third parameter of the three-dimensional environment map.

To render an object with this approximation, at each vertex compute $\hat{r}_v$ and compute the offset vector by adding $\theta_{i/\text{off}}$. Place the texture-coordinate representation of $\hat{r}_v$ in the first two texture coordinates, then compute $\hat{n} \cdot \hat{r}_v$ and place it in the third texture coordinate. The factor $\hat{n} \cdot \hat{r}_v$ in Equation 2 can be either incorporated into the environment map or assigned as the color at the vertices.

5.2 Single 2D Lobe Approach

In this approximation we only have a single filtered two-dimensional environment map, which was computed using the following filter:

$$E_{\text{glossy2D}}(\hat{r}_v) \quad = \quad \int_{\Omega} p(\hat{r}_v) E(\hat{l}) \, d\sigma(\hat{l}). \qquad (3)$$

As you can see the weight $k(\theta_o) = k(\hat{n} \cdot \hat{r}_v)$ is not included in the environment map, and neither is the factor $\hat{n} \cdot \hat{r}_v$ (which has to be used because we are dealing with an arbitrary isotropic BRDF).

At each vertex, we assign the weight $k(\theta_o)(\hat{n} \cdot \hat{r}_v)$ as the color. This takes care of the weight $k(\theta_o)$ and the factor $\hat{n} \cdot \hat{r}_v$. Now, we render the object using the two-dimensional environment map. Alternatively we can put the weights $k(\theta_o)$ in a texture map and use a two-pass rendering method, but as the $k(\theta_o)$ usually vary gradually, the first method was sufficiently accurate for the BRDFs we tested.

5.3 Multi-Lobe Approach

For a multilobe approximation we have several three-dimensional environment maps $E_{\text{glossy}}^l(\hat{r}_v, \hat{n} \cdot \hat{r}_v)$, each of has been blurred with a different set of lobes $p_{\theta_o}^l(\vartheta_i)$, as explained in Section 3.

For each environment map we basically run the same rendering algorithm that we described for the single lobe approach, and sum the results (using compositing or the accumulation buffer). The only additional difference is that we have to offset $\hat{r}_v$ by both $\theta_{i/\text{off}}$ and a non-zero $\varphi_{i/\text{off}}$.

6 Results

We have validated our technique with several examples, including Ward's model, the HTSG model, and measured car lacquer. Our tests have shown that our multilobe approximations yield RMS errors equivalent to the RMS errors for separable approximations with a similar number of terms [13]; the RMS errors were measured between the original BRDF and the approximated BRDF. However, since only positive lobes were used, negative residual error cannot be corrected and after six to eight lobes the error begins to increase rather than decrease.

Three test cases are shown in Figures 9–18, where they are compared with renderings using the actual BRDF filtered against the same environment map on a per-pixel basis. Note that we are testing the error of the BRDF approximation, *not* the error of the environment map reflectance approximation. In all cases we used a view-independent dual parabolic environment map of an office scene shown in Figure 8.

The first example applies our technique to the measured Cayman car lacquer from the Computer Graphics Group at Cornell. The results for the single lobe method can be seen in Figure 10 and for the single 2D lobe method in Figure 11. A rendering with the true BRDF (filtering is done for every pixel) is shown in Figure 9. Slices of the prefiltered environment map for the single lobe approximation can be seen at different elevation angles in Figure 8. The 3D texture map used had a resolution of $128 \times 128 \times 16$ slices in the z (elevation angle) direction. You can see that the sharpness and the color of the environment maps changes with elevation angle. This is visible on the lid of the teapot; the reflection in the 2D approximation is blurrier than it should be, although otherwise the approximation is adequate.

The second wavelength dependent BRDF we tried was the HTSG model for rough copper [9]. The results can be seen in Figure 13 for the single lobe method and in Figure 14 for the single 2D lobe method (compare with Figure 12). A few slices of the prefiltered environment map for the single lobe approximation are depicted in Figure 8, where you can again see increased sharpness with decreasing elevation.

Now we would like to demonstrate the differences between the multiple lobe method, the single lobe method, and the two-dimensional lobe method. In Figure 15 – 18 you can see a side-by-side comparison of a teapot rendered with the same BRDF (Ward's model) using these methods.

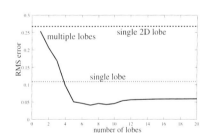

Figure 7: *RMS error for Ward's model.*

The relative mean square error for this BRDF using the different approximation methods is depicted in Figure 7.

These examples show that while the approximations are not exact, they are visually pleasing and adequate for real-time rendering applications. Two dimensional approximations will in general show more error, but in our tests were still visually close to the reflection generated by the original BRDF.

The rendering speed mainly depends on the graphics hardware, since only the texture coordinate generation needs to be done on the host. On an SGI Octane MXE we achieve 25 fps with the teapot model (4000 triangles) and a single lobe approximation. The three-lobe approximation is almost exactly three times slower. The teapot model with a single 2D approximation can be rendered with 33 fps.

7 Extensions

The greedy shaped lobe fitting algorithm may generate an inefficient approximation because it assumes that useful radially symmetric lobes are centered around peaks. Unfortunately, this assumption may be false.

First of all, measured BRDF data might have a peak somewhere that might be just a noisy data sample, but we want to maximize the total *volume*, of a lobe, not just its height. Secondly, BRDFs may contain radially symmetric lobes not centered around peaks, i.e. the centers might be "depressed". In this case the greedy fitting algorithm may use a large number of lobes to build a poor approximation when a single lobe would give a good approximation.

A more robust general-purpose fitting algorithm for radially symmetric lobes would be interesting. There are two possible approaches.

First, a heuristically-driven algorithm could be used that would look in several likely places (peaks, around the view direction for retroreflection, around the normal for generalized diffuse reflection, and finally around the reflected view direction), try to find a radially symmetric lobe for each of these vectors, and then pick the best one (in terms of maximum volume).

Secondly, a multiresolution search technique could be used. An exhaustive search could be made for the maximal volume radially symmetric lobe, but against a filtered and down-sampled version of the BRDF. Once one or more candidate lobes have been found, their positions and profile curves can be refined by increasing the resolution. This avoids the cost of exhaustively searching for all possible lobes at high resolution, but should give similar results.

Both these extension would still be greedy sequential algorithms, and so may not find optimal solutions. However, both approaches are fast and should robustly produce useful practical results.

Finally, the current technique can only handle anisotropic BRDFs by using many lobes and a 4D texture, which is inefficient. It would be interesting to use steerable filters [6] or spherical harmonics to implement anisotropic lobes to generalize the technique presented here.

Figure 8: *Parabolic environment maps of an office scene.*

Figure 9: *Teapot with the cayman car lacquer reflecting the office (original).*

Figure 10: *Teapot with the cayman car lacquer reflecting the office (3D).*

Figure 11: *Teapot with the cayman car lacquer reflecting the office (2D).*

Figure 12: *Copper teapot reflecting the office (original).*

Figure 13: *Copper teapot reflecting the office (3D).*

Figure 14: *Copper teapot reflecting the office (2D).*

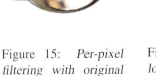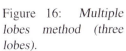

Figure 15: *Per-pixel filtering with original BRDF.*

Figure 16: *Multiple lobes method (three lobes).*

Figure 17: *Single lobe method.*

Figure 18: *Single 2D lobe method.*

Teapot with Ward's model ($k_d = 0.0, k_s = 0.80, \alpha_x = \alpha_y = 0.04$) reflecting the office.

126

8 Conclusions

We have presented a technique for representing arbitrary BRDFs using multiple radially symmetric lobes. This representation can be used to prefilter existing specular environment maps in order to render glossy surfaces at interactive rates on existing hardware. The straightforward greedy fitting algorithm we use is most appropriate for BRDFs with large peaks, but these are the BRDFs that produce recognizable reflections.

For several test BRDFs, objects rendered with environment maps that were filtered with our representation are visually convincing and can be rendered at real-time rates on appropriate hardware.

Our method is not restricted to a certain kind of isotropic BRDFs, since we can use a multilobe approximation, but memory requirements are excessive if many lobes are needed, making it unattractive. Therefore it is better to either restrict this method to BRDFs with almost radially symmetric lobes, which is true for many BRDFs, or to accept a loss in quality and use a single lobe or even a single 2D lobe only. Fortunately, our method enables the user to control the accuracy/memory ratio.

Cabral's technique turns out to be closely related to the technique presented here; in fact, our technique can be considered an alternative (and improved) implementation strategy for Cabral's technique. Cabral's method basically uses a sparse representation of the prefiltered environment map. However, we do not require per-frame warping, since we use view-independent environment maps, and we do not make the assumption of an orthogonal (constant) view direction. We have also gone farther in deriving multilobe representations of BRDFs.

Despite the different techniques used to store and reconstruct the prefiltered environment map data, our multilobe BRDF representations are compatible and have the same limitation to radially-symmetric lobes and to isotropic BRDFs.

Acknowledgements

Wolfgang Heidrich was very helpful in supplying code for rendering reflective objects using view-independent parabolic environment maps. He also supplied code for filtering environment maps.

The implementation of the He (HTSG) reflectance model was done by Glenn Evans at the University of Waterloo.

The core of this research was performed at the University of Waterloo, Canada, and was supported by a grant from the NSERC (the National Science and Engineering Research Council of Canada).

9 References

[1] R. Bastos, K. Hoff, W. Wynn, and A. Lastra. Increased Photorealism for Interactive Architectural Walkthroughs. *1999 ACM Symposium on Interactive 3D Graphics*, pages 183–190, April 1999.

[2] J. Blinn and M. Newell. Texture and reflection in computer generated images. *Communications of the ACM*, 19:542–546, 1976.

[3] B. Cabral, M. Olano, and P. Nemec. Reflection space image based rendering. In *Proc. SIGGRAPH*, pages 165–170, August 1999.

[4] P. Diefenbach and N. Badler. Multi-Pass Pipeline Rendering: Realism For Dynamic Environments . *1997 ACM Symposium on Interactive 3D Graphics*, pages 59–70, April 1997.

[5] A. Fournier. Filtering normal maps and multiple surfaces. Technical Report TR-92-41, University Of British Columbia, Department of Computer Science, 1992.

[6] W. Freeman and E. Adelson. The Design and Use of Steerable Filters. *IEEE Transaction on Pattern Analysis and Machine Intelligence*, 13(9):891–906, September 1991.

[7] N. Greene. Applications of World Projections. In *Proceedings of Graphics Interface '86*, pages 108–114, May 1986.

[8] P. Haeberli and M. Segal. Texture Mapping As A Fundamental Drawing Primitive. In *Fourth Eurographics Workshop on Rendering*, pages 259–266. Eurographics, June 1993.

[9] X. He, K. Torrance, F. Sillion, and D. Greenberg. A comprehensive physical model for light reflection. In *Proc. SIGGRAPH*, pages 175–186, July 1991.

[10] W. Heidrich. *High-quality Shading and Lighting for Hardware-accelerated Rendering*. PhD thesis, Universität Erlangen-Nürnberg, 1999.

[11] W. Heidrich and H.-P. Seidel. View-Independent Environment Maps. In *Eurographics/SIGGRAPH Workshop on Graphics Hardware*, pages 39–45, 1998.

[12] W. Heidrich and H.-P. Seidel. Realistic, Hardware-accelerated Shading and Lighting. In *Proc. SIGGRAPH*, pages 171–178, August 1999.

[13] J. Kautz. Interactive Reflection with Arbitrary BRDFs. Master's thesis, University of Waterloo, Waterloo, Canada, 1999.

[14] J. Kautz and M. McCool. Interactive Rendering with Arbitrary BRDFs using Separable Approximations. In *Tenth Eurographics Workshop on Rendering*, pages 281–292, June 1999.

[15] E. Lafortune, S.-C. Foo, K. Torrance, and D. Greenberg. Non-Linear Approximation of Reflectance Functions. In *Proc. SIGGRAPH*, pages 117–126, August 1997.

[16] D. Lischinski and A. Rappoport. Image-Based Rendering for Non-Diffuse Synthetic Scenes. *Nineth Eurographics Workshop on Rendering*, pages 301–314, June 1998.

[17] G. Miller, S. Rubin, and D. Ponceleon. Lazy Decompression of Surface Light Fields for Precomputed Global Illumination. *Nineth Eurographics Workshop on Rendering*, pages 281–292, June 1998.

[18] B.-T. Phong. Illumination for computer generated pictures. *Comm. ACM*, 18(6):311–317, June 1975.

[19] W. Stürzlinger and R. Bastos. Interactive Rendering of Globally Illuminated Glossy Scenes. In *Eighth Eurographics Workshop on Rendering Workshop*, pages 93–102. Eurographics, June 1997.

[20] D. Voorhies and J. Foran. Reflection Vector Shading Hardware. In *Proc. SIGGRAPH*, pages 163–166, July 1994.

[21] B. Walter, G. Alppay, E. Lafortune, S. Fernandez, and D. Greenberg. Fitting Virtual Lights for Non-Diffuse Walkthroughs. In *Proc. SIGGRAPH*, pages 45–48, August 1997.

[22] G. Ward. Measuring and modeling anisotropic reflection. In *Proc. SIGGRAPH*, pages 265–272, July 1992.

Adaptive Representation of
Specular Light Flux

Normand Brière   Pierre Poulin

Département d'informatique et de recherche opérationnelle
Université de Montréal

Abstract

Caustics produce beautiful and intriguing illumination patterns. However, their complex behavior make them difficult to simulate accurately in all but the simplest configurations. To capture their appearance, we present an adaptive approach based upon light beams. The coherence between light rays forming a light beam greatly reduces the number of samples required for precise illumination reconstruction. The light beams characterize the distribution of light due to interactions with specular surfaces (specular light flux) in 3D space, thus allowing for the treatment of illumination within single-scattering participating media. The hierarchical structure enclosing the light beams possesses inherent properties to detect efficiently every light beam reaching any 3D point, to adapt itself according to illumination effects in the final image, and to reduce memory consumption via caching.

Keywords: caustics, global illumination, ray tracing, wavefront, beam, shaft.

1   Introduction

Illumination defines how surfaces appear in an image, and therefore is considered an important area of image synthesis. Unfortunately, simulating in global illumination the multiple interactions of light in a general context represents a complex task to solve accurately and efficiently. This explains why so much research has been devoted to illumination.

Global illumination algorithms can be loosely separated in two categories: radiosity and path tracing. Radiosity techniques [6, 26] capture the infinite interreflections in diffuse polygonal environments. With recent advances in discontinuity meshing and clustering, they can handle larger and larger scenes. However these techniques mainly target diffuse interreflections, and they typically become much more expensive when extended to directional (specular) interreflections [24, 4].

Monte Carlo Path Tracing [22, 23] and bi-directional [27, 17] techniques solve the light transport problem for any geometry and any surface property. These sampling-oriented approaches compute the radiance along rays in the environment. While they can produce stunning results, they often exhibit noise due to insufficient sampling. Specular interactions are better handled because rays are more narrowly directed; diffuse interactions on the other hand may require many more rays to reduce noise. Although several efficient variance reduction techniques have been proposed [28], the coherence between adjacent samples is not guaranteed, which makes the reconstruction of the illumination prone to errors that appear in the form of noise.

Two-pass techniques [29, 25, 3, 32] have been introduced to exploit the best of both worlds. However while noise can be reduced significantly, it is still present in singular situations, such as small light sources and mirrors.

In this paper, we concentrate our efforts on capturing light emitted from point light sources and distributed within a scene via perfectly specular surfaces (that is the distribution of specular light flux). These effects are often associated with caustics.

1.1   Coherent Light Beams

In order to accurately simulate the light specular distribution, we construct a set of light beams. The concept of coherent 3D beams is not new in image synthesis. Heckbert and Hanrahan [12] use them to represent *exact* visibility after perfect reflections off polygonal surfaces (refractions are treated approximately). Each beam is clipped by any polygonal blocker. They propose to trace beams from a point light source to deposit illumination from the unclipped beams as *shading polygons* on diffuse polygonal surfaces for efficient rendering of indirect specular illumination.

This approach has been successfully applied by Watt [31] on a fine triangular mesh defining a surface of water. The light reaching a specular triangle refracts and settles onto diffuse polygons as a shading triangle. The resulting illumination on the shading triangle is computed as the irradiance on the specular triangle weighted by the ratio of the area of both triangles. To simulate the effect due to the presence of uniform participating media, *light beams* may be defined by linking a pair of specular and shading triangles, treating the attenuation along each light beam. Chuang and Cheng [5] can handle non-polygonal illuminated surfaces by searching the light beams within which any intersection point resides. Their light beams are enclosed in a hierarchy of bounding cones for more efficient point-in-beam detection. No participating media is treated. Instead of performing a scanconversion of the shading triangles, Nishita and Nakamae [19] also used light beams to treat uniform density participating media. Their triangular light beams originate from a pre-meshed ocean surface. They intersect all light beams with a plane for each scanline, and accumulate the contribution of each shading triangle. This results in an efficient rendering of underwater scenes provided that the camera lies under the ocean surface.

The light beams in the previous techniques are constructed from a set of pre-meshed surfaces. Their subdivisions must first be set to the desired accuracy. As caustics are highly localized effects, it is not obvious to estimate an appropriate level of detail. Also, these techniques can not in their current form handle caustics resulting from multiple interreflections and interrefractions.

An attractive approach samples the illumination by tracing photons from the light sources, and deposits them onto surfaces and/or in volumes. If only energy is associated to each photon [1, 11, 15, 30], reconstructing the illumination corresponds to solving a density estimation problem. By adding wavefront information to each photon [21, 7, 8], irradiance at any point along its path can be computed. Reconstructing the illumination then requires less samples in the filtering process. Another lower sampling solution is possible when considering adjacency information between the origins of the samples. Collins [7] exploited this adjacency information in order to determine the resolution of illumination maps associated with diffuse surfaces. Adjacency was used to estimate the wavefront on the intersected surface, and the kernel size and shape to distribute energy onto the elements of the illumination map on the surface. Only planar diffuse surfaces and no participating media were assumed.

Photon tracing techniques have proven to be both general and efficient, while capable of capturing many of the most complex illumination patterns. However, it is difficult to determine when the distribution of photons is sufficient for accurate illumination evaluation, how many of these photons to include in the filter kernel, and which photons really contribute within this kernel. This leads to possible illumination artifacts such as noise if the kernel is too small, or blur otherwise.

As suggested by researchers [14, 15, 16], one can gain in efficiency by replacing some of its generality to capture specific phenomena. In this paper, we focus on one such phenomenon: caustics.

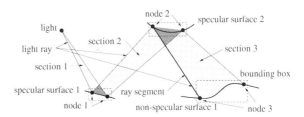

Figure 1: A 2D representation of a light beam.

Mitchell and Hanrahan [18] describe an accurate solution for solving this particular situation. Instead of sampling the illumination from the light source, they determine all light rays (Fermat critical paths) reaching any desired point in a scene. However this process requires a priori knowledge of interacting specular surfaces to avoid considering exponentially growing potential combinations.

To bypass this problem, we propose to calculate an approximation of the illumination produced by the specular flux rather than an exact characterization. We present in Section 2 an adaptive subdivision scheme to construct light beams issued from a point light source as samples of its specular distribution. It can handle any type of geometry (conics, bicubic patches, etc.) and generates coherent light beams from an arbitrary number of reflections and refractions. In Section 3, we explain how the flux density can be extracted from the light beams, and introduce extensions to participating media. Section 4 presents some techniques developed to reduce both memory and computing requirements. Finally extensions are discussed in Section 5, and we conclude by revisiting the achievements of our approach.

2 Light Beams

A light ray is traced from a point light source. It reflects or refracts onto various perfectly specular surfaces until it reaches a non-specular surface. The flux density at any point along this ray is a function of the propagated wavefront [21, 18, 7]. Infinitely many such rays would characterize the entire specular distribution of light in the environment.

In order to sample the light flux, we encode adjacency information in the form of *light beams*. A light beam is issued from a point light source and goes through a solid angle corresponding to three points on the *light image* (image as seen from the light source, illustrated in Fig. 10 (center)). The three *supporting light rays* are traced through the scene onto specular reflective or refractive surfaces until they reach a non-specular surface. At each interaction with a surface, the three intersection points are linked into a *node*, and this node is connected

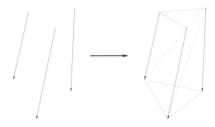

Figure 4: Quadtree element with four T-vertices and corresponding triangularization.

Figure 2: Supporting ray segments and corresponding light beam section.

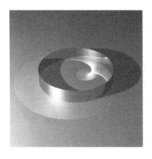

Figure 3: Left: caustic produced by a ring; Right: the corresponding mesh formed by the intersections of the reflected light beams with the floor.

to the previous node by ray segments forming a *section* of the light beam (Fig. 2). A section is built as a polyhedron with eight triangles. A light beam therefore consists of a linked list of triangular based sections. Fig. 1 illustrates (in 2D) elements of such a structure. Fig. 10 (left) illustrates it in an actual 3D scene. Fig. 3 shows the familiar caustic (cardioid) within a ring and a dimmed reflection outside the ring. The mesh is obtained by intersecting the light beams with the floor.

At this point, our light propagation process corresponds to the grid-pencil tracing described by Shinya *et al.* [20]. We therefore inherit advantages of their approach. To avoid high memory requirements, Shinya *et al.* deposit onto the polygonal surfaces the illuminance polygons carried by the light beams. Fortunately, by enclosing the light beams within a hierarchical structure, we will be able to use all information they provide thanks to a caching scheme. A volumetric representation has interesting properties and benefits such as the ability to treat participating media but also, to handle rough or bumpy illuminated surfaces.

2.1 Adaptive Refinements

We would like to keep the light distribution within a light beam as *coherent* as possible in order to approximate the light flux within a light beam only from the supporting rays. To ensure an appropriate distribution of light

beams, one can use a high basic subdivision for the light image, resulting in finer beams, and rely afterwards on re-unification of the light beams considered well enough approximated at a coarser level. This scheme based on uniform subdivision and adaptive re-unification provides a beam distribution which misses fewer features than purely adaptive subdivision for the same maximum subdivision level.

An adaptive subdivision of the light image is however more efficient. It can be performed according to various criteria such as the ordered list of objects encountered along the light rays defining a light beam (object paths), their directions, and the variation of the flux density (wavefront) along the light rays. By forcing a maximum difference of one subdivision level between neighbor light beams (balanced quadtree), it is easier to construct well behaved triangular light beams from quadtree elements since they are defined with at most four T-vertices (Fig. 4).

The center image of Fig. 10 shows the resulting balanced subdivision (started at a resolution of 8×8) when applying the criteria of object paths. In this case, no features have been missed and the resulting light beams represent our approximation of the specular light flux.

Adaptive subdivision schemes unfortunately do not guarantee that the light flux within a light beam is fully characterized by its supporting rays. Indeed for non-constant curvature surfaces, light may reflect outside of its beam. If these situations are detected, they should force a refinement. As a light beam becomes thinner, it better characterizes its light flux since its supporting rays usually converge to a single light ray.

2.2 Light Specular Distribution

At the end of this preprocessing step, we have a volumetric representation of the light flux via specular transfers in the scene. The light beams are themselves polyhedral, but because the supporting rays are defined by ray tracing (actually pencil tracing [21]), they can handle arbitrary reflection/refraction combinations for any type of primitive without requiring any surface meshing. This representation can be adapted according to discontinuities within the light flux, the light distribution within the light beams, and the participating media traversed.

Each point light within the scene can require up to six light images, defining a cube around the source. For a point light source distant with respect to the scene, the user can orient the light image according to the specular surfaces. The various parameters controling adaptive subdivision can be specified by the user.

3   Flux Density Computing

With a distribution of light beams, one can estimate the light flux at any 3D point P in the scene. Suppose P lies within a section of a light beam, and the light flux passing through the light beam is coherent. The flux density at P can be approximated from the information provided by the three supporting rays. The construction is illustrated in 2D in Fig. 5. We build a plane intersecting P and oriented along the average of the three supporting ray segments. The wavefronts are evaluated at the three intersection points P_i of the rays with this plane, and a barycentric interpolation of these wavefronts is assigned as the wavefront at P.

For some surfaces such as those modeled with a bump map, the wavefronts are not exact because a bump mapped surface does not correspond to a real surface. However they can provide a good approximation when the bump map has a low C^2 amplitude. Igehy [13] proposes to use the more general ray differentials to deal with such surfaces.

Another approximation of the flux density at P [31] is $E_P = I\Delta\omega/\Delta A$, where I corresponds to the intensity of the point light, $\Delta\omega$ to the solid angle at the light subtended by the light beam, and ΔA to the area of the triangle defined by the plane and the three ray segments. If P lies on a surface, the flux density E_P is multiplied by $\cos\theta$, where θ is the angle between the interpolated ray and the surface normal at P. The wavefront and triangle area approximations converge to the same result as the light beams are subdivided more finely. The triangle approximation can be used in all situations, but results in a more *blocky* appearance because no illumination is shared between adjacent illumination triangles. The wavefront approximation usually converges faster for it provides a continuous (C^0, but not C^1) illumination reconstruction.

Fig. 6 shows the main caustic produced by a glass sphere. The caustic in the image on the left is too small to observe the variations within the caustic region. The image on the right focuses on the caustic illumination. Colors have been scaled down in order to show the details in this small region. We used triangle areas to approximate the flux density. Fig. 7 shows the illumination pattern created by a point light source placed under a

Figure 6: Caustic under a glass sphere and a zoom on the illumination.

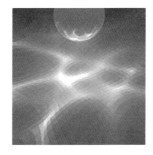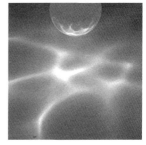

Figure 7: Reflection under a bump mapped sphere. Left: triangle area; Right: interpolated wavefront.

reflective bump mapped sphere. The direct illumination has not been not computed to display only the reflected illumination on the floor. The image on the left uses the triangle area approximation; the image on the right uses the wavefront barycentric interpolation.

3.1   Shadowing

Both techniques provide an approximation of the flux density at P *if* this light actually reaches P. However smaller objects may lie between the supporting rays without intersecting them. For more accurate shadowing during the rendering phase, the Fermat critical path is approximated by simply interpolating a light ray from the supporting light rays (Fig. 5). The shadow ray segment within a section uses the same barycentric weights at both adjacent nodes as we did for the interpolated wavefront. The resulting shadow ray is traced back to the light source through the specular interactions, and tested for occlusion with the entire scene.

On a concave shape, light beams might not reach the interior of its surface. To reduce illumination problems on concave shapes, each section of each light beam is extended in length to enclose as much as possible the intersected surface(s) (Fig. 8). The longer the extension, the less efficient the structure becomes because a point can then fall in more light beams. By tracing a shadow ray, we also make sure the illumination is properly reaching

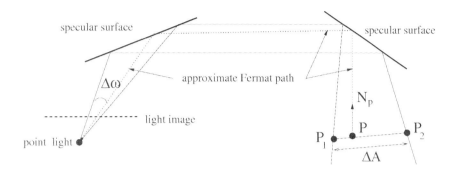

Figure 5: Computing the flux density at P.

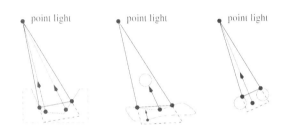

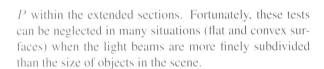

Figure 8: Extending a light beam section and tracing back shadow rays.

Figure 9: Disco era memories: sampled and analytical.

P within the extended sections. Fortunately, these tests can be neglected in many situations (flat and convex surfaces) when the light beams are more finely subdivided than the size of objects in the scene.

3.2 Shading

The flux density at P and its interpolated incident direction are inserted in the local reflection model to determine the light reaching the virtual camera. Therefore non-specular surfaces can have any reflection model. The total light contribution from P issued from all specular interactions is computed by summing up the contributions from all the light beams P lies within. Fig. 12 shows illumination produced by caustics reflected on a galleon and refracted within a pool of sharks.

The 3D nature of the light beams can take into account participating media attenuation and shading under the assumption of single scattering. Accumulated attenuation is stored at each intersection point of supporting light rays. One therefore needs only to compute the attenuation in the current section rather than along all the sections back to the point light source. The shadow ray is traced only in the current section, and its attenuation at the beginning of this section is interpolated from the attenuations of the supporting light rays. The storage re-

quired by the light beams is lower than the volumetric photons of Jensen and Christensen [16], although their technique allows for multiple scattering in participating media.

Fig. 9 shows a disco sphere in uniform density participating media. The image of the left shows a rendering using 100 sample points along eye rays. In this case, noise is still noticeable. However, if we compute the entry and exit points of eye rays with light beam sections, the shading equations resulting from uniform density media simplify, leading to a smoother rendering, as illustrated at the right. The direct illumination in Fig. 11 (center) is not included to display the fine light beams reflected in the uniform density media. Note that these light beams are also visible via reflection on the polygonized disco sphere. Fig. 11 (left) shows an image where the attenuation of the light due to non-uniform participating media is approximated by 10 samples along shadow ray segments.

4 Efficiency

Light beams offer various advantages to render specular indirect illumination. However it is critical to determine efficiently the light beams a point P lies into. We organize the light beams into a hierarchical structure to provide an efficient point-in-beam determination. Also, this hierarchical structure allows efficient caching of its elements. Therefore only a fraction of the total structure needs to be kept in memory at any given time. We detail in the following sections the advantages obtained with this hierarchical structure.

4.1 Hierarchical Point-in-beam

A typical scene with specular surfaces can result in thousands to millions of light beams per point light source. This requires an efficient hierarchical structure to identify the light beams enclosing a point P, which we refer to as *point-in-beam query*.

The intersection points of supporting rays forming the nodes of adjacent light beams are joined by a bounding box oriented along a global coordinate system. Two bounding boxes of consecutive nodes form a shaft [10] which corresponds to their convex hull. Adjacent light beams are enclosed by those shafts, and shafts are themselves organized into a hierarchy of shafts. The bounding boxes form as well an equivalent hierarchy. Similar structures have been used with success in previous applications [2, 9].

While shafts can give some indication about the light distribution, it is really in the enclosed light beams, down at the leaves of the hierarchy, that the flux is encoded. We use the hierarchy mainly to cull efficiently irrelevant light beams in order to determine a point-in-beam query logarithmically in the number of light beams.

4.2 Efficient Memory Management

The hierarchical nature of the structure also allows to free much of its information that can be recomputed when required. By storing only the ordered list of intersected objects (object path) for each light ray, we can rebuild efficiently and exactly any portion of the hierarchy. Because many point-in-beam queries often occur within the same 3D region, the localized behavior of caching the more recently requested portions of the hierarchy allows for efficient memory management.

Table 1 shows the impact on rendering time of reducing the memory requirements relative to keeping all structures (100%) in memory. We used different image resolutions of the sharks scene (Fig. 12 (right)). All light object paths as well as the entire bounding box hierarchy of the nodes are kept in memory. For reference, in our implementation, the data structure of a bounding box is about 10 times smaller than the data structure of a shaft joining two bounding boxes because of the various plane equations defining the shaft itself. Recomputing a light shaft corresponds to building it back from the bounding box hierarchy. Recomputing a light beam corresponds to retracing three light rays from their object paths to intersect the proper objects.

At a resolution of 256×256, keeping 10% of all light shafts requires only 1.06 more time than keeping everything, while keeping 10% of the light beams requires 1.25 more time. One can observe from this table that for this typical scene, keeping as little as 1% of the structures for both light beams and light shafts is still reasonable with respect to the rendering time. Keeping none (0%) of the structures means that every light ray is recomputed from its object path and every light shaft from its bounding boxes. In this case, rendering times only slightly increase with the resolution. In all other cases, caching efficiency increases with image resolution as more localized and coherent calculations are performed. This process allows us to construct more detailed light beams of complex light interactions within the same amount of memory space.

4.3 Wavelength Dependency

To capture wavelength-dependent phenomena, the light beam structure is extended to wavelengths. When a light beam traverses space where no interactions depend on the wavelength of the light carried within, the light beam remains the same as previously described. However when a light beam interacts with a refractive surface for instance, we construct new sections for a number of sampled wavelengths according to the spectrum of the light in the beam. The reconstructed shading at a point is then dependent upon the wavelength of all light beams it lies in. Fig. 11 (right) shows a crystal pyramid and the colored illumination (due to refraction) rendered at three sampled wavelengths. The *dispersion image solid* of Shinya *et al.* [20] would be applicable for more precise results.

4.4 Results

Table 2 gives some statistics for rendering the images in this paper. All renderings were computed on an SGI R10000 Impact at 195 MHz with 128 MB. The light image preprocessing lists the minimum and maximum resolutions of the adaptive subdivision, the number of light beams created, and the complete preprocessing time in seconds. The final rendering times of the images are given in minutes in the rightmost column. All renderings to gather the statistics were computed at a 512×512 resolution, 1 sample per pixel. All structures were kept in memory for the rendering of the entire image.

An important general observation about the light image preprocessing is that tracing the light rays and building the entire hierarchical structure represent typically a small fraction of the image rendering time. This indicates that we could continue to improve on the light beams distribution and therefore on the illumination details without much impact on the total rendering time. This favors a more sophisticated design for adaptive subdivision criteria and re-unification strategies.

Figure : Description	Light Image Preprocessing				Rendering Time (mins)
	Resolution		Beams ($\times 1,000$)	Time (secs)	
	Min	Max			
3 left : Ring	16×16	1024×1024	18	8	4
6 left : Glass sphere	128×128	128×128	16	47	63
6 right : Glass sphere: zoom					67
7 left : Bumped sphere: triangles	64×64	64×64	4	17	19
7 right : Bumped sphere: wavefronts					24
9 left : Disco sphere: 100 samples	16×16	256×256	23	50	3,200
9 right : Disco sphere: analytical					1,380
10 right : Mirrors	8×8	512×512	23	23	16
11 left : Smoke on cube: 10 samples	16×16	256×256	7.5	4	312
11 right : Refraction from pyramid	16×16	256×256	45	540	90
12 left : Galleon	256×256	256×256	65	840	132
12 right : Sharks	256×256	1024×1024	144	1020	120

Table 2: Statistics on some images displayed in this paper.

Image Resolution	Timings relative to full memory		
	0%	1%	10%
64×64	5.67 / 2.33	2.28 / 1.75	1.61 / 1.44
128×128	5.82 / 2.39	1.80 / 1.56	1.44 / 1.22
256×256	5.90 / 2.42	1.67 / 1.47	1.25 / 1.06

Table 1: Reduction of light beams / light shafts.

The second observation is that the *distribution* of the light beams in the scene has a major impact on the rendering time, often more than the scene complexity itself. For instance the sphere (Fig. 6) and the ring (Fig. 3) have about the same number of light beams, but the ones on the ring are well behaved and tightly distributed. The light beams refracted by the sphere are also narrowly distributed in the caustic region, but the ones reflecting on the sphere are spread all over the scene without contributing much to the illumination. This makes any hierarchical organization of the light beams fairly inefficient, as demonstrated in the rendering times about 17 times longer, even when zooming on the caustic region. We suggest in Section 5.2 that truncation of light beams carrying negligible flux density should bring much relief here.

As expected, attenuation in participating media requires also more computation. Again the nicely packed light beam distribution from the light to the cube of Fig. 11 (left) is rendered in far less time than the exploding light beams on the disco sphere of Fig. 9. In the latter image, as many as 100 samples along the eye ray still produce a noisy image while the analytical solution (en-

try and exit points of all intersected light beams with eye rays) is smooth and computed in less than half the time.

The relative slowness for rendering these two images is mainly due to the fact that we used a ray tracer to compute them. However, other rendering techniques, based upon scanconversion of light beam sections [19], might lead to more efficient rendering.

5 Extensions

In this section, we propose some ideas that can improve the quality of the rendering and reduce computation time. Although they have not been fully implemented, we feel confident these improvements will lead to better results.

5.1 Incremental Update of Light Beams

Our hierarchical structure inherits properties similar to those present in an interactive editor of a scene rendered via ray tracing [2]. For instance, when an object is modified interactively or in an animated sequence, the light beams that must be recomputed can be efficiently determined thanks to the hierarchy. They include changing surface reflection/refraction properties, geometry, and position/orientation.

Indeed if none of the light beams issued from a light image region are modified by a moving object, the indirect illumination carried by these beams will be identical at each frame and therefore does not need to be recomputed. The resulting images therefore exhibit no undesirable noise from its indirect illumination.

As shown in Table 2, building the light beam hierarchy is itself only a small portion of the total rendering time. However for a precise characterization of the light flux, with re-unification of a high resolution light image, the gain of these incremental updates can become significant.

5.2 Handling Degenerated Light Beams

The thinner a light beam, the better the approximation of its light flux. However there will always be light beams that do not intersect the same surface (on object silhouettes), or that spread over a large solid angle after interacting with a surface. We call these light beams *degenerated* as their insertion within the hierarchical structure can significantly reduce its efficiency. When the supporting rays of a light beam do not share the same object path, we should neglect its contribution to the indirect illumination. Indeed in this case, the flux is not properly defined and extracting information from that beam may produce undesirable artifacts. When such an incoherence in a light beam is detected, it is automatically subdivided in the preprocessing step. If the maximum subdivision level is sufficient, the neglected light beams should therefore not be noticeable.

We can also cut any light beam at a distance for which the flux density falls below a given threshold. Unless the light flux is reconcentrated in a small region, which can be verified, it should speed up the rendering by avoiding computing negligible illumination.

Unfortunately, these solutions do not prevent a potential explosion of higher levels of the hierarchy. Since the top level always encloses every light beam, it is likely that any bounding volume would cover the entire 3D space unless all light rays share the same object path. Rather than computing and testing degenerated bounding volumes, we propose instead using an independent hierarchy for each object path. By doing so, point-in-beam queries stay logarithmic provided that the number of object paths is very small compared to the number of light beams.

5.3 Importance-driven Subdivision Criteria

Assume the basic light beam subdivision is sufficient to characterize most specular transfers. One can easily project onto the image plane the three intersection points forming the final node of a light beam on the receiving non-specular surface(s). Assuming this triangle is not blocked, reflected, or refracted when projected on the image, this indicates the area of the image covered by this illumination triangle. If the projected triangle is not small enough, the light beam is subdivided.

We can also proceed by first determining all the intersection points used to construct a region of the final image. If many of these intersection points lie within the same light beam, one can decide to subdivide this light beam even further to more precisely capture its contribution to the illumination.

5.4 Almost Perfectly Specular Surfaces

The light beam structure characterizes light specularly reflected in the scene. This structure could reduce the list of potential combinations of specular surfaces reaching a 3D point. The optimization of Mitchell and Hanrahan [18] would thus avoid searching among all possible combinations of specular surfaces.

Although we developed the structure for perfectly specular surface interactions, it is possible to extend it to almost perfectly specular surfaces as long as the light distribution remains mostly directional. If we do so, the light distribution within a light beam is no longer as *regular*. However by sampling the contribution with rays back to the light source in some flavor of bi-directional technique [27, 17], we could simulate non-perfectly specular surface interactions.

6 Conclusion

We presented the use of a hierarchical light beam structure to capture the perfectly specular light flux. It provides accurate indirect specular illumination without some of the noise and blur artifacts that basic photon map techniques can exhibit (without the Monte Carlo phase).

Even though most of the techniques used here have been introduced in different contexts, we showed how they could be integrated into a hierarchy in order to handle some of the problems involved in complex light flux. Among the features investigated, our hierarchical structure allows for efficient capture of the 3D effects of participating media, incremental update of the structures in an animated sequence, memory space reduction via caching, and logarithmic detection of point-in-beam requests.

Some ideas to improve the efficiency and accuracy of the results have been proposed with importance-driven subdivision of the indirect specular light flux, and handling degenerate light beams and almost perfectly specular surfaces. Photon tracing techniques can not easily release memory, adapt the sampling distribution without bias, or be built incrementally for an animated sequence.

Our technique does not suit for rendering illumination effects where directionality is not a predominant factor. Such effects come from large extended light sources, volumetric multiple scattering, and indirect illumination due to interreflections on diffuse surfaces. However our approach shows nice properties to handle light specular interactions required to render illumination from caustics.

Acknowledgements

We acknowledge financial support from FCAR and NSERC. Special thanks to the anonymous reviewers for their numerous suggestions, and to Avalon Viewpoint Datalabs for making available the galleon and shark 3D models.

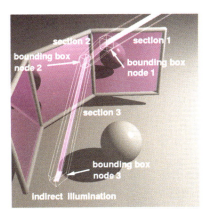 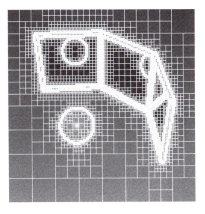 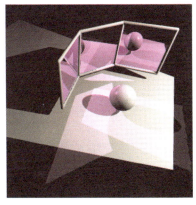

Figure 10: A 3D representation of light beams. Left: annotated 3D structure of shafts enclosing a light beam; Center: subdivided light image taken from the light source; Right: corresponding mirror reflections taken from the eye.

  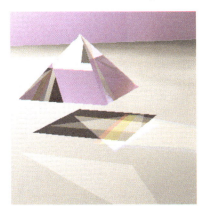

Figure 11: Left: non-uniform smoke with sampled attenuation; Center: uniform smoke illuminated with reflected beams only; Right: refraction at three wavelengths in a crystal pyramid.

Figure 12: Water worlds.

References

[1] J. Arvo. Backward ray tracing. In *SIGGRAPH '86 Developments in Ray Tracing seminar notes*, volume 12, August 1986.

[2] N. Brière and P. Poulin. Hierarchical view-dependent structures for interactive scene manipulation. In *SIGGRAPH 96 Conference Proceedings*, Annual Conference Series, pages 83–90, August 1996.

[3] S.E. Chen, H.E. Rushmeier, G. Miller, and D. Turner. A progressive multi-pass method for global illumination. In *Computer Graphics (SIGGRAPH '91 Proceedings)*, volume 25, pages 165–174, July 1991.

[4] P.H. Christensen, D. Lischinski, E.J. Stollnitz, and D.H. Salesin. Clustering for glossy global illumination. *ACM Transactions on Graphics*, 16(1):3–33, January 1997.

[5] J.H. Chuang and S.A. Cheng. Computing caustic effects by backward beam tracing. *The Visual Computer*, 11(3):156–166, 1995.

[6] M.F. Cohen and J.R. Wallace. *Radiosity and Realistic Image Synthesis*. Academic Press Professional, 1993.

[7] S. Collins. Adaptive splatting for specular to diffuse light transport. In *Fifth Eurographics Workshop on Rendering*, pages 119–135, June 1994.

[8] S. Collins. Reconstruction of indirect illumination from area luminaires. In *Eurographics Workshop on Rendering*, pages 274–283, June 1995.

[9] G. Drettakis and F.X. Sillion. Interactive update of global illumination using A line-space hierarchy. In *SIGGRAPH 97 Conference Proceedings*, Annual Conference Series, pages 57–64, August 1997.

[10] E.A. Haines and J.R. Wallace. Shaft culling for efficient ray-traced radiosity. In *Eurographics Workshop on Rendering*, pages 122–138, June 1991.

[11] P.S. Heckbert. Adaptive radiosity textures for bidirectional ray tracing. In *Computer Graphics (SIGGRAPH '90 Proceedings)*, volume 24, pages 145–154, August 1990.

[12] P.S. Heckbert and P. Hanrahan. Beam tracing polygonal objects. In *Computer Graphics (SIGGRAPH '84 Proceedings)*, volume 18, pages 119–127, July 1984.

[13] Homan Igehy. Tracing ray differentials. In *SIGGRAPH 99 Conference Proceedings*, Annual Conference Series, pages 179–186, August 1999.

[14] H.W. Jensen. Global illumination using photon maps. In *Eurographics Workshop on Rendering*, pages 21–30, June 1996.

[15] H.W. Jensen. Rendering caustics on non-lambertian surfaces. *Computer Graphics Forum*, 16(1):57–64, 1997.

[16] H.W. Jensen and P.H. Christensen. Efficient simulation of light transport in scenes with participating media using photon maps. In *SIGGRAPH 98 Conference Proceedings*, Annual Conference Series, pages 311–320, July 1998.

[17] E.P. Lafortune and Y.D. Willems. A theoretical framework for physically based rendering. *Computer Graphics Forum*, 13(2):97–107, June 1994.

[18] D.P. Mitchell and P. Hanrahan. Illumination from curved reflectors. In *Computer Graphics (SIGGRAPH '92 Proceedings)*, volume 26, pages 283–291, July 1992.

[19] T. Nishita and E. Nakamae. Method of displaying optical effects within water using accumulation buffer. In *Proceedings of SIGGRAPH '94*, Annual Conference Series, pages 373–381, July 1994.

[20] M. Shinya, T. Saito, and T. Takahashi. Rendering techniques for transparent objects. In *Proceedings of Graphics Interface '89*, pages 173–182, June 1989.

[21] M. Shinya, T. Takahashi, and S. Naito. Principles and applications of pencil tracing. In *Computer Graphics (SIGGRAPH '87 Proceedings)*, volume 21, pages 45–54, July 1987.

[22] P. Shirley. A ray tracing method for illumination calculation in diffuse-specular scenes. In *Proceedings of Graphics Interface '90*, pages 205–212, May 1990.

[23] P. Shirley, C.Y. Wang, and K. Zimmerman. Monte carlo techniques for direct lighting calculations. *ACM Transactions on Graphics*, 15(1):1–36, January 1996.

[24] F.X. Sillion, J.R. Arvo, S.H. Westin, and D.P. Greenberg. A global illumination solution for general reflectance distributions. In *Computer Graphics (SIGGRAPH '91 Proceedings)*, volume 25, pages 187–196, July 1991.

[25] F.X. Sillion and C. Puech. A general two-pass method integrating specular and diffuse reflection. In *Computer Graphics (SIGGRAPH '89 Proceedings)*, volume 23, pages 335–344, July 1989.

[26] F.X. Sillion and C. Puech. *Radiosity and Global Illumination*. Morgan Kaufmann, 1994.

[27] E. Veach and L. Guibas. Bidirectional estimators for light transport. In *Eurographics Workshop on Rendering*, pages 147–162, June 1994.

[28] E. Veach and L.J. Guibas. Metropolis light transport. In *SIGGRAPH 97 Conference Proceedings*, Annual Conference Series, pages 65–76, August 1997.

[29] J.R. Wallace, M.F. Cohen, and D.P. Greenberg. A two-pass solution to the rendering equation: A synthesis of ray tracing and radiosity methods. In *Computer Graphics (SIGGRAPH '87 Proceedings)*, volume 21, pages 311–320, July 1987.

[30] B. Walter, P.M. Hubbard, P. Shirley, and D.F. Greenberg. Global illumination using local linear density estimation. *ACM Transactions on Graphics*, 16(3):217–259, July 1997.

[31] M. Watt. Light-water interaction using backward beam tracing. In *Computer Graphics (SIGGRAPH '90 Proceedings)*, volume 24, pages 377–385, August 1990.

[32] K. Zimmerman and P. Shirley. A two-pass realistic image synthesis method for complex scenes. In *Eurographics Workshop on Rendering*, pages 284–295, June 1995.

Multiscale Shaders for the Efficient Realistic Rendering of Pine-Trees

Alexandre Meyer   Fabrice Neyret

iMAGIS[*]-GRAVIR / IMAG-INRIA
Email:{Alexandre.Meyer|Fabrice.Neyret}@imag.fr

Abstract

The frame of our work is the efficient realistic rendering of scenes containing a huge amount of data for which an a priori knowledge is available. In this paper, we present a new model able to render forests of pine-trees efficiently in ray-tracing and free of aliasing. This model is based on three scales of shaders representing the geometry (i.e. needles) that is smaller than a pixel size. These shaders are computed by analytically integrating the illumination reflected by this geometry using the a priori knowledge. They include the effects of local illumination, shadows and opacity within the concerned volume of data.

Key words: Shaders, levels of details, natural scenes, ray-tracing

1   Introduction

Natural scenes such as landscapes and forests are extremely complex in term of the number of geometric primitives that lies in the field of view. Trees belongs to this category of objects that have no defined surfaces, which makes most of the geometry inside the canope potentially visible and potentially enlightened. Ray-tracing such a scene is thus very costly and very subject to aliasing. On the other hand, geometric details like needles or leaves are so small that they usually cannot be seen except for the nearest trees. Boughs of leaves themselves merge with distance. It is thus tempting to replace the indistinguishable data by a fuzzy primitive that would reproduce the same photometric behavior that the group of geometry it represents. In this paper, we propose such primitives at several scales for the particular case of the pine-tree or fir-tree. This approach can certainly be extended to other kind of trees, or to other objects for which an a priori knowledge on the shape distribution exists.

2   Previous Work

Which aspects matter in the photometric behavior of a group of shapes ? The cumulated local illumination, the cumulated shadows, and the cumulated opacity. An a priori knowledge on the matter distribution will help to compute them. Conversely, the exact shape and location of single parts are unimportant as soon as they introduce no correlation in the visibility of parts that is not already captured in the a priori knowledge. We survey now the existing models which purpose is to represent the effects of the small scales and the rendering models of trees.

Surface shaders

Some primitives have been proposed early to figure small surface details without rendering explicitly their geometry: Blinn has introduced textures of Phong parameters [3] and bump-mapping [4] in this purpose.

Kajiya has introduced the idea of hierarchy of models [11]. In this paper, he suggests to switch from geometry to mapping of Phong parameters, then to reflectance model[1] according to the distance. Transitions from geometry to bump and from bump to reflectance have been proposed in [1, 5, 7].

Several reflectance models based on the surface micro-geometry have been developed [11, 24, 8, 17, 6, 10, 9]. Most of these models consist in proposing a representation of the matter distribution, then to integrate the local illumination while addressing the visibility of the details for the viewer and for the light (i.e. self-shadows).

Volume shaders

All the models above are designed for surface details. In the scope of 3D matter distributions, Blinn has early proposed a reflection model for volumes of dust [2] represented by micro-spheres. Stam has developed in [21] a stochastic model which allows the analytical integration of the stochastic distribution of matter to represent details in clouds. Kajiya introduced the volumetric textures [12]

_____

   [*] *iMAGIS* is a joint research project of CNRS/INRIA/UJF/INPG.
iMAGIS, INRIA Rhône-Alpes - ZIRST, 655 avenue de l'Europe, 38330
Montbonnot Saint Martin, France.

_____

[1] reflectance models are also named *shaders*.

138

in the scope of fur rendering. A shader (i.e. a local illumination model) is derived to integrate the light reflected on hairs represented by cylinders. This cylinder shader has been improved in [8] and Neyret has extended the volumetric textures representation in [14, 15] by introducing a shader able to integrate at one scale the shaders representing a thinner scale.

Contrary to the models of surface details, most of the 3D models presented above fail to address analytically the visibility of the details from the viewer or from the light. For instance the representation of the 3D microgeometry by a normal distribution in [14] cannot capture the visibility (otherwise the normal distribution should depend on the point of view), whereas the stochastic model of [22] can.

Dedicated tree rendering models

On the other hand, several models dedicated to an efficient representation and rendering of trees and forests have been proposed, using ray-tracing or real-time techniques [16, 23].

Reeves introduced the particles systems [19, 20]. This representation is dedicated to objects made of a huge amount of small long primitives that are drawn as simple strokes, well suitable for modeling trees. In his paper, the shadows are faked using a priori simple laws such as proportionality with depth inside a tree.

Max proposed in [13] a hierarchical representation of trees based on color-depth textures following the natural hierarchy of trees.

Early conclusions

To conclude at that point, we can tell that:

- shaders based on a normal distribution function difficultly account for the shadowing inside the small scale.
- shaders consisting in a sampled BRDF are more accurate, but cannot easily be parameterized.
- shaders consisting in analytical BRDF can be both visibility-compliant and parameterized but are not easy to derive.

Our key idea is that such analytical BRDF can be derived when strong a priori knowledge on the matter distribution is available. We think that the matter in trees is structured enough to offer such a possibility. In this paper we address needle-based trees such as pine-tree or fir-tree, as the a priori knowledge on needles distribution is strong.

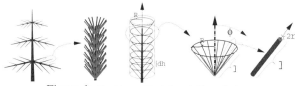

Figure 1: *Our hierarchical description of a tree.*

3 Contributions

3.1 Our model of pine-tree (see Figure 1)

- A tree is a set of branches and needles that we describe using an L-system [18].
- Branches are classical geometry (i.e. cylinders).
- Needles are cylinders, whose angle ϕ with the branch, length l, radius r, density (i.e. distribution) ρ change slowly along a branch so that they can be considered locally constant.
- The needles layer around the branch (i.e. the bough) is thus a cylinder of radius $R = l \sin(\phi)$.
- We assume that needles are spreaded on cones, with N needles per cone. The distance between cones along a branch is dh. As the gap between two needles end is $\frac{2\pi R}{N}$ and the gap between two cones is dh, it is reasonable to chose $dh = \frac{2.\pi.R}{N} = \sqrt{\rho}$. Whether it is the case or not, we have the relation $dh \frac{2\pi R}{N} = \rho$.

3.2 Multiscale rendering

Depending on the distance, the smallest primitive we consider is either the needle (level 1), the cone (level 2), or the bough (level 3). We render the scene using a simple cone-tracing: the conic ray is used to estimate the apparent size of primitives and to compute their coverage *alpha* to the pixel. We also use this cones for the shadow rays, assuming point light sources.

The main issue is to compute the global reflectance and opacity of a considered primitive, including the internal shadows. Since we use only conic rays, the rendering is processed with no oversampling at all.

Thus the main contributions of this paper are the multiscale representation that we detail in the next section, the three shaders we derive (detailed in sections 4, 5 and 6), and the method we use to solve the illumination integrals, in particular the geometric interpretation of the visibility and shadows in the level 3 model.

3.3 What we need to compute

In this section we estimate the requirement for the analytical computation of the three shaders. The results and the details of these successive integrations are the object of the three next sections. The $\vec{L}$ and $\vec{V}$ vectors are considered constant because light source and the viewer are far.

Figure 2: Left: *the continuous cone model.* Right: *the continuous bough model.*

Figure 3: A single needle.

Level 1 (needles)

To shade a needle, we need the amount of diffuse and specular light I_d and I_s reflected by a cylinder [12]. In [17] the integral is correctly expressed in pixel space. We use this form, with different bounds and a cheaper approximation for the specular integral.

We never compute explicitly the intersection of the needles with the cone-ray. We compute instead the intersection of a cone of needles, and we consider the needles that are on the visible part of the cone. Then we sum their illumination.

Level 2 (cones)

We consider that shading a cone of needles is equivalent to shading a continuous semi-opaque cone whose each point reflects the light as a local needle would (see Figure 2 left). The opacity A is the amount of the cone surface covered by needles, so is defined by $A = \frac{2Nr}{\pi R}$. The illumination is A times the integral in pixel space of the cylinder illumination on the visible part of the cone. The front and rear part are considered separately, and only a portion of these parts may be visible in a pixel. This integration is not trivial and requires several approximations.

Level 3 (boughs)

We consider that a bough to be shaded is equivalent to a semi-opaque anisotropic volumetric cylinder made of imbricated cones (see Figure 2 right). The illumination and opacity of front and rear parts of the cones correspond to the level 2 shader already derived (the front part of all the cones are equal, same for the rear parts). The volume model is both continuous and anisotropic: the opacity has to reproduce the same effect as the number of cones traversed by a ray while rendering at level 2, which is strongly dependent of the angle of the ray. The difficult part is the analytical volumetric integration of it, taking into account the visibility and the shadows. Assuming we can use a linear approximation [2] of the opacity composition law, i.e. $(1-A)^n \approx (1-n.A)$, we transpose this integral into a geometric form.

4 Cylinder illumination

We have to integrate the diffuse and specular components into screen space (i.e. we sum the contributions to the

---

[2] which is valid for $nA \ll 1$, i.e. if the bough is not too dense

---

pixel color and opacity). Either reflectance or illumination can be derived; one can trivially convert one into the other since we also compute the opacity.

- The diffuse reflectance toward the viewer is

$$R_d^{cyl} = \frac{\int_{cylinder} (N.L) \, \mathbb{1}_{(N.L>0)} (N.V) \, \mathbb{1}_{(N.V>0)} .dS}{\int_{pixel} (N.V) \, \mathbb{1}_{(N.V>0)} .dS}$$

Let c_v and c_l be the projections of V and L on the cylinder axis $\vec{a}$, i.e. $c_v = (\vec{a}.V)$ and $c_l = (\vec{a}.L)$ (see Figure 3).

Let V_p and L_p be the projections of V and L on the plane orthogonal to the cylinder, and s_v and s_l be their norm.

$$R_d^{cyl} = \frac{\int_{\alpha=\alpha_0}^{\alpha_1} s_l \cos(\alpha - \alpha_L) s_v \cos(\alpha - \alpha_V) d\alpha}{\int_{\alpha=\alpha_V - \frac{\pi}{2}}^{\alpha_V + \frac{\pi}{2}} s_v \cos(\alpha - \alpha_V) d\alpha}$$

with α_V and α_L the angles between a reference in the plane and respectively V_p and L_p. The bounds of visibility α_0 and α_1 are $\alpha_V - \frac{\pi}{2}$ and $\alpha_L + \frac{\pi}{2}$ if $L \times V$ has the same direction than $\vec{a}$. We introduce $\Delta\alpha = |\alpha_V - \alpha_L|$ and then

$$R_d^{cyl} = \frac{s_l}{4} (\sin(\Delta\alpha) + (\pi - \Delta\alpha)\cos(\Delta\alpha)) \tag{1}$$

- The specular reflectance toward the user is

$$R_s^{cyl} = \frac{\int_{cylinder} (N.H)^n \, \mathbb{1}_{(N.H>0)} (N.V) \, \mathbb{1}_{(N.V>0)} dS}{\int_{pixel} (N.V) \, \mathbb{1}_{(N.V>0)} dS}$$

with the half-way vector $H = \frac{V+L}{|V+L|}$ and n the specularity exponent.

Let H_p, c_h, s_h and α_V be defined like for L and V. Then

$$R_s^{cyl} = \frac{\int_{\alpha=\alpha_0}^{\alpha_1} s_h^n \cos^n(\alpha - \alpha_H) s_v \cos(\alpha - \alpha_V) d\alpha}{\int_{\alpha=\alpha_V - \frac{\pi}{2}}^{\alpha_V + \frac{\pi}{2}} s_v \cos(\alpha - \alpha_V) d\alpha}$$

It is well known that $\cos^n(x)$ is very similar to $e^{-\frac{n}{2}x^2}$ for n large (which is the case). Moreover the density of this function is concentrated on $x = 0$ (the standard deviation is $1/\sqrt{n}$, and n is generally greater than 100), so that $\cos^n(x - x_0) f(x) \approx \cos^n(x - x_0) f(x_0)$
Thus, we have

$$R_s^{cyl} \approx (s_h^n s_v \cos(\alpha_H - \alpha_V) \int_{\alpha=\alpha_0}^{\alpha_1} e^{-\frac{n}{2}(\alpha - \alpha_H)^2} d\alpha)/2s_v$$

Since $\int_{-\infty}^{\infty} e^{-\frac{1}{2}(\frac{x}{\sigma})^2} = \sqrt{2\pi}\sigma$, the integral above equals

$\sqrt{\frac{2\pi}{n}}$ if $\alpha_H \in [\alpha_0, \alpha_1]$ which is always the case. Thus

$$R_s^{cyl} \approx \frac{1}{2} s_h^n \cos(\alpha_H - \alpha_V) \sqrt{\frac{2\pi}{n}} \qquad (2)$$

• The opacity is the proportion of the needle apparent rectangle that falls in the pixel. If the needle is totally covered by the pixel, then

$$alpha^{cyl} = \frac{2 r . s_v l}{S_{pix}} \qquad (3)$$

where S_{pix} represents the surface of the ray-cone section at the primitive's distance. Thus the diffuse and specular illumination are $I_d = alphaR_d$ and $I_s = alphaR_s$.

5 Cone illumination

As discussed in section 3.3, we consider that the cone is a continuous semi-opaque surface of opacity A, whose each point of the surface reflects the light as a cylinder. Thus, we need to integrate the cylinder illumination into a cone of aperture ϕ for all the valid needle axis positions $\vec{a}_\theta$. In the polar coordinate system associated to the cone, we denote $L = (\theta_L, \phi_L)$, such that ϕ_L is the angle between L and the cone axis. Similarly we denote $V = (\theta_V, \phi_V)$.

• The diffuse illumination is given by:

$$I_d^{cone} = \frac{lA}{4} \int_{\theta=\theta_V-\frac{\pi}{2}}^{\theta_V+\frac{\pi}{2}} s_l s_v (\sin(\Delta\alpha) + (\pi - \Delta\alpha)\cos(\Delta\alpha))$$

where ls_v is the apparent length of a needle.

We cannot integrate analytically this formula. As such, we approximate $s_l s_v (\sin(\Delta\alpha) + (\pi - \Delta\alpha)\cos(\Delta\alpha))$ by using the function

$$F = s_l s_v (1/2 + \cos(\Delta\alpha)/2)(2 + (\pi-2)\cos(\Delta\alpha))$$

which has the same values and derivatives in 0, $\frac{\pi}{2}$ and π and which maximum error is less than 1%.
Since $\cos(\Delta\alpha) = \frac{(L_p.V_p)}{(|L_p|.|V_p|)} = \frac{(L.V) - c_l c_v}{s_l s_v}$ then
$\int F = (L.V + s_l s_v - c_l c_v).(2 + (\pi-2)(L.V - c_l c_v)/s_l s_v)$

Figure 4: Left: An example of F curve, for $L = (0, 1.2)$, $V = (1, 1.5)$ and $\phi = .5$. It is very smooth, despite its factors are quite more chaotic. Right: the FFT of this curve. Notes that the energy is clearly concentrated on the frequencies 0, 1 and 2, thus the motivation to fit F with a linear combination of 1, $\cos(\theta - \theta_A)$, $\cos(2(\theta - \theta_B))$. NB: the values at the extreme right are the mirroring due to the FFT.

When tracing this function with Maple for many values of the parameters L, V and ϕ, it appears that the curve is very smooth (Figure 4 left), and looks like a linear combination of 1, $\cos(\theta - \theta_A)$ and $\cos(2(\theta - \theta_B))$. The FFT evaluation on discretized curves shows that there is practically no energy out of the frequencies 0, 1 and 2 (Figure 4 right). As such, we try to fit such a curve to F from the location and value of its extrema. The first

factor capture most of the variations of F and is more easy to analyze, so to fit the curve we approximate F by $(L.V) + s_l s_v - c_l c_v$ which seems to have its extrema at the same θ value than F.
The term $c_l c_v - s_l s_v$ equals $\cos(\widehat{AL} + \widehat{AV})$ with $\widehat{AL}$ the angle between the vectors $\vec{a}$ and L, and $\widehat{AV}$ the angle between the vectors $\vec{a}$ and V. These angles vary smoothly between a minimum and a maximum while $\vec{a}$ rotates along the cone, so we model the variation of $\widehat{AL}$ by the form $A_L + B_L \cos(\theta - \theta_L)$ with $A_L = \max(\phi_L, \phi)$, $B_L = \min(\phi_L, \phi)$. We do the same for $\widehat{AV}$.
If we develop $\widehat{AL} + \widehat{AV}$ with this approximation we obtain the expression $A_\Sigma + B_\Sigma \cos(\theta - \theta_\Sigma)$ with
$A_\Sigma = A_L + A_V$, $B_\Sigma^2 = B_L^2 + B_V^2 + 2B_L B_V \cos(\theta_L - \theta_V)$,
$\cos(\theta_\Sigma) = (B_L \cos(\theta_L) + B_V \cos(\theta_V))/B_\Sigma$,
$\sin(\theta_\Sigma) = (B_L \sin(\theta_L) + B_V \sin(\theta_V))/B_\Sigma$

Figure 5: The two aspects for the curve $\cos(A_\Sigma + B_\Sigma * \cos(\theta - \theta_\Sigma))$, depending whether $A_\Sigma + B_\Sigma * \cos(\theta - \theta_\Sigma)$ crosses π (right) or not (left).

We can now search for the extrema of $F \approx (L.V) - \cos(\widehat{AL} + \widehat{AV})$. They correspond either to the extrema of $\widehat{AL} + \widehat{AV}$ or to the location for which $\widehat{AL} + \widehat{AV}$ crosses π. If $\widehat{AL} + \widehat{AV}$ does not cross π, F looks like a cosine function. If it does, F has a hat shape and looks like the combination of a cosine and a cosine at double frequency (see Figure 5). The similarity is high if ϕ_L and ϕ_V are not very close to ϕ. Thus, we can now obtain explicitly the extrema of the curve.
As we are precisely trying to fit F to the form
$(L.V) - (\lambda_0 + \lambda_1 \cos(\theta - \theta_m) + \lambda_2 \cos(2(\theta - \theta_m)))$
we just have to set the parameters from these extrema:
let $M = \cos(A_\Sigma - B_\Sigma)$ and $m = \cos(A_\Sigma + B_\Sigma)$.
Then $\theta_m = \theta_\Sigma$, $\lambda_1 = \frac{(m-M)}{2}$, $\lambda_0 = \frac{(m+M)}{2} - \lambda_2$, with $\lambda_2 = 0$ if no crossing of π occurs (both $A_\Sigma + B_\Sigma$ and $A_\Sigma - B_\Sigma$ are in $[0, \pi]$),
$\lambda_2 = \frac{\lambda_1 B_\Sigma}{4(2\pi - A_\Sigma)}$ in case of crossing of π ($A_\Sigma + B_\Sigma > \pi > A_\Sigma - B_\Sigma$), Now we can easily obtain the integral of F :

$$I_d^{cone} = \frac{lA}{4}(\pi(LV - \lambda_0) - 2\lambda_1 \cos(\theta_V - \theta_\Sigma)) \qquad (4)$$

where $\cos(\theta_V - \theta_\Sigma) = \frac{B_L \cos(\Delta\theta) + B_V}{\sqrt{B_L^2 + B_V^2 + 2B_L B_V \cos(\Delta\theta)}}$ and $\Delta\theta = \theta_L - \theta_V$.

• The specular illumination is given by

$$I_s^{cone} = \frac{lA}{2} \sqrt{\frac{2\pi}{n}} \int_{\theta=\theta_V-\frac{\pi}{2}}^{\theta_V+\frac{\pi}{2}} s_l s_h^n \cos(\alpha_H - \alpha_V)$$

with ls_v the apparent length of a needle. Once again, s_h^n is a function which density is concentrated on the location where $s_h = 1$, which occurs when $c_h = 0$, i.e. when H is orthogonal to the needle direction $\vec{a}$. Such a location $\theta_H^\perp$ only exists if $\phi_H \in [\frac{\pi}{2} - \phi, \frac{\pi}{2} + \phi]$, otherwise $I_s^{cone} = 0$.

If $\theta_H^\perp$ exists, we have again that $s_h^n f(\theta) \approx s_h^n f(\theta_H^\perp)$.
Since $s_l s_h \cos(\alpha_H - \alpha_V) = (V.H) - c_h c_v$, we finally have

$$I_s^{cone} \approx \frac{l.A}{2}\frac{2\pi}{n}(V.H)\varepsilon \tag{5}$$

where $\varepsilon = 1$ if $\phi_H \in [\frac{\pi}{2} - \phi, \frac{\pi}{2} + \phi]$ otherwise $\varepsilon = 0$.
Note that if both locations where H is orthogonal to $\vec{a}$ occurs on the same face (front or rear), we have that $\varepsilon = 2$.

- The opacity is given by $alpha^{cone} = A \int_{\theta=\theta_V - \frac{\pi}{2}}^{\theta_V + \frac{\pi}{2}} ls_v$

Since $s_v = \sin(\widehat{AV})$, we approximate $\widehat{AV}$ by $A_V + B_V \cos(\theta - \theta_V)$ in the same way that for the diffuse component. That is,

$$alpha^{cone} = l.A(\pi \cos(\phi)\cos(\phi_V) - 2\sin(\phi)\sin(\phi_V)) \tag{6}$$

6 Bough illumination

As stated in section 3.3, we consider that the bough is a volume having a cylindrical shape and an anisotropic opacity (as illustrated in Figure 6). We have to proceed to the analytical volume rendering of this cylinder.

Since the opacity A is not constant along the ray and the shadow ray, we have:

$$I = \frac{1}{S_{pix}} \int_{(x,y)\in\,pixel} \int_{z=near}^{far} A l^{cyl} e^{-\int_0^{l_z}\sigma} e^{-\int_0^{l_{shad}}\sigma} \tag{7}$$

with $e^{-\sigma} = T = (1-A)$ the anisotropic transparency, l_z the length of the ray within the volume and l_{shad} the length of the shadow ray within the volume.
We need now to explicit the opacity and to do some approximations to make the integral tractable.

6.1 Traversal of a 2D bough

Given an infinite 2D vertical field of parallel needles having a direction ϕ relatively to the top (see Figure 7 left). Let R be the field width, and dh the vertical distance between the needles. A ray in the direction ϕ_r relative to the top crosses the field.
The length of the ray within the field is $R/\sin(\phi_r)$
The step between the intersections is $\delta = dh\frac{\sin(\phi)}{\sin|\phi_r - \phi|}$
The average number of intersections is $\frac{R}{dh}\frac{\sin|\phi_r - \phi|}{\sin(\phi)\sin(\phi_r)}$
We denote $k(\phi_r, \phi)$ the quantity $\frac{\sin|\phi_r - \phi|}{\sin(\phi)\sin(\phi_r)} = |\frac{1}{\tan(\phi)} - \frac{1}{\tan(\phi_r)}|$
The opacity of the field along this ray is $1 - T^{\frac{R}{dh}k(\phi_r,\phi)}$
Let denote for short $k_r = k(\phi_r, \phi)$ and $\bar{k}_r = k(\phi_r, \pi - \phi)$
$\bar{k}_r$ corresponds to the traversal of a field which is symmetrical to the first relatively to the vertical.

A 2D bough is composed of two adjacent such fields, the right one with needles of orientation ϕ, and the left one with needles of orientation $\pi - \phi$ (as illustrated on Figure 7 left).
The total number of intersections along a ray is
$\frac{R}{dh}(k_r + \bar{k}_r) = \frac{R}{dh}\frac{\sin|\phi_r - \phi| + \sin|\phi_r + \phi|}{\sin(\phi)\sin(\phi_r)} = \frac{R}{dh}\frac{2}{\tan(\min(\phi,\phi_r))}$
This means that as long as the ray remains outside the

Figure 6: Left : We model a bough by a semi-opaque volumetric cylinder, which opacity is anisotropic in order to reproduce the variation of the number or intersection between a ray and the sub cones.
Right : Intersection of the plane P_x with one cone. We approximate the hyberbols by their asymptotes.

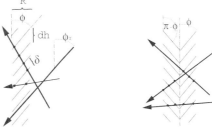

Figure 7: Left: 2D field of parallel 'needles'. Right: 2D bough. Note the variation of the opacity with the ray direction (mostly on left).

cone aperture (i.e. $\phi_r \in [\phi, \pi - \phi]$) the total opacity along the ray is constant, despite it is balanced differently between the front and the rear part. This is true either for a ray or a shadow ray: similarly for the light, in such condition the shadow casted by the bough is constant, while the light enters more easily in one side than in the other. If the ray is inside the cone aperture (above or below), the opacity increases up to 100% for $\phi_r = 0$ or π.

6.2 Extension to a 3D bough

Let us now come back to our regular bough. In 3D, if a ray crosses the axis of the bough, the situation is equivalent to the 2D situation above. But generally the ray does not cross the axis. Let consider the plane parallel to the cone axis and that contains the ray. Let x be its distance to the axis, thus we name the plane P_x. The intersection of the volume of the bough made of cones with the plane gives a set of hyperboles. We approximate these hyperboles by their two asymptotes (we can see on Figure 6 right that it is reasonable). In that way, the plane contains 'needles' having the same orientation ϕ and offset dh than in 3D, in a field of shrieked thickness $2R_x$ with $R_x = \sqrt{R^2 - x^2}$. So we can compute the number of intersections using the 2D formulas. To estimate the amount of light reaching a point on the ray, we consider a shadow ray starting at that point. Similarly, we introduce the plane parallel to the cone axis and that contains the shadow ray (Figure 8). The number of intersections can be obtained as for the main ray.

6.3 Traversal of a 3D bough

We can now come back to the volumetric integral 7. We choose the (x,y) pixel-surface parameterization so that the $\vec{x}$ axis is orthogonal to the cylinder. Thus x indexes the plane P_x (i.e. x is coherent with the previous section). In consequence we no longer need to integrate along the $\vec{y}$ axis, since the cylinder is homogeneous in this direction. Note that the albedo A in the equation should be corrected to A/δ, since no energy is gathered in the gap between two cones. Similarly on a differential length dl, the opacity is $e^{-\sigma dl} = T^{dl/\delta}$. We proceed to a variable change from (x,z) to (x,z') in the plane orthogonal to the cylinder. This means that we index a point on the ray by its projection on the orthogonal plane. The Jacobian of the transform is $\frac{1}{\sin(\phi)}$. The opacity associated to a differential length dl' on the plane is $T^{\frac{dl'}{\sin(\phi)\delta}} = T^{dl'\frac{k()}{dh}}$

6.4 Splitting the integral into regions

We know from the 2D case that the opacity along the ray is constant on the front half and on the rear half of the traversal (These two halves correspond to the two orientations of the needles in the plane P_x).

The disk has been split into two regions F_V and R_V, the front and the rear relatively to V. On each region $k()$ is constant. In section 5 we have also split the cones into a front face and a rear face, to evaluate the illumination. Let assume that I^{cyl} is constant in each of the two regions of the volume and let approximate it by the mean value I^{cyl}_{front} and I^{cyl}_{rear}. The integral becomes:

$$I = \frac{A}{2Rdh}\int_{x=-R}^{R}\left(k_v I^{cyl}_{front}\int_{z=-R_x}^{0} T^{\frac{k_v}{dh}(R_x+z)} T\int_{0}^{l_{shad}\frac{k()}{dh}} + \bar{k}_v I^{cyl}_{rear}\int_{z=0}^{R_x} T^{(\frac{k_v}{dh}R_x+\frac{\bar{k}_v}{dh}z)} T\int_{0}^{l_{shad}\frac{k()}{dh}}\right)$$

In order to get rid of the remaining integral in the exponent, we are now going to split again the disk to separate the front and the rear areas F_L and R_L relatively to L. However the shadow ray length that will appear depends on z on a complicated way, which makes the exponential tricky to integrate analytically.

In order to make the integral tractable, we use the linear approximation of the opacity composition law,

i.e. $(1-A)^n \approx (1-nA)$ which is valid if $nA \ll 1$, i.e. if the bough is not too dense.

Then $(1-A)^{n_1}(1-A)^{n_2} \approx 1 - n_1 A - n_2 A$, which ensures the separation of the factors. Thus the integral is defined as $I = I_{F_V} + I_{R_V} = \frac{A}{2Rdh}\left(I^{cyl}_{front}k_v I_{F'_V} + I^{cyl}_{rear}\bar{k}_v I_{R'_V}\right)$ with

$$I_{F'_V} = \int_{F_V}1 - A\int_{F_V}\frac{k_v}{dh}(R_x+z) - A\int_{F_V\times R_L}z_{shad}\frac{\bar{k}_l}{dh} - A\int_{F_V\times F_L}z_{shad}\frac{k_l}{dh}$$

$$I_{R'_V} = \int_{R_V}1 - A\int_{R_V}(\frac{k_v}{dh}R_x+\frac{\bar{k}_v}{dh}z) - A\int_{R_V\times R_L}z_{shad}\frac{\bar{k}_l}{dh} - A\int_{R_V\times F_L}z_{shad}\frac{k_l}{dh}$$

with $F_V \times R_L$ the region in R_L covered by shadow rays which origin is in F_V, and so on for the other composed regions (see on Figure 8 the representation of these surfaces).

6.5 Geometric integration

We can arrange this as:
$$I_{F'_V} = \pi\frac{R^3}{2} - A\frac{k_v}{dh}\frac{2}{3}R^3 - A\frac{k_l}{dh}\int_{F_V\times R_l}z_{shad} - A\frac{k_l}{dh}\int_{F_V\times F_L}z_{shad}$$

$$I_{R'_V} = \pi\frac{R^2}{2} - A\frac{k_v}{dh}\frac{4}{3}R^3 - A\frac{\bar{k}_v}{dh}\frac{2}{3}R^3 - A\frac{\bar{k}_l}{dh}\int_{R_V\times R_L}z_{shad} - A\frac{k_l}{dh}\int_{R_V\times F_L}z_{shad}$$

The four remaining integrals sum the length of the shadow rays starting in each point along the ray and included in the region in subscript, for each ray. Let consider for the moment only the integral along the ray. The shadow-ray sweeps an area while its origin follows the ray. The integral of its length value along the main ray has a strong connection with this surface: it is proportional to it, with a factor $\frac{1}{\sin(l_v)}$ where l_v is the angle between the projections L_P and V_P of L and V in the orthogonal plane. The proof is that if L_P is orthogonal to V_P, then the integral of the length is the regular surface measurement. Otherwise one can come back to this case with a change of variables, which the Jacobian is $\frac{1}{\sin(l_v)}$. So, to compute the integral along the ray, we have to measure the surface of each swept region S_1, S_2, S_3, S_4 using some geometric and trigonometric relations. Then we have to integrate the result for each ray. After some long and unpleasant derivations showing quite complicated formulas in the intermediate stages, we surprisingly found very simple and symmetric results (without any approximation):

$$\int S_1 = (1+\cos(l_v))\frac{R^3}{3}\sin(l_v)$$
$$\int S_2 = (1-\cos(l_v))\frac{R^3}{3}\sin(l_v)$$
$$\int S_3 = (1+\cos(l_v)/3)R^3\sin(l_v)$$
$$\int S_4 = (1-\cos(l_v)/3)R^3\sin(l_v)$$

The $\sin(l_v)$ factors disappear when multiplying by the Jacobian.

6.6 Resulting bough illumination

The opacity is derived trivially:
$$1 - \alpha_{F_V} = \frac{1}{2R}\int_{x=-R}^{R}A^{R_x\frac{k_v}{dh}} \approx 1 - \frac{AR}{dh}\frac{\pi}{4}k_v$$

i.e. $\boxed{\alpha_{F_V} = ak_v \;,\;\; \alpha_{R_V} = a\bar{k}_v}$ with $a = \frac{AR}{dh}\frac{\pi}{4}$

We introduce similarly the opacity for the light point of view: $\alpha_{F_L} = ak_l \;,\;\; \alpha_{R_L} = a\bar{k}_l$ and finally have $I = I_{F_V} + I_{R_V}$ with

$$\boxed{I_{F_V} = I^{cyl}_{front}\alpha_{F_V}\left(1 - \frac{8}{3\pi^2}\left(2\alpha_{F_V} + (1-\cos(lv))\alpha_{R_L} + (3-\cos(lv))\alpha_{F_L}\right)\right)}$$

$$\boxed{I_{R_V} = I^{cyl}_{rear}\alpha_{R_V}\left(1 - \frac{8}{3\pi^2}\left(4\alpha_{F_V} + 2\alpha_{R_V} + (1+\cos(lv))\alpha_{R_L} + (3+\cos(lv))\alpha_{F_L}\right)\right)}$$

We leave this formula into two separated parts, which allows to render a branch between them.

7 Results

Some resulting images are presented of Figure 9 and Figure 10. We have also compute an animation of the forest scene showing no aliasing artifact.

A major property of our model is the evolution of the cost when the number of needles vary, i.e. the complexity analysis in function of the number N of needles per cone and of the number $\frac{l}{dh}$ of cones on a branch per unit of length (these two numbers are proportional to the square root of the density of needles)[3]. The cost of one shadow ray should evolve the same. However a classical ray-tracer launches a shadow ray for each sample, while for our model the part of the shadow ray that is outside the bough is factorized.

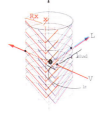 

Figure 8: Left: *The volume intersected by the vertical plane containing the ray looks like a 2D bough. Similarly for the shadow ray.* Right: *The volume of the bough cylinder seen in an orthogonal section. The surface of the four regions (see left Figure) $S_1 = F_V \times R_L$, $S_2 = F_V \times F_L$, $S_3 = R_V \times R_L$, $S_4 = R_V \times F_L$ are proportional to the integral of the length of the shadow rays for each possible origin on the ray (only the generic case is figured here). We have to integrate these surfaces for all x.*

We have compared the efficiency to a classical ray-tracer, Rayshade. On Rayshade side, it is important to know that there is a maximum amount of ray per pixel (which is 64), so that when a tree is far (i.e. less than 100 pixels high), Rayshade does not launch enough rays. It might seems efficient, but this is at the price of quality. The fact is that for a image with a lot of high frequencies as image of trees are, the aliasing is not very visible on a single image because it is hard to distinguish noise and information. But the aliasing is obvious during an animation.

The test scene consists of 80 fir-trees that are about 127 pixels high for the closest and 64 for the farthest (Figure 11).

Figure 9: Three fir-trees, from a very close to a far point of view.

---

[3]if N is multiplied by 2, the number of intersections for level 1 and the number of samples per pixel a ray-tracer should launch are multiplied by 2, while level 2 and level 3 are not affected at all. The same deduction could be done if dh is divided by 2

Figure 10: Trees on a hill.

Figure 11: The scene used for the benchmark.

Figure 12: The colors represent the level that is used in our method: red for level 1, green for level 2 and blue for level 3.

144

One fir generally contains 300 branches and about 28700 needles, thus the scene contains about 2 million of needles. Concerning one bough, a cone is 3.94 high, has a radius of 1.6cm, an aperture of $\pi/8$, and the offset between cones is 0.9cm. There are only 12 needles per cone for this tree, whose radius is 0.05cm and length is 4.25cm. On average 4.37 cones are imbricated, so that a ray passing through the axis and orthogonal to the branch would traverse on average 8.75 layers. We run our tests on an SGI Onyx2. The rendering time is 65.3 minutes with Rayshade and 8.1 minutes with our models. Thus our method is about 8 times faster than Rayshade. For landscapes, whose farthest trees are very small, rayshade cannot avoid aliasing due to its 64 samples per pixel limitation. If it could override this limit, the gain would greatly increase in the favor of our method.

8 Conclusion

We have introduced a set of three shaders able to represent at various scales the cumulated effects of the smaller scales without having to sample them, comprising the internal shadows, and taking the visibility into account. As all the required integrations are analytical, this provides at the same time efficiency and image quality (in particular, free of aliasing). However on the theoretical point of view, we would like to improve some of the approximations that have been done. Relaxing the low albedo hypothesis would be interesting either, e.g. using a polynomial law instead of a linear approximation.

The parameters of the shaders allow us to simulate various kind of pine-trees and fir-trees, and to modulate the characteristics inside a single tree (these modulations could be driven in time as well, e.g. to simulate the effects of the wind in a tree). We were able to derive these shaders because the objects we were interested in are very structured. Due to the extended use of the a priori knowledge, these three shaders can simulate nothing but trees made of needles. However, many objects in nature present one kind of structure or another, and even some similarities of structure, so it should be possible for each to derive shaders able to represent analytically each kind. The next step for us will be the simulation of other kind of trees, for which the structure is more stochastic (concerning the distribution and orientation of the leaves). Then it will be also interesting to handle larger scales, exploring larger structures than boughs inside and outside the trees...

Acknowledgments : We wish to thank Celine Loscos and Eugenia Montiel for re-reading this paper. Thanks to Pierre Poulin for discussing during this work.

References

[1] Barry G. Becker and Nelson L. Max. Smooth transitions between bump rendering algorithms. In James T. Kajiya, editor, *Computer Graphics (SIGGRAPH '93 Proceedings)*, volume 27, pages 183–190, August 1993.

[2] J. F. Blinn. Light reflection functions for simulation of clouds and dusty surfaces. In *Computer Graphics (SIGGRAPH '82 Proceedings)*, volume 16(3), pages 21–29, July 1982.

[3] James F. Blinn. Models of light reflection for computer synthesized pictures. In James George, editor, *Computer Graphics (SIGGRAPH '77 Proceedings)*, volume 11(2), pages 192–198, July 1977.

[4] James F. Blinn. Simulation of wrinkled surfaces. In *Computer Graphics (SIGGRAPH '78 Proceedings)*, volume 12(3), pages 286–292, August 1978.

[5] Brian Cabral, Nelson Max, and Rebecca Springmeyer. Bidirectional reflection functions from surface bump maps. In Maureen C. Stone, editor, *Computer Graphics (SIGGRAPH '87 Proceedings)*, volume 21(4), pages 273–281, July 1987.

[6] R. L. Cook and K. E. Torrance. A reflectance model for computer graphics. *ACM Transactions on Graphics*, 1(1):7–24, January 1982.

[7] Alain Fournier. Normal distribution functions and multiple surfaces. In *Graphics Interface '92 Workshop on Local Illumination*, pages 45–52, May 1992.

[8] Dan B. Goldman. Fake fur rendering. *Proceedings of SIGGRAPH 97*, pages 127–134, August 1997. ISBN 0-89791-896-7. Held in Los Angeles, California.

[9] Jay S. Gondek, Gary W. Meyer, and Jonathan G. Newman. Wavelength dependent reflectance functions. In Andrew Glassner, editor, *Proceedings of SIGGRAPH '94 (Orlando, Florida, July 24–29, 1994)*, Computer Graphics Proceedings, pages 213–220. ACM SIGGRAPH, July 1994.

[10] Xiao D. He, Kenneth E. Torrance, François X. Sillion, and Donald P. Greenberg. A comprehensive physical model for light reflection. *Computer Graphics (Proceedings of SIGGRAPH 91)*, 25(4):175–186, July 1991. ISBN 0-201-56291-X. Held in Las Vegas, Nevada.

[11] James T. Kajiya. Anisotropic reflection models. In B. A. Barsky, editor, *Computer Graphics (SIGGRAPH '85 Proceedings)*, volume 19(3), pages 15–21, July 1985.

[12] James T. Kajiya and Timothy L. Kay. Rendering fur with three dimensional textures. In Jeffrey Lane, editor, *Computer Graphics (SIGGRAPH '89 Proceedings)*, volume 23(3), pages 271–280, July 1989.

[13] Nelson Max. Hierarchical rendering of trees from precomputed multi-layer Z-buffers. In Xavier Pueyo and Peter Schröder, editors, *Eurographics Rendering Workshop 1996*, pages 165–174. Eurographics, Springer Wein, June 1996. ISBN 3-211-82883-4.

[14] Fabrice Neyret. A general and multiscale method for volumetric textures. In *Graphics Interface '95 Proceedings*, pages 83–91, May 1995.

[15] Fabrice Neyret. Modeling animating and rendering complex scenes using volumetric textures. *IEEE Transactions on Visualization and Computer Graphics*, 4(1), January–March 1998. ISSN 1077-2626.

[16] Tsukasa Noma. Bridging between surface rendering and volume rendering for multi-resolution display. In *6th Eurographics Workshop on Rendering*, pages 31–40, June 1995.

[17] Pierre Poulin and Alain Fournier. A model for anisotropic reflection. In Forest Baskett, editor, *Computer Graphics (SIGGRAPH '90 Proceedings)*, volume 24(4), pages 273–282, August 1990.

[18] Przemyslaw Prusinkiewicz, Aristid Lindenmayer, and James Hanan. Developmental models of herbaceous plants for computer imagery purposes. In John Dill, editor, *Computer Graphics (SIGGRAPH '88 Proceedings)*, volume 22, pages 141–150, August 1988.

[19] W. T. Reeves. Particle systems – a technique for modeling a class of fuzzy objects. *ACM Trans. Graphics*, 2:91–108, April 1983.

[20] William T. Reeves and Ricki Blau. Approximate and probabilistic algorithms for shading and rendering structured particle systems. In B. A. Barsky, editor, *Computer Graphics (SIGGRAPH '85 Proceedings)*, volume 19(3), pages 313–322, July 1985.

[21] Jos Stam. Stochastic rendering of density fields. In *Proceedings of Graphics Interface '94*, pages 51–58, Banff, Alberta, Canada, May 1994. Canadian Information Processing Society.

[22] Jos Stam and Eugene Fiume. A multiple-scale stochastic modelling primitive. *Graphics Interface '91*, pages 24–31, June 1991.

[23] Jason Weber and Joseph Penn. Creation and rendering of realistic trees. In Robert Cook, editor, *Computer Graphics (SIGGRAPH '95 Proceedings)*, pages 119–128, August 1995.

[24] Stephen H. Westin, James R. Arvo, and Kenneth E. Torrance. Predicting reflectance functions from complex surfaces. *Computer Graphics (Proceedings of SIGGRAPH 92)*, 26(2):255–264, July 1992. ISBN 0-201-51585-7. Held in Chicago, Illinois.

Anisotropic Feature-Preserving Denoising of Height Fields and Bivariate Data

Mathieu Desbrun[†][‡] Mark Meyer[†] Peter Schröder[†] Alan H. Barr[†]

[†] Caltech - [‡] USC

(a)   (b)

Figure 1: *Mars elevation map: (a) raw data, (b) smooth version after anisotropic diffusion. Notice how, with our non-uniform diffusion, the aliasing due to poor quantization is suppressed without altering the general topography of the surface (both pictures are flat-shaded).*

Abstract

In this paper, we present an efficient way to denoise bivariate data like height fields, color pictures or vector fields, while preserving edges and other features. Mixing surface area minimization, graph flow, and nonlinear edge-preservation metrics, our method generalizes previous anisotropic diffusion approaches in image processing, and is applicable to data of arbitrary dimension. Another notable difference is the use of a more robust discrete differential operator, which captures the fundamental surface properties. We demonstrate the method on range images and height fields, as well as greyscale or color images.

CR Categories: I.3.7 [Computer Graphics] Three-Dimensional Graphics and Realism; I.4.3 [Image Processing and Computer Vision] Enhancement.

Keywords: Anisotropic diffusion, Re-parameterization, Surface flows, Edge preservation, Image processing, Surface fairing.

1 Introduction

The problem of smoothing surfaces in computer graphics is closely related to the smoothing of images in computer vision. In both cases, we wish to smooth a 2-dimensional dataset, while preserving important features such as discontinuities. The discontinuities represent cliffs in height fields, and edges in images (edges in images arise when the associated height-field values—intensities of the image—change sharply with position).

To reduce the noise in images, early research has advocated the use of the laplacian as a local differential operator. Diffusing the signal using laplacian smoothing will reduce high frequency noise. Unfortunately, an unintended consequence is that the noise is diffused uniformly in screen space. Sharp edges and other fundamental features of an image are then lost, blurred away by the uniform diffusion. Consequently, anisotropic operators have been proposed. They can diffuse the signal non-uniformly to better preserve edges, while reducing noise in the signal.

The concept of noise removal with preservation of edges can be used for denoising textures acquired from images, or generalized for meshes to preserve features while removing small bumps, or even for reducing quantization effects in height fields. In this paper, we propose a technique for all these applications. Using robust differential geometry tools developed in the discrete domain for computer graphics, we define a non-linear anisotropic diffusion operator valid for any bivariate data (height fields, greyscale images, color images, tensor images). We explain the relations between our approach and previous work in image processing, and show results to demonstrate its reliability.

1.1 Anisotropic Diffusion in Image Processing

The first inhomogeneous diffusion model was introduced by Perona and Malik [PM90]. The idea was to vary the conduction spatially to favor noise removal in nearly homogeneous regions while avoiding any alteration of the signal along significant discontinuities (see [TT99] for an intuitive explanation of this technique). The change in intensity I over time was defined as:

$$I_t = div(\ g(||\nabla I||)\ \nabla I)\ \text{ with: } g(x) = \frac{1}{1 + \frac{x^2}{\alpha}}. \quad (1)$$

Many different variations on the conduction function g have been proposed [ROF92, ABBFC97, ALM92], and recently a higher order PDE has been introduced by Tumblin [TT99] in the context of displaying high contrast computer graphics pictures. Similar techniques have been used to visualize complex flow fields, as in [PR99]. All of these approaches rely on isophotes of the image (see Figure 2(a)): the anisotropic diffusion equation can be interpreted as a diffusion mainly in the direction tangential to each isophote. Therefore, discontinuities present in the orthogonal direction are not lost, as explained in [KDA97]. Typically, finite difference schemes are used to discretize the differential operators used.

Some of these approaches also use an inverse diffusion process orthogonal to the isophotes to enhance edges; this process, being very unstable by nature, requires a pre-smoothing of the gradient for the well-posedness of the problem.

However, in general, relying only on isophotes to restore a noisy image is questionable: non-uniform lighting (glares, specularity effects) often enhance our understanding of a scene while significantly affecting isophotes in complex ways. Other anisotropic diffusion models are therefore desirable.

1.2 Overview of Our Approach

In the remainder of this paper, we will develop a geometric framework for the denoising of images using a *surface-based* approach inspired by [DMSB99]. We will show how:

- a careful examination of the smoothing problem for surfaces in computer graphics,
- a straightforward adaptation to graph flows through reparameterization, and
- a penalization along edges

will allow us to define a *simple and very general denoising technique based on surface area minimization*. This will lead to 3D curvature-based models, mimicking diffusion with respect to the metric induced by the image itself instead of the usual screen space metric. Moreover, the numerical method to implement this technique will use this very nature of surface area minimization over the discrete data, ensuring a natural, accurate operator to integrate the resulting flow.

The generality of our framework enables us to use this technique on data of any dimensionality, such as greyscale or color images, with an overhead only linear in the dimension. We will also demonstrate how range images can be treated naturally with this method, offering better smoothing of a scanned surface than previous methods. More complex data, like flow fields or tensor images, can be treated in the exact same way by extending the concept of curvature for bivariate data in higher dimensions.

This paper is organized as follows: Section 2 establishes the main notation and discusses related work about surface flows. In Section 3, we derive a parameterization-independent flow for greyscale images before generalizing the approach to higher dimensional data such as color images (Section 4). We present a robust numerical scheme to integrate our flow in Section 5, then show results in Section 6 and conclude in Section 7.

2 Background on Surface Flows

A number of approaches for denoising in image processing research consider an image as a 2-manifold embedded in 3D: the image $I(x, y)$ is regarded as a surface $(x, y, I(x, y))$ in a three dimensional space, as depicted in Figure 2(b). Embedding the image in a higher dimension allows us to use richer and more meaningful differential operators. In this section, we review the different methods based on this idea, and give general definitions that we will build upon later.

2.1 Intensity as a 2-manifold

An image $I(x, y)$, usually considered as a function on a 2D plane (x, y), can also be regarded as a surface $(x, y, I(x, y))$ in a three dimensional space as depicted in Figure 2(b). The surface $S = (x, y, I(x, y))$ is sometimes called a Monge surface, or simply a *height field* as the intensity represents an elevation along the z direction of the (x, y, z) space. As we will see in the remainder of this

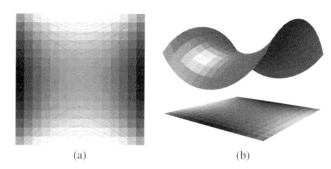

(a)   (b)

Figure 2: *The intensity map $I(x, y)$ of an image can be thought of as (a) a set of isophotes, or (b) a height field $(x, y, z = I(x, y))$.*

paper, considering an image as a surface, will allow us to use some well known differential geometry properties to design appropriate differential operators.

We will denote by **n** the normal of the surface S, and will use $\mathcal{W}$, the square root of the first fundamental form determinant of the surface [DHKW92, Gra98]. This latter quantity measures at a given point on the surface the area expansion between the parameter domain and the surface itself: a surface dA on the screen (parameter domain, also called screen space in our context) will then represent a surface area of $\mathcal{W} \, dA$ on the height field. Due to the simplicity of a height field, we can write:

$$\mathcal{W} = \sqrt{1 + I_x^2 + I_y^2} \qquad (2)$$

$$\mathbf{n} = \frac{1}{\mathcal{W}}(-I_x, -I_y, 1), \qquad (3)$$

where I_x (resp. I_y) is the first derivative of I with respect to x (resp. y).

2.2 Laplace-Beltrami Operator

As mentioned earlier, many recent approaches have focused on diffusing 2D isophote curves. For an image regarded as an embedding in 3D, a natural extension of this idea is to consider *surface diffusion*. The 2D curvature operator is then replaced by the mean curvature in 3D, denoted κ hereafter. A differential operator measures this mean curvature: the *Laplace-Beltrami operator*. Traditionally denoted Δ_g [DHKW92], this operator gives the mean curvature normal of the surface S:

$$\Delta_g S = 2\kappa \mathbf{n}.$$

Commonly used in differential geometry [DHKW92, Gra98], it is often referred as the natural generalization of the laplacian from flat spaces to general manifolds, as it uses the induced metric of the surface itself, not the metric of the parameter domain.

Almost all surface flow techniques consider this mean curvature normal for edge-preserving denoising, albeit in significantly varying ways. We briefly review these different flows used in image processing and vision, along with their motivations:

- Malladi and Sethian [MS96] proposed: $I_t = \mathcal{W}\kappa$ to implement the geometrically natural mean curvature flow. Contrary to the conventional laplacian filtering, it is an anisotropic flow more appropriate for a scale-space. They also derive a min/max flow, thresholding the curvature locally depending on local averages.

- Extending the Perona-Malik formulation for an intensity height field, Ford and El-Fallah [FEF98] proposed an inhomogeneous diffusion with a coefficient inversely proportional to the gradient magnitude:

$$I_t = div(\frac{1}{\sqrt{1 + I_x^2 + I_y^2}}(-I_x, -I_y, 1)^t).$$

Since this expression is actually the divergence of the unit normal **n** to the surface, we can reformulate it as:

$$I_t = -2\,\kappa.$$

They show how this flow provides good experimental results for noise removal with edge preservation, and give a FD (finite difference) algorithm to implement it using the Sobel operator for the evaluation of derivatives.

- Finally, Kimmel, Malladi and Sochen [KMS97, SKM98] proposed a framework for non-linear diffusion where equations are derived by minimizing a functional. Using the extended Polyakov action, which reduces to the surface area functional for 2D greyscale images, they obtained the Beltrami operator as the associated parameterization-independent Euler-Lagrange equation. To introduce an edge preserving flow, they proposed the following technique, called Beltrami flow:

$$I_t = -\Delta_g S \cdot \mathbf{e}_z = \frac{1}{\mathcal{W}}\kappa$$

where $\mathbf{e}_z$ is the unit vector in the z (intensity) direction. We will come back to this derivation in more detail in Section 3.2.1, as our derivation follows similar lines, although resulting in a different flow.

2.3 Discussion

In all previous methods, the mean curvature plays a central role. Curvature normal flow has a known connection to *surface minimization*: Lagrange already noticed that $\kappa = 0$ is the Euler-Lagrange for the surface area functional [DHKW92], meaning that the curvature normal flow minimizes surface area. But, to the authors' knowledge this property has not been used to derive a robust numerical scheme. We present in this paper both a geometrically-sound denoising flow based on surface area minimization and a discrete integration scheme following the geometric interpretation of the flow in a natural way. The next section explains the foundations of our new approach using greyscale images, while the rest of the paper will extend this method to color images and higher dimensional data.

3 Denoising of Greyscale Images

In this section, we present our first contribution in which we carefully derive a way to denoise greyscale images using surface considerations. We will show how it relates to previous work, and will demonstrate that this approach has desirable properties. Although we restrict ourselves to greyscale images in this section, the following derivation will be the backbone of our generalization to higher dimensional data.

3.1 Denoising Flow of a 3D surface

For better insight, we first explore the different methods to denoise a 3D surface. As we are about to see, crucial geometric properties have to be satisfied to achieve accurate results.

3.1.1 Curvature Flow of Arbitrary 3D Meshes

Recent work in computer graphics has demonstrated the efficiency of the mean curvature flow in removing undesirable noise from arbitrary 3D meshes [DMSB99]. Creating high-fidelity computer graphics objects using imperfectly-measured data from the real world requires an adequate smoothing technique. Earlier smoothing techniques, using a simple laplacian diffusion of the mesh, introduced large distortions in the geometry. In contrast, following

the mean curvature normal $2\kappa\mathbf{n}$ at each vertex of the surface is robust with respect to differences in sampling rate, as even highly irregular meshes can be smoothed appropriately (see Figure 3(c)). Even if diffusion is a close relative of curvature flow in terms of differential equations, practical experience demonstrates undeniable advantages in using curvature flow over simple diffusion.

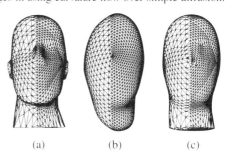

(a) (b) (c)

Figure 3: *Smoothing an irregularly sampled mesh: (a) Initial mesh, (b) Result of a laplacian smoothing assuming regular parameterization, (c) Result of a mean curvature flow as described in [DMSB99].*

3.1.2 Smoothing Shape vs. Parameterization

The reason for the superior performance of curvature flow over diffusion is the *parameterization-independent* nature of the Laplace-Beltrami operator. The laplacian of a mesh is always described with respect to a particular parameterization. The same geometric surface defined using another parameterization will result in a different laplacian vector. However, the notion of normal vector to a surface, or of mean curvature, is purely geometric, and as such, does not depend on the parameter space. The directions of the Laplace operator and of the Laplace-Beltrami actually coincide for the *conformal* parameter space [DHKW92]. This allows us to interpret the mean curvature normal $2\kappa\mathbf{n}$ as a special laplacian: it is a laplacian for a parameter space naturally *induced by the surface itself.*

These arguments explain a posteriori why any component in the tangent plane during the smoothing process would create distortion or local alteration of the shape of the triangulation [DMSB99]. Another insight into the nature of the tangent component can be gained if one considers a locally flat piece of a tesellated surface: any tangential component will introduce undesirable drift of the tesselation. The standard laplacian in effect fairs the parameterization of the surface as well as the shape itself. On the other hand, a purely geometric (i.e., parameterization independent) smoothing will produce the intended result of *smoothing only the shape* (notice that in Figure 3, the shapes of the initial triangles are preserved in the smoothed version).

3.2 Edge-Preserving Denoising

Starting with the denoising technique described above, we can easily introduce weights on vertices in order to preserve steep slopes of the height surface, important characteristics of the original image. Particular care must be taken to preserve the parameterization independent nature of the flow. This section explains how simple geometric considerations can be used to create a parameterization-independent, scale-invariant, edge-preserving smoothing.

3.2.1 Beltrami Flow

In the context of images, edges (i.e., sudden intensity changes) are fundamental. In denoising, any edge or boundary between different objects should be mainly preserved, while almost homogeneous regions should be smoothed quickly. Since edges in the image result in cliffs in the z direction for the corresponding height field, a first idea is to define the following flow (see Figure 4(a)):

$$I_t = 2\kappa \mathbf{n} \cdot \mathbf{e}_z$$

The normal to the surface near edges will be almost parallel to the screen, leading to little smoothing in those regions while more uniform regions will be denoised as before. Remembering Equ. (2) and (3), we find:

$$\mathbf{n} \cdot \mathbf{e}_z = \frac{1}{\mathcal{W}}, \qquad (4)$$

At this point, we recognize the Beltrami flow [KMS97]: $I_t = 2\kappa/\mathcal{W}$. However, in the rest of this section, we construct a more general approach by deriving a feature-preserving flow step by step.

3.2.2 Graph Flow

As we have briefly seen in Section 2.3, the Laplace-Beltrami operator is in a direction which minimizes surface area. Unfortunately, in the context of images, we can not easily "move" the sample points along the normal direction as it is generally not aligned with the image parameter directions. We would have to re-sample the surface back onto the pixel grid. Producing a *geometrically-equivalent flow* by only evolving the intensity field (therefore, constraining the sampling to remain the same) is then easier, and significantly faster. We will now introduce such a flow, referred to as "graph flow."

Suppose we have a surface $S(t)$ evolving in time, starting with a shape S_0. Let us define a potential $f(\mathbf{X}(t), t)$ in space such that the zero isosurface of f corresponds to S at every time t. As the evolving potential characterizes a moving isosurface, we can derive a simple differential equation satisfied by f. The path of a point $\mathbf{X}(t)$ during the evolution of the surface satisfies $f(\mathbf{X}(t), t) = 0$ for any time t, yielding:

$$\frac{\partial f}{\partial t}(\mathbf{X}(t), t) + \nabla f(\mathbf{X}(t), t) \cdot \frac{d\mathbf{X}(t)}{dt} = 0 \qquad (5)$$

Note that with this equation (the typical PDE used in the level-set literature) only the normal component of $d\mathbf{X}(t)/dt$ matters since it is dotted with the gradient of f, which is along the normal to the surface. An important consequence is that *only the normal component of a surface flow really affects the shape*: since any tangential component will not be accounted for in the PDE, the potential f will only evolve according to the normal component. Adding an arbitrary tangent component to a flow field will not perturb the evolution of a surface, just modify its parameterization (as mentioned in Section 3.1.2). The preceding remark allows us to construct different particle paths that lie on the same surface family. Note that in the case of mesh smoothing, we did not wish to allow the vertices of triangulated meshes to slide. Indeed, if the triangle vertices slide tangentially in the same surface family, the interior points of the triangle faces are not guaranteed to remain close to the surface: the triangles could cut deeply across the surface.

Since we want to obtain a mean curvature flow, the graph flow needs to match the mean curvature flow after projection onto the normal, as depicted in Figure 4(a). Since $\mathbf{e}_z$ projected onto the normal introduces a factor $1/\mathcal{W}$ (see Equ. (4)), we can obtain the equivalent graph flow:

$$I_t = -2\mathcal{W}\kappa \qquad (6)$$

This flow is the exact geometric equivalent of the mean curvature flow, but adapted for graphs (equivalent to the usual flow, followed by a re-sampling of the surface at the original pixel locations). Consequently, it satisfies the property of parameterization independence.

However, this flow still behaves inappropriately for height fields since edges will be smoothed significantly. No less it is an interesting anisotropic smoothing operator compared to standard laplacian smoothing (as noted by [MS96]).

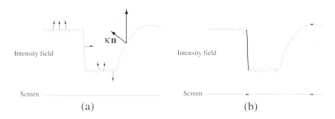

Figure 4: *(a): The left side indicates how normals are perpendicular to the screen in homogeneous, noisy areas, while parallel to the screen plane for edges. The right side shows how the graph flow is built out of the mean curvature flow by having the same magnitude once projected along the normal. (b): $\mathcal{W}$ measures the surface expansion between the parameter space (screen pixel) and the surface of the height field.*

3.2.3 Edge-Preserving Weighting

To further improve this flow and make it edge-preserving, we can now use a smoothing weight, dependent on the metric of the surface, in order to penalize the edges more than the flat regions. This corresponds to the soft constraints smoothing technique developed in [DMSB99], but this time, the appropriate smoothing factors are computed automatically, instead of being hand-chosen by the user.

Consider the term $\mathcal{W}$ (square root of the determinant of the surface metric): it measures the surface expansion between the parameter space (screen) and the surface itself (intensity field considered as a height field). Therefore, this term will be infinite along edges, while equal to one in flat regions as depicted in Figure 4(b). Its inverse is therefore a good candidate for an edge "indicator". This holds for any positive power of $\mathcal{W}$ as well. Since $\mathcal{W}$ is unitless this edge indicator is also scale-invariant. The complete edge-preserving flow can now be expressed as:

$$I_t = -\frac{2\kappa}{\mathcal{W}^\gamma} \qquad (7)$$

The coefficient $\gamma \geq 0$ determines the relative penalization of small jumps in intensity versus large jumps. Values less than one only penalize large jumps, while values larger than one penalize even small jumps. It controls the linearity of our edge-preservation metric: as such, γ can be described as an *edge contrast parameter*.

The flow derived above is quite general. For $\gamma = 0$, we find the same flow used by El-Fallah and Ford [FEF98]. For $\gamma = 1$, our formulation leads to the Beltrami flow, mentioned in Section 2.2. Other values of γ offer a whole new family of denoising flows, all having the properties of parameterization-independence, scale-invariance, and feature-preservation. In the next section, we propose to generalize the above derivation to nD data. In Section 5 we will present a natural and robust numerical scheme for this PDE, which will preserve the surface area minimization nature of the flow.

4 Denoising of Arbitrary Bivariate Data

Two-dimensional data often has more than one channel of information. Color images for instance have three channels per pixel: red, green, and blue. Although a straightforward channel by channel smoothing is easily achieved by the previous method, it may not lead to optimal smoothing. Independent changes in the red, green, and blue channels result in perceptually-strong color variations in the smoothed image. Therefore, smoothing in color should be performed in the rgb space where coupling between channels results in more natural color smoothing [Sha96]. Similarly, higher dimensional data should be smoothed in its respective space, not channel-by-channel. This section demonstrates that our previous approach can be extended easily to provide a denoising technique for higher dimensional data.

4.1 Graph Flow for Mean Curvature Smoothing

We now consider our bivariate multi-dimensional data as lying on 2-manifold embedded in nD. We can still define the Laplace-Beltrami operator as being the generalization of the mean curvature normal, or the generalization of the (parameterization-independent) surface area gradient. For the sake of simplicity, we will denote the Laplace-Beltrami operator as $\mathbf{B}$ from now on: $\Delta_g S = \mathbf{B}$. To make this flow a graph flow, we have to project this vector onto the subspace of free parameters, such as r, g, b in the case of color images. The orthogonal projection of $\mathbf{B}$ onto this sub-space is the vector $\overline{\mathbf{B}}$. It consists of the same coordinates as $\mathbf{B}$, except for the first two components (corresponding to the x and y axes of screen space) set to zero. Therefore, we need a vector in the direction opposite to $\overline{\mathbf{B}}$ to ensure a graph flow, but such that its projection onto $\mathbf{B}$ has the same magnitude as $\mathbf{B}$ to ensure the geometric equivalence:

$$-\frac{\mathbf{B} \cdot \mathbf{B}}{\overline{\mathbf{B}} \cdot \overline{\mathbf{B}}} \, \overline{\mathbf{B}}. \tag{8}$$

Applied to color images (5D space $(\mathbf{e}_x, \mathbf{e}_y, \mathbf{e}_r, \mathbf{e}_g, \mathbf{e}_b)$), the graph flow geometrically equivalent to a mean curvature flow is therefore:

$$\frac{d}{dt}\begin{pmatrix} r \\ g \\ b \end{pmatrix} = -\frac{\mathbf{B} \cdot \mathbf{B}}{\overline{\mathbf{B}} \cdot \overline{\mathbf{B}}}\begin{pmatrix} \overline{\mathbf{B}} \cdot \mathbf{e}_r \\ \overline{\mathbf{B}} \cdot \mathbf{e}_g \\ \overline{\mathbf{B}} \cdot \mathbf{e}_b \end{pmatrix}. \tag{9}$$

4.2 Edge-Preserving Flow

Following the same arguments as in Section 3, we now want to weight the features to favor smoothing of almost uniform regions. Thus, we need to find a way to measure discontinuities. Based on the same idea as in the greyscale case, we can use the ratio of surface expansion between the screen and the surface. It is directly measured by the ratio between the magnitudes of $\mathbf{B}$ and $\overline{\mathbf{B}}$, as cliffs are characterized by a normal parallel to the screen plane. Our multi-dimensional scale-invariant edge indicator can be written as: $\|\overline{\mathbf{B}}\|/\|\mathbf{B}\|$: the edge indicator will be valued 0 on sharp edges, and 1 in homogeneous regions. Adding an edge contrast parameter γ (slightly different than the previously defined γ, purely for aesthetic reasons), our feature-preserving flow becomes, for color pictures for instance:

$$\frac{d}{dt}\begin{pmatrix} r \\ g \\ b \end{pmatrix} = -\left(\frac{\|\overline{\mathbf{B}}\|}{\|\mathbf{B}\|}\right)^{\gamma}\begin{pmatrix} \overline{\mathbf{B}} \cdot \mathbf{e}_r \\ \overline{\mathbf{B}} \cdot \mathbf{e}_g \\ \overline{\mathbf{B}} \cdot \mathbf{e}_b \end{pmatrix}. \tag{10}$$

Notice that $\gamma = 0$ simplifies greatly to a Beltrami flow. The creation of higher dimension feature-preserving smoothing flows follows naturally.

4.3 Incorporating Perceptual Bias for Color

The (r, g, b) color space is not necessarily the most perceptually sound. Put simply, the human eye is not similarly sensitive to a change of red, green, or blue: what we visibly consider as a major color edge may not be considered as such in this color space, and vice-versa. Therefore, smoothing a color image in such a space may not lead to the most pleasant visual results.

Instead, we use the (L^*, U^*, V^*) color space to take some of the human color perception biases into account. This model has the advantage of being almost perceptually uniform for the human eye, and therefore, will appropriately define edges. Note that any other

model and/or linear combination of existing models is straightforward to implement in our framework as only the input has to be changed.

4.4 Tuning of Global Contrast

The framework defined so far has an additional degree of freedom: the scaling of intensity/colors. Colors are usually rescaled between 0 and 1, but the real color spectrum of the image is undetermined. Unless radiometric values of the image are available, we can arbitrarily choose a scale factor α to define the global contrast of the image. Note that our surface functional for a large value of α will be equivalent, for $\gamma = 0$, to a regularized version of the L_1 norm of the intensity: therefore, our flow will be equivalent to the total variation denoising approach of [ROF92]. On the other hand, a small scale factor will tend to create a flow based on the L_2 norm [Sha96] for the same γ [KMS97].

4.5 Discussion

We have defined a scale-invariant anisotropic flow to denoise any bivariate data while preserving features. It is based on surface area minimization, well-known in 3D to provide good denoising. As this method tends to minimize surface area in nD, the smoothing between data samples is treated in a non-linear way, significantly different from a channel-by-channel smoothing. In the special case of color images, color smoothing will induce an alignment of the gradient of each channel, which does not appear in a channel by channel smoothing. Our method also applies to higher dimensional data such as tensor or vector fields, providing an interesting framework to simplify complex fluid flows or MRI tensor images. However, a discrete implementation must be defined in order for the method to be practical. The next section addresses this point.

5 Implementation of our Flow

We now turn our attention to a practical and robust implementation of our feature-preserving flow. In this section we will derive a simple discrete form of the PDE and use it to reliably integrate the flow in time. The discretization is designed to preserve the surface area minimization nature of the flow.

5.1 Usual Implementation with FD

One can approximate the mean curvature directly by finite differences. Since the mean curvature is defined as:

$$\kappa = \frac{I_{xx}(1 + I_y^2) - 2I_{xy}I_x I_y + I_{yy}(1 + I_x^2)}{(1 + I_x^2 + I_y^2)^{3/2}},$$

a quick FD implementation can be derived for greyscale images. Kimmel [KMS97] also derived a FD numerical scheme for color images, but the complexity of the computations involved increases rapidly with the dimensionality of the data. Moreover we prefer to use a more natural discretization of the mean curvature, since it will guarantee good behavior as the discrete operator mimics the continuous case perfectly. We will also see that it can easily be extended to nD with a modest computational overhead.

5.2 Definition of Mean Curvature Normal

In differential geometry, the mean curvature normal is sometimes described as a geometric property of a surface. Around a point $\mathbf{P}$, the limit of the surface area variation with respect to $\mathbf{P}$ as we take a smaller and smaller piece of surface turns out to be the mean curvature at **P**. Therefore, the mean curvature normal can be defined through the following property [DMSB99]:

$$2\kappa\mathbf{n} = \nabla\mathcal{A}/\mathcal{A}, \qquad (11)$$

where $\mathcal{A}$ is a small area around **P**, and ∇ is the derivative with respect to **P**. Similarly, the vector **B**, generalizing the mean curvature normal in nD, can be expressed as:

$$\mathbf{B} = \nabla\mathcal{A}/\mathcal{A}. \qquad (12)$$

5.3 Definition of a Robust Discrete Operator in 3D

In [DMSB99], the authors showed a formulation of the surface area gradient of a piecewise linear 3D surface approximation (i.e., a triangle mesh) with respect to a given vertex. A direct derivation of the continuous case to the discrete case yields the formula:

$$\nabla\mathcal{A} = \frac{1}{2}\sum(cot\ \alpha_{ij} + cot\ \beta_{ij})(\mathbf{X}_i - \mathbf{X}_j), \qquad (13)$$

where $\mathbf{X}_i$ is a vertex of the mesh, $\mathbf{X}_j$ an immediate neighbor, and α_{ij}, β_{ij} the two opposite angles to the edge $\mathbf{X}_i\mathbf{X}_j$, as sketched in Figure 5. Notice that this gradient is zero for any flat piece of surface, regardless of the shape or the number of triangles in it.

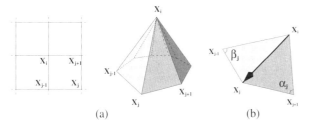

(a)   (b)

Figure 5: *A vertex x_i and its neighbors on the screen and on the surface (a), and one term of its curvature normal formula (b).*

The discrete operator has been proven robust and reliable even on irregular meshes. Fig. 6(a) and 6(b) exhibit two irregular meshes and their curvature plot using the previously discussed discrete curvature normal derivation. We observe a significantly reduced amount of noise compared to previous methods of approximating the mean curvature.

We believe that the good properties of this discrete form of the mean curvature are due to the preservation of the fundamental property of the operator: surface area minimization. This formulation

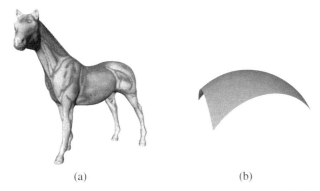

(a)   (b)

Figure 6: *Curvature plot (pseudo-colors representing magnitude of mean curvature normal) of two irregular meshes, proving the robustness of the discrete operator. (a) Model of a horse, and (b) piece of a unit discrete sphere, where the mean curvature approximation is equal to 1+/-2%*

is *conservative* in that sense. Hence, such a discretization will provide better results than regular FD schemes in the context of image denoising since area minimization is involved. Moreover, the extension to higher dimensional data spaces is straightforward as we are about to see.

5.4 Discrete Beltrami Operator in High Dimensions

Since the previous formulation for the surface area gradient is only valid in 3D, we must start with an extension for higher dimensional data spaces. For generality's sake, we will treat the nD case, and the color image case will only be a particular example.

5.4.1 Surface Area in nD

First, we must derive the expression for a surface area in nD. The area of a triangle formed by two vectors **u** and **v** in 3D is $2\mathcal{A} = ||\mathbf{u}\times\mathbf{v}||$. Being proportional to the sine of the angle between vectors, we can also express it as:

$$\begin{aligned}\mathcal{A}(\mathbf{u}, \mathbf{v}) &= \frac{1}{2}||\mathbf{u}||||\mathbf{v}||sin(\mathbf{u},\mathbf{v}) = \frac{1}{2}||\mathbf{u}||||\mathbf{v}||\sqrt{1 - cos^2(\mathbf{u},\mathbf{v})}\\ &= \frac{1}{2}\sqrt{||\mathbf{u}||^2||\mathbf{v}||^2 - (\mathbf{u}\cdot\mathbf{v})^2}.\end{aligned}$$

This latter expression is now valid in nD, and is particularly easy to evaluate in any dimension.

5.4.2 Derivation of the Area Gradient

Given the expression for the surface area of a triangle, we can formally derive the gradient of the area with respect to one of its vertices. We refer the reader to the appendix for the detailed derivation of the formula. It is shown there that the cotangent Equ. (13) is actually still valid *if we extend the definition of cotangent in nD as being*:

$$cot(\mathbf{u}, \mathbf{v}) = \frac{cos(\mathbf{u}, \mathbf{v})}{sin(\mathbf{u}, \mathbf{v})} = \frac{\mathbf{u}\cdot\mathbf{v}}{\sqrt{||\mathbf{u}||^2||\mathbf{v}||^2 - (\mathbf{u}\cdot\mathbf{v})^2}}.$$

With this definition, the implementation in nD space is straightforward and efficient, as dot products require little computation.

5.5 Practical Implementation for Denoising

The implementation of our scheme is now straightforward with the discrete operator we have just described. We will explicitly give the discretization for $\gamma = 0$ since these formulae are particularly simple. In the case of greyscale images, we change the intensity value I_i for every pixel according to:

$$\frac{dI_i}{dt} = \frac{1}{2\mathcal{A}}\sum(cot\ \alpha_{ij} + cot\ \beta_{ij})(I_j - I_i), \qquad (14)$$

where the total area $\mathcal{A}$ around a vertex is just the sum of the areas of all the triangles adjacent to this vertex. As in FD schemes, we sum the contribution for all eight immediate neighbors. The cotangent is implemented efficiently by computing the two adjacent 3D vectors forming the angle considered, and computing their dot product divided by the norm of their cross product.

For color images our edge-preserving flow becomes:

$$\frac{dr_i}{dt} = \frac{1}{2\mathcal{A}}\sum(cot\ \alpha_{ij} + cot\ \beta_{ij})(r_j - r_i)$$

$$\frac{dg_i}{dt} = \frac{1}{2\mathcal{A}}\sum(cot\ \alpha_{ij} + cot\ \beta_{ij})(g_j - g_i)$$

$$\frac{db_i}{dt} = \frac{1}{2\mathcal{A}} \sum (cot\ \alpha_{ij} + cot\ \beta_{ij})(b_j - b_i)$$

Note that the coupling between channels is incorporated in the cotangents. For data of different dimensionality the "feature-preserving" flow will be very similar to this previous set of equations.

5.6 Integration of the Flow

The implementation of the flow is done by integrating the last set of PDEs in time using either an explicit or implicit Euler scheme. The user can stop the smoothing when the data is sufficiently denoised. El-Fallah and Ford proposed an improvement on the integration by computing the time step to use according to the variation of the global area [FEF98]. Indeed, if the area of the whole image changes significantly during a time step, a lot of noise was present in the image, and it is safe to take a larger time step. When the area change starts to decrease, the image structure may be significantly affected by too large a time step, thus the time step should be reduced.

5.7 Discussion

We have derived a new discrete version of our differential denoising model. Building upon a classic curvature normal flow, we weight this smoothing process in order to preserve significant features of the data while still suppressing high frequency noise. This anisotropic smoothing flow is then implemented in a discrete setting with simple discrete-geometry tools. This numerical technique has two main advantages: it preserves the nature of the flow in a discrete way, and is easy to implement in any dimension. By varying the exponent γ, we can re-create existing flows or create entirely new flows. Additionally, we can easily extend these flows to arbitrary dimensions. The next section presents our first results obtained with the above numerical scheme.

6 Results

We tested our method on several datasets. We first used computer generated images with artificially added noise. In Figure 7(a-c) we can see that our method removes the noise from a simple greyscale image while retaining the edges present in the original image. Similarly, Figure 7(d-e) shows a smoothing for a simple color picture in the presence of large amounts of noise.

Next, we tested the method on "real world" images. The denoising technique performs well on classical test images, as demonstrated for instance in Figure 8. In Figure 10, we display a noisy image of a clock and its restored version, along with the height field representation of the images.

We also tried our technique on different depth data. Rather than using a 3D smoothing as in [DMSB99], we can take advantage of the fact that the error is only in the z direction. While former methods [Tau95, DMSB99] would make the assumption of an isotropic noise in space, our method applies better to this depth field as the noise (measurement error) mainly resides along the z axis. To demonstrate this advantage, we smoothed an elevation map of a section of Mars. Due to measurement errors and poor quantization of the original data, the height field is noisy as shown in Figure 1(a). After an anisotropic smoothing, we suppress the noise and most of the quantization effects, resulting in a smooth surface even with a flat-shaded rendering.

Finally, we demonstrate how our method behaves on range images in Figure 9. Given a noisy range image of a face, we can smooth the range image to reconstruct the face without visible noise while keeping the features in place. Once again, previous methods would have altered the shape since the assumption of isotropic noise in the data does not apply for range images.

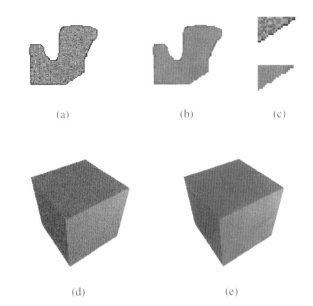

(a)   (b)   (c)

(d)   (e)

Figure 7: *Examples of denoising for computer-generated greyscale and color images (a&d: noisy images, b&e: denoised output, c: close-up of a and b).*

(a)   (b)

Figure 8: *(a) Noisy color image, (b) Denoising flow applied to (a), in 300 explicit iterations with dt = 1, γ = 0.*

7 Conclusions and Future Work

We presented a general framework for denoising of 2D data. Derived from smoothing of meshes in 3D, our approach proposes an anisotropic diffusion of data with convenient features: our method is robust, stable, feature-preserving, scale-invariant, and easily implemented for greyscale and color images, but also any forms of multi-channel bivariate data. We demonstrated how this approach provides an elegant way to smooth height fields and range images by taking into account the way these data were acquired: knowing that the noise is mainly in the depth approximation, our method provides more accurate results than previous 3D smoothing algorithms where the noise is treated as isotropic in space.

Our current work includes more testing of these previous denoising flows for different form of data (such as tensor images from MRI data), even for volumetric data, and irregular grids. We are also working on a denoising flow based on principal curvatures for the same applications.

Acknowledgments

The authors are thankful to Pierre Kornprobst for help in image processing; Andrei Khodakovsky for general assistance; Martin Rumpf for important insights; JPL for the Mars topography; and the anonymous reviewers for many helpful comments. This work was supported by NSF DMS-9872890, ACI-9721349, DMS-9874082, the Packard Foundation, Alias|Wavefront, the STC, and by the Academic Strategic Alliances Program of the Accelerated Strategic Computing Initiative (ASCI/ASAP) under subcontract B341492 of DOE contract W-7405-ENG-48.

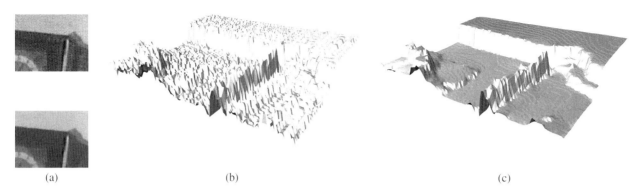

(a)   (b)   (c)

Figure 10: *Clock example: The initial image (a, top) contains a significant amount of noise as its height field (b) shows. Our denoising technique significantly reduces this amount of noise (a, bottom) while keeping the features in place (c).*

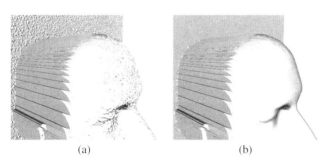

(a)   (b)

Figure 9: *(a) Head model obtained from a noisy depth image. (b) Reconstructed model after denoising (flat-shaded).*

References

[ABBFC97] G. Aubert, M. Barlaud, L. Blanc-Feraud, and P. Charbonnier. Deterministic edge-preserving regularization in computed imaging. *IEEE Trans. Imag. Process.*, 5(12), February 1997.

[ALM92] L. Alvarez, P.-L. Lions, and J-M. Morel. Image selective smoothing and edge detection by nonlinear diffusion (II). *SIAM Journal of numerical analysis*, 29:845–866, 1992.

[Bar89] Alan H. Barr. The Einstein Summation Notation: Introduction and Extensions. In *SIGGRAPH 89 Course notes #30 on Topics in Physically-Based Modeling*, pages J1–J12, 1989.

[DHKW92] Ulrich Dierkes, Stefan Hildebrandt, Albrecht Küster, and Ortwi Wohlrab. *Minimal Surfaces I*. Grundlehren der mathematischen Wissenschaften, Springer-Verlag, 1992.

[DMSB99] Mathieu Desbrun, Mark Meyer, Peter Schröder, and Alan Barr. Implicit Fairing of Irregular Meshes using Diffusion and Curvature Flow. In *SIGGRAPH 99 Conference Proceedings*, pages 317–324, August 1999.

[FEF98] G. Ford and A. El-Fallah. On mean curvature in non-linear image filtering. *Pattern Recognition Letters*, 19:433–437, 1998.

[Gra98] Alfred Gray. *Modern Differential Geometry of Curves and Surfaces with Mathematica*. CRC Press, 1998.

[KDA97] P. Kornprobst, R. Deriche, and G. Aubert. Nonlinear operators in image restoration. In *CVPR'97*, pages 325–331, Puerto-Rico, 1997.

[KMS97] R. Kimmel, R. Malladi, and N. Sochen. Images as embedding maps and minimal surfaces: Movies, color, and volumetric medical images. In *IEEE CVPR'97*, pages 350–355, 1997.

[MS96] R. Malladi and J.A. Sethian. Image processing: Flows under min/max curvature and mean curvature. *Graphical Models and Image Processing*, 58(2):127–141, March 1996.

[PM90] P. Perona and J. Malik. Scale-space and edge detection using anisotropic diffusion. *IEEE Transactions on Pattern Analysis and Machine Intelligence*, 12(7):629–639, July 1990.

[PR99] T. Preußer and M. Rumpf. Anisotropic Nonlinear Diffusion in Flow Visualization. In *IEEE Visuazliation'99*, pages 323–332, 1999.

[ROF92] L. Rudin, S. Osher, and E. Fatemi. Nonlinear total variation based noise removal algorithms. *Physica D*, 60:259–268, 1992.

[Sha96] J. Shah. Curve evolution and segmentation functionals: Applications to color images. In *IEEE ICIP'96*, pages 461–464, 1996.

[SKM98] N. Sochen, R. Kimmel, and R. Malladi. A geometrical framework for low level vision. *IEEE Trans. on Image Processing*, 17(3):310–318, 1998.

[Tau95] Gabriel Taubin. A Signal Processing Approach to Fair Surface Design. In *SIGGRAPH 95 Conference Proceedings*, pages 351–358, August 1995.

[TT99] Jack Tumblin and Greg Turk. LCIS: A Boundary Hierarchy For Detail-Preserving Contrast Reduction. In *SIGGRAPH 98 Conference Proceedings*, pages 83–90, 1999.

Appendix: Area Minimization in nD

In this appendix, we use Einstein summation notation for conciseness. For an introduction, see [Bar89].

Consider 3 points (P, Q, R) in a space of arbitrary dimension $n > 2$. As mentioned in Section 5.4.1, we can write the area formed by the triangle (A, B, C) as follows:

$$\mathcal{A}^2 = \frac{1}{4} \left(PQ_i PQ_i PR_j PR_j - PQ_i PR_i PQ_j PR_j \right).$$

Differentiating term by term with respect to P we get:

$$
\begin{aligned}
4 \frac{\partial \mathcal{A}^2}{\partial A_k} &= -\delta_{ik} PQ_i PR_j PR_j - \delta_{ik} PQ_i PR_j PR_j \\
&\quad -\delta_{jk} PQ_i PQ_i PR_j - \delta_{jk} PQ_i PQ_i PR_j \\
&\quad +\delta_{ik} PR_i PQ_j PR_j + \delta_{ik} PQ_i PQ_j PR_j \\
&\quad +\delta_{jk} PQ_i PR_i PR_j + \delta_{jk} PQ_i PR_i PQ_j \\
&= -2 PQ_k PR_j PR_j - 2 PQ_i PQ_i PR_k + PR_k PQ_j PR_j \\
&\quad + PQ_k PQ_j PR_j + PQ_i PR_i PR_k + PQ_i PR_i PQ_k \\
&= 2 \left[PQ_k (PQ \cdot PR - PR \cdot PR) + PR_k (PQ \cdot PR - PQ \cdot PQ) \right] \\
&= 2 \left[PQ_k (QR \cdot RP) + PR_k (PQ \cdot QR) \right]
\end{aligned}
$$

Additionally, we also have:

$$\frac{\partial \mathcal{A}^2}{\partial P_k} = 2 \mathcal{A} \frac{\partial \mathcal{A}}{\partial P_k}$$

Therefore, using Equ. 14, and if we define the cotangent of an angle between two nD vectors $\mathbf{u}$ and $\mathbf{v}$ as:

$$cot(\mathbf{u}, \mathbf{v}) = \frac{\mathbf{u} \cdot \mathbf{v}}{\sqrt{||\mathbf{u}||^2 ||\mathbf{v}||^2 - (\mathbf{u} \cdot \mathbf{v})^2}},$$

the gradient of the surface area can be expressed exactly as in Equ. (13), extending nicely the 3D case to nD.

A Fast, Space-Efficient Algorithm for the
Approximation of Images by an Optimal Sum of Gaussians

Jeffrey Childs   Cheng-Chang Lu   Jerry Potter

Department of Mathematics and Computer Science
Kent State University

Abstract

Gaussian decomposition of images leads to many promising applications in computer graphics. Gaussian representations can be used for image smoothing, motion analysis, and feature selection for image recognition. Furthermore, image construction from a Gaussian representation is fast, since the Gaussians only need to be added together. The most optimal algorithms [3, 6, 7] minimize the number of Gaussians needed for decomposition, but they involve nonlinear least-squares approximations, e.g. the use of the Marquardt algorithm [10]. This presents a problem, since, in the Marquardt algorithm, enormous amounts of computations are required and the resulting matrices use a lot of space. In this work, a method is offered, which we call the Quickstep method, that substantially reduces the number of computations and the amount of space used. Unlike the Marquardt algorithm, each iteration has linear time complexity in the number of variables and no Jacobian or Hessian matrices are formed. Yet, Quickstep produces optimal results, similar to those produced by the Marquardt algorithm.

Key words: *Gaussian approximations, geometric algorithms, surface fitting.*

1 Background

In the Gaussian decomposition of an image, we wish to find a minimum number of Gaussians whose sum approximates the image with a certain tolerance. Each Gaussian G_i has the form:

$$G_i(X,Y) = A_i e^{-[(X-x_i)^2 + (Y-y_i)^2]/2\sigma_i^2} \qquad (1)$$

where (X,Y) are pixel coordinates, A_i is the amplitude of

G_i, (x_i, y_i) is the mean (or position) of G_i and σ_i is the standard deviation (or scale) of G_i. Thus, an image can be represented by an array of these four parameters.

Gaussian representations have many promising applications. Gaussian parameters are promising for image transmission, since the Gaussians only need to be added together to reconstruct the image. In image transmission, they can be used for low to high resolution display, where the largest Gaussians are transmitted, added and displayed first, forming the basic structures of the image, while the smaller Gaussians are being transmitted. The smaller Gaussians, when added, fill in the details of the image. Hence, this type of representation allows simultaneous transmission and display from low to high resolution.

For motion analysis applications, Gaussian representation of objects can simplify computation, because a moving object can be simulated by adjusting the Gaussian parameters which represent it. In addition, Gaussians may be used to represent features of images, needed for image matching and recognition.

Once a Gaussian representation of an image is found, the Gaussians can be used, from then on, in a variety of ways. Finding the Gaussian representation, however, is not a trivial problem, and literature in the Gaussian decomposition of images is rather scarce. The greatest advances in optimality were made by Goshtasby and O'Neill [6, 7]. However, their method involves the Marquardt algorithm [10], a nonlinear least-squares approximation algorithm which requires enormous amounts of computations for practical image problems.

A further improvement in optimality was made by Childs *et al.* [3], by bounding Gaussian parameters intrinsically. In their work, which also uses the Marquardt algorithm, intrinsic boundaries were applied

154

to 1D signals to reduce the number of Gaussians used to represent them. Intrinsic boundaries for position are useful in this work, also, but those for amplitude and standard deviation are not used. The boundaries for position are set beyond the edges of a square image, at one quarter of the distance of one dimension, in pixels, of the image. In other work on Gaussian decomposition, Ben-Arie and Rao developed two very fast algorithms [1]. However, these methods are focused on speed rather than optimality. In contrast, this work attempts to improve the speed without sacrificing optimality. In the appendix of their work, as well as in a comment by Ferreira [5] on Wiener's earlier work, it was shown that any practical signal can be decomposed into a sum of Gaussians, given a tolerance.

In this work, a novel algorithm is introduced, which we call the Quickstep algorithm. It takes a global optimization approach to the number of Gaussians as originated by Goshtasby and O'Neill [6], yet it has a lower time complexity than the Marquardt algorithm.

2 Introduction

If we let a function f be defined as a sum of m Gaussians, such that

$$f(X,Y) = \sum_{i=1}^{m} A_i e^{-[(X-x_i)^2+(Y-y_i)^2]/2\sigma_i^2} \quad (2)$$

where the parameters are as defined in Equation 1, our goal is to find a function f with minimum m such that the signal is approximated by the sum of m Gaussians, i.e.

$$\max \{| P(X,Y)_j - f(X,Y)_j | : j=1,2,3,...,N\} < \varepsilon \quad (3)$$

where N is the number of pixels, $P(X,Y)_j$ is the data value at the jth pixel, $f(X,Y)_j$ is the value of the function of Equation 2 at the jth pixel, ε is a prescribed tolerance, and pixel j has coordinates (X,Y).

Let us define a vector b of length n, composed of Gaussian parameters, such that

$$b^{[n]} = (A_1, \alpha_1, \beta_1, \sigma_1, A_2,$$
$$\alpha_2, \beta_2, \sigma_2, ..., A_m, \alpha_m, \beta_m, \sigma_m). \quad (4)$$

where α_i and β_i are the intrinsic boundary counterparts to x_i and y_i, respectively [3]. The Marquardt algorithm attempts to make corrections to b to meet the prescribed tolerance by combining Newton's method [8] with the gradient method [4]. The gradient method determines the direction of correction, while the Newton method determines the amount of correction.

In every iteration of the Marquardt algorithm, a partial derivative of function f is taken with respect to every component of the b vector, at every point (X,Y), to form a Jacobian matrix of dimensions N x n. The transpose of the Jacobian is multiplied by the Jacobian to form a Hessian matrix. The Hessian is used, along with the gradient vector to solve a linear system of equations. The solution, with some modification, is used as the correction to the b vector to form a better fit between the sum of the Gaussians and the image being decomposed. A more detailed description is found in Marquardt's paper [10].

Hence, two major problems with the Marquardt algorithm are that (1) the number of computations within an iteration can consume much time and (2) the size of the matrices can consume much space for image decomposition. For example, in a small 16 x 16 image that may involve as many as 50 Gaussians, the Jacobian matrix would have over 50 thousand entries, making matrix multiplication time-consuming. Furthermore, if the reasonable method of Gaussian elimination is used to solve the linear system of equations, it would involve over eight million calculations. It would clearly be impractical to use the Marquardt algorithm for even larger images involving more Gaussians.

The decomposition method involves (for both Marquardt and Quickstep) selecting an initial Gaussian for the b vector first, and then letting the algorithm iterate, adjusting the b vector to minimize the error between the Gaussian and the image. If the tolerance ε is not met (see Inequality 3), another Gaussian is selected, concatenated to the b vector, and the algorithm runs again, refining all Gaussians in the set further. This continues until the tolerance is finally met. If many Gaussians are added to the set at once, there will probably not be a good initial fit between the Gaussian mass and the image, and it is more difficult for the algorithm to find an optimal fit, due to the high energy of the Gaussian mass. When the Gaussians are allowed to settle one by one, they have lower energy. This method was used in previous work [3, 6, 7] for optimality.

This problem is classified as a large-scale nonlinear least-squares approximation problem, for which the

Marquardt algorithm is not considered suitable for the reasons above. Current large-scale methods [2, 11] focus on approximating the Hessian matrix by other faster methods than matrix multiplication. For our application, however, we still find this unacceptable, as the formation of the Hessian matrix still requires at least $O(n^2)$ time, and the linear system of equations, which takes $O(n^3)$ time, does not benefit. It will be shown in the results section, that even if the formation of the Hessian matrix were instantaneous, the Quickstep method is still faster for practical image problems.

The contribution of this work is to provide a method which reduces the number of computations significantly, yet produces results that are similar in optimality to those produced by the Marquardt algorithm. The Quickstep algorithm is linear in the number of Gaussian parameters on each iteration. Each iteration takes a crude step towards the solution, requiring more iterations. However, each iteration is very fast so that the overall time is reduced substantially. The Quickstep method also has the advantage that it does not require large amounts of space to reach the solution, as the formation of the Jacobian matrix, the formation of the Hessian matrix, and solving the linear system of equations are all eliminated.

3 The Quickstep Algorithm

In practically any nonlinear least-squares algorithm, the initial selection of parameters is an important issue. A recent method for selecting initial parameters, which has proven quite successful, is the selection method used by Childs *et al.* [3]. It has been shown in their work, that for a signal composed of a set of Gaussians, a smaller set of Gaussians can often be found to approximate the signal, using this Gaussian selection method. Therefore, this selection method is also used in this work. To avoid computation inaccuracy, however, the selected standard deviation is no smaller than 0.4 and no larger than 100.0. The initial parameters, when determined, are concatenated to the b vector of Equation 4.

Quickstep makes use of the idea that these Gaussians can be truncated. Since a Gaussian decays so rapidly as the distance from its position increases, it makes sense to eliminate the insignificant computations at a certain distance from its position. The criterion that is used here is not the standard deviation, but the function value of the Gaussian, because this function value should be considerably less than ε (see Inequality 3). Therefore, the effective distance ξ from the position

of the Gaussian is defined as

$$\xi = \left\lceil \sqrt{2\sigma^2 \ln \frac{|A|}{\delta}} \right\rceil \qquad (5)$$

where δ is an absolute function value tolerance. This equation is easily derived from the 1D Gaussian function, setting its function value to δ and solving for $\xi = |X - x|$. The ceiling is used here since pixels have integral coordinates. For ease of implementation, computations are confined to a square of dimensions 2ξ instead of a circle of radius ξ. The notation ESA is used to refer to this "effective square area" of the Gaussian. The choice of δ for Equation 5 can be critical to how well this truncation method works. If δ is too small, no gain may be realized from using it. If δ is too large, it will prevent the algorithm from using a significant part of the Gaussian, increasing the number of Gaussians required. A good choice for δ seems to be $\delta = 0.05\varepsilon$, determined experimentally.

In the Quickstep algorithm, the gradient method [4] is used to determine the direction of correction for the b vector. Therefore, in an iteration of the Quickstep algorithm, the gradient vector g is created as

$$g^{[n]} = \sum_{j \in ESA_i} \left[P(X,Y)_j - f(X,Y)_j \right] \frac{\partial f(X,Y,b_i)_j}{\partial b_i},$$

$$\ell = 1,2,\ldots,n. \qquad (6)$$

where f and P are as defined in Equation 2 and Inequality 3.

The choice of scale is a very important problem. Without a properly chosen scale, the number of Gaussians to decompose a problem will increase sharply. The Quickstep method uses the diagonal of the Hessian that would be formed in the Marquardt algorithm to determine a scale, since this provides some important information without increasing the time complexity of an iteration. In Marquardt's original paper, the standard deviations of the parameters are used [10]. However, in Quickstep, when the diagonal Hessian is scaled, it becomes the identity matrix. Hence, the gradient vector is the solution. Since the scale is applied to both the gradient vector and the solution, it can be applied to the gradient vector twice. Hence, in Quickstep, the scale is used only on the gradient vector, and the variances of the parameters are used instead of the standard deviations, which avoids an expensive call to a square root

156

function. Hence, a scale vector s is created as

$$s^{[n]} = \sum_{j \in ESA_\ell} \left(\frac{\partial f(X,Y,b_\ell)_j}{\partial b_\ell} \right)^2, \quad \ell = 1,2,3,...,n$$

which should be computed at the same time as Equation 6, in order to prevent storing or recalculating the derivatives. The scale is then applied to the gradient vector g:

$$\hat{g}_\ell = \frac{g_\ell}{s_\ell} \qquad \ell = 1,2,...,n$$

The refinement correction to the b vector is now computed and stored to a trial vector t:

$$t_\ell = b_\ell + \frac{\hat{g}_\ell}{\eta} \qquad \ell = 1,2,...,n \qquad (7)$$

where

$$\eta = 1 + \frac{\lambda}{v}$$

where λ is initially 0.01 when the Quickstep algorithm starts up for a set of Gaussians, and v is more or less an arbitrary value, set to 10.0 in this work.

The trial vector t is processed a little more, depending on the type of element. Nothing is done to amplitude parameters. However, position parameters are normalized to equivalent values between 0 and 2π (for the sine function [3]); otherwise, their valid adjustments can be quite large, leading to inaccuracy in computations. In addition, the standard deviation is set to its absolute value (since it may become negative in the algorithm) between 0.3 and $100p$, where p is the number of pixels in one dimension of a square image. If the standard deviation adjusts outside these boundaries, it is set to the appropriate boundary value.

The next step is to calculate a sum-of-Gaussians matrix of the same size as the image or image section being decomposed (only the ESA's of the Gaussians need to be used here). This matrix is used as function f to calculate the sum-of-squares error Φ:

$$\Phi_{(k)} = \sum_{j=1}^{N} \left[P(X,Y)_j - f(X,Y)_j \right]^2 \qquad (8)$$

where P was defined earlier in Inequality 3, and $\Phi_{(k)}$ denotes the error Φ on the kth iteration of Quickstep. If $\Phi_{(k)} < \Phi_{(k-1)}$, then t becomes the new b vector, the new value λ is set as λ / v, and the Quickstep iteration repeats. If $\Phi_{(k)}$ is not lower, however, the search for a trial vector continues until Φ is lowered (assuming that Φ is not at the minimum error). If the search must continue for a suitable trial vector, the algorithm proceeds to adjust λ as in Marquardt's paper [10].

The test for convergence and other stopping conditions, as used in Marquardt's paper [10], are used as stopping conditions for Quickstep also. However, a stopping condition which needs further elaboration is when the number of iterations has reached a certain limit. Optimality seems to level off when 40 iterations has been reached. Many iterations, in both Quickstep and Marquardt, are idle iterations, in which insignificant decreases to error are made without any benefit in optimality, and putting a limit on the number of iterations removes many of the idle ones.

There is a stipulation in setting such a limit, however. Although the limit removes many idle iterations, it is difficult to predict when idle iterations eventually lead to significant iterations. In such cases, the algorithm "breaks new ground", that is, finds a steep path downhill. If the algorithm "breaks new ground", the count of iterations is restarted at 0, since such a steep path can lead to significant progress. New ground is considered to have been broken when $\Phi_{(k)} < 0.8\Phi_{(k-1)}$, determined experimentally.

The Quickstep algorithm assures convergence if no iteration limit is set, for three reasons: (1) the gradient method is used, (2) a trial vector is not accepted unless it leads to lower error, and (3) if no trial vector is ever accepted, eventually η reaches a number so large that, due to Equation 7, the trial vector approaches the b vector until the convergence test [10] is met.

The Quickstep algorithm uses the gradient method, like most nonlinear least-squares algorithms, but the Newton component [8] is reduced. The Newton component determines the amount of correction to the b vector very well, but it is responsible for the enormous amount of calculations in one iteration. In this work, a way is provided to quickly determine the correction size, which, though crude compared to the Newton correction size, still makes decent progress towards the solution. The result is that Quickstep requires more iterations to reach the solution, but an iteration of Quickstep is so fast that the overall time is dramatically reduced. Using the Quickstep method, the complexity of each iteration is reduced to $O(N + n\rho)$, where ρ is the average number of pixels in an ESA of a Gaussian.

It may be worth commenting that truncation of Gaussians can also be applied successfully to the Marquardt algorithm to increase the speed. In particular this does much to reduce the time for the matrix multiplication, since only the intersections of the ESAs need to be multiplied. However, the system of linear equations does not benefit from such truncation in the Marquardt algorithm, and therefore, the complexity of an iteration is not reduced as in Quickstep.

When the standard deviation of a Gaussian becomes the imposed minimum 0.3, the Gaussian can be used to approximate a pixel without having any significant effect on other pixels. Thus, a 16 x 16 image section, in the worst case, requires 256 "mutually exclusive" Gaussians for approximation. Though this type of approximation is undesirable, it shows that arbitrarily high frequencies can be approximated discretely. It also shows that noise in images will be included in the approximation. It is possible to use Gaussian decomposition for image smoothing, by eliminating Gaussians with small standard deviations, but this will remove some detail as well.

4 Results

The results in this section are limited to digital images. The use of the algorithm for continuous images would require that the image be first represented by a function, which is the goal of Gaussian decomposition in the first place (see Equation 2 and Inequality 3).

In this section, the performances of Quickstep and Marquardt will be compared. Therefore, the implementation of the Marquardt decomposition algorithm is described next. In this implementation, intrinsic boundaries are used as in Quickstep, for optimality, and the selection of initial parameters is the same as in Quickstep. The same adjustments on trial parameters (see previous section), are used to ensure accurate computations. In the Jacobian matrix multiplication, we make use of the fact that the resulting Hessian is symmetric, and therefore, only roughly half of the entries need to be computed. The system of linear equations was solved using Gaussian elimination with maximal column pivoting. The stopping conditions are the same as for Quickstep, except that the iteration limit is set at 10 for Marquardt and 40 for Quickstep (the reason for this will be explained later). However, if "new ground is broken", the iteration count is reset to 0 (see previous section). The tolerance ε is set at 10.0 for both

methods, which usually produces a good SNR rms; most of the points in the Gaussian approximation are usually well under the tolerance when the algorithms complete. The rest of the Marquardt algorithm is implemented as in Marquardt's original paper [10]. All experiments in this section were conducted on a 300 MHz PC.

In an initial experiment involving 30 random 16 x 16 images, Marquardt attained a total of 558 Gaussians for the image sections, requiring a total time of 5150 seconds, while Quickstep attained a total of 563 Gaussians in a total of 168 seconds. Each case usually had a different number of Gaussians for both Marquardt and Quickstep. Quickstep had increased the number of Gaussians in 9 of the cases, but decreased the number of Gaussians in 10 cases.

As mentioned earlier, in comparisons of Marquardt with Quickstep, the iteration limit is set at 10 for Marquardt, while it is set at 40 for Quickstep. The reason for setting an iteration limit in the first place is that it removes idle iterations which produce insignificant decreases in the error, and most of these occur in the later iterations. Since Quickstep requires more iterations to reach the solution, its iteration limit cannot be set to 10 without degradation of optimal performance. This is unfortunate because the lower the iteration limit is set, the faster the algorithm runs. For example, if the iteration limit is set at 10 for Quickstep, it requires a total of only 49 seconds instead of 168 seconds; however, the total number of Gaussians increases substantially to 596, an average increase of 1.1 Gaussians per test case. It is worth mentioning also that if the iteration limit is set at 40 for Marquardt, its total number of Gaussians only decreases by 3 to 555, yet its total time increases to a painful 15932 seconds. For these reasons, we feel that these different iteration limit settings allow for a fair comparison of the algorithms.

Current large-scale methods still try to speed up by approximating a Hessian matrix without doing a matrix multiplication [2, 11]. The Marquardt algorithm can also be sped up by using Gaussian truncation , done in our earlier experiments, which has a large effect on the matrix multiplication time. However, these methods do nothing to speed up an accurate solution to the linear system of equations. The total time spent in solving linear systems of equations in the Marquardt algorithm for the initial experiment was 470 seconds, about 2.8 times higher than the total time for Quickstep.

In a second more extensive experiment, the Lena standard image was divided into 16 x 16 sections and completely decomposed yielding 256 test cases of a variety of image sections, including high and low con-

(a)

(b)

(c)

(d)

Figure 1: (a). The original Lena image. (b). Lena constructed with Gaussians, decomposed with the Marquardt algorithm in 16 x 16 sections. (c). Lena constructed with Gaussians, decomposed with the Quickstep algorithm in 16 x 16 sections. (d). Lena constructed with Gaussians, decomposed with the Quickstep algorithm in 32 x 32 sections (shows a reduced blocking effect).

	Marquart	Quickstep	Quickstep
section size	16 x 16	16 x 16	32 x 32
iteration limit	10	40	20
total Gaussians	4617	4693	4332
maximum Gaussians in a section	61	62	197
total time for decomposition	95448 s	1561 s	3516 s
trial acceptance percentage	44.9%	47.7%	46.5%
average iterations per section	151	611	1234
SNR rms	30.7	29.8	32.3

Table 1: Comparison of decomposition methods.

trast, detailed and smooth. Figure 1a shows the original Lena image, while Figures 1b and 1c show the results for Marquardt and Quickstep, respectively. Table 1 shows how the decomposition methods compare. Although Table 1 shows slightly more Gaussians for Quickstep than Marquardt, Quickstep had a smaller number of Gaussians than Marquardt in 77 sections, with an average decrease of 1.7 Gaussians, while having a larger number of Gaussians in 89 sections, with an average increase of 2.3 Gaussians. Note, in Table 1,that the average trial acceptance percentage shows that Quickstep has a good ability to come up with trial vectors which reduce the error. Note, however, that Quickstep takes four times as many iterations to reach roughly the same optimal solution as Marquardt (to be expected from the iteration limits). It is apparent that while Quickstep takes steps to reduce the error, the steps it takes are rather crude compared to Marquardt. In spite of this increase in iterations, a striking feature of Quickstep is that it was sixty times faster in decomposing the image, giving rise to the name "Quickstep". For those sections which require few Gaussians, Quickstep and Marquardt had nearly the same speeds, but for those image sections requiring 50 or more Gaussians, Quickstep often achieved a speed 100 times faster than Marquardt, to be expected from the differences in the time complexities. Finally, the quality of results, SNR rms, is similar between the algorithms.

Note that there is a substantial blocking effect in Figures 1b and 1c, occurring mainly in the smooth regions of the image. This effect is largely due to our visual systems, which can perceive slight distortions in smooth regions much more easily than in detailed regions. Figure 1d uses 32 x 32 blocks in the Quickstep method, reducing the blocking effect. The price paid for this reduction, of course, is the increase in time shown in Table 1, in spite of the fact that the iteration limit was set lower at 20. The results in Figure 1d were produced for demonstration purposes only; the Marquardt algorithm was not used for this, since it would be hundreds, if not thousands, of times slower.

In spite of the reduction in the blocking effect in Figure 1d, note that some visual distortions still exist in the smooth areas. One way to improve the image quality would be to lower the tolerance ε (see Inequality 3), which was set at 10 gray scales for the results of Figure 1. This would, however, increase the number of Gaussians. Perhaps a better approach would be to decrease the tolerance for only smooth regions. It also appears that the tolerance can be increased for the detailed regions, providing a balancing effect in the number of Gaussians. This is to be a subject for future research.

Figure 2 shows a 128 x 128 BRDF image [9], which was interesting because of its smoothness and points of brightness. Figure 2a shows the original image while Figure 2b shows the Quickstep decomposition using a tolerance of 10 gray scales with the entire image block size. Note that the Gaussians

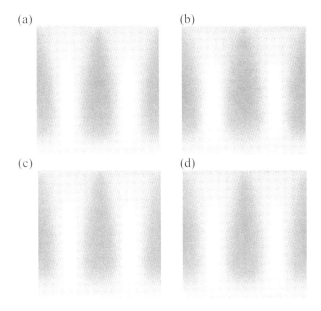

(a) (b)

(c) (d)

Figure 2: (a) Original BRDF image. (b)-(d). Constructed with Quickstep Gaussians at different tolerances. The solution for part (b) used a tolerance of 10 gray scales for 39 Gaussians, an SNR rms of 62.9, and a time of 325 s. The solution for part (c) used a tolerance of 8 for 46 Gaussians, an SNR rms of 93.2, and a time of 502 s. The solution for part (d) used a tolerance of 5 for 67 Gaussians, an SNR rms of 125.7, and a time of 850 s.

(a) (b) (c)

Figure 3: (a) Original solid triangle. (b) Marquardt solution, 26 Gaussians in 279 seconds. (c) Quickstep solution, 22 Gaussians in 4 seconds.

(a) (b) (c)

Figure 4: (a) Original line triangle. (b) Marquardt solution, 18 Gaussians in 183 seconds. (c) Quickstep solution, 20 Gaussians in 3 seconds.

(a) (b) (c)

Figure 5: (a) Original checkerboard. (b) Marquardt solution, 43 Gaussians in 1194 seconds. (c) Quickstep solution, 42 Gaussians in 20 seconds.

160

A	x	y	σ	A	x	y	σ
42.274208	12.203599	6.583468	7.200311	-138.774292	1.533950	1.532053	1.135911
43.400757	12.005547	6.820785	7.372244	-144.186066	15.474975	15.534304	1.752688
70.441765	11.396811	8.395815	10.301986	153.853256	9.906965	9.721567	15.381313
266.132111	7.506141	1.496234	0.570001	-226.461365	7.516838	15.506108	0.696704
-163.423981	11.431159	7.452995	8.088238	-169.637299	1.508797	9.492138	0.976500
318.471039	1.500715	7.505594	0.523438	-127.458023	7.247541	7.248353	1.094320
105.653259	9.611252	7.463912	1.520774	-164.261551	9.473604	9.484006	1.845971
182.185608	7.993632	9.074813	1.588626	-258.263092	9.489571	1.491194	0.592394
141.002945	15.503941	1.484623	1.454900	-233.087234	15.504033	7.516286	0.683021
176.595016	1.502229	15.495743	0.845721	-280.434479	7.506627	13.478838	0.556137
174.587067	15.493904	9.499632	0.893617	-276.227295	5.489450	13.484420	0.590671
313.620148	11.507056	15.504231	0.523847	-265.548615	9.494089	11.634647	0.420271
455.373016	11.532457	5.467762	0.416167	-268.916412	3.532081	11.522730	0.590058
511.010590	13.470234	3.530351	0.400589	-266.030731	3.611399	9.485515	0.533130
381.775269	11.592936	7.508440	0.394871	-284.022095	5.370478	7.518034	0.481777
465.260345	5.475596	11.524047	0.422260	-318.762756	11.554947	11.554553	0.464486
508.425995	3.507012	13.492288	0.423976	-368.327332	13.454527	13.452782	0.442399
441.056396	5.423644	9.497160	0.390403	-261.482300	5.456026	5.456465	0.584261
431.503571	3.502404	7.502584	0.452811	-345.473083	3.530949	3.530430	0.485007
396.376526	13.446114	9.497159	0.442155	-271.530792	7.518799	5.366188	0.493460
329.314117	3.506291	5.498511	0.515609	-263.843109	9.481397	3.522405	0.603679
317.646271	5.494154	3.509284	0.522677	-269.478210	11.517205	3.518836	0.596757
417.074951	7.498525	11.584785	0.391672	-277.096405	13.483739	5.491963	0.594079
418.942352	9.497097	13.497495	0.458514	-301.062653	13.482814	7.507129	0.536386
320.169495	11.502256	13.491319	0.524116	-251.241989	11.640913	9.494258	0.430138
302.156281	13.483729	11.508123	0.537596	226.632263	7.685505	9.437407	0.475072
315.037018	7.505332	3.510144	0.524875	208.890335	9.425779	7.682054	0.502574
358.022034	9.490659	5.400075	0.404291	-301.843292	3.607900	1.504779	0.449477
-212.223663	7.749088	7.731223	0.668982	-272.315552	15.494983	13.369817	0.420588
-213.701141	9.200408	9.267549	0.695086	-289.918518	1.505110	3.611056	0.456856
418.416382	1.501172	13.449910	0.432953	-280.464020	11.514410	1.492916	0.556433
381.748230	15.498572	3.603220	0.386795	-252.680649	13.359729	15.491117	0.425132
-58.661896	6.072452	7.875461	0.715204	-267.772858	5.464641	15.510127	0.573313
329.980164	1.496699	5.494276	0.510028	-268.120422	15.511187	5.466878	0.578068
370.436798	13.395384	1.502107	0.390808	-257.250610	1.495238	11.602804	0.522109
358.394714	3.556432	15.498575	0.460700	110.602249	1.484623	7.847948	0.378529
-63.836678	9.177217	11.012353	0.681923	79.193634	11.295532	7.749356	0.510608
314.962189	5.487666	1.494551	0.521280	79.568695	7.753181	11.298998	0.527986
308.281555	9.492308	15.499116	0.533067	55.679623	6.479113	9.261699	0.437128
288.189209	15.502576	11.565727	0.508811	39.449394	9.199624	6.398310	0.464254
-134.192871	15.503010	8.184283	0.300000	-18.759287	14.871377	10.357703	0.783934
-53.650463	7.808944	5.910851	0.627661	-16.998495	10.361329	14.967628	0.722080
-60.838818	10.877752	9.168189	0.699867				

Table 2: The Gaussians in the Marquardt solution used to form the checkerboard of Figure 5b. A tolerance of 10 gray scales is used, so a summation that is slightly negative should be set to 0 for image reproduction.

Table 3: The Gaussians in the Quickstep solution used to form the checkerboard of Figure 5c. For image reproduction, Gaussians should be truncated using Equation 5, with δ set to 0.5. A tolerance of 10 gray scales is used, so a summation that is slightly negative should be set to 0.

line up in the bright regions, producing a noticeable rounding effect. In this case, 10 gray scales is probably not an acceptable tolerance. Figures 2c and 2d show the results when tolerances of 8 and 5 are used, respectively. This was also done for demonstration purposes; Marquardt was not used for this because of the enormous amount of time it would take on a 128 x 128 block size.

Finally, Figures 3 through 5 show comparisons between Marquardt and Quickstep on some 16 x 16 artificial images. From these few results, we can conclude that Quickstep will sometimes attain smaller Gaussian solutions for artificial images. Tables 2 and 3 show the Gaussian solutions achieved by Marquardt and Quickstep, respectively, for the checkerboard image in Figure 5. In viewing these Gaussian solutions, one should keep two things in mind: (1) Gaussians with negative amplitudes will partially cancel Gaussians with positive amplitudes in summation, producing special surfaces, and (2) since the Gaussian approximations are used only for the discrete pixels, the Gaussians can do "whatever they want" between the pixels; it is not unusual for thin Gaussians to peak very high between pixels, with only its lower points being used in the discrete approximation. Note that, although the two solutions differ by only one Gaussian, the two Gaussian solutions are quite different. One suspects that there may be many such solutions. In a work by Childs *et al.* [3] it was shown that, for a signal composed of Gaussians, the same Gaussian solution is often not recovered. In fact, quite often, a smaller Gaussian solution is found.

Care should be taken to be taken to follow the directions under Tables 2 and 3, if the reader wishes to reproduce the results.

5 Conclusions

In Gaussian decomposition of images, Quickstep offers a much faster method to achieve optimal Gaussian representations than other methods currently available. The optimal Gaussian decomposition of images, previously considered a problem for supercomputers, is now within the grasp of the PC. This is due to a large reduction in the time complexity of an iteration. Newton's method can achieve very good steps towards the solution. In contrast, Quickstep takes rather crude steps towards the solution, but it takes them so quickly that the overall time is dramatically reduced.

Quickstep is based largely on the gradient method, but incorporates many components of the Marquardt algorithm to avoid the long convergence times characteristic of the gradient method. By using an appropriate scale and trying for larger step sizes, it is possible to reach the solution much faster.

Quickstep not only saves time, it also saves a great deal of memory space. Hessian matrices, in an application like this, can have up to hundreds of thousands of entries. Intermediate matrices are also often formed when solving a linear system of equations.

Quickstep also has the advantage of having less roundoff error for very large problems than Marquardt. One problem in solving large linear systems of equations is in the accumulation of roundoff error, which leads to inaccuracies of the solution and poor convergence. Quickstep, in comparison, can be expected to perform basically the same for even larger problems.

Gaussian representations have promising applications in computer graphics. Although it takes time to find a Gaussian representation of an image, once a Gaussian representation is achieved, the Gaussians can be added together quickly to reconstruct the image. Gaussians can be transmitted one at a time, from the most significant Gaussian to the least significant. The Gaussians that have been transmitted can be added to start constructing the image while the other ones are being transmitted. This allows low-to-high resolution display of images across the Internet, resulting in faster image recognition. Truncated Gaussians can be used to construct images even faster, because they only need to be added to the image in the truncated area. This is an important speedup since many Gaussians that fill in details of an image are small. Furthermore, moving images can be handled more easily, since it is only necessary to adjust the parameters, especially position parameters, of the Gaussians which represent them. Gaussians also make very good features for the coarse structures of an image, aiding in image recognition.

Practitioners are usually most interested in three areas: optimality, time, and quality of results. Regarding optimality, Marquardt may have a slight, though subjective, edge over Quickstep. However, in any event, it is justifiable to classify Quickstep as an optimal algorithm, since it can often achieve smaller Gaussian solutions than Marquardt. In fact, from the results in this section, Quickstep achieves a smaller solution than Marquardt about 30% of the time (Marquardt achieves a smaller solution than Quickstep about 34% of the time). Therefore, for those practitioners where optimality is most important (and time is not), it is recommended to use both Marquardt and Quickstep, and take the smaller Gaussian result of the two. The Gaussian solution can also be reduced by increasing the tolerance ε (see Inequality 3), to the point where the quality level is just acceptable.

Regarding time, Quickstep is unquestionably faster for large problems. However, one may want to consider the Marquardt algorithm if one has access to a parallel computer. The iterations cannot be put in parallel, and Marquardt takes less iterations to achieve a solution. It is currently not known how a Marquardt iteration will compare to a Quickstep iteration on a parallel machine. If Quickstep practitioners care little about optimality, the time can be further reduced by (1) decreasing the iteration limit and (2) increasing δ (see Equation 5). However, one should use care in adjusting these parameters; eventually, the algorithm will slow because of the sheer increase in the number of Gaussians.

Regarding quality, Marquardt and Quickstep are very close. For those practitioners for which quality is much more important than the number of Gaussians, the tolerance ε can be lowered. However, one should note that it is never necessary to set the tolerance below 0.5. When the tolerance is set at 0.5, the summation of the Gaussians result for a pixel can be rounded to produce the exact integral pixel value. Hence, such a Gaussian representation is lossless. However, one should also note that the number of Gaussians should increase substantially from a tolerance of 1.0 to a tolerance of 0.5, due to quantization effects. Using a tolerance of 0.5, even a very smooth image will have a blocked effect at the pixel level, due to its integral pixel values.

Quickstep is still in its early stages and there are many possibilities for improving the time further. Future research efforts should focus on reducing the time to form a sum-of-Gaussians matrix, as this process accounts for more than half of the time for the current implementation of Quickstep with truncation. This is presumably because the formation of the initial vectors does not need to be repeated when a trial vector fails, but the calculation of the sum-of-Gaussians matrix does repeat to check the error of other trial vectors. Reduction of the number of iterations, possibly by using a dynamic iteration limit, is another possibility for decreasing the time involved.

References

[1] J. Ben-Arie and K. R. Rao. Nonorthogonal signal representation by Gaussians and Gabor functions. In *IEEE Transactions on Circuits and Systems, Part II: Analog and Digital Signal Processing*, Vol. 42, pages 402-13, June, 1995.

[2] A. R. Conn, N. I. M. Gould, and P. L. Toint. A globally convergent augmented Lagrangian algorithm for optimization with general constraints and simple bounds. In *SIAM J. Numer. Anal.*, Vol. 28, No. 2, pages 545-72, April, 1991.

[3] J. Childs, C. C. Lu, and J. Potter. Intrinsic boundaries in Gaussian decomposition. In *Proceedings of IASTED*, pages 64-8, 1999.

[4] H. B. Curry. The method of steepest descent for non-linear minimization problems. In *Quarterly of Applied Mathematics*, pages 258-61, 1944.

[5] P. J. S. G. Ferreira. A comment on the approximation of signals by Gaussian functions. In *IEEE Transactions on Circuits and Systems, Part II: Analog and Digital Signal Processing*, Vol. 45, No. 2, pages 250-1, February, 1998.

[6] A. Goshtasby and W. D. O'Neill. Curve fitting by a sum of Gaussians. In *CVGIP: Graphical Models and Image Processing*, Vol. 56, No. 4, pages 281-84, July, 1994.

[7] A. Goshtasby and W. D. O'Neill. Surface fitting to scattered data by a sum of Gaussians. In *Computer Aided Geometric Design*, Vol. 10, pages 143-56, 1993.

[8] H. O. Hartley. The modified Gauss-Newton method for fitting of nonlinear regression functions by least-squares. In *Technometrics*, Vol. 3, No. 2, pages 269-80, 1961.

[9] J. Kautz and M. McCool. Interactive rendering with arbitrary BRDFs using separable decompositions. In *10th Eurographics Workshop on Rendering*, Springer-Verlag, Rendering Techniques '99, pages 247-60, 1999.

[10] D. W. Marquardt. An algorithm for least-squares estimation of nonlinear parameters. In *J. Soc. Indust. Appl. Math.*, Vol. 11, No. 2, pages 431-41, 1962.

[11] P. L. Toint. On large scale nonlinear least squares calculations. In *SIAM J. Sci. Stat. Comput.*, Vol. 8, No. 3, pages 416-35, May, 1987.

Oriented Sliver Textures:
A Technique for Local Value Estimation of Multiple Scalar Fields

Chris Weigle[1]   William Emigh[2]   Geniva Liu[3]   Russell M. Taylor II[1]   James T. Enns[3]   Christopher G. Healey[2]

[1]Department of Computer Science, University of North Carolina at Chapel Hill

[2]Department of Computer Science, North Carolina State University

[3]Department of Psychology, University of British Columbia

Abstract

This paper describes a texture generation technique that combines orientation and luminance to support the simultaneous display of multiple overlapping scalar fields. Our orientations and luminances are selected based on psychophysical experiments that studied how the low-level human visual system perceives these visual features. The result is an image that allows viewers to identify data values in an individual field, while at the same time highlighting interactions between different fields. Our technique supports datasets with both smooth and sharp boundaries. It is stable in the presence of noise and missing values. Images are generated in real-time, allowing interactive exploration of the underlying data. Our technique can be combined with existing methods that use perceptual colours or perceptual texture dimensions, and can therefore be seen as an extension of these methods to further assist in the exploration and analysis of large, complex, multidimensional datasets.

Keywords: computer graphics, human vision, luminance, multidimensional, orientation, perception, texture, scientific visualization.

1 Introduction

This paper describes a new texture generation technique designed to allow rapid visual exploration and analysis of multiple overlapping scalar fields. Our technique falls in the area of *scientific visualization*, the conversion of collections of strings and numbers (called datasets) into images that viewers can use to "see" values, structures, and relationships embedded in their data. A *multidimensional dataset* contains a large number of data elements, where each element encodes n separate attributes $A_1, ..., A_n$. For example, a weather dataset is made up of data elements representing weather station readings. Each element encodes a latitude, longitude, and elevation, a time and date readings were taken, and environmental conditions like temperature, pressure, humidity, precipitation, wind speed, and wind direction. An open problem in scientific visualization is the construction of techniques to display data in a multidimensional dataset in a manner that supports effective exploration and analysis [14, 20].

Previous work on this problem has suggested selecting n visual features (*e.g.*, spatial location, hue, luminance, size, contrast, directionality, or motion) to represent each of the n attributes embedded in the dataset. Although this technique can work well in practice, a number of limitations need to be considered:

- *dimensionality:* as the number of attributes n in the dataset grows, it becomes more and more difficult to find additional visual features to represent them.
- *interference:* different visual features will often interact with one another, producing visual interference; these interference effects must be controlled or eliminated to guarantee effective exploration and analysis.
- *attribute-feature matching:* different visual features are best suited to a particular type of attribute and analysis task; an effective visualization technique needs to respect these preferences.

The weather dataset (and numerous other practical applications) can be viewed as a collection of n scalar fields that overlap spatially with one another. Rather than using n visual features to represent these fields, we use only two: orientation and luminance. For each scalar field (representing attribute A_i) we select a constant orientation o_i; at various spatial locations where a value $a_i \in A_i$ exists, we place a corresponding *sliver texture* oriented at o_i. The luminance of the sliver texture depends on a_i: the maximum $a_{max} \in A_i$ produces a white (full luminance) sliver, while the minimum $a_{min} \in A_i$ produces a black (zero luminance) sliver. A perceptually-balanced luminance scale running from black to white is used to select a luminance for an intermediate value a_i, $a_{min} < a_i < a_{max}$ (this scale was built to correct for the visual system's approximately logarithmic response to variations in luminance [8]).

Figure 1a shows a uniformly-sampled 20×20 patch from a hypothetical scalar field. Values in the field are represented as greyscale swatches in Figure 1b. A constant orientation of 0° is used to represent values in the field (slivers rotated 0° are placed at the spatial locations for each reading in the field, shown in Figure 1c). Blending these two representations together produces the final image (Figure 1d), a layer of variable-lumi-

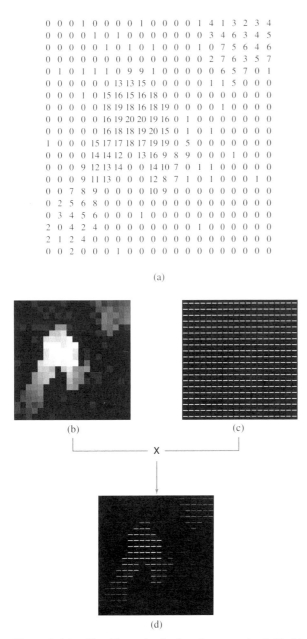

```
0  0  0  1  0  0  0  0  1  0  0  0  0  1  4  1  3  2  3  4
0  0  0  0  1  0  1  0  0  0  0  0  0  0  3  4  6  3  4  5
0  0  0  0  1  0  1  0  1  0  0  0  1  0  7  5  6  4  6
0  0  0  0  0  0  0  0  0  0  0  0  0  2  7  6  3  5  7
0  1  0  1  1  1  0  9  9  1  0  0  0  0  6  5  7  0  1
0  0  0  0  0  0 13 13 15  0  0  0  0  0  1  1  5  0  0  0
0  0  0  1  0 15 16 15 16 18  0  0  0  0  0  0  0  0  0  0
0  0  0  0  0 18 19 18 16 18 19  0  0  0  0  1  0  0  0  0
0  0  0  0  0 16 19 20 20 19 16  0  1  0  0  0  0  0  0  0
0  0  0  0  0 16 18 18 19 20 15  0  1  0  1  0  0  0  0  0
1  0  0  0 15 17 17 18 17 19 19  0  5  0  0  0  0  0  0  0
0  0  0  0 14 14 12  0 13 16  9  8  9  0  0  0  1  0  0  0
0  0  0  9 12 13 14  0  0 14 10  7  0  1  1  0  0  0  0  0
0  0  0  9 11 13  0  0  0 12  8  7  1  0  1  0  0  0  1  0
0  0  7  8  9  0  0  0  0 10  9  0  0  0  0  0  0  0  0  0
0  2  5  6  8  0  0  0  0  0  0  0  0  0  0  0  0  0  0  0
0  3  4  5  6  0  0  0  1  0  0  0  0  0  0  0  0  0  0  0
2  0  4  2  4  0  0  0  0  0  0  0  1  0  0  0  0  0  0  0
2  1  2  4  0  0  0  0  0  0  0  0  0  0  0  0  0  0  0  0
0  0  2  0  0  0  1  0  0  0  0  0  0  0  0  0  0  0  0  0
```

(a)

Figure 1. (a) a 20×20 patch of values from a scalar field; (b) the patch represented by greyscale swatches; (c) a collection of slivers oriented 0° at each data value location; (d) the greyscale map and slivers are combined to produce the final sliver layer

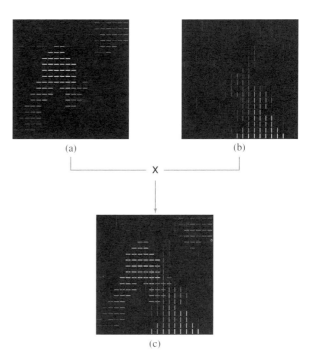

Figure 2. (a,b) two scalar fields represented with 0° and 90°, respectively; (c) both fields displayed in a single image, overlapping values show as elements that look like plus signs

nance slivers showing the positions and values of all the data in the original field.

Multiple scalar fields are displayed by compositing their sliver layers together. Figure 2a-b shows two separate sliver layers representing two scalar fields. The first field uses slivers oriented 0°; the second uses slivers oriented 90°. When a viewer visualizes both fields simultaneously, the sliver layers are overlayed to produce the single image shown in Figure 2c. This image allows the viewer to locate values in each individual field, while at the same time identifying important interactions between the fields. The use of thin, well separated slivers is key to allowing values from multiple fields to show through in a common spatial location. A viewer can use these images to:

- determine which fields are prominent in a region,
- determine how strongly a given field is present,
- estimate the relative weights of the field values in the region, and
- locate regions where all the fields have low, medium, or high values.

We continue with a discussion of related work, focusing in particular on the use of texture patterns for multidimensional data display. Next, we describe the psychophysical experiments we used to determine how to select perceptually salient orientations. Although our visualization technique is applicable to a wide range of practical applications, we were originally motivated by a specific problem: the display of multiple atomic surface properties measured with a scanning electron microscope. We conclude by showing how our technique can be used to visualize datasets from this domain.

2 Related Work

Several techniques exist for displaying multidimensional datasets on an underlying surface or height field.

A good overview of some of these techniques is presented in Keller and Keller [10]. Our work is most similar to methods that use textures or glyphs to represent multiple attribute values at a single spatial location. We therefore focus our study of previous work on this broad area.

Texture has been studied extensively in the computer vision, computer graphics, and cognitive psychology communities. Although each group focuses on separate tasks (e.g., texture segmentation and classification, information display, or modelling the human visual system), they each need ways to describe precisely the textures being identified, classified, or displayed. Statistical methods and perceptual techniques are both used to analyse texture [19]. Our focus in this paper is on identifying and harnessing the perceptual features that make up a texture pattern. Experiments conducted by Julész led to the texton theory [9], which suggests that early vision detects three types of texture features (or textons): elongated blobs with specific visual properties (e.g. colour or orientation), ends of line segments, and crossings of line segments. Tamura et al. [21] and Rao and Lohse [18] identified texture dimensions by conducting experiments that asked subjects to divide pictures depicting different types of textures (Brodatz images) into groups. Tamura et al. used their results to propose methods for measuring coarseness, contrast, directionality, line-likeness, regularity, and roughness. Rao and Lohse applied multidimensional scaling to identify the primary texture dimensions used by their subjects to group images: regularity, directionality, and complexity. Haralick et al. [3] built greyscale spatial dependency matrices to identify features like homogeneity, contrast, and linear dependency. Liu and Picard [13] used Wold features to synthesize texture patterns. A Wold decomposition divides a 2D homogeneous pattern (e.g., a texture pattern) into three mutually orthogonal components with perceptual properties that roughly correspond to periodicity, directionality, and randomness.

Work in computer graphics has studied methods for using texture patterns to display information during visualization. Grinstein et al. [2] built "stick-men" icons to produce texture patterns that show spatial coherence in a multidimensional dataset. Ware and Knight [26] used Gabor filters to construct texture patterns; attributes in an underlying dataset are used to modify the orientation, size, and contrast of the Gabor elements during visualization. Turk and Banks [24] described an iterated method for placing streamlines to visualize two-dimensional vector fields. Interrante [6] displayed texture strokes to help show three-dimensional shape and depth on layered transparent surfaces. Healey and Enns [4, 5] described perceptual methods for measuring and controlling perceptual texture dimensions during multi-dimensional visualization. van Wijk [25], Cabral and Leedom [1], and Interrante and Grosch [7] used spot noise and line integral convolution to generate texture patterns to represent an underlying flow field. Finally, Laidlaw described painterly methods for visualizing multidimensional datasets with up to seven values at each spatial location [11, 12].

Our technique is perhaps most similar to the stickman method used in EXVIS [2], or to the pexels (perceptual texture elements) of Healey and Enns [4, 5]. EXVIS shows areas of coherence among multiple attributes by producing characteristic texture patterns in these areas. We extend this technique by allowing a viewer to estimate relative values within an individual field, while still producing the characteristic textures needed to highlight interactions between different fields.

3 Orientation Categories

In order to effectively represent multiple scalar fields with different orientations, we need to know how the visual system distinguishes between orientations. In simple terms, we want to determine whether the visual system differentiates orientation using a collection of perceptual orientation categories. If these categories exist, it might suggest that the low-level visual system can rapidly distinguish between orientations that lie in different categories.

Psychophysical research on this problem has produced a number of interesting yet incomplete conclusions. Some researchers believe only three categories of orientation exist: flat, tilted, and upright [27]. Others suggest a minimum rotational difference d is necessary to perceive a spatial collection of target elements oriented tg in a field of background elements oriented bg (i.e., $d = |tg - bg|$). More recent work has shown that d is dependent on bg [15, 16]. For example, if the background elements are oriented $0°$ (i.e., horizontal or flat), only a small rotation may be needed to differentiate a group of target elements (e.g., $tg = 10°$ and $d = tg - bg = 10°$). On the other hand, a much larger rotational difference might be necessary to distinguish a target group in a sea of background elements oriented $20°$ (e.g., $tg = 40°$ and $d = tg - bg = 20°$). Based on these results, we seek to construct a function $f(bg)$ that will report the amount of rotational difference d needed to perceive a group of target elements oriented $tg = bg + d$ in a sea of background elements oriented bg.

3.1 Experiment Design

We began our investigation by attempting to construct a discrete function $f(bg)$ for 19 different background orientations of $0, 5, 10, ..., 90°$. The function f returns rotational differences in $5°$ intervals (e.g., $d = 5°$, $d = 10°$, $d =$

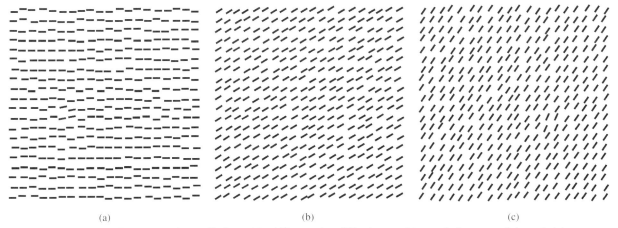

(a)   (b)   (c)

Figure 3. An example of three experiment displays: (a) a 10° target in a 0° background (target is five steps right and eight steps up from the lower left corner of the array); (b) a 30° background with no target; (c) a 65° target in a 55° background (target is six steps left and seven steps up from the lower right corner of the array)

15°, and so on). Our experiment was designed to answer the following questions:

- In a sea of background elements oriented bg, how much counterclockwise rotation d_{ccw} is needed to differentiate a group of target elements oriented $tg = bg + d_{ccw}$?
- How much clockwise rotation d_{cw} is needed to differentiate a group of target elements oriented $tg = bg - d_{cw}$?
- For a given background bg, do d_{ccw} and d_{cw} differ significantly?
- Do certain backgrounds (*e.g.*, the cardinal directions 0, 45, and 90°) have significantly lower d_{ccw} or d_{cw}?
- What is the maximum number of rapidly distinguishable orientations we can construct in the range 0–90°?

The initial experiment was divided into two parts: one to test background orientations from 0–45°, the other to test background orientations 45–90°. We describe trials in the 0–45° experiment. Apart from the specific orientations used, the design of the 45–90° experiment was identical.

During the experiment the background orientation was increased in 5° steps from 0° to 45°. This resulted in 10 different background subsections (0, 5, 10, ..., 45°). Every possible target orientation was tested for each separate background. For example, targets oriented 5, 10, 15, 20, 25, 30, 35, 40, and 45° were tested in a sea of background elements oriented 0°. Targets oriented 0, 5, 10, 20, 25, 30, 35, 40, and 45° were tested in a sea of background elements oriented 15°.

A total of 540 trials were run during the experiment (six for each of the 90 different background/target pairs). Each trial contained a total of 400 rectangles arrayed on a 20×20 grid. The position of each rectangle

was randomly jittered to introduce a measure of irregularity. Three trials for each background/target pair contained a 2×2 target patch (as in Figure 3a, c); the other three did not (as in Figure 3b). Twenty undergraduate psychology students were randomly selected to participate during the experiment (ten for the 0–45° experiment and ten for the 45–90° experiment). Subjects were asked to answer whether a target patch with an orientation different from the background elements was present or absent in each trial. They were told that half the trials would contain a target patch, and half would not. Subjects were instructed to answer as quickly as possible, while still trying to maintain an accuracy rate of 90% or better. Feedback was provided after each trial to inform subjects whether their answer was correct. The entire experiment took approximately one hour to complete. Subject accuracies (1 for a correct answer, 0 for an incorrect answer) and response times (automatically recorded based on the vertical refresh rate of the monitor) were recorded after each trial for later analysis.

3.2 Results

Mean subject response times $\overline{rt}$ and mean subject error rates $\overline{e}$ were used to measure performance. A combination of multi-factor analysis of variance (ANOVA) and least-squares line fitting showed:

1. A target oriented $d = \pm 15°$ or more from its background elements resulted in the highest accuracies and the fastest response times, regardless of background orientation.
2. $\overline{e}$ for backgrounds oriented 0 or 90° was significantly lower than for the other backgrounds.
3. $\overline{e}$ for targets oriented 0° or 90° was significantly higher than for the other targets, suggesting an asymmetry (good as a background, bad as a target) for these orientations.

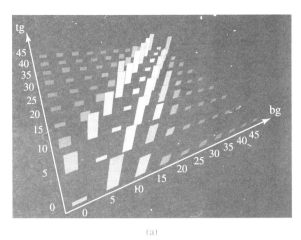

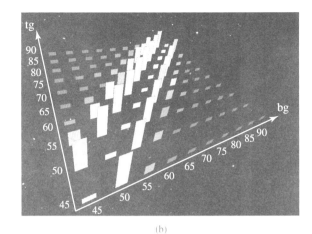

(a) (b)

Figure 4. (a) results for the 0–45° experiment, one strip for each background/target pair; the height of the strip represents $\bar{e}$ (taller for more errors), the brightness of the strip represents $\bar{rt}$ (brighter for longer response times); locations where $bg = tg$ (the diagonals on each graph) represent target absent trials; (b) results for the 45–90° experiment

4. There were no systematic differences in either $\bar{e}$ or $\bar{rt}$ between clockwise and counterclockwise rotations about any background orientation.

5. There was no significant difference in $\bar{e}$ between the 0–45° and the 45–90° experiments for corresponding background/target pairs, however, within the $d = \pm10°$ range $\bar{rt}$ was slower during the 45–90° experiment, compared to the 0–45° experiment.

Regardless of the specific background orientation being displayed, any target oriented $d = \pm15°$ or more from the background produced near-perfect accuracy and fast response times ($F(1, 90) = 8.06$, $p < 0.01$ and $F(1, 90) = 2.96$, $p < 0.05$ for $\bar{e}$ and $\bar{rt}$, respectively, in the $d = \pm15°$ range). This suggests that any target with an absolute rotational difference of 15° or more from the background can be rapidly and accurately perceived.

When background elements were oriented 0 or 90°, targets were detected more accurately ($F(9, 810) = 12.82$, $p < 0.001$ at $d = 5°$). On the other hand, targets oriented 0 or 90° were detected less accurately (*e.g.*, a 90° target in a background of elements rotated 85 or 80°, or a 0° target in a background of elements rotated 5 or 10°; $F(1, 162) = 48.02$, $p < 0.001$ at $d = 5°$; $F(1, 162) = 29.91$, $p < 0.001$ at $d = 10°$). This orientation asymmetry is documented in the psychophysical literature [22, 23]. In terms of visualization, it suggests we should treat the cardinal directions 0 and 90° carefully; although they produce less visual interference (*i.e.*, they act well as background orientations), they can be significantly more difficult to detect (*i.e.*, they act poorly as target orientations).

We found a small but statistically significant increase in $\bar{rt}$ during the 45–90° experiment ($F(1, 90) = 6.08$, $p < 0.05$ over the $d = \pm10°$ range, shown by brighter strips in Figure 4b). Since the overall pattern of response times between the two experiments is identical, we believe this result is due to a difference between subjects (*i.e.*, subjects in the 45–90° experiment simply needed more time to feel comfortable about the answers they gave). Even if the results are significant for all viewers, the small differences we encountered would not be important for applications that allow a viewer to spend time exploring an image. However, these differences could be important in real-time environments or during long viewing sessions. Additional experiments are needed to determine if any real differences in response times exist.

Two additional findings allow us to simplify our selection of orientations. First, there were no systematic differences in either $\bar{e}$ or $\bar{rt}$ between clockwise and counterclockwise rotations about any background orientation. In three cases (backgrounds of 55, 65, and 70°) clockwise rotations were significantly faster; in two other cases (backgrounds of 25 and 30°) counterclockwise rotations were significantly faster. Since subjects did not exhibit a consistent preference for either direction, we concluded that we can rotate the same amount in either direction to make a target patch salient from its background elements. Finally, there was no significant difference in $\bar{e}$ between the 0–45° experiment and the 45–90° experiment ($F(1, 18) = 0.157$, $p = 0.6893$). This means that, given a reasonable amount of time to search, accuracy in each set of backgrounds is statistically equal, and the two ranges can be considered mirror images of one another.

We conclude by noting that our experiments investigated how to *distinguish* multiple orientations from one another. This is a first step towards determining how many orientations the visual system can *identify* simultaneously (*i.e.*, the ability to identify the presence or absence of a sliver with a specific orientation). Our results provide a solid foundation from which to build future experiments that study the question "How many different orientations can I identify from one another?"

3.3 Emergent Features

An overlap between high-value regions in different scalar fields appears as a collection of slivers sharing common spatial locations. The overlapping slivers form shapes like plus, X, or star. It is often critical for viewers to be able to identify these overlapping regions. Although we did not conduct experiments on the perceptual salience of each type of overlap, the shapes they form fall into the broad category of *emergent features* [17]. An emergent feature is created by grouping several simpler shapes together. Although emergent features cannot always be predicted by examining the simpler shapes in isolation, they result in perceptually salient visual properties like intersection, closure, and shape (or curvature). We believe that all of the overlapping sliver types will produce at least one emergent feature (*e.g.,* every overlap will produce an intersection between the slivers). The emergent features make the locations of the overlapping regions salient from neighbouring, non-overlapping areas.

4 Implementation

Figure 1 shows the general process for creating one sliver layer. The slivers in Figure 1 are positioned on an underlying regular grid. In practice, however, we must jitter the placement of each sliver. This helps to prevent the technique from imposing any strong artificial structure on the data. Separating the slivers is also necessary to allow multiple slivers with different orientations to show through at common spatial locations. The base texture used to make the images in this paper is 10% sliver, 90% empty. We employed the image-guided streamline placement package of Turk and Banks [24] on a constant vector field to generate the base texture. Since we viewed this as a pre-processing step, the time used to build the base texture was not a critical concern.

Next, we assign an orientation to each scalar field in the dataset. Since slivers oriented 0–180° are mirror images of slivers rotated 180–360°, we restricted our selections to the 0–180° range. During implementation we assumed the experimental results from our 0–90° range were identical for orientations covering 90–180°. Anecdotal findings during the use of our system suggest this assumption is valid. We can immediately obtain 13 separate orientations by simply using a constant difference $d = 15°$. If we choose to treat the cardinal directions 0° and 180° as special background cases that only require targets with 5° of rotational difference, we can increase the number of separate orientations to 15.

Once an easily distinguishable orientation is assigned to each scalar field, the sliver layers can be constructed. The values in each field modulate the intensity of the slivers in the field's layer. In order to avoid an obvious artifact in the center of the final image, the centers of rotation for every layer are different. We accomplish this by translating each layer's texture centers to different points on a uniform grid. The layers are then overlayed on top of one another. The final texture is the per-pixel maximum of the overlapping sliver layers (using the maximum avoids highlights produced by averaging or summing overlapping luminances values).

We create only one base texture, rotating and translating it to form the other orientations. Alternatively, we could produce a separate base texture for each scalar field. The use of multiple base textures would prevent the appearance of regions with similar orientation-independent structures. Since we did not notice this phenomena in practice, we chose not to address this problem. Using a single base texture allows our technique to generate a 256×256 image with nine scalar fields at nine frames per second on a workstation with eight R10000 processors.

5 Practical Applications

The application for which this technique was originally developed is the display of multiple data fields from a scanning electron microscope (SEM). Each field represents the concentration of a particular element (oxygen, silicon, carbon, and so on) across a surface. Physicists studying mineral samples need to determine what elements make up each part of the surface and how those elements mix. By allowing the viewer to see the relative concentrations of the elements in a given area, our technique enables recognition of composites more easily than side-by-side comparison, especially for situations where there are complex amalgams of materials.

Figure 5a shows sliver layers representing eight separate elements: calcium (15°), copper (30°), iron (60°), magnesium (75°), manganese (105°), oxygen (120°), sulphur (150°), and silicon (165°). The orientations for each layer were chosen to ensure no two layers have an orientation difference of less than 15°. Figure 5b shows the eight layers blended together to form a single image. Figure 5c changes the orientations of silicon and oxygen to 90° and 180°, respectively, to investigate a potential interaction between the two (the presence of silicon oxide in the upper right, upper left, and lower left where regions of "plus sign" textures appear).

6 Conclusions and Future Work

This paper describes a technique for using orientation and luminance to visualize multiple overlapping scalar

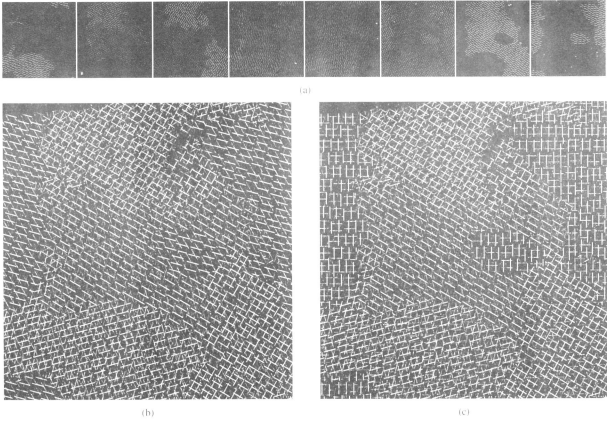

(a)

(b)　　　　　　　　　　　　　　　　　　　　　　　　　　(c)

Figure 5. (a) eight sliver layers representing calcium (15°), copper (30°), iron (60°), magnesium (75°), manganese (105°), oxygen (120°), sulphur (150°), and silicon (165°); (b) all eight layers blended into a single image; (c) silicon and oxygen re-oriented at 90° and 180°, respectively, to highlight the presence of silicon oxide (as a "plus sign" texture) in the upper right, upper left, and lower left corners of the image

fields simultaneously in a single image. Values in each field are represented by sliver textures oriented at a fixed rotation o_i. A sliver's luminance is selected based on the relative strength of the scalar field at the sliver's spatial location. We conducted psychophysical experiments to study how the low-level human visual system perceives differences in orientation. This knowledge was used to choose orientations for each field that were easy to distinguish. Our results suggest up to 15 orientations in the 0–180° range can be rapidly and accurately differentiated. The greyscale ramp used to assign a luminance to each sliver was also constructed to be perceptually linear. The result is an image that shows data values in each individual field, while at the same time highlighting important interactions between the fields.

Our technique varies a sliver's luminance, leaving chromaticity (hue and saturation) free for other uses. For example, an isoluminant, medium-intensity colour background will highlight slivers with high or low field values. If many fields have common values in the same spatial region, we can help to identify their individual boundaries by displaying some of the fields using

colour. Important fields can be shown in colour rather than greyscale to further enhance their distinguishability. Recent work in our laboratory has successfully combined sliver textures with perceptual colour selection techniques, thereby increasing the amount of information we can represent in a single display.

Orientation has been identified as a perceptual texture dimension, a fundamental property of an overall texture pattern. We can vary other perceptual texture dimensions of each sliver (e.g., their size or density) to encode additional data values. We want to note that we are forming a single texture pattern by varying its underlying texture dimensions. It is not possible to overlay multiple texture patterns (e.g., spot noise and slivers) to visualize multiple data attributes; in fact, the inability to analyse texture patterns displayed on top of one another was one of the original motivations for this work.

Finally, this paper focuses on 2D orientation. Future work will study the use of 3D orientation. The first question of interest is: "Which 3D orientation properties are perceptually salient from one another?" Research in the psychophysical community has started to address exactly this question. Once these properties are identified, we can conduct experiments to test their ability to encode information, both in isolation and in combination with one another. Three-dimensional orientation properties may allow us to represent 3D scalar volumes as clouds of oriented slivers in three-space. As with 2D slivers, we want to investigate the strengths and limitations of this type of technique vis-a-vis traditional methods of volume rendering and volume visualization.

References

[1] CABRAL, B. AND LEEDOM, L. C. Imaging vector fields using line integral convolution. In *SIGGRAPH '93 Conference Proceedings* (Anaheim, California, 1993), pp. 263–270.

[2] GRINSTEIN, G., PICKETT, R., AND WILLIAMS, M. EXVIS: An exploratory data visualization environment. In *Proceedings Graphics Interface '89* (London, Canada, 1989), pp. 254–261.

[3] HARALICK, R. M., SHANMUGAM, K., AND DINSTEIN, I. Textural features for image classification. *IEEE Transactions on System, Man, and Cybernetics SMC-3, 6* (1973), 610–621.

[4] HEALEY, C. G. AND ENNS, J. T. Building perceptual textures to visualize multidimensional datasets. In *Proceedings Visualization '98* (Research Triangle Park, North Carolina, 1998), pp. 111–118.

[5] HEALEY, C. G. AND ENNS, J. T. Large datasets at a glance: Combining textures and colors in scientific visualization. *IEEE Transactions on Visualization and Computer Graphics 5, 2* (1999), 145–167.

[6] INTERRANTE, V. Illustrating surface shape in volume data via principle direction-driven 3D line integral convolution. In *SIGGRAPH '97 Conference Proceedings* (Los Angeles, California, 1997), pp. 109–116.

[7] INTERRANTE, V. AND GROSCH, C. Visualizing 3D flow. *IEEE Computer Graphics & Applications 18, 4* (1998), 49–53.

[8] INTERRANTE, V., FERWERDA, J., GOSSWEILER, R., HEALEY, C. G. AND RHEINGANS, P. Applications of Visual Perception in Computer Grpahics. *SIGGRAPH 98 Course 32* (Orlando, Florida, 1992).

[9] JULÉSZ, B. A brief outline of the texton theory of human vision. *Trends in Neuroscience 7, 2* (1984), 41–45.

[10] KELLER, P. AND KELLER, M. *Visual cues: Practical data visualization.* IEEE Computer Society Press, Los Alamitos, California, 1991.

[11] KIRBY, R. M., MARMANIS, H., AND LAIDLAW, D. H. Visualizing multivalued data from 2D incompressible flows using concepts from painting. In *Proceedings Visualization '99* (San Francisco, California, 1999), pp. 333–340.

[12] LAIDLAW, D. H., AHRENS, E. T., KREMERS, D., AWALOS, M. J., JACOBS, R. E., AND READHEAD, C. Visualizing diffuse tensor images of the mouse spinal cord. In *Proceedings Visualization '98* (Research Triangle Park, North Carolina, 1998), pp. 127–134.

[13] LIU, F. AND PICARD, R. W. Periodicity, directionality, and randomness: Wold features for perceptual pattern recognition. In *Proceedings 12th International Conference on Pattern Recognition* (Jerusalem, Israel, 1994), pp. 1–5.

[14] MCCORMICK, B. H., DEFANTI, T. A., AND BROWN, M. D. Visualization in scientific computing—A synopsis. *Computer Graphics & Applications 7, 7* (1987), 61–70.

[15] NOTHDURFT, H-C. Orientation sensitivity and texture segmentation in patterns with different line orientations. *Vision Research 25* (1985), 551–560.

[16] NOTHDURFT, H-C. Texture segmentation and pop-out from orientation contrast. *Vision Research 31, 6* (1991), 1073–1078.

[17] POMERANTZ, J. R. AND PRISTACH, E. A. Emergent features, attention, and perceptual glue in visual form attention. *Journal of Experimental Psychology: Human Perception & Performance 15, 4* (1989), 635–649.

[18] RAO, A. R. AND LOHSE, G. L. Identifying high level features of texture perception. *Computer Vision, Graphics, and Image Processing: Graphical Models and Image Processing 55, 3* (1993), 218–233.

[19] REED, T. R. AND HANS DU BUF, J. M. A review of recent texture segmentation and feature extraction techniques. *Computer Vision, Graphics, and Image Processing: Image Understanding 57, 3* (1993), 359–372.

[20] SMITH, P. H. AND VAN ROSENDALE, J. *Data and visualization corridors report on the 1998 CVD workshop series.* Technical Report CACR-164 (sponsored by DOE and NSF), Center for Advanced Computing Research, California Institute of Technology, 1998.

[21] TAMURA, D., MORI, S., AND YAMAWAKI, T. Textural features corresponding to visual perception. *IEEE Transactions on Systems, Man, and Cybernetics SMC-8, 6* (1978), 460–473.

[22] TRIESMAN, A. AND GORMICAN, S. Feature analysis in early vision: evidence from search asymmetries. *Psychological Review 95, 1* (1988), 15–48.

[23] TRIESMAN, A. Search, similarity, and integration of features between and within dimensions. *Journal of Experimental Psychology: Human Perception & Performance 17, 3* (1991), 652–676.

[24] TURK, G. AND BANKS. D. Image-guided streamline placement. In *SIGGRAPH '96 Conference Proceedings* (New Orleans, Louisiana, 1996), pp. 453–460.

[25] VAN WIJK, J.J. Spot noise, texture synthesis for data visualization. In *SIGGRAPH '91 Conference Proceedings* (Las Vegas, Nevada, 1991), pp. 309–318.

[26] WARE, C. AND KNIGHT, W. Using visual texture for information display. *ACM Transactions on Graphics 14, 1* (1995), 3–20.

[27] WOLFE, J. M., FRIEDMAN-HILL, S. R., STEWART, M. I., AND O'CONNELL, K. M. The role of categorization in visual search for orientation. *Journal of Experimental Psychology: Human Perception & Performance 18, 1* (1992), 39–49.

Using a 3D Puzzle as a Metaphor for Learning Spatial Relations

Felix Ritter[1], Bernhard Preim[2], Oliver Deussen[1], and Thomas Strothotte[1]

[1] Otto-von-Guericke University of Magdeburg
Department of Simulation and Graphics
PSF 4120, D-39016 Magdeburg, Germany
{fritter, deussen, tstr}@isg.cs.uni-magdeburg.de

[2] MeVis gGmbH
Universitätsallee 29
D-28359 Bremen, Germany
bernhard@mevis.de

Abstract

We introduce a new metaphor for learning spatial relations—the 3D puzzle. With this metaphor users learn spatial relations by assembling a geometric model themselves. For this purpose, a 3D model of the subject at hand is enriched with docking positions which allow objects to be connected. Since complex 3D interactions are required to compose 3D objects, sophisticated 3D visualization and interaction techniques are included. Among these techniques are specialized shadow generation, snapping mechanisms, collision detection and the use of two-handed interaction.

The 3D puzzle, similar to a computer game, can be operated at different levels of difficulty. To simplify the task, a subset of the geometry, e.g., the skeleton of an anatomic model, can be given initially. Moreover, textual information concerning the parts of the model is provided to support the user. With this approach we motivate students to explore the spatial relations in complex geometric models and at the same time give them a goal to achieve while learning takes place. A prototype of a 3D puzzle, which is designed principally for use in anatomy education, is presented.

Keywords: Metaphors for spatial interaction, interactive system design, 3D interaction

1 Introduction

In many areas, learning involves the understanding of complex spatial phenomena. In engineering, the construction of machines has to be mastered as a prerequisite for maintenance purposes. To replace a part of a complex engine, a subset has to be decomposed in a well-defined sequence. The spatial composition of molecules is important in chemistry.

Probably the most complex system known to mankind is the human body. Therefore, medical students have considerable difficulties in imagining the spatial relations within the human body which they have to learn in anatomy. With interactive 3D computer graphics, based on high resolution geometric models, these spatial relations may be explored. To exploit this potential, dedicated 3D interaction and visualization techniques as well as convincing metaphors have to be developed.

The book metaphor as a general metaphor for the design of educational systems is well suited to structure the information contents, but is inadequate for learning spatial relations by itself. This is better performed by the atlas metaphor which offers more pictorial contents and is often based on 3D models which can be viewed from different directions [16]. In anatomy, for example, most of the systems available for learning spatial relations are based on this metaphor: Students explore geometric models and related textual information in a way inspired by a printed atlas. The leading example is the VOXELMAN [6] which additionally allows to remove parts of 3D models. Another more recent system is the ZOOM ILLUSTRATOR [14] which includes generated figure captions and sophisticated strategies to label 3D objects—both of which are inspired directly by anatomic atlases.

However, the atlas metaphor does not imply particular 3D interaction techniques. Though 3D interaction is provided to a certain extent, user studies have shown that students underutilize these possibilities or are even unaware of their existence [12]. Therefore, it is particularly useful to structure the user interface of such a learning system on the basis of a spatial metaphor and to provide specific tasks which necessarily include 3D interaction.

Based on the above observation, we introduce the metaphor of a 3D puzzle for learning spatial relations: Users compose specific geometric models from elementary objects. This idea was inspired by an empirical evaluation of the ZOOM ILLUSTRATOR with physicians and students of medicine [12]. Several students expressed the desire for more powerful 3D interaction like assembling parts of the model.

The paper is organized as follows: First we introduce the 3D puzzle metaphor and compare it with a related metaphor for spatial interaction. Then, the basic interaction tasks to be fulfilled by a learning system based on this metaphor are presented. In the next section, the requirements for the visualization and the 3D interaction techniques are discussed. We then focus on the realization of our 3D puzzle. An informal evaluation based on a scenario in medicine concludes the paper.

2 Metaphors for the Composition of 3D Models

Interactive systems, especially new and unfamiliar applications, should be based on metaphors [2]. Using metaphors helps interface designers to structure the design and supports users to handle the system. Metaphors should have their origin in daily life or in the work environment of the intended users. In the following we describe metaphors for the composition of 3D models. In particular we discuss the differences between the well-known construction-kit metaphor and our new 3D puzzle metaphor.

The Construction-Kit Metaphor: This wide-spread metaphor is used mainly in advanced CAD systems. Elementary objects are combined in varying ways to compose different models. The design of cars, for example, is based on various CAD models from different sources which are assembled into virtual prototypes using sophisticated 3D interaction techniques.

An interesting system based on this metaphor was developed in the VLEGO project [9]. Users take primitives, like LEGO bricks, and combine them at discrete, predefined positions and angles. Dedicated 3D widgets are provided for all 3D interaction tasks: composition, separation, picking, and copying. These 3D widgets can be handled with a 3D input device and for most of the 3D interaction tasks a two-handed interaction is suggested. Another example is Multigen's SmartScene product [11] which has been developed for construction and construction training in highly immersive environments.

In contrast to designing 3D-models using the construction-kit metaphor, learning of spatial relations requires the user to focus on unique parts which can be assembled in only one correct manner. Therefore, a new metaphor is required for the composition of complex models from unique elements.

The Metaphor of a 3D Puzzle: A 3D puzzle is a familiar concept for the composition of a *specific* 3D model. Consequently the puzzle metaphor is more appropriate for this task. Moreover, the clearly stated goal of the 3D puzzle—to assemble a given 3D model—motivates the user to focus on the spatial relations within this model.

This raises a question: Which aspects of a 3D puzzle can and should (from a user's point of view) be realized? In a puzzle, a set of elementary objects should be composed. The shape of these objects gives an indication as to which parts belong together. When working with dozens or even hundreds of objects, several deposits (e.g. tables) are used to sort and compose subsets. Obviously, when doing a puzzle one uses both hands and has all degrees of freedom of spatial interaction. In a puzzle, photos are provided to show how the final composed image (or 3D model) looks. These images motivate users and help them to perform the composition. These aspects should be included in a computer-supported 3D puzzle.

Our design has been guided by the metaphor of a 3D puzzle but differs in some major respects from real puzzles:

- Our system is intended to support learning rather than just providing entertainment.
- It is restricted as to what can be achieved in real time but offers additional possibilities in that the computer "knows" how the model should be assembled. This can be used to give guidance to the user.
- Textual cues can be integrated to provide additional information about the objects being composed.

In anatomy, for instance, objects have names, belong to regions and organ systems (e.g. an eye muscle), and have textual explanations as to their shape. This information may be exploited in order to place objects in the right position.

3 Interaction Tasks with a 3D Puzzle

In this section we describe the tasks which need to be accomplished in order to realize the metaphor of a 3D puzzle for learning spatial relations. Actually, there are two kinds of users:

- *authors* who prepare models
  The author segments the model or refines an existing structure, defines the position, shape, and color of docking points; and assigns related textual information. Furthermore, he or she decides on the level of difficulty (which objects are composed initially, which user support is made available, e.g. snapping).

- *students* who use the provided information space
  Students are able to adjust the level of difficulty in asking the system for assistance and additional information. They are, however, not allowed to change the structure of the prepared model itself.

In this paper we restrict ourselves to describing how students explore the information space and assume that it is carefully defined by an author. For students some typical interaction tasks include:

Recognition of objects: Two factors are crucial for the identification of objects: to be able to see an object from all viewing angles and to be able to inspect textual information as to spatial relations (e.g. name, description of shape). Therefore, direct manipulation of the camera is required to be able to inspect individual objects. From the experience Preim et al. described in [13] we hypothesize that visual and textual information mutually reinforce one another in their effect upon the viewer.

Selection of objects: The selection of 3D objects is the prerequisite for 3D interaction. Picking, typing the object name and choosing the name from a list are possible interaction techniques for this task.

Grouping of objects: The student must be able to create and manage subsets of the total set of objects. These subsets should be placed in separate views which

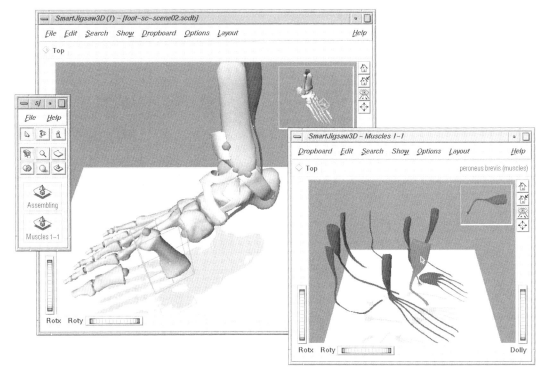

Figure 1: Overview of the interface: In the left view sinews and bones are composed, while in the right view muscles are randomly scattered. The small panel on the left provides an overview on all views.

can be named by the user. Within these views, 3D interaction is required to enable users to explore this subset. As not all views might be visible at the same time, an overview of existing views is crucial.

Transformation of objects: The transformation task includes translating and rotating 3D objects. Since this is the tasks the student is required to spend most of the time on, the success of learning the spatial relations highly depends on the selected interaction techniques.

Docking of objects: The final goal of exploring, selecting and transforming a set of 3D objects is to assemble objects at the "right" docking positions. Less obvious is that objects sometimes have to be separated. For instance, if objects in deeper layers must be assembled first but have been forgotten, objects in the outer areas may have to be decomposed to allow objects to be placed inside.

4 Visualization and Interaction Techniques

After describing the interaction tasks we now focus on what is necessary to support the user in perceiving the spatial relations.

4.1 Visualization of the 3D model

A 3D puzzle requires precise interaction in 3D and thus the simulation of depth cues and 3D interaction techniques similar to those in the real world. Humans perceive depth-relations particularly from the following depth cues [18]:

- shadows
- occlusion of objects
- partial occlusion of semi-transparent objects
- perspective foreshortening
- motion parallax
- stereoscopic viewing

Some of these depth cues, such as occlusion and perspective foreshortening, are part of standard renderers and are implemented in hardware. Shadow generation is usually not supported. In an evaluation, Wanger et al. [17] demonstrated that a shadow cast on the ground is the most important depth cue for distance estimation and shape recognition. Therefore, we developed a specialized view which provides shadow projection.

On graphics workstations with hardware-based alpha-blending, the display of semi-transparent objects and stereoscopic viewing is also feasible in real-time. As demonstrated in [7], motion parallax can be used most efficiently if the user has direct control over this effect. Thus we incorporated interaction techniques which allow the user the parallel manipulation of camera and objects. Even though user-controlled motion parallax is perceived, binocular disparity provides a strong additional depth cue [7].

4.2 Interaction with the 3D model

On the basis of a comprehensible rendition of objects, 3D interaction is possible. The design of 3D interaction techniques must take into account how humans interact in the real world. The following aspects are essential for interaction in the real world:

Collision detection: When one object touches another, it is moved away or will be deformed. Under no circumstances can one object be moved through another without deformation. We regard collision detection as one of the most important aspects of 3D interaction for the puzzle metaphor. However, this is a challenging task if complex non-convex objects are involved.

Two-handed interaction: People tend to use both hands if they manipulate 3D objects [3]. In medicine, two-handed interaction has been successfully applied, e.g., for pre-operative planning in neurosurgery. Hinckley et al. argue in [4] that for the interaction tasks involved (e.g. exploration of a brain with free orientation of head and cutting plane), the most intuitive handling can be achieved with two-handed 3D interaction where the dominant hand does fine-positioning relative to the non-dominant hand. In an empirical evaluation they demonstrated that physicians use these interaction techniques efficiently after only a short learning period.

Tactile feedback: When we grasp an object we receive tactile feedback which enables us to adapt the pressure to the material and weight of the object. Tactile feedback requires special hardware, such as data gloves with force feedback. To avoid the overhead with such an input device, we have not integrated this technique so far.

5   The Realization of the 3D Puzzle

The 3D puzzle incorporates the visualization and interaction techniques described in the section before. Our prototype is based on polygonal models (30,000 to 50,000 polygons segmented into 40 to 80 objects). The software is written in C++ using OPEN INVENTOR and OPENGL.

In addition to techniques required to enable users to compose models, some methods from technical and medical illustration have been added to further improve the understanding of spatial relations. In particular, students should be supported in the exploration of the final model before and during the composition. As mentioned above, the integration of names and short explanations is essential for the understanding.

For learning purposes it is also crucial that it is neither too easy nor too difficult to attach objects correctly. As the appropriate level of difficulty strongly depends on the task—the model to compose—and the user, enough flexibility must be provided to tailor the system.

The puzzle starts with two views: the *construction view* in which the user composes the model and a *deposit view* in which objects which do not belong to the construction view are randomly scattered. The initial position of the objects is adjusted such that they do not overlap (see Figure 1). In order to enhance the overview, an

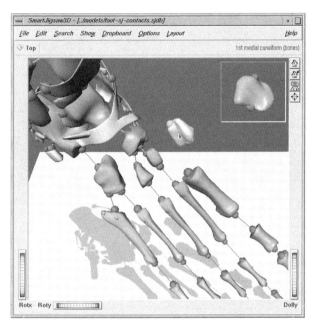

Figure 2: Exploded view of the partly composed model. Already connected docking points are interconnected by lines.

individual name can be assigned to each view, e.g. to circumscribe the subset of objects.

5.1 Recognition of objects

To improve the recognition of objects, we developed a shadow view with a light groundplane. This groundplane is scaled such that all objects cast a shadow on it whereby the orientation remains fixed with regard to the camera. Furthermore, we provide a detailed view like an inset in technical illustrations to allow the user to focus on the currently selected object. The object in this view is presented slightly enlarged without any occluding objects; it is rotated automatically to facilitate the perception of the shape (see the upper right of Figure 2).

To further support the recognition of objects, they are highlighted when touched by the pointing device. The object name and category (e.g. muscles) are displayed in the upper part of the viewer (see Figure 1). A double-click yields a short explanation as to the position and shape of this object. The structure of these explanations is inspired by anatomical atlases where this information is provided to support the understanding of the images.

In technical illustrations, exploded views are provided to improve the recognizability of objects and to enable users to become familiar with the spatial relations. In anatomy, exploded views reveal how bones are attached to each other—an important aspect (in manual drawings, as can be found in books, bones are deliberately separated). Exploded views are realized by scaling down all objects at their original positions, thus leaving empty space. The transition to this view is shown in a continuous change to be easily understood. As the connectivity and grouping of objects is known from the definition of contact points it can be considered in the generation of exploded views. We use this information to visually connect the docking points of the already composed objects by lines (Figure 2).

Motivated by the photos on the package of a real 3D puzzle which help the user to find the right place for a puzzle piece, we provide a *final view* where the model as such is displayed. The user may freely manipulate the camera and explode the model to explore insight objects.

We also integrated stereo-rendering which is realized as an extension of the Silicon Graphics X-Server and requires the use of shutter glasses to perceive the stereoscopic images.

5.2 Selection of objects

Selection by picking with a pointing device is the interaction inspired by the real 3D puzzle. Picking is useful but limited to objects which are visible and recognizable. Possible alternatives are selection by name or from a list. Since typing long anatomic names is tedious, an autocomplete mechanism is employed to expand names. When one of these textual interaction techniques is used, the selected object will be highlighted to provide feedback. If the object belongs to a view currently occluded it is sent to the front to make it visible. Moreover, the object might be occluded within its view. If this is the case, it is moved continuously towards the viewer until it is in front of other objects. In addition, semi-transparency can be used, so that all objects except the one selected by name are semi-transparent.

5.3 Grouping of objects

For the management of the objects, subsets can be created and attached to an unlimited number of 3D views. For this purpose, multiple selection of objects is possible. In addition, all objects in a region or category might be selected. The command "create view" opens a new view and moves all selected objects to this view while the relative position of the objects is preserved. An overview with icons for all views is presented to enable switching between them (recall Figure 1). In order to enhance the overview, an individual name may be assigned to each view. While the final view is read-only, objects can be exchanged between the other views by drag-and-drop (objects may be dropped either in the views or the corresponding icon in the overview).

5.4 Transformation of objects

The transformation of selected 3D objects is performed by direct manipulation of a surrounding 3D widget (Figure 3). This Transformer manipulator from OPEN INVENTOR makes it possible to translate and rotate the attached object with a 2D mouse. However, with a standard 2D mouse users often need to decompose 3D translations and rotations in sequential 2D transformations. It

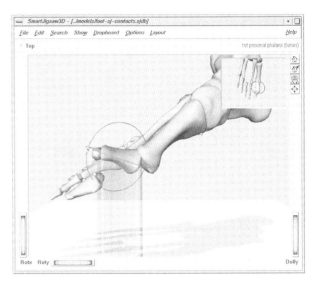

Figure 3: An object has been snapped at one docking point. The transformation is now restricted to the rotation to correctly orient this object.

is more effective to use several degrees of freedom (DOF) simultaneously like in reality. For this purpose a 3D mouse (Logitech Magellan) can be employed. To avoid unnecessarily complicated manipulations which may frustrate the user, the rotation of the objects is constrained to steps of 45 degrees. With this constraint users still have enough possibilities to rotate an object incorrectly. During transformation, the inset offers a different view on the manipulated object (see the upper right corner in Figure 3).

Collision detection

Collision detection prevents objects from being moved through others. When objects collide they are highlighted for a moment to provide visual feedback. If the user continues to attempt to move an object through another one, an acoustic signal is initiated and textual output is provided in the status line. We incorporated the software library V-COLLIDE [8] for collision detection, which accomplishes this test in a robust manner. The software also provides an interface which allows us to determine precisely on which objects the test is carried out. Thus, we restrict collision detection to the currently manipulated object, reducing the processing load considerably.

Since the objects in our puzzle cannot be deformed it is difficult to place an object immediately between two others. Normally, collisions cannot be avoided by the user in this case. Therefore, collision avoidance is disabled automatically if docking points are about to snap, but collisions are still detected and reported to the user.

Semi-transparent shadow volumes

A particularly useful technique for supporting the user during object translation is to connect the object and its casting shadow visually. The resultant shadow volume is

 Graphics **Interface** 2000

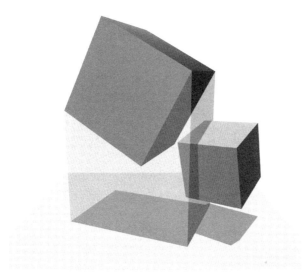

Figure 4: To ease the positioning task, a semi-transparent shadow volume is rendered for the manipulated object.

rendered by semi-transparent surfaces. As stated in Zhai et al. [18], semi-transparent volumes facilitate the perception of depth relations. Thus the correspondence of the object and the attached shadow volume helps to recognize the spatial relation between the object and its immediate neighborhood (see Figure 4 and Figure 3).

5.5 Composition and separation of objects

Objects are composed correctly if the docking points (e.g. spheres) touch each other. To ease this task, a snap mechanism is included (Figure 3). With snapping enabled, objects snap together if their distance is below a given threshold. If more than one docking point is in the immediate vicinity the behavior depends on the author's predetermination. If incorrect connections of objects have been permitted, the object snaps to the closest docking point regardless of correctness. Once an object is attached, the same algorithm prevents the user from detaching it inadvertently. With a quick movement, however, separation is possible. A technique we refer to as "reverse snapping" makes it difficult to attach an object to a wrong docking position. The opposite object acts repulsive by increasing the control-display-ratio for movements towards an inappropriate docking point. Currently, the author defines in the configuration whether or not these mechanisms are enabled.

Shape and color of the docking points give additional cues as to which objects can be connected. Unlike real puzzles where only two objects fit together, we found that providing the same docking points for well-defined groups and pairs of objects helps to transmit correspondences—and consequently spatial relations—in an easily understandable manner. Nevertheless, docking points should be simple to distinguish and simple in geometry, such as tetrahedrons, cubes or spheres.

5.6 Camera control

The virtual camera can be manipulated directly with the 3D mouse around a point of interest which is initially set to the center amid the objects. Additional control provide the OPEN INVENTOR widgets around the viewport. Wheel-widgets make it possible to change azimuth and declination angle and to zoom in and out. Camera control can be realized by intuitive two-handed interaction enabling the user to simultaneously rotate, zoom and pan.

5.7 Two-handed interaction

Our 3D puzzle supports the simultaneous use of two input devices—a 3D mouse and a 2D mouse. The use of these two input devices involves the user's bimanual motor skills enabling him or her to perform dependent subtasks in compound tasks [5].

In one configuration the 3D mouse is used exclusively to rotate the camera around a point of interest (POI) and to control the distance of the camera to this POI—a simultaneous manipulation of four degrees of freedom. The 2D mouse performs all other interactions like picking, selection from lists and the menu, and 3D transformations via the 3D widget. To provide intuitive interaction, people may use their non-dominant hand (NDH) for the camera manipulation task—an orientation task which is carried out with the NDH also in the real world—and the dominant hand (DH) to select certain objects from the scene. This separation of concerns is inspired by Leblanc et al. [10].

Another configuration enables the user also to control translation and rotation—including constraints—of a selected object with the 3D mouse. Here, the camera may be manipulated with the 3D mouse as long as there are no selected objects. Thus the user may explore the scene with the NDH, pick an object with the DH and rotate it with the NDH, finally placing it by translating the attached 3D widget with the DH.

6 Adapting the Level of Difficulty

Usually interactive systems should be as easy to operate as possible. However, with the 3D puzzle it should take some time to succeed because the time spent on solving this task is probably related to the learning success. On the other hand, users might become frustrated if it is too difficult to succeed [15]. There are two strategies by which the level of difficulty can be adapted: by "scaling" the task to be solved, and by providing support for solving the task.

To scale the task, the composition can be restricted to objects of certain categories (e.g. bones) and regions (e.g. eye muscles). Also, the composition can be performed at several levels. At the beginners' level, objects are rotated correctly when they are dropped to the construction view. The task is thus restricted to the correct translation of the object. To increase the level of diffi-

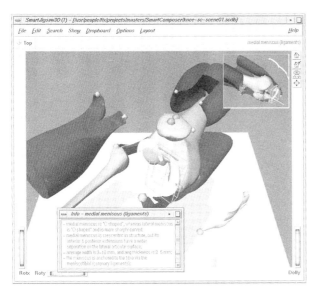

Figure 5: Assembling the right human knee. The system provides additional textual infomation to the selected item.

culty, rotation can be allowed but is constrained to steps of 45 degrees as mentioned before.

Additional support is provided by the display of textual information for a selected object (e.g. musculus procerus, eye muscle) and the mechanisms for snapping and reverse snapping.

7 Scenarios

Originally, the 3D puzzle was intended to enable students to explore and compose geometric models in their entirety, as it is required, for example, in anatomy. However, the 3D puzzle has some flexibility to restrict the task to subsets of the model. Moreover, the puzzle can also be used to decompose a model.

In anatomy, our system helps medical students in the preparation to the dissection of cadavers and can also be used to prepare for exams. As an example, Figure 1 showed the model of the right human foot where bones, sinews and muscles are to be connected. In Figure 5 a knee is assembled, which is a useful preparation to interventions in this area. The decomposition of models supports the rehearsal of surgical procedures and preparation tasks in which objects have to be removed to expose a particular part.

In car mechanic training the specific setup of complex engines has to be mastered. As an example we prepared the model of a six cylinder engine and discussed the scenario with mechanical engineers.

Another field where the 3D puzzle can help to ease the understanding of spatial relation might be chemistry. As stated in [1] the interactive work with complex molecules helps to gain new insights of molecular design. Puzzle pieces, such as proteins, might be composed in a specific way to form new drugs. In contrast to the other scenarios this has not been tested yet.

8 Informal Evaluation of a medical example

We have carefully discussed the 3D puzzle with two recently qualified physicians and four medical students who have some computer experience but had not used learning systems and 3D interaction before. Physicians are at first glance over-qualified as users of our system. However, as their anatomy courses date from former days the 3D puzzle can be used to refresh anatomic knowledge which is useful, for instance, to perform a certain intervention.

After a short introduction to the system's goal and functionality we asked all six candidates to explore a geometric model of a foot and finally to compose muscles and sinews onto the skeleton. For the composition snapping as well as collision avoidance was enabled and translation as well as rotation was required. After only a short time, the subjects were able to benefit from the 3D input device and used it in parallel with the 2D pointing device which seemed useful to them for zooming the camera and rotating the model at the same time.

Attaching the muscles and sinews—25 objects in total—to the skeleton took them approximately half an hour. This amount of time was deemed acceptable for this task.

For the composition it turned out that a frequent change between manipulating the viewpoint and transforming the selected object is necessary. The mode has to be changed which required the user to interrupt the manipulation. As a consequence, the mode may be switched with a button of the 3D input device and additionally in each view.

All subjects liked the management of the different deposits. Snapping was considered to be essential. Some of them also would like to have the system able to compose automatically a subset of the model in an animation and then do the same task themselves.

Furthermore, the evaluation turned out that the composite 3D widget used for translating and rotating objects (recall the left window of Figure 1) does not intuitively convey how to utilize it. Three subjects had difficulties to initialize rotation. For novice users, an explicit representation might be more appropriate. After a short explanation, however, all of them mastered all degrees of freedom to transform objects and succeeded in completing the puzzle having fun whenever they were informed that an object had been attached correctly.

9 Summary

We introduced the metaphor of a 3D puzzle for learning spatial relations and discussed its implication. The metaphor of a 3D puzzle guided our design and led us to incorporate advanced visualization and interaction techniques to enable students to compose 3D models. Furthermore, a prototype was developed and refined according to an informal evaluation to demonstrate the feasibility of this concept. With the metaphor of a 3D puzzle, users have a precise task involving spatial relations.

The puzzle task provides a level of motivation for learning which is hard to achieve with other metaphors. Different levels of difficulty are provided to accommodate users with different capabilities. The 3D puzzle of anatomic models is of interest for students of medicine, but also for students of physical education and physiotherapy who need an understanding of some structures inside the human body. The development of our system has been accompanied by informal usability tests which yielded promising results. We intend to perform a rigorous usability test. In particular, the use of two-handed interaction, the snapping mechanisms and the effects of the different levels of difficulty on the performance and satisfaction are being evaluated.

The 3D puzzle supports the perception of shapes, relative sizes, and other spatial relations at a glance. For educational or maintenance purposes a wealth of textual information, e.g., about objects and their meaning, about possible complications in repair tasks are required. Therefore, students benefit from the 3D puzzle *after* having a clear understanding of the object to be studied. Thus a 3D puzzle cannot replace traditional teaching materials and methods.

We will extend our system to adapt the level of difficulty automatically. For this purpose, it is recorded how many objects have been composed successfully, how often the user failed and how long it takes him or her. Techniques for the adaptation of the 3D puzzle might be derived from computer games where it is quite usual (and often attractive) that the level is adapted after successful completion of certain tasks.

References

[1] Brooks, F. P., M. Ouh-Young, J. J. Batter and P. J. Kilpatrick (1990): *Project GROPE: Haptic Displays for Scientific Visualization*, In: Proc. of ACM SIGGRAPH Conference on Computer Graphics, Dallas, TX, 177-185

[2] Erickson, Th. D. (1990): *Working with Interface Metaphors*, In: B. Laurel (ed.), The Art of Human Computer Interface Design, Addison-Wesley

[3] Guiard, Y. (1987): *Asymmetric Division of Labor in Human Skilled Bimanual Action: The Kinematic Chain as a Model*, Journal of Motor Behavior, Volume 19 (4), 486-517

[4] Hinckley, K., R. Pausch, J. C. Goble, and N. F. Kassell (1994): *Passive Real-World Interface Props for Neurosurgical Visualization*, In: Proc. of ACM CHI Conference on Human Factors in Computing Systems, Boston, MA, 452-458

[5] Kabbash, P., W. Buxton and A. Sellen (1994): *Two-Handed Input in a Compound Task*, In: Proc. of ACM CHI Conference on Human Factors in Computing Systems, Boston, MA, 417-423

[6] Höhne, K.-H., B. Pflesser, A. Pommert et al. (1996): *A Virtual Body Model for Surgical Education and Rehearsal*, Computer – Innovative Technology for Professionals, January, 25-31

[7] Hubona, G. S., G. W. Shirah and D. G.Fout (1997): *The Effects of Motion and Stereopsis on Three-Dimensional Visualization*, In: Proc. of the International Journal of Human-Computer Studies, Volume 47, 609-627

[8] Hudson, T.C., M.C. Lin, J. Cohen, S. Gottschalk and D. Manocha (1997): *V-COLLIDE: Accelerated Collision Detection with VRML*, In: Proc. of Symposium on the Virtual Reality Modeling Language

[9] Kiyokawa, K., H. Takemura, Y. Katayama, H. Iwasa and N. Yokoya (1997): *VLEGO: A Simple Two-handed Modeling Environment Based On Toy Block*, In: Proc. of Symposium on Virtual Reality Software and Technology, 27-34

[10] LeBlanc, A., P. Kalra, N. Magnenat-Thalmann and D. Thalmann (1991): *Sculpting with the 'ball and mouse' metaphor*, In: Proc. of Graphics Interface, Kelowna, B.C., 152-159

[11] Multigen Inc. (1997): *SmartScene User Guide 1.1*

[12] Pitt, I., B. Preim and S. Schlechtweg (1999): *Evaluation of Interaction Techniques for the Exploration of Complex Spatial Phenomena*, In: Proc. of Softwareergonomie, 275-286

[13] Preim, B., R. Michel, K. Hartmann and Th. Strothotte (1998): *Figure Captions in Visual Interfaces*, In: Proc. of ACM Workshop on Advanced Visual Interfaces, L'Aquila, Italy, 235-246

[14] Preim, B., A. Raab and Th. Strothotte (1997): *Coherent Zooming of Illustrations with 3D-Graphics and Textual Labels*, In: Proc. of Graphics Interface, Kelowna, B.C., 105-113

[15] Rappin, N., M. Guzdial, M. Realff and P. Ludovice (1997): *Balancing Usability and Learning in an Interface*, In: Proc. of ACM CHI Conference on Human Factors in Computing Systems, Atlanta, GA, 479-486

[16] Schiemann, T., J. Nuthmann, U. Tiede and K. H. Höhne (1996): *Generation of 3D anatomical atlases using the Visible Human.* In: Proc. of SCAR, Symposia Foundation, Carlsbad, CA, 62-67

[17] Wanger, L., J. Ferwerda and D. Greenberg (1992): *Perceiving Spatial Relationships in Computer-Generated Images*, IEEE Computer Graphics and Applications, Volume 12 (3), 44-58

[18] Zhai, S., W. Buxton and P. Milgram (1996): *The partial occlusion effect: utilizing semi-transparency in 3D human computer interaction*, ACM Transactions on HCI, Volume 3 (3), 254-284

Affordances: Clarifying and Evolving a Concept

Joanna McGrenere
Department of Computer Science
University of Toronto
Toronto, Ontario
Canada M5S 3G4
joanna@dgp.toronto.edu

Wayne Ho
User-Centered Design
IBM Software Solutions Toronto Laboratory
1150 Eglinton Ave. East, Toronto, Ontario
Canada M3C 1H7
who@ca.ibm.com

Abstract

The concept of *affordance* is popular in the HCI community but not well understood. Donald Norman appropriated the concept of *affordances* from James J. Gibson for the design of common objects and both implicitly and explicitly adjusted the meaning given by Gibson. There was, however, ambiguity in Norman's original definition and use of affordances which he has subsequently made efforts to clarify. His definition germinated quickly and through a review of the HCI literature we show that this ambiguity has lead to widely varying uses of the concept. Norman has recently acknowledged the ambiguity, however, important clarifications remain. Using affordances as a basis, we elucidate the role of the designer and the distinction between usefulness and usability. We expand Gibson's definition into a framework for design.

Keywords: Affordance, usefulness, usability, design.

1 Introduction

The *affordance* concept was popularized in the HCI community through Donald Norman's book *The Psychology of Everyday Things* (POET) [14]. The word *affordance* was new to the HCI vocabulary and the concept seemed somewhat novel: an affordance is the design aspect of an object which suggests how the object should be used [14]. It is not widely known that the word *affordance* was first coined by the perceptual psychologist James J. Gibson in his seminal book *The Ecological Approach to Visual Perception* [5]. Gibson and Norman appear at first glance to have similar definitions of the concept. Gibson intended an affordance to mean an action possibility available in the environment to an individual, independent of the individual's ability to perceive this possibility. Norman's definition spread quickly and some inherent ambiguities have lead to widely varying usage in the HCI literature. This inconsistent usage motivated a more thorough look at the similarities and important differences between the two definitions.

We first look at affordances as they were originally defined by Gibson. We turn next to Norman's introduction of affordances into the HCI community and his subsequent coverage of the concept. The differences between the two uses are identified followed by a brief survey of the use of the concept in the HCI literature. We clarify a number of ambiguities that remain today including the meaning of affordances in application software. Lastly we provide a design framework that extends Gibson's definition of affordances.

2 Gibson's Affordances

Gibson's academic career centered on the field of visual perception [5]. He deviated from the classical theories of perception that were based on physics and physical optics because he felt that physics provided an inappropriate frame of reference for visual perception. Gibson made it his life's work to describe an appropriate ecological frame of reference. He believed that studying the animal's visual perception in isolation from the environment that is perceived resulted in false understandings. Gibson claimed that we perceive at the level of mediums, surfaces, and substances rather than at the level of particles and atoms and, in particular, we tend to perceive what the combination of mediums, surfaces, and substances offer us. Thus "...the *affordances* of the environment are what it *offers* the animal, what it *provides* or *furnishes*, either for good or ill. [5, p.127]"

There are three fundamental properties of an affordance:

1. An affordance exists relative to the action capabilities of a particular actor.
2. The existence of an affordance is independent of the actor's ability to perceive it.
3. An affordance does not change as the needs and goals of the actor change.

To elucidate the first property Gibson gives the example of a horizontal, flat, extended, and rigid surface that affords support. A given surface that provides support for one actor, may not provide support for another actor (perhaps because of a differential in weight or size). There is only one surface in question here, yet the affordance of support exists for one actor whereas it does not exist for another. Note that the affordance is not a property of the experience of the actor but rather of the action capabilities of the actor. Also note that

180

even if the surface is not intended to provide support, if it does in fact support a given actor, then the affordance of support exists. The second and third properties point to the fact that an affordance is invariant.

Defined in this way, affordances cut across the subjective/objective barrier. They are objective in that their existence does not depend on value, meaning, or interpretation. Yet they are subjective in that an actor is needed as a frame of reference. By cutting across the subjective/objective barrier, Gibson's affordances introduce the idea of the actor-environment mutuality; the actor and the environment make an inseparable pair.

Gibson focussed his work on direct perception, a form of perception that does not require mediation or internal processing by an actor. Direct perception is possible when there is an affordance and there is information in the environment that uniquely specifies that affordance (see Figure 1[1]). For example, one will perceive that one can walk forward when one sees a solid, opaque surface that extends under one's feet. The affordance is walkability and the information that specifies walkability is a perceived invariant combination of a solid, opaque surface of a certain size relative to oneself. Direct perception depends on the actor's "picking up" the information that specifies the affordance and may depend on the actor's experiences and culture. Let us be clear, the existence of the affordance is independent of the actor's experiences and culture, whereas the ability to perceive the affordance may be dependent on these. Thus, an actor may need to learn to discriminate the information in order to perceive directly. In this way learning can be seen as a process of discriminating patterns in the world, rather than one of supplementing sensory information with past experience.

Given that the existence of an affordance and the information that specifies the affordance are independent, there are cases where an affordance exists but there is no information to specify the affordance. Take, for example, a hidden door in a paneled room. The door affords passage to an appropriately sized individual even though there is no information to specify that passage is in fact an action possibility. Here direct visual perception is clearly not possible.

There are two properties of affordances that Gibson implies but never directly states. The first is that affordances are binary; they either exist or they do not exist. For example, a stair is climbable by a particular individual or it isn't. Gibson does not address the gray area where an action possibility exists but it can only be undertaken with great difficulty: for example, a stair that

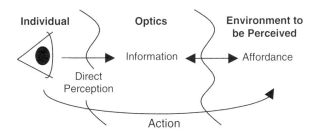

Figure 1: Direct perception is the act of picking up information to guide action.

is climbable but only with great difficulty. Second, Gibson implies that affordances can be nested when an action possibility is composed of one or more action possibilities. For instance, an apple affords eating, but eating is composed of biting, chewing, and swallowing, all of which are afforded by the apple. Gibson describes the environment as being composed of nested objects and he describes the nesting of information that specifies affordances but he never specifically uses the term *nested affordances.*

3 Norman's Affordances

Affordances, as Gibson described them, can be contrasted with Norman's affordances introduced in POET. Norman described affordances as follows:

> …the term *affordance* refers to the perceived and actual properties of the thing, primarily those fundamental properties that determine just how the thing could possibly be used. A chair affords ('is for') support and, therefore, affords sitting. A chair can also be carried. [14, p.9]

This quotation points to some apparent differences between Norman's affordances and Gibson's affordances. Norman talks of both perceived and actual properties and implies that a perceived property may or may not be an actual property, but regardless, it is an affordance. Thus, he deviates from Gibson in that perception by an individual may be involved in characterizing the existence of the affordance. Further, Norman indicates that an affordance refers primarily to the fundamental properties of an object. Gibson, on the other hand, does not make the distinction between the different affordances of an object. Another important difference is that for Norman there is no actor as a frame of reference.

Norman makes clear in an endnote in POET that he is deviating from the Gibsonian definition of affordances:

> The notion of affordance and the insights it provides originated with J.J. Gibson, a psychologist interested in how people see the world. I believe that affordances result from the mental interpretation of things, based on our past knowledge and experience applied to our perception of the things about us. My view is somewhat in conflict with

---

[1] This diagram is a simplification of Gibson's view of direct perception. See Gibson, 1979 [5] for a more complete description.

the views of many Gibsonian psychologists, but this internal debate within modern psychology is of little relevance here. [14, p. 219]

This quotation identifies another difference between Gibson and Norman. Gibson claims that the existence of affordances is independent of an actor's experience and culture. Norman, on the other hand, tightly couples affordances with past knowledge and experience. The frame of reference for Gibson is the action capabilities of the actor, whereas for Norman it is the mental and perceptual capabilities of the actor.

It is important to clarify Norman's position that affordances are perceived properties. He states that affordances "provide strong clues to the operations of things" [14, p.9] and that they "suggest the range of possibilities" [14, p.82]. He argues that when designers take advantage of affordances, the user knows what to do just by looking. Although complex things may require supporting information, simple things should not. If they do, then design has failed.

In more recent books, Norman stresses the importance of perceived affordances [15, 16, 17] and differentiates them from real affordances:

> It's very important to distinguish *real* from *perceived* affordances. Design is about both, but the perceived affordances are what determine usability. I didn't make this point sufficiently clear in my book and I have spent much time trying to clarify the now widespread misuse of the term. [17, p. 123]

This clarification will likely help to mitigate future misuse, but it still does not clearly separate the affordance from the information specifying the affordance.

In a recent article on the topic of affordances [18], Norman begins to separate affordances from their visibility and thus deviates from his original usage. Unfortunately, some misconceptions about affordances and the role of the designer remain in that article. We address these in the discussion section.

4 Highlighting and Interpreting the Differences

We will use what has become the canonical example of affordances in the HCI literature, namely the affordance of a door, to elucidate the differences between Gibson's and Norman's original use of the concept. Consider a door with no handle and no flat panel. Without prior knowledge of how the door operated, an actor would find it difficult to know the direction of opening. Following Gibson's definition, the fact that the door can be opened by a given actor is sufficient to determine that it has an affordance. (Perhaps the door can be pushed and it will swing away from the actor or the actor can grasp the door edges and pull.) There does not need to be any visual information specifying the correct

direction to the actor for there to be an affordance. According to Norman's use, on the other hand, the affordance would only exist if there was information to specify the possibility for action and the actor had learned how to interpret the information. In this case, there would need to be a door handle that signaled the direction of opening to the actor. If we were to redraw Figure 1 using Norman's definition, the two sections on the right, Optics and the Environment to be Perceived, would be collapsed into a single section.

Table 1 highlights the different meanings assigned to affordances by Norman and Gibson.

Gibson's Affordances
• Offerings or action possibilities in the environment in relation to the action capabilities of an actor
• Independent of the actor's experience, knowledge, culture, or ability to perceive
• Existence is binary – an affordance exists or it does not exist
Norman's Affordances
• Perceived properties that may or may not actually exist
• Suggestions or clues as to how to use the properties
• Can be dependent on the experience, knowledge, or culture of the actor
• Can make an action difficult or easy

Table 1: Comparison of affordances as defined by Gibson and Norman.

The most fundamental difference between the two definitions is that for Gibson an affordance is the action possibility itself whereas according to Norman's use it has been both the action possibility and the way that that action possibility is conveyed or made visible to the actor. Norman's "make it visible" guideline actually maps quite nicely to Gibson's statement that there must be perceptual information that specifies the affordance for the affordance to be directly perceived. We believe that this difference has caused confusion in the HCI community. In his original definition, Norman collapsed two very important but different, and perhaps even independent, aspects of design: designing the utility of an object and designing the way in which that utility is conveyed to the user of the object. Because Norman has stressed (but not entirely limited himself to) perceived affordances, he has actually favored the latter of the two. In Gibsonian terms, these two aspects are labeled: design of the affordances of an object and design of the perceptual information that specifies the affordances.

It is important to note that Norman and Gibson had two related yet different goals. Gibson was primarily interested in how we perceive the environment. He acknowledged that both people and animals manipulate (that is, design) their environment to change what it affords them, but the manner of manipulation was not his focus. Norman, on the other hand, is specifically interested in manipulating or designing the environment so that utility can be perceived easily. We speculate that, given Gibson's focus, he made the simplifying assumption that affordances are binary. Recall the example of a stair being climbable or non-climbable by a particular individual. Reality obviously isn't this black and white; a gray area exists that is meaningful to the stair climber. For a particular individual one stair may be climbable with great difficulty whereas a different stair may be climbable with ease. Gibson doesn't address this range; they are both climbable and thus they both qualify as affordances. From a design perspective, an affordance that is extremely difficult to undertake versus one that is undertaken with ease can hardly be put in the same category. In the design of everyday things, the goal should be to design information that uniquely specifies an affordance and also to design useful affordances that can be undertaken with ease.

Warren [26], an ecological psychologist, moves beyond binary affordances. He defines π numbers to be dimensionless ratios that provide measurements of the actor in relation to the environment. He has done detailed analysis of the affordance of stair climbability, for which he uses $\pi = R/L$ as the intrinsic measure, where R is the riser height of the stair and L is the climber's leg length. For climbers of different heights, Warren was able to determine a single optimal point (π_0) at which the energy expenditure required to climb through a given vertical distance is at a minimum and a single critical point (π_{max}) at which point a stair becomes impossible to climb bipedally. Using Warren's terms, the goal of design should be to achieve the optimal point for the target user.

5 Affordances as They Appear In the HCI Community

In order to understand how the affordance concept has been adopted by the HCI community we conducted a survey of the literature. We focussed mostly on the proceedings from the annual CHI conferences[2] because we felt these proceedings to be generally representative of the HCI literature. Nineteen papers were reviewed. The goal was to identify and loosely categorize how the term *affordance* has been used. Three high-level categories emerged:

- 8 papers adhering to Gibson's definition – an action possibility or offering [1, 2, 4, 6, 20, 22, 23, 27]

- 6 papers adhering to Norman's original definition – a perceived suggestion [3, 7, 8, 10, 13, 19]
- 5 papers deviating from both Gibson and Norman [11, 12, 21, 24, 25]

For reasons of brevity we only highlight a couple of papers in each category.

5.1 Gibson's Affordances - An Action Possibility

Papers that used Gibson's definition fall into two categories: the affordances of software applications [1, 2, 4, 23] and the affordances of physical objects [6, 20, 22, 27].

Action Possibility in Software Applications

Gaver [4] published the first paper in the CHI Proceedings that included the concept of *affordances*. This paper goes beyond the mention of affordances; it is specifically about affordances. Because Gaver's contribution is substantial, we discuss his work in depth at the end of this section. Another example of a paper in this category is by Smets, Overbeeke, and Gaver [23]. They show how the design of forms can convey complex non-visual information such as sound, taste, smell, and texture. They postulate that this research could be applied to the design of icons that represent complex information and activities and thereby improve the information that specifies the affordance.

Action Possibility in a Physical Object

Zhai, Milgram, and Buxton [27] document a study that strongly suggests that high-degree-of-freedom input devices should be designed so that they can be manipulated by the fingers because finger movements often provide more accurate control than do arm movements. Thus, these input devices should be shaped and sized so as to afford finger manipulation.

5.2 Norman's Affordance – A Perceived Suggestion

Mihnkern [10] describes affordances as the means of communicating a design model to the user. He says that when a metaphor is applied to a system, it gives the system a particular set of affordances and that the metaphor inevitably breaks down leaving some of the system's features affordance-less or invisible. [In Gibsonian terms, even if there is no information to specify the affordance, it still exists.]

Johnson [7] compares a number of techniques for panning, in particular, moving the scene under the window or moving the window over the scene (GUIs do the latter):

> … it is clear that the appearance of the touch-display can influence what people suggest [is the panning method]. This is what Gibson and, later, Norman refer to as an 'affordance': when an aspect of an artifact's design suggests how it is to be used. We thought that adding a brightly colored border around the displayed image might

---

2 Papers were selected using the ACM Digital Library and Gary Perlman's HCI Bibliography with the search string "affordance." All those papers that appear in the CHI proceedings have been reviewed and a few others were also selected based on availability.

suggest 'touch here' to users, and might therefore suggest Touch Edge panning (camera or background). [7, p.219]

5.3 Neither Gibson's nor Norman's Affordances

With the exception of the first paper in this category [11], the use of affordance in the papers is unclear [12, 21, 24, 25].

An Interface Object

Mohageg et al. [11] equates an affordance with an interface object: "all of this functionality is mapped onto a single affordance on the dashboard." [11, p.468] Here, they are referring to a virtual joystick.

Unclear Usage

Vaughan [25] provides a confusing account of affordances. She seemingly identifies the affordance of movement. She talks about the movement of a butterfly affording chasing and that when movement becomes more prominent the affordance of emotion becomes more evident. She cites Gibson, yet her use of affordances appears different from both Gibson's and Norman's.

5.4 Acknowledging Gaver's Contribution

As noted above, there are a number of authors who are aware that affordances originated with Gibson and have read Gibson's work. Yet most who cite Gibson and perhaps even quote him resort to using the meaning given by Norman. One author in particular, Gaver, makes a significant attempt to bring Gibson's ideas into the HCI community in his paper entitled "Technology Affordances", [4] which is illuminating and therefore needs to be outlined in some detail. This was the first paper in the CHI Proceedings that discusses affordances; but, it has gone largely unnoticed.

Gaver's discussion of the door example illustrates that his understanding of affordances differs from Norman's. Where Norman and all who followed talked about the affordance suggesting the action, Gaver talks about *the design that suggests* the affordance of the door. Here he uses the term *design* as the information that specifies the affordance. He uses the door example to demonstrate nested affordances, which he defines as "affordances that are grouped in space." The affordance of pulling a door handle is nested within the affordance of opening the door. Gaver recognizes the importance of distinguishing two aspects of design:

> Distinguishing affordances and the available information about them from their actual perception allows us to consider affordances as properties that can be designed and analyzed in their own terms. [4, p. 81]

Gaver identified apparent affordances:

> In general, when the apparent affordances of an artifact match its intended use, the artifact is easy to operate. When apparent affordances suggest different actions than

those for which the object is designed, errors are common and signs are necessary. [4, p.80]

These match what Norman has termed *perceived affordances*. Gaver provides a framework for separating affordances from the perceptual information available about them (Figure 2). Note that Gaver's perceptible affordance is not the same as his apparent affordance or Norman's perceived affordance, as we have shown by overlaying the latter two on Gaver's framework.

Perceptible Affordance and *Hidden Affordance* make sense but *False Affordance* is problematic. It is not the affordance that is false; rather, it is the information that is false. Gibson uses the term misinformation to describe this phenomenon. When misinformation is picked up by an actor, then misperception results. Gibson acknowledges that the "line between the pickup of misinformation and the failure to pick up information is hard to draw." [5, p.244]

Interestingly, Gaver does seem to contradict himself part way through his paper when he finally gives a concrete definition of affordances:

> The concept of affordances points to a rather special configuration of properties. It implies that the physical attributes of the thing to be acted upon are compatible with those of the actor, that information about those attributes is available in a form compatible with a perceptual system, and (implicitly) that these attributes and the action they make possible are relevant to a culture and a perceiver. [4, p.81]

Here he seems to be lumping in the information that specifies the affordance with the affordance itself. Gibson's affordances only cover the first of these three points.

Gaver then addresses the problem of complex affordances. He extends the notion of *affordances* to explicitly include exploration. He introduces the concept of sequential affordances, which refers to situations in which action on a perceptible affordance leads to information indicating new affordances (e.g.,

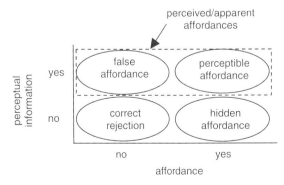

Figure 2: Separating affordances from the perceptual information that specifies affordances (adapted from [4]).

184

after mousing-down on the scrollbar, it can then be dragged). Sequential affordances explain how affordances can be revealed over time. As previously mentioned, Gibson implies the existence of nested affordances but never actually identifies them. Gaver, on the other hand, specifically defines nested affordances to be affordances that are grouped in space. He provides the example of manipulating the scrollbar widget as being nested within the affordance of scrolling within a window. Here Gaver is exploring affordances for low-level interaction in GUIs, which we deal with in greater detail in the next section.

6 Discussion

6.1 Does it matter?

In the end, does establishing a clear meaning of affordances really matter? We argue that it does matter. At the most basic level, establishing a concrete meaning will prevent widely varying uses of the term. Norman, in his latest article, also sees the need for clarification: "Sloppy thinking about the concepts and tactics often leads to sloppiness in design. And sloppiness in design translates into confusion for users. [18, p. 41]"

In the same way, we are motivated to further clarify affordances in terms of design, and specifically in the area of software design. To this end, we return to Gibson's definition of affordances and discuss its impact on design.

6.2 Usefulness *and* Usability

Clearly differentiating the two aspects of design is critical: designing affordances and designing the information that specifies the affordance should not be confounded. Said in another way, designing the utility of an object is related to but separate from designing the usability of an object. This is a distinction of usefulness versus usability [9].

The HCI community has largely focussed on usability at the expense of usefulness. Norman also emphasizes usability: "The designer cares more about what actions the user perceives to be possible than what is true" [18, p. 39]. A designer must also be concerned with creating the useful actions of the design, creating what is truly possible in the design. A useful design contains the right functions required for users to perform their jobs efficiently and to accomplish their goals. The usefulness of a design is determined by what the design affords (that is, the possibilities for action in the design) and whether these affordances match the goals of the user and allow the necessary work to be accomplished. The usability of a design can be enhanced by clearly designing the perceptual information that specifies these affordances. Usable designs have information specifying affordances that

accounts for various attributes of the end-users, including their cultural conventions and level of expertise. Of course, usability is also enhanced by following principles such as providing appropriate feedback, being consistent, and providing error recovery. Figure 1 can be redrawn to show the relationship between usefulness and affordances and the relationship between usability and the information specifying an affordance (see Figure 3).

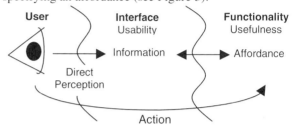

Figure 3: Usefulness and Usability.

6.3 Clarifying Affordances in Software Design

It is necessary to clarify the meaning of an affordance in the context of application software. There was considerable ambiguity on this in the reviewed HCI literature and there is additional confusion in Norman's latest article [18]. An affordance is an action possibility or an offering. Possible actions on a computer system include physical interaction with devices such as the screen, keyboard, and mouse. But the role of affordances does not end with the physical aspect of the system, as Norman implies [18]. The application software also provides possible actions. A word processor affords writing and editing at a high level, but it also affords clicking, scrolling, dragging and dropping. The functions that are invokable by the user are the affordances in software. Functions may include text-editing, searching, or drawing. The information that specifies these functions may be graphical (buttons, menus) or it may not exist at all.

Norman claims that a scrollbar is a learned convention and implies that it is not an affordance [18]. We disagree. The fact that the object affords scrolling is an affordance that is built into the software. The information that specifies this affordance is in fact a learned convention – we have all come to recognize a scrollbar.

In general, an underlying affordance or function can still exist regardless of correct interpretation or even perception by the user. A low-level user action triggers the execution of the function. The action could be the input of some obscure command (e.g., "ls -la") at a prompt or it could be clicking on a button in a GUI. In the first case, there is little or no information to specify the affordance. In the second case, there is some information. This case relies on the notion of nested affordances. The button has a clickability affordance, which is specified by a raised-looking push button. But users are not interested in clicking on a button for its own sake; they are interested in invoking some function. It is generally the icon or the label on the button that specifies the function to be invoked. Therefore, button clickability is nested within the affordance of function invokability. This is much the same as we would describe a piano as having an affordance of music playability. Nested within this affordance, the piano keys have the affordance of depressability.

It is important to note that affordances exist (or are nested) in a hierarchy and that the levels of the hierarchy may or may not map to system functions. In other words, affordances do not necessarily map one-to-one onto system functions. Taking a standard GUI-based word processor as an example, we can say that it affords document editing. Editing includes affordances for text addition and deletion, margin adjustment, font selection, and many others.

As Gaver identified, there are also sequential affordances, that is, affordances that are only available at certain points in time. Although such affordances also exist outside GUIs and applications, they are perhaps more obvious here given the dynamic nature of software and the ability to update the display quickly. The information that specifies an affordance can be updated as new affordances become available. Once a user clicks a visible button, a drop down menu may appear, from which the user can then make a selection. This is not to say that all applications update the visual information to specify the available affordances. The UNIX text editor vi, for example, gives the user no visual information about whether text entry is possible. In command mode, a user must first switch to input mode before entering text. It is impossible to discern from simply looking at the screen whether the system is in command mode or input mode.

6.4 Affordances as a Framework for Design

To use affordances to evaluate and improve design, it is useful to think of the degree of an affordance. To regard affordances as binary is to oversimplify them. Warren's [26] work on π numbers, and specifically the optimal and the critical points, began to address what we call the degree of an affordance. However, we still require language to describe affordances that exist between these two points and we need to incorporate the information that specifies the affordance. We can think of a two-dimensional space where one dimension describes the ease with which an affordance can be undertaken and the second dimension describes the clarity of the information that describes the existing

affordance. Each of these dimensions is a continuum. The goal of design is to first determine the necessary affordances and then to maximize each of these dimensions. If both dimensions are of equal importance for a given affordance, improvements in design should be seen to move along the diagonal given in Figure 4. Note that while determining the necessary affordances is related to usefulness, making an improvement in either of these dimensions is related to usability.

Personal customization of an interface provides a good example of how a user can improve the design of a system to make the affordance easier to undertake. For instance, a user may make an alias for a long command string (for example, turning "lpr –Pmyprinter" into "lpm") or may add a button to a toolbar for a frequently used command. Thus, an affordance is easier to undertake when the time to perform the action is reduced. It can also be made easier by increasing the physical comfort or reducing the exertion required. A command that requires a single key to invoke is physically easier than one that requires the simultaneous pressing of multiple keys.

By comparing a GUI to a command-line interface we can understand how the degree of information specifying the affordance can be varied. Command-line interfaces often provide little or no information about the options that are available to the user. GUIs, on the other hand, provide significant information. Despite the available information in a GUI, expert users tend to prefer command-line interfaces. Their preference can be understood in the context of this two-dimensional framework; it is faster to enter a short command via the keyboard than to move the hand to the mouse, position the pointer, and click. Expert users have committed these commands to memory and so the visual information is clutter and the mouse access is a slow-down. For novice users, having visual information and mouse access is easier than committing a series of command strings to memory. This same information

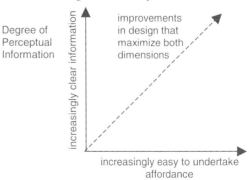

Degree of Perceptual Information

Degree of Affordance

Figure 4: Representing the affordance and the information that specifies the affordance on a continuum.

186

comes at the cost of making the affordance more difficult to undertake for expert users. Thus, the degree of an affordance exists relative to a particular user.

7 Conclusion

Without Norman's adoption of affordances in POET and his ongoing writing, affordances would likely be unfamiliar to many of us. It has been necessary for us to be detailed with respect to Norman's use of affordances because otherwise it would not be possible to sort out the misuse and the current confusions that remain. We applaud Norman's efforts in bringing this important concept to our community and continuing to clarify it.

As the concept of *affordances* is used currently, it has marginal value because it lacks specific meaning. Returning to a definition close to that of Gibson's would solidify the concept and would also recognize that designing the utility or functional purpose is a worthwhile endeavor in its own right. In order for the *affordance* concept to be used fully in the design world, however, Gibson's definition needs to incorporate the notion of varying degrees of an affordance. We have provided a framework for design that is based on this expanded notion of an affordance.

8 Acknowledgments

We are grateful to Kim Vicente for many engaging discussions on affordances and his thoughtful comments on earlier drafts of this paper. This research has been supported by the Centre for Advanced Studies at the IBM Toronto Laboratory and by NSERC.

References

[1] Ackerman, M.S., and Palen, L. (1996). The zephyr help instance: Promoting ongoing activity in a cscw system. *CHI 96 Conference Proceedings*, 268-275.

[2] Bers, M.U., Ackermann, E., Cassell, J., Donegan, B., Gonzalez-Heydrich, J., DeMaso, D.R., Strohecker, C., Lualdi, S., Bromley, D., and Karlin, J. (1998). Interactive storytelling environments: Coping with cardiac illness at Boston's Children's Hospital. *CHI 98 Conference Proceedings*, 603-610.

[3] Conn, A.P. (1995). Time affordances: The time factor in diagnostic usability heuristics. *CHI '95 Conference Proceedings*. 186-193.

[4] Gaver, W.W. (1991). Technology affordances. *CHI'91 Conference Proceedings*. 79-84.

[5] Gibson, J.J. (1979). *The Ecological Approach to Visual Perception*. Boston: Houghton Mifflin.

[6] Harrison, B.L, Fishkin, K.P., Gujar, A., Mochon, C., and Want, R. (1998). Squeeze me, hold me, tilt me! An exploration of manipulative user interfaces. *CHI 98 Conference Proceedings*, 17-24.

[7] Johnson, J.A. (1995). A comparison of user interfaces for panning on a touch-controlled display. *CHI'95 Conference Proceedings*, 218-225.

[8] Kohlert, D.C., and Olsen, D.R. (1995). Pictures and input data. *CHI'95 Conference Proceedings*, 464-471.

[9] Landauer, T.K. (1995). *The Trouble with Computers: Usefulness, Usability, and Productivity*, Cambridge, MA: The MIT Press.

[10] Mihnkern, K. (1997). Visual interaction design: Beyond the interface metaphor. *SIGCHI Bulletin*, 29(2), 11-15.

[11] Mohageg, M., Myers, R., Marrin, C., Kent, J., Mott, D., and Isaacs, P. (1996). A user interface for accessing 3D content on the world wide web. *CHI 96 Conference Proceedings*, 466-472.

[12] Moran, T.P., Palen, L., Harrison, S., Chiu, P., Kimber, D., Minneman, S., van Melle, W., and Zellweger, P. (1997). "I'll Get That Off the Audio": A case study of salvaging multimedia meeting records. *CHI 97 Conference Proceedings*, 202-209.

[13] Nielsen, J., and Wagner, A. (1996). User interface design for the WWW. *CHI 96 Conference Companion*, 330-331.

[14] Norman, D.A. (1988). *The Psychology of Everyday Things*. New York: Basic Books.

[15] Norman, D.A. (1992). *Turn Signals are the Facial Expression of Automobiles*. Reading, MA: Addison-Wesley.

[16] Norman, D.A. (1993). *Things That Make Us Smart*. Reading, MA: Addison-Wesley.

[17] Norman, D.A. (1998). *The Invisible Computer*. Cambridge: MA, MITPress.

[18] Norman, D.A. (1999). Affordance, conventions, and design. *Interactions*, 6(3), 38-42.

[19] Perkins, R. (1995). The interchange online network: Simplifying information access. *CHI'95 Conference Proceedings*, 558-565.

[20] Schilit, B.N., Golovchinsky, G., and Price, M. (1998). Beyond paper: Supporting active reading with free form digital ink annotations. *CHI 98 Conference Proceedings*, 249-256.

[21] Shafrir, E. and Nabkel, J. (1994). Visual access to hyper-information: Using multiple metaphors with graphic affordances. *CHI'94 Conference Proceedings*. 142.

[22] Sellen, A., and Harper, R. (1997). Paper as an analytic resource for the design of new technologies. *CHI 97 Conference Proceedings*, 319-326.

[23] Smets, G., Overbeeke, K., and Gaver, W. (1994). Form-giving: Expressing the nonobvious. *CHI'94 Conference Proceedings*, 79-84.

[24] Tamura, H., and Bannai, Y. (1996). Real^3 communication and aromatic group computing: HCI and CSCW research at Canon Media Technology Laboratory. *CHI 96 Conference Companion*, 131-132.

[25] Vaughan, L.C. (1997). Understanding movement. *CHI 97 Conference Proceedings*, 548-549.

[26] Warren (1995). Constructing an econiche. In J. Flach, P. Hancock, J. Caird, and K. J. Vicente (Eds.), *Global Perspectives on the Ecology of Human-Machine Systems*, (pp. 210-237). Hillsdale, NJ: Lawrence Erlbaum Associates.

[27] Zhai, S., Milgram, P., and Buxton, W. (1996). The influence of muscle groups on performance of multiple degree of-freedom input. *CHI 96 Conference Proceedings*, 308-315.

Are We All In the Same "Bloat"?

Joanna McGrenere
Department of Computer Science
University of Toronto
Toronto, ON Canada, M5S 3G4
joanna@dgp.utoronto.ca

Gale Moore
Knowledge Media Design Institute
University of Toronto
Toronto, ON Canada, M5S 2Z9
gmoore@dgp.utoronto.ca

Abstract

"Bloat", a term that has existed in the technical community for many years, has recently received attention in the popular press. The term has a negative connotation implying that human, or system performance is diminished in some way when "bloat" exists. Yet "bloat" is seldom clearly defined and is often a catch-all phrase to suggest that software is filled with unnecessary features. However, to date there are no studies that explore how users actually *experience* complex functionality-filled software applications and most importantly, the extent to which they experience them in similar/different ways. The significance of understanding users' experience is in the implications this understanding has for design. Using both quantitative and qualitative methods, we carried out a study to gain a better understanding of the experiences of 53 members of the general population who use a popular word processor, Microsoft Word, Office 97. As a result we are able to further specify the term "bloat", distinguishing an objective and subjective dimension. It is the discovery of the subjective dimension that opens the design space and raises new challenges for interface designers. There is certainly more to "bloat" than meets the eye.

Keywords: Complex software, bloat, creeping featurism, user experience, office applications, human-centred design, user study, evaluation, personalization.

1 Introduction

Over the past two decades desktop computing has become an integral part of the experience of work across economic sectors and occupations in the advanced economies. The spreadsheet was the first "killer app" for personal computers, followed shortly by the word processor, and the office suites of the late 1980s. These applications competed within their class in the marketplace in terms of the number of functions offered – a phenomenon that became known as the *Feature War*. The assumption was that the greater the number of features, the more useful, or at least the more marketable the application. These applications became increasingly complex in a number of ways. Not only were there more options available, but some of the options offered were sophisticated and required a more complete understanding of computers and traditional printing and publishing practices. Furthermore, the interface itself had become visually more complex, e.g., menus and submenus were growing longer. Simultaneously, there was an explosion in the size and diversity of the user population, many of whom were unfamiliar with either computers or printing or both. Technical developments such as the GUI, and attention to usability have led to improvements over the years, but the impact of this functionality explosion on the actual experiences of those using the tools has received little attention in the literature. However, we are encouraged by the National Academy of Sciences announcement that they are in the early stages of developing an agenda on what they call the "every-citizen" interface [9].

In the past few years, there has been considerable interest in the popular press and the computer world in what has been termed "bloat" or "bloatware" [7] and "creeping featurism"[10]. "Bloat" is a term that has been used in the technical community for some time. Software "bloat" has been defined as "the result of adding new features to a program or system to the point where the benefit of the new features is outweighed by the impact on the technical resources (e.g., RAM, disk space or performance) and the complexity of use" [11]. Creeping featurism, on the other hand, is the tendency to complicate a system by adding features in an ad-hoc, non-systematic manner [11]. One implication is that a bloated application is one in which there are a large number of unused features. In the popular press, "bloat" is often used as a catch-all phrase to suggest, negatively, that an application is filled with unnecessary features [1,3].

But, do users actually *experience* complex software applications in this way? (We define complex software as software with many features, most applications packages today.) We initially assumed that the "average" user must be struggling with applications such as word processors and spreadsheets. But, is this the case? And if it is, is this primarily related to unused functionality? Do people feel overwhelmed by the number and variety of choices in the interface, and if they do, how do they handle this? A goal of this paper is to specify more closely how users actually experience this complexity, and how they describe it. Our study of 53 Microsoft Word, Office 97 users from the general population provided an opportunity to explore these questions in detail.

First, we took a relatively straightforward quantitative approach, counting functions and defining software as "bloated" if a significant proportion of the functions available were not used by the majority of users. Second, we used qualitative methods to ground these data by placing them in the context of the users' narrative reports and questionnaire responses. Third, we evaluated and extended a study based on work done by Microsoft [7] which distinguished two profiles of users according to their perception of "bloat". We thus have several distinct methodological approaches, each offering a unique perspective on the problem. By triangulation of methods we are able to more fully understand the user's experience of complex software applications, and to gain insights that can be applied to interface design.

2   Previous work

To date, there has been no systematic study of how users experience complex software. Some early work has been done on logging the use of functions in UNIX [5, 6, 13]. This was followed by Carroll and Carrithers' now classic work on the "Training Wheels" interface for an early word processor. In this work they found that by blocking off all the functionality that was not needed for simple tasks, novice users were able to accomplish tasks both significantly faster and with significantly fewer errors than novice users using the full version [2]. Greenberg's work on Workbench for UNIX offered another solution. He labeled systems in which users use only a small subset of the command repertory as *recurrent systems* and created a reuse facility; this is a front end that collects the user's commands and then makes them easily accessible for reuse [5]. Linton's [8] recent work on word processors proposes a *recommender system* [12] that alerts users to functionality currently being used by co-workers doing similar tasks. All these researchers with the exception of Carroll and Carrithers have used software logging to capture their subjects' use of commands in the context of carrying out their everyday tasks. Results of these studies consistently show that users of complex software use very few of the commands available the majority of the time; informally this is called the 80/20 rule.

3   Study Design

3.1   Software Application Studied

The choice of a specific implementation of a word processor allowed us to control for one potential source of variation. Microsoft Word, Office 97, running on the PC was selected (MSWord). We used the number of functions available in an application as our indicator of complexity[1]. Because our primary question had to do with the users' perception of complexity, it was not sufficient to log the underlying commands invoked. We wanted to account for visual complexity and therefore defined a function as a graphical element on which the user could act, rather than an underlying piece of code. Functions are therefore action possibilities (affordances) that are specified visually to the user.

The following heuristics were developed to count the functions in the default MSWord interface:

- Each *final* menu item in the menus from the menu toolbar counts as 1. A menu item is not considered final if it results in a cascading menu.
- Each item on a toolbar counts as 1 (even if it provides a drop down menu – e.g., borders, styles, and font colour).
- Each button on a scrollbar counts as 1 except the scroll widget (which is composed of scroll left/up and scroll right/up buttons as well as the bar itself) which counts as 1.
- The selectable items on the status bar each count as 1.

Using these heuristics we counted 265 functions in the default MSWord interface. The second-level count included all options available on the first-level dialog boxes[2]–709 options available[3]. In this paper we report only on the first-level functions (n= 265).

3.2   Sample

The sample consisted of 53 participants selected from the general population. While this was not a simple random sample (and therefore it is not appropriate to use inferential statistics), participants were selected with attention to achieving as representative a sample of

---

[1] There are clearly other factors contributing to the experience of complexity, for example, the actual domain of the application can be inherently complex (e.g., engineering design is the domain of CAD software) or the structure of features within the interface can play a role (e.g., progressive disclosure). In this paper we focus specifically on the number of functions.

[2] First-level dialog boxes are those that are accessible directly from a menu item.

[3] Space limitations do not permit us to list the detailed heuristics used to count the dialog-box functions; these heuristics are considerably more complex than those of the main interface and are available from the authors. By comparison Gibbs reported that there were a total of 1033 functions in MSWord 97, but gave no source. Therefore, we do not know the method used to count the functions [4].

the general adult population as possible. That is, we paid particular attention to achieving representation in terms of variables such as age, gender, education, occupation and organizational status.

3.3   Instruments and Data collection

Functionality Interview

A researcher presented each participant with two series of printed screen captures. The first set successively revealed all the first-level functions on the default interface. The second set was a simple random sample of all the dialog box functions. For each function, participants were asked:

(1) Do you know what the function does? And if so,
(2) Do you use it?

Responses to question one were scored on a two-point scale: *familiar* and *unfamiliar*. Responses to question two were scored on a three-point scale: *used regularly*, *used irregularly*, and *not used*. Participants were told that familiarity with a function indicated a general knowledge of the function's action but that specific detailed knowledge was not required. A regularly-used function was defined as one that was used weekly or monthly and an irregularly-used function was one that was used less frequently.

We were particularly concerned with ecological validity, and the most valid way to assess the familiarity and use of functions by our participants would have been to have them use their own system while reporting familiarity and usage. However, we were concerned that if they had customized the interface in any way there was the potential to introduce error in the recording and make comparisons problematic. Our approach was to use colored screen shots of an out-of-the-box version of the word processor. We did, however, take screen captures from our participants' machines so that we could later assess the extent to which they had customized their interface.

To discourage guessing and to provide a measure of reliability, participants were told at the outset that they would be asked periodically to describe the action of any function with which they reported familiarity. Unreliable participants could in this way be identified and data discarded. Fortunately this did not turn out to be an issue in this study.

In-depth Interview

An in-depth interview was conducted with each participant to both ground and extend the quantitative work. Here specific issues that had been raised in the *Functionality Interview* were probed and participants were encouraged to talk more generally about their experiences with word processing in general, and MSWord, in particular.

The *Functionality Interview* and the *In-depth Interview* together required approximately one and a half hours of each participant's time.

Questionnaire

Prior to the interview each participant was given a poll-type questionnaire. This took approximately 30 minutes to complete. It included a series of questions on work practices, experience with writing and publishing, the use of computers generally, and the use of word processors specifically. A number of questions were designed to gather information for scale construction for the evaluation of Microsoft's profiling study. Basic demographic information, such as age, gender, education, and occupation was also requested. Throughout the questionnaire open-ended responses were encouraged and space provided.

3.4   How our work is differentiated from others

Our work can be differentiated from earlier research in a number of ways. First, we use multiple methods and the results show this provides us with a unique perspective for thinking about complex software. The different approaches do not provide conflicting answers, but rather help to elaborate an extremely complex question, each highlighting a specific dimension of the problem. Quantitative methods offer a detailed description of the feature space, questionnaire responses helped identify patterns and summarise the data, while the in-depth interviews allowed us to probe these summary statements in order to understand the users' actual experience and how it varied. Second, our data are self-reported—from questionnaires and in-depth interviews—in contrast with logging which has generally been the method of choice in computer science. It is important to note that while logged data report the functions actually used (at least as measured in terms of keystrokes), this method cannot distinguish between *familiarity* and *use*. Finally, while self-reported data are subject to the participant's ability to recall information, information on a function that is used irregularly could be missed if logging is not carried out for an extensive period of time. Thus, by using a variety of methods we compensate for the limitation of each method used on its own.

The next three sections present our findings and analysis.

4   Quantitative method: Software is "bloated" when a significant proportion of the functions available are not used by the majority of users

By this definition, MSWord is "bloated" indeed, as the pie charts illustrate (Figure 1). Compare the number of

190

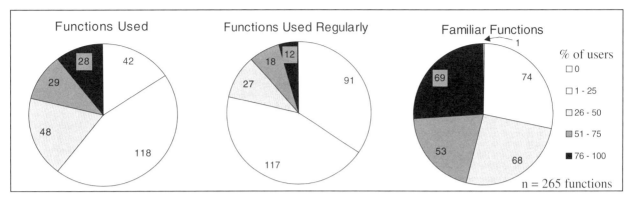

Figure 1: Number of functions that are "used", "used regularly", and "familiar" to our participants.

functions *used* by various percentages of the users and the functions *used regularly*. Of the 265 first-level functions, 15.8% (42) were not used at all and only 21.5% (57) were used by more than half of the participants. There were only 3.3% (12) functions that were used regularly by more than three quarters of the participants.

By looking at the number of functions with which users were *familiar*, however, we see that the distribution is much more even and that users were familiar with a great deal more than they actually used. Note that this familiarity data could not have been captured through logging. There was only one function that none of the users could identify, namely, *extend selection* (EXT) on the status bar. 28% (74) of the functions were familiar to 13 or fewer participants (1-25%), and 26% (69) of the functions were familiar to 40-53 (76-100%) of the participants. The high degree of familiarity points to one way in which this narrow definition of "bloat" may mask the actual experience of the user. Familiarity may lead to a certain level of comfort and so if users are familiar with functions, even if they do not use them, they may be less likely to perceive these unused functions as "bloat" rather than as functionality they simply do not use.

We can also look at the relationship between

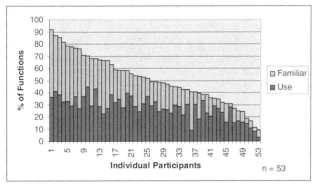

Figure 2: Percentage of functions "familiar" and "used" for each participant sorted in descending order of familiarity.

familiarity and *use* from the perspective of the individual user. Figure 2 shows a comparison for each participant between the percentage of functions with which they were familiar and the percentage actually used. On average, the Usage to Familiarity Ratio was 57% (standard deviation = 0.148).

Table 1 shows that a relatively low percentage of the functions were actually used. On average the participants used 27% of the functions, and were familiar with 51%[4]. There was greater variation in the number of functions with which participants were familiar (range from 9% to 92%) than the functions actually used (range from 3% to 45%). Figure 2 shows this graphically. However, this data cannot tell us whether each user experienced the unused functionality in the same way, or whether they experienced it as "bloat".

	First-level functions	
Average # familiar to participants	135	(51%)
Average # used by participants	72	(27%)
Average # used regularly	40	(15%)
Average # used irregularly	32	(12%)
Maximum # familiar to any participant	245	(92%)
Minimum # familiar to any participant	24	(9%)
Maximum # used by any participant	119	(45%)
Minimum # used by any participant	8	(3%)

Table 1: Means and ranges of "familiar" and "used" functions (n=53).

5 Qualitative Method: The Users' Experience

Our quantitative analysis showed that there was a great deal of unused functionality, but is this "bloat", or more neutrally, simply unused functionality? While our quantitative analysis highlights many interesting

---

[4] We found that participants' familiarity and usage at the dialog-box level was roughly half of what it was with the first-level functions: participants were familiar with on average 28% of the dialog box functions and used 13%.

aspects about the feature space, it cannot shed light on this question. Yet, the answer to this question has important implications for design. In this section we first focus on data from the questionnaire to answer the following questions:

1. To what extent did users report that they were satisfied or dissatisfied with their word processor?
2. Was concern with unused functionality a major source of dissatisfaction for users?
3. What other sources of dissatisfaction with their word processor did users report, and how can these be categorised?
4. Did users actually perceive that their word processing software as "bloated" and did they use this language?
5. What impact did unused functionality have on usability?

After answering these questions we turn to report what the users themselves said. We hear what frustrated them, how they responded to new versions of MSWord, and how in the final analysis they got their work done. It is important to note the ways in which these two methodologies complement each other, in particular how in-depth interviewing is able to deepen our understanding of users' experience and suggest design options that are masked by other methods.

5.1   Questionnaire

Participants were asked to rank on a Likert-type scale a series of 29 statements about their perception of using MSWord. Figure 3 shows the result for one of these questions, and is representative of the findings for statements on general satisfaction/dissatisfaction. Namely, the majority of the users reported "no opinion" to these statements and the rest of the users were almost evenly divided between those who agreed and those who disagreed.   However, when participants were asked in the interview to discuss these statements, they were, in general, more satisfied than the questionnaire responses indicated. Furthermore, the interviews

revealed that the major source of dissatisfaction was not about the large number of functions, or concern that the extra functions were getting in the way. Rather concern centered on factors such as poor implementation, unpredictability, and inconsistency.   Finally, with respect to "bloat", there was not a single person in our study who used the term, either in written comments on the questionnaire or in the interviews.

The responses to questions designed to assess the impact of a large number of functions on usability did, however, suggest that a problem exists. Examples of these are in Table 2 below. Users were almost evenly divided between those who agreed, disagreed or had no opinion when asked if they were overwhelmed by the number of interface elements. However, when asked specifically about the impact of excess functionality on their activities they were more clearly divided.

	Agree	No Op.	Disagree
I am overwhelmed by how much stuff there is. (n=51)	27.5%	39.2%	33.3%
I have a hard time finding the functions I need unless I use them regularly. (n=53)	58.5%	5.7%	35.8%
After using a new version for a short time, the commands and icons that I don't use don't get in my way. (n=51)	51.0%	17.6%	31.4%
Wading through unfamiliar functions can often be annoying/frustrating. (n=53)	62.3%	17.0%	20.8%

Table 2: Responses to statements about usability.

But how would users like to see excess functionality handled? Again, our participants were divided, and offered no easy solutions for designers (Table 3). Only 24.5% wanted to have unused functions removed entirely but 45% preferred to have unused functions tucked away. The fact that 51% wanted the ability to discover new functions as they use the application points to one underlying reason for users not wanting unused functions removed.

	Agree	No Op.	Disagree
I want only the functions I use. (n=53)	24.5%	9.4%	66.0%
I prefer to have unused functions tucked away. (n=53)	45.3%	15.1%	39.6%
It is important to me that I continually discover new functions. (n=53)	50.9%	18.9%	30.2%

Table 3: Users' preference for number of functions on the interface.

But why are some users not bothered by excess functionality while others are? This is, in part, we argue a reflection of the diversity among the users of word

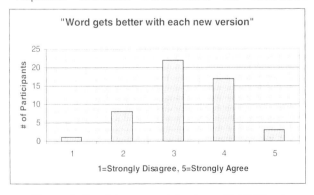

Figure 3: Participants satisfaction with MSWord.

192

processors in the general population. Furthermore, the power of today's word processor is that it is not necessary to be a technical expert to use it, however, lack of computing expertise may limit a user's ability to critique it.

A fascinating finding was that a specific occupational group, the secretaries and administrative assistants, reported the greatest satisfaction with their word processor. Initially we thought this might be explained by the fact that they would have received more training than members of other groups and were the heaviest users, but the results of the questionnaire did not support this. However, in the analysis of the transcripts from the in-depth interviews we did notice a pattern. When participants from this group were asked to say more about what they specifically liked about MSWord, or how it could be improved, they had difficulty giving precise answers. A number said that they simply accepted it as it was, or assumed that this was "just the way word processors are"! So, while this group included heavy users of word processors, they appeared not to have sufficient computing experience to think critically about this tool. When we looked at the technical experts, we found that not only did they report the greatest dissatisfaction, they were able to articulate this in terms of specific problems and underlying issues. The computer scientists, in particular, had a good understanding of what is possible in a software application and were less accepting of "bad" design or what they saw as "sloppy implementation".

These observations raise two points. First, designers should not automatically assume that users can answer their questions accurately (even if the questions are well designed). Second, there is a limitation to survey methodology if the goal is to understand user experience. We now turn to the users' own accounts given in the in-depth interviews. These more nuanced accounts of user experience suggest some new design ideas.

5.2   In-Depth Interview

Source of Dissatisfaction: Excess Functionality

In this section the users' speak. It is important to understand that the analysis that runs through this section comes out of a detailed reading and summarising of the transcripts from the in-depth interviews. The individual quotations have been selected both because they are representative of the analytical point we are making and for the way in which they give life to the issue.

A number of participants stated explicitly that their needs could be met by a "simpler" system. A senior technical expert commented:

"I want something much simpler… I'd like to be able to customize it to the point that I can eliminate a significant number of things. And I find that very difficult to do. Like I'd like to throw away the 99% of the things I don't use that appear in these toolbars. And I find that you just can't, there's a minimum set of toolbars that you're just stuck with. And I think that's a bad thing, I really believe that you can't simplify Word enough to do it."

By way of contrast, a junior technical expert suggested that he did not want a simpler system, but that he was concerned with the amount of screen real estate that these functions took up:

"I don't think they should be eliminated. It's always good to have them, but they shouldn't be given the same prominence or real estate on the screen as the other options."

An older office administrator who had once studied mathematics suggested that there was a need for a "light" version of the software not because of limited screen real estate but to prevent confusion:

"I think maybe what they could do is have different levels so you would not be bogged down with so many features, and if you don't need them all, they are just really in the way and they get cumbersome. They get into something you don't really want. So if they had something like Basic Microsoft Word, … that would be useful … for people who just do letters or something like that. I think that there is, in a way, too much there and that for a user like me it is, in fact, a disadvantage -- you get lost in it and when you need something very quickly, which is usual, whether one is typing a letter or a document, you don't have oodles of time to go exploring for three days. And then it takes you half an hour to do the thing… My background was mathematics, where you learn basic stuff and [then] you learn more difficult stuff and you build it. It goes very logically, whereas here you are just thrown in the middle of it and you flounder."

Several participants specifically said that they wanted all the functions present even if they did not use them because they might want them some day. This points to an underlying apprehension that functions that are not visible might get "lost" if they were tucked away. A young female lawyer who relies heavily on her secretary said:

"No, I think I prefer to have it there just in case there's an occasion when I'm here, she's [her secretary] not here and I want to do something. Then I'll just go in and do it. Like, an example would be, page numbering or making a list or using the automatic numbering or putting bullets in or some sort of formatting thing that I want to do if she hasn't done it and we've got to get the document out. So, no, I think it's fine how it is, and in fact, I sort of like to have the option. I wouldn't like to be treated like I only can work at a certain level. I prefer to have the option to work at a higher level if I choose to."

Others wanted all the features present specifically because they saw it as a sign of being up-to-date. A young female consultant said:

> *"And I always want the latest version whether I [laughs] you know, really use all the new stuff... I want it, whether I know what to do with it or not. [laughs] I understand why some people would only want to use what they have, 'cause that's what they're familiar with, but now you just can't be like that anymore."*

And others pointed out that reducing the functions would impede their ability to learn through exploration. A graduate student in the humanities said:

> *"Yes, it would probably be useful ... hmmm, I have two answers to that ... To some degree it would be useful to have a reduced set, but I like sometimes just playing around and discovering a function. So if you only have a reduced set then you don't have much chance to accidentally find a function and say "ah, this is what this does" but the results [of the functionality interview] show that I haven't been experimenting that much!"*

Not all the participants were concerned about the large number of functions. In fact, several were adamant that they liked to have them all. An entrepreneur and owner of a small successful IT company put it this way:

> *"And I know that in some software packages they try to create simple menus to allow you to decide what you want to see. I always default to the full set and the reason is that I feel comfortable with technology and I'd rather see the full extent of what's available, not just the sliver that is usable by me. I don't want to see a sliver or portion of it that has been determined statistically to be more useful for most users and think that I'm missing out on some features."*

Clearly there are conflicting views. The challenge to designers is to accommodate the diversity of user needs. In these quotations we begin to see what motivates users and how some of these motivations tie into underlying values, e.g., speed of accomplishing tasks, and the need to be seen as up-to-date. We also see how exploratory learning is one consequence of keeping all the functions at hand.

Additional Sources of Dissatisfaction
A source of dissatisfaction for some users was their perception that the multiple ways of executing an operation were confusing. In some cases this was because these variations did not produce the same result (e.g., print menu versus print icon) and users' perceived this as a sign of inconsistency. Others perceived the fact that variations produced the same result (save menu versus save icon) as a sign of unnecessary redundancy. A government policy analyst noted:

> *"It seems very redundant to have that many different ways of doing something, and it makes training very confusing when you're just starting up with the software."*

As we have noted there are several sources of dissatisfaction for users, and that excess functionality is seen as problematic by some. While different users "liked" or "hated" different features, there was almost universal distain for automatic features. For a variety of reasons, participants from across the occupational categories complained about these. As one technical expert exclaimed: *"Don't go there!"* or a librarian, commenting on AutoCorrect[5] put it this way:

> *"What I type is what I want, so I don't want the machine second guessing me."*

For others the problem was compounded because they did not know how to turn these automatic features off. A female consultant complained:

> *"With each new version there's a tendency for it to try and predict what you will do next. Drives me nuts! It's an advance that is totally annoying."*

But, even here there were a few who perceived that the automatic features that they used worked well and they considered them timesavers.

5.3 Summary
The analysis of the questionnaire data, informed by the in-depth interviews allowed us to further specify "bloat" by identifying an *objective* and a *subjective* dimension. There is a small subset of features that are not used or wanted *by any* user which we designate as *"objective bloat"*. The remaining features are divided into two sets which vary from user to user and are thus subjectively defined. One set includes those features that are not used *and* not wanted by an individual user - this is *"subjective bloat"* for that user. The second set includes those features that are wanted by that individual user, whether or not they are actually used. To refer to the unused functions in the second set as "bloat" is misleading as the user's experience of this unused functionality is not negative. In fact, users' responses both to the presence of unused functionality, and how they would like it handled varies widely. This discovery of set of unused features, both wanted and unwanted, that is subjectively defined by each user, opens the design space and raises new challenges for interface designers. There is certainly more to "bloat" than meets the eye. Some implications for design are discussed in Section 7 of this paper.

---

[5] This function corrects a word automatically while it is being typed.

194

6 Evaluating and Extending Microsoft's Study on User Profiling

The third method we used was user profiling which, like our second method, is qualitative in nature. In a workshop [5] Microsoft reported an unpublished study in which 12 members of a focus group were asked to define "bloat". Group members were asked to complete the statement *"My software feels bloated when..."* The sample is small and we have been unable to find information on how the group was chosen, but the results are intriguing. The Microsoft study reported that users can be categorized into one of two Profiles, A or B, depending on their perception of software as "bloated" or not. Profile A users prefer software that is complete, they will stay up-to-date with upgrades, they assume that all interface elements have some value, and they blame themselves when something goes wrong or when they can't figure out how to perform a specific task. Alternately, Profile B users prefer to pay for and use only what they need, they are suspicious of upgrades, they want only the interface elements that are used, and they blame the software and help system when they can't do a task. A user's profile was independent of expertise as it is traditionally defined in the HCI literature, a uni-dimensional construct which includes categories such as novice/beginner, intermediate, and expert. Microsoft's focus group included only intermediate and expert users.

The Microsoft profiling approach, although unpublished, represented a reasonable first attempt at understanding the perceptual component of "bloat". Our goal was to attempt to reproduce these findings in a more systematic study with a sample of users from the general population.

Our results showed partial support for the existence of the A and B profiles. We had to discard the questions on blame as few in our sample were willing to blame either the software or the company when they had problems, and even fewer were willing to blame themselves (3.8%)! On all the questions relating to

blame we had a high reporting of "no opinion", and at least two participants said that "blame" was very strong language and that they felt discomfort with the term. We have no explanation for why this was not a problem in the Microsoft group, other than a possible cultural one.

After removing blame we had three scales to construct. They are summarized in Table 4 along with the Cronbach's alpha (α), a reliability measure.

Functions	"The number of functions in the in interface does not make it difficult for me to find the function I am looking for." (# Variables = 3, α = .83)
Up-to-dateness	"I want my MS Word software to be up to date – I want the latest version." (# Variables = 3, α = .77)
Completeness	"I want a complete version of MS Word even if I don't use all the functions." (# Variables s = 6, α = .76)

Table 4: Summary statement for three scale variables (n = 50).

These three scales were then aggregated to comprise the final A/B Profile Scale (Cronbach's α of 0.81).

The distribution of the cases across the A/B Profile Scale revealed that while there were concentrations at both ends of the scale there was a substantial group near the center. We therefore divided the subjects into three groups, which we distinguished as Profile A, Neutral, and Profile B.

We found support for Microsoft's finding that the perception of "bloat" is independent of expertise (Figure 4). In addition, we found that it is independent both in terms of the number of functions used and in terms of the number of functions with which the user was familiar.

While there is some support for the A/B profiling, that is, the perception of "bloat" varied between groups of users, we wondered what else this profile might be capturing. First, we thought it might distinguish early from late adopters and that gender might play a role in

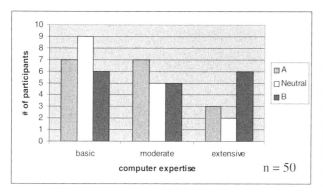

Figure 4: Distribution of computer expertise over the A/B Profile Scale.

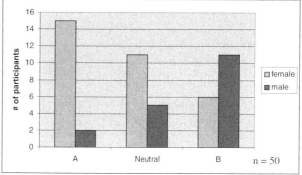

Figure 5: Distribution of gender on A/B Profile Scale.

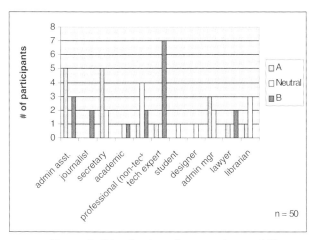

Figure 6: Distribution of occupation on A/B Profile Scale.

explaining the outcome. Figure 5 shows that there is indeed a difference based on gender, but contrary to our expectations it was the females who fell into Profile A, i.e., those wanting the most up-to-date, and complete version of the software. However, if we look at the distribution of the occupation of our participants (Figure 6), an alternate explanation is suggested. The gender difference also reflects differences in terms of their position in the division of labor.

The females cluster in administrative assistant and secretarial occupations, those for whom word processing may be the base of their craft knowledge and a source of status. Profile B includes the technical experts and one of the two academics, both groups who are less likely to have support staff and for whom word processing is yet another task. Also included in Profile B are the journalists and lawyers, all of whom have staff to format and/or edit their work. As they themselves are not responsible for the look and feel of the final product, they may not feel a need to upgrade. The academics and technical experts are most overburdened, responsible for both the creation and production of documents. Not surprisingly, perhaps they are the least interested in new versions of the software.

7 Bringing it All Together: Directions for Design

We had become concerned that the recent use of the term "bloat" in the popular press and more importantly in the technical community could suggest that widely used general applications, such as word processors, are filled with unnecessary features. We were especially concerned that the potential for these reports of user dissatisfaction could lead to the conclusion that users would be better served by simple or light versions of these applications. What was missing were the research studies that tested and evaluated these assumptions. It

was a goal of our study to begin to fill this gap, and to be able to understand more fully how users actually *experience* a complex application such as a word processor.

Our first objective was to see if the labeling of this complex software as "bloated" had any validity. If unused functionality is the metric, MSWord is clearly "bloated"—a little over 50% of the functionality with which users are familiar is actually used. And, while users are dissatisfied with a number of aspects of MSWord, not all this dissatisfaction centers on excess functionality.

"Bloat" can be further specified and defined in terms of *objective* and *subjective* "bloat". In terms of *"objective* bloat"—functions used by few users—we have the following design recommendations:

- Eliminate unused functions.
- Relocate functions used by few from high-level visibility in the interface. The determination of the exact "cut-off point" is likely application-specific.
- Prevent objective bloat. This requires a shift in design practice from programmer/marketing-centric to human-centered design. There is a need to recognize that there is a cost to the user of unused features. Each function should be evaluated carefully before it is added to the interface.

This leaves a subjectively defined group of unused functions. But this subset cannot de facto be defined negatively – this is not what all users told us. *Subjective* "bloat" is thus defined as the particular subset of functions that are not used and not wanted by an individual user. The fact that not all of an individual user's subset of unused functionality can be labeled as "bloat" was an unexpected finding of our study. *Subjective* "bloat" varies from user to user, so creating a simple or basic version by eliminating functions will inconvenience most users, albeit in different ways. To put it another way, my favourite function, may be your "bloat" and vice versa. We hope that this redefinition will encourage a more nuanced understanding of the richness of heavily-featured software applications and that a catch-all phrase such as "bloat" which distorts users' experiences, will no longer be used.

What is exciting is how this understanding opens the design space, challenging designers to accommodate both functionality that is used and functionality that is unused but nonetheless still wanted. The ultimate goal might be for each user to have an interface that includes functionality suited to his/her needs and desires, yet does not limit access to additional functionality. Although this goal is not likely achievable in its purest form, some progress can still be made.

Interface design has begun to acknowledge that "one-size-fits-all" interfaces may not in fact fit all. Facilities for customization and tailoring are included in most complex software applications, however the high overhead required to customize renders them neither effective nor adequate. We argue that the philosophy of design needs to move away from "enabling the customization of a one-size-fits-all interface" to supporting the creation of a personalizable interface. The personalization solution needs to be lightweight and low in overhead for the user, yet not limit or restrict their activities. We suggest that multiple interfaces may be one way to accommodate both the complexity of user experience and their potentially changing needs. Individual interfaces within this set would be designed to *mask complexity* and ideally to support learning. We recognize that continual access to the underlying formatted document or text needs to be preserved.

We are starting with a two-interface model for users who want a reduced function set. This group includes beginners as well as those users who regularly use only a few features, for example, the lawyers in our study. A simple toggle that enables the user to switch between the default interface and a reduced interface – for example the top 10% of functions used by all users – is the first approach. This gives a user access to a less complex interface while at the same time permitting the user to move readily to the more complex default version, if for example, a less frequently-used feature is required. As well, features can be added into the user's personal interface as desired. In this way the complexity is masked without limiting the user's access to the full system.

Simultaneously we are investigating an alternative approach—the creation of a set of interfaces. We are exploring a number of different bases for personalization to define these sets, e.g., psychological stereotypes, social roles, activities, and digital personae. Essentially we are arguing that not only has the time for "one-size-fits-all" interface design passed, but that "one-size-fits-one", or an interface for every user, even if possible, could also be limiting. It is only with a set of interfaces that we can begin to support the complexity and diversity of users' experience. The challenge is an exciting one as applications such as the word processor are used by millions and therefore potential impact of design changes is enormous.

8   Acknowledgements

We would like to thank CITO: Communication and Information Technology Ontario and IBM Centre for Advanced Studies who are supporting the *Learning Complex Software* Project of which this study is a part. We also thank Kellogg Booth and Ronald Baecker for commenting on earlier drafts of this paper.

References

[1] The bloatware debate (1998). *Computer World*, August 10, 1998.

[2] Carroll, J., and Carrithers, C. (1984). Blocking learner error states in a training-wheels system. *Human Factors*, 26(4), 377-389.

[3] Do computers have to be hard to use? Complex, volatile, frustrating; There must be a simpler way (1998). *New York Times*, May 28, 1998.

[4] Gibbs, W. (1997). Taking computers to task. *Scientific American*, July 1997, 82-89.

[5] Greenberg, S. (1993). *The Computer User as Toolsmith: The Use, Reuse, and Organization of Computer-based Tools*. New York: Cambridge University Press.

[6] Hanson, S.J., Kraut, R.E., and Farber, J.M (1984). Interface design and multivariate analysis of UNIX command use. *ACM Transactions on Office Information Systems*, 2(1), 42-57.

[7] Kaufman, L. and Weed, B. (1998). User interfaces for computers – Too much of a good thing? Identifying and resolving bloat in the user interface. *Conference Summary, CHI 98*, Workshop #10, 207-208.

[8] Linton, F., Joy, D. and Schaefer, P. (1999). Building user and expert models by long term observation of application usage. *User Modeling: Proceedings of the Seventh International Conference*. New York: Springer, 129-138.

[9] More *than Screen Deep: Toward Every-Citizen Interfaces to the Nation's Information Infrastructure*. (1997). Washington, DC, National Academy Press.

[10] Norman, Don. (1998). *The Invisible Computer*. Cambridge, MA: MIT Press, 80.

[11] *Online   Computing   Dictionary* http://www.instantweb.com/

[12] Resnick, P. and Varian, H.R. (1997). Recommender systems, *Communications of the ACM*, 40(3), 56-58.

[13] Whiteside, J. et al. (1982). How do people really use text editors? *Proceedings of the Conference on Office Automation Systems*, New York: ACM, 29-40.

Triangle Strip Compression

Martin Isenburg

University of North Carolina at Chapel Hill
isenburg@cs.unc.edu

Abstract

In this paper we introduce a simple and efficient scheme for encoding the connectivity and the stripification of a triangle mesh. Since generating a good set of triangle strips is a hard problem, it is desirable to do this just once and store the computed strips with the triangle mesh. However, no previously reported mesh encoding scheme is designed to include triangle strip information into the compressed representation. Our algorithm encodes the stripification and the connectivity in an interwoven fashion, that exploits the correlation existing between the two.

Key words: Mesh compression, connectivity encoding, triangle strips, triangle fans, stripification.

1 Introduction

Encoding the connectivity of triangle meshes has recently been the subject of intense study and many representations have been proposed [10, 11, 3, 7, 5]. The sudden interest in this area is fueled by the emerging demand for interactive visualization of 3D data sets in a networked environment (e.g. VRML over the Internet). Since transmission bandwidth across wide-area networks is a scarce resource, compact encodings for 3D models are needed.

For interactive visualization not only the speed at which a triangle mesh can be received is important, but also the speed at which it can be displayed. Here the bottleneck is the rate at which this data can be sent to the rendering engine. Each triangle of the mesh can be rendered individually by sending its three vertices to the graphics hardware. Then every mesh vertex is processed about six times, which involves passing its three coordinates and optional normal, colour, and texture information from the memory to and through the graphics pipeline.

A common technique to reduce the number of times this data needs to be transmitted is to send long runs of adjacent triangles. Such triangle strips [2, 15] are widely supported by today's graphics hardware. Here two vertices from a previous triangle are re-used for all but the first triangle of every strip. Depending on the quality of the triangle strips this can potentially reduce the number of vertex repetitions by a factor of three.

For rendering purposes, an optimal stripification covers the mesh with as few strips using as few swaps [2] as possible. Computing an optimal set of triangle strips is NP-complete [1]. Various heuristics for generating good triangle strips have been proposed by Evans et al. [2], Speckmann and Snoeyink [8], and Xiang et al. [16].

Given the difficulty of generating good triangle strips it would be desirable to do this just once and store the computed stripification together with the mesh. Especially for data sets with a large distribution (such as the models from the Viewpoint Datalabs collection [13]) it is worthwhile to provide a good pre-computed stripification.

Currently available mesh compression techniques do not support the encoding of stripified meshes. Obviously one can enhance any existing compression method by encoding the stripification separately and concatenating the results. However, such a two-pass technique adds unnecessary overhead—it does not exploit the correlation between the connectivity and the stripification of a mesh.

In this paper we introduce a simple and efficient scheme for encoding the connectivity and the stripification of a triangle mesh. Enhancing Triangle Fixer, our edge-based connectivity compression algorithm [4], we compress this information in an interwoven fashion, that fully exploits the existing correlation.

2 Connectivity Compression Techniques

Most efficient connectivity compression schemes for triangle meshes [10, 11, 3, 7] follow the same pattern: They encode the mesh through a compact and often interwoven representation of a vertex spanning tree and its corresponding dual, a triangle spanning tree. This is based on Turan's observation [12] that planar graphs can be encoded with a constant number of bits per vertex (bpv) when represented as a pair of spanning trees. Indexed triangle sets— the standard representation for triangle meshes— use at least $6 \log n$ bpv for the connectivity.

The Topological Surgery method [10] traverses the vertices of a mesh in a deterministic fashion (e.g. breadth or depth first search) and encodes the corresponding vertex and its dual triangle spanning tree separately. Run-length encoding both trees results in bit-rates around 4 bpv.

Touma and Gotsman's Triangle Mesh Compression scheme [11] records the degree of each vertex along a spiraling vertex tree. For branches in the tree they need an additional split code. This technique implicitly encodes the triangle spanning tree. They compress the resulting code sequence using a combination of run-length and entropy encoding and achieve bit-rates as low as 0.2 bvp for very regular meshes and between 2 and 3 bpv otherwise.

Both the Cut-Border Machine [3] and the Edgebreaker scheme [7] include triangle after triangle into a boundary while traversing a spiraling triangle spanning tree. At each step they record the adjacency relation between the included triangle and the boundary, which implicitly encodes the vertex spanning tree. Follow-up work by King and Rossignac [6] establishes the currently lowest known worst case bound of 3.67 bpv.

Inspired by Rossignac's Edgebreaker scheme [7], we propose an edge-based approach for connectivity compression, which—as we will see later—has a simple and natural extension towards the compression of triangle strips. This is accomplished by a design choice that is the crucial difference between our Triangle Fixer scheme and previous approaches [3, 7]. Our method slightly uncouples the traversal of the triangle spanning tree from the traversal of its corresponding vertex spanning tree. Triangles are included into a boundary without immediately specifying their adjacency relation.

3 Triangle Fixer

The Triangle Fixer scheme expects the input mesh to be a 2-manifold surface with boundary composed of consistently oriented triangles. This means that the neighbourhood of each vertex can be mapped to a disk or a half-disk. The input mesh might consist of several connected components and can have multiple holes or handles.

The connectivity of the input mesh is encoded as a sequence of labels T, R, L, S, E, H, and M. The total number of labels equals the number of mesh edges. For every triangle there is a label of type T, for every hole there is a label of type H, and for every handle there is a label of type M. The remaining labels R, L, S, and E describe how to 'fix' triangles and holes together.

Subsequently this sequence of labels can be compressed into a compact bit-stream by assigning a unique bit-pattern to every label. The correlation among subsequent labels can be exploited for more compact encodings with a simple order-3 adaptive arithmetic coder [14].

3.1 Encoding

The encoding process defines an *active boundary* in clockwise orientation around an arbitrary edge of the mesh. This initial boundary has two *boundary edges*; one of them becomes the *gate* of the boundary. The gate of the active boundary is the *active gate*.

In every step of the encoding process the active gate is labeled with either T, R, L, S, E, H, or M. Which label the

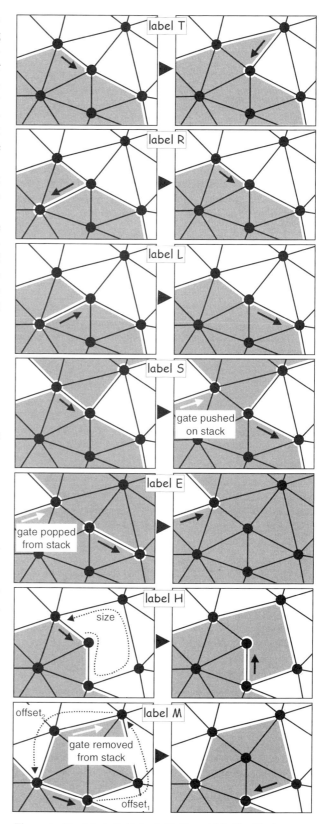

Figure 1: The labels T, R, L, S, E, H, and M. The black arrow denotes the active gate, the grey arrows denote gates in the stack.

active gate is given depends on its adjacency relation to the boundary. After recording the label, the boundary is updated and a new active gate is selected. Depending on the label the boundary expands (T and H), shrinks (R and L), splits (S), ends (E), or merges (M). An initially empty stack of boundaries is used to temporarily buffer boundaries. The encoding process terminates after exactly e iterations where e is the number of mesh edges.

In Figure 1 we illustrate for all seven labels the situation in which they apply and the respective updates for gate and boundary that they imply. They are as follows:

label T The active gate is not adjacent to any other boundary edge, but to an unprocessed triangle. The active boundary is extended around this triangle. The new active gate is the right edge of the included triangle.

label R The active gate is adjacent to the next edge along the active boundary with which it is 'fixed' together. The new active gate is the previous edge along the active boundary.

label L The active gate is adjacent to the previous edge along the active boundary with which it is 'fixed' together. The new active gate is the next edge along the active boundary.

label S The active gate is adjacent to an edge of the active boundary which is neither the next nor the previous. 'Fixing' the two edges together splits the active boundary. The previous and the next edge along the active boundary become gates for the two resulting boundaries. The first is pushed on the stack and encoding continues on the latter.

label E The active gate is adjacent to an edge of the active boundary which is both, the next edge and the previous edge. Then the active boundary consists of only two edges which are 'fixed' together. If the boundary stack is empty the encoding process terminates. Otherwise it continues on the gate of the boundary that is popped from the stack.

label H_n The active gate is not adjacent to any other boundary edge, but to an unprocessed hole. The active boundary is extended around this hole. Its size n (e.g. the number of edges around the hole) is stored with the label. The new active gate is the rightmost edge of the included hole.

label $M_{i,k,l}$ The active gate is adjacent to a boundary edge which is not from the active boundary, but from a boundary in the stack. 'Fixing' the two edges together merges the two boundaries. The boundary is removed from the stack. Its former position i in the stack and two offset values k and l (see Figure 1) are stored with the label. The new active gate is the previous edge along the stack boundary.

We use a simple half-edge data structure during encoding and decoding to store the mesh connectivity and to maintain the boundaries. Besides pointers to the origin, to the next half-edge around the origin, and to the inverse half-edge, we have two pointers to reference a next and a previous boundary edge. This way we organize all edges of the same boundary into a cyclic doubly-linked list.

3.2 Decoding

The recorded information (e.g. the sequence of labels) is sufficient to uniquely invert each boundary and gate update that was performed during encoding. We decode the mesh connectivity by processing the labels in reverse order, while performing the inverse of every label operation. Every update can be performed in constant time, which gives us linear time complexity. An exception is the inverse operation for label M, which requires the traversal of $k + l$ edges. However, labels of type M correspond to handles in the mesh, which are of rare occurrence.

	mesh characteristics				bits per vertex	
name	vertices	triangles	holes	hndls	fixed	aac-3
bishop	250	496	-	-	4.00	1.86
shape	2562	5120	-	-	3.99	0.77
triceratops	2832	5660	-	-	4.00	2.52
fandisk	6475	12946	-	-	4.00	1.67
eight	766	1536	-	2	4.09	1.43
femur	3897	7798	-	2	4.16	3.05
skull	10952	22104	-	51	4.22	2.96
bunny	34834	69451	5	-	4.00	1.73
phone	33204	66287	3	-	4.05	2.70
terrainSM	13057	25818	1	-	4.02	2.53
terrainLG	42943	85290	1	-	4.01	2.43

Table 1: Compressing connectivity with a fixed bit assignment scheme (*fixed*) and an order-3 adaptive arithmetic coder (*acc-3*).

3.3 Compression and Results

Triangle meshes of v vertices without holes or handles have $3v - 6$ edges and $2v - 4$ triangles. This means that $2v - 4$ labels are of type T and $v - 2$ labels of type R, L, S, or E. An encoding that uses 1 bit for label T and 3 bits each for the other labels guarantees a $5v - 10$ bit encoding.

We notice a correlation among subsequent labels that is consistent across our wide range of test models. Label R for instance is likely to be followed by label R, whereas label L is likely to be followed by another label of type L. We exploit this correlation for compression by making the bit assignment dependent on the last label. Using 1 bit for label T and a varying assignment of 2, 3, 4 and 4 bits for labels R, L, S, and E guarantees a $6v - 12$ bit encoding, while being in practice close to $4v$ bits. The table above describes the bit assignment we use.

after	TRLSE
T, R	1 2 4 3 4
L	1 4 2 4 3
S	1 4 3 4 2
E	1 2 4 4 3

The number of holes and handles of a mesh is generally small and so is the number of labels H and M. Since label T can never be followed by labels L or E, we encode label H with the label combination TL and label M with the combination TE. The associated integer values are compressed subsequently using a standard technique for encoding variable sized integers into bit-streams.

However, the correlation among subsequent labels also invites arithmetic encoding [14]. Experimental results for various meshes using a simple order-3 adaptive arithmetic coder are listed in Table 1. Since the input sequence to the arithmetic coder contains only five different symbols, it can be efficiently implemented using less than 4 KB of memory for the probability tables.

4 Triangle Strips

Supported in software and hardware, triangle strips are used for efficient rendering of triangle meshes. They reduce the data transfer rate between the main memory and the graphics engine by allowing the re-use of vertices for up to three consecutive triangles. This requires the graphics hardware to have a built-in buffer for two vertices, which is very common in today's graphic boards.

An OpenGL-style triangle strip is a sequence of m vertices $(v_0, ..., v_{m-1})$ that represents the sets of triangles $\{(v_i, v_{i+1}, v_{i+2})\}$ for even i and $\{(v_{i+1}, v_i, v_{i+2})\}$ for odd i with $0 \leq i < m - 2$. The distinction between odd and even assures a consistent orientation of all triangles.

Two triangle strips and the vertex sequences that represent them are shown in Figure 2. The strip on the left is called *sequential*, because it turns alternating to the right and to the left. The sequence of 9 vertices describes 7 consistently oriented triangles. The strip on the right is not sequential, because it contains consecutive turns in the same direction. Such a strip is is called *generalized*. Here 10 vertices are necessary to describe the 7 triangles. In order to use vertex v_2 in 4 consecutive triangles the degenerate zero-area triangle (v_2, v_3, v_2) needs to be inserted into the strip. The cost for such a *swap* operation is one vertex, which is cheaper than a restart that costs two vertices.

The problem of constructing good triangle strips has been considered in several papers [2, 8, 16]. The objective is to minimize the number of swaps and restarts, thereby minimizing the total number of required vertices. Since computing the optimal solution is an NP-complete problem [1], heuristic search strategies are employed. For polygon models that are not fully triangulated the *patchification* method by Evans et al. [2] gives good results. This technique lets the triangle strips dictate the way the poly-

gons are triangulated so that swaps are avoided.

Although the use of indexed triangle strips reduces the amount of data needed to represent the mesh connectivity by a factor between two and three compared to indexed triangle sets, it still needs at least $2 \log n$ bpv. For storage and transmission purposes it is often necessary to have a more compact representation of a mesh. However, current mesh compression techniques are not designed to encode stripified triangle meshes.

5 Triangle Strip Compression

The following is based on the observation that the stripification of a triangle mesh is uniquely defined by the set of *strip-internal* edges. These are edges that are shared by subsequent triangles in a strip. The set of strip-internal edges marks either none, one, or two edges of every triangle. A triangle without a strip-internal edge is a triangle strip by itself. A triangle with one strip-internal edge is either the start or the end of a strip. A triangle with two strip-internal edges is in the middle of a triangle strip.

It is necessary to distinguish the start from the end of a generalized triangle strip, because one direction sometime needs one fewer swap operation than the other. This can be computed in a single traversal of the triangle strip by counting the number of necessary swap operations.

Using one bit per edge (3 bpv) is sufficient to mark all strip-internal edges. Any previously reported mesh compression scheme could be combined with such an encoding of the stripification. However, this two-pass approach fails to exploit the redundancy between the connectivity and the stripification of a mesh: Every strip expresses the edge adjacency for each pair of subsequent triangles it contains. This local connectivity information also needs to be captured by the mesh compression scheme. Triangle Strip Compression specifies this information only once.

Our compression scheme follows the concept of encoding mesh connectivity through an interwoven representation of a triangle spanning tree and its dual vertex spanning tree. Instead of traversing a triangle spanning tree using a deterministic search strategy we let the underlying stripification be the guide. The adjacency information that is encoded while walking along a strip means progress for both the compression of connectivity and the compression of stripification.

5.1 Encoding

As in Section 3.1, the encoding process initially defines the active gate and the active boundary around some edge of the mesh. However, now this choice is not completely arbitrary. The edge must not be strip-internal.

Again the active gate is labeled at each step of the encoding algorithm. Instead of label T we use the four labels T_R, T_L, T_B, and T_E. This subclassification captures the

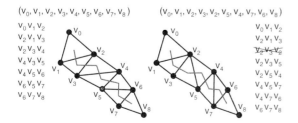

Figure 2: A sequential triangle strip (left) and a generalized triangle strip (right) with their corresponding vertex sequence.

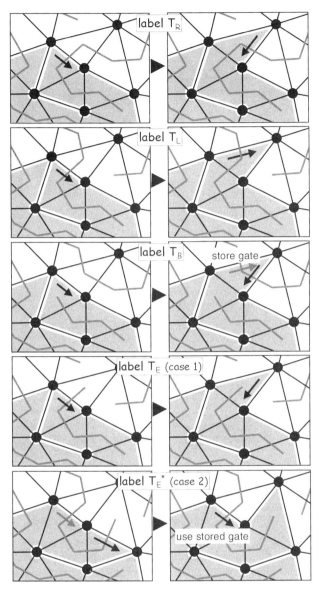

Figure 3: The labels T_R, T_L T_B, and T_E. The black arrow denotes the active gate, the dark-grey arrow denotes a stored gate.

label T_L The triangle strip leaves the included triangle through the left edge. The new active gate is this left edge.

label T_B The triangle strip leaves the included triangle through the right and the left edge, which means we just entered this triangle strip somewhere in its middle. Both directions need to be considered. Therefore the left edge is stored and the right edge is the new active gate.

label T_E (case 1) The triangle strip leaves the included triangle neither through the right nor through the left edge *and* this is the last triangle of this strip. The new active gate is the right edge.

label T_E^* (case 2) The triangle strip leaves the included triangle neither through the right nor through the left edge, *but* this is not the last triangle of this strip. Then there was a preceding label T_B. The edge that was stored with label T_B is the new active gate.

5.2 Decoding

As before, the labels are processed in reverse order and the inverse of each label operation is performed. However, one initial traversal of the labels in forward order is necessary. For every label T_B we count the number of encountered T_R labels before the first occurrence of a label T_E. We add 2 to the count and associate this value with the respective label T_E, marking it with a *.

When during the decoding process a label T_E^* with associated value w is encountered, we walk from the active gate w edges along the active boundary. The edge we arrive at is the new active gate and we continue normally.

This little variation becomes necessary to invert what happens during encoding: The first occurrence of a label T_E after a label T_B marks the completion of one end of a triangle strip. The active gate jumps to the edge that was stored with the preceding label T_B. The computed value expresses how many boundary edges were between the active gate and the stored edge at the time this jump occurred. The time complexity for decoding remains linear, since every triangle strip is traversed at most once.

The example in Figure 4 and 5 leads step by step through the encoding and decoding process of a small mesh with two triangle strips.

5.3 Compressing and Results

There is a very strong correlation among subsequent labels. We can observe long runs of labels R and L, and long sequences of alternating labels T_R and T_L. The simple bit assignment

after	T_R	T_L	T_B	T_E	R	L	S	E
T_R, T_E^*	2	1	–	2	–	–	–	–
T_L, T_B	1	2	–	2	–	–	–	–
T_E	4	5	3	6	2	7	1	7
R, E	7	6	5	7	1	4	3	2
L, S	6	7	5	7	4	1	3	2

scheme that is described in the table above exploits these dependencies and achieves bit-rates between 3.0 and 5.0 bpv. This bit allocation scheme is geared towards

stripification of the mesh. The four labels direct the way the encoding process traverses the mesh triangles so that it follows the underlying strips. Once a triangle strip is entered, it is processed in its entirety using these labels. The total number of edges that receive labels T_R, T_L, T_B, or T_E is equal to the number of mesh triangles. The labels R, L, S, E, H, and M are used and assigned as before.

Each of the four new label updates the boundary just like label T. The difference—illustrated in Figure 3—lies the way the active gate is updated. They are as follows:

label T_R The triangle strip leaves the included triangle through the right edge. The new active gate is this right edge.

mesh characteristics		corners of		bits per vertex	
name	strips	triangles	strips	fixed	aac-3
bishop	1	1488	498	2.98	1.78
shape	2	15360	5124	3.09	0.62
triceratops	144	16980	5948	4.12	3.49
fandisk	224	38838	13394	3.61	2.25
eight	24	4608	1584	3.46	1.78
femur	237	23394	8272	4.48	4.02
skull	600	66312	23304	4.74	4.18
bunny	1229	208353	71909	3.69	2.40
phone	1946	198861	70179	4.42	3.88
terrainSM	707	77454	27232	4.31	3.76
terrainLG	2404	255870	90098	4.41	3.83

Table 2: Compressing connectivity and stripification with a fixed bit scheme (*fixed*) and an arithmetic coder (*acc-3*).

long triangle strips with alternating left-right turns. The encodings become more compact with higher quality stripifications (e.g. fewer strips, fewer swaps).

The resulting compression rates (see Table 2) increase by at most 0.6 bpv for the fixed and 1.3 bpv for the arithmetic coder compared to those from Table 1. For very regular meshes the encodings are even more compact than before because such meshes can be decomposed into long sequential strips. Overall, the achieved compression rates for connectivity and stripification are significantly better than those of previously reported compression schemes for connectivity combined with an one bit per edge (3 bpv) encoding of the stripification.

We used version 2.0 of STRIPE [2] to stripify our example meshes. This software is designed for fast generation of triangle strips, hence the generated strips are not optimal. We would now like software that gives us higher quality strips at the expense of longer computation time.

6 Normals, Colours, and Texture Coordinates

Additional care needs to be taken when stripifying polygonal meshes that have multiple corner attributes per vertex. A corner is a vertex/triangle pair and corner attributes are typically vertex normals, colours, or texture coordinates. The idea of triangle strips is based on re-using the vertex data, which includes these corner attributes. Discontinuities in the model like a crease or a material change result in discontinuities in the corner attributes around a vertex. Good stripification software must assure that the triangle strips do not run across such discontinuities. Vertices have on average a set of three adjacent corners in a triangle strip and their attributes need to be consistent.

The above restricts the stripification process, but can be exploited for compressing the number of bits needed for mapping attributes to corners, which uses one bit per corner in the method by Taubin et al. [9]. Since the at-

tributes of all adjacent triangle corners within a strip are consistent, we need to specify them only once for such a *strip corner*. The number of different triangle corners for meshes with t triangles is $3t$. However, decomposed into s strips we need to distinguish only the $t + 2s$ strip corners for the mapping from attributes to corners (see Table 2).

7 Summary and Acknowledgments

Our main contribution is the compression of stripified meshes. We have extended Triangle Fixer to include information about a pre-computed set of triangle strips into the compressed representation of a mesh. Our algorithm fully exploits the existing correlation between connectivity and stripification of a mesh.

The new compressed format is especially useful for models with a large distribution. The computation of high quality stripifications is very expensive and, in particular for triangle meshes with corner attributes, not trivial. Once a good set of triangle strips has been computed, our technique allows to store and distribute it together with the model at little additional storage or processing cost.

Many thanks to Bettina Speckmann for discussions on triangle strips, to Xinyu Xiang for triangulating various models, and to Jack Snoeyink for reviewing the paper.

8 References

[1] F. Evans, S. S. Skiena, and A. Varshney. Completing sequential triangulations is hard. Technical report, Department of Computer Science, State University of New York at Stony Brook, 1996.

[2] F. Evans, S. S. Skiena, and A. Varshney. Optimizing triangle strips for fast rendering. In *Visualization'96*, pages 319–326, 1996.

[3] S. Gumhold and W. Strasser. Real time compression of triangle mesh connectivity. In *SIGGRAPH'98*, pages 133–140, 1998.

[4] M. Isenburg. Triangle Fixer: Edge-based connectivity encoding. In *16th European Workshop on Comp. Geom.*, pages 18–23, 2000.

[5] M. Isenburg and J. Snoeyink. Mesh collapse compression. In *Proceedings of 12th SIBGRAPI*, Brazil, pages 27–28, October 1999.

[6] D. King and J. Rossignac. Guaranteed 3.67v bit encoding of planar triangle graphs. In *Proc. of 11th CCCG*, pages 146–149, 1999.

[7] J. Rossignac. Edgebreaker: Connectivity compression for triangle meshes. *IEEE Trans. on Vis. and Computer Graphics*, 5(1), 1999.

[8] B. Speckmann and J. Snoeyink. Easy triangle strips for TIN terrain models. In *Proceedings of 9th CCCG*, pages 239–244, 1997.

[9] G. Taubin, W.P. Horn, F. Lazarus, and J. Rossignac. Geometry coding and VRML. *Proc. of the IEEE*, 86(6):1228–1243, 1998.

[10] G. Taubin and J. Rossignac. Geometric compression through topological surgery. *ACM Trans. on Graphics*, 17(2):84–115, 1998.

[11] C. Touma and C. Gotsman. Triangle mesh compression. In *GI'98 Conference Proceedings*, pages 26–34, 1998.

[12] G. Turan. Succinct representations of graphs. *Discrete Applied Mathematics*, 8:289–294, 1984.

[13] Viewpoint. *Premier Catalog (2000 Edition) www.viewpoint.com*.

[14] I. H. Witten, R. M. Neal, and J. G. Cleary. Arithmetic coding for data compression. *Comm. of the ACM*, 30(6):520–540, 1987.

[15] M. Woo, J. Neider, and T. Davis. *Open GL Programming Guide*. Addison Wesley, 1996.

[16] X. Xiang, M. Held, and J. Mitchell. Fast and efficient stripification of polygonal surface models. In *I3DG*, pages 71–78, 1999.

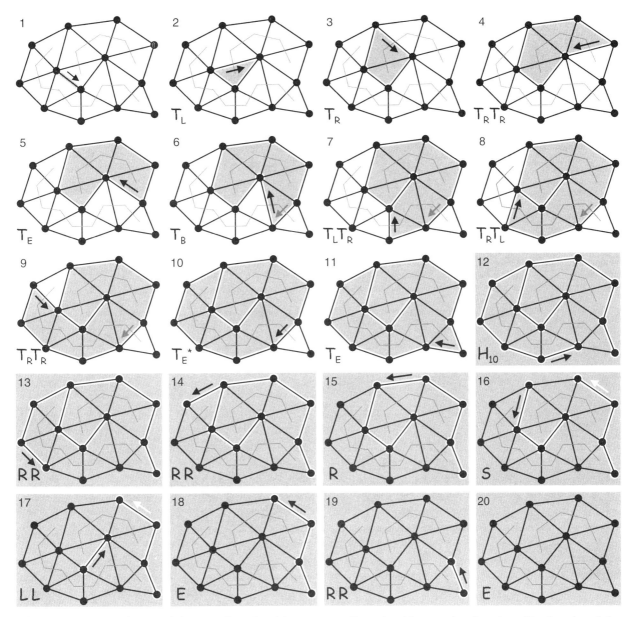

Figure 4: An example run of the encoding algorithm on a small mesh with two triangle strips. The interior of the active boundary is shaded dark, the active gate is denoted by a black arrow, a gate in the stack by a light-grey arrow, and a stored gate by a dark-grey arrow. The label(s) in the lower left corner of each frame express the performed update(s) since the previous frame. (1) Initial active boundary. (2-4) Boundary is expanded along the first triangle strip. (5) Reaching the last triangle of this strip. (6) Entering the second triangle strip in its middle. (7-9) Expanding this strip into one direction. (10) Finishing one side, the active gate jumps to expand other direction. (11) Finishing the other side. (12) Including a hole of ten edges. (13-15) Fixing the boundary with five R labels. (16) Splitting the boundary, one part is pushed on stack, continuing on other part. (17) Fixing the boundary with two L labels. (18) Ending this boundary, popping a boundary from stack. (19) Fixing the boundary with two R labels. (20) Ending this boundary, stack is empty, terminate.

Note: Instead of defining the initial active boundary around an edge we can also define it around a hole. In this example this would save us the label H_{10}. In general we want to define the initial active boundary around the largest hole of the mesh, which is also referred to as the boundary of the mesh.

204

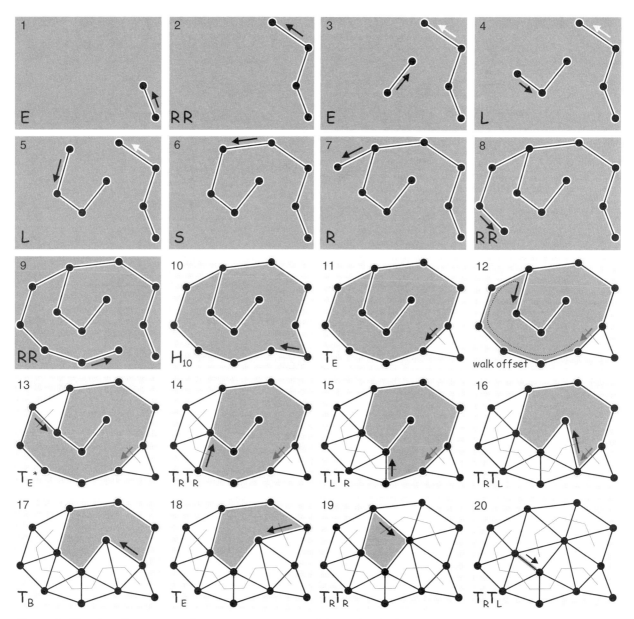

Figure 5: The decoding process that reconstructs connectivity and stripification of a mesh from the label sequence generated in Figure 4. The label(s) in the lower left corner of each frame indicate the inverted label operation(s) since the previous frame. In an initial forward traversal of the label sequence we mark the first occurrence of a T_E label after a T_B label with a *. Adding two to the number of T_R labels between T_B and T_E makes six, which is associated with the (now marked) label T_E^* (1) Creating a boundary of length two, undoing the last label E operation. (2) Expanding this boundary, undoing two label R operations. (3) Pushing the current boundary on the stack and creating a new boundary undoes another label E operation. (4-5) Expanding the boundary. (6) Merging the boundaries that were split by the S label. (7-9) Further expansion of the boundary. (10) Recreating a hole of size ten. (11) Recreating a triangle that starts the first strip. (12) Walking the offset associated with the marked label. (13) Recreating the first triangle at the other end of the strip. (14-16) Recreating six more triangles of this strip. (17) Finishing the first strip, by gluing its two sides together. (18) Recreating a triangle that starts the next strip. (19-20) Recreating four more triangles of this strip, terminate.

Incremental Triangle Voxelization

Frank Dachille IX and Arie Kaufman
Center for Visual Computing (CVC) and Department of Computer Science
State University of New York at Stony Brook
Stony Brook, NY 11794-4400

Abstract

We present a method to incrementally voxelize triangles into a volumetric dataset with pre-filtering, generating an accurate multivalued voxelization. Multivalued voxelization allows direct volume rendering of voxelized geometry as well as volumes with intermixed geometry, accurate multiresolution representations, and efficient antialiasing. Prior voxelization methods either computed only a binary voxelization or inefficiently computed a multivalued voxelization. Our method develops incremental equations to quickly decide which filter function to compute for each voxel value. The method requires eight additions per voxel of the triangle bounding box. Being simple and efficient, the method is suitable for implementation in a hardware volume rendering system.

Key words: Voxelization, volume filtering, hardware, incremental algorithm, cut planes

1 Introduction

Our interest in volume graphics [11] and voxelization is motivated by the recent proliferation of volume rendering algorithms, hardware (e.g., *VolumePro* by Mitsubishi Electric), and the increasing use of discrete volumetric representation in various important application areas. These include medical imaging (e.g., CT and MRI), scientific visualization, simulation (e.g., flight and mission simulation), computer-aided design, animation, and virtual reality. Volume graphics can be used in place of traditional geometric applications as well as those applications that intermix geometric objects with 3D sampled or computed datasets.

Traditional computational bounds to the use of volume graphics (i.e., memory storage, bandwidth, and processing) continue to be shattered, allowing mainstream use of volume graphics. Leading the way is a recently available PC-based hardware accelerator board for volume rendering, *Volume-Pro* [14], manufactured by Mitsubishi and based on the Cube-4 architecture developed at SUNY Stony Brook [15]. With the advent of widespread volume graphics, new applications and modalities will be forthcoming. In this paper, we seek to spur further development of volume graphics by providing efficient, simple methods to accurately voxelize geometric models and to implement cut planes efficiently.

The advantages of volume graphics are many-fold, the primary being that an object interior can be modeled and visualized and amorphous phenomena can be handled naturally. In addition, the uniformity of representation allows object independent processing based on sound theoretical techniques. In this way, various scanned physical phenomena and objects, synthesized data, and sampled geometric objects can be processed, combined, and rendered together into effective visualizations. Volumetric representations have the advantage of pre-filtering, so that subsequent rendering can proceed efficiently without aliasing. Volume graphics is also relatively insensitive to object and scene complexity; detailed polygon meshes or complex objects can be directly represented using a

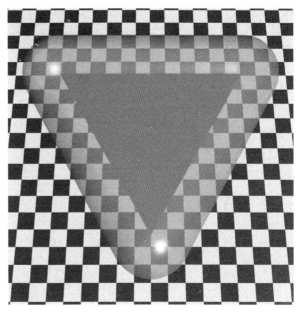

Figure 1: *The 3D region of influence around a triangle.*

finite volume, which can often be more compact. Furthermore, volumetric multiresolution pyramids allow antialiased rendering at various image sizes and are simple to generate, topology independent, and efficient for simplification [5]. Applications of pre-filtering are explored in Section 3.

Volume visualization is often enhanced by the combination of information from multiple data sources, both discrete and continuous. For example, medical visualizations can benefit from combining volumetric medical data with polygonal objects (e.g., prostheses, radiation therapy beams, and virtual scalpels placed within a sampled MRI or CT dataset). Geophysical visualizations can benefit from rendering analytical objects within a volume (e.g., oil drilling paths, pipeline placement, and man-made structures superimposed within a geophysical dataset).

To create these visualizations, it is necessary to combine volume rendering with traditional surface rendering. One approach is to render the surfaces into a z-buffer, then combine the z-buffer image with volume slices during texture map based volume rendering. However, this approach severely limits the quality and flexibility of the rendering and does not permit translucent surfaces without complicated sorting. Our preferred approach is to convert continuous surfaces into a discrete volumetric representation, called a voxelization [19]. The surfaces can be directly voxelized into the original volume and rendered with the usual means. If the surfaces are dynamic relative to the volume, they can be voxelized into a separate volume and combined only during rendering by interleaving volume samples in the direction of each image pixel (e.g., during ray casting).

Such applications and the new hardware driving them spur the development of efficient and accurate voxelization techniques. Cohen-Or and Kaufman [2] derived the theoretical properties of voxelizations in a raster grid of binary-valued voxels. Objects represented by a 3D grid of discrete values have topological properties analogous to their continuous counterparts. For example, a *6-connected* discrete 3D line is a set of voxels which are adjacent to another through at least one of the 6 voxel faces. A *6-tunnel-free* discrete 3D surface is a set of voxels which do not allow any 6-connected line to pierce it (i.e., the intersection of the two sets is not null).

Kaufman [8, 9, 10, 12] presented efficient methods to generate binary voxelizations of many geometric primitives. Huang et al. [6] detailed the accuracy (i.e., separability and minimality) properties of binary voxelizations of planar objects. However, a direct visualization of binary-valued voxels typically appears to be a set of cuboid bricks with hard, jagged edges. To avoid this image aliasing we use pre-filtering, in which scalar-valued voxels are used to represent the percentage of spatial occupancy of a voxel [19], an extension of the two-dimensional line anti-aliasing method of Gupta and Sproull [4]. The scalar-valued voxels determine a fuzzy set such that the boundary between inclusion and exclusion is smooth. Direct visualization from such a fuzzy set avoids image aliasing. Recent work on voxelization has focused on generating a distance volume for subsequent use in manipulation [1] or rendering [3].

Šrámek and Kaufman [17] showed that the optimal sampling filter for central difference gradient estimation in areas of low curvature is a one-dimensional oriented box filter perpendicular to the surface. Since most volume rendering implementations utilize the central difference gradient estimation filter and trilinear sample interpolation, the oriented box filter is well suited for voxelization. Furthermore, this filter is an easily computed linear function of the distance from the triangle. Their voxelization method was accurate, but did not address efficient methods for triangle primitive voxelization.

This paper proposes an efficient, incremental algorithm for multivalued triangle voxelization suitable for both software and hardware implementations. The term multivalued refers to scalar-valued voxels, as opposed to binary-valued voxels. Voxelization is conceptually similar to 2D rasterization, which is conventionally performed in hardware for sake of speed. 3D voxelization is more computationally intensive than 2D rasterization by one dimension, so it is important to consider a hardware solution. Our algorithm could be built into volume rendering hardware to voxelize polygons at interactive rates. The hardware could then provide combined visualization of continuous polygons and/or discrete volumetric data by combining the two volume datasets during rendering.

Conventional graphics hardware only rasterizes points, lines, and triangles; higher order primitives are expressed as combinations of these basic primitives. Similarly, we choose to voxelize only triangles since all other primitives can be expressed in terms of triangles. Polygon meshes, spline surfaces, spheres, cylinders, and others can be subdivided into triangles for voxelization. Points and lines are special cases of triangles so they can also be voxelized by this algorithm. To voxelize solid objects, we can first voxelize the boundary as a set of triangles, then fill the interior using a volumetric filling procedure.

Figure 1 shows the region which is affected by the multivalued voxelization of a triangle. All voxels within the translucent surface, which is at a constant distance from the triangle,

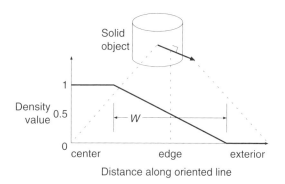

Figure 2: *Density profile of the oriented box filter along a line from the center of solid primitive outward, perpendicular to the surface. The width of the filter is W.*

must be updated during voxelization. Jones [7] presented a method for identifying this region around a triangle, voxelizing it, and repeating for an entire triangle mesh. His method located the minimum distance to the triangle by direct calculation for each voxel. Our method produces similar voxelizations using a more efficient incremental method.

Triangle rasterization methods have yielded some important algorithms which are extensible to triangle voxelization. Pixel Planes and Pixel Flow hardware [13] scan converts triangles with SIMD processors by computing three plane equations per pixel to determine whether or not it is inside the triangle. These equations, called *edge functions*, are linear expressions that maintain the distance from an edge by efficient incremental arithmetic. Shilling [16] used edge functions for antialiasing primitive edges. Our work extends this notion into three dimensions and applies antialiasing during the scan conversion of volumetric triangles.

2   Algorithm

The general idea of the algorithm is to voxelize a triangle by scanning a bounding box of the triangle in raster order. For each voxel in the bounding box, a filter equation is evaluated and the result is stored in memory. The value of the equation is a linear function of the distance from the triangle. The result is stored using a fuzzy algebraic union operator — the *max* operator. Thus, the complexity of the algorithm is $O(nk^3)$ where k is the average size in volume units of n triangles. The complexity has a lower bound of $\Omega(nk^2)$, since the triangles may be oriented perpendicular to a major axis and the thickness is constant.

2.1   Inclusion testing

The inclusion of a voxel in the fuzzy set varies between zero and one inclusive, determined by the value of the oriented box filter. The surface of the primitive is assumed to lie on the 0.5 density isosurface. Therefore, when voxelizing a solid primitive as in Figure 2, the density profile varies from a value of one inside the primitive to zero outside, and varies smoothly through the edge. For a surface primitive such as the triangle in Figure 3, the density is one on the surface and drops off linearly to zero at distance W from the surface. For the remainder of this paper, we only treat the voxelization of surfaces, not solids.

The optimum value for filter width W is determined to be $2\sqrt{3}$ voxel units [17]. Rendering from a multi-valued voxelized model is most often performed by ray tracing an implicit function $f() = 0.5$. This places an isosurface at the density value of 0.5, halfway between the minimum and maximum

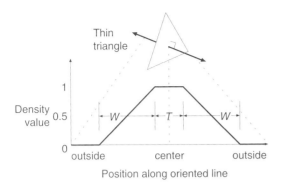

Figure 3: *Density profile of the oriented box filter along a line perpendicular to the triangle surface primitive.*

values. To resolve surface orientation, some for of shading (e.g., Phong) is applied based on an estimated gradient (normal) at the surface intersection. The oriented box pre-filter is designed to be combined with the central difference gradient estimation (i.e., $G_x = f(x + 1, y, z) - f(x - 1, y, z)$, etc.). Because the overall width of the central difference filter is at most $2\sqrt{3}$ units, a correct gradient is always found on the 0.5 density isosurface. Normally, the surface thickness T is zero unless thick surfaces are desired (see Figure 3). If more accurate shading is desired, an analytical normal could be computed using the original surface model, and stored at each grid point at a storage premium.

Based on a 0.5 density isosurface, the apparent thickness of a surface voxelization is $T + W$. By thresholding at 0.5 density, a 6-tunnel-free set of voxels is generated when $W \geq 1$ [6]. This property is useful for volumetric filling, (e.g., in order to generate solid objects).

All voxels with non-zero values for a triangle are within a bounding box $S = W + T/2$ voxel units larger in all directions than a tight bounding box. Therefore, the first step of the algorithm determines a tight bound for the triangle, then inflates it in all directions by S voxel units and rounds outward to the nearest voxels.

Figures 4 and 5 show the seven regions surrounding a triangle which must be treated separately. Each candidate voxel must be tested for inclusion within the seven regions, then filtered with a different equation for each region. In the interior region of the triangle (R1), the value of the oriented box filter is simply proportional to the distance from the plane of the triangle. In regions along the edges of the triangle (R2, R3, and R4), the value of the filter is proportional to the distance from the edge of the triangle. In regions at the corners of the triangle (R5, R6, and R7), the value of the filter is proportional to the distance from the corner of the triangle.

The regions are distinguished by their distance from seven planes. The first plane a is coplanar with the triangle and its normal vector **a** points outward from the page in Figure 5. The next three planes b, c, and d have normal vectors **b**, **c**, and **d** and pass through the corner vertices C_1, C_2, and C_3, respectively. The final three planes e, f, and g are perpendicular to the triangle and parallel to the edges; their normal vectors (**e**, **f**, and **g**) lie in the plane of the triangle and point inward so that a positive distance from all three planes defines region R1. All the plane coefficients are normalized so that the length of the normal is one — except for normal vectors **b**, **c**, and **d** which are normalized so that their length is equal to the inverse of their respective edge lengths. In that way, the computed distance from the plane varies from zero to one along the valid length of the edge. Table 1 summarizes the requisite condi-

Figure 4: *Illustration of the seven voxelization regions around a triangle. Each affected voxel is either closer to the triangle face, an edge, or a corner.*

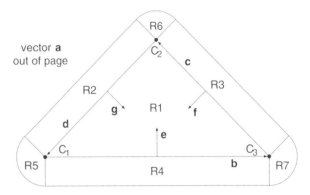

Figure 5: *2D illustration of the seven voxelization regions (R1-R7). The regions are delineated by seven planes a-g, whose normal vectors are shown.*

tions for inclusion in each region.

2.2 Distance from a Plane

For any planar surface, the distance of any point from the surface can be computed using the plane equation coefficients.

$$Dist = \frac{Ax + By + Cz + D}{\sqrt{A^2 + B^2 + C^2}}$$

which simplifies to $Dist = Ax + By + Cz + D$ when the coefficients are pre-normalized. This computation can be made incremental so that when stepping along any vector, the distance only changes by a constant. For example, if the distance from a plane is $Dist$ at position $[x, y, z]$, then stepping one unit distance in the X direction changes the distance to

$$\begin{aligned} Dist' &= A(x + 1) + By + Cz + D \\ &= Ax + By + Cz + D + A \\ &= Dist + A. \end{aligned}$$

Table 1: *The necessary (but not always sufficient) conditions for inclusion in a region based on the distances along seven plane normal vectors.*

Region	\multicolumn{7}{c}{Plane Normal Vector}
	a	b	c	d	e	f	g
R1	$(-S,S)$				$[0,\infty)$	$[0,\infty)$	$[0,\infty)$
R2	$(-S,S)$			$[0,1]$			$(-\infty,0)$
R3	$(-S,S)$		$[0,1]$			$(-\infty,0)$	
R4	$(-S,S)$	$[0,1]$			$(-\infty,0)$		
R5	$(-S,S)$	$(-\infty,0)$		$(1,\infty)$			
R6	$(-S,S)$		$(1,\infty)$	$(-\infty,0)$			
R7	$(-S,S)$	$(1,\infty)$	$(-\infty,0)$				

Define Plane(A, B, C, D);
Find triangle bounding box(bb);
$Dist = A{\times}bb.min.x + B{\times}bb.min.y + C{\times}bb.min.z + D$;
$xStep = A$;
$yStep = B - A{\times}bb.width$;
$zStep = C - B{\times}bb.height - A{\times}bb.width$;
For $z = bb.min.z$ to $bb.max.z$ with unit steps
   For $y = bb.min.y$ to $bb.max.y$
      For $x = bb.min.x$ to $bb.max.x$
         store $f(Dist)$ in $[x, y, z]$
         $Dist = Dist + xStep$;
      end For
      $Dist = Dist + yStep$;
   end For
   $Dist = Dist + zStep$;
end For

Algorithm 1: *Incremental algorithm for computing the distance from a plane.*

In general, stepping along any vector $\mathbf{r} = [r_x, r_y, r_z]$, the distance from the plane changes by

$$Dist' = Dist + \mathbf{r} \odot [A, B, C]$$

where $\odot$ indicates the dot product. While scanning the bounding box of the triangle, the distance from the plane of the triangle can be computed incrementally with just a single addition per voxel (see Algorithm 1). This incremental algorithm is a 3D extension of the edge function used by Schilling [16].

The Y-step is more complicated than the X-step because it not only steps one unit in the Y direction, but it also steps back multiple units in the X direction, exactly like a typewriter glides back to the left margin of the paper *and* advances the line with one push of the return key. Similarly, the Z-step combines stepping back in both the X and Y directions and stepping forward one unit in the Z direction. This simple preprocessing step ensures efficient stepping throughout the entire volume. If numerical approximation issues arise, then it is possible to store the distance value at the start of each inner loop and restore it at the end, eliminating numerical creep due to roundoff in the inner loops.

For multivalued voxelization, seven plane distances are required, so seven additions are required per voxel to compute the plane distances. Other computations per voxel include incrementing the loop index, comparisons to determine the appropriate region, and, if necessary, computations to determine the density.

2.3 Distance from a Triangle

In region R1, the density value of a voxel is computed with the box filter oriented perpendicular to plane a. Given a distance $DistA$ from plane a, the density value V is computed using:

$$V = 1 - \frac{|DistA| - T/2}{W}.$$

In region R2, the density is computed using the distance from planes a and g:

$$V = 1 - \frac{\sqrt{DistA^2 + DistB^2} - T/2}{W}.$$

Similarly, region R3 uses planes a and f, and region R4 uses planes a and e. Region R5 uses the Pythagorean distance from the corner point C_1:

$$V = 1 - \frac{\sqrt{(C_1^x - x)^2 + (C_1^y - y)^2 + (C_1^z - z)^2} - T/2}{W}.$$

Likewise, regions R6 and R7 use corner points C_2 and C_3, respectively.

2.4 Shared Edges

At the shared edge of adjacent triangles, we want to avoid cracks. Fortunately, the oriented box filter guarantees accurate filtering of the edges for any polyhedra, provided we correctly compute the union of the voxelized surfaces. Multivalued voxelization is based on fuzzy algebra, in which true/false Boolean decisions are abandoned in favor of scalar values indicating a continuously variable percentage of truth, or in our case, occupancy. The union operator can be defined [19] over multivalued density values $V(x)$ with $V_{A \bigcup B} \equiv max(V_A(x), V_B(x))$. Other Boolean operators are available; however, the *max* operator preserves the correct oriented box filter value at shared edges. At the edge of a triangle, the oriented box filter generates a cylinder on the 0.5 density isosurface (see Figure 4). If an edge is shared between two triangles, then the two coincident edge cylinders are superimposed yielding a smooth transition between them. Unfortunately, the *max* operator can introduce discontinuities at polygon intersections (e.g., a triangle piercing another).

The *max* operator permits us to voxelize triangles in any order without consequence. The implication of using *max* in our algorithm is that we must read the current voxel value from memory, then possibly modify it and write it back to memory. Thus, a maximum of two memory cycles are required per voxel, although this is true for any algorithm that voxelizes in a separate pass for each primitive.

3 Pre-filtering

Voxelization is a pre-filtering operation; the representation is filtered during generation so that aliasing is avoided during rendering. Pre-filtering is a powerful tool that allows complex calculations to take place off-line so that subsequent rendering from multiple viewpoints is optimized. Here we present two techniques that can be performed with our voxelization method.

Pre-filtering can be used to generate a series of volumes [5] of different resolutions (see Figure 6). This technique is useful for rendering images of different sizes; the size of the volume is chosen to correspond to the size of the final image. In this way, aliasing is avoided at all image resolutions and no unnecessary work is performed in rendering parts of the scene not visible at the image scale. Furthermore, low resolution volumes generated by our method provide accurate topology of the model.

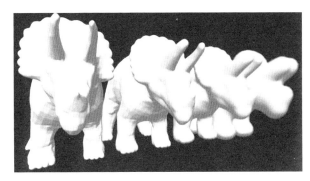

Figure 6: *Multiresolution triceratops voxelizations: maximum dimensions of 512, 256, 128, and 64 voxels.*

Figure 7: *Pre-filtered helicopter blade with motion blur efficiently rendered in a single pass at the same speed as without motion blur.*

Pre-filtering can additionally be used to model motion blur. As an object sweeps past a camera, it sweeps out a complex volume during the time the shutter is open, causing motion blur. To accurately render this, conventional rendering techniques actually render multiple images and blend them into a single image. This is accurate, but very slow. With pre-filtering, we can perform the sweeping operation once, during voxelization, so that motion blur can be rendered in the same time as regular volume rendering. This only works for certain cases where the motion is constant, (e.g., the same direction and/or rotation). A good example of this is a helicopter blade which spins at a constant speed during flight. We voxelized the blade spinning at the rate of 5Hz for an animation frame rate of 30Hz. That means that the blade sweeps out an arc of $\frac{5}{30}(2\pi)$ radians each frame. We voxelize by integrating the voxel density over the time of the frame. Because the inner portion of the blade sweeps out a smaller volume, the average density is much higher than the outer portion, where each voxel is occupied only a small portion of the time. The volume rendering transfer function is set so that the lower density values are less opaque and higher density values are more opaque. This correctly gives the visual impression of higher opacity near the center and lower opacity near the edge. The resulting image is shown in Figure 7.

4 Implementation

4.1 Software

The algorithm and volume rendering routines are implemented in object oriented C++. However, the inner loop of the algorithm avoids using C++ classes for a significant performance increase.

The efficiency can be further increased by limiting the amount of unnecessary computation. Specifically, the bound-

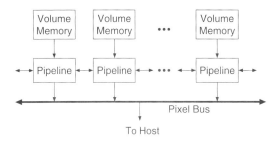

Figure 8: *The parallel, distributed architectural organization of the Cube-4 volume rendering accelerator.*

ing box often contains a greater percentage of voxels unaffected by the triangle than affected by it. Efforts to obtain a tighter bounding box generally increase the complexity of the algorithm. Therefore, such optimizations only increase efficiency when the size of the triangles is large (e.g., edges longer than 100 voxels). The bounding box can be made tighter by recursively subdividing the triangle when edge lengths exceed some constant.

A software implementation allows optimizations that are not possible in hardware. In software, usually a single comparison per voxel is all that is necessary since most of the voxels are unaffected by the voxelization of a single triangle. For a voxel to be considered, the distance from plane a must be less than or equal to S units. Therefore, a simple rejection test is used to eliminate most voxels from consideration. By eliminating most computation early, time spent traversing empty space is minimized and most of the time is spent computing the filter function.

The memory access patterns can be optimized for optimum cache coherence by reordering the computation. In our case, the triangles can be divided into volumetric groups suitable for the cache of the target platform. For example, with a 512KB cache and 1-byte voxels, the triangles could be voxelized into 64^3 sub-blocks of the volume, one sub-block at a time.

4.2 Hardware

With the advent of volume rendering hardware such as *VolumePro* [14], real-time volume visualization will soon be available for practical use. To visualize intermixed polygons and volumes, the polygons can be voxelized into the target volume and rendered in a single pass. If the polygons move with respect to the volume, then voxelization should occur in a copy of the original volume, so as not to corrupt the data. The multivalued voxelized polygon voxels can be tagged to distinguish them from volume data. In this way, polygons can be colored and shaded separately from other data.

The algorithm is efficiently implemented in the distributed pipelines of the Cube-4 volume rendering system. This algorithm adds just a small amount of hardware to the existing pipelines and performs accurate multivalued voxelization at interactive rates (see Section 5). Multiple Cube-4 pipelines work in parallel to retrieve voxels from distributed memories and perform ray casting in real time (see Figure 8). The volume is raycast beam-by-beam, one slice at a time into a buffer which eventually becomes the *Base Plane* (see Figure 9). After raycasting is complete, the *Base Plane* is 2D warped to the *Image Plane*. A primary advantage of the Cube-4 volume rendering algorithm is that the volume data is accessed coherently in a deterministic order. This feature allows orderly scanning of a bounding box similar to the software implementation with deterministic memory access.

The overall voxelization pipeline is shown in Figure 10.

210

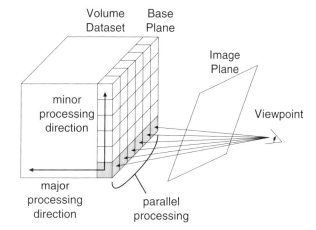

Figure 9: *Processing geometry of Cube-4. Processing occurs in slice order, beam by beam, then the* Base Plane *is 2D warped to the* Image Plane.

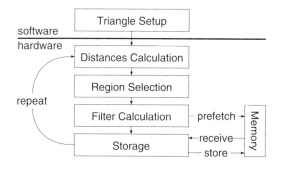

Figure 10: *An overview of the hardware voxelization pipeline.*

If on-the-fly voxelization is important, then there would be separate pipelines for volume rendering and voxelization. If voxelization could occur in a separate pass, then these two pipelines would be rolled into one, with the voxelization pipeline re-using most of the hardware from the volume rendering pipeline. The setup for each triangle occurs on the host system, much like setup is performed on the host for 2D rasterization. Per pipeline, this algorithm requires the use of 28 registers, 7 comparators, 12 adders, 3 multipliers, and one lookup table (LUT).

In the first hardware stage of the pipeline, the distances from the seven planes are computed. Seven simple distance units are allocated with four registers for each of the seven planes. One register holds the current distance from the plane and the other three hold the increments for the X, Y, and Z-steps. During each clock cycle of voxelization, the pipeline steps either in the X, Y, or Z direction, so the current distance is updated according to the direction of movement.

Since the hardware for looping through the volume is already built into the volume rendering pipeline, it is re-used here to scan the bounding box of the triangle. It is important to note that the hardware is a systolic array built with p parallel pipelines. The pipelines always operate on contiguous voxels in a beam, so it is necessary that the bounding box edges be a multiple of p. This potentially leads to inefficient load balancing, but p is typically small (i.e., four or eight).

After the seven plane distances are calculated, the values flow down the pipeline where tests are done in the next pipeline stage to determine in which region the current voxel

resides. Only seven comparators are needed to decide the outcome of the truth table (see Table 1), due to the mutual exclusion of some cases. For instance, in Figure 5 if you are on the negative (lower) side of plane b, then it is not necessary to test the distances from plane f or g depending on the value of the distance from plane e.

The next pipeline stage, which computes the filter function, is only activated if the current voxel is within S voxel units of the triangle. Otherwise, the current voxel is unaffected by the triangle and different regions require different calculations, ranging from a simple linear expression to a complex Pythagorean distance evaluation. Since hardware must be able to handle all cases equally well, it must be able to perform a square root approximation by means of a limited resolution LUT. Luckily, the range of inputs and outputs is small, so the size of the required LUT is tiny by most standards. Furthermore, the Cube-4 hardware has several LUTs available for volume rendering which can be re-used for voxelization. Instead of providing three separate units to compute the expression: $V = 1 - (\sqrt{Dist} - T/2)/W$, it is more efficient to roll all the calculations into one LUT. In this case, the input is $Dist^2$, defined over [0,12], and the output is the density value V in the range [0,1].

Due to the mutual exclusion of the seven regions, it is sufficient to provide hardware for only the most complex filter calculation. The most complex calculation is the corner distance computation of regions R5, R6, and R7 which requires 5 adders and 3 multipliers in addition to the already mentioned square root LUT. The line distance computations in regions R2, R3, and R4 are simpler, requiring only 1 adder, 2 multipliers, and the square root LUT. Region R1 requires a single multiply to obtain the distance squared, which is the required input to the LUT.

The final stage of the pipeline computes the *max* operation using the current voxel value and the computed density estimate. The *max* operator is simply a comparator attached to a multiplexor such that the greater of the two values is written back to memory. Since most voxels in the bounding box are not close enough to the triangle to be affected by it, memory bandwidth will be saved by only reading the necessary voxels. Further savings can be reached by only writing back to memory those voxels that change the current voxel value. Since there is some latency between asking for and receiving word from memory, the voxel should be fetched as soon as possible in the pipeline and the results queued until the memory is received. The final stage is write-back to memory, which can be buffered without worry of dependencies.

4.3 Cut Planes

During volume rendering, the distance units of the voxelization pipeline are unused. Each of the seven units could be used to implement cut planes that divide the volume into regions, positive and negative. The voxels in the intersection of the positive-valued regions are rendered visible while all other voxels are rendered invisible. Two such planes can be used as the yon and hither clipping planes. The remaining five planes could be arbitrarily oriented by the user for isolating a region of interest. For proper anti-aliasing, the oriented box filter is applied to the opacity using a non-zero width W.

Alternately, the visible region can be defined using only a single thick plane ($T \gg 1$). Again, the final opacity is determined by modulating with the value of the oriented box filter. In this way, it is possible to perform oblique multiplanar reformatting, useful in the medical field. Using this new definition, the yon and hither clipping planes can be implemented using a single thick cutting plane, located halfway between the clipping planes. The remaining 6 plane distance units can be used

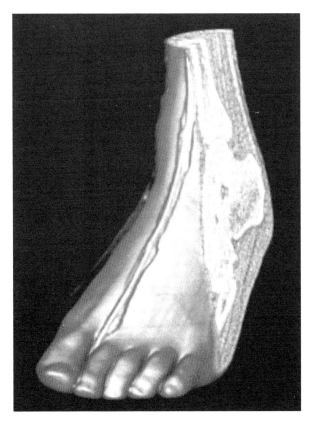

Figure 11: *Cross-section of a CT visible female foot rendered using our incremental cut plane algorithm.*

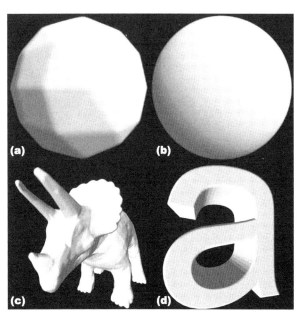

Figure 12: *(a) 128 triangle approximation of a sphere voxelized into a 256^3 volume in 1.8 s, (b) 32768 triangle approximation of a sphere voxelized into a 256^3 volume in 16.7 s, (c) 5660 triangle model of a triceratops voxelized into a $175 \times 229 \times 512$ volume in 5.8 s, (d) 1352 triangle model of the letter "a" voxelized into a $123 \times 256 \times 256$ volume in 5.3 s.*

for arbitrary region cutting. We simulated Cube-4-like object order volume rendering including an incremental cut plane. Figure 11 shows the CT foot of the visible female efficiently cut away to reveal inner structure.

5   Results and Discussion

The algorithm has been implemented on a 195 MHz MIPS R10000 and tested with various datasets (see Table 5). This algorithm has also been implemented and tested as part of a full-featured voxelization system [18]. The incremental voxelization method produces accurate, multivalued voxelization of triangles. The primary result is that voxelization proceeds at a high rate — often on the order of thousands of triangles per second. The rate varies with the average triangle size and their orientation. Sphere-3, shown in Figure 12a, is an approximation of a sphere with 128 triangles using three levels of recursive subdivision from an octahedron. Sphere-7 (see Figure 12b) is a better approximation of a sphere generated by four levels of recursive subdivision of Sphere-3.

The use of edge functions to compute distances has proven to be fast and easy to implement, even in hardware. The last column of Table 5 estimates the time required to voxelize the object in hardware, assuming a hardware fill rate of 2.5 Megavoxels/sec. This estimate is based on current *VolumePro* hardware which is capable of rendering a 256^3 volume at 30Hz (recall that voxelization requires up to twice the memory bandwidth of rendering).

Most of the voxelizations were at a medium resolution (i.e., at least 256 voxels), but a few were at a low resolution for comparison with prior work. Jones [7] voxelized objects into a 60^3 volume, taking on the order of 100 triangles per second. By comparison, our method in software voxelizes the same num-

ber of triangles into a similarly sized volume approximately one order of magnitude faster with a similar machine. Compared to Wang and Kaufman's method [19], ours provides at least one order of magnitude speedup for triangle primitives, but actually performs slower voxelizing solid primitives such as spheres and cones, which are approximated by a large set of triangles instead of a single implicit function. Such primitives are better voxelized using direct methods appropriate for each primitive, as in [18].

Other models voxelized were a triceratops model and the letter "a" (see Figures 12c and 12d). At a high resolution, the voxelized triceratops model appears as if it were an antialiased polygonal rendering. Pre-filtering is one of the advantages of voxelization followed by volume rendering compared to polygonal rendering, as shown in Section 3.

Since this is a rasterization method, the quality of the voxelization is directly related to the quality of the input triangle mesh and the desired resolution. Model meshes need not be manifold or otherwise structured, unless volumetric filling is employed. Degenerate triangles form either a line or a point which are handled as a special case using only three or one of our defined regions, respectively.

6   Acknowledgments

This work has been supported by NSF grant MIP9527694 and ONR grant N000149710402. The authors wish to thank Justine Dachille, Milos Šrámek, Kathleen McConnell, and the anonymous reviewers for their help and comments.

References

[1]   D. E. Breen, S. Mauch, and R. T. Whitaker. 3D scan conversion of CSG models in distance volumes. In *1998 Volume Visualization Symposium*, pages 7–14. IEEE, Oct. 1998.

212

Table 2: *Results of voxelization of various geometric objects in software and hardware (estimated).*

Model	Number of Triangles (triangles)	Maximum Dimension (voxels)	Average Tri Size (voxels^2)	Software Time (s)	Software Throughput (tris/sec)	Software Fill Rate (Mvox/sec)	Hardware Time (ms)
Triceratops	5660	512	127.2	27.3	204	5.6	629
Sphere-3	128	256	1028	1.9	67	8.0	61
Sphere-7	32768	256	5.7	22.8	1437	2.8	255
Text	1352	256	164.5	5.8	231	3.4	74
Triceratops	5660	105	4.6	5.0	1100	2.5	50
Sphere-7	32768	60	0.2	14.6	2243	2.5	148

[2] D. Cohen-Or and A. Kaufman. Fundamentals of surface voxelization. *Graphical Models and Image Processing: GMIP*, 57(6):453–461, Nov. 1995.

[3] S. F. F. Gibson. Using distance maps for accurate surface representation in sampled volumes. In *1998 Volume Visualization Symposium*, pages 23–30. IEEE, Oct. 1998.

[4] S. Gupta and R. F. Sproull. Filtering edges for gray-scale displays. In *Computer Graphics (SIGGRAPH '81 Proceedings)*, volume 15(3), pages 1–5, Aug. 1981.

[5] T. He, L. Hong, A. Varshney, and S. W. Wang. Controlled topology simplification. *IEEE Transactions on Visualization and Computer Graphics*, 2(2):171–184, June 1996.

[6] J. Huang, R. Yagel, V. Filippov, and Y. Kurzion. An accurate method for voxelizing polygon meshes. In *1998 Volume Visualization Symposium*, pages 119–126. IEEE, Oct. 1998.

[7] M. W. Jones. The production of volume data from triangular meshes using voxelisation. *Computer Graphics Forum*, 15(5):311–318, Dec. 1996.

[8] A. Kaufman. An algorithm for 3D scan-conversion of polygons. In *Eurographics '87*, pages 197–208, Aug. 1987.

[9] A. Kaufman. Efficient algorithms for 3D scan-conversion of parametric curves, surfaces, and volumes. In *Computer Graphics (SIGGRAPH '87 Proceedings)*, volume 21(4), pages 171–179, July 1987.

[10] A. Kaufman. *Volume Visualization*. IEEE Computer Society Press, Los Alamitos, CA, 1991.

[11] A. Kaufman, D. Cohen, and R. Yagel. Volume graphics. *IEEE Computer*, 26(7):51–64, July 1993.

[12] A. Kaufman and E. Shimony. 3D scan-conversion algorithms for voxel-based graphics. In *Proceedings of 1986 Workshop on Interactive 3D Graphics*, pages 45–75, Oct. 1986.

[13] S. Molnar, J. Eyles, and J. Poulton. PixelFlow: High-speed rendering using image composition. In *Computer Graphics (SIGGRAPH '92 Proceedings)*, volume 26, pages 231–240, July 1992.

[14] H. Pfister, J. Hardenbergh, J. Knittel, H. Lauer, and L. Seiler. The VolumePro real-time ray-casting system. *Proceedings of SIGGRAPH 1999*, pages 251–260, Aug. 1999.

[15] H. Pfister and A. Kaufman. Cube-4 - A scalable architecture for real-time volume rendering. In *1996 Volume Visualization Symposium*, pages 47–54, Oct. 1996.

[16] A. Schilling. A new simple and efficient anti-aliasing with subpixel masks. In *Computer Graphics (SIGGRAPH '91 Proceedings)*, volume 25, pages 133–141, July 1991.

[17] M. Šrámek and A. Kaufman. Alias-free voxelization of geometric objects. *IEEE Transactions on Visualization and Computer Graphics*, 5(3):251–267, July 1999.

[18] M. Šrámek and A. Kaufman. vxt: A C++ class library for object voxelization. In *International Workshop on Volume Graphics*, pages 295–306, Mar. 1999.

[19] S. W. Wang and A. Kaufman. Volume-sampled 3D modeling. *IEEE Computer Graphics and Applications*, 14(5):26–32, Sept. 1994.

Dynamic Plane Shifting BSP Traversal

Stan Melax

BioWare

Abstract

Interactive 3D applications require fast detection of objects colliding with the environment. One popular method for fast collision detection is to offset the geometry of the environment according to the dimensions of the object, and then represent the object as a point (and the object's movement as a line segment). Previously, this geometry offset has been done in a preprocessing step and therefore requires knowledge of the object's dimensions before runtime. Furthermore, an extra copy of the environment's geometry is required for each shape used in the application. This paper presents a variation of the BSP tree collision algorithm that shifts the planes in order to offset the geometry of the environment at runtime. To prevent unwanted cases where offset geometry protrudes too much, extra plane equations, which bevel solid cells of space during expansion, are added by simply inserting extra nodes at the bottom of the tree. A simple line segment check can be used for collision detection of a moving object of any size against the environment. Only one BSP tree is needed by the application. Successful usage within commercial entertainment software is also discussed.

Key words: collision detection, BSP tree, video game.

1 Introduction

Simulating an object as a point is a popular technique to reduce the complexity of various math and physics problems. Fast collision detection is important for interactive 3D applications that wish to maintain a high frame rate. Not surprisingly, one popular method of doing collision detection of an object with an arbitrary polygonal environment is to approximate the object as a point. The reason the object does not intersect the environment's geometry is because the object does its collision detection with an approximate offset surface - an "expanded" or "scaled" copy of the geometry where the interior walls have been moved inward, exterior walls shifted outward, the floors raised, and the ceiling lowered. Note that by environment we are referring to a large, detailed, 3D model that is rigid (static).

As the object moves from one position, v_0, to another, v_1, the motion line segment, (v_0, v_1), is checked against the offset surface to determine if it has collided. If a collision has occurred, there are a number of options for correcting the object's position. One possibility is to place the object at the point where the segment impacts the geometry. If the object is a freely moving physical body then its velocity can be mirrored to simulate an elastic collision. If the object is the user's avatar, the object can be easily made to slide along the plane of impact. This prevents the user from getting stuck when navigating near walls.

Note that just treating an object as a point is not a sufficient method for fast collision detection. An arbitrary polygonal environment can contain thousands of polygons. Therefore the geometry should be represented in an efficient spatial structure such as a binary space partitioning (BSP) tree.

A disadvantage of this offset surface technique is that it requires an additional copy of the environment's geometry for each object shape/size. If an object is allowed to change orientation, then there are further symmetry restrictions on the object's collision envelope. Typically, the environment's geometry is offset using a standard-sized sphere or cylinder for reference.

Our primary interest in this problem started with characters navigating a 3D environment in a video game. We do not want anything coming within a cylinder around the character. Prior to using the technique presented in this paper, the environment's geometry was offset to reduce these cylinders down to a point. In an effort to provide a content-rich game, we have many different sized characters. The memory requirement for having multiple copies of the environment's geometry was a problem. In addition to characters, our game also creates many small artifacts to make special effects such as explosions and debris. These small artifacts require fast collision detection as well. Creating another BSP tree for every particle size is just not feasible.

This paper presents dynamic plane shifting BSP traversal, a technique to overcome this single size limitation. Collision detection is still done using a fast line segment check. The environment is represented with only one standard BSP tree that was constructed without any regard for what shapes it would be doing collision detection with. We modify the plane equations of a BSP tree during the collision detection traversal. When BSP trees are constructed, we insert additional beveling nodes to limit the influence of solid volume cells when expanded. Our method will give a reasonable approximation for collision detection of an arbitrary convex shaped object moving along a linear path.

2 Related Work

Among the fastest collision detection algorithms are those specifically designed for pairs of moving convex polyhedra [Cohen95, Mirtich97]. Our environment has complex geometry. If it were broken down into convex polyhedra, there would be a large number of pieces to deal with. While our object is moving, the environment we deal with is static. Therefore, a BSP-based approach to collision detection is the best option available for our problem.

Merging BSP trees [Naylor98], or OBB trees [Gottschalk96] does provide accurate collision detection for arbitrarily shaped objects. However, the cost of such algorithms is a concern. Experimentation [Gottschalk96] has demonstrated fast collision detection (4ms) between two objects with 143690 polygons each. Unfortunately, such performance is not guaranteed. The very same research includes a smaller example with a 4780 object next to a 44921 polygon object and yet it runs 20 times slower (100ms) on a computer twice as fast. Similar work [Klosowski96] reports a series of individual query costs instead of just the averages. This reveals significant variation in the cost from one collision query to the next. The worst case happens when the objects are closer and there are more contacts. In a real application this worst case would be compounded further by the collision resolution mechanism. The collision query would have to be repeated until nonintersecting positions are found for the two objects. Video games have to maintain an interactive frame rate without any stalling. Extra time is not available when collisions/contacts occur. The majority of the CPU resources are being used by other parts of the application. Typically there are many moving objects being processed per frame. Some of these objects are in continual contact with the environment. Environments consist of tens of thousands of polygons. While our algorithm does not utilize all the details of the object's geometry, it is able to consistently meet our performance objectives. Our method is much faster since only a line segment is merged with the BSP tree.

Without additional volume extrusion over the path of travel, merging trees only produces interpenetration information. More processing is required to determine time and place of impact. With a large enough time step it is possible to pass through objects. Our technique extrudes the object's geometry (a point) from one point in time to another. This produces a line segment. A single query of this segment against the BSP tree indicates a time and place of the collision. There is no possibility of passing through matter.

The idea of using an offset surface for collision detection with an object's reference point (such as its center) goes back to early video games on the Apple 2 and Atari 2600. The combination of this with BSP trees was used in the popular video games Doom and Quake [Carmack]. Instead of having multiple BSP trees and restricting the possible dimensions of collidable objects, we accommodate different sized objects with only one BSP tree.

Accurate offset surfaces can be generated by Minkowski summation or polyhedral convolution [Basch96]. These procedures can significantly increase the number of faces. In practice, it is common to create approximate offset surfaces by moving existing faces and vertices. We were doing this previously. The error in this method is a bit worse than approximating an object with its convex hull. Normally, there are 3 nondegenerate cases of impact [Baraff97] for a pair of convex objects a and b: 1) vertex of a with face from b, 2) vertex of b with face from a, and 3) edge from a with edge from b. By treating our object as a point, the only contact that it can experience is a vertex on the object with a face of the environment. Similar errors are also present in the new technique presented in this paper. Beveling is used to improve the approximation.

Beveling geometry to limit its protrusion when scaled or expanded is not a new idea. Early polyline drawing algorithms would do this when drawing thick lines. This technique has been applied to boundary representations (the set of polygons describing a model) when expanding the geometry. From what we understand of the source code available, Quake's BSP precompiler [Carmack] does something like this to generate its offset surface for player collision. Quake's compiler then builds an additional BSP tree for this expanded geometry. Instead of the order: 1) bevel, 2) expand, 3) compute BSP tree, our order of operations is: 1) compute the BSP tree, 2) bevel, 3) expand. Because beveling comes after computing the tree, our beveling step is applied to the solid cell leaf nodes of the tree. Since expansion is the last step in this process, we are able to do this dynamically at runtime.

3 Dynamic Plane Shifting BSP Algorithm

The standard algorithm for colliding a ray with a BSP tree is a recursive function that starts at the root. If the segment lies on one side of the node's plane then the segment is passed down to the corresponding subtree. Otherwise the segment crosses the plane so it is split. The first piece of the segment is checked. If it fails to collide then the second piece of the segment is checked against the other subtree. If a solid leaf node is reached then the algorithm returns a collision with impact equal to the start of the subsegment that reached the leaf.

Here, in more detail, is our revised algorithm that dynamically alters the plane equations:

Graphics **Interface** 2000

```
HitCheckBSP(node n,vector v0,vector v1)
  int hit = 0
  vector w0,w1
  if n is an empty leaf
    return 0
  if n is a solid leaf
    Impact = v0
    return 1
  if dot_product(n->normal,v1-v0) > 0
    if rayunder(n shift up,v0,v1,&w0,&w1)
      hit = HitCheckBSP(n->under,w0,w1)
      if hit==1
        v1 = Impact
      if rayover(n shift down,v0,v1,&w0,&w1)
      hit |= HitCheckBSP(n->over,w0,w1)
    return hit
  else
    same thing, but in the other direction
End
```

The function `rayunder` returns true if part of (v_0,v_1) lies under the supplied plane. The portion of the line segment under the plane (cropped if necessary) is returned in (w_0,w_1). The function `rayover` has similar functionality. Unlike the previous algorithm, the segment is not divided into two disjoint pieces - the subsegments passed down into the subtrees will overlap. Even if a collision occurs in the first subtree, it may still be necessary to check the other subtree (after adjusting the segment endpoint) since an impact may occur sooner.

Notice that the plane is translated twice when we visit a node. The offsets are specified at runtime and may depend on the plane's normal. Furthermore, the upward and downward offsets do not have to be equal. There are various options available. We describe spherical, cylindrical, and general convex expansion. If the planes are translated by a constant factor d, then the colliding object is a virtual sphere of radius d. This is implemented by simply adding (or subtracting) d to the constant component, D, of the node's plane equation $Ax+By+Cz+D=0$. It is also easy to construct a formula to fit a cylinder. The plane is offset by the dot product of the plane normal with the vector from the cylinder's reference point to where the plane rests tangent to the cylinder's rim. Spherical or cylindrical expansion is fast and adds very little overhead to the collision detection.

Another appropriate amount to offset the plane is:

$$d = \max_{v \in vertices} \{n.normal \bullet v\}$$

The maximum is taken over the vertices of the object. Obviously, the vertex that determines this maximum will be on the convex hull. Therefore it can be found in $O(sqrt(num\_hull\_vertices))$ using gradient descent, or in $O(lg(num\_hull\_vertices))$ by exploiting a DK hierarchy [Dobkin85]. Finding the maximum with the normal negated determines the amount to offset the node's plane in the downward direction. By using a vertex on the model, we have a point of impact (other than the

object's reference point) in the event of a collision. Impulses and rendering effects can be applied to this point.

Note that we have not yet pursued rotation with our collision detection technique. With rotation the offsets would be different for point v_0 than for v_1 since they occur at different instance in time.

For collision purposes, BSP trees made from solid geometry are more efficient since the polygons can be ignored. BSP trees representing polygon soup must store the polygons at nodes in the tree. Our plane shifting gives no indication how to alter polygons, and our beveling step relies on the solid/empty status of the leaf cells. Therefore, we do not claim that our method will even work with polygon soup.

4 Why This Works

To analyze the algorithm, it helps to understand what a BSP tree represents. A BSP tree decomposes space into convex cells, which are either solid or empty. Each cell corresponds to a leaf node of the BSP tree. Its solid/empty status depends on which side of its parent's plane equation it resides. The cell is defined by the plane equations of the nodes on the path from its parent node up to the root of the tree. Some of these planes may not actually touch the cell.

In standard BSP algorithms, as the line segment (our object extruded over time) is passed down the tree to a leaf node, it is clipped according to the node's plane equations along the way. What reaches a leaf node is the intersection of the cell with the original line segment given to the root of the BSP tree.

When we move the planes, what reaches a cell will be the portion of the segment that intersects the expanded cell (planes moved outward). According to our algorithm, if anything reaches a solid cell, then a collision has occurred. The boundary of the union of all the expanded solid cells effectively simulates an approximate offset surface.

5 Potential Inaccuracy and Beveling

As mentioned previously, our technique (and similar techniques that simulate the object as a point) are subject to a certain degree of inaccuracy. This is illustrated in Figure 1. Two spheres, A and B, collide with the geometry below them. Using the center of each sphere is its reference point, the geometry is offset outward as represented by the dotted lines. The center of each sphere rebounds off these offset planes. As sphere A moves along its trajectory, the collision occurs before its perimeter contacts the surface. For comparison, sphere B will rebound with an appropriate impact point and direction of deflection.

216

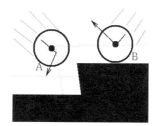

Figure 1: Collision using offsets

Most of the time, the protrusion of solid cells is tolerable, but the error starts to increase dramatically as the angle between adjacent planes approaches 180 degrees. We reduce this problem by beveling the solid cells of the BSP tree.

Figure 2 shows an example by looking at a small part of a BSP tree. Plane *C* divides a solid cell from an empty cell. The solid cell is beveled with two planes (*D* and *E*) by inserting extra nodes at the bottom of the tree.

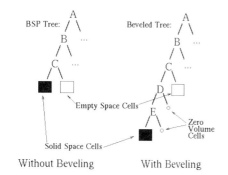

Figure 2: Bevel effect on BSP tree

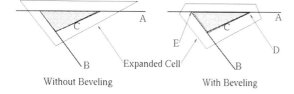

Figure 3: Bevel effect on plane shifting

Figure 3 shows the difference made by the added nodes. When the cell is expanded, it no longer protrudes as far as it did without the extra nodes.

When compiling a boundary representation into a BSP tree we are already keeping track of the volume of space at each node. This was originally done to help evaluate candidates when selecting the next partitioning plane [Berg93,Naylor98,Paterson90]. At the solid leaf nodes, these volume cells are inspected for neighboring faces (planes) that intersect at angles greater than 90 degrees. For every such case where the dot product of the two plane normals is less than zero, an additional

node is inserted into the BSP tree. This added node's plane normal is half way between the two plane normals and is coplanar with the intersection of the two planes (the edge between the two faces). The resulting tree represents the same initial boundary representation, but it contains extra empty cells of zero volume. In addition to sharp edges, sharp spikes (vertices) may also need to be beveled.

Although it may not always seem necessary, this beveling step is very important, even if the initial boundary representation contains no acutely convex angles. Our initial experiments in altering the plane equations, where we had not included the beveling step, were unsuccessful. The movement of characters in our video game was blocked in the strangest places as if someone had randomly placed invisible walls in the scene. This happens because the BSP compilation process splits polygons and creates cells with sharp angles in unexpected places. Beveling solved this problem and made the dynamic plane shifting technique viable.

Additional beveling can improve accuracy, but there is the cost of adding nodes to the tree. Extra memory and performance costs are analyzed in a later section.

6 Performance Justification

We have added some additional steps to the BSP traversal. Clearly, it will be faster to have a BSP tree based on offset geometry instead of dynamically shifting planes in the BSP. The reason for using our technique instead is because the BSP tree adapts to different sizes so only one tree is needed. To justify using our technique, it remains to be shown that it maintains a performance advantage over the alternative (single tree) method, which is to merge the object's geometry with the environment's BSP tree.

We could compare performance with a complicated model for the object, but that would give our technique an unfair advantage. Our algorithm's approximation to collision detection cannot be better than checking the convex hull of the object against the environment. Therefore let us assume our object is a convex polyhedron.

So far we have been talking about collision detection of moving objects. This is easy for a point since its motion can be represented as a line segment. Extruding a 3D model would make this discussion difficult. In this analysis we give up our temporal advantage and consider a stationary object. The query asked of both algorithms is whether or not an object interpenetrates the environment.

The algorithm for merging a BSP tree with a convex polyhedron (for the purposes of detecting interpenetration) is as follows:

```
M(node n, polytope p)
  if n is leaf
    return (n is solid)?1:0
  if p is completely over n->plane
    return M(n->over,p)
  if p is completely under n->plane
    return M(n->under,p)
  else
    (pa,pb) = Slice(p with n->plane)
    return M(n->over,pa) | M(n->under,pb)
End
```

The function `Slice` partitions the polyhedron into two disjoint pieces on opposite sides of the specified plane.

To determine if a stationary object interpenetrates the environment, our algorithm checks a point (instead of a line segment) against the BSP to see if it falls into any expanded cells. (Note that now $v_0=-v_1$.) Previously we have discussed our algorithm in terms of altering the planes. For purposes of comparison, it is easier to study the *dual* of our technique. It is not hard to see that our algorithm is equivalent to:

```
F(node n, polytope p)
  if n is leaf
    return (n is solid)?1:0
  if p is completely over n->plane
    return F(n->over,p)
  if p is completely under n->plane
    return F(n->under,p)
  else
    return F(n->over,p) | F(n->under,p)
End
```

The only difference between our technique, `F()`, and merge, `M()`, is that `Slice()` is not used. If any of the polyhedron lies on one side of the plane, then the entire polyhedron is passed down to the corresponding subtree. Slicing a polyhedron is significantly more expensive than the simple dot product and comparison used to determine where a vertex sits relative to a plane. Therefore, much better performance is possible by avoiding this operation.

Figure 4: Sample environment geometry

We did a performance test to support our claim that slicing adds a significant cost to BSP traversal. Sample geometry for testing was made by booleaning a number of simple shapes together. The resulting 774-face boundary representation was used to generate a BSP tree with 665 nodes (including leaves). A large cube with side length equal to half the sample geometry's width was placed at the center. We tested traversal with and without the slicing step. For both algorithms we did not stop at the first intersection and return true. All intersections were computed. Times in microseconds (not milliseconds) are reported in Table 1.

Algorithm	M() merge	F() no slice
Time	14312	261

Table 1: Cost of slicing vs. not slicing

The no-slice method, `F()`, finds all cells that intersect the cube. There is the possibility of error in that additional cells may be reported. Merging the cube with the environment computes exact interpenetrating information. Its equivalent to doing a solid geometry boolean operation. Merge performed 109 slices. We slice convex polyhedrons by creating a duplicate and then cropping them both. To compensate for this duplicate effort, the time reported for the merge technique is half of its actual time. We tried to make our crop algorithm efficient. Compiler optimization was enabled. Better performance may have been possible with more low-level optimization. The 50-fold difference in time seems to indicate that slicing has a significant cost.

The entire analysis in this section has been possible since we only considered stationary objects. Another strong argument for dynamic plane shifting is that it is trivial to generalize to moving objects - the point becomes a ray. Working with a moving volume requires either adding timesteps to maintain accuracy and resolve collisions, or adding a system of extruding a volume over the motion path that can extract a time of impact when a collision occurs. Both options would require significant overhead. Clearly, better performance is possible by approximating the object as a point.

7 Performance Overhead

Using the sample geometry from the previous section, we perform some more tests to measure the beveling and tree traversal overheads. As shown in Figure 5, the number of nodes added because of beveling increases as we decrease the allowable angle between cell faces. At a 90-degree limit we double the number of nodes. The impact on performance is minor since the collision detection algorithm is in $O(lg(n))$. Performance of standard ray and point intersection tests (for zero volume objects) will not increase by more than a few percent.

218

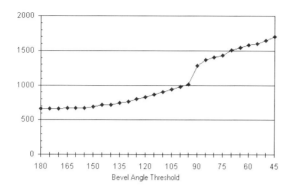

Figure 5: Size of tree vs. bevel angle

For objects, which use the dynamic plane shifting technique, there is an added cost. Additional nodes will be visited due to the bi-directional shifting of the node's plane equations. Using our sample environment, the number of nodes visited for a given object size is shown in Figure 6. For each given diameter, a number of stationary spheres were generated randomly within the volume. The average number of nodes visited during BSP collision check is reported. The diameter is expressed as a percentage of the size of the environment. As expected, the number of nodes visited increases with the given size. An object as large as the environment will touch every node in the tree. Clearly dynamic plane shifting works best for colliding objects that are small relative to the size of the environment.

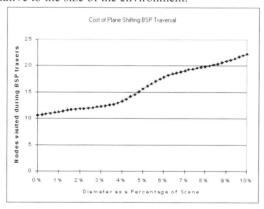

Figure 6: Nodes visited vs. object size

8 Application

We have employed our dynamic plane shifting algorithm in MDK2 [Bioware2000], a 3D video game our company will soon be publishing. It replaced our previous system that used multiple BSP trees. The movement and environment interaction of the characters is the same as before. Furthermore, we are now able to introduce more characters and objects of varying sizes, Figure 7.

Figure 7: MDK2 characters

Solid cells were beveled to ensure at most a 95-degree difference in adjacent planes. With this beveling threshold, an extent can still be expanded further than the amount the planes are moved. Since our technique is an approximation, it is beneficial to minimize error where it is most important. There is gravity in MDK2 which means the characters move along the ground. Therefore, for any solid cell that was not topped with a nearly level plane, we added a node with plane normal $z=1$ and made it concurrent with the highest vertex in that cell. (Note, Quake's system also adds axial planes to its brushes.) The extra horizontal beveling plane eliminated very rare but obscure cases where a solid cell would protrude through the floor when expanded. Gameplay improved as well. A character can now walk along a ridge without constantly fighting gravity even when the ridge was constructed without a flat top.

Even with all the beveling there still is some error in the system. Measuring a difference between the true offset surface and the apparent collision surface from plane shifting would not give a practical evaluation of our technique. The game was subjected to extensive review by internal testing, by our publisher's beta testers, and by Sega's quality assurance department. There were some cases where artwork had been modified to improve accuracy. Overall, in MDK2, our dynamic plane shifting technique achieved the quality standards required for a published entertainment title.

Our trees were typically between 2 and 2.5 times the size of the non-beveled tree. This is comparable to the results from the small sample geometry that was presented in the previous section. Having a larger tree is worth the extra space cost. With over a dozen different sized characters in the game, storing an extra tree for each character would not have been feasible.

When we replaced our multiple tree collision detection with our dynamic plane shifting solution, we did not detect a difference in the overall performance of the program. Most of the computing resources go into other areas such as animation, AI, physics, and rendering. Collision detection is a small fraction of the work. Furthermore, many of the BSP queries are for particle, bullet, line-of-sight, lens flare, and shadow checks. These require little or no geometry expansion. The variance in the overall time per frame made it impossible to measure a performance overhead this way.

It was necessary to measure the performance times in isolation to provide a clearer picture of the overhead of the dynamic plane shifting technique. We present results using the player's characters, which are larger than most objects and consequently should have higher overheads. Movement updates for the characters occur each frame. In the part of the code where the player's collision check is made, we inserted code for 3 methods of collision detection: regular BSP collision (labeled Ray), spherical offset, and cylindrical offset. Each method received the same input parameters, including the player's current position and desired new position for that frame. To ensure accurate timing, each method repeated its calculation 100 times every frame. Nothing but BSP traversal code contributed to the times. The game was played for at least 2 minutes with the player character constantly moving. The average times for each method were recorded. This was done for 3 finished levels within our game. The reason for using completed artwork is because early prototype content tends to contain less detail that would have resulted in fewer BSP cells being reached by an expanded volume. Testing was done on a Pentium 3 PC computer. The algorithms tested were all unoptimized C code. The average times in microseconds of each technique for the 3 tests is shown in Table 2.

Character	Ray	Sphere	Cylinder
Max the Robot	20	51	66
Doctor Hawkins	11	27	38
Kurt Hectic	19	44	64

Table 2: Average collision query time (microseconds)

As expected, the previous method is faster than dynamically shifting the plane equations. The bounding cylinders had less volume than the bounding spheres and yet they did not perform as well. This is probably due to the cylinder offsets being computed on the fly. Our results here show that the collision detection can be 2.5 to 3.5 times more expensive. Putting these results in context, at 30 FPS, each frame allows 33000 microseconds. We felt an additional 20 to 50 microseconds for a character's collision detection was worth the flexibility of allowing different sized characters and objects in our game.

Since this is an interactive application, the collision detection algorithm must provide consistent performance. Good average times are meaningless if the worst case is orders of magnitude more expensive. Figure 8 shows the collision times over a series of 200 frames where the Doctor character was running and jumping around in a room with stairs, corners, ledges, and other objects. There is variation in the sample times, but it is within a small constant. These fluctuations are not large enough to affect the framerate of the program.

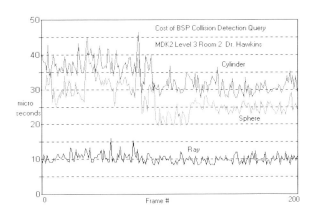

Figure 8: Variation in algorithm performance

Introducing dynamic plane shifting had other benefits. Previously we were having problems with offset surfaces. Our artists preferred to model game content in 3D Studio Max. Unlike Quake editors, which build content with intersecting convex brushes, we generate our BSP trees from 2-manifold geometry. Offsetting a boundary representation often creates self-intersections that corrupt our BSP compiler. Using dynamic plane shifting replaced this system and proved to be more robust.

As CPU speeds improve, it will eventually be practical to use a more accurate algorithm, such as merging BSP trees, for important collision detection tasks such as characters colliding with the environment. Using the object-as-a-point approximation will still be useful for less important artifacts in a 3D application. For example, our system can also support collision detection for hundreds of non-zero volume particles while maintaining the desired frame rate.

9 Conclusion

This paper addresses the problem of providing fast detection of various sized objects colliding with a static polygonal environment. Representing the object as a point makes it possible to do collision detection much faster than having to deal with the object's geometry. We no longer require an extra copy of the environment's geometry for every possible object size. Dynamic shifting of the plane equations during BSP tree traversal lets us adapt to any sized object. Beveling solid cells prevents geometry from protruding too far. Since the object is represented as a point, there is some inaccuracy in the collision detection. This error also existed in the previous system where we used multiple BSP trees. We have shown that our technique maintains a performance advantage over merging. In our practice, we have found the technique to be as accurate as using multiple trees, without losing the ability to do fast collision detection required by our application.

220

10 Future Work

Our dynamic plane shifting technique only addresses the issue of linear translational movement. General 3D rotation is becoming more commonplace in 3D applications. A change in orientation poses some challenges. The amount that the planes are offset depends on the orientation. If the orientation changes during a collision query then so can the offset. Currently, our algorithm does not take this into account.

The performance overhead of our technique is mostly due to the extra nodes visited. This is influenced by the object size with respect to the size of the cells of the BSP tree. For larger objects it may not be necessary to go to the entire depth of the tree. Multiresolution with BSP trees has already been used in other applications [Naylor98]. It may be possible to apply similar simplification to our collision detection algorithm.

Doing solid geometry boolean operations on BSP trees can provide a modifiable environment experience for the user. This technique will not work when multiple BSP trees are used to represent the environment. Since plane shifting BSP traversal only uses one tree, it may be possible to allow dynamic modification provided the result of the boolean can be beveled as necessary.

Acknowledgements

Special thanks to John Carmack of Id Software for confirming our description of Quake's system. David Falkner wrote the cylinder expansion routine and helped with the performance testing. Credit also goes to the rest of the MDK2 team at Bioware for testing the practical application of this technique. This paper would not have been possible without the help of Jean Melax.

References

[Baraff97] David Baraff, Andy Witkin. *Physically Based Modeling: Principles and Practice.* SIGGRAPH Course notes, 1997.

[Basch96] J. Basch, L. Guibas, G. D. Ramkumar, L. Ramshaw. *Polyhedral Tracings and their Convolution.* Algorithms for Robotic Motion and Manipulation, 1996.

[Berg93] M. de Berg, M. de Groot, M. Overmars. *Perfect Binary Space Partitions.* Canadian Conference on Computational Geometry, 1993.

[Bioware2000] Bioware, Shiny, and Interplay: *MDK2.* Sega and PC Video Game, 2000.

[Carmack] John Carmack, M. Abrash. *Quake's BSP compiler.* Id Software.

[Cohen95] Jonathan D Cohen, Ming C Lin, Dinesh Manocha, Madhav Ponamgi. *I-Collide, An Interactive and Exact Collision Detection System for Large-Scale Environments.* ACM Symposium on Interactive 3D Graphics (I3DG), pp 189-196, 1995.

[Dobkin85] D. Dobkin, D. Kirkpatrick.: *A Linear Algorithm for Determining the Separation of Convex Polyhedra.* Journal of Algorithms 6, pp 381-392, 1985.

[Gottschalk96] S. Gottschalk, M. C. Lin, D. Manocha. *OBB-Tree: A Hierarchical Structure for Rapid Interference Detection.* SIGGRAPH, pp. 171-180, 1996.

[Klosowski96] J. Klosowski, M. Held, J.S.B. Mitchell, H. Sowizral, K. Zikan: *Efficient Collision Detection Using Bounding Volume Hierarchies of k-DOPs.* SIGGRAPH Visual Proceedings, 1996.

[Mirtich97] B. Mirtich: *V-Clip.* Technical Report 97-05, Mitsubishi Electric Research Laboratory, 1997.

[Naylor90] Bruce F. Naylor, John Amanatides, William Thibault. *Merging BSP Trees Yields Polyhedral Set Operations.* SIGGRAPH, pp 115-123, 1990.

[Naylor92] Bruce F. Naylor. *Interactive Solid Modeling via Partitioning Trees.* Graphics Interface, pp 11-18, 1992.

[Naylor98] Bruce F. Naylor. *A Tutorial On Binary Space Partitioning Trees.* Computer Games Developer Conference Proceedings, pp 433-457, 1998.

[Paterson90] Michael S. Paterson and F. Frances Yao, *Efficient Binary Space Partitions for Hidden-Surface Removal and Solid Modeling.* Discrete and Computational Geometry, vol 5, pp 485-503, 1990.

[Torres90] Enric Torres, *Optimization of the Binary Space Partitioning Algorithm (BSP) for the Visualization of Dynamic Scenes.* Eurographics 1990.

Model Simplification Through Refinement

Dmitry Brodsky
Department of Computer Science
University of British Columbia

Benjamin Watson
Department of Computing Science
University of Alberta

Abstract

As modeling and visualization applications proliferate, there arises a need to simplify large polygonal models at interactive rates. Unfortunately existing polygon mesh simplification algorithms are not well suited for this task because they are either too slow (requiring the simplified model to be pre-computed) or produce models that are too poor in quality. These shortcomings become particularly acute when models are extremely large.

We present an algorithm suitable for simplification of large models at interactive speeds. The algorithm is fast and can guarantee displayable results within a given time limit. Results also have good quality. Inspired by splitting algorithms from vector quantization literature, we simplify models in reverse, beginning with an extremely coarse approximation and refining it. Approximations of surface curvature guide the simplification process. Previously produced simplifications can be further refined by using them as input to the algorithm.

1 Introduction

Many of today's applications require simplification of polygonal models at interactive speeds. Modeling applications must simplify and display extremely large models at interactive rates. In visualization applications isosurfaces from high dimensional data sets must be computed, simplified, and rendered in close to real-time. In dynamically modifiable virtual environments, newly generated surfaces are typically over-tessellated and must be simplified for display at interactive speeds. As the size of polygonal models balloons simplification algorithms have to scale gracefully to handle these extremely large models.

An ideal simplification algorithm for these applications would possess several characteristics. Most importantly, the algorithm must guarantee displayable results within a specified time limit. Second, the algorithm must provide good control of output model size if results are to be displayable. It is also very important that the output model quality remains reasonable, despite stringent time constraints. If time demands require the output of a crude simplification, then the algorithm should allow for later refinement of that output. Finally, for interactive display it would be useful if the algorithm produced a continuous level of detail hierarchy instead of several discrete levels of detail.

Most existing simplification algorithms are far too slow to be used in interactive applications. Some vertex clustering algorithms [15, 18] are very fast, but control of output quality and size is quite poor. Moreover this output is difficult to refine and to organize into a continuous level of detail hierarchy.

Our algorithm, *R-Simp*, was inspired by splitting algorithms from the vector quantization literature [6]. The algorithm simplifies in reverse from coarse to fine, allowing us to guarantee a displayable result within a specified time limit. At every iteration of the algorithm, the number of vertices in the simplified model is known, enabling control of output model size. We use curvature to guide the simplification process, permitting preservation of important model features, and thus a reasonable level of output model quality. Performing simplification in a reverse direction makes it possible to refine intermediate output as long as some state information is saved. Finally with its divide and conquer approach, R-Simp can easily be extended to create continuous level of detail hierarchies. R-Simp's complexity is $O(n_i \log n_o)$, where n_i is the size of the input model and n_o is the size of the output model. This enables R-Simp to scale linearly with respect to input size for a given output size. With all these traits, R-Simp is well suited for simplification of large models in interactive environments.

We also look to vector quantization to form a taxonomy of existing simplification algorithms. In sections 2, 3 and 4 we review vector quantization, related research, and curvature. The details of the algorithm are discussed in section 5. In section 6 we examine the performance of the algorithm and compare it to QSlim [5] and a vertex clustering algorithm [18]. Sections 7 and 8 present other possible applications of R-Simp and conclusions.

2 Vector quantization

Vector quantization (VQ) is the process of mapping a vector in a large set $S \subset \mathbb{R}^n$ into a smaller set $C \subset \mathbb{R}^n$. More precisely, a quantizer is a function $Q : \mathbb{R}^n \rightarrow C$ where $C = \{\vec{v}_i \in \mathbb{R}^n | 1 \leq i \leq N\}$. C is called the *codebook*.

The challenge is finding C such that it optimally represents all vectors in $S \subset \mathbb{R}^n$. The codebook C partitions the set S, since each $\vec{v}_i$ represents multiple vectors from S. A single partition of S is called a *cell* and $\vec{v}_i$ is the *centroid* of the cell. The difference between a vector $\vec{v}_i$ and an input vector $\vec{u}$ is called *distortion*. When the distortion for an input vector $\vec{u}$ is minimal for all $\vec{u} \in S$ then the codebook is called optimal.

In [6], Gersho and Gray present four basic types of VQ algorithms. Using these four types we will create a taxonomy of existing simplification algorithms.

Product code algorithms use scalar quantizers that are independently applied to each input vector element.

In *pruning* algorithms, the codebook initially contains all the vectors in the input set S. The codebook entry that increases distortion least is removed; removals continue until the desired codebook size is reached. Alternatively, the codebook is initially empty, and each of the input vectors is considered in succession. If representing any vector with the current codebook would result in distortion over a given threshold, the vector is added to the codebook.

Pairwise nearest neighbor algorithms also set the initial codebook to contain all the vectors in S. All possible cell pairs are considered and the pair that introduces the least distortion is merged. Merging continues until the desired codebook size or distortion tolerance is reached.

In *Splitting* algorithms, the codebook initially contains a single cell. The cell with the most distortion is located and then split. Splitting continues until the required distortion or codebook size is reached.

3 Vector Quantization and Simplification

Simplification relates to quantization as follows: a centroid equates to a primitive (vertex, line, or polygon) or a set of primitives in the simplified model. For most vertex merge algorithms, the centroid is a single vertex and associated faces. A cell equates to a set or cluster of faces in the original model. There are a few ways in which model simplification differs from vector quantization. For example in model simplification, two disjoint faces do not make up an ideal cluster, while in image quantization a cluster with two separate pixels is perfectly acceptable. We cannot review every known simplification algorithm; a fairly comprehensive survey is available from Garland and Heckbert [8].

Rossignac and Borrel [18] proposed an algorithm that applies a product codes technique to the model vertices. Cells are formed with a uniform voxelization; the centroid is usually chosen as the mean of the vertices in each cell (weighted averages or maxima are common alternatives). Only a linear pass through the vertices is required

to simplify the surface. The result is an extremely fast algorithm that produces poor simplifications. He et al [7] proposed a similar and slower algorithm that makes use of a low pass three dimensional filter. Low and Tan [15] developed a vertex clustering algorithm that non-uniformly subdivided the model's volume. Cells are centred on the most important vertices in the model.

The simplification algorithms taking the pruning approach are generally not as fast as the product code algorithms, but they produce better simplifications. Two such algorithms [9, 13] work by growing coplanar patches. When a face cannot be added to a patch without violating a co-planarity threshold, it is re-triangulated with fewer polygons and added to the codebook. Other algorithms [20, 21] work by removing or pruning away single vertices. The algorithm described in [20] simply removes a vertex whose surrounding faces are relatively coplanar and re-triangulates the created hole, while the algorithm described in [21] adds a completely new set of vertices and tries to prune away as many of the old vertices as possible.

There are many algorithms, commonly called vertex merge or edge collapse algorithms, that use the pairwise nearest neighbour approach [1, 3, 5, 10, 11, 14, 17]. These algorithms tend to produce the best simplification results but are often quite slow. The algorithms assign weights to each vertex merge and use a priority queue to locate the merge with minimum cost. They merge the vertices (merge the cells), recompute the affected vertex pairs, and iterate. The algorithms continue until the required model size or error tolerance is reached. The algorithms differ in how they assign weights to a vertex merge and how they determine the location of merged vertices (calculate centroids).

To our knowledge R-Simp is the only simplification algorithm based on the splitting technique. In R-Simp we treat simplification as quantization of face normals as opposed to colour (x, y, z instead of R, G, B). Our goal when splitting is to create cells containing the most planar surface possible (the variation in face normals is small). Thus, cells that contain little curvature are split less than cells that contain more curvature.

4 Curvature

One common measure of surface curvature is called *normal curvature* [16]. Normal curvature is the rate of change of the normal vector field U on a surface S in direction $\vec{u}$, where $\vec{u}$ is a unit vector tangent to the surface S at point p. There are two important normal curvature extrema called *principle curvatures*, these are the maximum (k_1) and minimum (k_2) values of normal curvature. The directions corresponding to these principle curvatures are called *principle directions*.

Since these curvature measures are defined for infinitely small patches, they provide a good description of the local surface around a point. However, they do not work well for larger surface patches with multiple scales of curvature. (e.g. asphalt looks flat from a distance but can feel quite rough close up). R-Simp requires measures of orientation change, curvature, for large patches. We will use the term *normal variation* to refer to orientation change in large patches.

5 The R-Simp algorithm

Unlike other algorithms, R-Simp starts with a coarse approximation of the model and refines it until the desired model complexity is reached. The algorithm begins with the triangulated model in a single cluster (a cluster is a collection of faces from the original model). The initial cluster is then divided into eight sub-clusters. These eight sub-clusters are then iteratively divided until the required number of clusters (vertices) is reached. Clusters are chosen for division based on the amount of normal variation on the surface in the cluster.

The R-Simp algorithm can be broken down into three stages.

- **Initialization:** In this stage we create global face (`gfl`) and vertex (`gvl`) lists, as well as vertex-vertex and vertex-face adjacency lists. We also create the eight initial clusters.

- **Simplification:** In this stage the model is simplified. The simplification consists of four steps:

  1. Choose the cluster that has the most face normal variation.

  2. Partition (split) the cluster based on the amount and direction of the face normal variation.

  3. Compute the amount of face normal variation in each of the sub-clusters.

  4. Iterate until the required number of clusters (vertices) is reached.

- **Post Processing:** For each cluster that is left, compute a representative vertex (centroid). Re-triangulate the model.

5.1 Data structures

The principle data structure in this algorithm is the `Cluster`. It stores all the information necessary to determine face normal variation and to compute the representative vertex. It contains two arrays of indices, for vertices (`vl`) and faces (`fl`), that index into two global lists of the vertices and faces from the original model (`gfl`

and `gvl`). The `Cluster` also contains the mean normal ($\vec{mn}$) that is the area-weighted mean of all the face normals in the cluster and is computed by Equation 1.

$$\vec{mn} = \sum_{i}^{N} \vec{n}_i a_i \qquad (1)$$

where N is the number of faces in the cluster, $\vec{n}_i$ is the normal of face i, and a_i is the area of face i. The `Cluster` also holds the mean vertex (mv) for the cluster, the amount of normal variation (nv), and the total area of the faces in the cluster.

Two other important data structures are the `Face` and the `Vertex` data structures which make up `gfl` and `gvl` respectively. The `Face` contains a list of vertices that make up the face, its normal, the face area, and its midpoint. The `Vertex` contains adjacency information for all the vertices and faces adjacent to it.

The vertices in the `Face` data structure are indices into `gvl`. The adjacency lists for the faces and the vertices in the `Vertex` data structure are also indices into `gfl` and `gvl`.

5.2 Initialization

During the initialization stage `gfl` and `gvl` are constructed and the initial eight clusters are created. The initial clusters are created by partitioning the model using three axis aligned planes that are positioned in the middle of the model's bounding box. We then compute the amount of face normal variation in each of these clusters (see Section 5.3). These eight clusters are then inserted into a priority queue sorted by the amount of face normal variation.

5.3 Choosing the cluster to partition

In the simplification stage of our algorithm the first step is to choose a cluster in which the face normals vary the most (the cluster at the head of the queue). We compute the amount of face normal variation using the area-weighted mean ($\vec{mn}$) of the face normals.

The flatter the surface, the larger the magnitude of $\vec{mn}$. If all the faces are coplanar, the magnitude of $\vec{mn}$ will equal the area of the surface in the cluster. We define this component cp of our face normal variation measure as follows:

$$cp = \frac{\|\vec{mn}\|}{\sum_{i}^{N} a_i} \qquad (2)$$

Even if the surface in a cluster is extremely small it can contain a large amount of curvature. In order to prevent small, highly curved details (e.g. a small spring in an engine) from dominating the simplification we must make our normal variation measure (nv) sensitive to size. To

224

do this, we scale cp by the ratio of the surface area in the cluster to the model surface area:

$$nv = \frac{\sum_i^N a_i}{\sum_i^M a_i}(1 - cp) \qquad (3)$$

where M is the number of faces in the model. We complement cp so that nv increases as face normal variation increases. In the remainder of this paper the term "normal variation" refers to variation of face normals.

5.4 Describing the pattern of normal variation

The next step is to describe normal variation in the chosen cluster. We follow Gersho and Gray [6] who suggest principle component analysis (PCA) [12] as a way of determining how to split cells when using a splitting algorithm. In PCA a covariance matrix is formed from the data set of interest. The eigenvectors of this matrix are aligned according to the pattern of variation in the data set. Garland [4] showed that if the covariance matrix is formed with normal vectors, the eigenvectors are generally related to the principal directions of normal curvature. Specifically, the largest eigenvalue and corresponding eigenvector represent the mean normal of the surface. Usually the second and third largest eigenvalues and corresponding eigenvectors represent the directions of maximum and minimum curvature.

The covariance matrix $\mathcal{A}$ around the mean $[0, 0, 0]$ is defined by:

$$\mathcal{A} = \sum_i^N \vec{n}_i \vec{n}_i^T \qquad (4)$$

We compute the eigenvalues and eigenvectors using the Jacobi method.

5.5 Partitioning the cluster

Partitioning the cluster consists of four steps. First, we must determine how many planes to use to partition the cluster. Second, we must orient the planes. Finally, we must position the planes and create new sub-clusters.

A cluster is partitioned into two, four, or eight sub-clusters depending on the amount of curvature. Let c_{mn}, c_M and c_m equal the eigenvalues in descending order (the second and third largest eigenvalues relate to k_1 and k_2, the magnitudes of principle curvature). Let $\vec{c}_M$ and $\vec{c}_m$ represent the corresponding eigenvectors (these are related to the directions of maximum and minimum curvature).

If all eigenvalues are of similar magnitude the pattern of normal variation is unclear. We test for this by comparing the eigenvalues as follows: both $c_M < 2c_m$ and $c_{mn} < 2c_M$ must be true. In this case we partition the cluster into eight sub-clusters. One partitioning plane is

perpendicular to $\vec{c}_M$, the second plane is perpendicular to $\vec{c}_m$, and the third plane is perpendicular to $\vec{mn}$.

Otherwise, if $\frac{c_M}{c_m} <= 4$ then the surface is most likely hemispherical since there is significant curvature in both the minimum and maximum directions of curvature. In this case we partition the cluster into four sub-clusters. One partitioning plane is perpendicular to $\vec{c}_M$ and the other plane is perpendicular to $\vec{c}_m$.

In all remaining cases $\frac{c_M}{c_m} > 4$ and the surface is most likely cylindrical since most of the curvature is in one direction. In this case we partition the cluster into two sub-clusters. The partitioning plane is perpendicular to $\vec{c}_M$.

We must now position the partitioning planes in the cluster. Ideally the surface should be partitioned along any ridges or through any elliptical bumps. However, locating such features is difficult, instead we do the following: first we compute the vector $\vec{c}_{M\perp}$, which is the projection of $\vec{c}_M$ onto P_{mn}, the plane defined by $\vec{mn}$ and the cluster's mean vertex (mv). We then project the midpoint of all the faces in the cluster onto P_{mn} and find the mean of all projected midpoints that fall within 2.5 degrees of $\vec{c}_{M\perp}$. The resulting point is the position for the partitioning plane(s).

Sub-clusters are created by partitioning the vertices in a cluster. The membership of a vertex depends on which side of the partitioning plane(s) it falls on. The faces follow the vertices to the sub-clusters. A face may belong to two or three clusters if the vertices of the face fall into different sub-clusters.

Even if the entire model is topologically connected, a given cluster may contain two or more disconnected components. Approximating these components with a single vertex can introduce severe distortion. We have found it useful to perform a topology check to determine if a new cluster contains topologically disjoint components.

The topology check is a breadth first search on the vertices and edges contained in a cluster. We use a bit array to record the vertices visited during the search, making it linear in complexity. If the cluster contains disjoint components, each component is placed into a separate cluster. Although this topology check increases the overall simplification time, the resulting increase in quality of the simplification is considerable.

5.6 Post processing

Once the simplification stage is finished two tasks remain. The first is to compute the location of the representative vertex (v) for each cluster. The second is to re-triangulate the output surface.

To represent a cluster's faces as accurately as possible, v should be as close as possible to all the faces. [5, 14, 17] all minimize the summed distance from the planes containing the cluster's faces. [5, 14] minimize the squared distance:

$$Q(v) = v^T \mathcal{A} v + 2\vec{b}^T v + c \qquad (5)$$

Where $\vec{n}_i + d_i = 0$ is the plane equation for face i, $\mathcal{A}$ is as previously defined, $\vec{b} = \sum_i^N d_i \vec{n}_i$, and $c = \sum_i^N d_i^2$.

Since Q is a quadratic then $Q(v)$ is minimum when its partial derivatives equal zero. This occurs when:

$$v_{min} = -\mathcal{A}^{-1} \vec{b}^T \qquad (6)$$

We re-triangulate using a method similar to that used by [18]. After v_j is computed for each cluster, the v_js are output to a simplified vertex list `svl`. In `gvl`, all vertex references contained in (`vl`) of cluster j are pointed at the new entry in `svl`. We then traverse the global face list `gfl`. Any face referencing three different vertices in `svl` is retained and output to the simplified face list `sfl`. All other faces have degenerated into lines or points and are discarded.

6 Results

Simplification algorithms are usually judged by two criteria. The first criterion is speed, the time required to simplify a model. The second and more difficult to measure criterion is quality. Intuitively speaking, quality of a simplification is its appearance or its geometric accuracy.

In the following subsection we present execution times for two different input models. We also present quality results, including images allowing for comparison of appearance and geometric accuracy measured with the *Metro* [2] tool.

6.1 Performance

Five different models were used in our comparisons. All models were simplified on a 195 MHz R10000 SGI Onyx2 with 512 MB of main memory.

We compared R-Simp to two other simplification algorithms. We chose the fastest vertex clustering algorithm and the fastest vertex merge algorithm. The first is Rossignac and Borrel's [18] vertex clustering algorithm (with unweighted centroid calculations). The second, QSlim [5], is one of the fastest vertex merge algorithms.

Figure 1 compares the performance of R-Simp to QSlim and vertex clustering with the Stanford bunny. R-Simp is considerably faster than QSlim; it is able to produce a simplified model of up to 20000 polygons before QSlim removes a single face. R-Simp's complexity is $O(n_i \log n_o)$ where n_i is the input model size and n_o is the output model size. Thus R-Simp is linear for a fixed output size. The speed of vertex clustering is not related to output size.

Figure 2 shows how the size of the input model affects simplification time. The dragon was initially simplified

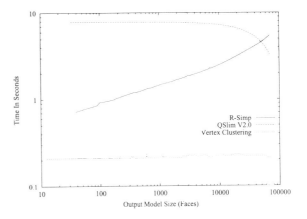

Figure 1: The effect of output model size on simplification time for the Stanford bunny.

using QSlim to various sizes. These models were then simplified by R-Simp, QSlim, and vertex clustering to 2100 polygons. As the graph shows, the larger the input model, the longer it takes to simplify. However, QSlim's curve is significantly steeper than R-Simp's. Vertex clustering is fastest but is affected by input size.

To compare model quality we took seven models and simplified them. Table 1 summarizes the results. The table shows the mean Hausdorff distance between the original and the simplified surface as a percentage of the diagonal of the bounding box of the original surface [2].

Figures 3a-h show the original bunny and dragon models and the corresponding simplifications produced by all three algorithms.

6.2 Discussion

As we noted earlier, in applications where the model is created in response to user input pre-computation is not possible. Models must be simplified at interactive rates. Applications that deal with extremely large models must ensure that the simplification algorithm is able to produce simplifications in reasonable time.

Algorithms useful for such applications should possess several characteristics:

- *Interactive response*: Most importantly, algorithms should be able to guarantee displayable results within a specified time limit. R-Simp's speed and coarse to fine pattern of simplification make it ideal for this application. Vertex clustering is even faster although precise control of execution time is difficult. Because QSlim is slower and simplifies from fine to coarse it cannot make any time guarantees.

Model	Input # Faces	Output # Faces	Vertex Clustering		R-Simp		QSlim	
			Error	Time (s)	Error	Time (s)	Error	Time (s)
Bunny	69451	1600	0.302%	0.09	0.155%	1.58	0.071%	7.85
Cow	5782	1600	0.256%	0.03	0.118%	0.12	0.060%	0.45
Dragon	871306	2100	0.428%	0.29	0.241%	18.9	0.175%	129
Horse	96966	1600	0.266%	0.05	0.147%	2.29	0.052%	11.5
Chair	2481	800	0.658%	0.00	0.215%	0.05	0.019%	0.17
Torus	20000	400	0.460%	0.05	0.265%	0.32	0.160%	1.74
Spring	9386	800	1.012%	N/A	0.594%	0.13	0.295%	0.75
Mean			0.483%	0.09	0.242%	3.34	0.119%	21.6

Table 1: *Simplification error and time of R-Simp, QSlim, and vertex clustering. The error is the mean surface deviation between two surfaces measured as a percentage of the sampling bounding box diagonal [2].*

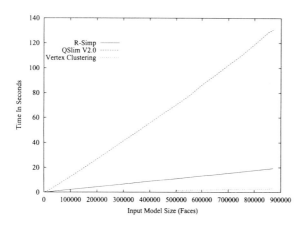

Figure 2: *The effect of input model size on simplification time. Output model size is 2100 polygons.*

- *Control of output model size*: Control of output model size is important if results are to be displayable. R-Simp and QSlim provide a straight forward way to control the output model size but most vertex clustering algorithms do not. In these algorithms one can only specify the number of voxels; the number of vertices and faces will typically be much smaller. Thus, if displayability is to be guaranteed, quality suffers.

- *High output quality*: Algorithms should output models of the best possible quality despite time constraints. QSlim clearly generates the best quality models. R-Simp's output quality is not as good, vertex clustering is worst.

- *Iterative improvement*: When time constraints require the output of a crude simplification, it should

be possible to refine the result after the time demands have been met. R-Simp's coarse to fine pattern of simplification makes this fairly simple; one must only save the priority queue of clusters. With QSlim there is no need for refinement, the more important question is whether the time constraints could be met. Vertex clustering uses a one pass, one resolution approach and thus refinement is not possible.

- *Continuous level of detail*: Many interactive applications require level of detail hierarchies. Both R-Simp and QSlim are able to produce hierarchies but much of the hierarchy initially output by QSlim will not be displayable in interactive settings. Vertex clustering cannot produce hierarchies without fundamental changes to the algorithm.

- *Scalability*: Simplification algorithms need to scale gracefully so that they are able to handle extremely large models. QSlim's complexity is $O(n \log n)$ in input while R-Simp's is linear for a fixed output size.

To summarize, QSlim generates the best quality models but it is not suitable for interactive applications because it is too slow and cannot guarantee displayable results in a fixed time. Vertex clustering algorithms are extremely fast but generate poor quality models and do not provide an easy way to control output model size. We believe R-Simp's time guarantees and quality/speed tradeoff make it ideal for use in interactive applications.

R-Simp can simplify any model, regardless of topology or manifold characteristics. In output it can simplify topology and thus does not guarantee topology preservation.

7 Future work and other applications

The quality of R-Simp's simplifications might be improved by adding a look-ahead feature, comparing the normal variation before and after the cluster split. It should also be possible to modify R-Simp to consider boundaries as well as face and vertex attributes (e.g. colour) during simplification. For large environments consisting of many objects, it should be possible to add a distance threshold to the topology check, so that disjoint but neighbouring objects remain in the same cluster and are merged.

To enable management of the quality/speed tradeoff, R-Simp might be used as part of a two stage simplification process. If speed is particularly important, vertex clustering could be used to simplify the model to a medium level of complexity and the result input to R-Simp. If quality is important, the output of R-Simp could be input to QSlim.

We have already discussed the use of R-Simp for level of detail hierarchies. The bounding box around the clusters in these hierarchies can be used to speed up collision detection. We have experimented with such bounding boxes as an error measure during simplification and found no loss in quality or speed. For view based level of detail control, the error measure should limit the distance between the simplified and original surfaces.

Since R-Simp simplifies in a coarse to fine direction, it should be well suited for application in progressive transmission of 3D models. Approximations of previously uncompressed models could be transmitted quickly.

8 Conclusion

We presented R-Simp, an algorithm that simplifies 3D models in reverse and is well suited for interactive applications such as generation of iso-surfaces. Given a limited amount of time most other algorithms cannot guarantee displayable results or results of reasonable quality. R-Simp also allows iterative improvements, precise control of output size, and construction of level of detail hierarchies.

Acknowledgments

We would like to thank Oleg Verevka for suggesting the comparison of quantization to model simplification and Carolina Diaz-Goano for her mathematical assistance. We are grateful to Alex Brodsky for all his helpful and insightful comments and to Greg Turk for his comments, geometry filters, and models. This research was supported by an NSERC grant: RGPIN203262-98.

References

[1] Maria-Elena Algorri and Francis Schmitt. Mesh simplification. *Computer Graphics Forum*, 15(3):C77–C86, 1996.

[2] P. Cignoni, C. Rocchini, and R. Scopigno. Metro: measuring error on simplified surfaces. Technical report, Istituto per l'Elaborazione dell'Infomazione - Consiglio Nazionale delle Ricerche, 1997.

[3] Jonathan Cohen, Dinesh Manocha, and Marc Olano. Simplifying polygonal models using successive mappings. In *Proceedings IEEE Visualization'97*, pages 395–402, 1997.

[4] Michael Garland. *Quadric-Based Polygonal Surface Simplification*. PhD thesis, Carnegie Mellon University, 1999.

[5] Michael Garland and Paul S. Heckbert. Surface simplification using quadric error metrics. In *SIGGRAPH 97 Conference Proceedings*, pages 209–216, 1997.

[6] Allen Gersho and Robert M. Gray. *Vector Quantization and Signal Compression*. Kluwer Academic Publishers, Norwell, Massachusetts, 1992.

[7] Taosong He, L. Hong, A. Kaufman, A. Varshney, , and S. Wang. Voxel-based object simplification. In *Proceedings IEEE Visualization'95*, pages 296–303, 1995.

[8] Paul S. Heckbert and Michael Garland. Survey of polygonal surface simplification algorithms. Technical report, Carnegie Mellon University, 1997. Draft Version.

[9] P. Hinker and C. Hansen. Geometric optimization. In *Proceedings IEEE Visualization'93*, pages 189–195, 1993.

[10] Hugues Hoppe. Progressive meshes. In *SIGGRAPH 96 Conference Proceedings*, pages 99–108, 1996.

[11] Hugues Hoppe, Tony DeRose, Tom Duchamp, John McDonald, and Werner Stuetzle. Mesh optimization. In *SIGGRAPH 93 Conference Proceedings*, pages 19–26, 1993.

[12] I. T. Jolliffe. *Principle Component Analysis*. Springer-Verlag, New York, 1986.

[13] Alan D. Kalvin and Russell H. Taylor. Superfaces: Polygonal mesh simplification with bounded error. *IEEE Computer Graphics and Applications*, 16(3):64–77, 1996.

[14] Peter Lindstrom and Greg Turk. Fast and memory efficient polygonal simplification. In *Proceedings IEEE Visualization'98*, pages 279–286, 1998.

[15] Kok-Lim Low and Tiow-Seng Tan. Model simplification using vertex-clustering. In *1997 Symposium on Interactive 3D Graphics*, pages 75–82, 1997.

[16] Barret O'Neill. *Elementary Differential Geometry*. Academic Press Inc., New York, New York, 1972.

[17] Remi Ronfard and Jarek Rossignac. Full-range approximation of triangulated polyhedra. *Computer Graphics Forum*, 15(3):C67–C76, C462, 1996.

[18] Jarek Rossignac and Paul Borrel. Multi-resolution 3D approximations for rendering complex scenes. In *Modeling in Computer Graphics: Methods and Applications*, pages 455–465, 1993.

[19] Dieter Schmalstieg. Lodestar: An octree-based level of detail generator for VRML. In *VRML 97: Second Symposium on the Virtual Reality Modeling Language*, pages 125–132, 1997.

[20] William J. Schroeder, Jonathan A. Zarge, and William E. Lorensen. Decimation of triangle meshes. *Computer Graphics*, 26(2):65–70, 1992.

[21] Greg Turk. Re-tiling polygonal surfaces. *Computer Graphics*, 26(2):55–64, 1992.

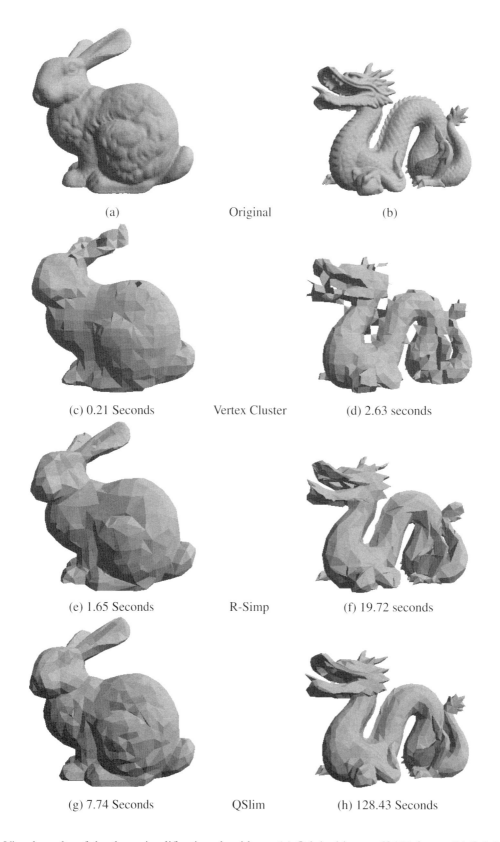

Figure 3: *Visual results of the three simplification algorithms.* (a) *Original bunny 69451 faces.* (b) *Original dragon 871306 faces.* (c)(e)(g) *are 1900 faces.* (d)(f)(h) *are 2500 faces.*

Author Index

Banks, David 3
Baraff, David 27
Barr, Alan 145
Bartram, Lyn 11
Bodenheimer, Bobby 53
Brière, Normand 127
Brodsky, Dmitry 221
Brostow, Gabriel 53
Childs, Jeffrey 153
Courty, Nicolas 69
Dachille, Frank 205
Desbrun, Mathieu 145
Deussen, Oliver 171
Emigh, William 163
Enns, James 163
Fraser, Julie 19
Golam, Ashraf 45
Gutwin, Carl 19
Healey, Christopher 163
Heidrich, Wolfgang 87
Ho, Wayne 179
Hodgins, Jessica 53,61
Inkpen, Kori 103
Isenburg, Martin 197
Ishii, Hiroshi 1
Jaksetic, Patricija 111
Kaufman, Arie 205
Kautz, Jan 119
Kokkevis, Evangelos 35
Lefebvre, Laurent 77
Liu, Geniva 163
Ljungstrand, Peter 111
Lu, Cheng-Chang 153
Marchand, Eric 69

McCool, Michael 119
McGrenere, Joanna 179,187
Melax, Stan 213
Metoyer, Ronald 61
Meyer, Alexandre 137
Meyer, Mark 145
Moore, Gale 187
Neyret, Fabrice 137
O'Brien, James 53
Potter, Jerry 153
Poulin, Pierre 77,127
Preim, Bernhard 171
Redström, Johan 111
Ritter, Felix 171
Schirmacher, Hartmut 87
Schroeder, Peter 145
Scott, Stacey 103
Seidel, Hans-Peter 87
Shoemaker, Garth 103
Singh, Karan 35
Smith, Jeffrey 27
Strothotte, Thomas 171
Taylor, Russell 163
Terzopoulos, Demetri 43
Uhl, Axel 11
van der Veer, Gerrit 95
Vertegaal, Roel 95
Vidimce, Kiril 3
Vons, Harro 95
Watson, Benjamin 221
Weigle, Chris 163
Witkin, Andrew 27
Wong, Kok Cheong 45

Graphics **Interface** 2000

Graphics **Interface** 2001

University of Alberta
Edmonton, Alberta, Canada
16–18 May 2001

Call for Papers

GI 2001 will be a unique event presenting the latest results in computer graphics and human-computer interaction. It offers three days of invited speakers, posters, and refereed paper presentations. A banquet and electronic theatre will provide additional opportunities to meet speakers and other attendees for informal discussion in a social setting.

This year will be the 27th annual Graphics Interface. It is the oldest regularly scheduled computer graphics and human-computer interface conference in the world. Graphics Interface has established a reputation for a high-quality technical program and excellent invited speakers. Full details can be obtained through the Graphics Interface web site at www.graphicsinterface.org.

GI 2001 will be held at the University of Alberta, in Edmonton, Canada. Edmonton is a beautiful Canadian city located on the North Saskatchewan River. It is served by Air Canada, Canadian, Northwest and Horizon Airlines. As the location for the University of Alberta and the provincial capitol, Edmonton has a thriving intellectual and cultural life. Spring will be at its full force in May, and the beauty of the river park, with its hundreds of miles of paths, will be at its peak.

Conference and Program Chairs
John Buchanan, Electronic Arts Canada
Benjamin Watson, Northwestern University

Posters Chair
Torsten Moeller, Simon Fraser University

Videos Chair
Dave Forsey, Radical Entertainment

Important Dates
Papers Due .... 19 November 2000
Decision for Papers .... 8 February 2001
Posters Due .... 26 March 2001
Videos Due .... 26 March 2001
Final Submission Due .... 2 April 2001
Decision for Posters .... 16 April 2001
Decision for Videos .... 16 April 2001

Program Committee
Kadi Bouatouch, IRISA, Rennes
Chris Bregler, Stanford University
Bill Buxton, Alias Wavefront & U. Toronto
Sheelagh Carpendale, University of Calgary
Mario Costa Sousa, University of Alberta
Deborah Fels, Ryerson Polytechnic University
Dave Fracchia, Mainframe Entertainment
Carl Gutwin, University of Saskatchewan
Jessica Hodgins, Georgia Institute of Technology
Yoshi Kitamura, Osaka University
Michael McCool, University of Waterloo
Bob Lewis, Washington State University
Mikio Shinya, NTT, Japan
Thomas Strothotte, University of Magdeburg & SFU
Wolfgang Stuerzlinger, York University

For the latest information on the call for papers, the submission process, and the 2001 conference, visit the Graphics Interface web site at:

www.graphicsinterface.org

This conference is sponsored by the Canadian Human-Computer Communications Society.

Graphics **Interface** 2001

Submissions

Contributions are solicited describing unpublished research results and applications experience in all areas of computer graphics and human-computer interaction, specifically including the following:

Image synthesis & realism	User interfaces & modeling	Image-based rendering techniques
Shading & rendering algorithms	Windowing systems	Hardware techniques
Geometric modeling & meshing	Computer cartography	Computer supported cooperative work
Computer animation	Image processing	Interaction techniques
Medical graphics	Graphics for CAD/CAM	Graphics in education
Computer-aided building design	Graphics & the arts	Industrial & robotics applications
Visualization	Graphics in business	Graphics in simulation
Mobile computing	Haptic interfaces	Human interface devices

Papers, formatted as they would appear in the final proceedings, must be received by **19 November 2000**. Submissions will be entirely electronic in the form of PDF files; please visit the Graphics Interface web site for a detailed description of the submission process and format requirements. In exceptional cases, traditional hardcopy submissions will be accepted; first contact one of the conference co-chairs. Refereeing will be double blind. Only the title, without any indication of authorship or author location, should appear on the manuscript body. A separate file (sheet) should contain the manuscript title, abstract, and the full names, postal addresses, phone numbers, fax numbers, and email addresses for all authors. One author should be designated the contact author for subsequent correspondence regarding the paper. Accepted papers will be published in an archival-quality proceedings to be distributed by both ACM and Morgan-Kaufmann.

Notification of acceptance or rejection will be emailed to the contact author by **8 February 2001**. The final versions of accepted papers are due **2 April 2001**. Each paper will be allotted up to eight (8) pages in the proceedings free of charge. Extra charges will be made for pages exceeding the limit and for colour pages. All printing will be done on an offset press using a high-resolution imagesetter and CMYK process colour, directly from electronic files (PDF) submitted by the authors. Exceptionally good papers will be considered for publication in journals; arrangements exist for the best graphics papers to be considered by Computer Graphics Forum and for the best human-computer interface papers to be considered by Behaviour & Information Technology.

Conference Co-Chair Addresses

John Buchanan
Electronic Arts Canada
4330 Sanderson Way
Burnaby, BC Canada
V5G 4X1
Phone: +1 604-419-3037
Fax: +1 604-729-6370
Email: juancho@ea.com

Benjamin Watson
Department of Computer Science
Northwestern University
1890 Maple Ave
Evanston, Illinois 60201, USA
Phone: +1 847-467-1332
Fax: +1 847-491-5258
Email: watsonb@cs.nwu.edu